EDUCATIONAL MEDIA AND TECHNOLOGY YEARBOOK

Michael Orey, Jo McClendon, and Robert Maribe Branch, Editors

2005 Edition Volume 30

Published in cooperation with the Association for Educational
Communications and Technology

LIBRARIES
U N L I M I T E D
A Member of the Greenwood Publishing Group

Westport, Connecticut • London

Library of Congress Cataloging-in-Publication Data

Educational media and technology yearbook.—Westport, CT : Libraries Unlimited,
   A Member of the Greenwood Publishing Group, Inc. 1985-
   v.-
   Annual
   2005- vol. 30
   Published in cooperation with the Association for Educational Communications and
   Technology, 1985-
   Continues: Educational media yearbook
   ISBN 1-59158-207-5
   LB1028.3.E372   2005   85643014
   British Library Cataloguing in Publication Data is available.

ISBN: 1-59158-207-5

First published in 2005

Libraries Unlimited, 88 Post Road West, Westport, CT 06881
A Member of the Greenwood Publishing Group, Inc.
www.lu.com

Printed in the United States of America

The paper used in this book complies with the
Permanent Paper Standard issued by the National
Information Standards Organization (Z39.48-1984).

10 9 8 7 6 5 4 3 2 1

Copyright Acknowledgments

The editors and publisher gratefully acknowledge the following sources for use of materials contained in this text.

American Association of School Librarians and the Association for Educational Communications and Technology, "Information Literacy Standards for Student Learning." Chicago: ALA, 1998. Copyright © 1998 by the American Library Association and the
Association for Educational Communications and Technology.

Association of College and Research Libraries. "Information Literacy Competency Standards
for Higher Education." Chicago: ALA, 2000. Copyright © 2000 by the American Library
Association and the Association for Educational Communications and Technology.

Contents

Part Three
Leadership Profiles

Part Four
Organizations and Associations

Part Five
Graduate Programs

Part Six
Mediagraphy

Preface

This is the fourth year for which I have been an editor and the second where I am the senior editor. I go to several conferences each year and try to go to as many sessions as I can. What I try to do is to get a sense for what the trends are in the field. This year, I have found that there is a growing and continuing interest in online learning—not just because of the hype, but because people with real distance learning needs are recognizing the importance and utility of online delivery. As a consequence, I have included two sections in the "Trends and Issues" section that deal with online learning. Perhaps as a consequence to the online learning movement, another trend I found was that there is a renewed interest in multicultural perspectives. Because people from various countries and subcultures within a country come together in an online class, cultural differences are encountered by teachers and students alike. Also, because of the war in Iraq and the increased threat of terrorism, multicultural understanding has become more than just something nice to do. Our (the world's) survival depends on it.

The audience for the *Yearbook* consists of media and technology professionals in schools, higher education, and business contexts. Topics of interest to professionals practicing in these areas are broad, as the table of contents demonstrates. The theme unifying each of the following chapters is the use of technology to enable or enhance education. Forms of technology represented in this volume vary from traditional tools such as the book to the latest advancements in digital technology, while areas of education encompass widely ranging situations involving learning and teaching.

As in prior volumes, the assumptions underlying the chapters presented here are as follows:

- Technology represents tools that act as extensions of the educator.
- Media serve as delivery systems for educational communications.
- Technology is not restricted to machines and hardware but includes techniques and procedures derived from scientific research about ways to promote change in human performance.
- The fundamental tenet is that educational media and technology should be used to

  1. achieve authentic learning objectives,
  2. situate learning tasks,
  3. negotiate the complexities of guided learning,
  4. facilitate the construction of knowledge,
  5. support skill acquisition, and
  6. manage diversity.

The *Educational Media and Technology Yearbook* has become a standard reference in many libraries and professional collections. Examined in relation to its companion volumes of the past, it provides a valuable historical record of current ideas and developments in the field. Part One, "Trends and Issues," presents an array of chapters that develop some of the current themes just listed, in addition to others. Part Two, "School and Library Media," concentrates on chapters of special relevance to K–12 education, school learning resources, and school library media centers. In Part Three, "Leadership Profiles," the authors provide biographical sketches of the careers of instructional technology leaders. Part Four, "Organizations and Associations in North America," and Part Five, "Graduate Programs in North America," are, respectively, directories of instructional technology-related organizations and institutions of higher learning offering degrees in related fields. Finally, Part Six, "Mediagraphy," presents an annotated listing of selected current publications related to the field.

The Editors of the *Yearbook* invite media and technology professionals to submit manuscripts for consideration for publication. Contact Michael Orey (morey@coe.uga.edu) for submission guidelines.

Michael Orey
Senior Editor

Contributors

Adekunle Akinyemi

Lilia Ana Alfaro Guevara

Barbara Bichelmeyer

Kay Bishop

Byron R. Burnham

John K. Burton

Gail Bush

Rebecca P. Butler

Jody Charter

Lloyd S. Curtis

Jean Donham

Lesley Farmer

Karen Ferneding

Andrew Gibbons

Katherine L. Hayden

Ellen S. Hoffman

Antonette W. Hood

Stephanie Huffman

Dave S. Knowlton

Annette Lamb

Miriam B. Larson

Barbara B. Lockee

Betty Marcoux

Marcia A. Mardis

Michael Molenda

David Richard Moore

Wayne Nelson

Ross A. Perkins

Thomas C. Reeves

Wendy Rickman

Wilhelmina C. Savenye

L. Bill Searcy

Berhane Teclehaimanot

Peter A. Theodore

Glenda Thurman

Mike Tillman

Penelope Walters Swenson

Part One
Trends and Issues

Introduction

Michael Orey

This is the fourth edition of the *Yearbook* for which I have served as the editor of the Trends and Issues section. One of the first things I did in this capacity was to break it up into sections. Each year, I go to the Association for Educational Communications and Technology and other conferences, where I try to take the pulse of what is happening in the field. Each of the major categories covered at these conferences then have representative chapters in the *Yearbook*. In addition, I always include chapters in which others try to analyze trends in the field. This year one chapter is featured in the general trends area, a follow-up to the previous edition's chapter. The other sections include Design, Online Learning Theories and Technologies, and Multicultural Perspectives in Online Learning.

Design is a constant in the field of instructional technology. It is unusual to think of this foundational idea as a trend, but the chapters in this section show where design is leading us in the future. The last topic, multiculturalism, is becoming particularly important because of the diversity of cultural perspectives that are found in online classes, particularly as more international students are included. I included Online Learning Theories and Technologies because of what one author of this edition said in her presentation at a conference I attended (Alfaro Guevara, 2003, personal communication). When describing the technology of online learning, she described this as the "sexy" part of the field of instructional technology. Her passion, however, was in theories that helped determine how those technologies are used. She referred to the theories as the "romantic" part of the field. Many of us in the field (including myself) are constantly looking at the new and cool technologies, and these are what often get us excited. Yet I quickly return to the theories that help me think about how these new technologies can be used for learning. I think the terms *sexy* and *romantic* work well to describe this difference.

TRENDS

Michael Molenda and his colleagues have provided the *Educational Media and Technology Yearbook* with the seventh lead chapter in the Trends section. This year he authored the chapter in collaboration with Barbara Bichelmeyer, and together they paint a snapshot of what is going on in the field. Molenda and Bichelmeyer provide a very real view on what is happening in instructional technology in schools, higher education, and business and industry within the United States.

DESIGN

In general, there are a collection of theories in our field that can be described as inquiry based. Most of these can also be thought of as constructionist in nature. Wayne Nelson and Dave S. Knowlton make use of a popular theory that has been called both "Learning by Design" and "Learning through Design." These authors have done what we all should do: they have used a constructionist model to teach teachers how to teach using a more constructionist perspective.

Whereas Nelson and Knowlton focus on design from a theory perspective, Miriam B. Larson and Barbara B. Lockee talk about the influence of culture on design and the training of designers. They consider how the employer environment affects instructional designers. Multiple contexts and cultures exist in the education and training world. Part of the teaching of instructional designers ought to allow these students to immerse themselves in multiple settings to help them learn which best suits their skills.

David Richard Moore reminds us of the complexity of determining what individual learners know. His ideas about allowing for a range of answers rather than a discreet response to a question has potential for instruction design that better meets the needs of individual learners.

ONLINE LEARNING THEORIES AND TECHNOLOGIES

The chapters in this section represent some of the most popular theories for online learning during this time: WebQuests, constructionism, and learning communities. All describe activities that would represent good teaching practice whether a class is taught online or face-to-face.

Penelope Walters Swenson and Lloyd S. Curtis describe how they use literature to help students understand the history of education in the United States. One of the most important ideas to come from this chapter is in noting how the method could be equally effective online or in a face-to-face classroom.

Katherine L. Hayden and Antonette W. Hood provide an additional perspective on building online learning communities (from those included in last year's edition of the *Educational Media and Technology Yearbook*). The authors cover the various online technologies that are available today and how each can be used to help create a learning community in the online class. After careful analysis of the technologies, they collected data on the extent to which these have helped develop learning communities.

Stephanie Huffman, Glenda Thurman, Jody Charter, and Wendy Rickman suggest that good teaching is good teaching, regardless of how it is delivered. They make useful points about online teaching practice that should be helpful to anyone who teaches online, but most of these would also benefit other teachers as well.

Annette Lamb and Berhane Teclehaimanot look at what has been done with WebQuests in the decade since they were first introduced. They track all the changes in this method over this period including those made by the originator of the idea and others who have adopted it. In addition, they review the impact of this method learning.

In their chapter, Peter A. Theodore and L. Bill Searcy describe how bulletin board discussions facilitate reflective thinking among education students. Wilhelmina C. Savenye examines the use of video for learning, particularly for preservice education majors. She clearly describes the importance and richness of video to present classroom technology integration cases. She also presents data to support how important this is to both graduates and undergraduates.

Lloyd S. Curtis and Penelope Swenson also examine the use of video. They detail all the technologies that are available to deliver video and point out that many people, particularly in rural areas, still do not have access to broadband. This can create yet another aspect of digital divide.

MULTICULTURAL PERSPECTIVES IN ONLINE LEARNING

Lilia Ana Alfaro Guevara presents a clear picture of how important it is to help inservice teachers in Mexico. She also shows how complex this is to accomplish and how online technologies can help make it happen. She clearly articulates a need, but the constraints of the Mexican infrastructure may make online learning projects difficult to carry forward.

There is a great deal of discussion about being sensitive to cultural differences in classrooms (online or otherwise). Adekunle Akinyemi describes how his culture requires the separation of men and women in the learning process. From a more Western worldview, this is an uncomfortable issue. In most cases, we want to respect differing cultural views, but is it possible to do so when another's worldview is in opposition to your own?

Finally, Ross A. Perkins, Barbara B. Lockee, and John K. Burton describe a Malawian perspective that is strikingly different from a Western viewpoint, such that it helps to clarify the importance of culture in today's global community. It also describes the interactions between people from Virginia Tech and Mzuzu University.

Michael Orey

Issues and Trends in Instructional Technology: Slow Growth as Economy Recovers

Michael Molenda and Barbara Bichelmeyer
Indiana University

This is the seventh in a series of reviews of issues and trends begun in 1998. The year since the previous review was written (Molenda, 2004) has seen an improvement in the U.S. economy after several years of recession. State tax revenues in the first quarter of 2004 increased dramatically over the year before (Jenny, 2004), signaling an easing of the budgetary crises that many states faced. Increased government and corporate revenues are expected to trickle down to improve the ability of schools, colleges, and businesses to acquire new technological hardware and software.

Schools, colleges, and businesses also continue to expand their information and communications technology (ICT) infrastructure by upgrading to broadband capacity and building wireless networks to complement their wired networks. The year 2004 could be considered the watershed year in which instructor access to networks became truly pervasive in schools and colleges. Does pervasive access mean pervasive instructional use? Hardly. Indeed, the story of this year's review is the examination of how and why the various ICT delivery systems were being used or ignored in the corporate, higher education, and K–12 school sectors.

As in previous reviews (Molenda & Sullivan 2002, 2003; Molenda, 2004), this review traces developments in three of the largest sectors in which ICT is employed—corporate training and development, higher education, and K–12 education. In addition to the economic forces just mentioned, there are, of course, internal dynamics within each organization influencing whether and how instructional technologies are used. This review shows how the adoption and use of ICT within these sectors has progressed in light of the changing circumstances of the past year.

OVERALL DEVELOPMENTS

Pervasiveness emerges as a major theme in this year's review. In schools and colleges, not only is everyone constantly within range of computer networks, but computing also pervades all functions of these institutions, from teaching and learning to administration to residential life. In schools, testing is becoming more dependent on technology as is instruction; in a number of school districts, virtual schools are coming to be as important to the mission as traditional schools.

Convergence is a second theme that cuts across sectors and across technologies. Analog media such as slides and video are now incorporated inside digital delivery systems, as, for example, in the case of streaming video on the Web. Functions that were once available only in separate devices—telephone, radio, television, calculating, text messaging—are now converging into a single handheld instrument. Likewise, instructional methods that were once considered separate—face-to-face classroom, video, Web-based—are converging into hybrid or blended learning formats.

Let's see how these themes play out in each sector, one at a time.

CORPORATE TRAINING AND DEVELOPMENT

Although business was beginning to expand in 2004, the national economy in the previous two years was still in recession. In that period, there was a startling decline in the number of small and medium-sized businesses. For the first time in a generation, the total corporate spending for training actually declined for two years in a row—2002 and 2003. The purchase of off-the-shelf training materials suffered the largest decline of all sectors of spending on corporate education (Galvin, 2003).

Issue 1: Use of Technology-Based Media for Delivery of Instruction

Classroom instruction vs. computer-based. We have been tracking the results of the annual survey of corporate training conducted by *Training* magazine since 1997, so it is possible to track longitudinally the trends in the use of various media and methods over this seven-year period.

Despite many earlier predictions to the contrary, face-to-face classroom instruction is still the most universally applied format of training, being used "always" or "often" at 91 percent of companies (Galvin, 2003, p. 31). As is shown in Figure 1, the proportion of organizations using classroom training has hovered around the 90 percent range since 1997, with no noticeable trend. Note that the data from 1997 to 2000 are not directly comparable to those from 2001 and after. In the former period, the question asked was simply, "Do you use this method or not?" whereas in the latter period, the question was phrased as "Do you use this method always, often, seldom, or never?"

Figure 1. Percentage of organizations using live classroom. (In 1997–2000, shows those who use "ever." In 2001–2003, shows those who use "always" or "often.") Source: Galvin, 2003.

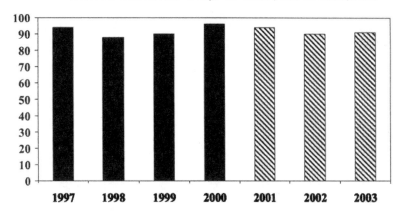

In terms of the percentage of *time spent in training,* instructor-led, face-to-face classroom instruction occupied 69 percent of all training time in 2003, a decline of 5 percent from the previous year. Another 10 percent of time was spent in classrooms with remote instructors, an increase of 3 percent since the previous year. Participation in computer-based learning occupied 16 percent of time, an increase of 4 percent over the previous year (Galvin, 2003, p. 22).

The proportion of time spent in technology-based training has been increasing slowly for several years, now showing a trend that has not been consistent in previous years. Because the proportion of time spent in face-to-face instruction has hovered around the 70 percent level for many years and yet the number of organizations making major use of Internet-based delivery and other technology-based delivery has grown dramatically over this period, one could conclude that technology-based training is *replacing* traditional classroom instruction to a small degree, but is *supplementing* it to a very high degree.

Traditional media. Print materials—manuals and workbooks—remain high in popularity, being used "often" or "always" at 79 percent of all businesses (Galvin, 2003, p. 30). As is shown in Figure 2, the use of print materials has remained around the 80 percent range since 1997, with a small tick downward in the past year.[1]

Figure 2. Percentage of organizations using workbook/manual. (In 1997–2000, shows those who use "ever." In 2001–2003, shows those who use "always" or "often.") Source: Galvin, 2003.

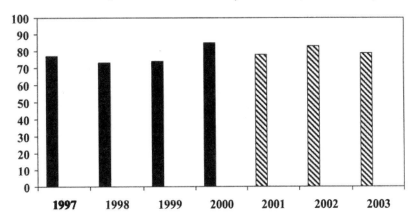

The popularity of print materials suggests that independent self-study might be a rather commonly used method of instruction. Actually, self-study as a method was not included as an option in the *Training* surveys until 2002, when "self-study non-computer" was used always or often at 25 percent of businesses, falling to 23 percent in 2003. The other category, "self-study Web-based," was used always or often at 36 percent of responding companies in 2002, rising to 44 percent in 2003 (Galvin, 2003, p. 31). This suggests a trend away from print-based and toward Web-based self-study.

Videotapes are used always or often at 52 percent of responding organizations (Galvin, 2003, p. 30). As is shown in Figure 3, this figure has declined substantially from the previous year.

Compared with videotapes, it has been less common for audiotapes to be used as the primary delivery system for prerecorded training modules or courses. Consequently, it is understandable that the reported usage of audiocassettes dropped markedly when the question was changed in the 2001 *Training* survey from "Do you use …?" to "How often do you use …?" As shown in Figure 4, only 7 percent of companies used audiocassettes "always" or "often" in 2002, and that figure declined to 4 percent in 2003, whereas in previous years the reported usage rate was in the 40 percent range. Some of the drop may also be accounted for by a change in media format; it may be that when audio materials are used, they are now more likely to be stored and used in some digital format rather than in tape format.

---

1. Note that the data from 1997 to 2000 are not directly comparable to those from 2001 and after. In the former period, the question asked was simply, "Do you use this method or not?" whereas in the latter period, the question was phrased as "Do you use this method always, often, seldom, or never?"

Figure 3. Percentage of organizations using videotapes. (In 1997–2000, shows those who use "ever." In 2001–2003, shows those who use "always" or "often.") Source: Galvin, 2003.

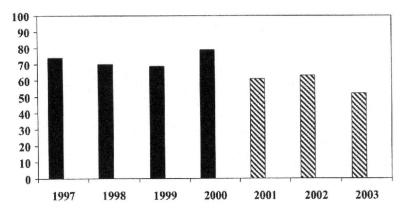

Figure 4. Percentage of organizations using audiocassettes. (In 1997–2000, shows those who use "ever." In 2001–2003, shows those who use "always" or "often.") Source: Galvin, 2003.

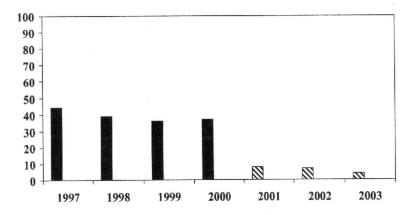

The use of slides and overhead transparencies has not been tracked consistently over the years, but these media formats seem to be receding slowly as they are replaced by computer-based display media.

The use of games and simulations that are not computer-based has declined a bit, being used "often" or "always" at 25 percent of companies (Galvin, 2003, p. 31). As is shown in Figure 5, the reported adoption of non-computer-based games and simulations has been in the 30 percent range since 1997, with no consistent trend downward until the past year.

Figure 5. Percentage of organizations using games/simulations. (In 1997–2000, shows those who use "ever." In 2001–2003, shows those who use "always" or "often.") Source: Galvin, 2003.

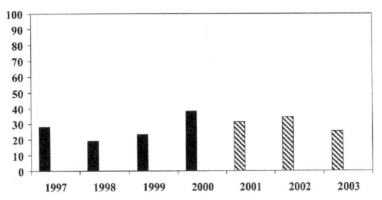

Telecommunications media. A small proportion of organizations use broadcast or satellite television to disseminate training programs to multiple sites. Some 20 percent of respondents reported using broadcast or satellite television in the period of 1998–2000. When the *Training* survey changed the question to measure *frequency* of use, it was found that only five to ten percent of companies were using this delivery method "always" or "often" in 2001 and 2002, rising slightly to 12 percent in 2003 (Galvin, 2003, p. 30), as shown in Figure 6.

Figure 6. Percentage of organizations using broadcast or satellite TV. (In 1997–2000, shows those who use "ever." In 2001–2003, shows those who use "always" or "often.") Source: Galvin, 2003.

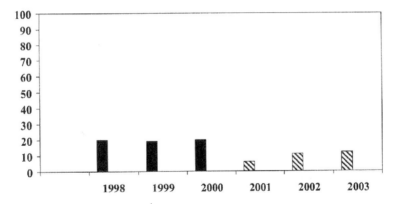

Two-way videoconferences distributed over satellite, cable, or the Web are used always or often for training at 22 percent of all organizations (Galvin, 2003, p. 30), as shown in Figure 7. This indicates an increase over each of the past three years. However, two-way videoconferences are not used for a large proportion of training time except in the military services. They tend to be used as supplements to other forms of training or for special purposes, such as the introduction of new products or the rollout of new tools at organizations with widely scattered locations.

Figure 7. Percentage of organizations using videoconferencing. (In 1997–2000, shows those who use "ever." In 2001–2003, shows those who use "always" or "often.") Source: Galvin, 2003.

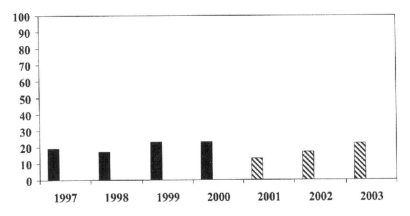

Computer-based media. Computer-based delivery systems have played a gradually expanding role in training over the past decade. In the early 1990s, this meant modules delivered via floppy disk or local network (LAN). Since then, computer-based material is more likely encountered by means of CD-ROM or DVD modules or, more likely, by connecting to the Internet or organizational intranet. In the 2003 *Training* survey, 45 percent of companies report using instruction in digital storage media "often" or "always," as shown in Figure 8, a small increase over the previous year. However, 63 percent used Internet or intranet delivery, as shown in Figure 9, a major increase over the previous year (Galvin, 2003, p. 30). Although both ways of delivering computer-based training seem to be increasing in popularity, the big growth is in the Web-based area.

Figure 8. Percentage of organizations using digital storage media—diskette, CD, or DVD. (In 1997–2000, shows those who use "ever." In 2001–2003, shows those who use "always" or "often.") Source: Galvin, 2003.

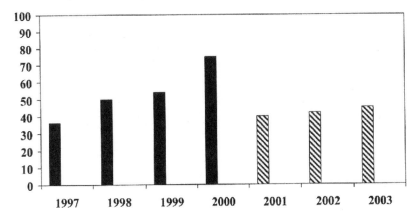

Figure 9. Percentage of organizations using Internet or intranet. (In 1997–2000, shows those who use "ever." In 2001–2003, shows those who use "always" or "often.") Source: Galvin, 2003. *Note:* In 2001, Internet and intranet listed separately; combined total is shown.

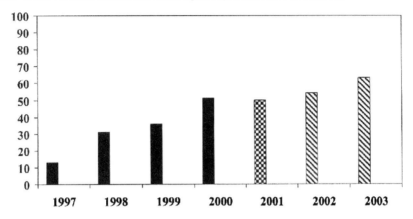

Games and simulations are often seen as ideal pedagogical methods for learning to make decisions about complex business problems, for practice under realistic conditions, or for repetitive drills on facts or concepts to be memorized. By using the computer to present the problems and select appropriate responses, more sophisticated programs can be run faster and less expensively. Considering these potential advantages, it is perhaps surprising to see that computer-based games and simulations are used "always" or "often" within only about 10 percent of responding organizations (Galvin, 2003, p. 31), as shown in Figure 10. Non-computer-based games and simulations are used about three times as often.

Figure 10. Percentage of organizations using games/simulations, computer based. (In 1997–2000, shows those who use "ever." In 2001–2003, shows those who use "always" or "often.") Source: Galvin, 2003.

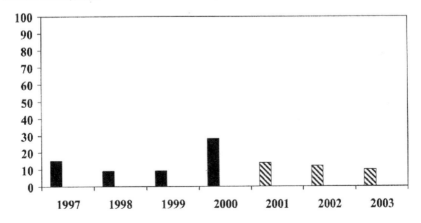

More advanced applications, put under the rubric of "virtual reality," have been tracked by the *Training* survey since 1997. There has been little growth reported in this cutting-edge area. Virtual reality programs are used "always" or "often" in only about 3 percent of organizations (Galvin, 2003, p. 31), as shown in Figure 11.

Figure 11. Percentage of organizations using virtual reality. (In 1997–2000, shows those who use "ever." In 2001–2003, shows those who use "always" or "often.") Source: Galvin, 2003.

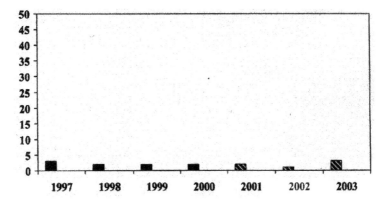

Taken together, ICT delivery now accounts for roughly a quarter of the time spent in training. This represents an unusually large jump in one year and the acceleration of what had been a rather weak trend.

Consistent with this trend, the traditional audiovisual media used in face-to-face instruction show a pattern of slow decline, although video materials continue to be widely used.

The largest constraint to the expansion of e-learning is the global business cycle, in a downward drift since 2001, but showing signs of recovery in 2004. E-learning initiatives require substantial front-end investments in hardware and software as well as in development time and talent. E-learning remains a tempting prospect for improving return-on-investment (ROI) in training. There does not seem to be a simple recipe for substituting "cheap" e-learning for "expensive" face-to-face instruction, however. E-learning obviously works equally well for instruction that is merely knowledge transmission, but for more advanced skills or skills in the affective and motor domains, more sophisticated pedagogical methods are necessary, both for face-to-face and for ICT-based instruction. For advanced skills, the secret still lies in involving learners in engaging, challenging problems and guiding their budding abilities to solve those problems. To the extent that e-learning can provide such an interactive learning environment, it will succeed and find an eager market.

Unfortunately, e-learning courses often suffer a high dropout rate, indicating both that trainees often enter with insufficient reason for staying and that the instructional methods they encounter fail to hold them. A text-heavy, didactive approach is commonly found in e-learning courses, which contrasts sharply with the problem-based, inductive approach advocated for adult learners seeking usable skills.

Issue 3: Challenges to Existing Paradigms

Blended learning. In everyday parlance, trainers have tended to classify learning events into discrete categories: face-to-face classroom instruction, online learning, self-directed study, action learning, and so on. In fact, though, corporate training programs increasingly consist of hybrids, for example, face-to-face classroom meetings interspersed with Web-based team projects; satellite video conferences followed by small-group discussions at remote sites; on-the-job action learning plus mentoring via e-mail. Combining conventional and online methods has come to be recognized as a "third path," referred to as blended learning. The advantages of combining formats are obvious. Online activities offer self-pacing, standardization of information dissemination, and rapid deployment of new material, whereas face-to-face learning allows practice with feedback, team building, networking, and the other functions that are tied to people's emotional responses. There is a growing consensus that the future belongs to blended approaches. The strong foothold of this new paradigm is indicated in the findings of the *Training* magazine Industry Report for 2003 (Galvin, 2003), discussed earlier. The survey shows face-to-face instruction still dominating the time spent in training *at the same time* as e-learning formats are taking off in terms of more and more frequent use. How can both modes be flourishing? By being used as complements to each other—blended learning.

Since 2002, the *Training* survey has included self-study as a separate instructional mode. As shown in Figures 12 and 13, the use of non-computer-based self-study declined between 2002 and 2003, but the use of Web-based self-study grew from 36 to 44 percent, making it one of the most widely used learning modes. This is a concrete indicator of the trend toward blending Web-based materials with other methods, such as live classroom training.

**Figure 12. Percentage of organizations using self-study, noncomputer "always" or "often.")
Source: Galvin, 2003.**

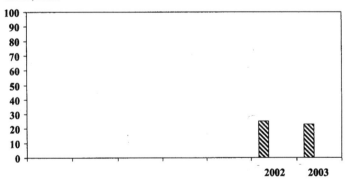

**Figure 13. Percentage of organizations using self-study, Web-based "always" or "often.")
Source: Galvin, 2003.**

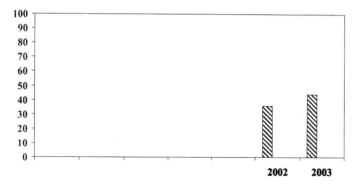

In addition to combining various types of instructional media and methods, blended solutions also tend to include noninstructional cognitive supports, such as online help systems or printed job aids. Thus, the line between instructional and noninstructional interventions is becoming blurred, as is the line between conventional and digital instruction.

Performance improvement. The profession formerly known as training has been in a prolonged state of identity crisis, driven primarily by economic pressures that have forced corporations to be increasingly conscious of the costs and benefits of all their processes. Top-level managers are willing to pay only for operations that actually yield results, which conventional training often does not. There is not yet a clear consensus on a name or conceptual framework for the new profession. However, one of the leading contenders is the concept of performance improvement (PI), which grew out of the instructional technology field (Molenda & Pershing, 2004). The gist of PI is that the ultimate purpose of training is to enhance performance in the workplace, which can best be accomplished by combining instruction with other interventions, such as incentives, job redesign, and job aids.

In the most recent examination of the future of the training profession, Galagan (2003) observes that "performance improvement is both time-tested and newly appealing to organizations fed up with training programs that don't change anything that matters" (p. 30). Respondents to a survey associated with Galagan's article favored "workplace learning and *performance*" as a new name over "training and development" and "human resources development" (p. 29). The time may finally have arrived for a paradigm shift in the field formerly known as training.

HIGHER EDUCATION

As in the corporate sector, the use of instructional technology in the higher education domain is affected by external economic forces as well as internal sociocultural influences. The downturn of the national economy beginning in 2000 and continuing through 2003 led to severe shortfalls in state tax revenues, which led to tightening of budgets at most state-supported universities, which in turn forced cutbacks in planned upgrades or expansions of academic computing. Although the business cycle began improving in 2004, those improvements had not begun to ripple into college and university budgets.

Economic forces have not favored instructional technology thus far. Investment in new technology tends to be driven by payoffs, particularly economic payoffs. Organizations implement technology with the hope that it will increase their benefits or decrease their costs. In the case of higher education, information technology has begun to pay off in terms of administrative costs and improvement of student services at a more affordable cost. Information technology has not proven to be a cost-reducer on the educational side of operations, however. Indeed, as long as universities are organized as they are (teacher-centered decision making, professors as independent operators, decentralized academic fiefdoms), there is little possibility to reduce instructional costs. So instructional technology advocates are left with the claim that benefits increase: greater numbers of students reached; more satisfied students; more content and productive faculty, and the like. This benefits argument is not as potent at the economic one, so the provision of technology support tends to be lower than in other parts of the administration.

The tempo of change in instructional practice, including what tools will be used, is driven much more by the dynamics of sociocultural forces within colleges and universities themselves: by whom instructional decisions are made, whose interests are primary, and how rewards are allocated. In American colleges and universities, these forces are generally conservative of traditional practices and values, thus putting a brake on major change in teaching–learning arrangements.

Issue 1: Use of Technology-Based Media for Delivery of Instruction

Classroom media: Traditional audiovisual media. Many college and university instructors still prefer to use analog media—audio and video cassettes, overhead transparencies, 2 x 2–inch slides, and the like—for various reasons including legibility, reliability, familiarity, and a large installed base of materials. Administrators, on the other hand, tend to prefer digital media. They are seeking standardization to allow compatibility within and across departments. Standardization would allow updating and expanding of existing materials without having to start all over, as is the case with analog media. As in the corporate sector, the dream is an enterprisewide database for all the institution's instructional media.

Because digital media are viewed as the way of the future, there is little research on the extent to which analog media are still used. However, an informal survey of university media service centers indicates such usage is still common, for example:

- Overhead projectors—virtually every classroom is equipped with a projector, and instructors still use them, although no usage statistics are kept. Many instructors, especially younger ones, use PowerPoint™ presentations instead of or in addition to overheads.[2] Nonetheless, attempts to remove the overheads and substitute document cameras meet faculty resistance. The authors have witnessed this themselves. When a new building for the Education Department was furnished, the dean insisted on equipping the largest classroom only for digital media, prohibiting electrical outlets in the front of the room just to be sure that overheads could not be used. The faculty dragged in overhead projectors and found extension cords to reach the side outlets.

- Slide projectors—circulation of projectors is declining, but projectors tend to be built into classrooms and labs in departments that make heavy use of slides, such as biology, veterinary medicine, optometry, fine arts, classics, and drama. These fields rely on visual images, and high resolution is often a priority. It is difficult to match the sharpness of optical images with digital projection. In addition, such departments often have large collections of slides, including of historic subjects, which simply can't be replaced by newer digital media.

- 16mm films are still used, mainly in film-studies classes, but a small number of instructional films are used in other classes.

- Video recordings in VHS format are still widely used, with thousands of bookings annually at universities with large central collections. Circulation has been steady for about ten years. As VHS video recordings have become less expensive, many individuals and departments own their own copies; showings of these do not appear on campus circulation records.

- DVD recordings are growing in popularity, slowly replacing the VHS format, although their total circulation figures are only a quarter of those of VHS videos at the present time. Many of the VHS titles that are now used by faculty are not available in DVD format; furthermore, libraries and media centers cannot afford to replace their already large collections of VHS recordings. Consequently, VHS will continue to be used for many years to come.

As noted, VHS, overhead, and slide formats are going to continue to be significant vehicles for instructional presentations for the foreseeable future. We can foresee a coming hardware crisis, as slide and VHS equipment ceases to be available in the marketplace. Campus media service centers are going to be hard-pressed to provide the equipment needed to keep showing the software on which the faculty rely.

---

2. Although this has not been documented with formal research, there is growing anecdotal evidence of student malaise with PowerPoint™ overuse. Some of the malaise is attributable to the monotonous series of bulleted lists that are all too easy to create with the PowerPoint™ software.

Classroom media: computer-based digital media. In our 2002 annual review (Molenda & Sullivan, 2002) we reported that the pace of faculty adoption of computer-based media appeared to be slowing. According to the annual surveys of the Campus Computing Project between 1997 and 2000, faculty adoption of certain computer-based teaching applications—such as course Web pages and use of Internet resources—grew each year during that period. The percentage increase was *smaller* each succeeding year, however, indicating plateauing of the adoption rate.

Unfortunately, the Campus Computing Project has not continued to measure these indices and has focused on other topics in information technology. This lack of attention may be an indication of a slackening interest in classroom media within the academic computing community. In fact, in the 2004 EDUCAUSE survey, e-learning, distributed learning, and course management systems have slipped from near the top to near the bottom of the list of concerns of information technology professionals (Spicer et al., 2004). In any event, there are no national data comparable to those of the Campus Computing Project. It is possible, however, to get a picture of how usage of digital media has evolved by piecing together a sampling of internal university reports. Four reports were found (Indiana University—Bloomington, University of Wisconsin System, Wright State University, and City College of San Francisco), which are summarized in Figures 14 and 15.

Figure 14. Percentage of faculty using various instructional technology applications. Source: Distributed Education Committee, 2002.

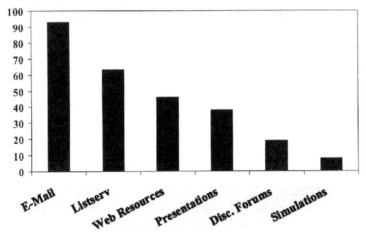

Generalizing from these selected cases, we can project that around 90 percent of all faculty exchange e-mail with students; some 60 percent use class listservs; about one-half assign the use of Web resources; upward of 40 percent show digital presentations; about 20 percent provide online discussion forums; and between 10 and 30 percent provide online simulations or lab experiments.

Figure 15, showing comparative data from 1998 and 2002, also reinforces our earlier hypothesis that the curve of adoption has slowed in recent years, as the growth rates were higher in the years before 1998. This is mentioned specifically in the City College of San Francisco (CCSF) report:

> there were significant gains in use and interest between 1997 and 1999, but the ensuing two years showed a much flatter trajectory…. There has been no increased interest in using listservs or presentation software….the use and interest in computer lab assignments and computer lab classes remained virtually unchanged. (*Research & Planning Briefs*, 2003)

Figure 15. Percentage of faculty using various instructional technology applications. Source: Achieving Excellence Accountability Report, 2003–2004.

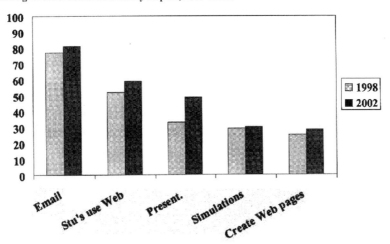

A number of other interpretations may be drawn from these findings. First, they indicate that faculty incorporation of computer media in their teaching can be viewed as a wide spectrum of adoption decisions, not a single yes–no decision. Second, consistent with earlier national survey findings, a decade after the Web became widely available to students and faculty, barely half the faculty are incorporating Web resources into their courses.

Third, it can be inferred that uses requiring a greater change from familiar practice will be incorporated less readily. Most faculty already use e-mail as a matter of daily routine, so it's not surprising that some 90 percent extend this use to their teaching. Setting up and using distribution lists requires a bit more time and effort, so use of listservs drops to the 60 percent range, and so on with the other applications shown in Figures 14 and 15. At the other end of the spectrum is the use of online simulations and lab experiments, which require considerable investment of time and special expertise, hence attracting a much lower rate of adoption.

Finally, one could hypothesize that there is an inverse correlation between adoption and likelihood of making a major impact on learning improvement. The most popular uses entail reading or viewing informational presentations, and the least popular require active engagement, negotiating understanding, and seeking patterns in complex problem-solving spaces. Small improvements in instruction come easily; major advances require greater investment of time and resources, and possibly structural change.

Course management systems. Software systems specifically designed to manage course content and course activities have become a mainstay at most colleges and universities. By 2002, more than three-quarters of all colleges and universities had adopted a standard course management system (CMS; Campus Computing Project, 2002), and by 2004 such systems could be considered to be ubiquitous. One brand, Blackboard, dominates the market. Its success in capturing this market enabled Blackboard, Inc. to become a publicly traded stock in mid-2004. Although Blackboard has become the de facto standard for CMS, a number of universities—including Indiana, Michigan, Stanford, and MIT—are working together to establish an "open source" standard to compete with the proprietary one. Their Sakai Project has the goal of enabling faculty and developers at all universities to create instructional materials that are transportable within and among universities.

The existence of a CMS motivates faculty to create content to make use of this delivery system. Having created ingenious learning activities, they want to be able to reuse them each semester and to adapt them over time. Eventually they may wish to share lessons or parts of lessons with others. These "reusable learning objects" can only be shared if they are created using standards and methods common to other users. Although few faculty are consciously aware of or interested in "reusable learning objects," they find themselves becoming creators and users of them. Thus, what has been a topic of theoretical and technical concern for a decade—without much practical payoff in higher education—is becoming a topic of urgent importance (Metros & Bennett, 2004).

Distance education. Around the time of the dot-com collapse, the most highly touted American university distance education (DE) initiatives had already crashed in flames, and in 2004 the major British effort, UK eUniversities Worldwide or UKeU, was dismantled. As further indication of the fading of the land-rush mentality, in EDUCAUSE's annual survey of top issues facing administrators, for "issues with a high potential for becoming significant in the coming year," distance education dropped from first place in 2001 to off-the-chart in 2004 (Spicer et al., 2004). Nevertheless, many more modest distance education ventures continue to grow steadily.

Of all residential four-year colleges and universities and two-year community colleges, more than two-thirds now operate distance education programs (more than 90 percent for major public universities). Among these dual-mode institutions, DE enrollments grew by an average of more than 25 percent from 2003 to 2004, according to Primary Research Group (2004). A significant finding of this survey is that the audience for such programs seems to be shifting. DE programs initially targeted such "nontraditional" niche groups as single mothers, employed adults, people with disabilities, and those living in remote areas. By 2004, these programs were becoming more fully integrated into the universities' traditional programs and now draw many students who are already enrolled in regular on-campus courses of study.

Among dual mode institutions, an operational model that appears promising is the consortium approach—having a common portal, sharing course development and marketing costs, but facilitating enrollment at any one of the participating schools. More than thirty states have formed such distance learning consortia, and some have experienced growth far above the average for individual institutions. For example, in 2003–2004 New York State's SUNY Online had more than 70,000 enrollments, an increase of 32 percent over the prior year; UMassOnline enrolled 15,000, also up 32 percent. Illinois's Virtual Campus had more than 125,000 enrollments, an increase of 54 percent.

One factor impelling universities to develop online programs is the pressure from proprietary institutions such as University of Phoenix Online and Jones International University, which have achieved enrollments larger than any individual universities, and have demonstrated that online-only universities can be profitable, a goal that is still elusive for most dual-mode institutions.

Issue 2: Constraints on Acceptance and Use of Technology

Administrative issues—funding. The financial picture of higher education was summarized by the executive director of the Western Interstate Commission for Higher Education (WICHE): "American higher education is confronting a perfect storm of more limited public resources, increasing demand, and an increasingly difficult-to-serve customer base of poor and minority students" (Symonds, 2003, p. 74). This financial climate of falling state government revenues, leading to falling state university budgets has led to more and more severe cuts to academic computing budgets. In 2003, 41 percent of all institutions reported cuts (higher for public universities), up from 33 percent in 2002 and 18 percent the year before that (Campus Computing Project, 2003).

In this time of tight budgets, administrators find themselves in an "arms race" with other colleges and universities, requiring increased investments in services such as wireless access. This is true even of the elite liberal arts colleges—all of the top liberal arts colleges are fully wired and racing to keep up with amenities offered by the competition (Smallen,

2004). Students have these digital amenities at home and expect to find them at college. Nearly 80 percent of all campuses have wireless LANs (up from 30 percent in 2000). Only a small proportion of these cover the whole campus; on average, about one-quarter of the campus has wireless access (Campus Computing Project, 2003).

"Going wireless" is just one of the current funding challenges. Institutions continue to struggle with the battle of bandwidth, attempting to keep up with the enormous traffic loads caused by student downloading of music and video. Universities are pursuing more rigorous enforcement of copyright claims, downloading quotas, and user charges in an effort to manage this problem.

With lowered incomes and rising infrastructure demands, it is not surprising that for the past two years in a row "funding information technology" has been the number one issue of concern among information technology administrators (Spicer et al., 2004). This climate obviously imposes constraints on resources available for the sorts of faculty development and technical support needed to promote deeper and wider use of technology in the teaching–learning enterprise.

Administrative issues—productivity. Closely related to the funding issue is that of achieving productivity improvements. Ultimately, any investment must be judged according to its contribution to productivity, and that includes the adoption of instructional technologies. There are several ways of measuring productivity and several ways of comparing decreased costs and increased benefits. So far, instructional technology innovations have not garnered a track record of either clearly lower cost or clearly increased student learning. One possibility is promoting the notion of indirect benefits, such as increased student satisfaction. That is, one could argue that better discussion opportunities, enhanced feedback, and easier access to updated grades improve the student's educational experience. This benefits the institution by increasing student retention and improving the whole educational climate.

There are projects, however, notably the Pew Program in Course Redesign, that have compiled an impressive track record of using technology to redesign courses that are both less expensive and more effective. The features that account for the success of these remarkable courses are familiar to instructional technologists: whole course redesign, active learning instructional methods, computer-based learning resources, a mastery learning framework, on-demand help, and alternative staffing (Twigg, 2003). These course design models could help turn the productivity argument from a constraint to an advantage.

Faculty acceptance. As discussed earlier, instructors have a tendency toward conservatism in selecting teaching methods. The burgeoning of course management systems (CMS) and administrative promotion of these systems has triggered an interesting payoff for improved teaching. Most large universities now support a primary CMS and have pressed individual instructors to at least post their syllabus and some course materials on the system. As it is now playing out, this simple adoption seems to serve as a wedge that expands to encompass more and larger changes. Professors report that they tend to use the CMS more and more extensively because they gradually see more potential uses of its features. It begins with the content presentation tools, and for some it ends there. Many users go on to make use of the discussion forums, quiz tools, and grade book. Usage of the features of the CMS has a cascading effect (Morgan, 2003). On the other hand, other professors, a minority, stop or even regress in their CMS adoption. They often resent the time required to load and reload course materials. Some find the CMS structure to be inflexible and inadaptable to their preferred teaching approach (Morgan, 2003).

Issue 3: Challenges to Existing Paradigms

Ubiquitous computer networking. Quantitative changes sometimes become qualitative changes. Over the past twenty years, the surging growth of the Internet, the relentless wiring of campus networks, and more recently the overlay of wireless networks has made virtually every higher education institution a "network of networks." This process has progressed to the point that the everyday functioning of colleges is *dependent* on the functioning of its networks. Students, faculty, and staff can no longer do their work without the campus network. This dependency signals a qualitative change: the institution has been transformed, intentionally or not (Stunden, 2004).

This transformation of the communication system has made possible the unbundling of the rights and responsibilities of the faculty, emphasizing the roles of course manager and coach and making possible the outsourcing of roles such as lesson designer–producer and information dispenser. There becomes a technological imperative to carry out the unbundling, to find the cheapest labor source for each of the constituent roles. The same is true for students (who may be affiliated with two or more colleges at a time), other staff, and administrators. People's long-held, comfortable roles are changing.

At a deeper level, technological transformation is challenging the very meaning of a college. Cyber universities such as University of Phoenix Online and Jones International University bring into question the notion of having a campus—and even of having a faculty. Institutions will have to examine deeply what their values and mission are, and they may find themselves evolving into a more diverse set of institutions than we have now. Rather than a unitary model of what a college is, there will be multiple models. The landscape could look quite different in the next generation.

K–12 EDUCATION

It would be impossible to tell the story of technology integration in K–12 education during the past year without putting it into the context of President George W. Bush's "No Child Left Behind" (NCLB) initiative, because this law has been the signature element of the federal government's education agenda since its signing in 2002 and therefore the lens through which most K–12 developments, including the use of technology, must be viewed. State and local funding for technology, already stressed by tax revenue declines, was further stressed by the diversion of funds to testing programs.

Issue 1: Use of Technology-Based Media for Delivery of Instruction

Computer-based assessment. As it happens, the focus of technology-based media in K–12 education during the past year has not been on the use of computers for instruction, but rather on the use of computers as a tool for the *assessment* of instruction. This shift in view of technology use, a direct result of the NCLB legislation, was highly controversial and became a campaign issue for the 2004 presidential election. One of the key issues in the controversy over the legislation was the major emphasis on test scores and testing processes to measure whether schools achieved "Adequate Yearly Progress" in student achievement as required by NCLB (Austin, 2004).

As might have been expected, one solution proposed to address the problems of testing for Adequate Yearly Progress was computer-based assessment and recordkeeping. The emphasis on the computer as a tool of assessment and accountability was shown by the titling of *Education Week*'s annual Technology Counts report as "Pencils Down: Technology's Answer to Testing" ("Pencils Down," 2003). This special issue included articles that explored the drivers and restrainers for computerized testing (Olson, 2003), the problems and promise of computer adaptive testing for K–12 schools (Trotter, 2003), students' use of online test-preparation materials for advanced placement tests and college-entrance exams (Borja, 2003), the role of computers in testing children with disabilities (Goldstein, 2003) and in classroom assessment (Galley, 2003), as well as the economic boon of computer-based assessment to for-profit companies that have a presence in the marketplace of education (Walsh, 2003).

Schools' needs for large-scale, high-stakes testing stimulated a vibrant commercial market. Mergers and acquisitions between K–12 education companies were up from 27 in 2002 to 34 in 2003 ("More Education Companies," 2004). To procure "eduTest," a computer-based assessment system, Plato Learning acquired Lightspan in one of the major deals of 2003. Plato Learning also acquired NetSchools Corporation, a curriculum standards management company, in 2003.

Like its for-profit counterparts, the National Center for Education Statistics (NCES) also explored the potential of computers for testing and measurement during this period. The NCES engaged in the Technology-Based Assessment (TBA) Project, the primary purpose of which was to explore how the use of computers would "enhance the quality and efficiency of educational assessments" for the National Assessment of Educational Progress (NAEP; NCES, 2004). Also known as "the Nation's Report Card," NAEP is a nationally representative assessment that has been administered periodically since 1969 to measure student performance in reading, mathematics, science, writing, history, civics, geography, and the arts. During 2003–2004, the NCES engaged in a three-phase process of pilot testing, pretesting, and field testing several components of the TBA, including assessments for math, writing, and problem solving.

The need for and consequences of accountability as defined in the NCLB legislation were hotly debated in the professional and popular literature, with a supportive position taken by Chester E. Finn Jr. and William J. Bennett in an opinion piece in the *Wall Street Journal* titled "No standards without freedom" (2003), which identified one key value of the accountability movement as its provision of "private alternatives to failing public schools" (p. A14). A rejoinder by Alfie Kohn ran in the *Kappan* (2004) titled "Test Today, Privatize Tomorrow: Using Accountability to 'Reform' Public Schools to Death," which claimed that the high-stakes testing initiative at the heart of NCLB has already begun to undermine public education.

Traditional audiovisual media. There are few sources of current information on a national level regarding the usage of noncomputer media in the schools. NICEM, which operates a national database of audio and video materials, continues in operation after more than 35 years. It has a catalog of more than 440,000 titles and adds 20,000 new titles a year. So, clearly, audiovisual materials continue to be produced and used in classrooms.

While the interests of federal-level politicians and policy makers were focused on issues of accountability and the role that computers may take in addressing accountability, the primary source of funding for media/technology centers came from local and state governments, and funding from those sources has decreased during the past two years (National Association of Media & Technology Centers [NAMTC], 2003).

The predominant media formats in the collections of members of NAMTC continue to be analog, particularly videocassettes. Their collections include (from greatest to least) videocassettes, multimedia, curriculum materials, professional books, digital video disks, and CD-ROMs. However, purchases of some types of digital media during the past two years outpaced purchases of most types of analog media. Although videocassettes still represent the greatest expenditure, expenditures for this analog medium were closely followed by expenditures for several types of digital media including Internet resources, DVDs, and multimedia.

Computer-based media. The constraints on local education spending due to the sluggish national economy were reflected in school administrators' estimates of expected spending for 2002–2003 (Market Data Retrieval, 2003). Projected technology spending for hardware, software, and staff development dropped 25 percent in one year, to $89 per student. To compare, projected technology spending was $118 per student in 2001–2002.

Four measures of leading-edge technologies in schools showed significant growth during 2003, including the presence of DVD drives, laptops, wireless networks, and high-speed Internet access (Market Data Retrieval, 2003). The presence of DVD drives in schools increased 67 percent in one year, with half of all U.S. public schools having DVD drives in the school. The number of schools using high-speed Internet connections such as T1, T3, or cable modem increased from 75 percent to 80 percent of all public schools.

Schools, like universities, are going wireless. The percentage of schools with wireless networks nearly doubled, from 15 to 27 percent. Additionally, 43 percent of schools reported having some wireless laptop computers, up 7 percent from the previous year, with the actual number of laptops in those schools averaging about 22 (Park & Staresina, 2004). The proliferation of laptops has been hampered by the downturn in state education budgets. Early in the decade, there was a boomlet in state programs to provide every student with a laptop, but that movement has stagnated with the budget crunch.

The oft-cited student-per-Internet-connected computer was 4.3:1, much improved from 5.6:1 the previous year ("Global Links," 2004). Along the way, however, the federal E-Rate program, begun in 1996 to fund computer infrastructure in poor and rural schools, has come under increasing scrutiny for its susceptibility to fraud. Many computer suppliers have sold schools equipment they did not need, overcharged them, and then even inflated the bills submitted to the government authority even further. In June 2004, the U.S. House of Representatives was engaged in an investigation of fraudulent practices in the E-Rate program, with major cases erupting in Puerto Rico and in Milwaukee, New York, and other cities. In the largest fraud case, NEC Business Network Solutions pleaded guilty and agreed to pay $21 million in fines and restitution. At least one school information technology director has been convicted of collusion in such fraud (Richtel & Rivlin, 2004). Professional organizations, including the International Society for Technology in Education (ISTE) and the Consortium for School Networking (CoSN) were obliged to undertake public relations efforts to save the E-Rate program.

Emerging digital technologies. Handheld personal computers, referred to as pocket PCs or personal digital assistants (PDAs), have progressed beyond the experimental stage to significant use in the classroom. Nationally, about 8 percent of schools provide PDAs for teachers and 4 percent provide them for students (Park & Staresina, 2004). Handhelds have been adopted on a large scale in a number of school districts and are finding "niche" purposes that they serve well. For teachers, they are especially useful for lesson preparation and classroom management, for example, taking attendance. For students, handhelds are used as digital readers and graphing calculators, for word processing and spreadsheet creation, and for specific instructional activities, such as concept mapping (ISTE, 2004).

Video games, the high-technology application that children know best, are still far from being adapted to constructive educational use. The potential is well established, but creation of appropriate software is still an extremely expensive proposition, too expensive for commercial producers to undertake in view of the small size of the market. Indeed, overall sales of educational PC software have actually been dropping in recent years. With development costs so high and potential sales so low, truly educational video games are still a distant prospect.

Teacher computer use. What do teachers *do* with the computer hardware and software to which they have access at work? In recent years Internet communication and search functions have been used at a slowly increasing rate, with the most common uses continuing to be gathering information for lesson plans, communication with colleagues, administrative record keeping, and communicating with parents (U.S. Department of Education Policy and Program Studies Service, 2003).

Directly instructional uses are less common. Although about one-half of all teachers (55 percent) report that they use computers for instructional purposes at least once a week (69 percent of elementary teachers and 43 percent of secondary teachers), those uses tend to be rather marginal. The two most popular activities assigned to students are "to improve their computer skills" and "to have free-time, as a reward." Next most popular are drill-and-practice exercises and doing word processing. More innovative activities tend to be assigned by only a small fraction of computer-using teachers, as indicated in Figure 16.

Student computer use. In fact, K–12 students primarily access and use technology *at home* rather than at school. Seventy percent of students in grades 7–12 and 57 percent of students in grades 4–6 who participated in a NetDay survey conducted in late October 2003 reported that their home was the primary access point for using technology to complete schoolwork.

Figure 16. Teachers' *frequent* use of technology with students for different instructional purposes. Source: U.S. Department of Education Policy and Program Studies Service, 2003.

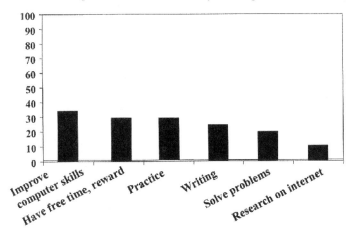

Students typically learn about new technology and Internet resources primarily from friends, parents, and through personal online exploration, rather than from a class or a teacher recommendation. The Internet tools that students use most frequently are e-mail, search engines, instant messenger, and online games. Seventy-nine percent of students in grades 7–12 have their own e-mail address, and 70 percent have instant messenger accounts. Almost half (45 percent) of students in grades 4–6 have an e-mail account, whereas 29 percent of students in grades K–3 have an e-mail account (NetDay, 2004).

When at school, students in grades 4–12 use computers predominately in a computer lab (64 percent). Students in grades 4–12 most commonly use computers at school to find information, visit class or school Web sites, and to take tests. Students in grades K–3 use technology to play learning games, create pictures, and practice spelling and reading, and these younger students primarily access technology in their own classrooms (NetDay, 2004).

Computer access is the overarching obstacle to using technology more at school, according to students who participated in the NetDay survey. Lack of time during the school day, slow Internet access time, school filters and firewalls, not enough computers in the school, and having computers that are not functional were the most frequently reported obstacles by students in grades 7–12 (NetDay, 2004).

Equity in access. The percent of Technology Literacy Challenge Funds that were apportioned to high-poverty school districts declined significantly between 1997 and 2000, with the poorest half receiving 80 percent of funds in 1997, but by 2000 the percentage of funds apportioned to this group had dropped by 30 percent to the point at which funding was equal to their proportion of the population (U.S. Department of Education, 2003).

During the 2003–2004 school year, most school districts faced stagnant or declining technology budgets, contributing to a growing gap between "have" and "have not" schools.

On the other hand, the money gap is not completely synonymous with a gap in services. A recent survey of school technology decision makers reveals that visionary leadership and local community support can influence how those funds are expended. Through careful prioritizing, some schools have been able to channel funds into activities that have helped improve teaching and learning (CoSN, 2004).

Another study showed that teachers in high-poverty schools appear to use computers differently from teachers in other schools, creating another equity gap related to technology use. Seventy percent of teachers in high-poverty schools use technology to teach basic skills and facts through drills, tutorials, and learning games, compared with 54 percent of teachers in other schools (U.S. Department of Education, 2003).

Issue 2: Constraints on Acceptance and Use of Technology

Professional development. Given that computers and the Internet are almost universally available in schools, one might assume that the challenge of technology integration is to build capacity to use these technologies for instructional purposes. Because a major key to increasing capacity is to build the technology skills of teachers, the NCLB Act of 2001 requires states to allocate 25 percent of federal technology dollars to professional development. However, only 15 percent of schools' technology budgets were spent on staff development in 2003 ("Pencils Down," 2003).

The greatest professional development need identified by teachers is for the integration of technology into instruction. Virtually all teachers say that they would be willing to engage in additional professional development on the topic of educational technology, but what they mean is learning how to integrate technology into instruction (80 percent), not just learning basic computer skills (37 percent; U.S. Department of Education, 2003).

In lieu of or in addition to professional development, teachers are using other strategies to learn about technology (see Figure 17): 95 percent report that they teach themselves to use computers; 88 percent learn from other teachers at school; 78 percent learn from family and friends; and 50 percent learn from their students. In an indication that children of the Information Age are now reaching adulthood, 13 percent of teachers say they have learned technology use from their own K–12 schooling (U.S. Department of Education, 2003).

Figure 17. How teachers learned to use technology. Source: U.S. Department of Education Policy and Program Studies Service, 2003.

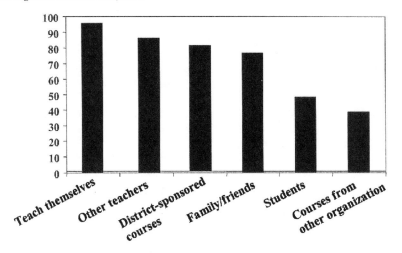

Barriers to use of technology. Time continues to be the greatest barrier to teachers' integration of technology into instructional and professional activities. Lack of time to develop activities is a constraint reported by 68 percent of teachers. Issues of access also create barriers to computer use: teachers report not having enough computers (47 percent), lack of student access to computers outside of school (46 percent), and lack of access to appropriate materials (37 percent; U.S. Department of Education, 2003).

Figure 18. Teachers' reports of barriers to use of educational technology. Source: U.S. Department of Education Policy and Program Studies Service, 2003.

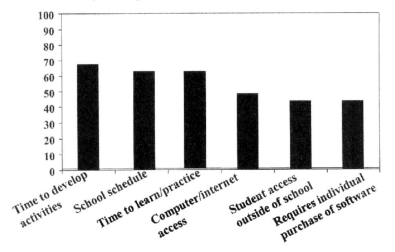

Technology support. The lack of technical support for computers is one additional barrier to teachers' integration of computers into their professional and classroom activities. Although virtually all teachers report that technology support of some sort is available to help them with computer integration, only half report that their needs for technical support are met fairly or extremely well (U.S. Department of Education, 2003). A full-time technology coordinator is present in only 16 percent of schools; a full-time teacher who also has the title of technology coordinator is present in 21 percent of schools; a district-level coordinator only is available to 17 percent of schools; and the library/media specialist serves as technology coordinator for 14 percent of schools. In all other cases, the level of technology support is informal or ad hoc ("Pencils Down," 2003).

Issue 3: Challenges to Existing Paradigms

Virtual schools. The number of states that allow virtual charter schools tripled between 2002 and 2004. In 2002, twelve states had established online high school programs (Trotter, 2002, p. 16). A year later more than 40,000 students attended approximately 2,400 publicly funded virtual schools and virtual charter schools in 37 states (Fording, 2004). "From a federal standpoint, virtual schools and distance learning is one of the top technology issues we are focused on," according to one federal official (Fording, 2004, p. 2). Some school districts are creating virtual schools to compete with for-profit competitors, because many states mandate that state funding follows students when they transfer to a charter school, thus siphoning millions of dollars out of the public schools. Public school administrators are also discovering that online classes serve several subgroups of students who have traditionally posed a challenge to regular schooling—students with emotional and behavioral disorders or health problems, students who drop out or are expelled, and pregnant or parenting students.

As the number of states allowing virtual charters schools has grown during the past two years, the number of questions and concerns about these types of schools has also grown. Concerns include isolation of students who take online classes, the lack of activity involved in virtual classes, lack of access to these classes for all students, and the policy barriers to distance learning given the historical locally controlled nature of K–12 schools (Fording, 2004). School leaders have expressed numerous questions about virtual learning environments, including the development of content, policies and management issues, technology support, as well as support for teachers and parents.

The two most fundamental concerns about virtual schools are the same concerns expressed about traditional schools: issues of cost and quality. Initial reports regarding both of these measures do not reflect favorably on virtual schools. Test results from the states of Pennsylvania and Ohio for 2003 show that virtual school students scored below state averages on a majority of proficiency tests, did not meet state standards, and did not match the achievement levels of their peers attending traditional schools (Gartner, 2004a).

Regarding comparative costs, virtual schools do not appear to be much cheaper to operate than traditional schools, even though virtual schools do not require expenditures for the physical infrastructure required by traditional schools (Gartner, 2004b). Despite having a ratio of between 40 and 50 students to one teacher, the for-profit virtual school Connections Academy has lost money in Florida. A vice president of for-profit K12 Virtual Academy estimates that states need to allocate approximately $5,000 per student to adequately support virtual schools and at that level of funding, "the profit is in the curriculum" (p. 1). Legislators and education departments in several states, including Florida, Ohio, Idaho, and Pennsylvania, have questioned the amounts that for-profit companies charge to operate schools and want more oversight authority regarding how funding for virtual schools is spent by these for-profit companies (Gartner, 2004b).

Some educators have expressed concerns about the close relationships between the nonprofit school boards that oversee the schools and the for-profit companies that manage school budgets because "none of the states with virtual schools prevent board members from having ties to school-management companies or even from serving in dual roles" (Gartner, 2004b, p. 3). As discussed previously in this chapter, Kohn (2004) expressed a similar concern in his rejoinder to Finn and Bennett about the relationships between education officials and for-profit companies at the federal level, arguing that the emphasis on assessment by education officials in the Bush administration masked the administration's goal of privatizing public education. Kohn's cynicism regarding Bennett's own motives seems to be justified, given that Bennett (who was the secretary of education for George H. W. Bush) founded and is on the board of directors of K12, one of the for-profit virtual academies that has been the focus of state legislators' concerns regarding cost accounting for virtual schools.

Effectiveness of technology. The emphasis on accountability coupled with tight state budgets has led administrators and policy makers in education back to the question of return on investment for technology expenditures. Meta-analyses of the effects of technology by McCabe and Skinner (2003); by Waxman, Lin, and Michko (2003); and by Kulik (2003) indicate small but positive effects on student achievement of various types of technology, for example, computer-simulated frog dissection, interactive CD-ROM storybooks, computer-based basic skills development, and the Plato Learning System.

Although there appears to be some positive effect on learning from the use of computer technologies, this association is tenuous at best, and those who are looking for evidence of a positive effect between educational technology and student achievement must continue the search. Some technology proponents, however, are beginning to question whether evidence of this association really matters (McCabe & Skinner, 2003), noting that educational researchers are not looking for positive effects of other technologies such as books and pencils on achievement. There are other benefits of technology integration (such as increased employment opportunities for students with computer skills), and technology can influence teachers and students in ways other than achievement, such as student engagement and school climate.

NCLB and the new National Educational Technology Plan. The NCLB legislation mandated the development of a new National Educational Technology Plan to "inform and guide policymakers in their efforts to ensure that schools will be able to use technology to support high-quality teaching and learning for all students" (Culp, Honey, & Mandinach, 2003). U.S. Department of Education policymakers in the Office of Educational Technology spent a fair amount of time in 2003 working to develop that plan, which is likely to shape the direction of education technology integration efforts at the federal and state levels for some years to come. In a report commissioned to contribute to the development of the new National Educational Technology Plan, Culp et al. (2003) summarize what they believe should be the focus of educational technology policy in the near future:

> educational technologists have begun to understand with more nuance that technology needs to work in concert with other factors like effective leadership, instructional priorities, and the day-to-day demands of classroom practice. The most recent policy reports begin to address these needs, and are once again placing technology in the context of broader educational challenges that are of immediate concern to educators and which technology may be well positioned to address, such as the need to make productive use of assessment data; to provide increasingly individualized and flexible but sustained and substantive professional development; and to create administrative efficiencies that support educators in day-to-day work with students and colleagues. These are some of the most promising links between education and technology. (p. 22)

To summarize, this planning document emphasizes the use of technology to facilitate assessment, professional development, and administrative efficiency. We have already noted the increasing role of technology in education assessment. If the Office of Educational Technology takes on the additional priorities of efficiency and professional development in the next National Educational Technology Plan, it appears that the next phase of technology integration in education will focus on administrative support rather than on teaching and learning.

CONCLUSION

During the period covered in this review, schools, colleges, and businesses were still suffering from the budget exigencies inflicted by the recession of 2000–2003. Corporate training budgets actually contracted two years in a row. In schools and colleges, many information technology operations absorbed budget cuts, although the majority managed to avoid service reductions. Information technology infrastructure continued to expand nevertheless, so that access to networks became virtually ubiquitous.

On the other hand, instructional use of ICT advanced at a decreasing pace, a trend that has been notable for about three years. Use of traditional audiovisual media has been stagnant for a decade, while use of digital media is growing, but slowly—a few percent a year. Growth in instructional use of digital media was a bit faster in the corporate domain, but slower in the higher education domain.

Put together, these trends tell us that pervasive access to information technology infrastructure does not guarantee its use in teaching. Infrastructure is a necessary, but not a sufficient, condition for use. Human factors such as resistance to practices that require new ways of working and the need for specialized training impinge on trainers', teachers', and professors' use of ICT. Because of these human factors, as they play out in training and education, it is inevitable that technology use lags behind technology availability.

REFERENCES

Achieving Excellence Accountability Report 2003–2004. (2004). Madison: University of Wisconsin System. Retrieved June 4, 2004, from http://www. uwsa.edu/opar/achieve04/ae04.pdf

Austin, A. (2004, April 8). Will "failing" schools trip Bush campaign? *The Christian Science Monitor*, pp. 11.

Borja, R. (2003, May 8). Prepping for the big test. Technology Counts 2003. *Education Week, XXII*(35), 23–26.

Campus Computing Project. (2002). *Campus portals make progress; technology budgets suffer significant cuts.* Retrieved June 24, 2004, from http://www. campuscomputing.net/

Campus Computing Project. (2003). *Campus policies address digital content and copyright; wireless networks show big gains.* Retrieved May 21, 2004, from http://www.campuscomputing.net/summaries/2003/index.html

Consortium for School Networking. (2004). *Digital leadership divide.* Washington, DC: Author. Retrieved June 24, 2004, from http://www.cosn.org/resources/grunwald/digital_leadership_divide.pdf

Culp, K., Honey, M., & Mandinach, E. (2003). *A retrospective on twenty years of education technology policy.* Washington, DC: U.S. Department of Education, Office of the Educational Technology. Retrieved April 20, 2004, from http://www.nationaledtechplan.org/participate/20years.pdf

Distributed Education Committee. (2002). *Distributed Education at Indiana University Bloomington.* Retrieved November 8, 2003, from http://www.iub. edu/~bfc/BFC/circulars/02-03/B13-2003.htm

Finn, C. E., & Bennett, W. J. (2003, December 23). No standards without freedom. *Wall Street Journal*, pp. A14.

Fording, L. (2004, March 30). Education, 21st century-style. *Newsweek.* Retrieved April 7, 2004, from http://msnbc.msn.com/id/4633126/

Galagan, P. (2003, December). The future of the profession formerly known as training. *T+D, 57*(12), 26–38.

Galley, M. (2003, May 8). The teacher's new test. Technology Counts 2003. *Education Week, XXII*(35), 31–33.

Galvin, T. (2003, October). 2003 industry report. *Training,* 21–45.

Gartner, J. (2004a, March 15). Sketchy grades for cyber schools. *Wired.* Retrieved April 7, 2004, from http://www.wired.com/news/print/0,1294,62662,00. html

Gartner, J. (2004b, April 1). Virtual-school costs under siege. *Wired.* Retrieved April 7, 2004, from http://www.wired.com/news/print/0,1294,62890,00. html

Global links: Lessons from the world. Technology Counts 2004 report. (2004, May 6). *Education Week* XXIII(35).

Goldstein, L. (2003, May 8). Spec. ed. Tech sparks ideas. Technology Counts 2003. *Education Week, XXII*(35), 27–29.

International Society for Technology in Education. (2004). *Pocket PC computers—A complete resource for classroom teachers.* Washington, DC: Author.

Jenny, N. W. (2004, June). *State tax revenue recovery gathering steam.* Fiscal Studies Program, No. 6. Albany, NY: Nelson A. Rockefeller Institute of Government.

Kohn, A. (2004, April). Test today, privatize tomorrow: Using accountability to "reform" public schools to death. *Phi Delta Kappan, 85*(8), 569–577.

Kulik, J. A. (2003). *Instructional technology and school reform models.* Ann Arbor: University of Michigan Office of Evaluations and Examinations. Retrieved April 5, 2004, from http://www.plato.com/downloads/papers/ paper_meta-analysis.pdf

Market Data Retrieval. (2003). *Technology in Education, 2003.* Market Data Retrieval. Retrieved May 3, 2004, from http://www.schooldata.com/mdrtechhilites.asp

McCabe, M., & Skinner, R. (2003, May 8). Analyzing the tech effect. Technology Counts 2003. *Education Week, XXII*(35), 50–52.

Metros, S. E., & Bennett, K. A. (2004, May 25). Learning objects in higher education: The sequel. *EDUCAUSE Center for Applied Research (ECAR) Research Bulletin.*

Molenda, M. (2004). Issues and trends in instructional technology: Bad economy slows technology investment. In M. Orey, M. A. Fitzgerald, & R. M. Branch (Eds.), *Educational media and technology yearbook 2004* (Vol. 29). Englewood, CO: Libraries Unlimited.

Molenda, M., & Pershing, J. A. (2004, March–April). The strategic impact model: An integrative approach to performance improvement (PI) and instructional systems design (ISD). *TechTrends, 48*(2), 26–33.

Molenda, M., & Sullivan, M. (2002). Issues and trends in instructional technology: Hitting the plateau. In M. A. Fitzgerald, M. Orey, & R. M. Branch (Eds.), *Educational media and technology yearbook 2002* (Vol. 27). Englewood, CO: Libraries Unlimited.

Molenda, M., & Sullivan, M. (2003). Issues and trends in instructional technology: Treading water. In M. A. Fitzgerald, M. Orey, & R. M. Branch (Eds.), *Educational media and technology yearbook 2003* (Vol. 28). Englewood, CO: Libraries Unlimited.

More education companies playing "let's make a deal." (2004, April 14). *Education Week, 24,* pp. 8.

Morgan, G. (2003, May). *Faculty use of course management systems.* EDUCAUSE Center for Applied Research. Retrieved May 3, 2004, from http://www.educause.edu/asp/doclib/abstract.asp?ID=ERS0302

National Association of Media & Technology Centers. (2003). *Bi-annual membership survey results.* Retrieved March 16, 2004, from http://www.namtc.org/pages/member_survey_all.html

National Center for Education Statistics. (2004, April 22). *Technology-Based Assessment Project.* Retrieved April 15, 2004, from http://nces.ed.gov/nationsreportcard/studies/tbaproject.asp

NetDay. (2004, March). Voices and views of today's tech-savvy students: National report of NetDay Speak Up Day for Students 2003. Retrieved April 18, 2004, from http://www.netday.org/speakupday2003_report.htm

Olson, L. (2003, May 8). Legal twists, digital turns. Technology Counts 2003. *Education Week, XXII*(35), 11–15.

Park, J., & Staresina, L. N. (2004, May 6). *Education Week.* Retrieved June 7, 2004, from http://www.edweek.org/sreports/tc04/article.cfm?slug=35tracking. h23

Pencils down: Technology's answer to testing. Technology Counts 2003 report (2003, May 8). *Education Week, XXII*(35).

Primary Research Group. (2004). *The Survey of Distance & Cyberlearning Programs in Higher Education,* 2004 edition. New York: Author.

Research & Planning Briefs. (2003, January 27). San Francisco: City College of San Francisco. Retrieved May 28, 2004, from http://www.ccsf.edu/Offices/ Research_Planning/pdf/brf01273.pdf

Richtel, M., & Rivlin, G. (2004, May 28) NEC unit admits it defrauded schools. *New York Times,* pp. C1, C7.

Smallen, D. L. (2004, January/February). A liberal arts IT odyssey. *EDUCAUSE Review*, 29–41.

Spicer, D. Z., DeBlois, P. B., & the EDUCAUSE Current Issues Committee. (2004) Fifth annual EDUCAUSE survey identifies current IT issues. *EDUCAUSE Quarterly, 27*(2), 1–23.

Stunden, A. (2004, May). The network: Enterprise technology underpinning. *Syllabus, 18,* 26.

Symonds, W. C. (2003, April 28). Colleges in Crisis. *Business Week,* 72–78.

Trotter, A. (2002, May 9). E-learning goes to school. *Education Week,* 13–18.

Trotter, A. (2003, May 8). A question of direction. Technology Counts 2003. *Education Week, XXII*(35), 17–21.

Twigg, C. A. (2003, September/October). Improving learning and reducing costs: New models for on-line learning. *EDUCAUSE Review*.

U.S. Department of Education, Office of the Under Secretary, Policy and Program Studies Service. (2003). *Federal funding for educational technology and how it is used in the classroom: A summary of findings from the Integrated Studies of Educational Technology.* Washington, DC. Retrieved April 18, 2004, from http://www.ed.gov/rschstat/eval/tech/iset/summary2003.pdf

Walsh, M. (2003, May 8). Marketing to the test. Technology Counts 2003. *Education Week, XXII*(35), 35–38.

Waxman, H. C., Lin, M. F., & Michko, G. M. (2003). *A meta-analysis of the effectiveness of teaching and learning with technology on student outcomes.* Naperville, IL: Learning Point Associates. Retrieved May 12, 2004, from http://www.ncrel.org/tech/effects2/waxman.pdf

"Learning through Design" as a Strategy for Faculty Development: Lessons Learned in a Teacher Education Setting

Wayne Nelson and Dave S. Knowlton
Southern Illinois University Edwardsville

Across the academy, preparing faculty members to teach is a pressing need. A doctoral degree in a discipline does not necessarily prepare a faculty member to teach effectively in that discipline (Soder, 1996). We extend Soder's point to note that faculty members also may be unprepared to deal with areas related to teaching, such as the design of curriculum or the development of instructional materials. In most disciplines, new faculty members tend to deal with these issues by recalling their own graduate school experience. That is, they teach the way that they were taught, and they develop curriculum and materials that are markedly similar to those that they encountered in their own doctoral programs. "Teach the way you were taught" may have been a useful heuristic at one time, but as society moves further from the Industrial Age and deeper into the Information Age, curriculum goals, course materials, and pedagogy must change to reflect the evolving demands of the workplace (Knowlton, 2003). In our situation within a school of education, changing the ways that new teachers are trained requires a change among faculty members who prepare these preservice teachers for practice.

We begin this chapter by explaining why traditional approaches to faculty development often are problematic in helping faculty members improve their skills and capabilities. Then we describe one approach for overcoming some of these problems, namely, principles of a "Learning through Design" model, and we offer a detailed account of how our institution is using these principles to organize the professional development of faculty members. We conclude by reporting some of the potential problems of the "Learning through Design" model as a faculty development initiative, and we make recommendations to other faculty development administrators who plan on adopting this model in their own faculty development efforts.

PROBLEMS WITH TRADITIONAL FACULTY DEVELOPMENT

Because of the need for faculty to improve teaching skills, universities often provide a wide variety of faculty development opportunities. Traditional faculty development approaches are sometimes problematic, however. For example, faculty members have few incentives and little time to invest in professional development efforts (Weiss, Knowlton, & Knowlton, 2000). Even when they take the time to participate, faculty members sometimes establish roadblocks that impede the success of faculty development activities (Sigsbee & Speck, 1999). Or worse, some faculty members may feel that pedagogical development (or technology integration) is not worth the effort because, in the words of one faculty member, "teaching is like breathing" (Weiss et al., 2000). Even when faculty members recognize the scholarship of teaching and its difficulties (Boyer, 1990), they often are pulled in other directions because scholarly activities involving research and publishing are valued more highly at many academic institutions.

Another reason that traditional approaches to faculty development are often problematic is because workshops and seminars tend to be isolated, generic, and decontextualized. Rarely do faculty development specialists provide scaffolding to prepare faculty for the workshops, and the cost of follow-up support is usually prohibitive. Isolation and decontextualization is heightened over time when one faculty development seminar or workshop is unrelated to the next—or at least the same faculty members do not attend each workshop. Finally, the models of instruction used for many faculty development efforts are not conducive to helping faculty members change their approach to teaching and technology integration. How many times have you seen "workshops" where someone lectures and demonstrates how, for example, a spreadsheet might be used to create a simulation, and the workshop facilitator finishes by saying, "Now go use this tool in your classes with your students"?

LEARNING THROUGH DESIGN AND THE DESIGN STUDIO

Because of the problems with traditional faculty development, a new approach to faculty development was implemented as described here. With the luxury of extensive resources and personnel provided through a Preparing Tomorrow's Teachers to Use Technology grant (PT3), the model for faculty development was organized around the metaphor of design studios, employing principles of Learning through Design (Davis, 1998; Mishra, Koehler, Hershey, & Peruski, 2001) as a means of helping faculty members integrate technology into their teaching. Through integrating technology, these faculty members also would be effectively modeling technology integration strategies for students. In this section, we describe the theoretical underpinnings of Learning through Design and design studios. In the next section, we describe our application of Learning through Design as a faculty development initiative.

Design has been described as the search for solutions to unstructured and "wicked" problems (Rittel, 1984). These problems are solved through a systematic approach of creating artifacts to achieve emergent goals that are continually generated and refined throughout the design process (Lawson, 1990; Malhotra, Thomas, Carroll, & Miller, 1980; Mayer, 1989; Newell & Simon, 1972). Others view design as an experiential learning process by which an individual constructively shapes the problem and solution through cycles of situated action and reflection (Schon, 1991; Suchman, 1987). When viewed as a social process, however, design becomes a collaborative activity in which conversation, argumentation, and persuasion are used to achieve consensus about perspectives and actions that might be taken to solve a design problem (Lave & Wenger, 1991; Stumpf & McDonnell, 1999). With this view, the design process involves both shared and distributed cognition (Lanzara, 1983); through conversation and representations, the design team develops a shared understanding of the problem. Because of the power of shared cognition, the design team is more likely to reach a viable solution through their individual and collaborative efforts (Hutchins, 1991; Walz, Elam, & Curtis, 1993).

Design is increasingly seen as an activity that can be used to facilitate learning in a variety of content areas and contexts (Perkins, 1986). Design tasks support a kind of learning-on-demand, where learning goals emerge from the situation at hand, rather than being contrived by a teacher and presented through an artificial context (Nelson, 2003). Designers collaborate in diverse ways during design tasks and often are required to reflect on where they are and where they are going. As a result, new opportunities for inquiry, participation, and conversation occur as the design process unfolds. In this respect, design supports self-organized learning for both individuals and groups (Thomas & Harri-Augstein, 1985). Learners must accept responsibility for their own learning by identifying their own purposes, setting goals for learning, implementing learning strategies, and identifying appropriate resources and tools (Fiedler, 1999). From students learning through the design and production of multimedia (e.g., Kahn & Taber Ullah, 1998) to students learning science by constructing and testing solutions to problems (e.g., Harel & Papert, 1991), project-based and problem-based learning that incorporate design tasks have become effective models for promoting learning.

To organize and manage Learning through Design activities, educators have adopted the model of design studios common in the practices of the visual arts, architecture, and other fields that emphasize design (Orey, Rieber, King, & Matzko, 2000). Studios provide an open learning environment where participants use design tools and processes to complete various real world—and often self-selected—projects. In most studios, participants make regularly scheduled presentations of their work in progress. These presentations allow participants to give each other suggestions and constructive criticisms of the design process and resulting artifacts. This collaborative atmosphere lends itself well to the self-organized and self-paced learning that occurs in studio design activities. Facilitators can help participants establish individual and small-group goals through the use of performance contracts (Rieber, 2000). The facilitator can also moderate peer critiques, where participants offer feedback to their peers. When asked, the facilitator may even offer assistance and critique.

LEARNING THROUGH DESIGN AS FACULTY DEVELOPMENT

Learning through Design supports many of the principles of adult learning recognized by various theorists (see Knowles, 1989); therefore, it can be easily adapted to faculty professional development efforts. For readers to understand our application of Learning through Design as a faculty development initiative, we describe the context in which we applied Learning through Design principles. Then, we describe the process of engaging faculty in design projects. Finally, we offer two examples of projects being developed by design teams.

Faculty Development Context

The Learning through Design model was employed within the School of Education at Southern Illinois University, Edwardsville as part of our PT3 program efforts. Specifically, Learning through Design was used by teams of faculty members who were involved in a two-year, field-based certification program that was delivered completely at partnership schools. The primary responsibility of the faculty members was to supervise preservice teachers who assisted inservice teachers in K–12 classrooms. These faculty members also delivered weekly content seminars where preservice teachers were given opportunities to discuss various theories and methods. "Courses" were nonexistent. Instead, various content areas such as educational psychology, educational foundations, special education, along with general and discipline-specific methods classes, were completely integrated across the two-year program. Preservice teachers prepared portfolios to demonstrate their growth and competence in standards set by state and national certification and accreditation agencies.

We felt the design studio model was particularly appropriate for our faculty development goals for several reasons. First, the faculty participants possessed varying levels of skill development with respect to technology utilization and integration. Second, the faculty participants were already organized as teams to deliver the teacher education program at partnership schools. Therefore, they had developed a high degree of camaraderie and were accustomed to collaborating. Third, a small core of faculty members who were highly skilled and experienced with various learning technologies were available to act as facilitators, or "lead designers" for each team. (The second author of this chapter is one of these lead designers.)

Implementation Process

We needed to implement our PT3 faculty development activities to meet several goals. First, we sought to assist our teacher education faculty members to develop the skills necessary to model technology integration strategies effectively for the preservice teachers whom they supervised. Second, we needed to provide faculty development opportunities that would ultimately allow faculty members to design effective learning activities to support the goals of our teacher education partnership programs.

Our implementation of the Faculty Technology Design Studio was designed to meet these goals. The Faculty Technology Design Studio process began by inviting faculty from the School of Education and the College of Arts and Sciences to attend a kickoff meeting where the Design Studio concept was shared, along with information related to the Illinois teacher certification standards for technology integration and utilization. Eight design facilitators and three project staff members, all of whom were members of the School of Education faculty and highly successful with technology integration, were called on to facilitate the design studio activities as "lead designers." They challenged the thirty-seven faculty participants to identify opportunities for technology integration in their teaching activities, especially activities that might model appropriate practices or help preservice teachers meet some of the new state certification standards. After much collaboration and discussion, more than fifteen design projects were identified and described in written "design briefs," produced either by individuals or by small groups of faculty who shared similar visions for technology integration.

Following the kickoff meeting, PT3 grant staff and administrators reviewed the design briefs to identify available technologies and determine support personnel that could be assigned to assist with the design projects. The PT3 grant staff also offered informal feedback to each team's lead designer, who continued meeting with the faculty participants to refine and elaborate the designs. Based on this feedback, each team designed, developed, and implemented a technology-based project within the context of their partnership schools.

Example Projects

In the confines of a short chapter, we cannot provide an overview of all fifteen projects, so two projects that exemplify the diverse strategies that were designed to integrate technology will be highlighted. First, one team of faculty worked with preservice teachers to design and publish a research journal focused on teaching activities within the partnership school. Each preservice teacher was required to submit at least three manuscripts for the journal, and the inservice teachers and university faculty served as editors for the journal. An online article submission system was developed, along with facilities for editors to communicate with students regarding revisions to the manuscripts. In addition, an artist worked with the editorial staff to create graphics for the journal, which was published as a traditional paper product, as well as in an electronic version.

In another Design Studio project, a team of faculty developed Web-based instruction designed to explore various concepts of educational psychology and educational foundations. Inservice teachers were videotaped as they taught their K–12 students. Faculty members then prepared content that elaborated on the principles being illustrated by the video cases. Preservice teachers were able to access the video cases through the Web, participating in asynchronous discussions about the cases, as well as submitting their own analyses of the cases. In addition, the inservice teachers shown in the video and university faculty were participants in the discussions, allowing preservice teachers to ask questions about the video cases and, presumably, identifying issues for further learning and discussion. These are two examples of the many design projects currently being completed. Faculty are participating not merely as designers but also as developers wherever possible, thereby increasing their technology skills while working on something of utility for their teaching and their students' learning.

LESSONS LEARNED AND ADVICE FOR OTHERS

At the time of writing, the two-year cycle of our teacher education partnership curriculum has not ended, and the design projects are at various stages of completion and implementation. Therefore, formative evaluation of this faculty development initiative is ongoing. Informally, though, we have been pleased with the results, while acknowledging some shortcomings in our application of Learning through Design. From these shortcomings, we offer recommendations for improving a "Learning through Design" faculty development initiative.

Involve All Partnership Personnel

As faculty teams determine the direction of their design projects, they should actively strive to involve both preservice teachers and inservice teachers (not to mention school-site administrators) in the design process. To ignore the need for creating broad involvement among stakeholders is to deprive some of these stakeholders of the opportunity to experience the design process fully. For example, the team designing video case studies delivered the project to preservice teachers as a multimedia, Web-based video. By using this video, preservice teachers see that faculty members have developed multimedia instruction, but the students have learned little about the process of developing the multimedia. These preservice teachers have seen the products of integration, but not the processes that led to the integration.

One way that we intend to overcome this potential problem is to have faculty members serve as lead designers for both the preservice and inservice teachers as they solve design problems of their own. That is, right now, faculty members are learning about design by becoming designers. As these projects culminate, we will urge these faculty members to engage the preservice and inservice teachers that they serve in design projects. With this tactic, we are hoping that the inservice teachers will be inspired to engage their K–12 students in design projects as well. This trickle down effect ultimately will involve all levels—from university faculty through K–12 students—in the Learning through Design process.

Provide Participant Incentives

Earlier we mentioned some drawbacks of traditional faculty development models. We suggested that lack of time and incentive often lead university faculty members to avoid faculty development opportunities. To some extent, the Learning through Design model overcomes these barriers. Because the design of the project is shared across a team, the workload is divided. Similarly, we believe—and our informal conversations with participating faculty confirm—collaborative efforts are more motivating and educational. Thus, the opportunity to work within a team is an incentive. Also, because the projects met a real need related to curriculum development, incentives for faculty members to participate may have been higher.

Despite improvement in these areas, we see the need to increase incentives even more if the cost of design is to be worth the benefits. Some evidence suggests, for example, that many faculty members invested a large amount of time in the design projects and suggested the need for release time to design and implement the projects efficiently. In addition, the need for design teams to develop a shared vision for the project increases the amount of time they must invest.

Perhaps opportunities for release time are an incentive; however, monetary support (salary or "in-kind" resources) provide powerful incentives, particularly for well-conceived and ambitious design projects. Administrators should also help faculty participants understand the possibility for publishing and research opportunities related to their design projects. Perhaps most important, faculty development administrators should communicate the viability of design projects to administrators at all levels, from department chairs to chief academic officers. As a result, design projects are more likely to be treated with seriousness in tenure and promotion applications. Creating buy-in among administrators provides additional incentives for faculty members to pursue design with a seriousness of purpose and a high degree of scholarly integrity.

Scaffold Progress and Celebrate Success

Many of the design teams worked well together and were easily able to meet design and development deadlines. Other design teams were not as successful. One way to overcome this problem might be to have lead designers assist team members with developing time lines and devise an effective division of labor among team members. Lead designers also might facilitate a continued narrowing of the scope of the design project. Faculty development administrators should also keep open lines of communication with the lead designers and team members to solicit feedback and information by e-mail or electronic bulletin board. Furthermore, administrators can provide opportunities for collaboration and the sharing of ideas across design teams.

Part of scaffolding the progress of design teams is to provide opportunities to celebrate successful design and implementation of projects. To this end, administrators might sponsor a "showcase," where K–12 students, preservice teachers, inservice teachers, and university faculty come together to demonstrate and share the results of their design activities. A secondary benefit of such a showcase would be to provide opportunities for faculty members who did not participate to see the results of the faculty development initiative. These nonparticipating faculty might be more likely to participate in the future once they have taken part in the showcase as a spectator.

Evaluation of Projects and Assessment of Designs

We believe in the virtues of Learning through Design, and we argue that faculty who are engaged in design processes will develop new knowledge and skills. Still, administrators would do well to assess faculty participants' growth as a result of the design initiative. We suggest a multilevel evaluation that not only evaluates outcomes—new knowledge and skills—but also that assesses social processes and faculty members' opinions of the faculty development initiative. Faculty development administrators should concern themselves with optimal learning environments. By evaluating the social processes as well as outcomes and opinions, new information can be gained about the best way to integrate future Learning through Design initiatives.

Not only faculty members' knowledge, skills, and attitudes should be assessed, but the actual design projects as well. That is, each design team should evaluate the degree to which the design process and resulting artifacts actually solved the original problem articulated by faculty members in their design briefs. Such an evaluation should include data from the intended audience of the designed artifacts. For example, the team that designed the education journal might survey preservice teacher participants about their attitudes toward writing the journal articles. These preservice teachers might also be asked to share their opinions about the degree to which the writing of articles actually changed their "practice" in the classroom.

CONCLUSION

We have described how our institution implemented a Learning through Design faculty development initiative. Based on our experiences, we have made recommendations to other faculty development administrators who may have an interest in implementing a Learning through Design approach. Inherent to our perspective is the idea that faculty members should be provided autonomy to pursue their own interests in design projects. It is the role of faculty development administrators to frame those pursuits in ways that will allow faculty members to achieve success. We hope the experiences chronicled here will provide a basis for such efforts.

REFERENCES

Boyer, E. L. (1990). *Scholarship reconsidered: Priorities of the professoriate.* Princeton, NJ: Carnegie Foundation for the Advancement of Teaching.

Davis, M. (1998). Making a case for design-based learning. *Arts Education Policy Review, 100*(2), 7–14.

Fiedler, H. S. D. (1999). *The studio experience: Challenges and opportunities for self-organized learning.* Retrieved January 19, 2005, from http://itech1.coe.uga.edu/studio/fiedler.html

Harel, I., & Papert, S. (Eds.). (1991). *Constructionism.* Norwood, NJ: Ablex.

Hutchins, E. (1991). The technology of team navigation. In L. B. Resnick, J. M. Levine, & S. D. Teasley (Eds.), *Perspectives on socially shared cognition* (pp. 283–307). Washington, DC: American Psychological Association.

Kahn, T. M., & Taber Ullah, L. N. (1998). *Learning by design: Integrating technology into the curriculum through student multimedia design projects.* Tucson, AZ: Zephyr Press.

Knowles, M. (1989). *On becoming an adult educator.* San Francisco: Jossey-Bass.

Knowlton, D. S. (2003). Preparing students for educated living: The virtues of problem-based learning across the higher education curriculum. In D. S. Knowlton & D. C. Sharp (Eds.), *Problem-Based learning in the information age* (pp. 5–12). San Francisco: Jossey-Bass.

Lanzara, G. F. (1983). The design process: Frames, metaphors and games. In U. Briefs, C. Ciborra, & L. Schneider (Eds.), *Systems design for, with and by the users.* Amsterdam: North-Holland.

Lave, J., & Wenger, E. (1991). *Situated learning: Legitimate peripheral participation.* Cambridge, MA: Cambridge University Press.

Lawson, B. (1990). *How designers think* (2nd ed.). London: Architectural Press.

Malhotra, A., Thomas, J., Carroll, J., & Miller, L. (1980). Cognitive processes in design. *International Journal of Man-Machine Studies, 12*, 119–140.

Mayer, R. E. (1989). Human nonadversary problem-solving. In K. J. Gilhjooley (Ed.), *Human and machine problem-solving.* New York: Plenum.

Mishra, P., Koehler, M. J., Hershey, K., & Peruski, L. (2001, November). Learning through design: Faculty development and on-line course development. Paper presented at the Seventh Sloan-C International Conference on Online Learning: Emerging Standards of Excellence in Asynchronous Learning Networks, Orlando, FL.

Nelson, W. (2003). Problem solving through design. In D. S. Knowlton & D. C. Sharp (Eds.), *Problem-based learning in the information age* (pp. 39–44). San Francisco: Jossey-Bass.

Newell, A., & Simon, H. A. (1972). *Human problem solving.* Englewood Cliffs, NJ: Prentice Hall.

Orey, M., Rieber, L., King, J., & Matzko, M. (2000, April). *The studio: Curriculum reform in an instructional technology graduate program.* Paper presented at the annual meeting of the American Educational Research Association, New Orleans, LA.

Perkins, D. N. (1986). *Knowledge as design.* Hillsdale, NJ: Erlbaum.

Rieber, L. P. (2000). The studio experience: Educational reform in instructional technology. In D. G. Brown (Ed.), *Best practices in computer enhanced teaching and learning* (pp. 195–196). Winston-Salem, NC: Wake Forest Press.

Rittel, H. W. (1984). Second-generation design methods. In N. Cross (Ed.), *Developments in design methodologies.* Chichester, UK: Wiley.

Schon, D. (1991). *The reflective practitioner: How professionals think in action.* New York: Teacher's College Press.

Sigsbee, D. L., & Speck, B. W. (1999). The generative process in faculty development activities. *Perspectives, 29*(1), 41–66.

Soder, R. (1996). Teaching the teachers of the people. In R. Soder (Ed.), *Democracy, education, and the schools* (pp. 244–274). San Francisco: Jossey-Bass.

Suchman, L. (1987). *Plans and situated actions: The problem of human/machine communication.* New York: Cambridge University Press.

Stumpf, S. C., & McDonnell, J. T. (1999, April). Relating argument to design problem framing. Proceedings of the 4th Design Thinking Research Symposium, Cambridge, MA.

Thomas, L., & Harri-Augstein, S. (1985). *Self-organised learning.* London: Routledge.

Walz, D., Elam, J., & Curtis, B. (1993). Inside a design team: Knowledge acquisition, sharing and integration. *Communications of the ACM, 36*(10), 63–77.

Weiss, R. E., Knowlton, D. S., & Knowlton, H. M. (2000, November). *Faculty attitudes and understandings about online learning technologies.* Paper presented at the annual meeting of the Mid-South Educational Research Association, Bowling Green, KY.

Workplace Cultures: Preparing Instructional Designers for Varied Career Environments

Miriam B. Larson and Barbara B. Lockee
Virginia Polytechnic Institute and State University

Those who practice the art and science of instructional design are being prepared through an ever-increasing variety of academic disciplines. It seems that everyone is jumping on the bandwagon, incorporating instructional design preparation programs, tracks, or courses in their programs of instructional systems and technology, educational psychology, human performance technology, training and development, human resource development, organizational development, and information technology, to name the most common.

Graduates from these programs compete for jobs in a variety of career environments, including higher education, business and industry, K–12 education, government and military, health care, nonprofit, and more. To add to the competition for jobs, more and more individuals are obtaining training and certifications from corporate universities, professional organizations, and private companies. How can traditional instructional design and technology (IDT) programs distinguish their graduates and prepare them to compete in this ever-expanding market? One way is to customize the preparation for the career environment or work place where the student intends to practice instructional design. How should programs seek to customize preparation? They can focus on ways to incorporate the *context* and the *culture* of the intended career environment into the instruction.

CONTEXT

The idea of "context" gained increased attention from the instructional design community in the years following 1989, when Brown, Collins, and Duguid introduced educators to the concept of situated learning. They submitted that many traditional teaching practices result in inert or unusable knowledge, or the inability of students to use what they know in relevant situations. Brown et al., (1989) argued that learners are often unable to solve complex, real-world problems because they have learned rules and algorithms in school in a de-contextualized way: "To learn to use tools as practitioners use them, a student, like an apprentice, must enter that community and its culture. Thus, in a significant way learning is . . . a process of enculturation" (p. 33).

Context is, then, an essential element of situated learning (Driscoll, 2002), and it can be defined as the "whole situation, background or environment that is relevant to a particular event," (Tessmer & Richey, 1997, p. 87). A learning system context consists of "those situational elements that affect both the acquisition and application of newly acquired knowledge, skills or attitudes" (p. 87). Learning and performance are embedded in contextual factors such as political or physical factors of the support environment, the social interaction, and the interaction of cultural factors (Driscoll, 2002), and all these factors interact to influence learning (Tessmer & Richey, 1997). Specific methods, such as apprenticeships, role-play, and simulations, can be used to situate learning within a relevant context.

Situated learning had a big impact on the IDT community when it was introduced, and during the 1990s substantial research was devoted to testing the new theory (Driscoll, 2000). By 1997, Winn reported that a growing body of evidence supported the theory that what a student actually learns is determined more by the situation in which learning takes place (the environment) than what the student brings to learning (prior knowledge and cognitive abilities). Situated learning is still characterized as an emerging theory today, however, as it gains prominence the importance of context is being given more attention.

Tessmer and Richey (1997) point out that while context has been shown to have a complex and powerful influence on successful learning, it is ignored or deemphasized in most classic ID models. ID models have traditionally been based on the premise that instructional solutions are "environmentally neutral" (p. 85) and applicable to all settings.

Contextual knowledge implies "knowing why, when, and where to employ specific concepts, rules, and principles" (Tennyson, 1992, p. 38), and it "represents a more complete understanding of human behavior, which is necessary for defining an educational learning theory" (p. 39). Knowing why, when, and where to employ IDT concepts, rules, and principles is a characteristic of expert instructional designers. It is also a worthy goal for students planning to practice IDT. What does context consist of for the IDT student? Relevant IDT context refers both to the context of instructional design and the context of the career environment in which the student will practice.

INCORPORATING INSTRUCTIONAL DESIGN CONTEXT

Advanced study in any field implies a desire to emulate expert practice in that discipline. IDT graduate students are no exception. Their desire to develop the skills of an expert can be facilitated through immersion in the culture of ID practice (Cennamo & Holmes, 2001). Relevant IDT context, therefore, involves authentic experiences that immerse learners in the IDT community of practice. Immersion of this sort can be accomplished through assistantship and collaborative design experiences, but it is also facilitated when IDT educators "practice what they preach" and model the practices, thinking processes, and problem-solving strategies they promote. Cennamo and Holmes cite methods to accomplish this development of expertise including "modeling, coaching, scaffolding, articulation, reflection, and exploration" (p. 46).

Rowland, Fixl, and Yung (1992) outlined three important elements necessary to move the novice IDT student more directly from everyday problem-solving processes to skilled design processes: "learning in context, modeling of expert thought processes, and reflection" (p. 37). They linked these practices to develop an apprenticeship model of learning. These new designers will learn their craft more readily and more completely, however, if IDT educators go beyond merely incorporating the context of instructional design and seek ways to also include the context of the student's intended career environment.

INCORPORATING THE CONTEXT OF THE CAREER ENVIRONMENT

Tessmer and Richey (1997) state that "successful instructional designs must be, to some extent, situation-specific. Effective instruction is context-rich" (p. 89), accounting for the learners' immediate and future work environments and organizational structures. Contextualizing the instruction to the future work environment "makes abstract concepts more concrete, promotes understanding and retention, as well as facilitates reinforcement and transfer of training" (p. 90).

When instruction is situated in either the target work environment or an approximation of that environment, students perceive the utility of the instruction to their future career goals. Clark, Dobbins, and Ladd (1993) found that the perceived career value of a particular training program was directly linked to learning motivation. In other words, when learners consider the material they are learning to be relevant to their career goals, they are motivated to learn. Bohlin and Milheim (1994) concur, writing, "the instruction must have perceived relevance to the immediate or long-range personal needs of the learner. These personal needs can be met by matching the instruction to learners' goals, [and] making the benefits clear" (p. 71).

Others agree. In a study designed to explore the relationship between academic preparation and professional ID practice in business and industry, Julian (2001) found that "because the field of ID has become so rich and varied in terms of settings in which it is

practiced, we can no longer discuss the profession without consideration of the environment of practice" (p. 16). Consequently, the study of IDT should be situated in the environment of practice, both the instructional design environment and the career environment, as
matched to the students' career goals.

Suggestions for ways to incorporate workplace context go back over two decades. In
1981, Rossett generated a list of authentic learning experiences for IDT students for purposes of strengthening the link between the academic world and the community. The methods she suggested included training students in problem solving by engaging them in
authentic opportunities to meet community needs on real-world projects, internships, and
other occasions for collaboration between the community and the universities. These methods were reemphasized in the early to mid-1990s by IDT educators who emphasized that
these experiences would provide students with opportunities to learn problem solving in
authentic contexts under the guidance of experts (Ertmer & Cennamo, 1995; Quinn, 1995;
Rowland, 1994; Tripp, 1994).

Tripp (1994) suggested the use of a "design studio" to incorporate an apprenticeship
experience into the IDT student's education, featuring real-world problem solving without
the associated risks or pressures. New ideas for authentic, situated experiences grew from
constructivist theory and situated learning, which emphasized new approaches for conveying problem-solving skills for ill-defined problems, complex problems, and learning tasks
(Driscoll, 2000). These ideas for authentic, real-world experiences include use of real ID
projects from visiting experts or community–university collaborative projects, design competitions where students work on projects for nonprofit or community organizations,
real-world case studies from a variety of career environments, and internships and apprenticeships in the student's choice of career environment (Cennamo & Holmes, 2001; Ertmer
& Cennamo, 1995; Ertmer & Quinn, 2003; Julian, Larsen, & Kinzie, 1999; Kapp &
Phillips, 2003; Kinzie, Hrabe, & Larsen, 1998; Quinn, 1994, 1995; Rossett, 1981;
Rowland, 1994; Rowland, Parra, & Basnet, 1994).

In a study to assess the affect of ten situational factors on the use of the steps in the
ISD model, Holcomb (1993) found that situational factors did, indeed, have a significant
effect on the subjects' design practices. She recommended that courses designed to develop
students' ID skills should include consideration of such situational factors as time and
money limitations, student expectations, target population size and characteristics, and
organizational payoff.

One way to make the context of the intended career environment apparent to students
is to emphasize the competencies that are peculiar to that environment. A study by Branch,
Moore, and Sherman (1988) found that distinct business and academic markets for IDT
professionals do exist. Furthermore, competencies can be identified for a variety of career
environment that are either unique or are particularly important to successful instructional
design practice in those environments. Making students aware of such competencies and providing them with learning experiences and opportunities to develop those competencies will
produce graduates who are better prepared for their career environment of choice (Branch et al.,
1988). Table 1 lists competencies emphasized in specific career environments.

Instructional methods, content, and opportunities that provide authentic experiences
for IDT students can accomplish the goal of incorporating both design context and career
environment context into their academic experience. Such methods support the concept of
situated, authentic environments, providing relevance for students as they prepare for professional practice (Rowland, 1994). Context is only part of the equation, however, and students can be trained also to consider culture as they contemplate their career goals.

Table 1. Unique or Emphasized Areas of Competency for Specific Career Environments

Career Environment	Area of Competency and Specific Skills
Business and Industry	The Basics: ability to think, write, and communicate orally and to make wise and wide use of instructional design and technologies
	Communication Competence (writing and technical writing, public speaking and presentation skills, ability to justify and communicate a sound business case for training solutions)
	Interpersonal Relationship Competence (motivation, coaching, persuasion, leadership, negotiation, team skills, cross-cultural awareness)
	Analytic Competence (critical thinking, problem definition and problem solving, performance gap analysis and strategy/intervention application, business research skills)
	Project Management Competence (project/resource management, contracting and outsourcing skills, customer-oriented outlook)
	Business Competence (systems thinking, organizational and industry knowledge, change management and coping, global solutions, cost-benefit analysis and return on investment studies, knowledge of business trends such as performance improvement and emotional intelligence)
	New Technology Literacy and Competence (knowledge of recent technologies, evaluation of new technologies, online teaching/designing, and distance education abilities)
Higher Education	Teaching experience
	Interpersonal skills
	Knowledge and/or experience in advanced multimedia technologies and computer-based instruction
	Expertise and track record in research
	Knowledge of and experience in applying learning theories to instructional designs
	Production of grant proposals
	Knowledge and/or experience in telecommunications and distance learning
K–12 Education	Knowledge and skills to meet federal and state standards
	Library media specialists require information specialist skills, resource selection skills, and cooperative planning skills
Military	High level of training and familiarity with technologically advanced systems
	Knowledge of technological simulation systems
	Training methods for digitized tasks
	Knowledge of Distributed Mission Training (DMT), combining live, virtual, and constructive simulation
	Knowledge or experience in program evaluation and needs assessment
	Knowledge of adult learning

Career Environment	Area of Competency and Specific Skills
Government	Training for learners with less formal education preparation
	Knowledge of federal and state codes and regulations
	Ability to apply for and obtain federal- and state-funded grants
	Project management, oversight and evaluation of training consultants and services
	Contracting IDT services
	Knowledge of adult learning

From American Association of Librarians and Association for Educational Communications and Technology, 1998; Andrews, Moses, & Duke, 2002; Association for Educational Communications and Technology, 2000; Austin, 2002; Downs, Jenkins, Repman, & Carlson, 2002; Duderstadt, 2001; International Society for Technology in Education, 2001; International Technology Education Association, 2003; Kennedy, 1999; Liang, 1999; McCabe & McCabe, 2000; Moallem, 1995; Morlan & Lu, 1993; Richey, Fields, & Foxon, 2001; Roseman, 2001; Rossett, 2000; Ruckdeschel, Yarter, Riveccio, Cortes, & Cookson, 1998; Surry & Robinson, 2001.

CULTURE

So what is *culture* and what does the term *workplace culture* mean? Culture is an aspect of context (Tessmer & Richey, 1997), and the terms are sometimes used interchangeably. King (1998) defines culture as "those behaviors and beliefs that guide an organization's actions and can be described as its values, heroes, rites and rituals, and communication" (p. 33). These shared beliefs are often reflected in an organization's policies and actions. For example, an organization with a learning culture is committed to supporting the transfer of learning, and continuous learning is recognized at the organizational level (Tessmer & Richey, 1997). King (1998) gives examples of items that can describe the culture of an organization, including its system of rewards and recognition, the leaders' expectations and support for training, and the formal structures and policies that guide the activities of the organization. For example, some environments value individual creativity and others stress conformity; some are decentralized and others are centralized; some stress employee empowerment and others adhere to a strict approval cycle.

Powell (1997) defines culture as

the sum total of ways of living, including values, beliefs, aesthetic standards, linguistic expression, patterns of thinking, behavioral norms, and styles of communication, which a group of people has developed to assure its survival in a particular physical and human environment. (p. 15)

Countries, communities, organizations, communities of practice, and workplaces all have cultures.

Each workplace has its own unique culture that consists of the values, beliefs, attitudes, assumptions, and customs characteristic of that particular environment. Although each workplace culture is unique, the culture of workplaces are more likely to be similar *within* a career environment than *across* career environments. For example, the definition of "success" used in a Fortune 500 company will probably be closer to that used in a sole proprietorship (because both organizations are in the business and industry career environment) than to the definition used at a research university (from the higher education career environment).

In business and industry, the organizational environment is typically a company culture, often referred to as *corporate culture* (Tessmer & Richey, 1997). McBer and Company, a Boston-based organizational consultant, developed a list of six key cultural factors about which companies typically have a written or unwritten statement: conformity, responsibility, standards, rewards, clarity, and team spirit (Heritage & Davidson, 2002). Although these cultural factors often differ between businesses, they are significantly different and sometimes not even a factor in other career environments. Cabral-Cardoso (2001) indicates that individuals with different values are attracted to different organizations. Therefore, if individuals take time to reflect on their own values and become informed about the culture of the organizations to which they are applying, they are more likely to be satisfied with and successful in the position they take.

INCORPORATING THE CULTURE OF THE CAREER ENVIRONMENT

The phenomenon of culture frames all activities that occur within a community or organization. Meaning and purpose are socially constructed through negotiations among present and past members of a community (Brown et al., 1989). When students do not consider differences in culture before graduation, they may end up in an organizational culture that is inconsistent with their own values, beliefs, and principles. Trimby (1982) cautions that the IDT graduate should be aware of potential differences between academia (or *formal education*) and business and industry (*training situations*). She strongly recommends that the factors on which the two environments differ be considered and weighed prior to making a career decision. Bartell (2001) states that it is at the level of culture that problems should be addressed for culture is the "origin of the most fundamental, underlying beliefs that guide human behavior in an organization" (p. 357).

When individuals first begin a career or a new job, there may be aspects of the workplace culture that they have not anticipated. If totally unprepared, these aspects of the culture may become "issues," requiring the individual to expend more effort than desired to adjust to the culture. The greater the difference in culture between the individual's previous environment and the new environment, the greater the potential for this type of stress. For example, such stress is likely if a recent graduate goes from an academic environment where individuals are encouraged to set goals independently and define strategies for achieving them to a workplace where the schedule, projects, and methods are rigorously dictated and monitored. Table 2 illustrates the type of cultural aspects that can become issues for individuals.

A recent mail and online survey of practicing instructional designers, conducted by contacting members of three professional organizations (Association for Educational Communications and Technology, International Society for Performance Improvement, and American Society for Training and Development), was conducted to determine whether any of the cultural aspects listed in Table 2 had been "issues" for the participants when they first entered professional practice (Larson, 2004). An "issue" was defined in the survey as an aspect of the workplace culture that requires an individual to expend more effort than desired to adjust to their surroundings. Examples include the value placed on timeliness; beliefs about the amount of autonomy employees can handle; attitudes toward risk; assumptions about priorities, deadlines, and work ethic; and dress customs (formal vs. informal).

Table 2. Aspects of Workplace Culture

General Category	Cultural Variables
Level of Autonomy and Independence	Amount of freedom given to set goals Amount of freedom given to set priorities and deadlines Amount of freedom given to make decisions
Work Assignments	Trade-offs between quality, timeliness, and cost in work assignments Quality standards for work assignments Flexibility of established deadlines for work assignments Expectations of time between project start and completion Accountability for work assignments Workload Stability of work assignments Freedom to express creativity through work assignments Availability of project resources for work assignments
Work Relationships	Type and amount of collaboration and teamwork with coworkers Verbal and nonverbal interpersonal communication Written communication Flow and clarity of communication in work relationships The nature of management styles (e.g., directive vs. participative) Formal versus informal authority and reporting structures
Workplace Political Climate	The nature of internal workplace politics Freedom to challenge or criticize decisions of supervisors Effect of national politics on reporting structures and resources
Working Conditions	Expectations regarding conformity to established norms Employer or coworker attitudes regarding discrimination Employer's concern for employee quality of life and job satisfaction Established or acceptable dress Flexibility of hours and schedule Expectations for work completion and overtime Expectations of appropriate work ethic and its demonstration Practices and expectations regarding meetings and their conduct Employer attitudes toward change, innovation, and risk Amount of freedom given to express individuality Job security Employer emphasis on established rules and procedures (bureaucracy)

General Category	Cultural Variables
Reward Systems	Rewards systems such as salary, vacation, and other benefits
	Employer support of continuing education and professional development
	Availability of opportunities for advancement
	Recognition and occupational prestige
	Measures and methods of employee assessment
	Types of incentives and disincentives
Alignment of Personal Values and Beliefs with That of the Work Environment	Emphasis on or attitude toward knowledge sharing
	Emphasis on or attitude toward protection of proprietary information
	Emphasis on group versus individual problem-solving processes
	Status of intellectual property rights
	Emphasis on knowledge creation versus knowledge consumption.
	Emphasis on knowledge as a means-to-a-goal versus as an end-in-itself
	Emphasis on learning to meet individual's goals, as opposed to meeting the goals of the organization
	Assumptions concerning the nature of truth and reality

From Bartell, 2001; Cabral-Cardoso, 2001; Grimwald, 2001; Tasker & Packham, 1993; Trimby, 1982.

The mail portion of the survey gleaned a response rate of 32.0 percent. Results of the two versions of the online survey and the mail survey were combined, and eight aspects of workplace cultural were consistently identified as issues by at least 40 percent of respondents who had received their degrees in the last ten years. Those aspects and the percentage of respondents for whom they were issues include the following:

- the nature of internal workplace politics (59.1%)
- trade-offs between quality, timeliness, and cost in work assignments (46.6%)
- freedom to challenge or criticize the decisions of supervisors (46.0%)
- availability of project resources for work assignments (44.3%)
- directive versus participative management styles (43.2%)
- the amount of freedom given to make decisions (42.0%)
- employer attitudes toward change, innovation, and risk (40.9%)
- workload (40.9%)

For five of these cultural aspects, over half the respondents indicated they had not been prepared for a given aspect of their preparation program. Those aspects and the percentage of respondents who indicated they were issues but were not prepared for them are as follows:

- freedom to challenge or criticize the decisions of supervisors (74.4% not prepared for this)
- availability of project resources for work assignments (68.4%)
- the nature of internal workplace politics (69.2%)

- directive versus participative management styles (64.9%)
- workload (52.8%)

Other aspects that rated highly as issues were:
- Flow and clarity of communication in work relationships
- Employer emphasis on rules and procedures (or bureaucracy)
- Availability of opportunities for advancement
- Employer's concern for employee's quality of life and job satisfaction

As is suggested by this list of potential cultural workplace issues, many aspects of culture deal with the affective domain. Tennyson (1992) reports research indicating that the affective domain may actually dominate the cognitive domain. Affective variables include such items as motivation, feelings, attitudes, emotions, anxiety, and values. Tennyson stresses that when educators plan instruction to provide a knowledge base, they should also consider the affective component.

How can affective components and culture be incorporated into IDT preparation? They must be considered both in the examples used and in the ID procedures themselves. Summers, Lohr, and O'Neil (2002) suggest that because "the cues in the corporate world look very different to the novice designer than the cues they received in their academic preparation" (p. 27), training cues need to match closely to the cues in the work setting. Thomas, Mitchell, and Joseph (2002) further emphasize that culture is so much a part of the construction of knowledge that it should "underpin not only the analysis phase but all phases of the design process" (p. 41).

To ensure that culture is considered in the instructional design process, Thomas et al., (2002) recommend the use of an iterative approach to the traditional ADDIE (Analyze, Design, Develop, Implement, and Evaluate) instructional design model, along with a *cultural* dimension. They proposed that this cultural dimension have three parameters: intention, interaction, and introspection. The intentional parameter would involve reflection to make ensure that the designer considers and makes their personal cultural bias explicit. The interaction parameter emphasizes the collaboration of designer, subject matter expert (SME), and end user throughout the model phases to facilitate the melding of culture into the end product. Finally, the designer must engage in introspection to ensure that their own thoughts, beliefs, attitudes, desires, and feelings toward the cultures represented are identified and considered. "The designer's world view cannot be divorced from his societal context; therefore, it becomes critically important that the designer becomes introspective in his approach when designing instruction" (Thomas et al., p. 44). The core of the *societal context* and *worldview* refer to the individual's (and the organization's) value system (Tasker & Packham, 1993).

The differences in value systems between career environments can be substantial. Tasker and Packham (1993) define *value* as something with "personal meaning which is derived from what is of value and gives purpose to individuals or groups" (p. 128). Table 3 provides a listing of the values common to different career environments, illustrating the potential for incompatibility. Tasker and Packham use the term *incommensurable* (p. 135) to describe the value systems of industry and academia, and they warn that these differences must be acknowledged, respected, and made explicit to avoid destructive conflict where the interests of industry and universities meet.

Table 3. Comparison of Cultural Aspects of Different Career Environments

	Higher Education	Business and Industry	Military	Government
Purpose and Goals	To generate knowledge through collaboration between scholars, not competition, and in such a way that society as a whole benefits To educate learners and expand the boundaries of knowledge through disciplined inquiry	To generate profit for private gain, usually in competition with other companies To increase productivity and maximize the financial position of organizations	To protect, defend, and preserve the country	Deriving its just powers from the people, governments are instituted to protect the rights of the people; to secure the "unalienable rights" of life, liberty, and the pursuit of happiness
Contextual Features	Resist change Authority diffused to individual faculty members and committees for decisions Highly traditional	Definite and precise deadlines	When not at war, in training Strong hierarchical structure	Pervasive influence of politics Frequent change in political leadership and policy direction Absence of well-defined measures of success Democratic accountability Rules of procedures

Basic Values	Academic freedom of scholars and the institution Academic rigor Disinterested pursuit of knowledge Intellectual integrity and freedom of expression in teaching and research Take the time to do it right Inquiry-oriented culture	Capitalist values Pragmatism Time is money Transferable intellectual and social skills Outcomes-based culture	Duty, honor, country Discipline and integrity Competence, physical courage, moral courage, teamwork, confidence, trust, delegation, cooperation	Public service Security Respect for the law and democratic institutions Political neutrality and provision of impartial advice Integrity and pride in work Fair, honest, and impartial treatment of people Public accountability and probity Commitment to the principles of equity and merit Ethical behavior Workplace free from harassment
Stereotype Others Have of Them	Researchers aren't doers They can't meet deadlines They're too theoretical and don't have any practical experience Don't know how to speak or write plain English	Not creative Only interested in the bottom line Work tends to be boring with no opportunity for creativity	Blood-thirsty warmongers Low intellectual abilities Rigid and trapped in bureaucracy	Questionable talent because after a trial period of employment, employment laws make it difficult to remove a government worker who is not producing Mired in bureaucratic red tape

From Clark, 2001; Davidson-Shivers, 2002; Durzo, 1981; Knowles, 1977; Leveson, 2000; Stolovitch, 1981; Tasker & Packham, 1993.

Cultural differences between career environments are further support by Barnum's (1979) study. He compared an academic theoretical model of ID with an applied, pragmatic design from business and industry. Barnum found that the models resulted from "two radically different environments, an idealistic, academic approach and a heavily pragmatic, training product marketing approach" (p. 269).

The point is that differences in cultural factors between career environments may have a significant impact on the ability of IDT students to transfer their skills from the academic environment to other career environments (Summers et al., 2002). In the case of business and industry, Leveson (2000) states, "because of the differences in the cultural contexts of academia and work, an automatic transference of skills cannot be assumed" (p. 161). The research suggests, however, that IDT educators may be able to provide limited acculturation through situated methods and learning experiences (Summers et al.).

CONCLUSIONS

The challenge to be met is the design of learning environments that allow students to develop their own interests, yet provide students with comprehensive skills that can be applied in a wide range of potential contexts (Carver, Lehrer, Connell, & Erickson, 1992, p. 402). Tessmer and Richey (1997) report that the instructional design literature contains little information on how to identify and accommodate context. However, the literature also reports success in preparation attempts when instructors include practice using ill-defined problems in authentic settings using such strategies as case studies, real-world experiences, studio experiences, and more (Carr-Chellman, 1999; Julian et al., 1999).

REFERENCES

American Association of School Librarians and Association for Educational Communications and Technology. (1998). *Information power: Building partnerships for learning.* Chicago: American Library Association.

Andrews, D. H., Moses, F. L., & Duke, D. S. (2002). Current trends in military instructional design and technology. In R. A. Reiser, & J. V. Dempsey (Eds.), *Trends and issues in instructional design and technology* (pp. 211–224). Upper Saddle River, NJ: Merrill Prentice Hall.

Association for Educational Communications and Technology. (2000). *NCATE Program Standards for Initial & Advanced Educational Communications & Technology Programs.* Washington, DC: Author.

Austin, A. E. (2002). Preparing the next generation of faculty: Graduate school as socialization to the academic career. *Journal of Higher Education, 73*(1), 94–122.

Barnum, T. M. (1979). An analysis of instructional systems design as reflected in formal education, industry, and military institutions: Theory vs. application (Doctoral dissertation, Northern Illinois University, 1979). *Dissertation Abstracts International, 40*, 3061.

Bartell, S. M. (2001). Training's new role in learning organizations. *Innovations in Education and Teaching International, 38*(4), 354–363.

Bohlin, R. M., & Milheim, W. D. (1994). *Applications of an adult motivational instructional design model.* In Proceedings of the 1994 National Convention of the Association for Educational Communications and Technology, Nashville, TN, February 16–20, 1994, pp. 69–78. (ERIC Document Reproduction Service No. ED373704)

Branch, R. C., Moore, D. M., & Sherman, T. M. (1988). Evaluating potential instructional technology and design professionals for academic and business settings: Criteria for decision-making. *Educational Technology, 28*(10), 34–37.

Brown, J. S., Collins, A., & Duguid, P. (1989). Situated cognition and the culture of learning. *Educational Researcher, 18*, 32–42.

Cabral-Cardoso, C. J. (2001). Too academic to get a proper job? The difficult transition of PhDs to the "real world" of industry. *Career Development International, 6*(4), 212–217.

Carr-Chellman, A. A. (1999). I have a problem! The use of cases in educating instructional designers. *TechTrends, 43*(6), 15–19.

Carver, S. M., Lehrer, R., Connell, T., & Erickson, J. (1992). Learning by hypermedia design: Issues of assessment and implementation. *Educational Psychologist, 27*(3), 385–404.

Cennamo, K. S., & Holmes, G. (2001). Developing awareness of client relations through immersion in practice. *Educational Technology, 41*(6), 44–49.

Clark, C., Dobbins, G., & Ladd, R. T. (1993). Exploratory field study of training motivation. *Group and Organization Management, 18*(3), 292–307.

Clark, I. D. (2001, February). Distant reflections on federal public service reform in the 1990s. In *Public service management reform: Progress, setbacks and challenges*. Canada: Office of the General Auditor of Canada. [WWW document]. Retrieved January 19, 2005, from http://www.oag-bvg.gc.ca/domino/other.nsf/html/01psm_e.html

Davidson-Shivers, G. A. (2002). Instructional technology in higher education. In R. A. Reiser, & J. V. Dempsey (Eds.), *Trends and issues in instructional design and technology* (pp. 256–268). Upper Saddle River, NJ: Merrill Prentice Hall.

Downs, E., Jenkins, S. J., Repman, J., & Carolson, R. (2002). Essential instructional design competencies for library media specialists. *Proceedings of SITE, 2,* 949.

Driscoll, M. P. (2000). *Psychology of learning for instruction* (2nd ed.). Boston: Allyn and Bacon.

Driscoll, M. P. (2002). Psychological foundations of instructional design (pp. 57–69) In R. A. Reiser & J. V. Dempsey (Eds.), *Trends and issues in instructional design and technology.* Upper Saddle River, NJ: Merrill Prentice Hall.

Duderstadt, J. J. (2001). Preparing future faculty for future universities. *Liberal Education, 87*(2), 24–31.

Durzo, J. J. (1981). Through the looking glass: Images of business and academe. *NSPI Journal, 20*(1), 6–7, 28.

Ertmer, P. A., & Cennamo, K. S. (1995). Teaching instructional design: An apprenticeship model. *Performance Improvement Quarterly, 8*(4), 43–58.

Ertmer, P. A., & Quinn, J. (2003). *The ID casebook: Case studies in instructional design* (2nd ed.). Upper Saddle River, NJ: Merrill Prentice Hall.

Grimwald, A. (2001). Industry vs. academia: Survey results, March 2001. *The Scientist, 15*(8), 28. Retrieved April 4, 2001, from http://www.the-scientist.com/yr2001/apr/survey_010416.html

Heritage, G., & Davidson, S. (2002). Recruiter smarts—XIV: Successful job requirements—the missing links, part II. Retrieved January 19, 2005, from the Monster.com Web site: http://hr.monster.com.sg/articles/7108/

Holcomb, C. (1993). The effects of project situational factors on the implementation of instructional design activities in a corporate training setting (Doctoral dissertation, University of Missouri—Columbia, 1993). *Dissertation Abstracts International, 55,* 851.

International Society for Technology in Education. (2001). *Educational computing and technology literacy: Initial endorsement guidelines.* Retrieved January 19, 2005, from http://cnets.iste.org/ncate/

International Technology Education Association. (2003). *Advancing excellence in technological literacy: Student assessment, professional development, and program standards.* Reston, VA: Author.

Julian, M. F. (2001). Learning in action: The professional preparation of instructional designers (Doctoral dissertation, University of Virginia, 2001). *Dissertation Abstracts International, 62,* 136.

Julian, M. F., Larsen, V. A., & Kinzie, M. B. (1999). *Compelling case experiences: Challenges for emerging instructional designers.* Bloomington, IN: AECT. (ERIC Document Reproduction Service No. ED436129)

Kapp, K. M., & Phillips, T. L. (2003). Teaching the business of instructional technology: A collaborative corporate/academic partnership. *TechTrends, 47*(1), 46–51.

Kennedy, H. (1999, November). Simulation reshaping military training: Technology jumping from teenagers' computers to pilots' cockpits. *National Defense Magazine*. Retrieved November 8, 2003, from: http://www.nationaldefensemagazine.org/article.cfm?Id=113

King, J. V. (1998). Practitioner perceptions of critical data for analysis of three types of training (Doctoral dissertation, University of Northern Colorado, 1998). *Dissertation Abstracts International, 59,* 2459.

Kinzie, M. B., Hrabe, M. E., & Larsen, V. A. (1998). An instructional design case event: Exploring issues in professional practice. *Educational Technology Research & Development, 46*(1), 53–71.

Knowles, M. S. (1977). *The modern practice of adult education: Andragogy versus pedagogy.* New York: Association Press.

Larson, M. B. (2004). IDT professional preparation and Work Environment: Professional preparation of instructional design and technology graduates for different work environments. Unpublished doctoral dissertation, Virginia Tech, Blacksburg.

Leveson, L. (2000). Disparities in perceptions of generic skills: Academics and employers. *Industry & Higher Education, 14*(3), 157–164.

Liang, C. C. (1999). Benchmarking competent instructional media designers in the corporate world. *Educational Media International, 36*(4), 317–320.

McCabe, L. L., & McCabe, E. R. B. (2000). *How to succeed in academics.* San Diego, CA: Academic Press.

Moallem, M. (1995, April). *Analysis of job announcements and the required competencies for instructional technology professionals.* Paper presented at the Annual Meeting of the American Educational Research Association, San Francisco, CA. (ERIC Document Reproduction Service No. ED405355)

Morlan, J. E., & Lu, M. (1993, January). *A survey of media and instructional technology competencies needed by business, industry, health professions, agencies, military trainers, and independent contractors in Northern California, USA.* In the proceedings of selected research and development presentations at the convention of the Association of Educational Communications and Technology, New Orleans, LA. (ERIC Document Reproduction Service No. ED362188)

Powell, G. (1997). Understanding the language of diversity. *Educational Technology, 37*(2), 15–16.

Quinn, J. (1994). Connecting education and practice in an instructional design graduate program. *Educational Technology Research & Development, 42*(3), 71–82.

Quinn, J. (1995). The education of instructional designers: Reflections on the Tripp paper. *Performance Improvement Quarterly, 8*(3), 11–117.

Richey, R. C. (Ed.), Fields, D. C., & Foxon, M., with Roberts, R. C., Spannaus, T., & Spector, J. M. (2001). *Instructional design competencies: The standards* (3rd ed.). Syracuse, NY: ERIC Clearinghouse on Information & Technology. International Board of Standards for Training and Performance Improvement (IBSTPI).

Roseman, T. O. (2001). Information technology (IT) and its impact on the direction of policy development and scope of naval military education and training, 1985–2000 (Master's thesis, Loyola University Chicago, 2001). *Masters Abstracts International, 40,* 34.

Rossett, A. (1981). Instructional technology as link between university and community. *NSPI Journal, 20*(1), 26–28.

Rossett, A. (2000). What's academia got to do with it? An informal tour of what managers are seeking from entry-level instructional technologists. *TechTrends, 44*(5), 32–35.

Rowland, G. (1994). Educating instructional designers: Different methods for different outcomes. *Educational Technology, 34*(6), 5–11.

Rowland, G., Fixl, A., & Yung, K. (1992). Educating the reflective designer. *Educational Technology, 32*(12), 36–44.

Rowland, G., Parra, M. L., & Basnet, K. (1994). Educating instructional designers: Different methods for different outcomes. *Educational Technology, 34*(6), 5–11.

Ruckdeschel, C., Yarter, M., Riveccio, M. A., Cortes, I., & Cookson, M. S. (1998). Beyond instructional systems: A performance technology degree. *Performance Improvement, 37*(3), 22–26.

Stolovitch, H. D. (1981). Preparing the industrial and educational developer: Is there a difference? *NSPI Journal, 20*(1), 29–30.

Summers, L., Lohr, L., & O'Neil, C. (2002). Building instructional design credibility through communication competency. *TechTrends, 46*(1), 26–32.

Surrey, D. W., & Robinson, M. A. (2001). A taxonomy of instructional technology service positions in higher education. *Innovations in Education and Teaching International, 38*(3), 231–238.

Tasker, M., & Packham, D. (1993). Industry and higher education: A question of values. *Studies in Higher Education, 18*(2), 127–136.

Tennyson, R. D. (1992). An educational learning theory for instructional design. *Educational Technology, 32*(1), 36–41.

Tessmer, M., & Richey, R. C. (1997). The role of context in learning and instructional design. *Educational Technology Research & Development, 45*(2), 85–115.

Thomas, M., Mitchell, M., & Joseph, R. (2002). The third dimension of ADDIE: A cultural embrace. *TechTrends, 46*(2), 40–45.

Trimby, M. J. (1982). Entry level competencies for team members and supervisors/managers on instructional development teams in business and industry (Doctoral dissertation, Michigan State University, 1982). *Dissertation Abstracts International, 43,* 0346.

Tripp, S. D. (1994). How should instructional designers be educated? *Performance Improvement Quarterly, 7*(3), 116–126.

Winn, W. (1997). Advantages of a theory-based curriculum in instructional technology. *Educational Technology, 37*(1), 34–41.

A Software Architecture for Guiding Instruction Using Student's Prior Knowledge

David Richard Moore

CONSTRUCTIVISM AND PRIOR KNOWLEDGE

"The most important single factor influencing learning is what the learner already knows, ascertain this and teach him accordingly" (Ausubel, 1968, p. 18). This quote is the core definition of constructivist teaching methods. Building instruction on prior knowledge respects what is known about how the brain works and how knowledge is represented in the brain (Zull, 2002). To implement Ausubel's advice, a teacher must have an accurate conception of their student's knowledge base and must be prepared to act on this information in an efficient and individualized manner. Obtaining an accurate description of a current knowledge base requires students to represent publicly what they know (Richmond, 2001). Teachers must use these representations to infer the students' state of knowledge.

Solving a problem or accomplishing a task provides evidence that students have a degree of functional understanding; however, other techniques such as strategic questioning can provide further evidence that a student's conceptualization is useful when applied to a similar class of problems. No preassessment approach is perfect or complete. For example, a student may be able to perform a particular narrow task even while being misinformed of the underlying principle that would allow knowledge to be transferred to other settings and used to solve other problems. The consequence of this incompleteness is that an overvaluing of understanding occurs and the difficult work involved in developing broader and more accurate mental models may not commence.

Multiple-choice questions are compelling assessment instruments, particularly as the number of students in a class or workshop increases or as the volume of topics and instructional goals increase. Their ability to sample efficiently a large group of students on a large number of topics is attractive. The efficiency of multiple-choice testing lies in its discrete nature, which makes scoring relatively easy, particularly with automated scoring technologies such as the Scantron system. Multiple-choice question techniques have already benefited from technological advances such as Internet-based Course Management Systems, which allow questions to be delivered outside of class and allow data to be graded and collated instantly. Russell (2002) confirms this when stating "By eliminating the need to distribute, collect, and then scan paper-based tests, the Internet can streamline distribution, administration and scoring into a seamless and nearly instantaneous process" (p. 65). The logistical advantage of this type of learning makes it the logical choice in many instructional settings, and thus it is the focus of this chapter.

LIMITATIONS OF MULTIPLE-CHOICE QUESTIONS IN SAMPLING PRIOR KNOWLEDGE

The efficacy of multiple-choice questions is often disputed. Many believe that the technique is less effective than more qualitative techniques such as the essay or short-answer-type questions (Hillis, 2001). Creating quality multiple-choice questions is challenging, but this shouldn't imply that such questions could not be created. Evidence suggests that most types of learning goals, including higher-order objectives, can be assessed through well-crafted questions. These questions have been shown to have similar validity and reliability as other techniques (Haladyna, 1994). Nevertheless, multiple-choice questions have several limitations.

Quality multiple-choice questions often require learners to make a potentially unwarranted claim: that they believe one answer alternative is entirely correct and that the other choices are entirely incorrect. Students must commit themselves to a response, which may mask their level of uncertainty. In other words, they may guess, and guessing may skew assessment results and hide valuable information about the student's state of comprehension. The result is that the student's mental model may remain inadequately sampled—or worse, missampled—leading to instructional interventions and adjustments that are unneeded or inappropriate.

We all operate in our day-to-day lives with a remarkably large degree of uncertainty about what we know and what we don't know; the result is an enormous degree of intellectual caution (Norman, 1983). This caution may lead to performance hesitation, which may be wholly appropriate in some situations and dangerous in others. Even when a person's knowledge base is comprehensive and accurate, people will often unnecessarily hesitate in developing conclusions. In other words, people's lack of intellectual confidence results in their being unable to take full advantage of the knowledge they do have. Discrete multiple-choice testing may mask this uncertainty and result in an overestimation of one's knowledge and in unwarranted confidence or may lead to the underestimation of one's knowledge, resulting in an inability to take action. Both circumstances may make it difficult to identify appropriate, efficient, and effective remediation.

ADMISSIBLE PROBABILITY MEASURES

Multiple-choice questions are usually presented as shown in Table 1. An alternative method for displaying the question in Table 1 can be seen in Figure 1. Figure 1 presents an equilateral triangle; each corner corresponding with an alternative answer.

Table 1. Standard Multiple-Choice Presentation

What area would suffer an infarction following occlusion of the right coronary artery near its origin by a thrombus?
A. Lateral wall of the right ventricle and the right atrium*
B. Lateral left ventricle
C. Anterior left ventricle

Adapted from Haladyna (1994, p. 74).
* Correct answer.

Unlike the multiple-choice question, in Figure 1 students have a number of alternatives that allow them to express their knowledge base with a great deal more accuracy (Bruno, 1987; Klinger, 1997). The geographic area within the triangle provides alternatives with relative distances between available distracters. With this system, test takers not only can express their belief about the correct answer but also express their confidence in that answer. The triangle allows learners to express their understanding by selecting a point between conceptual possibilities. This system is referred to an *admissible probability measure* or an *admissible scoring system*. As Landa (1976) states, an admissible probability measure (APM) "enables and encourages the student to give honest answers to all questions, freely and frankly identifying the gaps in his knowledge" (p. 14).

In Figure 1, points A, B, and C represent a student's absolute certainty in the selected answer; point D represents complete uncertainty; points E, F, and G represent an understanding that two alternatives are equally as likely to be correct, whereas the third alternative is definitely not believed to be correct; points H, I, and J are associated with points A, B, and C, respectively, and represent the belief that one of those alternatives is likely to be correct, but the student is not confident in the selection or, in other words, he or she is experiencing doubts (Bruno, 1987; Klinger, 1997). Assuming A is the correct answer, student S1 has selected point A, and student S2 has selected point D. Student S1 is essentially correct and completely confident in her response whereas student S2 is unable to express a preference between the choices. If these students had been forced to choose, it is likely that student S1 would have recorded the correct answer and Student S2 would have been forced to guess, possibly skewing the instruments reliability and validity. A similar assessment triangle has been used in the original PLATO computer instructional system (Landa, 1976). The advantage of this system is that not only is confidence in an answer expressed, the relative correctness of all the distracters is expressed as well.

Figure 1. Multiple-choice alternative.

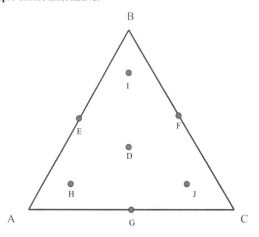

An appropriate weighting system needs to be implemented to provide incentives for students to evaluate appropriately the risk associated with their decision and accordingly reflect their mental models. Without this weighting system, students have no incentive not to guess, and consequently the testing instrument may not produce distinguishable results from other methods. The weights assigned to each coordinate must encourage honest appraisal of one's knowledge base. PLATO IV, one of the initial experimental programs in computer-based instruction, used a logarithmic weighting system for implementation of the APM. This implementation of the logarithmic scale was derived from analyzing risk and designed to ensure that selecting an end point or closely positioned coordinates would only benefit the students if they were 90-percent certain of the correctness of their response (Landa, 1976).

Klinger (1997) summarizes the weights as ensuring "that on the average any response pattern that differs from an expression of one's true knowledge yields lower scores" (p. 3). In other words, guessing, which reduces the validity of the instrument, is to be discouraged. This logarithmic weighting system has been validated and seems to provide credit satisfactorily to students who honestly and accurately appraise their own knowledge and their associated confidence in that knowledge (Bruno, 1987).

In practice a correct answer would receive 24 points, whereas a response that indicates that all alternatives are equally likely would receive 0 points; selecting a wrong alternative would receive –76 points. Thus, a student who guesses wrongly not only will not receive points but points will be taken away. Figure 2 demonstrates the relative weights assigned to each point as a function of distance from the extremes, that is, the distance between the correct answer and an incorrect answer. The slope of the line becomes steeper as the selected response moves farther from the answer to provide the appropriate risk incentive. A student receives a modest incentive for selecting the correct answer but has a strong incentive not to select an incorrect answer. These steps should encourage a more modest expression of one's knowledge. It is possible, however, that individuals may differ in their level of risk assessment. Differences in gender, cultural background, and experience require further investigation in determining the applicability and utility of this tool to those groups.

Figure 2. Slope of scoring weights.

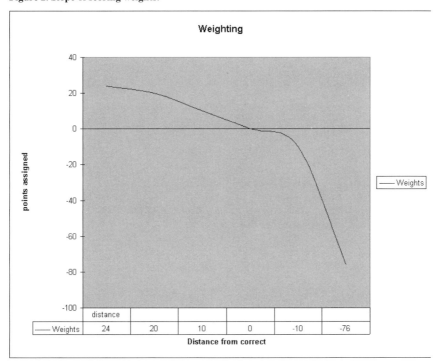

Although powerful, this technique may require students to undergo training on how the technique works. When students engage in multiple-choice tests, it is assumed that they behave in a rationale manner and that they access their relative risk preferences when selecting an answer. Risk assessment may change dramatically when students engage in an area-based admissible scoring system. Students need to be aware of the implications of guessing wrongly and the virtue of selecting a coordinate that reflects the true state of their knowledge. To this effect, students should have ample opportunity to take practice area-based admissible scoring system tests and carefully review the evaluation process so they have a full understanding of the implications of the choices they make.

A variation of this type of "admissible scoring system" can be created that allows a student to select any coordinate within the assessment triangle instead of being restricted to discrete points on the corners and edges. Appropriately designed software is indispensable in collecting and collating this data. Figure 3 presents an interface for collecting this type of nondiscrete response. The student uses the cursor to select any point within the triangle, and that point is then correlated with the appropriate weighting score (Moore, 2004). Assuming point A is the correct answer, Figure 3a shows a response that reveals the learner is relatively uninformed, whereas Figure 3b shows a response that reveals the learner is relatively misinformed. Any point within the triangle can be assessed and assigned a value. Figure 4 demonstrates the pseudo-code used to create this interface.

Figure 3. A: Uninformed selection. B: Misinformed selection.

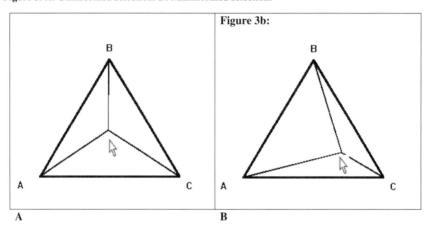

Essentially, the code is defining the area of the screen in which the triangle exists and testing to see whether the cursor is within that area (the "Test" command is similar in function to the more familiar "if–then" conditional statement). The next step is to determine the length of the line with the end points from the correct answer to point selected as illustrated in Figure 5.

Figure 4. Pseudo-code for enhanced admissible probability measure interface.

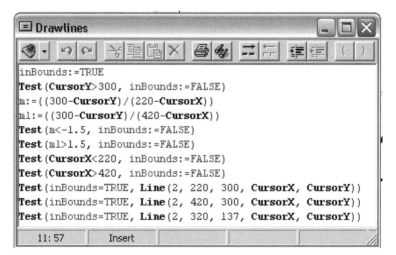

The length of that line segment is then associated with the appropriate logarithmic weighting. Without software, this extension of the APM technique would be impractical. This example was mocked up in Authorware; however, the procedure is based on simple geometry and is easily transferable to another programming environment.

Figure 5. Identify distance from point of origin.

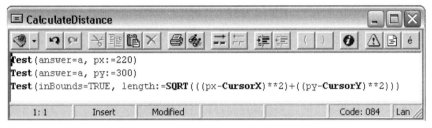

USING THE APM TO GUIDE CONSTRUCTIVIST TEACHING

Bruno (1987) has suggested that the areas within the assessment triangle may broadly correlate with the qualitative terms informed, partially informed, uninformed, partially misinformed, and misinformed. As a consequence, this information may be used to guide the selection of instructional activities, particularly using constructivist instructional theories that value a student's prior knowledge state. A student who selects the correct answer not require additional remediation, whereas a student who reports that he or she is informed but not 100 percent confident may be brought along with some encouragement; both of these circumstances are easily addressed. The next best scenario is when students report that they are uninformed or that they believe that each alternative answer is equally likely. In this case, a generic treatment might be appropriate to guide instructional activities. Being misinformed, of course, is the state in which, unfortunately, students are inappropriately confident in an erroneous conceptualization, and this state actively inhibits further learning because the mind is prevented from finding or creating consistent patterns.

Table 2. Knowledge and Instructional Interventions

Informed	Learners are confident in their answer, and their conception matches that of the larger intellectual community. No additional intervention is required. If this is a stable response, students may proceed to other learning objectives.
Partially Informed	Learners seem to know the correct answer; however, they are not confident in their response. In knowledge domains that require quick decisions (medical, military, etc.), this lack of confidence could become a problem. An appropriate instructional intervention would include confirming the learners understanding and reinforcing it.
Uninformed	In this case, Learners do not have a preference from the choice given. In this situation, the nature of the alternatives should be reviewed. A standardized intervention that explains the facts, concepts, and principles involved following established instructional design principles would be appropriate.

Partially Misinformed	Learners in this case are fortunate compared with those who have a complete misunderstanding because they have self-identified a problem with their conceptualizations (otherwise their level of confidence in their response would be stronger). An instructional intervention is similar to one for the completely misinformed; however, the instructor may expect resistance to change to have less influence in this case.
Misinformed	In this case, learners have acquired a misunderstanding. It is likely that this state of affairs prevents additional knowledge acquisition in a particular domain because of the difficulties in generating consistency. An appropriate instructional intervention may include the active identification and isolation of the misunderstanding. The false nature of the conceptualization must be exposed before new material is presented.

Being uninformed is preferred over being misinformed because in the case of the former, it is hypothesized that prior knowledge in the domain in question hasn't been solidified. Zull (2002) describes a model of brain activity that supports the idea that learning has a tangible physical manifestation in the form of neural connections and the relative strength of those neural connections. It is argued that these connections are semipermanent structures that remain despite the influence of new learning. When new learning occurs, new connections are made that with use should be strengthened to the point that older neural paths are eventually ignored and subsumed into the new structure. Zull (2002) indicates that this process is not immediate, and there is often a likelihood of a relapse or reemergence of neural connections. If this description of brain activity and structure is accurate, then it may be assumed that something that has been learned incorrectly, leading to one being misinformed, would be more difficult to correct than in a case were there are no strong neural connections. It is easier to build new connections than attempt to tear down those that are malformed. Table 2 illustrates the differing states of knowledge with possible instructional interventions.

CONCLUSION

This brief chapter has introduced the concept of an area-based admissible scoring system and presented a basic software architecture for creating an interface to such a system. By gathering the data that an instrument such as that presented allows, instructors can better evaluate their students' current understanding and conceptualizations while still benefiting from the efficiency of computer scored multiple-choice testing systems. Instructors, when using preassessments, have had to interpret data that was skewed based on all or nothing responses. As a result, they have been provided with little guidance for their instructional interventions. By using the system presented in this chapter, instructors can collect appropriate data, classify students, and adjust their instructional interventions accordingly.

REFERENCES

Ausubel, D. P. (1968). *Educational psychology, a cognitive view*. New York: Holt, Rinehart and Winston.

Bruno, J. E. (1987). Admissible probability measures in instructional management. *Journal of Computer-based Instruction, 14*(1), 23–30.

Haladyna, T. M. (1994). *Developing and validating multiple-choice test items*. Hillsdale, NJ: Erlbaum.

Hillis, P. (2001). Devising new history examinations for Scottish schools. Retreived January 19, 2005, from the Australian History Teacher Web site: http://www.pa.ash.org.au/afssse/members/htaa/journal/aht01.pdf

Klinger, A. (1997). *Experimental validation of learning accomplishment.* Presented at the ASEE/IEEE Frontiers in Education Conference, July 11, 1997. Retrieved January 19, 2005, from fie.engrng.pitt.edu/fie97/1271.pdf

Landa, S. (1976, March). CAAPM: Computer-aided admissible probability measurement on Plato IV (R-172-ARPA). Santa Monica, CA: Rand.

Norman, D. A. (1983). *The design of everyday things.* New York: Basic Books.

Moore, D. R. (2004, March). *Using technology to collect and assess non-discrete multiple-choice data.* Paper presented at the 2004 Society for Information Technology and Teacher Education, Atlanta, Georgia.

Richmond, B. (2001). *An introduction to systems thinking.* Hanover, NH. High Performance Systems.

Russell, M. (2002). *How computer-based technology can disrupt the technology of testing and assessment in technology and assessment: Thinking ahead.* Proceedings from a workshop of the National Research Council, Washington, DC.

Zull, J. E. (2002). *The art of changing the brain.* Sterling, VA: Stylus.

Creating an Online Constructivist Learning Environment: A Work in Progress

Penelope Walters Swenson
California State University—Bakersfield

Lloyd S. Curtis
Central Arizona College

Kristie, a student in an education masters program, stated emphatically, "I had vowed that I would never take an online class. I heard the horror stories. But I was stuck. I could not graduate without this course, and it was online." Kristie was computer literate and an excellent student in her face-to-face courses. After five weeks in the online course, Kristie sent the professor an e-mail. "I never thought an online course could be so creative and so exciting." What had Kristie expected?

The online course landscape is littered with electronic workbooks. Students are told, "Read this. Fill in that. Make a few comments online or by e-mail. Take a test to demonstrate competencies. Get credit for the course." Although there are face-to-face courses that are similarly uninspired, online courses are subject to increased discussions of quality and effectiveness (Commission on Institutions of Higher Education, n.d.).

It is no surprise that online courses often have a higher dropout rate than do face-to-face courses. Still, the demand for them is increasing. How do we increase participant satisfaction and encourage learning at a level that is equal to or better than the face-to-face course? All too often, the work of an online course is insular, isolated, and nearly devoid of the human touches. Such courses lack the spark that identifies vibrant learning communities. Distance education courses, however, need not be flat, dispassionate, or unengaging. They can and—with some exceptions such as technical skill certification—should be laden with experiences and active learning.

What are the successful strategies?

- Constructivist learning environments
- Creation of dynamic learning experiences
- Personalizing courses and adding the human touch
- Compelling activities
- Encouraging and supporting student responsibility for learning
- Developing an active learning community
- Enhancing emotional intelligence

A WORK IN PROGRESS

At California State University, Bakersfield, Foundations of American Education is a required course in the Master of Arts in Education with concentration in Curriculum and Instruction program. It also is the prerequisite for the Educational Administration program. Foundations of American Education can be taught, online or face-to-face, as essentially a social history course with philosophy and other social sciences sprinkled throughout, yet it needs to be more. If the point of this course is to help individuals become better teachers or administrators, active engagement with the past and relating it to the present is paramount.

As we reviewed the required courses and assessed the reasons for requiring them, we found many students viewed the Foundations course as "just another history course" and a hurdle to jump over rather than a course with meaningful contribution to their lives and careers. We determined that our students needed to understand a period of history and its impact on the children of the time. We also believed the students would be able to use their newly developed framework to better understand other historical events and even develop greater empathy for today's children and youth from a variety of cultures and backgrounds.

Students in the course are from somewhat diverse backgrounds. Some have families that have lived in the United States for at least four generations, but a substantial minority are immigrants or first- and second-generation residents. Their residences range from upscale neighborhoods to the barrio. Most of the students have been schooled primarily in the United States, although not all in California and not all in middle-class settings. The participants in the course include recent college graduates and teachers with substantial experience in the classroom. They also range in age from early twenties to mid-fifties. A shared experience appeared necessary to give students a common understanding of the historical challenges facing a minority child. Developing such an experience presented challenges. We wanted students to move out of the "what do I have to do to get an A" model into a questioning, reflecting, and building experience.

Constructivist Learning Environments (CLEs) immerse students in a case, situation, or problem. Through that immersion, the students explore their prior knowledge, gain new knowledge, and create new understandings. CLEs must be engaging and filled with richness of experiences, information, and activity. Students explore and manipulate the environment, pressing beyond trying to determine what the professor wants them to know into developing multiple perspectives on a problem. According to Jonassen (n.d.), "Understanding any problem requires experiencing it and constructing mental models of it." The CLE should be dynamic and encourage independent and collaborative work. It also should be constructed to provide reflective times. Also critical to an effective CLE is providing timely opportunities for participants to express their learning, questions, and reflections.

For the initial shared experience, we considered films, plays, and stories that would fit in the context of the history and conflicts covered in the course. Film or video, although potentially engaging, could be a challenge for distant learners who might not be able to find the same video. Similarly, a play would not be available, except in print, to all of the enrolled students. A highly available book written for middle-grade students seemed to provide what we sought. Mildred Taylor's Newbery Award–winning book *Roll of Thunder, Hear My Cry* is the story of the Logan family, African Americans in rural Mississippi during the early 1930s. Chapter 1 introduces the characters and gives a description of place and circumstance that personalizes life in those times. Additionally, this chapter focuses on tensions and conflicts between emotions and realities experienced by the characters as the black school is given worn, castoff texts from the white school. An added benefit is that the book is inexpensive and available in many bookstores and in school and public libraries.

Class participants are assigned to read Taylor's Chapter 1. They describe, in three to ten words, the emotional impact of the book on each of four pivotal characters, two adults and two children. The word lists generated by the participants are from the position of being bystanders. At this time in the CLE, the students are observers, not participants in the drama. Their descriptions are posted anonymously, although the student's name is listed as having entered the posting area on a separate list for recordkeeping purposes. Anonymity is employed in the hope that the participants will be honest in their posts, rather than seeking to be politically correct or in line with what they think the instructor wants. Unlike in a face-to-face setting, the word lists the students post are not connected to their faces and the stereotypes, prejudices, and assumptions that follow such cues as appearance, age, race, and status.

At the beginning of the next week, the anonymous lists for each of the characters are posted to a location where they can be viewed by the entire class. Participants are challenged to read the lists and told, "Please relate your initial reaction to the word lists generally. Please hold any comment on the reactions of others until next weekend." The reactions are varied, but many comments focused in on the specific word choices and how similar they were for the two children and the wide range of interpretation regarding the reactions of the two adults. Although the word arrays in the word lists were anonymous, their reaction statements are attached to individual names, as are the subsequent series of responses to the "gut reactions." In those responses, students grappled with the characters and reactions. One student commented:

> There were so many emotions that swirled around those old books. I think that the lists really captured the complexity of such a situation, and by dividing up the characters we were able to identify the different feelings that could occur depending on how one viewed the situation. I think that the words listed captured the dynamic quality of the situation as well as allowing us to examine perhaps how characters could feel so differently about a set of books. Also, it is interesting to think about how a simple set of books can hold so much history and culture, not so much in their text, but in the way that they are used.

Another said, "Similar words, some surprises, wondered if we all read the same passage especially for Daisy Crocker." Yet another noted, "My initial response as I read each list was that I felt as though I was reading a recipe for hopelessness. As I close comment right now I am rediscovering that words alone can in fact illustrate great suffering."

After posting the initial reactions, participants were asked to respond to the postings of at least two others. The responses were respectful and thoughtful. Typical of these posts are comments like these:

> C__, I agree with you on the many different ways Mrs. Logan's and Daisy's characters were portrayed. I had never stopped to think of Daisy as "thankful." I guess that's why we all have different opinions. Thanks.

> R__, I also found it exciting that many of us had the same reactions in describing the characters' feelings. I noticed that many of the words I used were also used by our classmates.

Many of the participants are struck by the similarities they found in what they thought and the thoughts of others. Some are touched by a word choice and wondered why they had not found that perfect word. Still others are impressed with the variety of interpretations of the characters. The variation is particularly evident in the reactions to Daisy Crocker, a teacher who seeks to get along and does not challenge the circumstances. Although some participants see her as lacking courage and integrity, others view her as doing what she needed to serve the children.

The next part of the experience places the students into the position of county superintendent, a character not developed in the book. Mary Logan, however, is a prominent figure in Chapter 1 and throughout the book. At this point, the students become participants in the drama. Students are asked to write what they think a white county superintendent of schools would say in response to a question. Students post to a site created for this purpose their response, in the voice of that white superintendent, to Mrs. Logan's question, "What happened that enabled us to get those texts, and what is your plan for their use?" Students create their responses without seeing the paragraphs others develop. One student had the superintendent say the following:

Mrs. Logan, these books have been donated to Great Faith Elementary and Secondary School by the county. They may look a little rough around the edges, but you folks should be thankful you have them. There's a lot of useful information here. The school was just going to throw them out, but now your students here can use them. You should consider yourself fortunate to get these books. I'm sure you and the other teachers will put them to good use.

After the superintendent statements are posted, they are moved to the open site where comments can be made. Participants are asked to comment on at least two posted statements. Responding to the typical post in the previous extract, a student says, "It is interesting how people say similar things about the superintendent and Mrs. Logan. It seems that the idea of 'you should be thankful' is common." Through the voice of the superintendent, participants give their insights into the scenario and the history surrounding the roles individuals assume.

While the instructors read the statements and comments, there is a conscious effort not to enter the discussions. Participants are encouraged to develop their own meaning from the experiences rather than seeking clues and cues from the instructor about how to think and how to react. As one student noted, "This was such an interesting project. I like reading everyone's responses."

Another student reflected on the superintendent statements and sees great variety in them. She says,

I was surprised to see how many different types of responses were written. Some people made the superintendent sympathetic, others made him patient and professorial, still others made him ambivalent but influenced by a charitable community member, and yet others, like myself, made him bigoted.

The instructors' minimalist approach to guiding discussion and postings for the course encourages each student to form his or her own reactions to the shared information and experience and take responsibility for one's ideas and emotions. The constructivist instructor may guide but moves away from giving knowledge. The students are constructing knowledge, modifying their earlier assumptions, and exploring alternative viewpoints.

The initial scene for the CLE is rural Mississippi. Some of the participants know more about Central California than Mississippi, so another scene is introduced that is set just a few miles east of Bakersfield, California. During the late 1930s, the Dust Bowl drought, combined with other effects of the Great Depression, brought thousands of families from Oklahoma to Central California where they competed for several hundred jobs in the fields. The Okie children who came with their families to the region were shunned by school districts and they lived in difficult circumstances, often in camps with poor sanitation, little food, and few other facilities. Students are given an article, "Bringing the Story Home," about the Kern County Schools superintendent who championed the cause of these poor children who needed a school and so much more. After reading about Leo Hart, students compare the situations of the children, seeking any parallels and considering differences. They then submit a substantive post and reply to the posts of at least two others. The responses range from mentioning that discrimination was not just based on racial issues to considering capitalism, elitism, and power. With little active involvement from the professor, lively, intelligent, and searching dialogue ensues on the Web site.

A student commented,

She [Mary Logan, mother and a teacher at the black school] has her pride and dignity, but I believe that her battle is harder. I don't think that she would have been able to accomplish as much as Leo Hart did, not because of her personal abilities, but because of her skin color.

Responding to this post, another student replied, ". . . good point about not being able to accomplish as much due to the color of her skin. But, at least she did do something FOR the children and sticking out her neck. It is wonderful to hear positive stories about people that have helped our world."

Yet another student looked at herself, and her attitudes as she wrote,

> I guess the sad reality is that we don't care for people that are different than us. We get upset, as teachers, at those that are more challenging than what is considered the "norm." I have yet to hear a teacher say that they would like to have more of those hard to handle children, or to have more slower learners. I . . . went into the office at the beginning of the school year and complained because I had the majority of the low readers in my class. We would like to think of ourselves as civilized and compassionate, and yet to some extent, we are still discriminatory.

This student became highly reflective and concerned about her own prejudices. Furthermore, she felt comfortable enough within the group that she expressed her thoughts even with her name attached.

Later in the course, through the other assignments and experiences, the learning from the *Roll of Thunder* CLE keep bubbling to the surface. A reflective post about the integration of Central High in Little Rock, Arkansas, stated:

> When Elizabeth [Eckford in the famous picture] walks past the National Guardsmen, she reminds me of Mary [mother and teacher at the black school in *Roll*]. She makes a stand with her presence in a quiet way, but in another way, it is a loud presence. It took courage for her to attend an "all white school." She had to face all her white peers as they entered the school and I'm sure they didn't have a nice thing to say. . . . I could have never survived being in that kind of situation and I give her credit for being brave and courageous.

We posit that through the initial use of the CLE, students begin to personalize the history, first relating it to the experiences of the children and adults of Taylor's book, then to themselves. The *Roll of Thunder* CLE provides a scaffold, developing experience and insight. The students have new lenses through which they can view other culture clashes within the history of U.S. education and those existing within their own schools. As evidenced by one of the student comments quoted earlier, perhaps some students even began recognizing those culture clashes within their own schools and the damaging impact those clashes have on children.

Within the CLE, students develop a new sense of reality. They create a community wherein they can and do discuss sensitive issues without assumptions based on what they thought the professor wanted or their colleagues would accept from them. They explore, collaborate, share, and build. In so doing, they construct new meaning and increase understanding both of the past and of the present. Students made narrative comments on an anonymous exit survey about the experience:

". . . it helped me understand . . . more clearly. It put me in their shoes."

"I think that in order to avoid negative situations that happened in the past, one must be able to feel what the situations might have done to people. Having emotions about a situation will impact whether or not it will happen again."

After reviewing the student postings and replies to colleagues, we found they demonstrate the following:

- Active engagement
- Acknowledgment and appreciation for diverse perspectives
- Understanding of how an individual's motivations within a highly charged political, social, and emotional atmosphere could be interpreted both positively and negatively
- A variety of emotions regarding prejudice and perceived wrongs directed toward children
- An understanding of the roles people play to survive
- Willingness to make judgments on the motivations of people, then suspend those judgments as another perspective emerged
- Curiosity about historical events
- Reflection on personal attitudes and personal goals
- Desire to be just, fair, and compassionate

Hew, Hur, Jang, and Tian (2004) proposed eight events of instruction within constructivist learning, providing an effective means to review a CLE through looking at these events, beginning with gaining the attention of learners and moving through to ongoing engagement within communities of practice. Although the latter is difficult within a quarter or semester, the informal feedback indicates many participants do continue to think about the *Roll of Thunder* CLE and talk about their insights.

We are continuing research on the use of this Constructivist Learning Environment and seeking to demonstrate how such environments can enrich humanities and social science courses. We also are endeavoring to demonstrate experiences that are best conducted online, exploring those pedagogies that help create dynamic, meaningful online courses. We currently have two more online groups engaged in this course. Thus far, their responses are similar to those of the earlier groups.

REFERENCES

Commission on Institutions of Higher Education. (n.d.). *Best practices for electronically offered degree and certificate programs.* Retrieved April 7, 2004, from http://www.neasc.org/cihe/best_practices_electronically_offered_degree.htm

Hew, K., Hur, J., Jang, H., & Tian, L. (2004). The eight events of instruction: An instructional method based on the constructivist paradigm. *Information Technology & Teacher Education Annual: Proceedings of SITE 2004, 4110–4115.*

Jonassen, D. (n.d.). *Welcome to the design of constructivist learning environments (CLEs).* Retrieved April 15, 2003, from http://tiger.coe.missouri.edu/%7Ejonassen/courses/CLE/index.html

The E-Environment:
A 21st-Century Approach to Building Community

Katherine L. Hayden and Antonette W. Hood
California State University—San Marcos

In the past two decades, there have been some sweeping changes in the use of technology as a means of course delivery at colleges and universities. Whole programs of study are now offered completely through electronic environments, and much of the professoriate have scurried to stay abreast of this trend. Social and educational demands have prompted institutions to provide students with a variety of learning opportunities and have seemingly ensured a place for electronic course delivery in higher education.

Electronic teaching and learning (ETL) utilizes a wide variety of e-tools to access courses and programs supported by e-environments (Hood & Hayden, 2004). Online course content and activities, videoconferencing experiences, and a variety of other real-time (synchronous) and choice-time (asynchronous) learning opportunities now occupy considerable space in the course listings of college catalogues. Higher education faculty members are bombarded by vendors offering online resources and services. Conference sessions are replete with suggestions and scenarios of effective uses of educational technology.

Students who have access to the educational opportunities offered in e-environments are able to participate in virtual communities that expand their learning at times and in places beyond the limitations of the traditional campus classroom. Dede (1995) and Witherspoon (1997) suggest that distance education and the use of online technology provides learners with a sense of community. To build community, course designers must plan interactive and collaborative experiences and activities that bond individuals. Designers must understand and effectively utilize characteristics of electronic discourse that enhance communication and build community.

E-ENVIRONMENTS

> The web is a distributed multimedia environment, which potentially can provide a truly integrated teaching and learning system to educators. (Witherspoon, 1997)

E-environments that include the use of effective electronic communication tools provide students with global access to peers, mentors, and experts. E-environments such as videoconferencing, Tapped In, and WebCT enable students to transition from traditional classroom experiences and local learning groups to broader venues (Gottschalk, 2003).

> Distance education technologies are enabling students in rural communities to reach out to those in urban areas; they are enabling students in wealthy [school] districts to interact with those less well endowed; they are enabling students of one racial background to collaborate on multicultural projects with those from another. (Poole, 1997, p. 206)

Today, distance education technologies continue to meet that goal through interactive E-environments, and the use of E-tools.

THE BENEFITS OF E-TOOLS

> Information infrastructures will provide channels for delivering . . . technol-
> ogy-intensive learning experiences just-in-time, anyplace, and on-demand,
> enabling partnerships for effective K-12 [and higher] education among
> schools, parents, businesses, communities, and the media. (Dede, 1995, p. 1)

E-tools support interactive online activities that meet diverse learning needs and personalize learning pathways in electronic environments. According to the publishers of
WebCT (2003),

> Virtual learning programs address educational needs and provide several im-
> portant benefits, including:
>
> Extending educational access and ensuring equity for all students cost-effectively;
> Assisting educators in enhancing students' academic performance; and
> Introducing technologies that support, rather than distract, educators.

Educational Access

Issues of educational access are often resolved through the use of e-tools. Common
issues include campus parking, space constraints, transportation difficulties, class scheduling conflicts, and family needs and child care (Barton, 2003). Virtual learning programs
have provided students with the opportunity and flexibility to participate in learning at convenient times that accommodate personal schedules. This learning can take place at a variety of remote sites, such as satellite campuses, local public libraries, and private homes.

Student Performance

Online virtual connection with students allows instructors to monitor students' progress continuously and to individualize their learning. Conducting ongoing, interactive virtual conversations with students enhances the mentoring process. It enables instructors to
differentiate and be supportive of students' diverse learning needs.

Support for Educators

WebCT provides educators with e-tools that can support their teaching. Students
have the opportunity to ask questions at any time, and instructors are not left wondering between class meetings whether students understand basic course content or assignment directions. Feedback can be provided individually at times outside of scheduled class hours.
Announcements can be posted between class sessions, as can additional information to follow-up class discussions and activities. Instructors also have the flexibility to schedule online advising sessions at times convenient to both instructor and student.

By design, the e-tools of WebCT allow educational communities to develop. In the
public forum of the Discussion Board, for example, interactive dialogue among course participants and the instructor can take place. Common and diverse philosophical and pedagogical stances can be openly discussed, and like-minded and contrary interactions that
characterize the discourse of any learning community can emerge. In the traditional classroom, time constraints would not allow for this to occur. Professors arrive with time-certain
agendas that rarely build in sufficient time for extended discussion opportunities.

These technology experiences prepare students for engagement in lifelong learning
and the acquisition of essential 21st-century skills. Many researchers (e.g., Andres, 1995;

Dede, 2004; Dwyer, 1994; Hayden & Hood, 2003; Schrum, 2004) concur that these experiences provide skills that enable students to lead productive lives in a global, digital, information-based future society.

DESIGNING ETL ENVIRONMENTS

> Communities of learners [students and instructors] . . . in cyberspace are . . .
> able to communicate their feelings, needs, and passions through their writings
> . . . eloquently and sincerely. (Nevin, Hood, & McNeil, 2002, p. 146)

Electronic teaching and learning (ETL) environments are generally characterized as *synchronous* (real-time participation) or *asynchronous* (different or choice-time participation). In their examinations of ETL, some researchers (e.g., Beck, 2002; Nevin et al., 2002) sought to create online communities within these ETL environments that would be comparable to those formed in traditional classrooms. What they discovered was that participants in these two settings (online vs. face-to-face) approach activities differently. Class discussions in campus-based classes were often brief, and the critical thinking of course participants was not supported by opportunities for students to use course resources to respond fully to the occasional class commentary. Conversely, students engaging in asynchronous online class discussions (using the Discussion Board in WebCT, for example) could use supplementary resources to enrich their responses. They could also take advantage of the luxury of reflection and respond or participate in asynchronous discussions following thoughtful consideration of a discussion prompt. Successful ETL communities that develop between and among students and instructors provide students with "more time to reflect before jumping in, and because a sense of anonymity promotes risk-taking, student responses [tend] to be much more thoughtful" (Beck, 2002, p. 9). Students' communication is also "richer, deeper, more open, and more frequent than that of their face-to-face counterparts" (Nevin et al., 2002, p. 138).

Experiences common to traditional (face-to-face) learning environments are not always transferable to online communication experiences. This does not presuppose, however, that outcomes will always be less satisfying or less effective in traditional classes.

Online Chat

Another synchronous 3-environment used in ETL is online chat. In this synchronous communication environment, course designers often create class discussions and activities that imitate the real-time element of the traditional classroom. In other words, participants are able to have dialogue that simulates face-to-face conversation. Online chat is a feature of Tapped In® (http://tappedin.org/tappedin/), which is "an international professional support system for teachers" (Bull, Bull, & Kajder, 2004, p. 36). An added benefit of online chat is that it also provides participants with opportunities for *virtual anonymity*. Nevin et al., (2002) suggest that the opportunity for virtual anonymity is an element of online communication that increases communication by students who are otherwise quiet in the classroom. Students reported that they became more willingly and actively engaged in chat when their presence and presentation were within the written discourse of their online classes.

In online chats, the playing field is leveled in terms of the opportunity to respond and length of response. According to Hood and Hayden (2004), conversation is able to flow "without being influenced by the occasional student who might otherwise dominate a classroom discussion. The equal opportunity to be *heard* positively contributes to the building of community in the virtual classroom, and the sense of belonging is more satisfying" (p. 5). In their Tapped In commentary, Bull et al. (2004) suggest that students and teachers are able to find out about the elements and benefits of effective online communities. Specifically, participants in Tapped In "discover what it means to critique ideas, and how it is that we facilitate active talk and learning within electronic spaces" (p. 37). They suggest that the Tapped In Discussion Board is useful as "both a space for individual expression and a place where the group's voice is gathered and amplified. Authentic discussion should allow students to test new ideas and push the thinking of their peers" (p. 37). Tapped In chats provide a forum for virtual, collaborative work and study groups, social interactions, peer mentoring opportunities, and, consequently, community building. An additional desirable feature of Tapped In chat is that the transcripts of each discussion are "automatically generated and e-mailed to participants" (pp. 35–36).

Videoconferencing

Another synchronous model of electronic teaching and learning is videoconferencing. This model is gaining momentum with expanded bandwidth available today. In this e-environment, participants at geographically distant locations are able to communicate in real time with the use of audio, video, and other media to simulate real-time conversations. According to McCracken (2001), videoconferencing is an electronic environment that promotes continuous discussion and has the potential to simulate interactions that occur in traditional classrooms. McCracken found that the "collective synergy, created through opportunities for continuous exchange, application, and self-assessment, is critical to realizing learning effectiveness in virtual environments" (p. 1).

Online chat and videoconferencing enable students to participate in learning experiences despite barriers of distance and time. Through these synchronous e-environments, students and their instructors build interactive communities as they communicate with each other in real time (Hayden, 1999; Nicholson & Bond, 2003).

Synchronous E-Environments

In designing synchronous e-environments, it is important that instructors thoughtfully consider the selection and appropriateness of the e-tools and activities included in their courses. Typically, designers choose tools that are available from a menu offered through educational software, such as WebCT. Among these common E-tools are Class Mail, Discussion Board, Calendar, Syllabus, Assignments, Quizzes, and Content Modules. Course participants access these e-tools at different times, according to their personal schedules. There are several advantages to using e-tools. Twigg (2001), for example, notes that although assignments and activities may have specific due dates, the barrier of real-time participation in class discussions and certain postings is eliminated. The paperless assignments that students submit electronically also conserve resources, and barriers of time and cost are minimized.

The Study

Investigators have developed ETL activities in their distance education courses offered through the College of Education at Cal State—San Marcos. The following courses have been included in their research:

- Instruction of Students with Special Learning Needs
- Using Data-Based Instruction
- Language and Literacy for Education Specialists
- Issues and Research in Educational Technology
- Technology Tools for Teaching and Learning
- Teaching and Learning in Elementary Schools

As part of their courses, the researchers included the use of WebCT, Tapped In, and videoconferencing seminars involving guest speakers and participants (see Figure 1).

Figure 1. Videoconferencing session from a remote site.

The ETL strategies and activities studied by the investigators within the e-environments of their courses explored strategies to develop and maintain communities of learners. Through the use of interactive technologies, students and teachers were involved in group and individual synchronous and asynchronous discussions, commentary, assignment presentations, and other collaborative activities.

As facilitator-participants in their courses, the investigators allowed interactive communities to develop through activities that promoted common interests, purpose, and interactions between and among students and instructors.

Purpose of This Study

The purpose of this study was to examine the effectiveness of e-tools within the e-environments of courses taught by the researchers. They hoped to identify ways in which the use of ETL strategies and activities promote the development and maintenance of communities of learners within e-environments. The investigators examined the following:

- Characteristics inherent in electronic communication tools

- Strategies and activities used in electronic communication

- Communication enhancements used by course participants and facilitators

- Other ways in which communities of learners develop in E-environments

Methodology

Research has shown that many learners prefer online classes because they are able to connect with mentors, advisors, faculty members, and peers (e.g., Bull et al., 2004; McCracken, 2001). To examine how communities develop and are sustained, the investigators asked their current and former students to complete a confidential survey about their experiences in using videoconferencing and Web-based technologies during 2002 and 2003. The surveys defined community as a *sense of belonging developed by participants in a learning group facilitated by an instructor.*

The surveys included four questions for which students used a five-point Likert scale. The survey also included four open-ended questions. Seventy-six students completed the surveys, and responses provided data regarding their perceptions of specific strategies, behaviors, and characteristics of e-environments that promote the development of dynamic, interactive communities of learners. Participants were asked to respond to questions about their experiences using online communication tools in courses taught by the researchers. The Likert scale used the following ratings: 1 = *weak,* 2 = *adequate,* 3 = *strong,* 4 = *very strong,* and 5 = *no opinion.*

Findings

In analyzing the surveys completed by students who had participated in their distance education courses, the researchers obtained averages for the responses to each question. The responses for *no opinion* were not included in the analysis. Review of the open-ended statements gave further insight into the perceptions of the students related to the course activities.

Question 1. Participants were asked to rate the extent to which characteristics inherent in online communication tools lead to building community. Average ratings for the following characteristics were as follows:

- opportunities for threaded discussions (3.0)
- opportunities for private communication (2.9)
- opportunities for public communication (3.1)
- access to people outside of the course (2.2)

Participants indicated that threaded discussions and public communication were strong characteristics that lead to building community. Although access to people outside the course received an adequate rating, the researchers realized that the entire participant pool did not have the same access (to people outside the course), because some courses did not offer this feature.

Through the use of Tapped In, students in one of the courses had been involved in virtual chats in a community open to educators throughout the world. Although the course participants developed presentations for sharing their research and issues on topics from the course, they also had the opportunity to attend sessions offered in the community of educators. They felt the experiences enhanced their learning through the chat tool and the Tapped In e-environment.

Question 2. Participants were asked to rate the extent to which certain strategies and activities used in online communication tools lead to building community. Average ratings for the following strategies and activities were as follows:

- prompts/topics from course content (2.9)
- interesting/controversial/timely instructor prompts (2.8)

- interesting/controversial/timely student comments (3.1)
- individual course assignments (2.0)
- group course assignments (3.0)

   Looking at the results of Question 2, the researchers noted that four of the five strategies and activities averaged between 2.8 and 3.1 (with 3.0 considered strong). Individual course assignments, on the other hand, received a 2.0, which was a considerably lower rating than that of the other strategies and activities. Student comments to open-ended questions further explained how they enjoyed working in groups and sharing their thoughts, rather than working individually and isolated from other course participants.

   Question 3. Participants were asked to rate the extent to which the use of certain *communication enhancements* (e.g., use of props, symbols, visual referents, and oral and written language) lead to building community. Averages for the following communication enhancements were as follows:

- punctuation (2.3)
- capitalization for emphasis (2.6)
- "Netiquette" (2.7)
- symbols (emoticons) to create expressions (2.6)
- clear, explicit, descriptive language (3.3)
- visuals (3.3)

   Responses to Question 3 indicated that the participants' use of visuals and clear, explicit, descriptive language in online activities lead to building their sense of community. The visuals were an important element in the videoconferencing sessions experienced by some participants. Through clear, explicit descriptive language, the sessions became an opportunity to meet experts in areas related to the course. Without the open opportunity to connect with experts outside the course, the students would not have had this enriched experience.

   Question 4. Participants in the courses were asked to consider other ways in which communities of learners develop online (in addition to the statements offered in the survey). The researchers examined students' responses to the open-ended prompts provided on the survey. For example, students were asked to describe characteristics of the online communication tools or online experiences that facilitated their sense of membership and belonging in their course. The following are samples of responses to those prompts:

- The base teams we have worked in provide a sense of membership and belonging. Each member's opinion is valued, and each has the ability to be a facilitator/member.
- Participating in Tapped In sessions gave me a sense of membership by networking with teachers across the nation.
- I was able to communicate with my cohort five thousand miles away.

   Online learning communities, described in the students' responses, are environments in which students were able to demonstrate course competencies collaboratively while building interdependent relationships with peers.

DISCUSSION AND RECOMMENDATIONS

   Becoming a member of a community of learners allowed students to better understand the value of community in their personal and professional lives. The feedback provided by students clearly identified the chat tool Tapped In as a valuable e-environment for group discussions and experiences that brings students in contact with a larger community of educators (SRI International, 2003).

The e-tools used through WebCT provided opportunities for collaboration and communication. Connecting with people beyond the course and sharing ideas through discussions and group activities expanded the students' learning community and enriched their academic experience.

Although the use of videoconferencing seminars was considered valuable for sharing ideas, responses indicated a need for more interactivity among participants during each session. This research has provided important insights into the effects of strategies and collaborative online assignments related to building community. The researchers have made modifications in their courses based on the findings of this study, and they are currently developing new courses that incorporate the highest ranked ETL strategies and activities (i.e., they have expanded the number of online sessions in their courses and included more group activities). The investigators plan to continue to survey their students and reflect further on how the use of ETL strategies and activities promotes a sense of community.

REFERENCES

Andres, Y. M. (1995). Collaboration in the classroom and over the Internet. Article originally published in *Electronic Learning,* March 1995. Available: http://www.gsn.org/teach/articles/ (September 9, 2003).

Barton, D. (2003). Teaching online in the early 21st century—using technology to enrich the learning experience. In *E-Learn 2003 World Conference on E-Learning in Corporate, Government, Healthcare, & Higher Education* (pp. 875–878), proceedings of the Association for the Advancement of Computing in Education meeting, November 2003, Phoenix, AZ.

Beck, E. (2002). The mysterious territory of distance learning. *Thought and Action: The NEA Higher Education Journal, XVIII,* 77–89.

Bull, G., Bull, G., & Kajder, S. (2004, February). Tapped In®: The new incarnation of this resource is now available. *Learning and Leading with Technology, 31(5).* Retrieved March 5, 2004, from http://www.iste.org/LL.

Dede, C. (1995, October). Testimony to the U. S. Congress. House of Representatives, Joint Hearing on Educational Technology 21st century. Retrieved September 9, 2003, from http://www.virtual.gmu.edu/SS_research/cdpapers/congrpdf.htm

Dede, C. (2004, March). *Distributed-learning communities as a model for educating teachers.* Presented at the Association for the Advancement of Computing in Education (AACE): Society for Information Technology & Teacher Education (SITE) 15th International Conference, Atlanta, Georgia.

Dwyer, D. C. (1994). Apple classrooms of tomorrow: What we've learned. *Educational Leadership, 51(7),* 4–10.

Gottschalk, T. H. (Ed.). (2003). Distance education: An overview. Retrieved November 6, 2003, from http://www.uidaho.edu/evo/dist1.html

Hayden, K. L. (1999). Videoconferencing in K–12 education: A Delphi study of characteristics and critical strategies to support constructivist learning experiences. (Doctoral dissertation, Pepperdine University, 1999). *Dissertation Abstracts International, 60,* 06A.

Hayden, K. L., & Hood, A. W. (2003, November). *Collaborative online activities that promote a sense of community: Perceptions of graduate students.* Presented at the Association for the Advancement of Computing in Education (AACE): World Conference on E-Learning in corporate, Government, Healthcare, & Higher Education (E-Learn). Phoenix, AZ.

Hood, A. W., & Hayden, K. L. (2004, March). *Enhancing communication and community in electronically delivered coursework: Responding to students' perspectives.* Presented at the Association for the Advancement of Computing in Education (AACE): Society for Information Technology in Teacher Education (SITE) 15th International Conference, Atlanta, GA.

McCracken, H. (2001). The importance of learning communities in visual learning environments. Retrieved October 31, 2002, from http://www.ipfw.edu/as/tohe/2001/Papers/mccracken.html

Nevin, A. I., Hood, A. W., & McNeil, M. E. (2002), Creating community in online (electronic) environments. In H. Christiansen & S. Ramadevi (Eds.), *Reeducating the educator: Global perspectives on community building.* Albany: State University of New York Press.

Nicholson, S. A., & Bond, N. (2003) Collaborative reflection and professional community building: An analysis of pre-service teachers' use of an electronic discussion board [Electronic version]. *Journal of Technology and Teacher Education, 11*(2), 259–279. Retrieved March 5, 2004, from http://dl.aace.org/13568

Poole, B. J. (1997). Education for an information age: Teaching in the computerized classroom (2nd ed.). San Francisco: McGraw-Hill.

Schrum, L. (2004, March). *Student achievement and success in online environments: Research into characteristics and strategies.* Presented at Association for the Advancement of Computing in Education (AACE): Society for Information Technology & Teacher Education (SITE) 15th International Conference, Atlanta, GA.

SRI International. (2003). Tapped In®. Retrieved September 9, 2003, from http://ti2.sri.com/tappedin/index.jsp

Twigg, C. A. (2001). Innovations in online learning: Moving beyond no significant difference. Troy, NY: Center for Academic Transformation (sponsored by a grant from the Pew Charitable Trusts). Retrieved January 30, 2004, from http://www.center.rpi.edu/PewSym/Mono4.html

WebCT. (2003). WebCT learning transformations: Opportunities for secondary education leveraging virtual learning programs. Retrieved March 24, 2004, from http://www.webct.com

Witherspoon, J. P. (1997). Details and serendipity: Observations about effective distance education. Distance Education Report. Retrieved April 26, 1997, from http://www.catalog.com/_de/jwinter.html

E-Learning Best Practices:
Strategies and Tips for the Online Instructor

Stephanie Huffman, Glenda Thurman, Jody Charter, and Wendy Rickman
University of Central Arkansas

There are many myths about teaching and learning online utilizing both synchronous and asynchronous formats. Many faculty argue both vehemently and emotionally that students cannot learn as much, as well, or as effectively in an online environment as in the traditional classroom. This is simply not true. Research has demonstrated in general that students engaged at a distance learn as well and as effectively as students in a traditional classroom (Moore & Thompson, 1990). As with all teaching, the key to success lies with the instructor being prepared, knowing the classroom environment, communicating with students, creating stimulating assignments, and providing timely feedback.

The use of any form of instructional technology in teaching must begin with the learner in mind. The focus of this yearbook chapter is on how instructors can use e-learning strategies effectively through the decisions they make and the way in which each structures the online environment. Practical tips and strategies for instructors on course shell content development, synchronous and asynchronous communication formats, student motivation, and simulations and interactive games are the thrust of this piece, thus providing guidance on extending the class discussion beyond time and place.

CONTENT DEVELOPMENT

Principles of Teaching/Learning

The same principles for effective teaching and learning utilized in a traditional classroom can be applied to the online environment. Instructors should organize the course shell to encourage active learning and student involvement. High expectations communicated throughout the course aids in guiding student achievement. Just as in a traditional classroom, time on learning tasks should be emphasized in the online classroom. Respect for diversity and differing learning styles is the protective environmental umbrella allowing equal opportunities for all students (Crys, 1997).

It is important to communicate and connect teaching and learning goals and objectives in many ways to increase student understanding. The connection of new information to prior knowledge provides links in learning goals and objectives (Lever-Duffy, McDonald, & Mizell, 2003). Utilize cooperative learning and appropriate practice activities for the transfer and application of skills. It is vital that the instructor articulate his or her philosophy and model of teaching and learning (Norton & Wiburg, 2003).

Instructional Design

When organizing an online course, books and articles recommend application of the principles of instructional design to develop the elements of the course in a systematic fashion (The Ultimate WebCT Handbook, 2002; Teaching Online: Best Practices and Tips, 2003). The instructional design model used here is a modification of one found in Turner and Riedling (2003).

The model begins by identifying instructional goals and objectives, continuing to the design of an assessment of student performance, which is based on the stated objectives. The next two design steps aid in choosing content for online courses by selecting both resources for the course and developing strategies, activities, and "best tools" that will accommodate the chosen resources (Drummond, 2002). The last two steps of the model implement what has been designed and the evaluation of how well the implementation functioned. Do not forget the evaluation of student perception of the implementation.

The first suggested step in organizing any course is to identify the goals and subsequent objectives to be achieved by the students. These will be the foundation of all of the instructional design activities. They will also provide a core for the course syllabus, one of the documents that structures or organizes the course. It is recommended that professional standards of content areas found in professional organizations such as those of Association for Educational Communications and Technology, American Association of School Librarians, or textbooks be reviewed to determine appropriate objectives for any specific course designed.

The second suggested step in organizing any course is the creation of the assessment of student performance, based on each objective designed for the course. Assessments can take the form(s) of an assignment, exam, portfolios, performance evaluations, journals, reflective papers, and Web site development (Hanna, Glowacki-Dudka, & Conceição-Runlee, 2000). Provide the three parts of an assignment that will communicate expectations: course objectives, a description and guidelines, and a rubric for grading.

Next, it is recommended that "best practices" and "available online tools" be selected in developing the content. The consideration of content in the form of readings and other resources are excellent additions to the course. Permission to use copyrighted materials must be obtained. Selected readings, Web sites, and institutional resources such as online access to library resources for the course can also be added.

At this point, the information to organize the course content and course outline is available to complete a syllabus. If software includes a calendar, general deadlines can be posted. A time line for the course can also be created that includes dates, readings, class topics or activities, assignments given, and assignment deadlines. This type of time line organizes the whole course chronologically.

Now implement the design and keep notes on how each segment functions. This allows for evaluation of the progress of each element of the course. One form of evaluation is surveying the students using a Lickert scale. Have the students check how well they feel they can perform each course objective. Once evaluations are done, review what changes should occur and begin a revision cycle through the instructional design process to improve the course and keep it fresh.

Through this design process, the course has been organized to include content, readings, and resources such as a syllabus, time line, assignments, and course evaluation. Built into most course shells (e.g., WebCT and BlackBoard) are content development tools. These tools consist of, but are not limited to, the content model tool, the syllabus tool, the quiz and survey tool, the assignment box tool, the photo gallery tool, the audio and video tools, and the student Web page development tool. Adding content is similar in nature to that of a Web page. The same file types are used and links are embedded to provide structure and flow from one area to another. It is vital that the design and layout be easily understood. Students should not have to struggle to find the content needed.

SYNCHRONOUS AND ASYNCHRONOUS COMMUNICATION TOOLS

Once the initial planning issues have been considered, just as in traditional instructional design, the next step is to examine the supporting technologies that are available. In the field of distance education, such technologies fall into two broad categories: technologies that support synchronous distance education and those that support asynchronous distance education. Synchronous distance education is instruction that occurs at the same time or real time, although typically not in the same geographic location. In contrast, asynchronous distance education is time altered; meaning that teacher and student can participate at differing times (Newby, Stepich, Lehman, & Russel, 2000).

Various modes of communication are built into course shells. The most common being the discussion board or bulletin board, e-mail, chat, whiteboard, and the calendar tool. The discussion board, e-mail, and calendar tool are all forms of asynchronous communication. The chat tool and whiteboard are used for synchronous instruction.

Regardless of the level of expertise, a few basic principles must be followed to promote successful use of communication tools: (1) answer e-mail promptly, (2) use open-ended questions for greater participation on the discussion board, (3) frequently review and redirect the dialogue of students on the discussion board, (4) always define the purpose of each discussion despite the communication tool utilized, (5) set rules for chat room use, (6) act quickly to suppress inappropriate or harsh language used by students, (7) spice up the chat room or discussion board by inviting experts to contribute to the conversation, (8) allow the use of emoticons in the chat room (see Table 1), (9) encourage reflective thinking and writing, and (10) use the calendar tool as a guide for organizing the entire class (Teaching Online, 2003).

Table 1. Basic Emoticons

Symbol	Meaning	Symbol	Meaning	Symbol	Meaning
:-)	Happy face	:-(	Sad Face	:'-(	Crying
:-X	Writer lips are sealed	>:->	Really devilish remark	:-/	Skeptical
:-D	Laughing	;-)	A wink	:-l	Indifference
:->	Sarcastic remark	:-&	Tongue tied	:-O	Surprise

STUDENT MOTIVATION

One of the biggest problems facing a distance education instructor is how to motivate students. The lack of shared physical local each class period unnerves many instructors. This contact acts as reassurance but according to research does not necessarily motivate students. Students are not motivated by instructors.

Instructors have the power to design and develop an exciting and stimulating environment, one in which students want to learn a new skill (Morrison & Lowther, 2002). For students to be motivated, three questions must be answered: why, what, and how. Students need to know *why* they should learn something new, *what* benefits are provided from the learning, and *how* it applies to their future (Crys, 1997). The trick to answering these questions is in linking the learning to the student.

Explicit language must communicate expectations of learning as a result of attending and participating in a class. Utilize student guides and handouts to help students see connections and relationships among ideas. Share the inner self and expose passions, beliefs, and excitement about the subject matter. Explain how vital the topic is to the student's future as a professional. Employing humor, stories, analogies, and provocative statements adds spice to the mix and shakes things up. The utilization of various forms of media (video, audio, print, and interactive Web sites) provides multiple modes of delivery for multiple modes of learning (Lockard & Abrams, 2004). Remember, in the end it all comes back to *why*, *what*, and *how*.

SIMULATIONS

Simulations were introduced to the educational market in the 1970s and 1980s as large-size boxes of tools allowing students to achieve various learning objectives. Often the students were asked to assume roles. Taking part in this way helped students "see" some of society's issues as multifaceted problems. In the game Redwood, the user may have been a member of the lumber industry or a preservationist. In following the character's role, the user learned more about the point of view of the person whose role was represented, but also about the view of the "other fellow."

According to Tip 132 of *147 Practical Tips for Teaching Online Groups* (Hanna et al., 2000), "Simulations are dynamic, interactive, task-driven exercises that allow students to experience a concept. They use goal-based scenarios based on real-life situations in which individuals and groups must understand their tasks and successfully interact in order to achieve their objective."

Online teaching allows for simulations, but generally those created and planned from the instructor's standpoint rather than buying into commercial kits or software. In many subject areas, those commercial packages are available. Nonetheless, their use still requires an instructor who learns by experimenting to make the simulation more user-friendly online.

The discussion board is one avenue for conducting a simulation either synchronously or asynchronously. With multiple "threads" created by the instructor, roles can be assigned. Students begin by downloading an agenda or a listing of events that mock how events would presumably take place in real life. An example of a simulation exercise online is a "mock hearing." The focus is on a policy-making body, in which a moderator is responsible for maintaining the agenda. The participating online students are made aware of an appropriate order in which to post thoughts or replies after reading carefully to absorb what others have said.

As in real life, there can be an "agitator" or "complainant" to further complicate the event. If a vote is to be taken, which in reality would be of an anonymous nature, a "thread" in the discussion board allows for an anonymous vote. The moderator or facilitator can be given several threads as needed for introducing the group, reminding others of the agenda, calling time (or the agenda can specify time limits), calling for a vote, reporting the vote, and final interactions with the group. This type of simulation has been used in the library media and information technologies area to heighten awareness in graduate students of challenged materials hearings that take place in many school districts in the United States.

The "hearing" follows school policy, that is, the board-approved Challenged Materials or Reconsideration Policy. Students, of course, must be aware of the contents of such policies previous to taking part in the simulation. The use of the Course Content downloading function and the chat room for clarifications, exceptions, and differences between policies can be explored. Also, "expert guest chatters" can be invited to participate. Experts can also be asked to help the instructor evaluate the completed simulation.

GAMING

Classroom games for learning go back to the one room schoolhouse. The spelling bee tested students in a fun way by allowing a break in routine through *standing up* and *circling* the classroom. Active participation and involvement kept most learners' attention.

Difficult words dropped the least prepared back to their desks, while spelling opportunities were posed to the remainder of the group. In time, the group lessened to two or three as the tension in the classroom grew. Few extrinsic rewards were involved; the spelling bee winner instead was graced with wild applause.

In today's online classroom, there is an emoticon for applause. This emoticon is two parentheses clashing: (). Heightened applause merits several clashing sets of parentheses. Online students enjoy games as much, perhaps even more, than traditional classroom students. Gaming activities, however, require a good deal of preparation done by the instructor as well as students who feel confident in taking part. Tip 19 from *147 Practical Tips for Teaching Online Groups* reminds that "Team-based learning requires rich communication [between instructor and students] above all" (Hanna et al., 2000). In other words, "time on task" by students studying and working with the information involved in the game is needed before the event. This tip reminds that gaming, which can be used for problem solving, project development, and encouragement of discussion as well as cognitive learning must take place in a learning environment of both knowledge and trust.

One example of a teaming approach is the quiz bowl. Academic quiz bowls of one type or another are used by school systems and by individual classrooms. Local public television stations also encourage academic achievement by broadcasting quiz bowl tournaments. A quiz bowl can be used within the online classroom by simply dividing the chat list into two "teams" omitting the instructor who pitches questions. Team spirit is heightened by students coming up with team names and by fellow team members who claim points for a question missed, limiting humiliation. Questions must be kept short if they are keyed in for those without online audio. Answers must be short in nature. This is not the place to use case studies or essay questions. Anything requiring more than two lines of keying to answer is not appropriate for an online quiz bowl.

A content area that lends itself well to cognitive learning is that of federal copyright laws. There is a massive amount of "basic" information to learn in this area that is necessary to assimilate a sufficient backdrop for dealing with frequent changes in court decisions and legislation. The content area of copyright allows for several "rounds" of a quiz bowl spread over a semester. As teams change for each round, every student would have a chance to contribute to a winning team.

As with any instructor-led gaming, students need to be involved in the statistics of the game. One instructor cannot keep up with the questions, student playing order, and other demands necessary to the game. Students should be trusted to keep score. Both teams must agree on the final score with the members of the winning team collecting their huge intrinsic prize: the respect of the teacher and the other team. Clipart-type certificates saved as .pdf files are a nice surprise when filled in by the instructor and dropped into the current champions' e-mail boxes the next day.

CONCLUSIONS

Classroom success is dictated by the preparation and organization of the instructor. The successful classroom is dependent on the instructor being prepared, knowing the classroom environment, communicating with students, providing feedback, and creating stimulating assignments that link knowledge and learning together regardless of the classroom setting. Physical location of both classroom and student in relation to the instructor is irrelevant.

The key to online learning is to be more aware of the classroom environment when organizing the instruction. Content development must revolve around those learning goals and objectives for the student. Assignments and activities must be stimulating and reality based to keep the student involved and motivated. The use of simulations and games are encouraged. Assessment must be communicated in advance and related to course objectives. The use of rubrics, handouts, and study guides aides in the students' ability to make connections within the content. Communication tools are abundant and relevant to both synchronous and asynchronous settings. Often these resources provide a means of effective feedback for both the instructor and students in a timely, if not real-time, manner.

When developing an online course the instructor must keep the learner in mind. Instructional technology is just one more tool for the aiding learning regardless of the location of the classroom. Content organization, stimulating assignments and activities, communication with the student, and student motivation are the focus of any classroom environment. Effective use of e-learning strategies will consistently aid instructors in the decisions guiding the structure and environment of their online classroom.

REFERENCES

Crys, T. E. (1997). *Teaching at a distance with the merging technology: An instructional systems approach.* Las Cruces: New Mexico State Printing and Duplication Center.

Drummond, T. (2002). A brief summary of the best practices in teaching. Retrieved March 30, 2004, from http://northonline.sccd.ctc.edu/eceprog/bstprac.htm

Hanna, D. E., Glowacki-Dudka, M., & Conceição-Runlee, S. (2000). *147 practical tips for teaching online groups essentials of web-based education.* Madison, WI: Atwood.

Lever-Duffy, J., McDonald, J., & Mizell, A. (2003). *Teaching and learning with technology.* New York: Allyn and Bacon.

Lockard, J., & Abrams, P. D. (2004). *Computers for twenty-first century educators.* New York: Allyn and Bacon.

Newby, T. J., Stepich, D. A., Lehman, J. D., & Russell, J. D. (2000). *Instructional technology for teaching and learning: Designing instruction, integrating computers, and using media.* Upper Saddle River, NJ: Prentice Hall.

Norton, P., & Wiburg, K. M. (2003). *Teaching with technology: Designing opportunities to learn.* Belmont, CA: Wadsworth.

Moore, M. G., & Thompson, M. M. (1990). *The effects of distance learning: A summary of literature* (ACSDE Research Monograph No. 2). University Park: American Center for the Study of Distance Education, Pennsylvania State University.

Morrison, G. R., & Lowther, D. L. (2002). *Integrating computer technology into the classroom.* Upper Saddle River, NJ: Prentice Hall.

Teaching online: Best practices and tips. (2003). Retrieved March 30, 2004, from the John Jay College Web site: http://blackboard.jjay.cuny.edu/faculty/teachonline.html.

Turner, P. M., & Riedling, A. M. (2003). *Helping teachers teach.* Westport, CT: Libraries Unlimited.

The Ultimate WebCT Handbook. (2002). Atlanta: Georgia State University.

A Decade of WebQuests: A Retrospective

Annette Lamb
Indiana University and Purdue University at Indianapolis

Berhane Teclehaimanot
Carver Teacher Education Center, University of Toledo

Ten years have passed since the word "WebQuest" was conceived by Bernie Dodge, a professor at San Diego State University. Through the work of Dodge and thousands of his followers, WebQuests have influenced the way millions of students and their teachers use the Internet. Although other approaches to classroom Internet integration focused on searching for information, Dodge's model stressed the evaluation, analysis, and transformation of information. Rather than using the Web to collect a hodgepodge of facts and opinions, this engaging, inquiry-based approach to teaching and learning promotes the kind of meaningful and authentic learning experiences that achieve the high-level of student thinking educators have sought for decades.

The purpose of this chapter is to provide a retrospective examination of the first decade of the WebQuest. The chapter begins with a description of the WebQuest approach and a discussion of the theoretical foundations. The next section traces the evolution of the WebQuest phenomenon. Factors that contribute to the success of the approach conclude the article.

WEBQUEST DEFINED

Known as the "father of the WebQuest," Dodge defined a WebQuest as an "inquiry-oriented activity in which some or all of the information that learners interact with comes from resources on the Internet" (Dodge, 1995a). In addition, Dodge distinguished between short-term and long-term WebQuests. In a short-term WebQuest, the goal is knowledge acquisition and integration, whereas in a long-term WebQuest, learners analyze and transform knowledge into something that is understandable by others.

In addition to these basic definitions, Dodge (1995a) outlined what he viewed as the critical attributes of a WebQuest, including an introduction that sets the stage of the activity; a doable, interesting task; a set of information resources; a clear process; guidance and organizational frameworks; and a conclusion that provides reflection and closure. Noncritical attributes included group activities, motivational elements, and interdisciplinary approaches.

WebQuests provide "an authentic, technology-rich environment for problem-solving, information processing, and collaboration" (Teclehaimanot & Lamb, 2004, p. 1). Often written by preservice teachers in university courses and by inservice teachers as part of a workshop, most WebQuests follow the original template designed by Dodge (1995b). For example, *Paper or Plastic: An Internet WebQuest on Recycling* (Crandall, Kinney, Taylor, & Trauth, 2002) was designed and updated by undergraduate teacher education students. This WebQuest asks learners to reflect on whether to choose paper or plastic bags at the grocery store. The introduction poses the question, "Have you ever wondered if you are making an informed decision or even the right decision?" Students take on the role of the paper advocate, plastic advocate, recycling pessimist, or concerned citizen as they explore this issue. Internet resources are preselected in each category to help the learner gather relevant information. Guiding questions are used to facilitate data analysis and synthesis. Working together, students create posters that can be displayed at their local grocery store sharing their conclusions.

The WebQuest page (webquest.sdsu.edu) at San Diego State University has received more than five million visitors since 1998. Rarely has an educational approach gained so much attention. Teacher education programs and professional development workshops around the world require students to develop WebQuests (Stinson, 2003).

THEORETICAL FOUNDATIONS FOR THE WEBQUEST

What Theories and Practices Support the WebQuest Approach?

The WebQuest concept is rooted in a multifaceted collection of educational theories and popular practices. According to March (2003/2004),

> well-designed WebQuests promote dependable instructional practices by combining research-supported theories with effective use of essential Internet resource, produce open-ended questions, and offer authentic tasks that motivate students. Moreover, they allow students to develop expertise in a subject from within a situated learning environment and off opportunities for transformative group work. (p. 42)

In a 2004 e-mail interview of a teacher educator from the United Kingdom, Tony Fisher stressed that WebQuests map easily onto the pedagogical principles that underpin quality teaching. With an emphasis on flexibility, adaptability, explicability, transferability, and improvablity, WebQuests tied in well with the resource-based materials and emphasis on social constructivism that were popular as the Internet emerged as a tool for educators in the 1990s.

A learner-centered approach to teaching, WebQuests draw on the following areas: constructivist philosophy; thinking, understanding, and transformational learning; authenticity and situated learning environments; inquiry-based learning; scaffolding; differentiation; cooperative learning; and motivation, challenge, and engaged learning. A brief overview to each area is now provided, along with its application to WebQuests.

CONSTRUCTIVIST PHILOSOPHY

Many educators have connected WebQuests with the constructivist approach to learning (Benz, 2002; Dutt-Doner, Wilmer, Stevens, & Hartmann, 2000; March, 1998b). The constructivist philosophy incorporates a variety of theories regarding teaching and learning. According to Jonassen, Peck, and Wilson (1999), constructivist learning emphasizes the five attributes of meaningful learning, including intentional learning, active learning, constructive learning, cooperative learning, and authentic learning. For example, a constructivist classroom might place learners in problem-solving situations with scaffolding to support their learning. As students become more self-sufficient, the support is gradually removed (Tiene & Ingram, 2001). Rich, authentic resources, practical experience, and anchored instruction are all central to this educational approach.

The constructivist movement of the 1980s and 1990s was perfect for nurturing the WebQuest concept. A Web-based learning environment provides teachers with unprecedented access to a breadth of resources (March, 1998b). In this environment, the Internet becomes a tool that facilitates information exploration and knowledge construction. McKenzie (2001) stresses that students must find meaning to create insight. Answers to essential questions can't be found; they must be invented by synthesizing many examples and perspectives to build their personal understandings.

THINKING, UNDERSTANDING, AND TRANSFORMATIONAL LEARNING

For more than half a century, educators have used Bloom's (1956) *Taxonomy of Educational Goals* to classify intellectual objectives. Although much of the evidence is anecdotal, Web-based resources and activities have been found to deepen student background knowledge and understanding of content (Tancock, 2002). In a recent interview, Dodge stated that in today's world, knowledge is more than remembering, "it's remembering plus learning to transform information. It's making people producers of information" (Geraghty, 2004b).

McTighe and Wiggins (1998) argue that understanding is different from knowledge. Doing well on tests of knowledge doesn't mean that students have deep understanding or will be able to transform this knowledge to new situations. In their book *Understanding by Design,* McTighe and Wiggins outline a multifaceted view of understanding, including explanation, interpretation, application, perspective, empathy, and self-knowledge. These six facets represent the kinds of performance students can do and insights they may possess. According to Gardner (1991), performances of understanding occur when students flexibly apply information and skills to new situations.

Although addressing these understandings can be difficult, WebQuests provide an excellent instructional environment for student learning. Lipscomb (2002) points out that students have a difficult time achieving historical empathy. Through a Civil War WebQuest incorporating role-playing and journal writing, eighth-grade students achieved varied degrees of historical empathy.

WebQuests provide students with intellectual challenges by fostering critical thinking. From the beginning, a focus on thinking skills has been an integral part of the WebQuest philosophy (Dodge, 1995a; Dudeney, 2003; Vidoni & Maddux; 2002). Marzano's (1992) work is often cited when identifying the types of thinking expected of students. His categories include comparing, classifying, inducing, deducing, analyzing errors, constructing support, abstraction, and analyzing perspectives.

The focus on high-order thinking and understanding match the emphasis of the WebQuest on transformational learning. Dodge (1998b) terms these transformation activities as "tasks for Bloom's penthouse" including assignments such as synthesizing conflicting opinions, combining multiple sources of data to discover something new, developing a unique solution to a specific problem, or defining a stance and defending it. Kelly (2000) notes that students found the "thinking" required in a WebQuest assignment more difficult than completing worksheet blanks. Students also commented, however, that they had a better understanding of subject matter when required to participate in high-level activities.

A well-designed transformational experience provides a foundation of background knowledge and skills, then asks learners to synthesize information, make inferences, and make meaningful decisions. According to March (2003/2004), the key to an effective WebQuest is whether "newly acquired information undergoes an important transformation within learners themselves" (p. 42). For example, students might apply lessons from global problems to a local situation, make predictions from a particular perspective, or argue for the best alternative solution.

AUTHENTICITY AND SITUATED LEARNING ENVIRONMENTS

Students need a context for learning. Dewey (1933) stressed the importance of context when he stated that understanding something "is to see it in its relations to other things: to note how it operates or functions, what consequences follow from it, what causes it" (p. 137). Creating a meaningful context for learning is key to an effective WebQuest. This involves providing students with (1) a motivating setting and interesting mission; (2) a logical, guided process that facilitates meaningful student work; and (3) assessments and culminating activities that help students reflect on their work. March (2000a) suggests that the best WebQuests contain three Rs: real, rich, and relevant.

Authentic assignments, activities, assessments, and audiences are the cornerstone of many WebQuests. Dudeney (2003) speculates that authenticity leads to more effort, greater concentration, and a real interest in task achievement. Others have connected the use of primary sources to the development of meaningful critical thinking skills (Vidoni & Maddux, 2002).

Educators across academic areas have found that WebQuests provide an excellent tool for exploring content-area information. Peterson, Caverly, and MacDonald (2003) point out that WebQuests provide a new instructional opportunity for developing academic literacy skills. Marco (2002) found that WebQuests are an excellent way to provide authentic language experiences for students learning English as a second or foreign language.

A real-world connection is an important key to meaningful, contextual learning. Learning scenarios should be as close as possible to real-world situations found by workers, scholars, and other professions that might attack a similar problem (Bloom, Madaus, & Hasting, 1981). Whether working with the local chamber of commerce on promotional projects, providing nutrition information to area restaurants, conducting oral histories, or building Web sites for local nonprofit agencies, students need authentic audiences.

WebQuests engage students in authentic assignments, activities, and assessments. According to Perkins and McKnight (2003), students and teachers like the authentic nature of the WebQuests that incorporate primary source materials and real-world problems. By providing students with up-to-date information and authentic simulation tasks, Marco (2002) states that questions help students develop critical reading and synthesis skills.

Authentic reading and writing experiences are a major benefit of the WebQuest approach. Tancock (2002) found that WebQuests required students to use of variety of authentic reading skills and strategies including skimming, scanning, and interpreting directions. They also had to learn efficient navigation and remember where resources were located. Snider and Foster (2000) found that writing for authentic purposes is an important element of an effective WebQuest.

Many educators advocate the use of interdisciplinary approaches to engage students learning (Dutt-Doner et al., 2000; Vidoni & Maddux, 2002). By addressing learning outcomes across content areas, teachers can make more effective use of time and resources (Lamb, 2003). Interdisciplinary learning involves students in applying concepts from various subjects in real-world tasks. WebQuests are motivating for students because they can combine student enthusiasm with technology with "real-world" experiences that transfer beyond the school setting (Watson, 1999).

INQUIRY-BASED LEARNING

Inquiry is the process of formulating questions, organizing ideas, exploring and evaluating information, analyzing and synthesizing data, and communicating findings and conclusions. Inquiry-based learning is a powerful strategy for learning (Brooks, Nolan, & Gallagher, 2001; Lim, 2001; Milson, 2002; Vidoni & Maddux, 2002). The structure of the WebQuest is based on inquiry-based learning (Dodge, 1995b; Jakes, Pennington, & Knodle, 2000). According to Callison (2003), information inquiry is an interactive process involving questioning and exploring, assimilation and inference, and reflection.

WebQuests are a Web-based, information inquiry approach. Lamb, Smith, and Johnson (1997) noted that the most successful Web-based learning experiences were those in which the teacher acted as a facilitator, paying careful attention to the students and guiding them through critical stages of their inquiry projects.

SCAFFOLDING

WebQuests help teachers guide students through a learning experience. They facilitate high-level thinking by breaking a task down into meaningful chunks and providing support for success at each stage in learning (March, 1998b). Benz (2003) identified proper guidance and scaffolding as keys to promoting the type of learning that goes beyond "transmission-of-knowledge" often found in a traditional classroom.

Scaffolding is the process of organizing an event to facilitate student success in a learning experience. Students work within their ability and are given "scaffolds" to help them complete complex tasks. The scaffolds involve providing limited choices, good directions, demonstrations, and other methods to reduce frustration and increase success (Chatel, 2003; Wood, Bruner, & Ross, 1976; Wood & Middleton, 1975). Scaffolding in WebQuests allows students to solve problems and complete tasks that would be beyond the ability of students without assistance. Carefully designed scaffolds can help differentiate instruction in a class with varied learning styles and needs. For example, concept mapping is often used in WebQuests to help visualize information (Chandler, 2003).

Dodge (2001a) describes scaffolding as a "temporary structure used to help learners act more skilled than they really are" (p. 58). Because scaffolding is intended to be temporary, Dodge stresses the need to fade support as students gain experience and skills.

In a WebQuest, scaffolding can take many forms, including resource links, compelling problems, templates for student production, or guidance for specific skills (Dodge, 1998b). Specifically, Dodge outlines three basic types of scaffolds: reception scaffolds, transformation scaffolds, and production scaffolds (Patterns Summer Symposium, 2000).

DIFFERENTIATION

One of the primary benefits of a WebQuest learning environment is the ability to address individual differences. Students can work at their own pace or as part of a team. Resources can be provided at different reading levels, depth of detail, and varied communication channels (i.e., text, audio, visual) to meet the interests and learning needs of each member of the class. Milson (2002) found that students of varying academic ability levels are able to complete WebQuests. These students approach the investigation differently, however, depending on ability.

Techniques of differentiation offer a variety of ways to address readiness levels, interests, and learning profiles (Tomlinson, 1999). For example, teachers can vary the content, process, and product of instruction to meet particular needs. The learning styles of all children can be addressed through choice of activities, peer assistance, pacing flexibility, and multiple channels of communication (Perkins & McKnight, 2003). Teachers of English as a second language (Dudeney, 2003) have used adapted WebQuests as a way to include their students in regular education classroom activities. Kelly (2000) has found that WebQuests work well with special needs students in a regular classroom. Tools such as e-mail for homebound students and read-aloud software for students with visual challenges make learning more accessible. Teachers can build accommodations into WebQuests such as varied forms of readability (i.e., larger text, simple directions). In this way, students are able to work on higher-order thinking skills with their peers without disabilities.

COOPERATIVE LEARNING

Whether working as teams or role-playing in a group, WebQuests often incorporate a cooperative element (Milson & Downey, 2001). Perkins and McKnight (2003) found that teachers like the way WebQuests engage students in learning through collaborative, problem-based activities. According to Gardner (1991), students must be able to view problems and solutions from different perspectives. Group work assists students with understanding. Monroe (2003), however, found that boys and girls work differently in groups. Whereas girls' interactions were generally cooperative and focused on task-related activities, boys' interactions were disputations related to power.

Cooperative learning environments can challenge students to seek out new ideas, build content connections, work with others, and develop flexible communications through collaborative, generative, and interactive projects (Lamb, 2003). Kelly (1999) found cooperative learning and technology beneficial for inclusion students. When using WebQuests along with other innovative, technology-rich approaches, eighth-grade inclusion students improved their reading levels.

Beekeeper, artist, president, and coach are just a few of the roles found in WebQuests. In the article "Role-Playing Software and WebQuests," Brucklacher and Gimbert (1999) describe how role-playing can be used for cooperative learning. WebQuests tackle large, complex topics that would be difficult for students to address individually. By working together, learners can take different perspectives, debate ideas, and work together to solve problems (March, 1998b).

MOTIVATION, CHALLENGE, AND ENGAGED LEARNING

Some students find school boring and without meaning. Motivation is particularly important to young adolescents who are quick to question the importance of school assignments (Lipscomb, 2003). Keller's *ARCS Model of Motivational Design* (1983) describes the importance of student attention, relevance of activity to needs, confidence in achieving success, and a sense of satisfaction. According to Brooks and Brooks (1999), students can be challenged by engaging them in active questioning, exploring new information, examining contradictions, and researching ideas that challenge their current views. WebQuests can provide the type of challenges that motivate students (Lipscomb, 2003; Marco, 2002). Tancock (2002) found that allowing choices in Web resource exploration creates high interest among students.

WebQuests promote independent students who are responsible for their own learning (Perkins & McKnight, 2003). According to Kelly (2000), students enjoyed the WebQuest environment because it "made sense" to them. Marco (2002) states, "WebQuests fit well in a learner-centered curriculum that seeks to help students develop autonomous learning" (p. 24).

WebQuest learners are given a meaningful central question or problem, real resources to explore and gather insights, a significant role to play, and the opportunity to share their understandings in an authentic way (March, 1998b). These are the types of strategies that increase student motivation and promote engaged learning.

EVOLUTION OF THE WEBQUEST

What Sparked the WebQuest Phenomenon and Caused It to Spread So Quickly?

In the 1990s, educators were seeking a way to make sense of the vast information resources rapidly becoming available to their students through the Internet. Like Dodge, a growing number of educators were gaining access to tools such as e-mail, Web sites, and videoconferencing. They wanted to go beyond the "scavenger hunt" approach to Internet integration. Rather than having students answer low-level questions such as "What's the longest river in the world," scholars were seeking ways to promote higher-order thinking through inquiry-based activities (Lamb, 2004). Educators wanted students to transform what they learned into meaningful understandings rather than a series of facts. McKenzie (1997) referred to these as the "why? how? which?" questions of inquiry and learning. These types of questions required students to collect evidence, reason, and draw conclusions.

Dodge, with encouragement from educators around the world, created an approach to technology-rich learning that revolutionized the use of Internet in the classroom. In a 2004 e-mail interview with Midge Frazel, the educational technology consultant reflected on her introduction to Bernie Dodge at a national conference in the late 1990s. "It was one of those 'techno-moments' where a bridge is formed between a traditional situation and a virtual meeting.... I was touching an inventor, just as if I was shaking hands with Edison."

The following chronology discusses the major advances in the evolution of the approach along with variations and popular applications over the past decade.

1995—THE BIRTH OF THE WEBQUEST

In preparation for a university course, Dodge developed a technology-enhanced activity called *Investigating Archaeotype* (Dodge, 1996b) to help graduate students learn about a software simulation program through reading documents, interviewing the designers in a virtual chat, and videoconferencing with a teacher using the software. The culminating activity involved making a decision regarding software purchase in a real-world setting. The activity generated much deeper, multifaceted discussions than traditional approaches (Dodge, 1996a; Starr, 2000).

Dodge began brainstorming names for this new approach to technology-rich learning. After finding no matches in a Web search for the word "WebQuest," the new term was born. Dodge wrote a draft of the foundational document called *Some Thoughts about WebQuests* in February 1995. Portions were later published in the *Distance Educator* (1995b) and provide the framework for the WebQuest approach.

Also in early 1995, the Department of Educational Technology at San Diego State University became involved with the SBC (formerly Pacific Bell) Education First Initiative. Three people were selected for fellowships including Tom March, who worked closely with Dodge to refine the WebQuest approach. The goal of the project was to create high-quality educational applications for K–12 schools, community colleges, and public libraries. They sought to design resources that educators could quickly and easily implement in the classroom or library with little training. Under the supervision of Dodge, March developed the first WebQuest designed for use outside San Diego State University, *Searching for China: WebQuest.*

In the summer of 1995, March published one of the first articles that discussed the WebQuest concept within the context of types of Web-based applications for educators. In addition to the WebQuest, March identified a variety of ways that educators could address learning goals through the use of Web-based activities including topic hotlist, multimedia scrapbook, treasure hunt, and subject sampler.

After their first experiences with WebQuests, Dodge and March spent a year discussing "best practices" related to Web-based activities to refine the concept. They explored multiple examples and discussed the critical attributes along with nonexamples of WebQuests "emphasizing the importance of combining authentic tasks with Internet resources to develop critical thinking skills" (March 2003, p. 42). Later, rubrics were designed to help others evaluate WebQuests (Dodge, 2001b; March, 1998a, 2000b).

1996—WEBQUEST: THE BUZZWORD

By 1996, educators at the K–12 level began to discover the potential of WebQuests. In a 2004 e-mail interview, Kathy Schrock stated, "at the time it [the WebQuest] seemed to have been created for use with college students. Bernie and I soon became e-mail buddies, talking about its use in the K–12 environments." As Schrock began working with teachers to develop WebQuests, she saw them as an excellent tool for teaching and learning across grade levels. Her online article and presentation titled *WebQuests in Our Future: The*

Teacher's Role in Cyberspace (Schrock, 1996, 2004) focused on the use of WebQuests in the K–12 environment.

From the beginning, Dodge emphasized the importance of active learning in WebQuests and hoped to provide easy-to-apply frameworks for understanding the approach. Three domains were identified to assist teachers in dealing with the prospect of developing Web-enhanced learning environments: inputs, transformations, and outputs. Inputs included articles, resources, experts and other information sources. Transformations were high-level activities such as analysis, synthesis, problem solving, and decision making. Finally, output included products such as presentations, reports, and Web publishing (Dodge, 1996a).

Launched in 1996, the Filamentality Web site was a major step forward in the dissemination of online resources to support the development of WebQuests and other Web-based materials in K–12 classrooms. Funded through the Education First Initiative, the project provided examples, tools, and resources to guide educators through the process of developing a WebQuest. The WebQuest *Look Who's Footing the Bill!* developed by Tom March (1996) was the first example of a QuickQuest using the tools of Filamentality.

In December 1996, *Classroom Connect* declared the WebQuest a "quiet revolution," "innovative approach," and "hot buzzword." The cover article titled *Using WebQuests in the K–12 Classroom* (1996/1997) attracted the attention of many educators seeking practical, effective ways to integrate the Internet into the classroom. In addition, it provided a list of examples to explore, a sample, and template.

1997—THE WEBQUEST CONCEPT SPREADS

The Department of Education's Technology Innovation Challenge Grant program (1995–2000) provided fertile ground for the exploration of the WebQuest concept. Schools and universities across the United States included the idea in proposals for courses and professional development activities. In particular, the San Diego Unified School District grant projects, Triton and Patterns Projects (projects.edtech.sandi.net) were developed with support from a multipartner educational collaborative including San Diego State University. Teachers participated in professional development activities and developed curriculum units focusing on standards-based technology integration.

In addition to the Department of Education national grants, many schools districts funded projects through the Technology Literacy Challenge Funds administered at the state level including Salt Lake City Schools in Utah, Macomb Intermediate School District in Michigan, and Montgomery County Intermediate Unit in Pennsylvania.

Under the direction of Bernie Dodge, the creation of WebQuests became an integral part of this program. Materials such as *A WebQuest about WebQuests* (Dodge, 1998c) and *Building Blocks for a WebQuest* (1997) were developed to support these professional development efforts. These materials were quickly embraced by other professional development projects across North America.

Educators began noticing how the WebQuest format could be applied to a variety of subject areas and theoretical approaches. For instance, in 1997, Lamb et al. used an early WebQuest titled *Nonprofit Prophets* by Tom March as an example of how this inquiry approach promoted information literacy through meaningful, engaging, and authentic project-based learning.

1998—COLLECTIONS EMERGE

By 1998, WebQuests had become a way for teachers from all grade levels and subject areas to share their enthusiasm, experiences, and products. Although many individual Web pages were already posted at the San Diego State University, Dodge's introduction of *The WebQuest Page* Web site in February 1998 generated dozens of Web site awards. In June

1998, Tom March moved to Australia and launched Ozline.com. WebQuests were also becoming popular in Canada.

Educators began hearing about workshops where they could learn about effective Internet integration. At these workshops, teachers often produced WebQuests that were posted on the Internet for others to examine and use. This cycle of workshops, project postings, and sharing has continued for nearly ten years.

Collections of WebQuests generated by university courses, conference workshops, and other professional development activities began to emerge. Arizona State University, Bridgewater State College, Louisiana State University, New Mexico State University, and Indiana University posted these types of teacher-produced collections. According to Yoder (1999), "this proliferation of curricular materials convinced many teachers that it was all right to publish their own WebQuests for others" (p. 6).

Many grant projects began using the WebQuest approach as a focal point for teacher training for technology integration. For instance, the Teach the Teachers Collaborative involves teachers from the Los Angeles Unified School District in summer workshops including WebQuest development. The WebQuests generated through these types of grants were often disseminated as WebQuest collections. For example, the EMPOWER project in Evansville, Indiana, teamed high school teachers and high school students for the development of WebQuests (Lamb, 1998). In 1998, Dodge focused on the importance of scaffolding for higher-level learning. These ideas were later incorporated into WebQuest workshops (Patterns Summer Symposium, 2000) focusing on reception, transformation, and production scaffolds.

The *Taxonomy of Information Patterns* was created to illustrate different ways that information could be visualized (Dodge, 1998a). Types of information patterns included cluster, hierarchy, Venn diagram, time line, flowchart, concept map, causal loop diagram, comparison matrix, and inductive tower.

At the same time, Tom March was working on the "group process" aspect of WebQuest development. The original *Searching for China* WebQuest was revised to include individual group roles and a real-world feedback element (About WebQuests, 1995). The *Tuskegee Study WebQuest* (1996) was designed to help students understand tragedies such as the Tuskegee Study and was updated in 1998 to incorporate the idea of group process through looking at different perspectives. Transformation builders were later integrated into the group process stage in the *Little Rock Nine WebQuest* (March, 1999).

1999—TOOLS FOR REPLICATION

During 1999, a number of resources were developed to make the process of designing and developing WebQuests easier. WebQuest templates provided an easy way to create a WebQuest (*WebQuest Training Materials,* 2004). At first, a single-page format was posted. Over time, more complex templates were added including a version with frames and rollover text navigation.

Tools such as the *WebQuest Process Checklist* (Dodge, 1999b) helped designers to be certain that they were including adequate scaffolding for students. The Web page *Fine Points* provided fourteen ideas for polishing WebQuests (Dodge, 1999c). Finally, a series of *Process Guides* provided help for students completing activities such as brainstorming, building consensus, and using primary source documents (McDowell, 1999).

An emphasis on WebQuest tasks was the next expansion to the WebQuest approach. Through exercises such as the *WebQuest Task Design Worksheet* (Dodge, 1999a), educators could use the *WebQuest Taskonomy* (Dodge, 2002b) to design a doable and engaging task that requires students to think. These tasks included retelling, compilation, mystery, journalistic, design, creative product, consensus building, persuasion, self-knowledge, analytical, judgment, and scientific. In addition to task identification, emphasis was placed on the design of effective evaluation including rubrics.

These templates, generators, and other tools made creating a WebQuest realistic for people with limited instructional design and technology skills. Although templates were available, some teachers continued to find developing and uploading Web pages a barrier (Summerville, 2000). Perkins and McKnight (2003) found that teachers with experience building Web pages were significantly more likely to use WebQuests.

2000—COLLABORATION AND GLOBAL IMPACT

WebQuests take time and expertise to develop. As the popularity of WebQuests has grown, educators increasingly have sought the support of each other. Many developers include their e-mail address in their Web sites. This allows teachers to make connections, share experiences, and develop collaborative efforts (Yoder, 1999).

Teacher teams have been found to be an effective way to design, develop, and manage WebQuests. For example, Kelly (2000) encouraged regular education and special education teachers to team in the development of WebQuests that are flexible enough to address special needs.

The school library is a logical focal point for WebQuest activities. For example, a middle-grade library served as the location of a mock science museum for a WebQuest on the solar system (Minkel, 2000). Braun (2001) encouraged teachers and librarians to work together. Librarians can ensure that quality Web-based materials are carefully selected to support information needs. In addition, they can assist teachers in helping students develop knowledge, skills, and attitudes needed to become effective users of information. The article titled *Sherlock Holmes on the Internet: Language Arts Teams Up with the Computing Librarian* by Truett (2001) is another example of this type of collaboration. Collaboration of this type extends to higher education. For example, a New York community college librarian worked with an English professor to develop a literature assignment (Spanfelner, 2000).

Collaboration extends beyond the walls of individual buildings. A Yahoo Groups discussion group on WebQuests was launched in August 1999 as a "forum for sharing ideas, insights, problems and solutions for those using the WebQuest model in their teaching." This was the first of many outreach programs that reached locations involved in WebQuest development including Australia, Brazil, New Zealand, South Africa, and the European Union.

WebQuestUK (2004) is an example of the many countries around the world that began to embrace the WebQuest concept. The United Kingdom version associates Web resources with the UK National Curriculum. The Netherlands also has a WebQuest resource (http://www.webkwestie.nl/).

WebQuests are now available in dozens of languages around the world. Marco (2002) suggests that WebQuests "can be effectively used as activities for a content-based approach to English for Specific Purposes (ESP) instruction" (p. 20).

2001—THINKING AND TRANSFORMATION

From the beginning, Dodge and March encouraged the use of WebQuests to promote high-level thinking and transformational learning. Porter (2001) applied three broad categories and assessment strategies to the use of technology including literary uses, adapting uses, and transforming uses. New learning experiences and roles for students that would be impaired or difficult without technology were considered transforming uses. Porter used the example of a project in which students maintained a community Web site in Spanish to support the local chamber of commerce while also gaining language credit.

In preparation for a new Web site titled *BestWebQuests.com*, March (2002) reviewed the contents of WebQuest directories to identify the best in WebQuests. He found many excellent projects. He stated, however, that in more than half the WebQuests "knowledge isn't used to create new meaning or construct knowledge, isn't transformed or applied to a new situation."

Dodge distinguished between WebQuests and other Web-based activities such as treasure hunts. In a 2000 interview, Dodge states that

> A WebQuest is built around an engaging and doable task that elicits higher order thinking of some kind. It's about doing something with information. The thinking can be creative or critical, and involve problem solving, judgment, analysis, or synthesis. The task has to be more than simply answering questions or regurgitating what's on the screen. Ideally, the task is a scaled down version of something that adults do on the job, outside school walls. (Starr, 2000)

In his article "FOCUS: Five Rules for Writing a Great WebQuest," Dodge (2001a) offered suggestions in how to design effective WebQuests. He states that the "ideal of engaging higher-level thinking skills . . . seems to resonate with many educators" (p. 7).

2002—ADAPTING WEBQUESTS

After seven years, many WebQuests were available through the Internet. At the same time, many teachers found that developing a quality WebQuest was time-consuming. Perkins and McKnight (2003) suggested that teachers preview existing WebQuests and consider how the teaching strategies would work with their students.

Lamb (2000) identified four ways to build a WebQuest learning environment including using existing resources, adapting or modifying a WebQuest, creating a new WebQuest, or coproducing materials. For example, a teacher could adapt a WebQuest by incorporating resources at varied readings levels, building in additional content, exploring different perspectives, or adding multimedia elements (Lamb, 2004).

Dodge (2002a) identified a series of steps in adapting or enhancing a WebQuest including (1) choose a standard or topic, (2) search for existing WebQuests, (3) determine if you can use one as is, (4) select those with high potential, (5) identify changes needed, (6) get author permission, (7) download the WebQuest, (8) modify and enhance, (9) evaluate and revise as needed, and (10) publish and share.

According to Teclehaimanot and Lamb (2004), those interested in adapting a WebQuest may wish to (1) identify supplemental Web resources to enhance a WebQuest, (2) mix and match elements from a number of different projects, (3) adjust the content for a different grade level or purpose, (4) modify the focus to a related topic or region, or (5) extend an incomplete or dated project.

2003—WEBQUESTS AS A VIRUS

From the beginning, Dodge welcomed ideas that would enhance the use of WebQuests in the classroom. In a recent presentation titled *WebQuests and other Viruses*, Dodge (2003) compared the approach used to disseminate the WebQuest idea to a virus that catches on quickly and mutates along the way.

Many educators have refined the original WebQuest format. For example, March (2002) places emphasis on involving students in asking and answering questions rather than completing tasks. He also incorporated role-playing, background information, and real-world feedback elements into his projects.

Some of the WebQuest variations strive to meet the unique needs of particular set of learners. For example, the goal of the TalenQuest is to customize the WebQuest concept for foreign language learning and teaching (Koenraad & Westoff, 2003). Faculty in the Netherlands identified additional essential features needed for language-based WebQuests.

Taking a constructivist approach to teaching and learning can put students in the role of WebQuest designer (Hill, Wiley, Nelson, & Han, 2003). A growing number of educators have found that students benefit from the development of WebQuests for a particular audience (Perkins & McKnight, 2003; Van Leer, 2003). Student WebQuest development can help students and teachers to think differently about students and technology. For example, Peterson and Koeck (2001) involved students in constructing WebQuests in a chemistry course. This approach was found to be effective in engaging students in problem solving, promoting interdisciplinary thinking, and using technology as a communication tool.

Although people are most familiar with WebQuests presented as Web pages, alternative media formats have grown in popularity. For example, Microsoft Word can be used to present the assignment including links and worksheets. This document can then be stored on a disk, CD, network server, or the Web. In the same way, Microsoft PowerPoint, HyperStudio, and other multimedia tools can be used as the "starting point" for Web-enhanced, inquiry-based learning activities. A PowerQuest (created in PowerPoint) or HyperQuest (created in HyperStudio) is sometimes used to introduce the class to the general assignment then placed on the network so students can easily access the activities. Regardless of the format, the key to a powerful inquiry-based learning environment is the assignment, resources, and assessments.

The ways that people have chosen to interpret the WebQuest approach have not always been positive. Many educators have expressed concerns about the varying quality of WebQuests (Perkins & McKnight, 2003). Thousands of WebQuests are posted on the Internet, but few actually fit the basic criteria of a WebQuest. Philip Benz, a foreign language instructor in France, shared his experiences with WebQuests on the Yahoo Groups forum. His understanding of the WebQuest concept evolved over time as he became more aware of the theories behind them. Once he grasped the main concepts, he began adapting the model to fit his needs as a foreign language instructor (Benz, 2003).

The WebQuest Portal was introduced in 2003 as a tool to promote conversations about using and extending the WebQuest model. This Web site includes collaborative tools, training materials, templates, and a database of examples. In an effort to focus on quality examples, a new section was added to the WebQuest portal highlighting two categories of WebQuest examples: "top" and "middling." Exemplary WebQuests are placed in the "top" area, and those with good ideas that don't necessarily meet the established criteria are considered "middling."

In addition, other resources have been integrated into the WebQuest Portal to support relationships among WebQuest developers, researchers, and users. For example, monthly live chats on Tapped In (tappedin.org) are announced, a threaded discussion board provides separate sections for specific topics such as research and subject area applications, and a community-authored Weblog is used to share news and information.

2004—QUALITY EXTENSIONS AND ENHANCEMENTS

Recently, Dodge and others have begun formalizing some of the variations that have been identified. For example, Think, Construct, and Communicate (2004) is a project of the European Schoolnet established to promote cooperation among schools in Europe. They are working cooperatively on building WebQuest projects as well as developing guidelines for "best practice" of WebQuest use.

Many content-area experts are investigating ways to enhance the use of WebQuests in their fields. For example, social studies and language arts are the two areas where WebQuests have become the most popular. Literature-based WebQuests incorporate "book(s) as a focal point for reading-centered, online learning activities." (Teclehaimanot & Lamb, 2004, p. 1). Emphasis may be placed on characters, plot, theme, setting, genre, or authors depending on the particular learning outcome. Teachers often combine WebQuests with the literature circle approach to reading.

Drawing on the design pattern idea used in previous enhancements, Dodge recently introduced new templates that streamline WebQuest design (*WebQuest Design Patterns,* 2004). Each design pattern has proven to be instructionally solid, focuses on a unique instructional purpose, and can easily be adapted to incorporate different subject matter content. After reading the description and instructional purpose, developers can explore the examples and download the easy-to-modify templates. For instance, the "simulated diary" design pattern directs students to "write a daily account from the point of view of a particular individual in a specific time and place." Sample topics include a journey to Japan, the caste system in India, and a Civil War journal.

2005—THE PHENOMENON CONTINUES

The WebQuest phenomenon continues to spread. Between 1998 and 2000, visitors at the San Diego State University WebQuest page rose from 200 to nearly 2,000 per day (Dodge, 2004). More than five million people have visited the entry page since 1998.

In a recent interview, Bernie Dodge stated that the "WebQuest is changing the role of the teacher from dispenser of knowledge to facilitator of learning" (Geraghty, 2004a).

WHY WEBQUESTS? ISSUES IN DEVELOPMENT AND USE

With all of the educational approaches, initiatives, and mandates of the past decade, what made WebQuests unique, accessible, and ultimately successful?

WebQuests are built on a strong, theoretical foundation emphasizing the authentic needs and motivations of learners, a structured yet flexible environment for learning, and the power of technology. Their popularity spans all ages and subject areas. Some believe the focus on student motivation to learn gives the approach its global appeal (Geraghty, 2004a). This combination of theory, practical applications, and global appeal all contribute to the popularity of WebQuests.

The following section explores the growing research base associated with WebQuests. Next, the connection to standards and learning outcomes is explored. Followed by a discussion of management and use of WebQuests. The section concludes with a focus on technology and resources.

Growing Research Base

With increasing concerns regarding accountability, many educators have identified the need for additional research into the use of WebQuests in teaching and learning (Monroe, 2003; Perkins & McKnight, 2003). Although educators have enthusiastically embraced the WebQuest concept based on its practical application of educational theory, few experimental research studies have been published demonstrating its impact on learning.

Much of the research related to WebQuest applications has been in the area of case studies and teacher action research projects (Delisio, 2001; Dunne, 2000). In the last several years, however, an increasing number of studies have been conducted on the effectiveness of WebQuests as a tool for inquiry-based learning (Arbaugh, Scholten, & Essex, 2001; Brucklacher & Gimbert, 1999; Perkins & McKnight, 2003; Kelly, 1999, 2000).

Recently, studies in a wide range of grade levels and subject areas have pointed to the success of WebQuest use in areas such as higher education (Peterson et al., 2003; Pohan & Mathison, 1998), social studies (Milson, 2001), math (Monroe, 2003), English and language arts (Snider & Foster, 2000; Spanfelner, 2000; Tancock, 2002; Truett, 2001) and English as a second language (Marco, 2002). In a review of the literature, Hill et al. (2003) stated that the "research related to teacher-directed implementation indicates that WebQuests are a success" (p. 444).

Standards and Learning Outcomes

Over the past several years, educators have become increasingly concerned about addressing challenging student standards. According to Copper and Smarkola (2001), "WebQuests are potentially effective, ready-made learning resources that may enable teachers to move in a positive direction toward the vision of technology-enhanced educational practice described in the National Educational Technology Standards" (p. 2). Teachers using WebQuests have sought alternative ways to demonstrate student performance. For example, Kelly (2000) found that after a WebQuest activity, student writing samples reflected deeper thought.

WebQuest development begins by considering the purpose of the activity including the specific learning outcome and standards to be addressed (Garry & Graham, 2002; Lamb, 2003). What should students be able to do or talk about when they've completed the activity? Although addressing specific standards may be at the core of most learning activities, other factors such as developing problem solving skills and information fluency are also important considerations. For example, Kelly (2000) stressed the importance of maintaining flexibility to address special needs of students.

WebQuests naturally reach across curriculum areas, so teachers can often draw on content area, information, technology, and life skills standards when designing technology-rich learning environments (Lamb, 2003). Before using a WebQuest in the classroom, teachers must carefully evaluate the entry skills of their students to determine whether they have the skills necessary to be successful (Garry & Graham, 2002). If not, scaffolding will need to be embedded to support student learning.

Information skills. Although resources vary, the need for information skills remains the same across topics and content areas (Peterson et al., 2003). Milson (2002) found that students' strategies for collecting and organizing information often involve using the "Path-of-Least-Resistance" rather than the most effective methods. Teachers can successfully guide students to more productive approaches for information use through the use of WebQuests and other structured learning materials.

Reading skills. Reading is a critical skill whether using print or technology-based materials. Tancock (2002) found that reading problems experienced by children were intensified when gathering and applying Web-based information. Because the WebQuest was motivating, however, students were willing to ask for adult assistance. Interestingly, the high-ability students were energized by the challenge of the Web-based reading. In a study of English as a second or foreign language, Marco (2002) found that

> through extensive reading, students acquire the vocabulary related to a topic
> of their discipline. By using authentic texts to perform real world tasks students become aware of concepts such as purpose and audience and see the
> utility of studying a second or foreign language. (p. 25)

Writing and communication skills. The introduction of technology has made final products more visually appealing, but it has also made plagiarism easier. For example, Tancock (2002) found that regardless of how many lessons stressed summarizing skills, most students ended up copying information for the PowerPoint products developed within their WebQuest. According to Lamb (2003), the solution to the "copy and paste" crisis is the transformation of our assignments. Rather than writing a term paper or making an oral report, quality WebQuests require students to connect their understanding of content knowledge to new situations through original products for authentic audiences. Rather than writing a book review, ask students to critique the reviews of others. Instead of writing a book about big corporations, hold a debate about the pros and cons of Walmart coming to

town. The most effective WebQuest communication products provide students with opportunities to analyze, synthesize, and evaluate information and alternative perspectives.

Management and Use of WebQuests

Integrating WebQuests into the classroom involves access to technology and good
classroom management skills. Perkins and McKnight (2003) conducted a survey focusing
on the concerns of teachers related to WebQuest use. They found that teachers of all ages,
genders, backgrounds, and school situations were using WebQuests. Novice WebQuest users were most concerned about learning about WebQuests and how they affect teaching,
whereas regular users were interested in innovative applications.

Although a digital divide continues to exist, access to technology has increased dramatically over the past decade. In 1998, March (1998a) identified technology access as the
greatest hurdle to implementing WebQuests. In addition, technical skills have been a problem for some students and teachers. According to Perkins and McKnight (2003), some
teachers express concerns about student lack of keyboarding and other technical skills.

Classroom management is a concern of educators (Dutt-Doner et al., 2000; Perkins &
McKnight, 2003). In some cases, problems relate to general classroom issues such as managing multiple groups working at different speeds, whereas other concerns relate to managing computer use. The problem is sometimes lack of computers or difficulty in helping
students when everyone has a computer. Garry and Graham (2002) recommend carefully
examining the role of technology in the WebQuest. They advocate a balance between
computer time and other activities.

Time is the most common concern of educators using WebQuests in the classroom
(Dutt-Doner, et al, 2000; Lipscomb, 2002; Perkins & McKnight, 2003). Some teachers
have questioned whether the instructional time was worth the educational gains. Others expressed concern about the time to develop a quality WebQuest.

Information overload is a concern of many teachers who like the structured nature of
WebQuests (Chatel, 2003; Ficklen & Muscara, 2001; Perkins & McKnight, 2003). The educators view preselected links as an efficient use of student time. They also like the way students stay on track and focused on relevant resources and information.

Technology and Resources

A quality WebQuest makes good use of information resources. In some cases, a
book, map, photograph, or hands-on experiment is the best tool for data gathering. However, Internet resources provide access to information that would not be available other
ways. Although it may not be possible to take a class field trip to visit a volcano or ancient
historical ruins, students can explore these locations through text, visuals, and audio on the
Internet. The school library may not hold the most recent census data, but a government
Web site contains both popular and obscure reports. Milson (2002) found that students have
differing perceptions of the value of print and electronic resources. Many students prefer
print resources to Internet resources.

Although some Web-based research approaches ask students to use search engines
on the Internet to locate information, a WebQuest provides a structured set of materials that
guides students through the exploration of relevant, timely resources (Vidoni & Maddux,
2002).

Some educators have pointed out teacher concerns related to Internet use (Levin &
Arafeh, 2002) and specifically WebQuest use (Dutt-Doner et al., 2000; Perkins &
McKnight, 2003; Summerville, 2000; Yoder, 1999). Levin and Arafeh (2002) found that
the quality of Internet-based assignments varies widely and that planning is critical to
success.

Although Websites may be pre-selected, students can still end up with poor-quality or inappropriate information. WebQuests are dependent on the stability of Web sites used as resources. Many teachers find that Web links provided in WebQuests are no longer active. This "link rot" is a common complaint of teachers (Perkins & McKnight, 2003; Summerville, 2000). According to Teclehaimanot and Lamb (2004), supplemental Web resources can be identified to enhance dated WebQuests. They can also be used to differentiate instruction to meet individual needs.

CONCLUSION

Educational systems around the world have been under tremendous pressure to meet the needs of today's diverse learners. In a world where students are increasingly cynical and unmotivated, WebQuests provide an engaging, challenging learning environment.

According to March (2003, p. 42), the best WebQuests inspire students to "see richer thematic relationships, to contribute to the real world of learning, and to reflect on their own metacognitive processes."

An ever-expanding community of educators has grown around the WebQuest concept. At the same time, a body of evidence supporting the effectiveness of this approach is being established. As global access to high-speed Internet, wireless technology, and easy-to-use multimedia authoring tools continues to grow, the opportunities for teaching and learning through technology will continue to evolve, challenging teachers to facilitate learning experiences that promote transformational learning through the use of WebQuests.

REFERENCES

About WebQuests. (1995). *SBC Knowledge Network Explorer.* Updated February 23, 2004. Retrieved January 19, 2005, from http://www.kn.pacbell.com/webquests.html

Arbaugh, F., Scholten, C. M., & Essex, N. K. (2001). Data in the middle grades: A probability WebQuest. *Mathematics Teaching in the Middle School, 7*(2), 90–95.

Benz, P. (2002, December). *The English multiverse—WebQuests.* Retrieved from January 19, 2005, http://www.ardecol.ac-grenoble.fr/english/tice/enwebquests.htm

Benz, P. (2003). Message of 1051 of 1068. *Yahoo Groups: WebQuest.* Retrieved January 19, 2005, from http://groups.yahoo.com/group/webquest/message/1051

Bloom, B. S. (Ed.). (1956). *Taxonomy of educational objectives: Classification of educational goals. Handbook 1: Cognitive domain.* New York: Longman, Green.

Bloom, B., Madaus, G., & Hasting, J. T. (1981). *Evaluation to improve learning.* New York: McGraw-Hill.

Braun, L. W. (2001). In virtual pursuit [Electronic version]. *Library Journal, 126*(17), 32. Retrieved January 19, 2005, from http://www.findarticles.com/cf_dls/m1299/11_47/80851841/p1/article.jhtml

Brooks, D. W., Nolan, D. E., & Gallagher, S. M. (2001). *Web-teaching: A guide to designing interactive teaching for the World Wide Web* (2nd ed.). New York: Kluwer Academic/Plenum.

Brooks, J. G., & Brooks, M. G. (1999). *In search of understanding: The case for constructivist classrooms.* Alexandria VA: Association for Supervision and Curriculum Development.

Brucklacher, B., & Gimbert, B. (1999). Role-playing software and WebQuests—What's possible with cooperative learning and computers. *Computers in the Schools, 15*(2), 37–48.

Building blocks of a WebQuest. (1997). Retrieved January 19, 2005, from http://projects.edtech.sandi.net/staffdev/buildingblocks/p-index.htm

Callison, D. (2003). *Key words, concepts, and methods for information age instruction: A guide to teaching information inquiry*. Baltimore: LMS Associates.

Chandler, H. (2003). Concept mapping: WebQuests in Social Studies. *Media & Methods, 39*(3), 38–39.

Chatel, R. G. (2003). Developing literacy in the technical age: Expanding the boundaries of reader-text interactions. *New England Reading Association Journal, 39*(2), 67–73.

Cooper, R. A., & Smarkola, C. (2001). WebQuests: Online inquiry instructional activities for teachers. *MARTEC Technobrief*, 117. Retrieved January 19, 2005, from http://www.temple.edu/martec/technobrief/tbrief17.html

Crandall, A., Kinney, M., Taylor, S., & Trauth, B. (2002). *Paper or plastic: An Internet WebQuest on recycling*. Retrieved January 19, 2005, from http://oncampus.richmond.edu/academics/education/projects/webquests/paper/

Delisio, E. R. (2001). Technology in the classroom: WebQuest sends student back in time. *Education World*. Retrieved January 19, 2005, from http://www.educationworld.com/a_tech/tech073.shtml

Dewey, J. (1933). *How we think: A restatement of the relation of reflective thinking to the educative process*. Boston: Henry Holt.

Dodge, B. (1995a). *Some thoughts about WebQuests*. Updated May 5, 1995. Retrieved January 19, 2005, from http://edweb.sdsu.edu/courses/edtec596/about_webquests.html

Dodge, B. (1995b). WebQuests: A technique for Internet-based learning. *Distance Educator, 1*(2), 10–13.

Dodge, B. (1996a). *Active learning on the Web (K–12 version)*. Presentation to the faculty of La Jolla Country Day School, August 20, 1996. Retrieved January 19, 2005, from http://edweb.sdsu.edu/people/bdodge/active/ActiveLearningk-12.html

Dodge, B. (1996b). *Investigating Archaeotype: A WebQuest*. Updated February 29, 1996. Retrieved January 19, 2005, from http://web.archive.org/web/19980121013443/edweb.sdsu.edu/edweb_folder/Courses/EDTEC596/WebQuest1.html

Dodge, B. (1998a). *A taxonomy of information patterns*. Updated July 18, 1998. Retrieved January 19, 2005, from http://projects.edtech.sandi.net/staffdev/tpss98/patterns-taxonomy.html

Dodge, B. (1998b, June). *WebQuest: A strategy for scaffolding higher-level learning*. Presented at the National Educational Computing Conference, San Diego, CA. Retrieved January 19, 2005, from http://webquest.sdsu.edu/necc98.htm

Dodge, B. (1998c). *A WebQuest about WebQuests*. Retrieved January 19, 2005, from http://webquest.sdsu.edu/webquestwebquest.html

Dodge, B. (1999a). *WebQuest task design worksheet*. Retrieved January 19, 2005, from http://projects.edtech.sandi.net/staffdev/tpss99/taskmastery.html

Dodge, B. (1999b). *WebQuest process checklist*. Retrieved January 19, 2005, from http://projects.edtech.sandi.net/staffdev/tpss99/processchecker.html

Dodge, B. (1999c). *Fine points: Little things that make a big difference*. Retrieved January 19, 2005, from http://projects.edtech.sandi.net/staffdev/tpss99/finepoints/index.htm

Dodge, B. (2001a). FOCUS: Five rules for writing a great WebQuest. *Learning & Leading with Technology, 28*(8), 6–9, 58.

Dodge, B. (2001b). *WebQuest rubric*. Retrieved January 19, 2005, from http://webquest.sdsu.edu/webquestrubric.html

Dodge, B. (2002a). *Adapting and enhancing existing WebQuests*. Retrieved January 19, 2005, from http://webquest.sdsu.edu/adapting/index.html

Dodge, B. (2002b). *WebQuest taskonomy: A taxonomy of tasks*. Retrieved January 19, 2005, from http://webquest.sdsu.edu/taskonomy.html

Dodge, B. (2003, November). *WebQuests and other viruses*. Keynote address presented at the Association for Educational Communications and Technology Conference, Anaheim, CA.

Dodge, B. (2004). *WebQuest.org*. Retrieved January 19, 2005, from http://webquest.org

Dudeney, G. (2003, March). The quest for practical Web usage. *TESL-EJ, 6*(4). Retrieved January 19, 2005, from http://www-writing.berkeley.edu/TESL-EJ/ej24/int.html

Dunne, D. W. (2000). Technology in the classroom: Cinco de Mayo WebQuest includes a fiesta! *Education World*. Updated April 28, 2003. Retrieved January 19, 2005, from http://www.education-world.com/a_tech/tech019.shtml

Dutt-Doner, K., Wilmer, M., Stevens, C., & Hartmann, L. (2000). Actively engaging learners in interdisciplinary curriculum through the integration of technology. *Computer in the Schools, 16*(3/4), 151–166.

Ficklen, E., & Muscara, C. (2001). Harnessing technology in the classroom. *American Educator, 25*(3), 22–29.

Filamentality Web site. (1996). Updated February 26, 2004. Retrieved January 19, 2005, from http://www.kn.pacbell.com/wired/fil/

Gardner, H. (1991). *The unschooled mind: How children think and how schools should teach*. New York: Basic Books.

Garry, A., & Graham, P. (2002, April 1). How to succeed with WebQuests. *Teaching and Learning*. Retrieved January 19, 2005, from http://www.techlearning.com/db_area/archives/WCE/archives/adampary.htm

Geraghty, C. L. (2004a, February 2). Bernie Dodge puts his life online. *SDSUniverse*. Retrieved January 19, 2005, from http://www.sdsuniverse.info/people_content.asp?id=13409

Geraghty, C. L. (2004b, February 2). Learning (and teaching) in the technological age. *SDSUniverse*. Retrieved January 19, 2005, from http://www.sdsuniverse.info/story.asp?id=13378

Hill, J. R., Wiley, D., Nelson, L. M., & Han, S. (2003). Exploring research on Internet-based learning: From infrastructure to interactions. In D. H. Jonassen (Ed.), *Handbook of research on educational communications and technology* (2nd ed.). Bloomington, IN: Association for Educational Communications and Technology.

Jakes, D. S., Pennington, M. E., & Knodle, H. A. (2000). *Inquiry-based learning and the Web: An epaper*. Retrieved January 19, 2005, from http://www.biopoint.com/inquiry/ibr.html

Jonassen, D. H., Peck, K. L., & Wilson, B. G. (1999). *Learning with technology: A constructivist perspective*. Upper Saddle River, NJ: Prentice Hall.

Keller, J. M. (1983). Motivational design of instruction. In C. M. Reigeluth (Ed.), *Instructional design theories and models*. Hillsdale, NJ: Erlbaum.

Kelly, R. (1999). Getting everybody involved: Cooperative PowerPoint creations benefit inclusion students. *Learning & Leading with Technology, 27*(1), 10–14.

Kelly, R. (2000). Working with WebQuests: Making the Web accessible to students with disabilities. *Teaching Exceptional Children, 32*(6), 4-13. Retrieved January 19, 2005, from http://www.teachingld.org/pdf/teaching_how-tos/ working_with_Webquests.pdf

Koenraad, T. L. M., & Westoff, G. J. (2003, September). *Can you tell a LanguageQuest when you see one? Design criteria for TalenQuests*. Paper presented at the 2003 Conference of the European Association for Computer Assisted Language Learning. University of Limerick, Ireland. Retrieved January 19, 2005, from http://www.feo.hvu.nl/koen2/Home/TQPinball/index-l.htm

Lamb, A. (1998). *EMPOWER: State of Indiana technology literacy challenge grant project*. Retrieved January 19, 2005, from http://www.evsc.k12.in.us/schoolzone/schools/EMPOWER/empower.html

Lamb, A. (2000). Internet expeditions. *Eduscapes*. Retrieved January 19, 2005, from http://www.eduscapes.com/sessions/travel/

Lamb, A. (2003). Extreme thinking: Transforming traditional student projects into effective learning environments. *Educational Technology, 43*(4), 31–40.

Lamb, A. (2004). From potential to prosperity: Twenty years of online learning environments. In G. Kearsley (Ed.), *Online learning: Personal reflections on the transformation of education.* Englewood Cliffs, NJ: Educational Technology.

Lamb, A., Smith, N., & Johnson, L. (1997). Wondering, wiggling, and weaving: A new model for project- and community-based learning on the Web. *Learning and Leading with Technology, 24*(7), 6–13.

Levin, D., & Arafeh, S. (2002, August 14). *The digital disconnect: The widening gap between internet-savvy students and their schools.* Washington, DC: Pew Internet & American Life. Retrieved January 19, 2005, from http://www.pewinternet.org

Lim, B. R. (2001). *Guidelines for designing inquiry-based learning on the Web: Online professional development of educators.* Doctoral dissertation, Indiana University, Bloomington. (UMI Number: 3024215)

Lipscomb, G. (2002). Eighth graders' impressions of the Civil War: Using technology in the history classroom. *Education, Communication & Information, 2*(1), 51.

Lipscomb, G. (2003). I guess it was pretty fun: Using WebQuests in the middle school classroom. *Clearing House, 76*(3), 152–155.

March, T. (1995, July/August). What's on the Web: Sorting strands of the World Wide Web for educators. *Computer-Using Educator's Newsletter.* Revised October 2001. Retrieved January 19, 2005, from http://www.ozline.com/learning/webtypes.html

March, T. (May 1996). *Look who's footing the bill! a WebQuest.* Updated May 30, 2001. Retrieved January 19, 2005, from http://www.kn.pacbell.com/wired/democracy/debtquest.html

March, T. (1998a). *WebQuest rubric.* Updated January 6, 2004. Retrieved January 19, 2005, from http://www.ozline.com/webquests/rubric.html

March, T. (1998b). *Why WebQuests?* Updated January 6, 2004. Retrieved January 19, 2005, from http://www.ozline.com/webquests/intro.html

March, T. (1999, January). *Little Rock Nine WebQuest.* Updated December 22, 2003. Retrieved January 19, 2005, from http://www.kn.pacbell.com/wired/BHM/little_rock/

March, T. (2000a). The 3 R's of WebQuests. *Multimedia Schools, 7*(6), 62–63.

March, T. (2000b). WebQuests 101. *Multimedia Schools, 7*(5), 55–58.

March, T. (2002). *About best WebQuests.* Updated 2004. Retrieved January 19, 2005, from http://www.bestwebquests.com/about/default.asp

March, T. (December 2003/January 2004). The learning power of WebQuests. *Educational Leadership, 61*(4), 42–47.

Marco, M. J. L. (2002, July). Internet content-based activities for English for special purposes. *English Teaching Forum,* 20–25.

Marzano, R. J. (1992). *A different kind of classroom: Teaching with dimensions of learning.* Alexandria VA: Association for Supervision and Curriculum Development.

McDowell, D. (1999). *Process guides.* Retrieved January 19, 2005, from http://projects.edtech.sandi.net/staffdev/tpss99/processguides/index.htm

McKenzie, J. (1997). Creating research programs for an age of information. *From Now On, 7*(2). Retrieved January 19, 2005, from http://fno.org/oct97/question.html

McKenzie, J. (2001). From trivial pursuit to essential questions and standards-based learning. *From Now On: The Educational Technology Journal, 10*(5). Retrieved January 19, 2005, from http://www.fno.org/feb01/pl.html

McTighe, J., & Wiggins, G. (1998). *Understanding by design*. Alexandria VA: Association for Supervision and Curriculum Development.

Milson, A. J. (2001). Fostering civic virtue in a high-tech world. *International Journal of Social Education, 16*(1), 87–93.

Milson, A. J. (2002). The Internet and inquiry learning: integrating medium and method in a sixth grade social studies classroom. *Theory and Research in Social Education, 30*(3), 330–353.

Milson, A. J., & Downey, P. (2001). WebQuest: Using Internet resources for cooperative inquiry. *Social Education, 65*(3), 144–146.

Minkel, W. (2000). Solar system WebQuest. *School Library Journal, 46*(11), 34.

Monroe, E. E. (2003, June). *The nature of discourse as students collaborate on a mathematics WebQuest*. Paper presentation at the National Educational Computing Conference in Seattle, WA.

Patterns Summer Symposium. (2000). Retrieved January 19, 2005, from http://projects.edtech.sandi.net/staffdev/patterns2000/

Perkins, B., & McKnight, M. (2003, February). *What are teacher's attitudes toward Web Quests as a method of teaching?* Paper presented at the Eastern Educational Research Association Conference, Hilton Head, SC. Retrieved January 19, 2005, from http://arachne.cofc.edu/faculty/Perkins/PerkinsEERA%20WQPaper.doc

Peterson, C., Caverly, D. C., & MacDonald, L. (2003). Developing academic literacy through WebQuests. *Journal of Developmental Education, 26*(3), 38–39.

Peterson, C. L., & Koeck, D. C. (2001). When students create their own WebQuests. *Learning & Leading with Technology, 29*(1), 10–15.

Pohan, C., & Mathison, C. (1998). WebQuests: The potential of Internet-based instruction for global education. *Social Studies Review, 37*(2), 91–93.

Porter, B. (2001). *Evaluating student computer-based products*. Sedalia, CO: Bernajean Porter.

Schrock, K. (1996). WebQuests in our future: The teacher's role in cyberspace. *Kathy Schrock's Guide for Educators*. Retrieved January 19, 2005, from http://web.archive.org/web/19970619021119/www.capecod.net/schrockguide/webquest/webquest.htm

Schrock, K. (2004). WebQuests in our future: The teacher's role in cyberspace. *Kathy Schrock's Guide for Educators*. Revised Edition. Retrieved from http://kathyschrock.net/slideshows/webquests/frame0001.htm

Snider, S. L., & Foster, J. M. (2000). RESEARCH—Stepping stones for linking, learning and moving toward electronic literacy: Integrating emerging technology in an author study project. *Computers in the Schools, 16*(2), 91.

Spanfelner, D. L. (2000). WebQuests, an interactive approach to the Web. *Community & Junior College Libraries, 9*(4), 23–28.

Starr, L. (2000). Technology in the classroom: Meet Bernie Dodge—the Frank Lloyd Wright of learning environments! *Education World*. Updated December 5, 2003. Retrieved January 19, 2005, from http://www.education-world.com/a_tech/tech020.shtml

Stinson, A. D. (2003). Encouraging the use of technology in the classroom: The WebQuest connection. *Reading Online, 6*(7). Retrieved January 19, 2005, from http://www.readingonline.org/articles/art_index.asp?HREF=stinson/

Summerville, J. (2000). WebQuests: An aspect of technology integration for training preservice teachers. *TechTrends, 44*(2), 31–35.

Tancock, S. M. (2002). Reading, writing, and technology: A healthy mix in the social studies curriculum. *Reading Online, 5*(8). Retrieved January 19, 2005, from http://www.readingonline.org/articles/art_index.asp?HREF=tancock/index.html

Teclehaimanot, B., & Lamb, A. (2004). Reading, technology, and inquiry-based learning through literature-rich WebQuests. *Reading Online*, 7(4). Retrieved January 19, 2005, from http://www.readingonline.org/articles/art_index.asp?HREF=teclehaimanot /index.html – peer-reviewed journal

Think, construct, and communicate. (2004). Retrieved January 19, 2005, from http://cfievalladolid2.net/thinkweb/

Tiene, D., & Ingram, A. (2001). *Exploring current issues in educational technology*. Boston: McGraw-Hill Higher Education.

Tomlinson, C. A. (1999). *The differentiated classroom: Responding to the needs of all learners*. Alexandria, VA: Association for Supervision and Curriculum Development.

Truett, C. (2001). Sherlock Holmes on the Internet: Language Arts teams up with the computing librarian. *Learning & Leading with Technology, 29*(2), 36–41.

Tuskegee study WebQuest. (1996). Updated February 4, 2003. Retrieved January 19, 2005, from http://www.kn.pacbell.com/wired/BHM/tuskegee_quest.html

Using WebQuests in the K–12 classroom. (December 1996/January 1997). *Classroom Connect, 3*(4), 1, 4–6.

Van Leer, J. (2003). Teaching information and technology literacy through student-created WebQuests. *Multimedia Schools, 10*(2), 42–45.

Vidoni, K. L., & Maddux, C. D. (2002). WebQuests: Can they be used to improve critical thinking skills in students? *Computers in the Schools, 19*(1/2), 101–117.

Watson, K. L. (1999). WebQuests in the middle school curriculum: Promoting technological literacy in the classroom. *Meridian: A Middle School Computer Technologies Journal, 2*(2). Retrieved January 19, 2005, from http://www.ncsu.edu/meridian/jul99/webquest/index.html

WebQuest design patterns. (2004). Retrieved January 19, 2005, from http://webquest.sdsu.edu/designpatterns/all.htm

WebQuest training materials. (2004). Retrieved January 19, 2005, from http://webquest.sdsu.edu/LessonTemplate.html

WebQuestUK. (2004). Retrieved January 19, 2005, from http://www.webquestuk.org.uk/

Wood, D., Bruner, J. S., & Ross, G. (1976). The role of tutoring in problem solving. *Journal of Child Psychology and Psychiatry, 17,* 89–100.

Wood, D., & Middleton, D. (1975). A study of assisted problem solving. *British Journal of Psychology, 66,* 181–191.

Yoder, M. B. (1999). The student WebQuest: A productive and thought-provoking use of the Internet. *Learning & Leading with Technology, 26*(7), 6–9.

Using Computer-mediated Bulletin Board Discussions to Facilitate Critical and Reflective Thinking among Teacher Education Students in a Professional Development School

Peter A. Theodore and L. Bill Searcy
Southern Illinois University at Edwardsville

One of the primary goals of our teacher education program is to produce "inquirer-professionals," teachers who are able to think critically and reflectively about their own practice to continually improve that practice. A considerable body of theory and research indicates that this sort of thinking is facilitated by interaction—that people are stimulated to think by engaging in discussion with others. There is also a lot of support for teacher education students doing a good deal of their learning in the field—working in K–12 classroom settings more and being with their peers in college classes and seminars less. The dilemma this creates is related to the perennial problem of teacher isolation. To the extent that teacher education students are placed in K–12 classrooms, they have less opportunity to engage in discussion with their peers, with a concomitant loss of what that discussion could do for them in terms of stimulating critical and reflective thinking about their practice.

One possible way out of this dilemma involves the use of computer-mediated bulletin board discussions. If teacher education students in K–12 classrooms are able to participate in an ongoing electronic discussion with their colleagues, it may be possible to have the best of both worlds—to have the experience of being in K–12 classroom settings while being able to discuss that experience with peers who are similarly placed. The present study involves just such a situation. Thirty-one undergraduate teacher education students were placed in K–5 classrooms in two elementary schools that were professional development schools for the university. These undergraduates met once a week in a seminar but had the opportunity to participate in an ongoing discussion with their peers that was available twenty-four hours a day, seven days a week, via computer. In this chapter, we examine how this computer-mediated bulletin board discussion facilitated critical and reflective thinking among these teacher education students.

THE CONTEXT

A cohort of thirty-one elementary education majors were assigned to complete their preservice professional education requirements in two elementary schools in an urban school district identified by the university as professional development schools. These teaching partners spent two years in the same schools with responsibilities progressing through observing, assisting, teaming, and full teaching responsibility. All coursework for the professional sequence was presented on site over the two years. Teaching partners were supervised by two university faculty who also taught the courses. The two university faculty were in the school buildings interacting with teaching partners, mentor teachers, students, and building administrators for a minimum of one day a week.

During the first year, teaching partners spent two full days in the classroom with a four hour seminar held once a week. It was through this seminar that content in educational psychology, educational foundations, and teaching methodology was taught. The second year teaching partners were assigned to a classroom five days a week and continued the seminar. Throughout the two years, teaching partners rotated through a variety of grade-level assignments and were mentored by the classroom teachers to whom they were assigned.

The university faculty involved with this cohort decided to use WebCT bulletin board as one teaching tool for the two-year experience. Teaching partners were given training on how to use WebCT, as well as the expectation to respond on the bulletin board on a regular basis. University faculty used the bulletin board to pose questions to teaching partners about the content of the seminars as well as their classroom experiences. They also responded to teaching partners' questions and responses. Teaching partners responded to the faculty questions, posed questions of their own, and responded to each other in a variety of ways.

COMPUTER-MEDIATED COMMUNICATION AND THINKING

Terms such as *thinking, critical thinking, reflective thinking,* and *reflection* are variously defined throughout the research literature, and there seems to be no clear consensus concerning just what these terms mean (Gipe & Richards, 1992; Hatton & Smith, 1994). Despite the lack of a single, agreed-on definition for any of these terms, there seems to be a lot of agreement that the development of critical and reflective thinking is important in teacher education and that computer-mediated communication can facilitate this development (Andrusyszyn & Davie, 1997; Harrington & Hathaway, 1994).

Faculty members working with teacher education students placed in classrooms have utilized electronic mail to have discussions with them that were seen to be "critical to their development as professionals" (Schlagal, Trathen, & Blanton, 1996). Other faculty working with prospective teachers have found the discussion enabled by an e-mail listserv to be "custom-made for reflection" (Elias & Brown, 2001). Furthermore, faculty members have found that a Web-based discussion environment helped them to "examine processes of student learning" (Russell & Daugherty, 2001).

QUALITATIVE ANALYSIS OF THE BULLETIN BOARD TRANSCRIPTS

The transcript of the WebCT bulletin board discussion, which consisted of 650 posts totaling 291 pages of text (more than 110,000 words), was subjected to a qualitative analysis, following established qualitative research procedures (Glesne & Peshkin, 1992; Marshall & Rossman, 1994; Strauss & Corbin, 1990). The initial phase of the analysis was performed by the first researcher and involved repeated readings of the transcript, identifying themes that emerged from the data and developing codes based on those themes. The coding system was refined during the process of repeated readings.

No attempt was made in the current research to arrive at a precise, or objective, definition of *thinking* or to distinguish between such varieties of thinking as *critical* and *reflective*. The initial analysis of the transcript of the bulletin board discussion was deliberately undertaken without any categories, or codes, decided in advance because the goal of the research was to discover any number of ways that the bulletin board discussion might help preservice teachers relate the theory they were learning to their practice in classrooms.

In the initial analysis of the bulletin board transcript, one of the things that was noted was a student making connections, thinking an issue through. It seemed that the act of thinking about an issue, perhaps struggling with it, was relevant to making connections between theory and practice, so the code "TH," for thinking, was added to the developing set of codes. After the first researcher had coded the entire transcript, the second researcher was given the set of codes that had been developed, including the code for thinking and was provided with a brief description of what the first researcher meant by each of the codes. The second researcher then independently coded the transcript. After this coding by the second researcher, the first and second researcher met and extracted from the transcript all those posts that they had both independently coded as exhibiting thinking, ignoring any posts that had been coded by one but not the other. Thus, in place of an attempt to define thinking objectively, what was achieved was an intersubjective definition. *Thinking* was deemed to occur in those posts where two researchers, working independently, saw evidence of thinking. This process identified 131 student posts as exhibiting thinking.

These 131 posts were then subjected to a process of analysis similar to what had been done with the entire transcript. The first researcher read the posts, developed codes, and coded the posts. Seven codes were developed in this process. This set of seven codes was then given to the second researcher, who independently coded the 131 posts. After both researchers had independently coded the 131 posts, they met and compiled those excerpts from the posts that they had independently coded similarly, eliminating those posts that only one researcher had given a particular code. This resulted in approximately 28 pages of student contributions to the bulletin board discussion, divided into seven categories according to the codes that had been developed. Each researcher then independently reread these 28 pages to attempt to see what story might emerge from these data regarding how the students' participation in the bulletin board discussion facilitated their thinking. The researchers then combined what they found into the present chapter.

THINKING ABOUT TEACHING

When the university faculty analyzed how the WebCT discussions were being used, they discovered one thing teaching partners used the bulletin board for was to explain their thinking about various aspects of their teaching experiences. They used the discussions to interact with each other, to agree or disagree with statements made by colleagues. They sometimes supported their thinking through examples from their own personal histories as well as ongoing classroom examples. At times, the discussions were used to attempt to make connections between theory and practice.

INTERACTION

Teaching partners interacted with each other through WebCT almost as though they were conversing in person. Sometimes those interactions were directed to individuals, and sometimes the response was directed to the larger group through the individual. As with any conversation, these interactions were used to agree with and support each other, to raise questions about the issues, and to give advice and directions.

One of the clearest and simplest indicators of interaction was that students frequently addressed one another by name, as in the following examples (names used here are pseudonyms):

> Amelia, it seems to me that the best thing for the students is to put aside personal feelings about "errors" and to score the test as it is intended to be scored. Perhaps it is the term "error" that bothers you more than the scoring technique.

> bill i have noticed the same things. the children get really excited when you mention that we are going to do science next. but the minute you mention doing math or reading they moan and groan. i think that the reason is just as you mentioned. they can use imaginations and at times the exercises will allow them to touch and see things that they have never seem before and at times things that we cannot control or explain. who knows why, but if someone as a solution to making reading and math just as exciting, share with us all because i'm sure all of us would like to know how.

> Carmen—I have the same problem in the library and the classroom. If I allow the students to talk then someone else yells at them to be quiet. I have also had other teachers tell me that I need to have better control over the students if I don't stop their talking. This often happens when my mentor leaves the class-

room. Once the students have their assignment I do not mind if they aren't ab-
solutely silent—but they are reprimanded later by someone else. It is a
frustrating situation.

I also believe that these kids need some time to just chat. They are hounded to
be quiet as soon as they enter the school, when they go to lunch, and every-
where else. One of my students said that at her old school the girls could at least
talk in the bathroom. I think that is sad. Look at (or listen to) us in seminar! We
talk every time there is a break in the action (and often when there is not).

Another indicator of interaction in these posts was the use of second-person, imperative verbs, as in the following examples:

go see it, it is really neat

Maybe share a time when you were depressed and explain how you overcame it

Think about how YOU would want to be treated and work from there

Look at (or listen to) us in seminar!

Interaction was also indicated by students posing questions to one another, as in the
following examples:

Have you thought about talking about depression with her?

Better yet, how do we deal with this when higher authorities turn the other way?

It seems clear that students perceived themselves as in interaction with one another
when they participated in the bulletin board discussion, and thus that this electronic discussion could provide that "discussion with others" that could stimulate critical and reflective
thinking. What remains to be explored is just *how* critical and reflective thinking is facilitated by participation in the bulletin board discussion.

CONCRETE EXPERIENCE

According to constructivist theories of education since Piaget, children's thinking develops as children interact with concrete materials. Much of the discussion on the bulletin board by
our teacher education students concerned the use of "manipulatives" with children learning
mathematics. It occurred to one researcher as he read the student posts that the teacher education students were using their own experiences in classrooms as manipulatives of a sort. These
teacher education students were discussing concrete experiences they had in classrooms and
were using those concrete experiences to facilitate their thinking about education.

One issue that may not be foremost in the minds of prospective teachers but that becomes salient once someone is actually in the classroom, especially the elementary classroom, is the problem of time and scheduling—the problem of "fitting in" all the various
subjects one is supposed to teach. Following are two students' posts to the bulletin board
that show the students thinking about this issue, using their own experience in the classroom as a sort of manipulative, a concrete context they can "use" to think about the problem
of time in the classroom.

Each day I find myself torn between moving on or allowing extra learning
time. Usually things like english and spelling don't spark too much extra interest from the children, but I have noticed science, reading, and social studies
do. I know that for the most part now I have to follow my mentor's schedule,
but I don't know what to do when I get my own class. (Message 386)

I also feel rushed. I feel as if I get to school and the next thing you know is your going home. These days go by so fast. I feel as if in the younger grades especially that it is better to expand on the information that might take more time. In kindergarten, we do not always get through everything in a day because we do expand. Most of the time it is the first time these children are learning this, so it is better to take it slow and with more details. If we do not get to something we save it for the next day. (Message 388)

In these excerpts, we can see the teacher education students bringing their separate classroom experiences into the common forum of the bulletin board discussion. To be involved in discussion together, people have to have something to talk *about*. Often, in university classrooms, this "something" is an assigned reading—all of the students are expected to read the assigned material, and this common text becomes the basis for class discussion. We did have assigned readings that we discussed in seminars with our teacher education students, and on occasion references to these readings found their way to the bulletin board. Much more common, however, were student references to their individual experiences in classrooms. These experiences were both something students had in common and something unique to each student. They were "in common" because all of the students were placed in a classroom in one of the two professional development schools. They were "unique" because each student was in a different classroom.

STUDENT STRUGGLES

The following two excerpts are part of a student discussion on the bulletin board about the use of math manipulatives. These excerpts show the students struggling with the problems that arise in an actual classroom and trying to reconcile these problems with their conviction that the use of the manipulatives is important to help the children they are teaching understand certain concepts. (Names are pseudonyms.)

I taught a lesson on apples dealing with math. I had little beads that the students had to use to count on the apple tree. The students did learn what they suppose to but I saw a lot of students playing and dropping the beads. Even though the students are distracted by manipulatives, I found that it is . . . another way to teach. Every child is different. With the lesson, I went back the next day and took another approach to solving problems. I do realize that students are active and they need manipulative type of activities. It is a way to be active and doing something constructive where learning can take place also. The students who were not following, I asked the students to show me what they understand. In the other classes I have had, it has not been as complicated. I did notice how students who are active tend to do well with manipulative activities. (Message 299)

Most of our students play with the math manipulatives, too. I had a student make a gun out of the cubes just like Denise did. I like the idea of using math manipulatives, but as a teacher you have to be all over the class at all times because the students do not use them right. In my mind the whole idea of math manipulatives is that the kids experiment with them hands-on to learn more about the math lesson. This is the way the teacher hopes it would go, but it doesn't. We have a handful of students that use the manipulatives correctly, and these are the same kids that already understand the lesson. The students that do not get it, are building guns and animals etc. So in our class we walk the students through exactly what is to be done, but to me this takes away from the whole purpose of the manipulatives which is to let the students experiment on their own. I am confused as well about the use of manipulatives in the classroom. I just feel like the students that need to learn, are learning nothing with the manipulatives. It is just a fun time to build cool things. (Message 345)

INFORMATION FOR SUPERVISORS

For the two of us who were supervisors/instructors for these teacher education students, posts such as those included here provided valuable windows into our students thinking. The previous two posts in particular, for example, provided us with the following information:

1. Our students had certain beliefs about why manipulatives were valuable and how they were supposed to work.

   "I do realize that students are active and they need manipulative type of activities"

   "It is a way to be active and doing something constructive where learning can take place also."

   "I did notice how students who are active tend to do well with manipulative activities."

   "In my mind the whole idea of math manipulatives is that the kids experiment with them hands-on to learn more about the math lesson."

2. At the same time, our students had some doubts about how well the use of manipulatives worked in an actual classroom setting.

   "The students did learn what they suppose to but I saw a lot of students playing and dropping the beads."

   "Most of our students play with the math manipulatives, too. I had a student make a gun out of the cubes"

   "I like the idea of using math manipulatives, but as a teacher you have to be all over the class at all times because the students do not use them right."

   "We have a handful of students that use the manipulatives correctly, and these are the same kids that already understand the lesson. The students that do not get it, are building guns and animals etc."

   "I am confused as well about the use of manipulatives in the classroom. I just feel like the students that need to learn, are learning nothing with the manipulatives. It is just a fun time to build cool things."

Having this sort of information from our students enabled us to reteach the use of manipulatives with mathematics education, building on what the students already understood and specifically addressing the concerns they had made evident on the bulletin board discussion. The students' discussions of their experiences in K–5 classrooms as they attempted to put what they were learning into practice created a connection between the K–5 classrooms and our seminar time, enabling both settings to work together synergistically toward the education of our teacher education students.

CONCLUSIONS AND RECOMMENDATIONS

Our research indicates that computer-mediated bulletin board discussions can be a useful tool to help preservice teacher education students think critically and reflectively about their practice. Two key factors that can facilitate thinking—interactive discussion and concrete experiences—are brought together by the bulletin board discussion. Students can be placed in classrooms where they have the opportunity to have concrete teaching experiences, while they are connected to an ongoing discussion with their peers and the faculty, allowing them to engage in interactive discussion about those experiences.

The use of computer-mediated bulletin board discussions allowed these preservice teachers to use the manipulatives, that is, the real classroom experiences, and to receive and provide support for one another throughout the process. It wasn't necessary for our students to wait a week or more to share their experiences and get needed feedback from faculty and peers. They were able to share their experiences and their questions almost immediately. While interacting through the bulletin board discussions, they shared common understandings, agreed and disagreed on issues and practice, sought and received help, and raised questions of themselves and each other—just as they did during their face-to-face discussions. The bulletin board discussions allowed for continuation and expansion of ideas.

An added benefit for us as faculty was how our participation in the discussion allowed us to monitor the effectiveness of our own teaching. In essence, the posting informed our teaching. We could determine whether our students needed reteaching or expanded depth over particular topics. Their questions gave us guidance in topics that needed to be addressed, whether or not those topics were planned for our next meeting. The result was our being able to model student-centered instruction for our teacher education students.

The use of computer-mediated bulletin board discussions was an important strategy toward our goal of producing teachers who are "inquirer-professionals." It allowed our preservice teacher education students the opportunity to keep in touch while participating in elementary classrooms. Their bulletin board discussions served as documentation of how they were thinking: it provided a window into their thought process in ways not possible through occasional classroom discussions or writing assignments. Their postings were an ongoing record of what they were doing and what they thought about doing it—while they were doing it. Thus, the concrete context of the classroom interfaced with ongoing discussions, which resulted in the desired outcome: critical and reflective thinking.

Did participating in these bulletin board discussions make critical thinkers out of those who were not already able to think that way? Probably not. It did, however, provide a medium for preservice teachers to use and expand their skills in reflecting on their practice, something few of them had had the need to do before. It provided extended discussion time for students to dig into topics they felt were important, as well as topics determined by faculty to be important. Along with that, it served as a tool for us as faculty to assess our students' ability to think critically and to reflect.

We found the strategy to be highly successful and would recommend the use of computer-mediated bulletin board discussions be used for any type of extended field work in teacher education. Preservice teachers need to be trained in how to use the program chosen for the bulletin boards, and decisions need to be made about when and how often they will post. Although faculty may occasionally want to post questions about specific topics covered in classes or seminars, the value of this type of discussion is that it allows students to talk about what is important to them as a result of their own experiences. So, rather than control the topics, faculty should model how to raise questions from practice and how to interact in meaningful ways through this medium. The result can be rich discussions focusing on practice and reflection.

REFERENCES

Andrusyszyn, M. A., & Davie, L. (1997). Facilitating reflection through interactive journal writing in an online graduate course: A qualitative study. *Journal of Distance Education, 12*(1/2) 103–126.

Elias, D., & Brown, D. (2001). Critical discourse in a student listserv: Collaboration, conflict, and electronic multivocality. *Kairos, 6*(1) Retrieved January 19, 2005, from http://english.ttu.edu/kairos/6.1/index.html

Gipe, J. P., & Richards, J. C. (1992). Reflective thinking and growth in novice's teaching abilities. *Journal of Educational Research, 86*(1), 52–57.

Glesne, C., & Peshkin, A. (1992). *Becoming qualitative researchers: An introduction.* White Plains, NY: Longman.

Harrington, H. L., & Hathaway, R. S. (1994). Computer conferencing, critical reflection, and teacher development. *Teaching and Teacher Education, 10*(5), 543–554.

Hatton, N., & Smith, D. (1994). Reflection in teacher education: Towards definition and implementation. *Teaching and Teacher Education, 11*(1), 33–49.

Marshall, C., & Rossman, G. B. (1994). *Designing qualitative research* (2nd ed.). Thousand Oaks, CA: Sage.

Russell, D., & Daugherty, M. (2001). Web crossing: A context for mentoring. *Journal of Technology and Teacher Education, 9*, 433–446.

Schlagal, B., Trathen, W., & Blanton, W. (1996). Structuring telecommunications to create instructional conversations about student teaching. *Journal of Teacher Education, 47*(3), 175–183.

Strauss, A., & Corbin, J. (1990). *Basics of qualitative research: Grounded theory procedures and techniques.* Newbury Park, CA: Sage.

Learning Technology Integration from Video Cases: Development and Research Issues

Wilhelmina C. Savenye
Arizona State University

The work reported in this chapter was supported in part by grants from the U.S. Department of Education. The opinions expressed are solely those of the author. The author would like to acknowledge the contributions of James Middleton, Thomas Brush, Ann Igoe, Martha Mann, Cumali Oksuz, Terri Kurz, Jiahong Li, Everett Louis, Praveen Puligundla, and Gloria Llama to the projects on which this work is based.

OVERVIEW

Recently, several researchers have begun to develop video cases to aid teachers in learning about technology (cf. Hayek, 2002). Talley (2002) observes that a few of these projects include teacher interviews; reflection by the teacher, as well as experts; and teacher-developed lesson plans and materials (Savenye et al., 2002). Other researchers are developing means for teachers to share discussion about the video cases (Ginsburg, 2002). Barab and his colleagues (Barab, MaKinster, Moore, Cunningham, & the ILF Design Team, 2001) in their use of video cases have extended these discussions to the formation of online communities to support teachers in discussing and applying their virtual visits to each other's classrooms. Strength of such learning communities appears to have a relationship with learning achievement (Moller, Harvey, Downs, & Godshalk, 2003).

In this chapter, we describe a video case project, funded by a Preparing Teachers to use Technology (PT3) grant. In this project, which is completing its third year, a series of research studies have been undertaken with the final studies to be completed in the summer and fall of 2004. This chapter focuses on one case study. In this study, four video cases were examined in depth by graduate students in two courses. Attitudes toward the cases were examined, as were learning and implementation issues and suggested revisions for supporting preservice and inservice teachers who will use the video cases in the future.

PERSPECTIVE

Research on preservice preparation of teachers continues to show that teachers do not feel prepared to integrate technology effectively into their instruction (Schrum, 1999; Strudler & Wetzel, 1999; Topp, Mortensen, & Grandgenett, 1995). That teachers need such preparation is apparent; Bare and Meek (1998) report that 78 percent of K–12 schools have access to network resources, and school district leaders believe their students must have access to and use technology (Brush, 1999; Brush & Bannon, 1998). There is also a national call for preservice education programs to play an increasingly more important role in educating our teachers, and therefore our nation's students (Bransford, Brown, & Cocking, 2000). Yet technology integration is complex, and teachers with little classroom experience typically have no context in which to apply what they may learn in university computer courses.

One solution to developing complex knowledge and problem-solving skills in education and other professions has been the use of cases. Case-based instruction provides learners with models or descriptions of complex problems that the learners are asked to analyze and solve (Stepich, Ertmer, & Lane, 2001). Jonassen and Hernandez-Serrano (2002) propose that developing problem-solving and case-based reasoning skills can be fostered by the use of stories. These researchers argue that stories enable learners to see how experts model their struggle to solve problems, helping learners develop principles that they can use in making decisions in complex environments. They suggest, too, that stories in such cases can take the place of experience and thus support learners in developing from novices into experts.

The form that cases take may vary. In the past, cases were often presented in text form. As Hill and Hannafin (2001) have noted, however, digital environments afford educators the opportunity to foster teaching and learning using digital resources. Videotaped examples of teachers and classrooms have occasionally been used over the past several decades; however, digital video technologies and the Web provide teacher educators the chance to build more dynamic resource-based learning environments.

THE PT3-FUNDED VIDEO CASES FOR TEACHING PROJECT

In response to the needs of preservice teachers, the PT3 program is an initiative of the U.S. Department of Education designed to improve teacher preparation programs to allow educators to integrate technology more effectively into their teaching.

Arizona State University was awarded a PT3 grant to develop a project involving a collaboration among universities, schools, state agencies, and industry. The technology skills and processes the preservice teachers learn are based on state recommendations and the International Society Technology in Education (2000–2002) standards. Hill and Hannafin (1997) have noted that developing resource-based learning environments is a complex endeavor and that learners may become "lost" in these environments. They add that such learning environments require significant resources to aid learners, and that such resources may take the form of tools, scaffold, and so on (2001). In our project, we are attempting to support learners in this type of learning environment.

The Teaching Practices Video Case Project

As part of this project, we have developed a set of video cases, which forms the basis of an online-resource-based learning system. The approach has been to "capture" an entire technology-based lesson, edited to about twenty minutes, as well as reflective interviews of the teacher and all the lesson materials. For instance, in our project, as we evaluate our video cases, the interface, and the open-ended learning system we developed, we are investigating the effects of our externally imposed contexts, compared with the contexts various learners bring to the project materials.

We have also developed an extensive set of tools for preservice teachers (and, later, inservice teachers) to use in accessing, manipulating, and evaluating the materials in the database, and we are collecting data regarding the effectiveness of these tools. These tools include a description of the lesson, teacher biography, lesson plan, links to state standards, the teacher-developed lesson materials, and a prelesson and postlesson reflective interview with the teacher.

The model teachers used a systematically designed lesson plan format to ensure that each lesson includes everything another teacher would need to deliver it (cf. Dick & Carey, 2000; Sullivan & Higgins, 1983). The reflective interviews and commentaries assist preservice and other teachers in learning about technology integration and their changing roles when using technology. They also learn how to think about instructional design for video, online, Web-based, computer-based, and distance technologies (cf. Eastmond & Ziegahn, 1995; Hirumi & Bermudez, 1996).

We are also developing two types of expert commentaries, one on the use of educational technology in each lesson and one on the content pedagogy the teacher used. Finally, we are investigating several types of scaffolding to support the teachers as they use our database.

The process of developing the video cases has evolved to be robust and replicable, but not easy (Kurz, Llama, Savenye, & Li, 2003; Li et al., 2003; Llama, Kurz, & Savenye, 2003; Oksuz, Savenye, & Middleton, 2003). Teachers who use technology in exemplary ways are nominated to be part of the project. Each nominated teacher is interviewed and observed, and his or her possible lesson discussed, before final selections are made. In addition to the lesson plan and materials, documents collected include parental, teacher, and materials use consent forms. Two to three staff members, including well-trained graduate students, do the taping during real classes. They use two cameras and both a wireless lavalier microphone for the teacher and a shotgun microphone for the students. Teachers are interviewed using a standard set of questions, which they receive ahead of time, before they teach the lesson, and again immediately, if possible, after teaching the lesson.

The lesson video is edited to about 20 minutes, now in several short chunks to correspond to common lesson segments, and compressed before uploading to the Web. Also uploaded are the interviews and lesson materials. After the videos are prepared, the teacher is asked to provide a commentary, as are technology and content/pedagogy experts.

So far twenty video cases have been developed, and we are seeking funding to develop more. The lessons in the cases cover the full range of grade levels, from kindergarten to high school, and represent a wide range of content areas, including language arts, math, science, social studies, and even multimedia journalism. We have also attempted to provide teachers with role models who show good methods for helping all students learn; special education and lower-ability students are represented, as are high-achieving and gifted students. Students and teachers of diverse ethnic and cultural backgrounds are included, as are students and teachers in richer, average, and poorer schools.

The Prototype Teacher Video Cases

In developing the first four prototype video cases for the formative evaluation studies, we strove to include a wide range of content and grade levels. Teacher A video case showed a fifth/sixth-grade class of higher-ability students learning about Archimedes' spiral in an interdisciplinary approach to math, science, and a bit of history. Teacher A began her lesson by asking students inquiry-based questions to help them recall their earlier lesson on natural spirals. She had developed a PowerPoint presentation that included graphics and an animation to show past and present uses of an Archimedes screw. She had also designed her own Quicktime movie to show students the procedures they would be using in this class to build their own Archimedes spirals. While half the students were creating their spirals, the other students worked in cooperative groups to complete Internet-based challenges in which they learned more about uses of these spirals and the math and science behind them. In the pre- and post-lesson interviews, Teacher A described her expectations of what students would learn and how she planned to assess their learning, the state standards being learned, and advice for other teachers who would use this lesson.

The prototype video case of Teacher B (Figure 1) showed a second-grade teacher helping her students learn about suffixes and prefixes. She began her lesson by having her students play an engaging game in which students walked around to other students to find prefixes and suffixes that those students carried on signs to match their root words. Teacher B also used a SMART Board to show how to identify and use prefixes and suffixes. The lesson concluded with students working cooperatively at the computer to build a PowerPoint slide showing a word that had a suffix or prefix.

Figure 1. Teacher B video case.

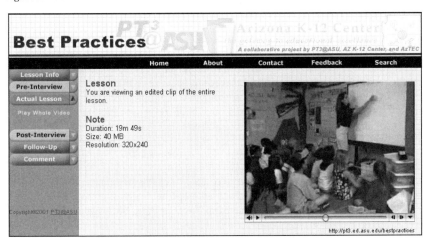

The final two prototype video cases represented high school learning. Teacher C's video case showed a language arts teacher working with a mixed-level class of eleventh and twelfth grade students who were learning about myth, story, and research and writing skills using the mystery of King Arthur and Camelot. She began her lesson also by questioning her students about their perceptions of myth and about King Arthur. Students immediately became engaged in the lesson. Then as a whole class they viewed a PowerPoint presentation that piqued students' interest in various aspects of the King Arthur legend, but also showed students the learning tasks they would carry out over the next several days. Students were challenged to work in small groups using the Internet to answer questions about the legend and to propose their own answers to the mysteries involved. The teacher had focused the students' searches by preparing a Web site that included links to use in beginning their search. Students later used Inspiration software and PowerPoint to develop and present reports of their investigation to the class.

The Teacher D prototype video case showed a high school physics teacher who is well known for his inquiry-based approaches. He had written grants to build his classroom lab with computers equipped to help students conduct various types of experiments, analyze their experimental data, and develop their reports. In this video case, he initially introduced the students to the concepts they would be investigating, acceleration and force. He showed a video that he had developed to help introduce the topic and then tasked them with their set of experiments. His students then rotated in small groups through the various experimental stations, collecting data to verify their hypotheses. The lesson concluded with the students presenting their reports to their classmates. The prototype video cases described here can be found at the following sites:

- A: http://pt3.ed.asu.edu/bestpractices/sutton/index2.html
- B: http://pt3.ed.asu.edu/bestpractices/zia2/index2.html
- C: http://pt3.ed.asu.edu/bestpractices/crane/index2.html
- D: http://pt3.ed.asu.edu/bestpractices/dukerich/index2.html

All video cases will later be linked from our main Web site at http://pt3.ed. asu.edu/index.html.

FORMATIVE EVALUATION OF THE TEACHING PRACTICES VIDEO CASE PROJECT, WITH A FOCUS ON LEARNING, ATTITUDES, AND IMPLEMENTATION ISSUES

Formative evaluation of the Arizona project is being accomplished in a series of studies. The earliest phase of formative evaluation took the form of a Web usability study, using a think-aloud approach, observations, and in-depth interviews with five learners (Corry, Frick, & Hansen, 1997; Kinzie & Julian, 1999–2000). In the usability study, we found that there were problems with our basic database-driven approach to delivering the videos over the Web, resulting in only a few users being able to access the videos at a time. We also discovered, and subsequently revised, a few navigation errors in the original Web pages.

The next phase of the evaluation involved a small pilot group of six preservice teachers who used one of the video cases, that of Teacher A, on their own and then completed an attitude survey and a technology integration lesson-planning task (Savenye et al., 2003).

The focus of this section is on the third phase of our formative evaluation, an in-depth case study of nineteen graduate students, mostly inservice instructors and instructional designers-in-training, who aided us in improving the scaffolding, attitudinal, and implementation aspects of the first four prototype video cases, delivered either via CD or over the Web. In two subsequent studies, currently being completed, we are collecting data on the attitudinal and learning value of the video cases for 54 and 240, preservice teachers, respectively, using two technology-integration learning tasks, mostly in whole-group rather than individual class settings. Some preliminary comparisons with the graduate student case-study data is also discussed briefly here.

METHODS

Participants

The case study was conducted in two phases, with nineteen graduate students participating. In the spring of 2003, five of the nine participating students were enrolled in a required core course on design of computer-based instruction in an educational technology graduate program, and four were enrolled in an online elective course on teaching with technology that was open to any education graduate students. In the spring of 2004, the ten participating graduate students were all enrolled in the latter online course on teaching with technology.

More of the participants (fourteen) were women than men. The students ranged in age from eighteen to over forty-one, with about half being between twenty-three and thirty, eight over thirty, and two under twenty-three. Almost all the graduate students represented education programs, with almost half (nine) in the educational technology program.

All the participants said they owned a computer and had used computer-based lessons before, although most (fifteen) had not used video cases before. Their ratings of their own level of computer expertise ranged from "2 or some experience" to "5 or expert," with an average rating of 3.6.

Procedures

In the spring of 2003, eleven graduate students in the two courses viewed the prototype video case for Teacher A, who taught the advanced math and science lesson on Archimedes' spiral to sixth-graders. They viewed the lesson on CD, on their own time, for extra credit and completed the survey in paper-based form. Most of these students (seven) said they viewed the CD on their home computer, whereas three used a computer at their work, and one used a computer in a university lab.

In the spring of 2004, ten graduate students viewed three more prototype video cases, this time as a required assignment in their fully online course on teaching with technology. They viewed the video cases in their intended format, via the Web. As in 2003, more of these participants (five) viewed the video cases on their home computer, with three using a work computer and two using a university lab computer. These graduate students also completed their surveys online. They chose from among the four prototype video cases; none chose the video case for Teacher A used in 2003. Four students chose to view the video case for Teacher B, who taught second-graders a language arts lesson on base words, prefixes, and suffixes. Five students chose to view the video case for Teacher C, who taught eleventh- and twelfth-grade high school students a language arts lesson on King Arthur. Finally, two students chose to view the video case for Teacher D, who taught the high school physics lesson on acceleration and force.

Instrument

After using the video case, the students completed a two-part survey designed to measure their attitudes and learning. The first part of the survey consisted of thirty-seven Likert-scale-type items. The first eleven items consisted of the demographic questions.

The second section of this part of the survey included seven items to measure student satisfaction with the video case, and the third included twelve items assessing their perceptions of what they learned about technology integration. The final section asked participants to rate the value of specific components of the video case. All the "rating" items employed a five-choice Likert-type scale, with 5 or A indicating *Strongly Agree,* and 1 or E indicating *Strongly Disagree.*

Questions in Part Two of the survey asked students 1) prompted questions that called for them to write a detailed description of the Archimedes lesson, focusing on how the teacher integrated technology; 2) to write their own idea for a detailed lesson plan integrating the same or other technologies; 3) what they liked best and least about the video case; and 4) their suggestions for improving the scaffolding or guidance to be included in this and other video cases.

RESULTS

Graduate Students' Attitudes Toward the Four Prototype Video Cases

Mean attitude scores for graduate students by teacher video case viewed are presented in Table 1. As can be seen, student attitudes toward using the four video cases were generally positive. No grand mean scores on any of the attitude items (items 12–37) fell below neutral, that is, 3.0, or *neither agree nor disagree.* The graduate students were most positive overall about using technology. Their grand mean response to item 30, "I plan to use technology in my classroom," was 4.8, with 5 indicating *strongly agree.* Similarly, in response to item 21, "technology can help me help my students to learn," the average rating was 4.7, and to item 22, "technology enhanced the students' learning in this video case," the average rating was 4.6.

Table 1. Arizona Mean Attitude Scores of Graduate Students for Video Case Viewed

	Teacher A	Teacher B	Teacher C	Teacher D	Grand Means
	Grades 5/6 Math and Science	Grade 2 English	H.S. English	H.S. Physics	
Satisfaction					
12. This video case is good.	4.6	4.3	4.8	4.5	4.6
13. This video case is high in quality.	4.1	3.5	4.4	3.5	3.9
14. This video case will be useful to elementary teachers.	4.4	4.3	4.4	3.0	4.0
15. This video case will help teachers better learn to integrate technology.	4.0	4.3	4.6	3.5	4.1
16. This video case was easy to use.	4.0	3.3	4.8	4.5	4.2
17. This video case was easy to navigate.	4.1	4.3	5.0	5.0	4.6
18. The menus and submenus were clear.	4.3	4.0	5.0	5.0	4.6
(Grand means by teacher/case)	4.2	4.0	4.7	3.4	—
Learning How to Integrate Technology					
19. I learned a lot about how to integrate technology in a MATH/SCIENCE lesson.	3.8	2.3	2.8	4.0	3.2
20. I learned a lot about how to integrate technology in general in my classroom.	3.8	4.0	4.6	4.5	4.2

	Teacher A	Teacher B	Teacher C	Teacher D	Grand Means
22. Technology enhanced the students' learning in this video case.	4.6	4.0	4.6	5.0	4.6
23. This video case helped me learn to incorporate technology in my classroom.	4.0	4.3	4.6	4.5	4.4
24. I feel prepared to teach other lessons using the technologies I saw in this lesson in my classes.	3.8	5.0	4.4	2.0	3.8
25. I feel confident in my ability to try other lessons integrating different forms of technology as a result of viewing this video case.	3.6	3.5	4.4	3.0	3.6
26. I am interested in learning more about technology as a result of viewing this video case.	4.6	4.3	5.0	3.5	4.4
27. This teacher was a good teacher.	4.6	4.5	4.6	4.5	4.6
28. This teacher used technology well to aid student learning.	4.4	4.0	4.8	4.5	4.4
29. I would use more video cases like this in the future when they are available.	4.2	3.8	4.8	5.0	4.5
30. I plan to use technology in my classroom.	4.7	4.8	4.8	5.0	4.8

	Teacher A	Teacher B	Teacher C	Teacher D	Grand Means
Grand means by teacher/case	4.2	4.1	4.5	4.2	—
31. The LESSON INFORMATION section of the video case was valuable in learning about technology integration.	3.6	3.8	4.0	2.0	3.4
32. The LESSON MATERIALS section of the video case was valuable in learning about technology integration.	4.2	4.3	4.6	3.5	4.2
33. The TEACHER BIOGRAPHY was valuable in learning about technology integration.	3.0	3.3	3.0	2.0	2.9
34. The PREINTERVIEW with the teacher was valuable in learning about technology integration.	4.0	4.3	4.4	3.5	4.1
35. The video of the ACTUAL LESSON was valuable in learning about technology integration.	4.7	4.5	4.6	4.0	4.5
36. The POSTINTERVIEW with the Teacher was valuable in learning about technology integration.	4.0	4.3	4.6	4.0	4.3

	Teacher A	Teacher B	Teacher C	Teacher D	Grand Means
37. The FOLLOW-UP commentary with the TECHNOLOGY EXPERT was valuable in learning about technology integration.	4.0	N/A	4.6	N/A	(4.3)
(Grand means by teacher/case)	3.9	4.1	4.3	3.2	—

Note: Mean scores range from 5 (*Strongly Agree*) to 1 (*Strongly Disagree*).
Teacher A: Sixth-grade advanced math/science, $n = 9$ (one student skipped item 24; evaluated on CD on paper-based survey).
Teacher B: Second-grade language arts, $n = 4$ (evaluated on Web using online survey).
Teacher C: high-school language arts, $n = 5$ (evaluated on Web using online survey).
Teacher D: high-school physics, $n = 2$ (evaluated on Web using online survey).

With regard to satisfaction with the cases, the graduate students' ratings of the clarity and navigation in the cases, although quite positive, were mixed. They gave the highest ratings in this section to item 17, "the video case was easy to navigate," and item 18, "the menus and submenus were clear" (both 4.6); however, their rating on item 16, "this video case was easy to use," was somewhat lower (4.2).

Although these participants were positive in response to item 12, "this video case was good" (also 4.6), they were least positive about the quality of the video case, responding to item 13, "this video case is high in quality" with an overall rating of 3.9 across the four cases.

In addition to their positive attitudes about using technology overall, with regard to the second area on the survey, learning how to integrate technology, participants also indicated positive attitudes toward the teacher (item 27, mean of 4.6) and his or her use of technology to aid student learning (item 28, mean of 4.4). The graduate students also indicated a desire to use more video cases like the one they had viewed (item 29, mean of 4.4), noting the attitude that the video case had helped them learn to integrate technology into their classroom (item 23, mean of 4.4) and an interest in learning more about technology as a result of using the video case (item 26, mean of 4.4).

The picture is not completely rosy, however. These participants were least positive overall about their feelings of preparedness and confidence. Their overall response across the four video cases to item 23, "I feel prepared to teach other lessons using the technologies I saw in this lesson in my classes," was 3.8; to item 25, "I feel confident in my ability to try other lessons integrating different forms of technology as a result of viewing this video case, " the response was 3.6.

Overall, the video case component rated most highly was the video of the actual lesson (4.5), followed by the postinterview, and of the two videos that included them, the follow-up commentary by experts (4.3). Participants were least positive about the value of the teacher biography (2.9), and, interestingly, in light of suggestions they made in Part 2 of the survey, the lesson information (3.4).

All the participants rated the teacher whose case he or she viewed as "good" (item 27; C = 4.6, A = 4.6, B = 4.5, D = 4.5). Overall the participants tended to rate highest across all three areas—satisfaction, learning to integrate technology, and the video case components—Teacher C's video case, the high school lesson on King Arthur. Although still rated positively, they tended to rate Teacher D's video case, the high school physics lesson, among the lowest; it should be noted, however, that only two participants viewed this case, and the difficult content may have influenced attitudes.

Preliminary Comparison of Graduate Students' Attitudes and Undergraduate Students' Attitudes Toward Teacher A Video Case

The next phase of our evaluation involves fifty-four undergraduate students who viewed the video case for Teacher A on Archimedes' spiral as part of a whole-class activity (in several smaller sections of a large class), with their instructor showing the video using the CD. Although these are preliminary data, we found it useful to compare the data from these undergraduate, preservice teachers, with those from the graduate students, who are mostly inservice teachers, college faculty, or instructional designers. For this comparison, we looked at just the items measuring satisfaction and learning to integrate technology, items 12 through 30.

As can be seen in Table 2, the responses of the fifty-four preservice teachers were again positive overall and were not so different on many items from the responses of the nine graduate students who also viewed the video case for Teacher A, with most average ratings being within .2 or .3 of each other on most of the items. As did the graduate students, the undergraduates indicated their most positive attitudes toward technology for learning, with their highest average rating being for item 21, "technology can help me help my students learn" (4.5). They, too, rated Teacher A as a good teacher (4.4) and felt that this teacher used technology well to aid student learning (4.5).

The undergraduates were slightly more positive about the quality of the video case than were the graduate students. This may be related to their possible comfort with using technology like these video cases because their highest satisfaction rating was on item 17, "this video case was easy to navigate" (4.4).

In contrast to their attitude toward the ease of using the video case, these 54 undergraduates indicated that they felt as ill prepared to use technology for teaching as did the graduate students. Their lowest attitude ratings, too, were on item 24, "I feel prepared to teach other lessons using the technologies I saw in this lesson in my classes" and item 25, "I feel confident in my ability to try other lessons integrating different forms of technology as a result of viewing this video case" (both 3.4).

With important implications for our project focused on preservice teachers, the attitudes that differ the most among these undergraduate preservice teachers and the more experienced graduate students involved their plans to use technology in their classrooms (item 30; undergraduate, 4.3, graduate 4.7) and interest in learning more about technology as a result of the video case (item 26; undergraduate, 3.9, graduate, 4.6).

Graduate Students' Perceptions and Suggestions for Improvement and Scaffolding: Open-Ended Responses

The graduate students responded to several open-ended items on the attitude survey. Their responses were highly detailed, which may be indicative of their experience in teaching, doing instructional design, and using technology. All nineteen graduate students accurately described the lesson the teacher they viewed had taught, including the lesson objectives, activities, and technologies used. (All nineteen also developed their own lesson plan around a technology of their choice.)

Table 2. Arizona Comparison of Mean Attitude Scores of Graduate Mostly Inservice and Undergraduate Preservice Teachers for Teacher A's Video Case

	Graduate (Mostly Inservice Teachers)	Undergraduate (Preservice Teachers)
Satisfaction		
12. This video case is good.	4.6	4.3
13.This video case is high in quality.	4.1	4.3
14. This video case will be useful to elementary teachers.	4.4	4.2
15. This video case will help teachers better learn to integrate technology.	4.0	4.1
16. This video case was easy to use.	4.0	4.3
17. This video case was easy to navigate.	4.1	4.4
18. The menus and submenus were clear.	4.3	4.2
Grand means	4.2	4.3
Learning How to Integrate Technology		
19. I learned a lot about how to integrate technology in a MATH/SCIENCE lesson.	3.8	3.9
20. I learned a lot about how to integrate technology in general in my classroom.	3.8	3.7
21. Technology can help me help my students to learn.	4.8	4.5
22. Technology enhanced the students' learning in this video case.	4.6	4.2
23. This video case helped me learn to incorporate technology in my classroom.	4.0	3.9
24. I feel prepared to teach other lessons using the technologies I saw in this lesson in my classes.	3.8	3.4
25. I feel confident in my ability to try other lessons integrating different forms of technology as a result of viewing this video case.	3.6	3.4
26. I am interested in learning more about technology as a result of viewing this video case.	4.6	3.9
27. This teacher was a good teacher.	4.6	4.4
28. This teacher used technology well to aid student learning.	4.4	4.5
29. I would use more video cases like this in the future when they are available.	4.2	4.0
30. I plan to use technology in my classroom.	4.7	4.3
Grand means	4.2	4.0

Note: Mean scores range from 5 (*Strongly Agree*) to 1 (*Strongly Disagree*). Both groups evaluated Teacher A's video case. Graduate students ($n = 9$) evaluated the case on CD, individually. Undergraduate students ($n = 54$) evaluated the case after their teacher showed it on CD to the whole class (missing data from one undergraduate student on items 27–30; means calculated on these with $n = 53$).

The participants indicated that what they liked best about the video case they viewed was the real video of a real teacher, seeing the link between the lesson plan and the video, the variety of technologies demonstrated, the interdisciplinary nature of the lesson they viewed, the teacher's skill such as in guiding student inquiry, the value of the pre- and post-lesson interviews, and the step-by-step or well-organized nature of the lesson. In an interesting contrast with opinions of other respondents, several indicated that the video case they viewed was easy to use and navigate. Participants also listed particular features of the video case they liked, such as the Archimedes animation, the subtopics, or the Imovie.

Technical issues dominated the discussion of what they liked least about the video case they had viewed. For instance, students mentioned problems with the size of the video files and their slowness to load, video and sound quality, their wish that the lesson video was accessible in smaller chunks, fonts that were difficult to read, submenu bars covered by video clips, no narrative, and commentaries, links, and resources they would like.

Although some said that no improvements were needed, many participants provided thoughtful suggestions for improving this video case and others. Their suggestions included adding interviews with students and seeing more of their work, providing expert commentaries on pedagogy and technology, and adding more explanations such as "the math behind it" for video case A. They also suggested providing more detailed overviews for both the lesson and the video case early on, improving video and sound quality, adding connections, making files that are quicker to download and larger, and suggestions for improving ease of navigation, especially among components of the case but also across the video cases on the Web.

We asked these graduate students, in particular, to help us develop scaffolding or guidance for these video cases. Although some said no guidance was needed, their suggestions included providing many types of resources and links; more information about students' reactions and learning achievement, as affected by the technologies; warm-up exercises; many forms of explanations, such as overviews, pop-up bubbles, outlines, and alt tags; more directions; additional background information on the lesson; contact information for the teacher; index or search tools for the technologies across lessons; and worksheets, tests, and activities (which actually were in the video case, indicating possible problems with navigation or searching).

Participants added a few more suggestions when asked for final comments. Several wrapped up their comments by making positive remarks, such as "great concepts," "video case is excellent for teacher professional development and an incentive to integrate technology," "enjoyed it," and "hope current teachers can use it."

IMPLICATIONS

Video cases are expensive and time-consuming to develop. Although they hold great potential as teaching tools for preservice and inservice teachers, more research is needed regarding their most effective design, as well as their use.

Recently, we have initiated a collaboration with colleagues who have developed a PT3-funded video case project at the University of Hawaii (Ho, 2003, 2004; see the ETEC-Connections Web site [http://www.Hawaii.edu/etec]) and who are conducting research on the effects of these video cases on motivation, based on the work of Keller (1983, 1987). The cross-fertilization of our projects even at this formative stage has led us in Arizona to plan to develop our video cases in short "ad" form to help publicize their availability on the Web, to serve as "trigger videos" (which the Hawaii researchers also plan to do), and to serve as "teasers" in methods classes to entice more faculty and students, as well as practicing teachers, to use them. We also intend to deliver the video cases in a wider variety of formats, including CD, DVD, and, probably, videotape. We plan to extend our collaboration further with technology integration projects using video case methodologies across the country.

A sticking point for us at this stage is how to better extend the use of the video cases into our methods courses in education. We can turn to the work of Krueger, Boboc, and Cornish (2003), and their InTime project for a possible model for how to accomplish this. The InTime researchers have developed a database of more than six hundred videos, mostly shorter in length, accompanied by narrative, various methods to use the cases, a discussion forum and a tool for enabling methods faculty to build their own teaching case from those in the database.

Overall, the video cases in our PT3-funded projects appear to be motivating and enjoyable for both preservice and inservice teachers to use. Happily, many of the technical suggestions made by the students who used the four prototype cases have been addressed in subsequent cases. For instance, camera movement has been minimized; additional lights are often used, if needed, in the classrooms, and two microphones are now used to record both the teacher's and the students' voices. The evaluation results confirmed the importance of expanding the use of commentaries, such as the technology expert's commentary shown in Figure 2.

Figure 2. Example of expert commentary.

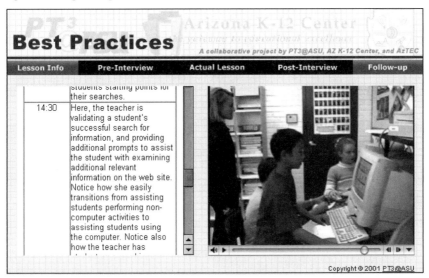

In the Arizona cases, however, we plan to seek further funding to incorporate more substantive suggestions from our evaluation study into the database and upcoming video cases and to conduct more controlled research investigating the effects of various scaffolding strategies. Another concept we may pursue is that proposed by Bransford et al. (2000), who suggest that multiple model lessons in video format be developed and studied for common curriculum units.

In summary, improvements will be made in technology delivery, scaffolding, and better integration into the teacher-education curriculum. A tough issue that remains to be investigated is how best to deliver video and video cases in online formats so that learners can not only access them easily, but so that they can become engaged in deeper learning with them as well. It has become clear to us that video cases serve to motivate and energize preservice and inservice teachers. They can be jumping-off points for discussions, serve as models for lesson planning, and provide new ideas for teachers about the possibilities technologies provide for fostering student learning. Videos appear to be best used as part of a suite of tools, however, the makeup of which remains to be determined.

We anticipate that access to the video cases, lesson materials, reflective interviews, and commentaries, by PT3 teachers both involved in our projects and across other states, will enhance teachers' success in integrating technology into their classrooms. Their use of technology will go beyond using computers as tools to allowing their students to learn in innovative ways using a full range of technologies (Figure 3).

Figure 3. Example of students engaged in learning with technology.

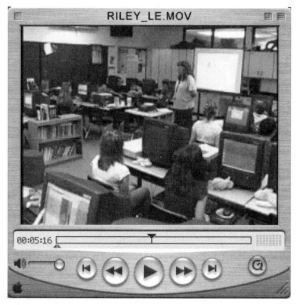

REFERENCES

Barab, S. A., MaKinster, J. G., Moore, J. A., Cunningham, D. J., & The ILF Design Team. (2001). Designing and building an on-line community: The struggle to support sociability in the Inquiry Learning Forum. *Educational Technology Research and Development, 49*(4), 71–96.

Bare, J., & Meek, A. (1998). *Internet access in public schools* (Report No. NCES98-031). Washington, DC: National Center for Education Statistics.

Bransford, J. D., Brown, A. L., & Cocking, R. R. (Eds.). (2000). *How people learn: Brain, mind, experience, and school.* Washington, DC: Committee on Developments in the Science of Learning and Committee on Learning Research and Educational Practice, Commission on Behavioral and Social Sciences and Education, National Research Council.

Brush, T. (1999). Technology planning and implementation in public schools: A five-state comparison. *Computers in the Schools, 15*(2), 11–23.

Brush, T., & Bannon, S. (1998). Characteristics of technology leaders: A survey of school administrators in the United States. *International Studies in Educational Administration, 26*(2), 47–56.

Corry, M. D., Frick, T. W., & Hansen, L. (1997). User-centered design and usability testing of a Web site: An illustrative case study. *Educational Technology Research and Development, 45*(4), 65–76.

Dick, W., & Carey, L. (2000). *The systematic design of instruction* (5th ed.). New York: Scott Foresman.

Eastmond, D., & Ziegahn, L. (1995). Instructional design for the online classroom. In Z. Berge & M. Collins (Eds.), *Computer mediated communication and the online classroom* (Vol. 3, pp. 59–80). Cresskill, NJ: Hampton Press.

Ginsburg, L. (2002, March). *Captured wisdom.* Paper included in the Proceedings of the annual convention of the Society for Information Technology and Teacher Education (SITE), Nashville, TN.

Hayek, D. (2002, March). *InTime: A video archive for integrating best practice technology into classroom curriculum.* Paper included in the Proceedings of the annual convention of the Society for Information Technology and Teacher Education (SITE), Nashville, TN.

Hill, J. R., & Hannafin, M. J. (1997). Cognitive strategies and learning from the world wide Web. *Educational Technology Research and Development, 45*(4), 37–64.

Hill, J. R., & Hannafin, M. J. (2001). Teaching and learning in digital environments: The resurgence of resource-based learning. *Educational Technology Research and Development, 49*(3), 37–52.

Hirumi, A., & Bermudez, A. (1996). Interactivity, distance education and instructional systems design converge on the information superhighway. *Journal of Research on Computing in Education, 29*(1), 1–16.

Ho, C. P. (2003). *Distance learning and online instruction at the University of Hawaii. Supplement to the Bulletin of the Research Institute of Bukkyo University* (comparative study on school-based teacher education curriculum in Japan and U.S.A.), 25–34.

Ho, C. P. (2004). Instructional strategies and learning objects for Pacific-delivered courses. In K. Kondo (Ed.), *NIME 2003 Symposium: Vol. 44. Networks without borders: Toward cross-cultural learning communities*, 104–117.

International Society Technology in Education. (2000–2002). *ISTE NETS: National educational standards for teachers.* Retrieved May 21, 2004, from http//cnets.iste.org/teachers/

Jonassen, D. J., & Hernandez-Serrano (2002). Case-based reasoning and instructional design: using stories to support problem solving. *Educational Technology Research and Development, 50*(20), 65–77.

Keller, J. M. (1983). Motivational design of instruction. In C. M. Reigeluth (Ed.), *Instructional design theories and models: An overview of their current status.* Hillsdale, NJ: Erlbaum.

Keller, J. M. (1987). *IMMS: Instructional materials motivation survey.* Tallahassee: Florida State University.

Kinzie, M. B., & Julian, M. F. (1999–2000). Usability guidelines. Retrieved July 19, 2002, from http://kinzie.edschool.virginia.edu/Uiguide.html

Krueger, K., Boboc, M., & Cornish, Y. InTime: Online video resources for teacher educators featuring technology integration in preK–12 classrooms. In M. A. Fitzgerald, M. Orey, & R. M. Branch (Eds.), *Educational media and technology yearbook* (Vol. 28, pp. 183–197). Westport, CT: Libraries Unlimited.

Kurz, T., Llama, G., Savenye, W., & Li, J. (2003, November). *The beginnings of a case: The Best Practices project.* Paper presented at the annual convention of E-Learn, Phoenix, AZ.

Li, J., Middleton, J., Oksuz, C., & Savenye, W., Louis, E., & Kurz, T, (2003, November). *Digitizing classroom video: Technical considerations in video editing.* Paper presented at the annual convention of E-Learn, Phoenix, AZ.

Llama, G., Kurz, T., & Savenye, W. (2003, November). *Video case instruction for pre-service teachers.* Paper presented at the annual convention of E-Learn, Phoenix, AZ.

Moller, L. A., Harvey, D., Downs, M., & Godshalk, V. M. (2003). Identifying factors that affect learning community development and performance in asynchronous distance education. In M. A. Fitzgerald, M. Orey, & R. M. Branch (Eds.), *Educational media and technology yearbook* (Vol. 28, pp. 139–151). Westport, CT: Libraries Unlimited.

Oksuz, C., Savenye, W., & Middleton, J. (2003). *Developing a video case for educators: Major aspects and some basic considerations.* Paper presented at the annual convention of E-Learn, Phoenix, AZ.

Savenye, W., Brush, T., Middleton, J., Blocher, M., Horn, P., Oksuz, et al. (2002, April). *Improving teaching with technology: The "Best Practices" digital video project.* Paper presented at the annual convention of the American Educational Research Association, New Orleans, LA.

Savenye, W., Brush, T., Middleton, J., Igoe, A., Horn, P., Oksuz, C., et al. (2003, April). *Developing and evaluating online teacher video cases for learning technology integration.* Paper presented at the annual convention of the American Educational Research Association, Chicago, IL.

Schrum, L. (1999). Technology professional development for teachers. *Educational Technology Research and Development, 47*(4), 83–90.

Stepich, D. A., Ertmer, P. A., & Lane, M. M. (2001). Problem-solving in a case-based course: Strategies for facilitating coached expertise. *Educational Technology Research and Development, 49*(3), 53–69.

Strudler, N., & Wetzel, K. (1999). Lesson from exemplary colleges of education: factors affecting technology integration in pre-service programs. *Educational Technology Research and Development 47*(4), 63–81.

Sullivan, H., & Higgins, N. (1983.) *Teaching for competence.* New York: Teachers College Press.

Talley, S. (2002, March). *Video cases.* Paper included in the Proceedings of the annual convention of the Society for Information Technology and Teacher Education (SITE), Nashville, TN.

Topp, N. W., Mortensen, R., & Grandgenett, N. (1995). Building a technology-using facility to facilitate technology-using teachers. *Journal of Computing in Teacher Education, 11*(3), 11–14.

What Works: Video for Online Presentation, Formats, Methods, and Notes from the Field

Penelope Walters Swenson
California State University—Bakersfield

Lloyd S. Curtis
Central Arizona College

Online courses have the potential to be flat and rather lifeless. Engaging students is made more difficult because of the text-driven nature of online class work. Students want and need involvement in the course. They want a human side to most courses, yet this is difficult to achieve except through the online conversation. We were seeking a means to jump-start this engagement. Some students mentioned that even a picture of the instructor would help.

We did not want long copies of lectures or flat photographs. We determined that short video clips could help humanize the course and present capsules of information in a format other than reading. We set about to develop video clips that could be integrated into the course and used to meet course objectives.

Since the advent of the graphical browser, an immersive multimedia environment has been the dream of most multimedia designers. As the technology available to Web developers has become more sophisticated, a number of options for production of multimedia content have been developed. The approaches range from simple animations constructed using the animated GIF format to elaborate vector- and raster-based constructs requiring additional functionality be built into or added onto an existing browser.

That is not to say that the plethora of options has left designers with singular clear choices in presentation. Numerous formats exist for Web-based presentation, each with its own advantages and disadvantages, each with its own following and specific authoring environments. This chapter attempts to explain the factors that contribute to the selection of a format for online video production and the major formats in use in multimedia for presentation of video for online courses and presentations. It also touches on the positives and negatives and our personal experiences and observations on these formats.

EQUAL ACCESS FOR SOME?

One of the most important aspects of video production for the World Wide Web is in making the materials accessible to the target audience. In the case of many corporate entities, this is not an issue. A corporation that sells primarily to businesses can make the assumption that their target audience has a minimum connection speed. This allows them to create multimedia productions that may or may not be accessible to those on slow dial-up connections. Although this may be fine for corporate sites, it is not a strategy that works well in an educational distance learning environment.

In many areas of North America, and indeed the world, dial-up connections account for a large percentage of Internet access. With 56K modems standard for most dial-up connections, it is easy to assume that the lowest potential transfer rate for data between a Web server and a client would be well defined. Unfortunately, this is not the case. There is the "high-speed dial-up" that uses caching of frequently visited Web sites, but this is a minor factor in the equation. Many times the actual connection and transfer speed is dictated by other factors. In many areas of the country that are rural, for example, phone company equipment, switches, and wiring may date back fifty years. Because this equipment was intended to handle voice communication and not to accommodate data, the actual throughput may range anywhere from 20K up to near the maximum of 56K. Obviously, this has the effect of limiting the amount of data that can be transferred to and from students' computers.

In urban areas, other options may be available, including DSL, cable, satellite, and even wireless high-speed access. The widespread availability of broadband can eliminate, or at least make it possible to dictate, the size constraints on video for use in some courses. If the online course is strictly regional, such as a training event for faculty or a course designed for a specific entity that exists within a limited geographic boundary, then designing for the lowest common denominator becomes easier. Much as with corporate entities, it may be possible to predict what sort of connection speeds can be expected on student computers, even going so far as to require a minimum connection speed.

The temptation is to set minimum connection speeds as a requirement for students to enroll in distance education courses, and many institutions of higher educational do impose such restrictions. Although this is possible in some areas, it may not be in others. It is important, however, to ensure that whatever the situation in terms of connection speeds, all students have access.

If we are to make the assumption that it is the responsibility of education providers to meet the needs of the community, it is important to design multimedia content that is accessible to all students. Working at an institution that has both rural and urban settings, the authors found it is important to provide multiple versions of a video, ranging from that designed to be accessible on a 28.8K modem connection, to one designed for a 56K connection, to one that can be accessed through a faster connection such as DSL or cable modem. Only through this level of effort will all students have access.

VECTOR VERSUS RASTER AND RESOLUTION

Before exploring the various aspects of video formats and development environments must come a basic understanding of the terms and concepts involved. It is important when dealing with video production to understand something of the constraints involved. Not only Internet access speed but the computer itself may limit one's ability to produce and deliver video in an online environment.

The first limitation involves the display of information. In terms of hardware, a computer monitor, regardless of size, presents a resolution of 72 dots per inch (dpi). This is in contrast to text graphics in magazines that typically use a resolution that is in the neighborhood of 300 dpi. Anyone who has ever printed out a graphic from a Web page can attest to the striking difference between the two. Already it can be seen that any video produced for a computer monitor will never rival what is available in print. This is a hardware-dictated limitation that controls how an image is viewed on the screen. For example, if an image is scanned at 144 dpi, it will be twice as large when viewed on the screen than one scanned at 72 dpi. Most modern graphics accommodate this limitation and make certain that the output is 72 dpi.

It is important to remember the 72-dpi limitation when planning for production of video that relies heavily on graphical elements such as filmed PowerPoint or overhead projector presentations. When graphics of this type are displayed on the screen, they will never come close to the original appearance. One work-around for this problem is to insert still images of presentation slides that occupy the entire frame rather than rely on the original video version. Slides produced in PhotoShop, for instance, can be inserted into a video and act as a static slide while the presenter provides the audio in the background.

Now we come to the question of how the graphical content being presented relates to the limitations of screen resolution on the computer monitor. Video intended for the Internet is by its very nature a raster-based technology, just as the monitor is. That is to say that the image is constructed of dots, or pixels. They are in rows and columns with each pixel having an x and y coordinate. Each pixel on the screen is individual. It can only exist in two states, on or off, and can only display a single color at one time. What this means to the viewer is that the resolution is fixed, with the best clarity available only when the image is viewed at 100 percent of the size in which it was produced. Thus, a video segment produced at 320 by 200 pixels will have the best clarity at 320 by 200.

Contrast this to a vector-based format. A prime example of this is Macromedia Flash. Vector-based formats use an x and y system, but are created, rather than by lighting pixels, by drawing lines between mathematical points. What results is an image independent of pixels that can be scaled to different sizes without a loss of visible quality. Although this applicable to graphical content, it cannot be used for video because video requires a specific resolution based on an x and y grid of pixels.

It is possible to view video at different sizes, but this affects the clarity of the image. For example, a raster image that is expanded to 200 percent will contain four visible pixels for every pixel available in the source at 100 percent. In practical terms, this means that for each pixel of a single color, there are now four pixels of that color. This results in a "blocky" appearance to the image. Conversely, reducing an image to 50 percent forces the video player to reduce four pixels into one. This causes a blurring of the image because only a subset of the available information can be seen on the screen. The best choice in creating video output intended for the Web is to create it at the resolution it is intended to be viewed. It also is important to remember that file sizes increase when more data are present, making it critical to plan ahead for the output size.

FORMATS

Numerous video formats are available for use on the Web. Some of the more popular formats are Windows Media™, Real Media™, and Quicktime™. Each has its own strengths and weaknesses; to discuss these formats, we need to know something about video formats in general.

When we speak of video formats, we are talking about the method used to display information on the screen or through the computer speakers. To make as much video and audio available as possible to the end user, the video and audio must be compressed into a file that is then decompressed when viewed. This is known as a codec (**C**ompressor/**Dec**ompressor). Codecs are algorithms for making raw video smaller. There are two means of compression. The first is lossless. When compressing video or audio, lossless compression loses no data. Once decompressed, the data contained in the file are is exactly the same as what it contained before compression. There is no degrading of the sound or image. This form of compression works simply by eliminating space in between data in the uncompressed file. Unfortunately, there is a natural limitation to the amount that any file can be compressed using a lossless method, because the total compressed file size can be no smaller than the sum of the data from the original file. The GIF image format is an example of a lossless compression scheme.

Lossy compression is the other system. Lossy compression removes data to further reduce or compress the file. This is done by removing data determined to be redundant during the compression process. The compression algorithm examines the uncompressed file and makes decisions about which data can be removed without significantly affecting the quality of the image. For example, if an image contains several adjacent pixels that are very close in color, the algorithm may reduce these to a single color. This makes it possible to reduce the file size because the file no longer has to keep track of as many color variations within a specific area of the image. Although the amount of compression possible may be attractive, when the file is uncompressed, the potential for degrading is significant. The JPEG or JPG image format is an example of a lossy compression scheme.

When considering formats, it is also important to think about the delivery method. Will the content be delivered using a streaming video server? Will it be delivered as complete files downloaded from the Internet? Or will it be made available in some other means, such as on CDs distributed to students? Anticipated delivery methods may well dictate how the video is produced. This consideration goes beyond issues associated with bandwidth, although bandwidth is important.

STREAMING VIDEO AND STATIC FILES

When offering video in an online or hybrid course, it is important to think about how the video will be presented. Currently, the two primary methods of delivering online video are downloadable files and streaming video. Although additional methods of delivery do exist, these involve distribution of physical media or disk images that students may write to CD or other physical media.

Streaming video requires proprietary formats and usually special server software. Streaming video has an advantage over downloadable video files in that the content can be delivered at the same time it is being downloaded. This being the case, in an ideal situation, video can be delivered without a substantial wait. Streaming video is an ideal format for delivery over the Web, or so it would seem.

In reality, the delivery of video through streaming can be problematic. Streaming video is dependent on the amount of data that can be transmitted across a connection at any time, and this is highly variable. Streaming media techniques attempt to anticipate fluctuations in delivery speed by downloading ahead, or "buffering" content when download speeds are high to ensure uninterrupted play when speeds diminish. This meets with mixed results. Often streaming media files will appear to stop for periods of time when data are being downloaded slowly and the data downloaded ahead of time in the buffer is exhausted. In a sense, streaming media sacrifices stability of video delivery for speed.

Nonstreaming formats have been around much longer. As the name implies, these formats must download in their entirety before being displayed. The major advantage of these formats is they are self-contained and do not need special software to be played. Another advantage is in the stability of the video. Because the video has already been downloaded, it does not suffer from breaks and pauses due to a lack of data being transmitted over a connection.

Of course, nonstreaming video has one drawback. It requires large files to be downloaded before viewing. This download can take a significant amount of time for a long video segment, and thus students may not immediately get the benefit of the video output. During this period of time, students must have something else that can engage them. The wait time can be obviated in several ways. One approach is to provide a companion CD or DVD in a course with a video component. This can be accomplished either by providing the CD or DVD itself through the mail or by making an image file for the video available online.

Although the process for creating a CD to be distributed though the mail may be familiar, the creation and distribution of CD or DVD images may not be. An image file is a literal snapshot of the entire CD or DVD. Image files can be generated using any of the popular CD burning software packages currently in production. CD image files are usually created in a format known as ISO9660, which can be read by almost any computer. DVD uses a different format known as UDF but maintains compatibility with ISO9660 so that data stored on a DVD can be read by a computer. This compatability allows a DVD to store large amounts of data that can be read by a computer with a DVDROM drive.

Once the CD or DVD image has been created, it can be uploaded to a Web or FTP server for distribution to students. Students can then use commonly available software to "burn" the image to a CD or DVD, thus creating a copy of the original. This saves duplication and mailing costs. The major drawback to this approach is the need for students to have access to a high-speed Internet connection while downloading the image, up to 470 megabytes for a CD image and up to 4.7 gigabytes for a DVD.

POPULAR FORMATS AND THEIR CHARACTERISTICS

The majority of formats in use on the Web are formats that can be streamed. The advantage to this was discussed earlier in the chapter. There are currently many competing standards in compressed video. The most common formats for streaming video and audio production are RealNetwork's Real Video, Apple's Quicktime, and the Microsoft Media Player formats. An evolutionary step over the MPEG 2 (MP2) standard, MPEG 4 (MP4), has recently been released. This streaming format has been adopted by both Apple and RealNetwork as a technology for their players. Additionally, the MP3 format is available to stream audio only. All of these formats provide different advantages, although all, except for MP3 and MP4, have the same basic features. Although MP4 holds a great deal of promise, it is not yet widely available in educational environments.

For the purpose of this chapter, we concentrate on a single authoring environment only, that of Adobe Premiere. The reason for this decision is that Premiere is capable of producing output in most of the popular formats and has a large feature set that is essentially a superset of consumer-level products. Many more very good environments exist for video production both at the professional and consumer levels. Frequently consumer-level products such as Roxio VideoWave™, Ulead VideoStudio™, MS Movie Maker™, and iMovie™ for Apple computers will serve perfectly as a means of transferring video to the Web. In addition these products do not have the steep learning curve hardware requirements, or the cost of professional-level products. The trade-off becomes a matter of ease of use and shallow learning curve for the relative novice against the expanded feature set and additional capabilities of the professional environment. Increasingly, as these products mature and expand, the consumer-level products are able to do most of what a moderately skilled user may wish to accomplish.

Video is captured in AVI format. AVI, being uncompressed video, takes up approximately 13 gigabytes of space for every hour of video. Compression schemes, depending on the format and level of compression, can reduce file size to something approach 1/100th the size of the original. This of course varies depending on the format, size of the video frame, and the level of compression.

For the purpose of this evaluation, we used existing footage of an ITV segment. The subject piece exported was a section of lecture to be used as the basis of a discussion exercise in a Foundations of American Education course. The source video, captured from ITV, was brought into the computer from a VCR through a Dazzle Hollywood DV - Bridge. The DV-Bridge converted the standard NTSC on VHS effective resolution of approximately 300 x 480 to an AVI format that is the same resolution as DVD (720 x 480). This would be a common input and output resolution from such a device, converting the video from a taped lecture to a standard high-quality format. Because the original resolution was lower than the conversion, errors and loss of clarity resulted. The video quality could not be any better than NTSC VCR quality because it originally came from videotape. Had the ITV video been available in higher resolution originally, the results could have been different.

The resulting raw video in AVI format, when properly edited, was four minutes, thirty-two seconds in length. The file was then output to a number of formats and the results compared for both audio and video quality. To ensure that the output could be used over a slower Internet connection, the only output formats that were used were those that supported 56-Kpb modems and lower and that could be delivered from a streaming video sever. As a basis for comparison, the source video in AVI format had the following characteristics. The video was 720 x 480. It had a rate of 29.97 frames per second (standard for American NTSC broadcasts) requiring an average data rate of 3.61 megabytes per second. The results of other formats are discussed subsequently.

The video was then output through the formats available in Premiere™, Quicktime™, Windows Media™, and Real Media™. The resulting file sizes varied depending on output size, compression methods, and the amount of compression used.

In terms of video quality, the larger the file size, the better the video appeared on the monitor in almost every circumstance. The largest output files intended for 56K modems approached 8 megabytes in size, with some variation. These exhibited slight artifacts and blurring from the compression; however, there was no discernible degradation in audio quality.

By contrast, the smaller files exhibited visible artifacts the smaller the video frame and the more compression used. The smallest output files, those output at a frame size of 160 x 120, were by far the most affected. Within this group, some were reduced to a file size of less than 300 kilobytes but suffered video and audio degradation to the point where they were essentially unusable.

RECOMMENDATIONS

None of the formats differed substantially from any other in terms of output quality. Real Media file sizes tended to be the smallest and suffered more video distortion and artifacts when highly compressed. On the other hand, audio did not suffer as much as it did in the others. Quicktime had larger file sizes overall but maintained better overall quality. Windows Media fell right in between in both categories.

Whatever format is used for streaming compressed video has inherent advantages and disadvantages. None of the formats performed, at least in these tests, did significantly better than any other. The key to providing video as a means of conveying information in an online course is understanding these limitations and gearing video production around specific use.

Humanizing online courses is a worthy goal. Using video segments shows great promise. Length is an issue. We found that a video segment of under five minutes is well received, despite minor technical problems, whereas longer segments increase the potential of difficulty and students appreciate them less. Providing for the range of download capacities is necessary and an effort that students will welcome.

Teachers' Training Online:
A Mexican Experience and Proposal

Lilia Ana Alfaro Guevara
National Minister of Education, Mexico

As individual societies and on a global scale, we are experiencing transformations as a result of the paradigm shift from the Industrial Age to the Information Age. These transformations have affected the economic, political, and social structures of the global economy (Rowley, Lujan, & Dolence, 1998). In an attempt to respond to these changes, Mexico is reshaping these structures to guide its educational system through the new focus on constructivism, which sees as the development of reflective reasoning, thoughtful assessment, and critical analysis as primary to educational goals, particularly those at the higher levels of education (Secretaría de Educación Pública [SEP], 2001).

According to the Organisation for Economic Co-operation and Development (OCDE; 1996), we are confronting a shift from the Industrial Age model of mass production to an Information Age model, with new interest in democracy, equal opportunity, and the generation of a workforce that can enable economic progress. Lifelong learning and continuing professional education is a part of this model, as is innovation in education through the use of technology. The Mexican government acknowledges that its society is in transition and that teachers' professional development should be transformed accordingly, leading to a more effective and flexible educational system based on equity, quality, and actualized knowledge (SEP, 2001).

The quality of education is a determining factor in a nation's competitiveness. To compete globally, Mexico needs to raise its educational standards. Several innovations to raise the quality of basic education at federal and state levels have been developed, one of these being the professional training of teachers and subsequent improvement of their working conditions and salaries. There has yet to be a systematic effort for teachers at middle- and higher-level education, however.

The Mexican National Educational Program 2001–2006 (SEP, 2001) is considering the participation of all public and private institutions in the elaboration of a master plan to implement new communication and information technologies in education—not just for teachers' distance training but for professional distance education of adults as well. However, few specialists are available in Mexico to lead the government to the most effective decisions and help overcome fears related to investing large portions of the budget in activities with benefits that won't be seen immediately. The challenge continues to be the development of teachers at higher levels of education who can help build intellectual capital for the transnational industries, assist in the transfer of technologies, and develop a productive citizenry.

Recognizing that teachers' active participation is a critical component of any formal education plan, it is necessary to update their skills without taking them out of the classroom or distracting them from their professional activities. With regard to higher education in Mexico in both private and public spheres, more than 50 percent of the teachers are not full-time employees at the universities or educational institutions where they teach, but work in other professional fields as well (SEP, 2002a). For this reason, they need access to professional development opportunities with flexible options and no restrictions of time and place.

These are among the main reasons to promote Web-based continuing education programs for teachers that can offer professional development as a dynamic process that extends from their initial preparation over the course of an entire career. Even for the part-time teacher, pursuing ongoing learning can contribute both to the second profession's knowledge base and to quality, effective teaching. For these reasons, the Mexican government is responsible for investment in continuing education for individual teachers and the profession as a whole and for establishing policies, resources, and organizational structures that guarantee ongoing opportunities for teachers learning face-to-face and at distance.

This chapter presents the efforts in Mexico to promote distance learning for secondary and university teachers using informatics and communication interactive technologies. It also discusses a proposal to create a national system of Web-based continuing education and training for teachers.

TEACHERS' TRAINING IN UNIVERSITIES AND INSTITUTIONS OF HIGHER EDUCATION IN MEXICO

Most of the actions related to continuing education of professional university and higher education teachers in Mexico have not been systematic and have had no precise goals, being disarticulated from the main purposes of the educational system. This situation, according to Eusee (1994), has affected the role of the teachers and their social function, leading to the need to redefine the objectives around their professional formation and continuing education. In the 1990s, Rodriguez (1994) discussed the need to analyze the training of teachers at the higher and middle-levels of education in Mexico in an attempt to introduce new practices and to break from the traditional face-to-face methods.

The National Educational Development Program of the Mexican government, established for the period of 1995–2000 (SEP, 1995), presented a proposal around the creation of the National System of Professional Development and Training for Mexican Teachers, including both face-to-face and distance education components, the latter distributed through satellite television (Edusat) and the Internet. The aim was to support the quality and efficient educational opportunities, as well as educational reforms, at the elementary, middle, and higher education levels. This proposal was not accepted, and efforts have recently been made only at the elementary level, with only minimal training provided for university and higher education teachers that consists largely of disarticulated, face-to-face efforts such as voluntary attendance at workshops, conferences, and seminars, together with the existence of isolated distance education programs.

Various other concerns have also been voiced, including the need to raise both teachers' standards and their salaries, to create national recruitment initiatives and scholarship programs to prepare teachers in fields where there are shortages, to expand teachers' education programs with the use of informatics technologies in high-need fields, and to create high-quality induction programs for beginning teachers. There is, however, no comprehensive, official data that can answer questions such as the following: Who trains university and higher level education teachers? How often should they receive training? Who determines the content of training? Why is the training that does exist held in short, isolated, face-to-face programs instead of through an organized online system with national common rules and objectives?

The Mexican National Educational Program 2001–2006 (SEP, 2001) mentions the importance of using information and communication technologies to change educational processes, as well as the need to have national, systematic, articulated continuing educational systems using these technologies. In particular, the importance of developing a profile for higher education and university teachers related to the use of these technologies, changing learning strategies, and maintaining continuing education to improve professional profiles was stressed. What remains clear at present is the need to treat inservice teachers' professional growth as a national process that can continue over time, offering regular and long-term support and the opportunity for teachers to reflect on their practice. At the same time, educational institutions and universities will continue promoting efforts on their own.

WEB-BASED CONTINUING PROFESSIONAL
EDUCATION FOR TEACHERS IN MEXICO

According to the National Association of Universities and Higher Education Institutions (Asociación Nacional de Universidades e Instituciones de Educación Superior [ANUIES], 2000), attempts to develop open and distance education in Mexico has a history of more than fifty years. For teacher training in particular, the Federal Institute of Teachers' Training was created in 1947 with the aim of preparing teachers through the use of open and distance education, using mostly print materials. The project was directed to elementary education teachers not just in Mexico, but throughout Latin America.

Another effort began in 1972 when the National Autonomous University of Mexico (Universidad Nacional Autónoma de México [UNAM]) created units for open and distance education for teacher training, later focusing on professional education in what they called the Open University System (Sistema de Universidad Abierta [SUA]). The first conducted distance education using print materials have evolved into what today is called the University's Coordination of Open and Distance Education (Coordinación de Universidad Abierta y Educación a Distancia [CUAED]), which is in charge of the development of continuing, open, and distance education for professional programs and some online teachers' development programs (UNAM, 2004). The United Nations Educational, Scientific, and Cultural Organization (UNESCO, 1997) has also noted that distance and open education projects in every country must be supported by national policies that can help to canalize efforts to benefit education and that they must be systematic to improve quality on institutions, to avoid duplication, and to promote cooperation and the creative use of technologies.

Since the 1970s, many Mexican private and public universities and higher education institutions have created distance and open education units (around 104 at present). Some of these direct their efforts to teachers' distance training, although there is little available at the university level. Such coursework has been managed variously over time by using printed materials, video and audio cassettes, telephone, fax, magnetic disks, satellite TV, educational software, and computer-mediated communication through the Internet. Some means of communication have included the use of EDUSAT, a national satellite television system, the national Mexican Technological Network (RTN), and other private transmission and delivery systems (ANUIES, 2000).

ANUIES (2004) has also described efforts to design and implement national programs of distance education. It notes the importance of developing quality and efficiency standards and suggests coordination of teachers' distance continuing education programs among affiliated institutions, recognizing the potential of Web-based opportunities which supports principles such as democracy and rights for universal access. Nevertheless, although such ideas remain untested in the real world, online teacher training has been promoted mostly by private institutions over the past year, together with a small number of public universities and associations, and this interesting market has yet to be fully pursued.

Although space does not allow mention of all the individual efforts of public and private institutions and universities to promote Web-based continuing education for teachers in Mexico, some are relevant and worth noting. The Technological Institute of Monterrey (Tec de Monterey), for example, is a private university that has been offering a program called PAHD, the purpose of which is to actualize skills and abilities for teachers at all levels, including higher education. An average of 8,234 teachers per year, from Mexico and throughout Latin America, have participated in the program. Distance Web-based post-graduate programs related to the improvement of education practices are also offered (*La internacionalización del Tec de Monterrey*, 2000).

La Salle University (ULSA), also a private institution, is involved with similar efforts through its department of distance education, which has organized some teacher training workshops through satellite videoconferences and more recently through the Internet (ULSA, 2004). The Metropolitan University (Universidad Autónoma Metropolitana [UAM]) in Mexico City, with both public and private financial support, is also starting to offer virtual programs directed to teacher training, although these are directed primarily to their own teachers (UAM, 2004). The Mexican Valley University (Universidad del Valle de México; (UVM), a private institution that belongs to Sylvan International Consortium, also offers workshops and postgraduate programs related to the improvement of the educational practice of universities teachers (UVM, 2004).

The Commercial Banking School (Escuela Bancaria Comercial; EBC), a private school, in collaboration with CDI International, is starting an Internet-based online training program called Effective Teaching and Training, hosted on the Confederation College Server (EBC, 2004). Another example of a private university is Las Americas University, located in Puebla City, which is also distributing continuing Web-based education for teachers.

Some public state universities are developing virtual spaces of information and management of the learning, using them sometimes for teacher training. Two examples are the State University of Guadalajara (*Universidad de Guadalajara,* 2004), with its Innova project, and Colima State University (UCOL, 2004). Also, in postgraduate studies, a federal program called the Master Program for Teaching basic Sciences (first financed and distributed at high-level technological institutes by the Subsecretary of Technological Education and Research), has with a mixed model of online activities and face-to-face sessions, reached more than three thousand higher education teachers around the country (CIIDET, 2003).

Additional efforts to support online courses for teachers at all educational levels have been made by the Latin-American Institute of Educational Communication (Instituto Latinoamericano de Comunicación Educativa [ILCE]), which has organized online workshops in recent years, some directed to higher education, and the National Courses of Teachers Actualization (CAN) project, online workshops directed mostly at elementary education teachers (ILCE-SEP, 2003).

On the other hand, as a part of the educational innovations that have been held at federal and state levels to raise the quality of education through professional training for teachers and to improve teachers' working and salary conditions, the elementary education sector now has a systematic and well-organized continuing educational program for teachers, which also has corresponding economical rewards, called Carrera Magisterial. This program manages some Web-based distance learning programs, financed by the federal and state governments, but it is primarily distributed via face-to-face workshops.

Not all Mexican and Latin American programs have been described here, but a lack of continuity and direction with regard to meeting common educational objectives continues to prevail. Teacher training is still conducted primarily in face-to-face programs and is measured by a national standard defined simply by the number of courses a teacher has taken. Such measures fail to have a significant impact on student achievement (Lopez Acevedo, 2002).

Financial issues have often been the excuse for the Mexico's failure to create national programs and virtual universities for teacher training in higher and university education. There are, however, national programs aimed at supporting the costs of enrichment for teachers in service in public middle and higher education (PROMEP—Programa de Mejoramiento de Profesorado) and in elementary education (PRONAP—Programa Nacional de Actualización Permanente de los Maestros de Educación Básica en Servicio). Established in 1996, these are supported by the National Minister of Education through its two main Subsecretaries, that in charge of higher education and scientific research activities (Subsecretaría de Educación e Investigación Científicas) and that responsible for technological higher education and its research and innovation activities (Subsecretaría de

Educación e Investigación Tecnológicas). It also has the support of the National Council of Science and Technology (Consejo Nacional de Ciencia y Tecnología) and the National Association of Universities and Higher Education Institutions. This program has been financing national courses, workshops, and postgraduate study for high-level public institutions and university teachers, held mostly face-to-face, according to the principles of the National Educational Program 2001–2006. It has acquired financial support and is aimed at financing and supporting efforts around the professional development of teachers to secure an efficient educational opportunity (SEP, 2002-b).

ANUIES (2000) has declared that Mexico should seek to develop teacher training through a national educational system that utilizes new technologies to prepare innovative teachers of high academic quality by 2020. Give the recent accomplishments of the various institutions described here and the possibility of financial support, it seems possible that such a system might be possible much sooner—by 2007.

A NATIONAL SYSTEM OF WEB-BASED CONTINUING PROFESSIONAL EDUCATION FOR HIGHER EDUCATION AND UNIVERSITY TEACHERS

All effective online programs require initial strategic planning to outline objectives and design a system directed to involve participants actively and connect them with communities for the exchange of experiences and ideas, using specialized materials and taking into consideration the personalization of the teaching and learning process. The time is right to rethink what must be done for teachers in Mexico who seek to continue their professional development; the possibility of creating a national system for teacher training and promoting Web-based continuing professional distance education for teachers present particularly relevant opportunities.

The first thing to consider are recent changes in Mexico as a nation that might affect a national teacher training system; the advantages and limitations of such a system within this context should be considered in the planning stages so that new roles and competencies can be incorporated into the teaching process of institutions of higher education and universities, in accordance with economical, social, politic, and intellectual needs of the country.

Figures 1 and 2 present some scenarios that are considered desirable, based on the work of authors such as Bates (2000), Rowley, Lujan, and Dolence (1998), Pallof and Pratt (1999), Didriksson (1998), Alfaro (2000), and Finnegan (1997). The figures attempt to envision the general and educational contexts for Mexico that may exist in 2007, the time when the national system of online teacher training may be consolidated, and to present a view of the desirable situation for the program.

Figure 1 shows four main categories—economy, society, politics, and knowledge—as they are envisioned for Mexico in 2007, considering the end of the forecasted period as well as the possible response of education to these conditions. Figure 2 forecasts the situation for teachers at universities and institutions of higher education in 2007, considering characteristics that must be taken into account to establish common national teacher training and Web-based continuing education programs.

Despite consensus among researchers, practitioners, and policy makers that the lack of teacher training is a problem for higher education and universities in Mexico, providing training opportunities is not an easy task. It becomes even more difficult if such opportunities must be systematic and organized and managed through the Internet at a distance.

Figure 1. A forecast of desirable scenarios for general and educational contexts related to economics, society, politics, and knowledge in Mexico for 2007.

Economy		Society	
• Reinforce global economy • Privatization • Competitiveness • Balance between private and public interests • Respond to instability • Development	• Globalization of education • Education responds to economic needs and the marketplace • Education serves the economy • New Educational models • More funding	• Social equity • International trends/ national traditions • Demand for comparable quality of life • Knowledgeable society • Lifelong learning	• Demand for better education • Reinforcement of values and traditions • Quality and efficiency of education • Learning to live globally
Knowledge		Politics	
• Students as skilled workers • Technology supporting education • National and international competence • Need to be highly educated	• Need for constructivist and actualized education· Flexible educational models • Scientific and technological development • Competitiveness	• Democracy • Equity • International approaches • Uncertainty • Lack of consensus • Transparency • Quality and innovation	• Democratic decisions in education • International intervention in education • Equal opportunities • Transparency of education policies

Figure 2. A forecast of desirable scenarios describing the challenges for teachers and teacher training for Mexico in 2007.

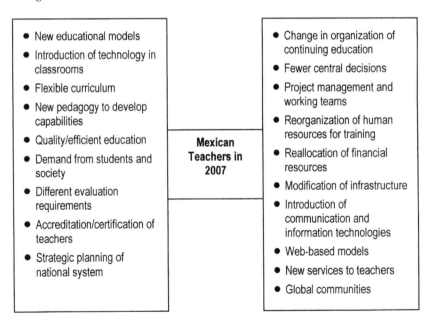

A number of factors influence the delivery of this kind of training, including limited financial resources, the organization of services, the lack of a research base, the high rate of teacher turnover, the conditions of preservice training and the minimal state policies and guidelines regarding standards for teachers certification. During the recent years, Mexican teachers have become more creative and assertive in addressing their own learning needs, and some have been actively involved in training activities through self-directed learning and peer coaching. Nevertheless, effective national programs are needed, based on systematic, identified needs and not on administrators' perceptions of what might be required. There is no doubt that changing teachers behavior through distance education environments requires the encouragement of collegiality and collaboration, as well as instructional designs with clear and precise educational foci that address the level of knowledge that needs to be communicated. Figure 3 proposes a possible focal point for developing a national system of Web-based continuing education and training for teachers.

Figure 3. A proposed educational focus for a national Web-based system for teachers' continuing education and training.

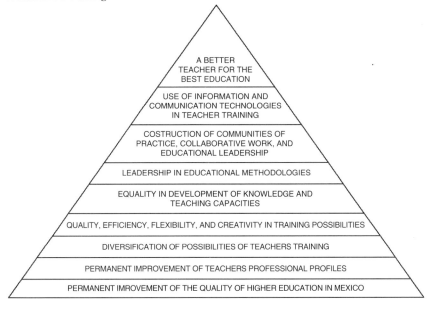

Programs within this system must be created with the following in mind: helping teachers learn; improving their reading and writing skills; developing teachers' informatics skills, creative thinking skills, and problem-solving abilities; promoting self-esteem, interpersonal skills, and organizational and planning effectiveness; and promoting cultural development and specialized knowledge. Recognizing that providing training services is complicated—more so if these are offered at a distance using interactive Web modalities—adequate training must be rethought and expanded on the basis of systematically identified needs. A successful endeavor will involve planning and decision making with the goal of creating and maintaining a positive climate for teachers to grow and change. Such programs must include an up-to-date knowledge base that offers continuity and follow-up training to ensure that skills are transferred to classroom settings and are ultimately reflected in the quality and efficiency of the country's education system. Considering these conditions, this chapter concludes by presenting a proposal for a strategic planning system to develop a national teacher training and Web-based continuing educational system.

A PROPOSAL FOR A STRATEGIC PLANNING MODEL

As Marquad and Kearsley (1999) note, the importance of integrating technology into learning is that it presents the possibility to enhance the speed and quality of the process and provide people with the power to manage knowledge through intelligent planning, organizational practices, and methodologies. Advantages of Web-based learning must be considered in the use of computer-assisted learning systems such as that proposed here. For example, Web-based learning offers the following benefits:

- It is available to learners on an as-needed basis.
- It allows users to work at their own pace.
- It is user-friendly.
- It is accessible over wide geographic areas.
- It can be learner-controlled and provide hands-on interactive learning opportunities.
- It is cost-effective.
- It can be adjusted to accommodate the motivation levels of diverse learners.
- It is safe and flexibile.
- It provides uniformity of content and delivery.
- It can be made to adjust to individual learning styles.
- It can address learners' mobility and usage concerns.
- It allows content to be updated continuously.

Implementation of Web-based learning programs must be accompanied by concrete strategic planning, however, to build general organizational and management conditions that ensure the success of formal learning systems.

Figure 4 details a strategic planning model to develop a national training and Web-based continuing education system for higher education and university teachers in Mexico. It describes seven strategic programs: planning, managing, and maintenance; technology selection, infrastructure, and student access; academic, pedagogical, and research requirements; support of change and innovation; cost and quality assurance issues; funding, alliances, and competition; and organization, policies, and procedures. The model has been designed considering the recommendations made by Moran (1998), Oblinger (1998), Holmberg (1999), Bates and Mingle (1998), Bates (2000), ANUIES (2000), and the A & M Center for Distance Learning Research (2001).

FINAL CONSIDERATIONS

Much remains to be done to develop continuing education for teachers in Mexico. It is clear that distance education may have the potential to update teachers' skills effectively without taking them out of the classroom for extended periods, although there are logistical and educational difficulties to confront. Developed countries are successfully using computer- mediated environments in the field of teachers' education, resulting in research that provides ideas and techniques of potential value for inclusion in Mexican distance education programs.

To close this chapter, some final considerations are shown on Figure 5. In accordance with the development of Mexican society and the country's economic and political practices, the Mexican education system is under pressure to devise complex and efficient educational practices and services to raise the quality of education and address deficiencies in teachers' professional options. Various players within the educational domain are committed to this goal, with teachers playing a major role. Although creating a Web-based training program for teachers is a challenging enterprise that requires cross-functional cooperation among governmental authorities and universities, the use of complex infrastructures and technologies, and the commitment of content experts, the goal of raising the quality of education and developing a better country makes this project a priority.

Figure 4. Proposal for a strategic planning model.

New Mission
To develop teachers who can use theory and technology practically and reflexively to develop a new way of thinking and understanding and who continuously review their educational practice.

New Vision
To have a distance training system by 2007 that all teachers can access using interactive communication and information technologies to improve teacher training through flexible programs.

Strategic Programs

1. Planning, Management, and Governance: Develop a multidisciplinary project management team and smaller working teams to provide assistance for elaborating plans, managing activities, and making decisions. **Goal:** 80 percent of teacher training activities will occur at a distance by 2007. **Step 1:** Selection of central and midlevel project management teams by federal authorities. **Step 2:** Develop a written strategic plan. **Step 3:** Establish appropriate timeline and process for annual project evaluation.

2. Technology Selection, Infrastructure, and Student Access: Selection of technology, infrastructure, and support staff, balancing administrative and academic needs and the need for students/teachers to have access to technology on and off campus. **Objectives:** Guarantee adequate hardware and software infrastructure with adequate networking and Internet access; retain technology support staff; ensure teacher access to technology; explore renovation of infrastructure. **Goals:** Provide teachers with a computer lab, expand general computer labs by at least 50 percent starting Year 2 of project, expand number of hours labs are available (at least 8 hours/day for teachers), assist teachers and students to acquire computers, have five-person support staff at each institution, have at least one space equipped for satellite and telecommunications, and augment infrastructure and services by 25 percent each year by 2007. **First step:** Create five-year plan for technology infrastructure.

3. Academic Pedagogical and Research Requirements: Reengineer teachers' education processes; challenge current pedagogical methods, the role of the academy, current expectations of teachers/students, and the way research is conducted and projects evaluated. **Objectives:** Reconsider didactic strategies, contents, and mechanics related to teacher training and adapt these to collaborative distance learning according to adult learning principles. **Step 1:** Create academic committee of education and technology experts to redesign didactic strategies. **Step 2:** reconsider plans, programs, and contents for each course, extended workshop, and master's degree program; establish principles to guide redesign. Training of participating academic personnel and hiring of full-time educational researchers to assist in research and design will take place.

4. Supporting System for Change and Innovation: Support environment of change to assist teachers in learning about technology and accepting new teaching methods utilizing technology. **Objectives:** Support teachers and academic and administrative staff in the use and acceptance of technologies; train academic and research staff in instructional design and course planning/management. **Goals:** Years 1–3, most academic staff, including virtual tutors, will be hired; by 2007, system will have its own academic tutorial and design staff trained and a program to establish promotion/acceptance of distance learning. **Step 1:** Reorganize teacher training programs, considering willingness to change, new models of teaching and learning with technology, principles of virtual tutoring in adult education, and skills to manage interactive technologies.

5. Funding Alliances and Competition: Build strategies for funding a distance learning system using external grants, reallocation of operating funds, and alliances and partnerships. **Objective:** Use methodology to reallocate internal funds without damaging primary activities, obtain external grants from international agencies, and obtain government financing. **Goals:** Obtain 100-percent financing for technology infrastructure from external grants during Year 1; begin reallocating resources by 20 percent each year to provide necessary materials and human elements for each project until the new training model is completely functioning.

6. Organization, Policies, and Procedures: Create organization to respond to administrative and academic procedures in teacher training with a central unit responsible for the project and project teams. **Goals:** Within five years, a mostly decentralized organization will manage distance learning, modify academic policies, and design/operate student computer service systems. A central technology support unit will be created.

Figure 5. Final considerations.

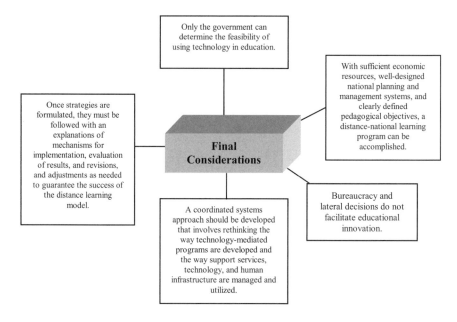

REFERENCES

A & M Center for Distance Learning Research. (2001). *Distance education administrators certification program.* Retrieved from http://www.cdlr.tamu.edu/education/training_programs/admin.asp

Alfaro, L. (2000). *Propuesta de apoyo a la Reforma de la Educación Superior Tecnológica en el Sistema Nacional de Educación Tecnológica con miras al año 2000.* Master's thesis, Universidad del Valle de México.

Asociación Nacional de Universidades e Instituciones de Educación Superior. (2000). *Plan maestro de educación superior abierta y a distancia.* Retrieved from http://www.anuies.mx/

Asociación Nacional de Universidades e Instituciones de Educación Superior. (2004). *Programa regional de educación abierta y a distancia.* Retrieved from http://anuies-rco.ucol.mx/educontinua/diatec2.pdf

Bates, A. W. (2000). *Managing technological change. Strategies for college and university leaders.* San Francisco: Jossey-Bass.

Bates, A. W., & Mingle, J. (1998). *The role of the Indiana Commission for Higher Education in promoting effective use of information technology resources* Indianapolis: Indiana Commission for Higher Education. Retrieved from http://www2.cstudies.ubc.ca:8900/EDST533/Readings/Indiana.html

CIIDET. (2003). *Maestría en ciencias en enseñanza de las ciencias.* Retrieved from http://204.153.24.32/.

Colima State University. (2004). *Centro de educación a distancia de la Universidad de Colima.* Retrieved from http://www.ucol.mx/

Didriksson, A. (1998). *Escenarios de la educación superior en México.* México: CISE-UNAM.

Escuela Bancaria Comercial. (2004). *Mexico—Effective teachers training. EBC.* CDI International/Confederation College. Retrieved from http://www.confederationc.on.ca/cdi/cdiInt/ourprojects_latinAmerica/

Eusse, O. (1994). Proceso de construcción del conocimiento y su vinculación con la formación docente. *Perfiles Educativos 63-194.* 31-42. México: CISE, UNAM.

Finnegan, D. (1997). Transforming faculty roles. In M. Peterson, et al. (Eds.). *Planning and management for a changing environment.* San Francsico: Jossey-Bass.

Holmberg, B. (1999). *Theory and practice of distance education* (2nd ed.). New York: Routledge.

Instituto Latinoamericano de Comunicación Educativa/Secretaría de Educación Pública (2003). *Cursos nacionales de actualización.* Retrieved from http://pronap.ilce.edu.mx/cursos/cna/paquetes_en:linea.htm

La internacionalización del Tec de Monterrey. (2000). *La internacionalización del Tec de Monterrey.* Retrieved from http://www.sistema.itesm.mx/vi/boletin/boletin2.PDF

La Salle University. (2004). *Centro de educación a distancia.* Retrieved from http://www.ulsa.edu.mx/

Lopez-Acevedo, G. (2002). *Determinants of technology adoption in Mexico* JEL Codes: L60 ; L20 ; J31 and J38. Retrieved from http://econ.worldbank.org/files/11791_wps2780.pdf

Marquad, M., & Kearsley, G. (1999). *Technology-based learning.* New York: American Society for Training and Development.

Moran, C. (1998). Strategic information technology planning in higher education. In D. G. Oblinger & Rush (Eds.), *The future compatible classroom.* Boston: Anker.

Oblinger, D. (1999*). Putting students at the center: A planning guide to distributed learning* (EDUCAUSE Monograph Series No. 1). Boulder, CO: EDUCAUSE.

Organisation for Economic Co-operation and Development. (1996). *Life-long learning for all.* France: Author.

Pallof, R., & Pratt, K. (1999). *Building learning communities in cyberspace. Effective strategies for on-line classroom.* San Francisco: Jossey-Bass.

Rodríguez, A. (1994). Problemas, desafíos y mitos de la formación docente. *Perfiles educativos 63.* México: CISE-UNAM.

Rowley, D., Lujan, H., & Dolence, M. (1998). *Strategic choices for the academy.* San Francisco: Jossey-Bass.

Secretaría de Educación Pública. (1995). *Programa de Desarrollo Educativo 1995–2000.* México: Author.

Secretaría de Educación Pública. (2001). *Programa Nacional de Educación 2001–2006.* México: Author.

Secretaría de Educación Pública. (2002-a). *Estadística básica del ciclo 2001–2002.* México: Author.

Secretaría de Educación Pública. (2002-b). *El Programa nacional de actualización permanente de los maestros de educación básica en servicio (PRONAP) y su influencia en el desempeño docente.* Retrieved from http://basica.sep.gob.mx/dgie/PDFs/IV-B-6-c-Pronap.pdf

United Nations Educational, Scientific, and Cultural Organization. (1997). *Aprendizaje abierto y a distancia. Perspectivas y consideraciones de política.* Madrid: Author.

Universidad Autónoma Metropolitana. (2004). *Coordinación de educación continua y a distancia.* Retrieved from http://xochitl.uam.mx/cecad/

Universidad de Guadalajara. (2004). *Proyecto Innova.* Retrieved from http://www.innova.udg.mx/modelo/index_e.cfm?seccion=BA

Universidad Nacional Autónoma de México. (2004). *Coordinación de Universidad y Educación a Distancia. Descripción.* Retrieved from http://www.cuaed.unam.mx/

Universidad del Valle de México. (2004). *Centro de alto desarrollo tecnológico y educación en línea (CADEL).* Retrieved from http://cadel.uvmnet.edu/

Web-based Learning and Cultural Interference: Perspectives of Arab Students

Adekunle Akinyemi

United Arab Emirates University, College of Education

INTRODUCTION

There are many learning platforms on the educational scene. The range and flavor of platforms vary from one geographic location to another and also from one level of education to another. Pedagogy and andragogy address themselves to different clients and age groups. The practice of traditional education cannot be described to have the same flavor from one cultural setting to the other in developing and developed countries. Traditions and conventions of the people go a long way in dictating patterns of educational practice. Cultural values and idiosyncrasies play a great role in the way different societies teach and learn in schools. It is common in underdeveloped countries to put female students at a disadvantage in how much or how far they can go in their educational pursuits. The Islamic practice of the *Puder* (confinement of women to the home) keeps the females at home, thus making it difficult for them to have equal exposure to education as that enjoyed by their male counterparts. The practice of early marriage of female children in some cultures further compounds the limitations women face in attaining an education. Proponents of virtual and Web learning platforms may argue that these limitations can in fact be overturned given the *anytime and anywhere* characteristics of Web learning.

Duncan Timms (2001) states that although e-learning is frequently promoted as a means of breaking down barriers between cultures but warns against the danger of ignoring cultural differences so as not to allow e-learning to become a potent form of cultural imperialism. Kelliny and Kelliny (2002) present as one of three challenges the need to overcome cultural barriers resulting from the differences between one's indigenous culture and the target cultures associated with the English language or the culture of cyberspace. These authors further pose a question similar to Timms' (2001): Is the Internet a tool for linguistic and cultural dominance, immersion or integration? Nonnative speakers of English have a limited access to the Internet in their mother tongue because of the linguistic barriers that restrict computer use to people with the ability to work in many languages (Kelliny, 2002, p. 145). In addition, the level of development of many nations, infrastructural limitations, and families' economic situation dictate the ability to afford computers and the Internet connectivity.

The goal of this chapter is to highlight some critical issues that came out of studies related to the adoption of Web platforms, WebCT and the Blackboard, in two Arab and Gulf universities. Although these pilot studies cannot be said to be conclusive, there is a need for large-scale studies on the wider implications of e-learning in higher education in the coeducational and non-coeducational setups. The two universities that provide the foci of this chapter are the Sultan Qaboos University (SQU) in Oman and the United Arab Emirates University (UAEU). Both are the premier universities of the two Arab countries in the Gulf region.

EDUCATIONAL SYSTEMS IN THE ARAB COUNTRIES

The educational system in Arab countries, as in other countries around the world, has the main purpose of inculcating knowledge and values that are germane to the needs of their societies. Religion is held in high esteem, and hence the existence of Islamism and the

Quranic schools, even before the advent of Western education. The peoples' culture and practice in general respect and honor women and protect them in many respects. This is why in many Arab countries, separate provisions and facilities are provided for children (male and female) in schools. The cultural practice in Arab societies at large permits such segregation in accordance with the religious doctrines.

Major differences exist in the structure and practice of higher education in the institutions that serve as pilots in this study. The SQU is coeducational, with the male and female students attending classes on the same campus. The UAEU has its male and female students on different campuses and so male and female students do not mix or take courses in the same classrooms. Even in the SQU case, which is coeducational, restrictions in the mixed mode of operations are in place. The typical classroom scene is that the class arrangements are naturally and automatically in two segments. Female students sit on one side of the class, away from their male counterparts. This is also in accordance with the Islamic doctrine and Arab culture. Even outside the classroom, special corridors and pathways are reserved for female students.

CULTURE AND WEB-BASED EDUCATION

The literature is replete with inconclusive evidence on the effects of interactions that take place in Web-based learning and the interference of cultures. Gunn, McSporran, Macleod, and French (2003) states that the interactions that take place through electronic channels lose none of the sociocultural complexity and gender imbalance that exist within the society. One of the questions posted in that report was how far gender imbalance in computer-supported learning reflect the values and norms of the culture in which they exist and how far can this be generalized across national and social boundaries. That report called for further research as to how instructional designers can increase the flexibility of courses to cope with aspects of culture and a people's values. Khakhar, Quirchmayr, and Wills (2001) state that sociocultural and ethical issues do affect Web-based instructions. They further report experience showing that materials and delivery methods transferred from one place to another may interfere with peoples' cultures and values when subject matter is assumed to be culturally neutral (e.g., technology and mathematics) but may not necessarily be. Materials used in Web education need to be relevant, appropriate, and in conformity with cultures and values of the citizenry of many nation.

The heart of any computer-based learning and instruction is interactivity. The learner should assume an active role during the course of instruction. Web-based learning can utilize one of several platforms for instructional delivery. In relation to these experiences in Oman and the UAE, two platforms, the Blackboard and the WebCT, were utilized. Both platforms have include similar features and elements, which are key to the focus of this chapter. The choice and decision as to which platform to adopt is generally institutional.

Every platform has tools with which learning is engineered. Tools such as e-mail, discussion, and chat are communication tools for interactions—teacher to students or student to student. Kearsley (2000) indicates that e-mail is the foundation for all forms of online learning and teaching; it is possible to use nothing more than e-mail in a course and still create a highly valuable learning experience. It is also recognized to be very cost-effective.

Threaded discussions are said to rank close in capability to e-mail for online education. Kearsley (2003) contends that although there are many variations of these features (elements), they all work in the same fashion. Topics and subtopics are created in which learners and teachers post messages to one another as desired or as preplanned by the teacher.

Interactions between the learner(s) and the teacher and among learners seem to be the bedrock of Web-based or online education. Interaction in the virtual realm is faceless and eliminates potential bias in terms of race, color, sex, religion, or other factors. A cultural conflict may thus emerge because interaction patterns among the male and female students cannot be easily controlled. Furthermore, religious barriers are known to collapse in the virtual realm.

Manninen (2001) reports that learning on the Web is usually a social and collaborative process. The social and interactive process may at times go too far for cultural and religious permissiveness as in the following extreme example cited by Manninen (2001): "Those who are still in doubt should read how Anna (almost) fell in love in a Web-course." This is kind of unrestrained interaction on the Web is definitely unacceptable (a taboo, *haraam* in Islam).

Similarly, Rheingold (1993) indicates that "People in virtual communities. . . exchange pleasantries . . . share emotional support . . . make plans . . . gossip . . . feud . . . fall in love . . . find friends . . . play games . . . flirt. . . . People in virtual communities do just about everything people do in real life but we have our bodies behind. You can't kiss anybody and nobody can punch you on the nose but a lot can happen within those boundaries." Arab culture certainly frowns at many of these things people are known to do and does not condone some of these activities on the Web.

SQU AND UAEU PRACTICE OF WEB EDUCATION

As noted earlier, these two Arab universities are structured differently. SQU is coeducational, and UAEU has separate campuses for the male and female students. SQU has embraced WebCT since the fall semester of 2001 and still uses the platform to date. UAEU has only recently stopped using WebCT and now uses Blackboard.

Being a multicampus institution of higher education, UAEU is not faced with the cultural interference dilemmas that manifest in coeducational settings. Male and female students do not interact with one another in the real or virtual realm during the learning process. Therefore, concerns in terms of interference with culture and religion by Web learning are not evident at UAEU because male and female students operate as different entities although under the same University governance.

The situation is different within the coeducational setup of SQU, however, where the WebCT is used. Akinyemi, Osman, and Al Kindi (2001) report some comments and perspectives of male and female students after going through the WebCT experience for the first time. Their experience with the communications tools (e-mail, discussions, chats, and bulletin board) provided them with the opportunity to interact with opposite-sex counterparts for the first time. Table 1 shows a sample of comments from both the male and female students. The social profile of the students makes this Web relationship and experience a unique one. If it were possible to measure the emotional effects of such interactions, one might be surprised at the results.

It is important to note reactions 4, 9, and 13. Although 4 and 9 relate to the pleasure and privilege of interaction, 13 represents a singular call for an Arabized e-learning platform. On the other hand, and most important, reaction 4 reflect some traces of excitement and joy of interacting with the opposite sex by some students. Also, one of the female students, in her informal reaction to the Web-based learning utilizing the WebCT, expressed a thanks to the lecturer for enabling her to experience interaction with the opposite sex (male counterparts) on the Web-based course. Because the cultural, social, and religious practices of Arabs and the Muslim–Islamic world forbid gender interaction or socialization patterns, such Web-based experiences can be viewed as a major cultural and religious interference, as *haram.*

Table 1. Sample of Students Comments about WebCT

1.	"The communication tools enriched my experience in the course."
2.	"I felt that the course materials are directed to me personally."
3.	"My self-confidence in using the Internet has improved significantly."
4.	"The WebCT method has brought together both sexes through interactivity, which is not normally the case in other courses."
5.	"Computer labs are always congested, and we had little time to use the computer."
6.	"There should be an assigned and dedicated time slot within the course for WebCT discussion."
7.	"Need for more content materials on the Web site."
8.	"It was nice to have been able to solicit other students' suggestions on various issues."
9.	"It was a wonderful opportunity to communicate with our male and female classmates."
10.	"WebCT encourages us to read additional materials and put it on the site for the course."
11.	"There should have been additional links to related sites for more information."
12.	"[There is a] Need for more laboratories for e-learning."
13.	"WebCT should be better equipped to handle courses in Arabic Language."

Source: Akinyemi et al. (2001).

CONCLUSION AND RECOMMENDATIONS

The world has become one global village. No one wants to be left behind, and in fact, no one can afford to lag behind others in the global train. The potent question now is "Where do we go from here?" This is the loaded question that requires attention as the use of technology continues to expand rapidly. The interactivity factor in Web-based learning poses a threat to the Arab culture and the religion of Islam. In view of some of the foregoing learner reactions and the uncontrollable, inevitable potential of virtual learning to interfere with cultures in coeducational institutions and settings, there is need for an action plan to control and contain the situation.

In this global era, can or should communication tools be completely eliminated from the Web-based learning structure? The obvious answer is "no." Can or should students' groupings be organized to avoid mixed (male–female) classes? This is perhaps possible and feasible. Can communications tools be structured and closely monitored to eliminate "love and romance" from Web sessions? This is also possible; however, it may not be possible to control this in the absolute sense. What cultural differences or context issues should be considered when developing online courses for multicultural cohorts? The need for and the contributions of research in this area are of utmost importance as e-learning becomes a global entity.

RECOMMENDATIONS

1. Higher education institutions in Arab countries should carefully structure Web-based education to eliminate interaction patterns that run counter to cultural and religious practice.

2. Coeducation institutions in the Arab world may need to increase their surveillance over the Internet and closely monitor their courses.

3. Phonographic and obscene sites must be blocked from the Internet so that learners are not distracted and contaminated with profane materials from the Internet.

4. Arab educators and professionals must embark on the design of an Arabized e-learning platform to reduce the English-language dominance of the existing platforms.

5. Intensive and aggressive research is needed on various facets of Web-based instruction with a special focus on protecting and preserving Arab sociocultural values and heritage.

6. Arab universities must form a strong consortium for collaboration and cooperation in the region on an Arabized e-learning practice that will protect and preserve the people's culture while ensuring its compatibility with the available and existing formats in other parts of the world.

REFERENCES

Akinyemi, A., Osman, M. T., & Al Kindi, M. (2001). Implementation and perspectives of WebCT at Sultan Qaboos University. Muscat, Oman: Center for Educational Technology, Sultan Qaboos University.

Gunn, C., McSporran, M., Macleod, H., & French, S. (2002). Dominant or Different? Gender issues in computer supported learning. *Journal of Asynchronous Learning and Networks, 7*(1). Retrieved from http://www.sloan-c.org/publications/jaln/v7n1/index.asp

Kearsley, G. (2003). Learning and teaching in cyberspace. Retrieved from http://home.sprynet.com/-gkearsley/chapts.htm

Kelliny, W., & Kelliny, I. M. (2002). Is the Internet a tool for linguistic and cultural dominance, immersion or integration? In W. W. H. Kelliny (Ed.), *European University Studies XXI Linguistics, Volume 12: Surveys in linguistics and language teaching III: E-learning and e-research.* New York: Peter Lang.

Khakhar, D., Quirchmayr, G., & Wills, C. C. (2001, October). *Critical factors in developing e-education frameworks.* Presented at "E-Learning in a Lifelong Learning Perspective," the 2nd WBLE conference, Lund, Sweden.

Manninen, J. (2001, October). e-myth and e-reality: Digging the fears, the dreams and the reality of virtual learning. Presented at "E-Learning in a Lifelong Learning Perspective," the 2nd WBLE conference, Lund, Sweden.

Rheingold, H. (1993). The virtual community. Reading, MA: Addison-Wesley. Retrieved from http://www.rheingold.com/vc/book/

Timms, D. (2001, October). eLearning—Back to the future? Presented at "E-Learning in a Lifelong Learning Perspective," the 2nd WBLE conference, Lund, Sweden.

Building Human Capacity in Malawi: Contextual Considerations in Instructional Technology Project Implementation

Ross A. Perkins, Barbara B. Lockee, and John K. Burton
Virginia Polytechnic Institute and State University

The scene that follows took place in a classroom as a group of U.S., Chinese, and Malawian students and professors collaborated to redesign distance learning courses for use in Malawi, Africa.

> Professor Black was sitting attentively as she always does when listening closely to someone speak. She was particularly attentive as Kondwani read the list of contextual elements that would help guide the redesign process. Despite his strong command of the English language—back home he is a language instructor—his manner of talking quickly combined with a Chichewa-British accent makes his words difficult to decipher if one is not looking straight at him. The other students sat quietly as he read his section of the report. He was sure to point out that a very important person in the distance learning assessment process is the invigilator—every distance center would have to have one. *Invigilator?* Maybe we had misunderstood what he said. A couple of the Malawian students nodded, silently agreeing that invigilators are important, so whatever he said, they understood it. The professor leaned toward the desk and poked her head forward as if to get closer to the same word that had stumped the rest of us. Others in the room seemed to have the same dialogue bubble over their heads asking, "What is that!?" Finally, the professor asked the question on all our minds. Kondwani, thinking perhaps we did not hear the word correctly, enunciated it, "Invigilator." She shook her head, and it was clear to him that only the Malawians understood what he meant. He then told us that an invigilator makes sure that students do not cheat on exams. One student spoke up, "You mean a proctor!" Herbert, who helped lead the Malawian team, smiled, wrinkled his nose a bit, and asked with a quizzical smile, "What's that?" After the misunderstanding was cleared up, we laughed and talked a few minutes about "crisps" vs. "chips," "torches" vs. "flashlights" and "gas" vs. "petrol" before getting back to Kondwani's report. (Adapted from Perkins, 2003)

The vignette provides a brief but poignant example of how divergent cultural understandings can make communication difficult even at a seemingly mundane level. This chapter describes how culture and context have influenced, and in some cases redirected, efforts in a human capacity project funded by the U.S. Agency for International Development (USAID). Following a brief overview of the project background, the authors provide a number of examples to illustrate how culture and context affect an instructional technology project taking place in Malawi, Africa.

PROJECT OVERVIEW

In its effort to provide the country of Malawi with quality basic education programs, USAID sponsors a program that links U.S.-based institutions of higher education with universities, educational organizations, and other institutions in Malawi. The program, known as UPIC, or University Partners for Institutional Capacity, "is a direct response to Malawi's critical need to establish high quality primary school teacher training and to build and maintain

150

capacity for productive education analysis and planning" (Ministry of Education Division of Planning, Task Force for Professional Enhancement and Training, & GABLE PPC [MEDP], 1999, p. 1). The "critical need" arises out of that country's overwhelmed primary, secondary, and tertiary level schools. The inadequate facilities and equipment notwithstanding, there is quite simply a lack of properly trained personnel. Development of the human resources and institutional capacity for maintaining the human resources is imperative, for without them, "there can be no hope for sustaining the educational reform efforts that are taking place in Malawi today" (MEDP, 1999, p. 2).

In response to the USAID call for proposals, Virginia Tech successfully earned two of three UPIC grants. One grant, known by the acronym ICET (Information Communications and Technology), has as its focus the development of human capacity in the ICT, not hardware and software purchases as the name might imply. This goal is reflected in the grant proposal,

> [the goal is to] prepare a group of Malawian educators to serve as instructional technology specialists with the skills not only to design and implement on-line programming regarding IT [instructional technology], but also to serve as technology trainers for other Malawian teachers. (Burton, Lockee, & Moore, 2001, n.p.)

The ICET activity partners Virginia Tech with a newer Malawian institution situated in the northern part of the country, Mzuzu University. Mzuzu's mission, which in many ways is similar to that of Virginia Tech's mission as a land-grant university, is "to provide high-quality education, training, research, and complementary services to meet the technological, social, and economic needs of individuals and communities in Malawi" (Ngwire & Kanjeza, 2000). Though the two schools can be contrasted in numerous ways, administrators from both institutions shared the vision set forth in the USAID proposal.

The initial plan was for a group of Malawian students to become full-time, on-campus students at Virginia Tech, where they would study instructional technology to receive a master's degree. This cadre of instructional technologists would then redesign a number of preexisting Web-based courses that make up the Instructional Technology Master's of Arts degree (ITMA) program. The revamped courses would compose a master's program offered in Malawi and accommodate up to eighty distance learners. These newly trained people would ostensibly have the ability to continue to build and expand access to a well-designed, distance teacher education curriculum in Malawi, thus helping fill the country's dire need for greater numbers of qualified teachers.

Because all courses were created by professors in the United States for a predominantly North American audience, it was clear from the beginning that some content redesign would necessary. However, there were a number of unanticipated events and circumstances that had ramifications on the instructional (re)design efforts and affected the project as a whole. The lessons learned to date clearly emphasize the importance of context.

CONTEXTUAL ISSUES AND CHALLENGES

Tessmer and Richey (1997) define context as "a multilevel body of factors in which learning and performance are embedded" (p. 87). The multilevel nature of context is discovered through what is known as either a context analysis or environmental analysis (Dean, 1994; Tessmer, 1990; Tessmer & Harris, 1992; Tiene & Futagami, 1987). Our collective experiences, which include informal and formal analyses of context, have provided much insight into the influence of context in the instructional design process, particularly related to design across and between greatly differing cultures. The following section identifies many of the situational factors encountered during the implementation of the project, and relates it to literature that specifically discusses context within the field of instructional technology.

Context Analysis

A context analysis may or may not include the same elements as the more commonly known needs assessment or needs analysis (e.g., Witkin & Altschuld, 1995). Eastmond's (1994) broad view of needs assessment, where he describes it as "a systematic inquiry into the most important needs to be met," (p. 88) underscores the similarity of the two analyses. Some would assert that the needs assessment tends to focus on "the exact nature of an organizational problem and how it can be solved" (Dick & Carey, 1996). The context analysis, on the other hand, is an examination of "physical and psychosocial factors that affect learning . . . a phenomenological approach to instructional design in that it seeks to describe the learning 'as it is' in the real world" (Tessmer & Harris, 1992, p. 15). This definition implies that the orientation is less on what needs to be learned and more on how what surrounds the teaching and learning situation affects and sustains (or diminishes) the educational process. The goal of the analysis is "to describe where an instructional product will be used, how it will be used, and how it will be sustained" (Tessmer, 1990). The foundational assumption behind the rationale of a context analysis is that it will improve the instructional design (ID) product (Tessmer & Harris, 1992). As part of the theoretical rationale for their model, Tessmer and Richey (1997) discuss general systems theory, communication theory, and psychological theory. Interestingly, Rogers (1995) calls diffusion a special instance of a general communication model. This relationship between context and innovations becomes all the more clear when one considers the importance of context factors in the design process. Because instructional design is, among other things, a "field of innovation" (Surry & Brennan, 1998), the designer is wise to keep in mind the relationship between environmental analysis, the ID process, and the ensuing communication, adoption, and implementation of the instructional product.

Emergence of a Design Culture

To speak of product improvement or evolution without noting the changes to the programs that create the products is to misrepresent the recursive nature of instructional design. The word "culture," already encumbered by hundreds of definitions (Lonner & Adamapoulos, 1997), no longer refers (in this case) to the broader cultures of Malawi and the United States. Instead, one can also consider the contexts and influences within the design culture itself. In our project, the design team comprised stakeholders representing each partner organization, therefore representing both Malawian and American perspectives. As in any international project, cultural differences provided challenges from which we were able to learn. First, and likely most interesting, language has been an issue although both constituent groups speak English. As Goodfellow, Lea, Gonzalez, and Mason (2001) determined, linguistic differences can influence the relationship that exists between international groups working on such collaborative distance education initiatives. Differing speech patterns between team members, as well as British versus American dialects, have presented challenges for both groups in terms of listening comprehension and written communication.

Cultural differences related to time also presented obstacles in terms of project progress. Americans are driven by the clock, and the planning and conduct of ID projects is no exception. According to the accounts of our Malawian colleagues, lifestyles are less constrained by time and the hour of the day. These differing perspectives caused challenges at first, but as team members have become more knowledgeable and familiar with each other, both groups realize the expectations of each culture and work toward sensitivity to these issues. The initial sense of "cultural otherness" (Goodfellow et al., 2001) has been largely overcome as the partner groups have greater awareness of lifestyle patterns and traditions.

What we found in our partnerships is the emergence of a design culture, one that shares values and perspectives of both its Malawian and U.S. constituents and whose members take into account multiple contextual elements. This culture gives us much confidence in the relevance of instructional programs we have produced.

Teaching and Instructional Design Issues

The matching of educational conditions to their proposed solutions happens less frequently than one might expect. Many who write about the diffusion of innovations in developing nations (innovations that often make up part of a distance education system) warn against the "foreign expert" who lacks real knowledge about the culture into which the innovation will be implemented (Abrahams, 1993; Chadwick, 1970; Ellsworth, 2000; Ely, 1989; Marchessou, 2000; Michele, 1987; Rogers, 1995; Shrestha, 1997). Chadwick (1970), uses the metaphor of a rescue helicopter to illustrate the typical consultant, who

> swoops in on a three day trip, has four meetings with educational officials, two parties with the education minister, and leaves behind a two page memorandum specifying all the "answers" needed by the country, with no recognition of the cultural, social, or political factors which may affect the problem. (p. 48)

The close interaction we have had with our Malawian colleagues since the grant's inception has given us insight into pertinent environmental factors. Although communication has not been perfect and clear in all instances, we feel a knowledge of each other's contexts has brought us closer to Rogers' (1995) notion of *homophily* (likeness between individuals who interact with each other). The "modification of wares according to local needs" (Shrestha, 1997, Part V, para. 62) can only occur when the promoters of such wares understand the end-user level (the individual) reaction to products and methods.

The Malawian educational system generally reflects the influence of the British system put in place during the colonial era, which ended in 1964. Little has changed with regard to education since Malawi became an independent country. Large numbers of students are served by few teachers typically through lecture-based instruction (K–16). Additionally, teachers of all grades are trained as subject matter experts as opposed to being prepared with generalizable skills, so the notion of instructional design and its related processes was a truly foreign approach to the creation of instructional programming for the Malawian team members. The Malawian culture emphasizes great respect for the classroom teacher; concurrently, teaching strategies are typically teacher-led. Because of the cultural expectations and large numbers of students, changes in teaching approaches would be difficult to operationalize. Project team leaders from Virginia Tech were responsible for teaching instructional design to the Mzuzu University team members while they were enrolled as students. Philosophical differences in the design of instruction had to be resolved so that the IT program to be delivered in Malawi would balance cultural tradition with effective practice.

Distance Delivery Issues

Bates (2001) offers a number of suggestions for addressing the issues that arise when one institution creates a distance education program to be used internationally. Included among them is the development of a close relationship between the exporting and importing institutions through active participation in course and policy creation; tailoring programs to local needs; assistance in building capacity in places where little human or technical infrastructure exists for the importer to create its own courses; and development of training programs for course developers to increase sensitivity to cultural issues. As described in the project overview, the proposed plan developed by the project partners was that team members would redesign Virginia Tech's ITMA program for use in Malawi and for delivery by Mzuzu University. This effort would begin Mzuzu's foray into distance education, and their leadership wished to implement the new program via the Internet.

The team's desire to demonstrate technological capacity quickly clashed with issues of feasibility and access. First, although Mzuzu has Internet connectivity on campus, such connectivity is not commonplace throughout the country. Lack of reliable electrical and telecommunications infrastructures, along with the related scarcity of computers, would not allow for the intentions of the team to be realized. The large-scale needs assessment team members conducted (Zozie et al., 2004) proved beneficial as it became clear that the online program would need to be transitioned to print-based instruction. Because the Malawian team members had computer and Internet access, they are also producing materials in electronic format for delivery via CD-ROM to other universities and teacher education colleges in Malawi. The team members have therefore gained experience in both print-based and computer-based programming for distance education. This dual development approach has been informative for all team members in terms of distance education design and delivery implications.

The role of cultural influences in the development of educational programs cannot be understated. As Trueba (1988) remarks, "the conditions for effective learning are created when the role of culture is recognized and used in the activity settings during the actual learning process" (p. 282). As predicted by and described in research on diffusion of innovations, programs that remain insensitive to local contexts (whether social or economic) are likely not to be adopted and most certainly not implemented (Brown, 1981; Rogers, 1995; Zaltman, Duncan, & Holbek, 1973). The concept of cultural distance (Wilson, 1999), which is implied in the work of others who research international aspects of distance education, describes the isolation the learner experiences when things like language, country-specific terms and expressions, and academic expectations do not match his or her own (Goodfellow et al., 2001). One must realize, however, that cultural issues do not, by themselves, constitute a sufficient context. Defined as "the circumstances in which an event occurs" (American Heritage Dictionary, 1993), context is created by numerous inputs (and outputs), some of which cannot be predicted.

Administrative and Policy Issues

Other unanticipated challenges that arose were related to university support for international projects. At Virginia Tech, the Office of Sponsored Programs provided assistance with USAID grant acquisition, but once the project funding was in place, little support was available to deal with the many factors that emerged during project implementation. For example, our project encountered unimaginable challenges for which support mechanisms did not seem to be in place. First, during the summer that our Malawian colleagues returned home to conduct a needs assessment for the project, two team members were in an automobile accident two days before returning to Virginia Tech for the fall 2003 semester. One of our team members was killed and the other was seriously injured, taking some months to heal sufficiently before he could return to the United States. In addition to the tremendous personal loss and emotional trauma the entire team suffered, the project director spent countless hours working toward restitution for the family of the deceased, as well as compensation and support for the wounded student as he recovered in Malawi. Making the process more difficult was the fact that the team members were in their home country when the accident occurred but working for the Virginia Tech USAID project. Policy issues seemed insurmountable at times, but through much persistence the necessary financial and medical support became available. Dealing with insurance coverage for team members, as well as for the project vehicle located at Mzuzu University in Malawi, required extensive research and a significant allocation of time on the part of the project coordinators.

Personnel Issues

Other administrative challenges arose during the implementation of the project. The initial agreement between Virginia Tech and Mzuzu University was that the team members from MU would be "released" to design and implement the new distance delivered IT program—in other words, it would become part of their job. Unfortunately, because of the scarcity of human resources in Malawi, the Mzuzu University team members returned to their standard responsibilities full-time upon graduation from Virginia Tech, making any work on the distance education project above and beyond their usual position requirements. Adoption of an innovation, which in this case is represented by a team of instructional technologist, can be based less on how effectively ideas about it are communicated and more on the adopter's capacity to accommodate the infrastructure and market characteristics of the innovation (Brown, 1981; Dzama & Osborne, 1999).

The Virginia Tech project director worked with Mzuzu University leadership to "buy out" some of the MU team members' time; however, their expectation was actual monetary compensation for the additional work. Because the implementation of federal grants like the USAID program are heavily regulated in terms of project expenditures, much negotiation has been necessary in the fiscal management of project activities in Malawi. As Bates (2001) indicates, the establishment of a strong relationship between the partnering distance education organizations is essential for such projects to be successful. Such a relationship allows for open discussion of sensitive issues such as fiscal operations and policies and also for the resolution of challenges that emerge related to such issues.

RECOMMENDATIONS

The authors have learned a great deal about the importance of contextual considerations related to collaborative international efforts for the design of distance education programs, based on our experiences in the project we describe here. Culture pervades every aspect of our work and social processes, and differences in context only ensure differing perspectives and philosophies. The following recommendations may apply to instructional design projects internal to the United States, but cross-cultural efforts will definitely benefit from these insights gained through our experiences.

First, it is imperative that all stakeholders understand and endorse the project goals and plans. Even in cases when agreement on these factors seems evident, it is still important to verify knowledge of the plan of action and each stakeholder's role in project activities and success. Insight into the project outcomes and the responsibilities of project personnel will contribute to the development of a collaborative environment that is based on trust and clear communication.

Also, expect (and plan for) the unexpected. How can this be done? Project leadership must remain flexible with regard to plans and expectations, as much so as the project will accommodate. The provision of alternative plans for distance program development and delivery may seem unnecessary, but if such plans help convey the necessity to manage change and to demonstrate flexibility, the effort will not be wasted.

Identify necessary support personnel to ensure project success. The range of experiences previously described related to all facets of such international projects should convey the importance of securing the services of supporting staff, such as travel, health, and risk management professionals.

Be prepared to go above and beyond. Cross-cultural projects such as the one described here require constant work, and international partnerships can be very demanding in terms of time and effort on the part of everyone involved. The multilevel factors that comprise context as defined by Tessmer and Richey (1997) require the attention and management of such international distance education projects to actualize a program that will effectively meet the needs of its intended learners.

REFERENCES

Abrahams, F. (1993). *The transfer of educational technology: An assessment and discussion of appropriateness in Africa and other selected developing countries.* Unpublished doctoral dissertation, Columbia University Teachers College, New York, NY.

American Heritage Dictionary (3rd ed.). (1993). Boston: Houghton Mifflin.

Bates, T. (2001). International distance education: Cultural and ethical Issues. *Distance Education, 22*(1), 122–136.

Brown, L. A. (1981). *Innovation diffusion: A new perspective.* London: Methuen.

Burton, J. K., Lockee, B., & Moore, D. M. (2001). *Proposal to develop the instructional technology skills of Malawi educators.* Unpublished manuscript, Blacksburg, VA.

Chadwick, C. (1970). Educational technology in international development education. (ERIC Document Reproduction Service No. ED046238)

Dean, G. (1994). *Designing instruction for adult learners.* Malabar, FL: Krieger.

Dick, W., & Carey, L. (1996). *The systematic design of instruction* (4th ed.). New York: HarperCollins.

Dzama, E. N. N., & Osborne, J. F. (1999). Poor performance in science among African students: An alternative explanation to the African worldview thesis. Journal of *Research in Science Teaching, 36*(3), 387–405.

Eastmond, N. (1994). Assessing needs, developing instruction, and evaluating results in distance education. In B. Willis (Ed.), *Distance education: Strategies and tools* (pp. 87–105). Englewood Cliffs, NJ: Educational Technology.

Ellsworth, J. B. (2000). Surviving change: A survey of educational change models. Washington, DC: Office of Educational Research and Improvement. (ERIC Document Reproduction Service No. ED443417)

Ely, D. P. (1989). The diffusion of educational technology in Indonesia: A multi-faceted approach. *British Journal of Educational Technology, 20*(3), 183–190.

Goodfellow, R., Lea, M., Gonzalez, F., & Mason, R. (2001). Opportunity and e-quality: Intercultural and linguistic issues in global online learning. *Distance Education, 22*(1), 65–84.

Lonner, W. J., & Adamapoulos, J. (1997). Culture as antecedant to behavior. In J. W. Berry, Y. H. Poortinga, & J. Pandey (Eds.), *Handbook of cross-cultural psychology: Theory and method* (Vol. 1, pp. 43–83). Boston: Allyn and Bacon.

Marchessou, F. (2000). Some ethical considerations in Ed-tech consultancies across borders. *Educational Technology, Research and Development, 48*(4), 110–114.

Michele, C. (1987). Educational radio and television—their transfer to developing societies. In R. M. Thomas & V. N. Kobayashi (Eds.), *Educational technology—its creation, development and cross-cultural transfer* (Vol. 4, pp. 125–143). Oxford, England: Pergamon Press.

Ministry of Education Division of Planning, Task Force for Professional Enhancement and Training, & GABLE PPC. (1999). *University partners for institutional capacity in education Malawi: Concept paper.* Unpublished manuscript, Lilongwe, Malawi.

Ngwire, F., & Kanjeza, D. (2000). Mzuzu University home page. Retrieved May 29, 2003, from http://www.sdnp.org.mw/webwshp/dkanjeza/

Perkins, R. A. (2003). *The role of context in instructional design: A case study examining the re-purposing of web-based master's degree courses for use in Malawi.* Unpublished doctoral dissertation, Virginia Polytechnic Institute and State University, Blacksburg, VA.

Rogers, E. M. (1995). *Diffusion of innovations* (4th ed.). New York: Free Press.

Shrestha, G. (1997). Distance education in developing countries (updated February 10, 2000). Retrieved December 18, 2001, from http://www.undp.org/info21/public/distance/pb-dis.html

Surry, D. W., & Brennan, J. P., II. (1998). Diffusion of instructional innovations: Five important, unexplored questions. (ERIC Document Reproduction Service No. ED422892)

Tessmer, M. (1990). Environment analysis: A neglected state of instructional design. *Educational Technology, Research and Development, 38*(1), 55–64.

Tessmer, M., & Harris, D. (1992). *Analysing the instructional setting.* London: Kogan Page.

Tessmer, M., & Richey, R. (1997). The role of context in learning and instructional design. *Educational Technology, Research and Development, 45*(2), 85–115.

Tiene, D., & Futagami, S. (1987). Designing effective educational multimedia projects: General guidelines for developing countries. *International Journal of Instructional Media, 14*(4), 282–292.

Trueba, H. T. (1988). Culturally based explanations of minority students' academic achievement. *Anthropology and Education Quarterly, 19*(3), 270–287.

Wilson, M. S. (1999). *Cultural discontinuities between West African adult learners and print-based distance instructional materials.* Unpublished doctoral dissertation, University of Oklahoma, Norman.

Witkin, B. R., & Altschuld, J. W. (1995). *Planning and conducting needs assessments.* Thousand Oaks, CA: Sage.

Zaltman, G., Duncan, R., & Holbek, J. (1973). *Innovations and organizations.* New York: Wiley.

Zozie, P. A., Sanga, M. W., Gwayi, S. M., Nyirongo, N. K., Perkins, R. A., & Lockee, B. B. (2004). Establishment of distance education for secondary school teachers in Malawi, Africa: A national needs assessment. In M. A. Fitzgerald, M. Orey & R. M. Branch (Eds.), *Educational media & technology yearbook 2004* (Vol. 29). Westport, CT: Libraries Unlimited.

Part Two
School and Library Media

Introduction

In 2004, the world continues to reverberate with the shock waves from the terrorist attacks of September 11, 2001, as well as continued strains from the Gulf War. The world has become accustomed to added security in airports, public facilities, and even schools. The Department of Homeland Security has become one of the most powerful arms of the U.S. government, establishing a system of security known and understood worldwide.

The economic picture for the nation at large may have improved with a slow upturn in the U.S. unemployment rate, but education has continued to reel from budget cuts and hiring freezes on both the K–12 and higher education levels. The acute need for media specialists has continued as new schools are built rapidly in population growth centers such as the southern United States. The result has been the establishment of temporary categories, special waivers, and training programs for teachers in all areas. This process has led to some confusion with the rapid change in hiring criteria and concern from school library media programs over the quality of staffing in the field.

All of these changes renew the need for school library media centers and their professionals to identify challenges, opportunities, and a new vision for service today and in the future, to create services for increasing student and teacher use of existing resources, to open an invitation to new populations, and to better understand our students, teachers, and staff. In short, the current trends in school library media centers require highly trained professionals who can identify needs, address them, and point out the critical role it plays to the success of students, teachers, schools, and communities.

Contributions to the 2005 *EMTY* School and Library Media Section have been extraordinary, resulting in twelve chapters. These have been divided into three sections: social, cultural, and political arenas; emerging trends in libraries; and roles for and in the media center.

The Social, Cultural, and Political Arena section begins with a chapter by Jean Donham outlining the mismatch between high school senior media experiences and college freshman's daunting challenge. "Your Seniors Are Our First-Year Students" makes a cogent argument for increasing student preparation for the critical thinking needed to manage independent research on the college level. The second chapter, "Multicultural Literature and the School Library Media Center," is by Kay Bishop. This chapter recognizes the guidelines in *Information Power* (AASL/AECT, 1988) and goes further to offer specific plans and actions for media specialists. Bishop explores the writer's perspective of insider and outsider in portraying cultural literature genuinely and warns that books should meet content standards as well as programmatic and curricular needs before being added to the collection. Indeed, she offers a list of evaluation criteria for multicultural literature. In conclusion, Bishop offers an excellent literature review of books, Web sites, and journals that can offer guidance when building a quality collection representing a broader demographic. The third chapter, by Rebecca Butler, is a valuable addition that tracks the development of the U.S. Homeland Security Department and its predecessors and through its growing implications for intellectual freedom. With the convoluted nature of mounting legislation, Butler's contribution gives a solid background for library professionals to help interpret the proposed bills increasing the power of homeland security measures (H.R. 4414) and its impending clash with the proposed Civil Liberties Restoration Act (Bill of Rights Defense Committee, 2004).

The second section explores emerging trends in libraries and media centers. Digital libraries represent a new and valuable resource for all information users. Mardis and Hoffman explain the uses of these new tools and talk about some of the concerns surrounding electronic resource access. Three exemplary digital libraries noted are the International Children's Digital Library (ICDL), Teacher's Domain (a part of the National Science Foundation's National Science Digital Library), and the Digital Library for Earth System Education (DLESE). By using the increased access to information via computers often located in the school library media center (Lance, Welborn, & Hamilton-Pennell, 1993), library professionals are challenged to teach evaluation techniques but have new opportunities for teacher collaboration as such quality online resources grow. Next, Lesley Farmer takes a critical look at teen perceptions of electronic reference services. As more students gain home access to the Internet, more of their research is conducted by accessing online resources. One critical way to increase the breadth and depth of information literacy training is by increasing access to experts in such a way as electronic reference. Farmer explores the added benefit of online reference services provided by such tools as digital libraries and what the issues are when outsourcing. The last chapter in Section Two is a level-specific electronic resource for teacher use. Tillman's "Kindergarten Teacher" represents how a comprehensive Web site can be tailored to the needs and interests of a narrow group. Such specific Web resources not only can encourage young children to learn, they can attract teachers who seek presorted and evaluated educational links for immediate use in the classroom. This trend for niche development represents a great area for service growth on the Web.

The third section, Roles For and In the Media Center, examines future needs in media center professional development. Using critical theory, Karen Ferneding expounds on her research involving school library media specialists and their critical view of technology in the school. What do library professionals think of computers in the work and learning space? She encourages us to continue to consider why we use technology and its implications for how we work, how we teach, and how we learn. Next, Betty Marcoux documents her research on examining how principals perceive school library media specialists. Her work suggests that administrators need a more thorough understanding of the current role and future implications for the position of school library media specialist. The last chapter in Section Three discusses the use of inquiry groups to help formulate the idea that the library is a place where critical thinking, curriculum planning, and teacher collaboration can begin allowing greater use of resources, improved communication with teachers, and perhaps increased critical thinking by students. Gail Bush encourages readers to use the inquiry method outlined to empower faculty, students, and staff for greater information literacy by providing a collaborative forum for problem inquiry and solution.

The authors of these chapters were invited to write for the *Yearbook* on the basis of presentations made at important professional and research conferences in late 2003 through mid-2004. These chapters represent research and prescriptive strategies that together exemplify the important trends and developments in the library media field this year. We hope that library media specialists, school administrators, higher education faculty, and school library media researchers will find useful information within them.

Jo McClendon

REFERENCES

American Association of School Librarians/Association for Education Communication & Technology. (1998). *Information Power: Building partnerships for learning.* Chicago: American Library Association.

Bill of Rights Defense Committee. (2004). 323 Civil liberties safe zones! [online]. Retrieved January 26, 2005, from http://www.bordc.org/

Lance, K. C., Welborn, L., & Hamilton-Pennell, C. (1993). *The impact of school library media centers on academic achievement.* Castle Rock, CO: Hi Willow Research.

Your Seniors Are Our First-Year Students

Jean Donham

Cornell College, Mount Vernon Iowa

The transition from high school to college can be an abrupt adjustment. Being a high schooler in June and a college student in August calls for social, psychological, and academic adjustments of major proportion. Although much attention is paid to the social transitions of living away from parents and learning to make decisions more independently, the academic adjustment can be great as well. Teaching styles of college professors are likely to be quite different from those of high school teachers. Common assumptions held by college professors about incoming students may result in unrealistic expectations about their background knowledge, their technical savvy, and their ability to take ownership for their own learning. Rarely does the literature about transition to college speak of the library and information literacy. Yet college work in most disciplines is likely to demand research work of students, and for the majority of them, the college library is likely to be overwhelming, whether visited physically or virtually, if for no other reason than the wider array of resources available there—to say nothing of the adjustment from Dewey to LC call numbers.

Information literacy can be a central theme that brings high school library media specialists and college librarians together to play a vital role in easing the high school to college academic transition. The competencies that make up information literacy are vital to student success. The AASL/AECT standards have led the way for all types of libraries in considering this important set of competencies (American Association of School Librarians/ Association for Educational Communications and Technology, 1998). College libraries are rapidly adopting the collegiate version of information literacy standards developed as the *ACRL Information Literacy Competency Standards for Higher Education* (Association of College and Research Libraries [ACRL], 2000). The time is ripe for thinking about information literacy in a K–16 context. As a point of beginning, college librarians would do well to familiarize themselves with the standards for K–12, and school library media specialists would benefit from reviewing the ACRL standards document.

A SHARED GENERATION

These days, both high school and college librarians are working with the same generation of students: "Millennials"—students born after 1982. This generation is profiled in *Millennials Rising; The Next Great Generation* (Howe & Strauss, 2000). Characteristics that authors Howe and Strauss attribute to this generation include *conventional, confident, sheltered, pressured, achieving,* and *team-oriented.* These qualities are worthy of attention as librarians consider how and what to teach them. In a recent interview, Strauss described Millennials as "very serious students relative to what came before." He goes on state,

> They are used to competing against their peers, even to the point of stress. They will appreciate being challenged and not look at that as a burden. They will want to get something out of college as a lifelong experience more than a cash value element.. . . They will listen when faculties tell them that we need to have a core curriculum because this is something that develops you into a fuller person. . .They tend to take more of the long view, which reflects their optimism. (Lowery, 2001, p. 9)

Members of this generation are described as individuals who trust authority more than recent generations have; their behaviors as a generation harken back to the "Great Generation"—the generation that fought World War II and believed in its government, trusted parents, and respected all authority figures (Leo, 2003). If this characterization is true, the value of information literacy should be a relatively easy "sell" to a generation of students who have high achievement motivation and are willing to invest their energy and time for the long term. This profile suggests that in both high school and college, librarians need to be prepared to instruct these students to meet their high standards of excellence in their work.

COMPARISON OF STANDARDS AASL/ACRL

Both the AASL and ACRL Information Literacy Standards offer clear guidance for teaching students the information search process. Both sets of standards emphasize teaching students to access information efficiently and effectively, evaluate information and its sources critically, and use it for a specific purpose. Table 1 displays the alignment of the two sets of standards. The AASL/AECT standards include a category not explicit in the ACRL Standards—Independent Learning. These three standards are aimed at dispositions toward information and research, rather than specific skills or knowledge. Although these may be among the most difficult to teach and assess, they have significant long-term importance. Otherwise, there is considerable common ground between the two sets of standards.

The definition of information literacy in the ACRL document states:

> Information literacy is a set of abilities requiring individuals to recognize when information is needed and [to] have the ability to locate, evaluate, and use effectively the needed information. (ACRL, 2000, p. 2)

Again, the parallel with the definition from AASL/AECT is clear:

> Information literacy [is] the ability to find and use information. (AASL/AECT, 1998, p. 1)

It is noteworthy that these definitions suggest an emphasis on the information, not on the technology used to access it. In some education sectors, there is confusion between computer literacy and information literacy, but these two organizations agree on the emphasis on finding and using information. At Cornell College, a campuswide commitment to teaching information literacy is grounded in the following definition of information literacy: the attainment of the skills, knowledge, and disposition that enable one to locate, evaluate, use, and communicate information effectively for the purposes of solving a problem or making a decision. This definition brings together the concepts of both AASL/AECT and ACRL documents.

Although these professional associations have chosen the label information literacy, the professional literature raises questions about whether literacy is an appropriate term (Snavely & Cooper, 1997). Other suggestions have ranged from *information fluency* to *information competence* to *library appreciation*. The term fluency carries connotations of a higher degree of facility than "mere" literacy. However, if one defines literacy as more than decoding text, but in fact as the process of making meaning out of textual or visual material, then indeed information literacy may be an appropriate term. These sets of standards urge that students learn to make appropriate meaning out of the information around them by not only accessing it, but evaluating it and applying it to specific purposes that call for analysis, interpretation, and communication. Agreement between school and college librarians on the term is worthy of note and holds promise for cooperative efforts.

Table 1. AASL/ACRL Standards

Information Literacy AASL	Information Literacy ACRL
Standard 1: The student who is information literate accesses information efficiently and effectively.	**Standard 1:** The information literate student determines the nature and extent of the information needed.
Standard 2: The student who is information literate evaluates information critically and competently.	**Standard 2:** The information literate student accesses needed information effectively and efficiently.
Standard 3: The student who is information literate uses information accurately and creatively.	**Standard 3.** The information literate student evaluates information and its sources critically and incorporates selected information into his or her knowledge base and value system.
Independent Learning	
Standard 4: The student who is an independent learner is information literate and pursues information related to personal interests.	**Standard 4.** The information literate student, individually or as a member of a group, uses information effectively to accomplish a specific purpose.
Standard 5: The student who is an independent learner is information literate and appreciates literature and other creative expressions of information.	**Standard 5.** The information literate student understands many of the economic, legal, and social issues surrounding the use of information and accesses and uses information ethically and legally.
Standard 6: The student who is an independent learner is information literate and strives for excellence in information seeking and knowledge generation.	
Social Responsibility	
Standard 7: The student who contributes positively to the learning community and to society is information literate and recognizes the importance of information to a democratic society.	
Standard 8: The student who contributes positively to the learning community and to society is information literate and practices ethical behavior in regard to information and information technology.	
Standard 9: The student who contributes positively to the learning community and to society is information literate and participates effectively in groups to pursue and generate information.	

Sources: American Association of School Librarians/Association for Educational Communications and Technology. (1998). *Information Literacy Standards for Student Learning.* Chicago: American Library Association.

Association of College and Research Libraries (2000*). Information Literacy Competency Standards for Higher Education.* Chicago: American Library Association.

Differences between the two sets of standards begin to show at the level of outcomes and indicators, where the level of complexity differs as it should. To illustrate this, consider the standard in both venues that describes accessing information efficiently and effectively, as summarized in Table 2. Although the parallels between the two standards are apparent, one can readily see in the table the ways in which the ACRL expectations build on the AASL ones.

Table 2. Accesses Information Efficiently and Effectively

AASL	ACRL
Standard 1—The student who is information literate accesses information efficiently and effectively.	Defines and articulates the need for information
Identifies a variety of potential sources of information	Identifies a variety of types and formats of potential sources for information
	Considers the costs and benefits of acquiring the needed information
	Reevaluates the nature and extent of the information need
Develops and uses successful strategies for locating information	Selects the most appropriate investigative methods or information retrieval systems for accessing the needed information.
	Constructs and implements effectively designed search strategies
	Retrieves information online or in person using a variety of methods
	Refines the search strategy if necessary
	Extracts, records, and manages the information and its sources

Sources: American Association of School Librarians/Association for Educational Communications and Technology (1998). *Information Literacy Standards fro Student Learning.* Chicago: American Library Association.

Association of College and Research Libraries (2000*). Information Literacy Competency Standards for Higher Education.* Chicago: American Library Association.

Examining these two sets of indicators suggests analogous processes being taught, but a progression of increasing complexity. What, then, might be taught at each level? Table 3 proposes some specific topics appropriate at high school with continuation and expansion of those topics in college-level information literacy instruction.

Table 3. Instruction at High School and College

High School	College
Using a general encyclopedia, textbook, or motion media to build background	Using subject encyclopedias and specialized reference materials to build background
Focusing a topic Formulating a researchable question Constructing a thesis statement	Formulating a researchable question Strategies for focusing a topic, e.g., browsing the journal literature on a broad topic, examining tables of contents of books, browsing related terms in an online database thesaurus Constructing a thesis statement
Keyword searching in an online catalog or a recommended subscription database Using truncation and Boolean logic in searches	Selecting an appropriate subscription database Searching databases with a controlled vocabulary; using a database thesaurus Using bibliographies of articles to lead to additional relevant documents
Evaluating citations for scope, relevance, availability, and authority Differentiating primary and secondary source documents	Evaluating citations for scope, relevance, authority Differentiating scholarly versus popular sources of information Gauging the practicality of interlibrary loan in terms of time (or money) as a factor in determining the importance of a potential information source Distinguishing between HTML and pdf. full-text format and the advantages of each Using a bibliographic management program like *RefWorks* or *EndNote*

Immediately evident is the fact that the topics suggested under the ACRL standard depend on students having experiences that have helped them develop the competencies described on the AASL side. For example, the step from a general encyclopedia to a subject encyclopedia or subject-specific reference book is clear. If students have learned that an encyclopedia is a reference book useful for building background, then the step to a subject encyclopedia or reference tool is small. Effectively using a controlled vocabulary in searching depends on students already knowing how to do keyword searching in contrast to the natural language searching they do on the Internet. Understanding Boolean logic will help them develop precision in search strings as they gain knowledge of controlled vocabularies and subject headings rather than keyword searching. Use of bibliographic management tools becomes more practical when students' research projects expand to semester-long or longer research projects in which they are trying to keep track of a large number of sources. Without a basic understanding of the library research process, they will have difficulty understanding the value of such a tool.

Building on what high school library media specialists teach, instruction in college information literacy contexts can avoid repeating what students already know and take them to higher levels of sophistication in their research strategies. Conversely, as high school librarians consider what students will learn in college, they can teach information literacy with an eye to what comes next. In addition, considering information literacy as a continuum that travels from high school to college underscores the need for adequately staffing high schools with professional library media specialists to deliver this instruction as a step toward preparation for post-secondary success. The more communication occurs between the professional associations and among local school and college librarians, the better the planning and the teaching.

Clearly, all students will not arrive at the college gate with the same competencies. Each high school is different, and each student's experiences within those high schools differ. However, the potential to improve students' knowledge at both levels is enhanced as librarians from both settings bring their ideas together. Too often, college librarians and college professors assume either too little or too much knowledge among entering first-year students. High school librarians can provide the "reality check" that helps collegians understand what secondary school library research experiences are typical or reasonable. Currently, a common myth exists, especially among college faculty, that because the Millennials have had access to computers much of their lives, they are skilled at information searching online. Conversation between high school and college librarians can provide the basis for an argument that there is a limited set of information literacy competencies that they tend to bring with them to college.

There is little doubt that today's college students have a high level of "screen literacy." Students who spend hours a day in front of one screen or another—television or computer—are bound to become adept at "reading the screen." According to *Kids & Media @ The New Millennium,* a comprehensive national analysis of children's media use published in 1999 by the Kaiser Family Foundation, American children aged eight to thirteen spent one hour per day at a computer or video game screen (Roberts, Foehr, Rideout, & Brodie, 1999). As a result of their time at screen, they seem able to scan a screen very efficiently to locate the button or link they are seeking. This adeptness has misled many to believe that this skill translates into information literacy. Unfortunately, there is much they do not know and that needs to be taught explicitly—and this constitutes the information literacy curriculum K–16. It is highly inappropriate to expect that they will learn everything they need to know to be effective adult researchers by the time they graduate from high school, but it is appropriate to expect them to have developed some identifiable competencies. It is the task of the college librarians and the faculty to assess what they know and build on it once they arrive.

Understanding University Success (Conley, 2003) outlines the knowledge and skills that university faculty believe students need to succeed in higher education. Expectations are described for English, mathematics, natural sciences, social sciences, second languages, and the arts. Information literacy skills, defined as research skills in this document, are included in both English and Social Sciences. Both sets of research expectations indicate that students ought to understand the research process, know how to find a variety of sources and use them properly. These expectations are directly compatible with the Information Literacy Standards of both the AASL and ACRL. Teaching faculty, then, seem to have the same ambitions for students as librarians and school library media specialists.

College classroom expectations are different from those of high school. That may sound like a simplistic statement, but it must be a well-understood assumption underpinning a college-level information literacy curriculum. At the high school level, most often —although not always—student library research calls for students to transmit information and ideas recorded by others. College teachers set an expectation that students will extend beyond *reporting* to *creating* knowledge. In the introduction to *Understanding University*

Success, Conley states that at the college/university level, "It is not enough to simply know something; the learner must possess the ability to do something with the knowledge" (2003, p. 9).

One of the greatest challenges facing librarians at both the high school and college level is developing in students the dispositions that lead to sincere and serious inquiry. Too often, as a result of "schooling," students see research assignments as something to get done, rather than as something to embrace and engage in intellectually. Everyone can envision the wondrous curiosity and enthusiasm that kindergarten children bring to school. The challenge of educators at all levels is to sustain that native curiosity and develop a disposition that causes students to invest intellectually in the research process. The AASL/AECT "Independent Learning" standards speak to the issue of developing positive dispositions toward research. Guiding students at both the high school and college levels toward these attitudes is no small undertaking, but together librarians at both levels might work toward such a goal.

Sometimes too close adherence to standards may cause us to lose sight of some important aspects or nuances of the information search process. Close reading of both sets of standards reveals that there are implicit values and concepts in the information literacy standards, but these may not always be forefront in the consciousness of library media specialists or college librarians. Focusing attention on these "between the lines" concepts and values can serve as conversation starters for discussion between high school and college educators and librarians. Consider these values and concepts as examples of such nuances:

1. *The importance of exploration.* In the Kuhlthau (1993) model of the information search process, Stage 3, after *Initiation* and *Selection*, is *Exploration*. This stage of the process is characterized by feelings of anxiety, doubt, and confusion in her model because the researcher is still somewhat naïve about the topic of choice; he or she still needs to learn about the topic—to *explore* it. Confidence cannot come until there is enough background knowledge to formulate a research focus. During that *Exploration* period, much hard work of the research process occurs. Rushed through this stage, students arrive at a topic that is too broad, a topic they don't really understand, or a topic that doesn't interest them. Librarians can work with teachers to encourage the investment of time in the *Exploration* stage to allow students to feel the frustration of this stage in part so that they can experience the sense of ownership, accomplishment, and relief once they arrive at the *Formulation* stage. It is the early phases of their research that set the stage for a meaningful inquiry that will lead them to construct meaning based on the information they gather.

2. *The benefit of strategic thinking and planning.* Expert researchers begin their investigation by building their background in the topic of choice and proceeding toward more focused sources of information as they refine their research question, build their understanding of the topic, and focus their information needs. For student library researchers, their experience at Web searching is likely to develop habits that are less strategic.

3. *The value of precision.* Natural language searching is the standard for the naïve searcher and is the approach most common to those whose principal research tool is the Internet. For more sophisticated databases, this approach will not yield relevant results. The precision that subscription databases offer is grounded in effective use of keywords and Boolean logic. At more sophisticated levels, these strategies are enhanced with controlled vocabularies often unique to discipline-specific databases.

4. *A critical disposition toward information.* There is little doubt about the need for healthy skepticism for a savvy information consumer today. With self-publication and special interests the norm on the Internet, learning to evaluate sources of information is essential. Explicit criteria that include authority and potential for bias should be a part of the vernacular among young researchers.

5. *Respect for the ethical use of information.* The copy-and-paste capabilities of today's technology have misled students into believing that if something *can* be done technically, it is acceptable. The extensive mass media discussion of music file-sharing has brought the copyright issue to the forefront in the culture of young people. Understanding the rationale behind copyright protection is a crucial first step toward compliance. High school classes teaching government and social issues can play a role in teaching concepts related to intellectual property and the constitutional foundation of copyright. Similarly, both high school and college librarians have a responsibility to teach students about copyright. Still, many students understand well the principle of least effort, and it is important to develop not only intellectual understanding of ownership of ideas but also the moral responsibility citizens have to uphold these principles. All educators share the responsibility for helping students grow in understanding and responsible behavior.

As high school and college librarians engage in dialog, concepts and values like these may offer good conversation starters.

Researchers at Stanford University have been engaged in The Bridge Project, studying high-school-to-college transition practices. In a report on this effort work, the summary states the following:

> The national debate about standards and education reform in general has been conducted primarily without coordination between K–12 and postsecondary education. If there are to be clearer and more consistent signals about what students need to know and be able to do to succeed in college, then linkages between K–12 and postsecondary education must be strengthened. (Venezia, 2003)

To improve the transition from high school to college, conversations need to occur in all sectors. AASL and ACRL have established a joint committee to address this topic at the association level. Locally, college librarians and school library media specialists can build communication channels through their respective state organizations or in less formal collaborations within local areas. The potential benefits of continued conversation include the following:

- Mutual advocacy for information literacy programs at both levels

- Exchange of teaching and resource ideas

- Opportunities for joint projects in such areas as resource allocation and sharing

- Cooperative assessment of student performance.

Initiating the conversation is the first step!

REFERENCES

American Association of School Librarians/Association for Educational Communications and Technology. (1998). *Information Literacy Standards for Student Learning.* Chicago: American Library Association.

Association of College and Research Libraries. (2000). *Information Literacy Competency Standards for Higher Education.* Chicago: American Library Association.

Callison, D. (2003, December). Information fluency. *School Library Media Activities Monthly, 20*(4), 38–39.

Conley, D. T. (Ed.). (2003). *Understanding university success; A report from Standards for Success.* Eugene, OR: Center for Educational Policy Research.

Howe, M., & Strauss, W. (2000). *Millennials rising; The next great generation.* New York: Vintage Books.

Kuhlthau, C. C. (1993). *Seeking meaning: A process approach to library and information services.* Norwood, NJ: Ablex.

Leo, J. (2003, November 3). The good news generation. *US News and World Report, 135*(15), 60.

Lowery, J. W. (2001, July–August). The Millennials Come to Campus. *About Campus, 6*(3), 6–12.

Roberts, D. F., Foehr, U. G., Rideout, V. J., & Brodie, M. *Kids & Media @ the New Millennium, A Kaiser Family Foundation Report.* Retrieved March 18, 2003, from http://www.kff.org/entmedia/1535-index.cfm.

Snavely, L., & Cooper, N. (1997, January). The information literacy debate. *Journal of Academic Librarianship, 23*(1), 9–14.

Venezia, A. (2003, winter). Connecting the systems: What can postsecondary education do to work with K–12 to help students better prepare for college. *Peer Review, 5*(2), 27–30.

Multicultural Literature and the
School Library Media Center

Kay Bishop

School Library Media Program, School of Informatics, University at Buffalo

There is a growing recognition that tomorrow's citizens need to acquire the knowledge, skills, and attitudes that are critical to function in a diverse complex world. With increasing cultural diversity in our schools, it is essential that school media specialists be knowledgeable about multiculturalism and how to incorporate multicultural literature into the various aspects of a media center program.

MULTICULTURAL LITERATURE ISSUES

Currently, there is not a consensus on the meaning of the term *multicultural literature*. To some, this term refers to the four most heavily populated groups of racially diverse persons living in the United States: African American, Asian American, Latino American, and Native American. Other definitions, however, include religious groups such as Jewish Americans or Amish. Some people include all world cultures in their understanding of multiculturalism, and others further widen their definition of multiculturalism to deal with any group of minorities to whom prejudice is exhibited, thus encompassing the gay and lesbian population and persons with disabilities. In reality, racial and cultural borders are blurring in the United States as more of the population becomes racially and ethnically mixed. Yet in all of these instances, the term refers to those who are outside the mainstream population.

School media specialists generally adhere to the principle of providing materials to meet the needs of all students; therefore, the variety of definitions for multicultural literature is not highly critical. In *Information Power: Guidelines for School Library Media Programs* a number of challenges facing school media specialists are discussed. Of particular value in relation to multicultural materials is the first challenge: "To provide intellectual and physical access to information and ideas for a diverse population whose needs are changing rapidly" (American Association of School Librarians/Association for Educational Communications and Technology [AASL/AECT], 1988, p. 3).

Another multicultural issue deals with the question of who is qualified to write about ethnic and cultural experiences. Should someone outside a culture or only a member of a particular ethnic group or culture write about that culture? This question has been addressed in many books and journal articles. Hazel Rochman in *Against Borders: Promoting Books for a Multicultural World*, notes, "only gifted writers can do it, write beyond their own cultures" (1993, p. 22). Sometimes this issue is discussed in relation to perspective:

> An inside perspective is one that portrays a cultural group from the point of view of one who is a member of the group. An outside perspective is the portrayal of a cultural group by one who is not a member of the group. An inside perspective is more likely to give an authentic view of what members of the cultural group believe to be true about themselves, whereas an outside perspective gives the view of how others see the particular group's beliefs and behaviors. This difference in voice determines how readers will perceive the culture depicted. (Yokota, 1993, p. 158)

The most hotly debated issue related to multicultural literature deals with the authen-ticity and accuracy of the materials. Although it has become trendy to include multicultural literature in libraries, media specialists must be knowledgeable in regard to evaluating multicultural materials, making certain they meet particular criteria in addition to those used to select good literature. A book should not be included in a collection simply because it is multicultural.

THE VALUES OF MULTICULTURAL LITERATURE

Many of the goals of multicultural education can be attained through multicultural literature. It is important that all young people, not just those from ethnic backgrounds, un-derstand the richness of the cultures that make up the United States, as well as the world. Each culture in the United States has made unique contributions to the American way of life, but frequently students are not aware of those contributions. Learning about the values and social customs of different cultures can promote increased appreciation, understand-ing, and sensitivity among students from various ethnic backgrounds.

Multicultural literature can provide opportunities to explore other cultures and hu-man experiences. Nonfiction materials can help students gain factual information about a culture. By reading fiction, students can vicariously identify with characters in the litera-ture and become emotionally sensitive to their circumstances. Both of these types of mate-rials can contribute to breaking down cultural barriers and dispelling prejudice.

When children from marginalized cultures see themselves represented in literature, it raises their self-esteem and helps them build positive self-concepts. Additionally, they are able to develop a pride in their heritage by gaining a better appreciation and understanding of who they are and the contributions made by individuals from their ethnic or religious backgrounds.

Students also learn about the commonalities of human experiences. They are able to understand and respect the ideas of universal rights and fundamental freedoms. This, in turn, prepares young people to live responsibly in a free society and contributes to peace and harmony among peoples.

EVALUATING MULTICULTURAL LITERATURE

When initially evaluating multicultural materials the literary elements of quality lit-erature should be applied. Discussions of these criteria can be found in books commonly used as textbooks in university courses dealing with children's literature (Huck, Hepler, Hickman, & Kiefer, 2002; Lukens, 2002; Norton & Norton, 2002; Sutherland, 1997; Tomlinson & Lynch-Brown, 2002). They include such criteria as well-developed charac-ters or meaningful themes. Additionally, there are specific criteria that should be applied to multicultural literature. The following are some questions that can be used to help evaluate multicultural literature:

- Does the text reflect an authentic portrayal of the group's way of life?
- Are the illustrations culturally accurate and nonstereotypical?
- Are characters from different cultures portrayed as individuals, without stereotyping?
- Does the book (or other material) show diversity within as well as across human cultures?
- Are issues presented in their true complexity as an integral part of the story?
- Is offensive language avoided?
- Does the dialect serve a legitimate purpose and is it accurate?
- Are factual and historical details accurate?

- Do people of color solve their own problems, rather than depending on white bene-
factors?
- Is the author qualified to write about the culture?

It is not vital that all multicultural materials deal with serious issues. People of color or persons from diverse religious and ethnic backgrounds should be present in as many books as possible. Nonetheless, we would not want young readers to think that every multi-cultural book deals with a social issue or is grim or depressing. Often, multicultural materi-als fall into two general categories: *culturally neutral* or *culturally specific*. In culturally neutral materials, the characters are from diverse backgrounds, but no particular social is-sue or concern is addressed. Examples of such books are Ezra Jack Keats's *A Snowy Day* and Faith Ringgold's *Tar Beach*. On the other hand, the characters in culturally specific materials are rooted in the culture, and social issues and themes are emphasized. Mildred Taylor's *Roll of Thunder, Hear My Cry* and Judith Ortiz Cofer's *An Island Like You: Sto-ries of the Barrio* are examples of culturally specific books. It is important that both of these types of multicultural literature be present in school media center collections (Bishop, 2003).

COLLECTION DEVELOPMENT AND MULTICULTURAL MATERIALS

Collection development of multicultural materials in a country that comprises many ethnic, racial, and religious cultures can be challenging. Not only is it necessary to include media that reflect the local demographics, it is also important to have items that provide stu-dents with the rich diversity of the United States and the world. Specific goals for creating such a collection should be included in a school media center's policy and procedures man-ual (Sharp, 1992). Media specialists should also make collection development selections that support the curriculum in their schools; thus, they should select multicultural materials that relate to themes that are presented in classroom lessons. The articles in the journal *Book Links: Connecting Books, Libraries, and Classrooms* (American Library Associa-tion) can be especially useful for this purpose. In addition to books, these articles frequently recommend videos and audiocassette titles.

Besides applying criteria to evaluate multicultural materials, school media special-ists can refer to bibliographic resources to help select quality multicultural materials for their collections. Some general multicultural resources that can be used include *Promoting a Global Community through Multicultural Children's Literature* (Teachers Idea Press, 2001) by Stanley F. Steiner; *Many Peoples, One Land: A Guide to New Multicultural Liter-ature for Children and Young Adults* (Greenwood, 2000) by Alethea K. Helbig and Agnes Regan Perkins; and *Multicultural Literature for Children and Young Adults: A Selected Listing of Books 1991–1996 by and about People of Color* (Wisconsin Department of Public Instruction, 1997).

Several resources focus on specific ethnic cultures as well. Sherry York's *Children's and Young Adult Literature by Native Americans* (Linworth, 2003) is a guide to help librari-ans, teachers, parents, and students locate books written by American Indians. This book includes publication and cataloging information, book review references, availability of tests from the Accelerated Reader or Reading Counts electronic reading programs, a list of American Indian storytellers and their Web sites, and brief biographies of authors and illus-trators. York provides similar types of information in her *Children's and Young Adult Lit-erature by Latino Writers* (Linworth, 2002). *The Coretta Scott King Awards Book: 1970-1999* (American Library Association, 1999) edited by Henrietta M. Smith features annotations of the award-winning titles, color illustrations from the books, and biographies of the authors. Critical evaluations of books by and about American Indians can be found in

Through Indian Eyes: The Native Experience in Books for Children (American Indian Studies Center, 1998).

The illustrations in multicultural picture books are the focus of Sylvia and Ken Marantz's *Multicultural Picture Books: Art for Understanding*, volumes I and II (Linworth, 1994, 1997). Stories and activities to promote literacy and cultural awareness are included in Tara McCarthy's *Multicultural Fables and Fairy Tales* (Scholastic, 1992). Mary Anne Pilger provides an index to multicultural projects in more than 1,700 books in *Multicultural Projects Index: Things to Make and Do to Celebrate Holidays Around the World* (Libraries Unlimited, 1998). More than a thousand titles are recommended in *Culturally Diverse Videos, Audios, and CD-ROMS for Children* (Neal-Schuman, 1999).

Numerous Web pages provide lists of multicultural materials for children and young adults. Information on some of these sites can be found in *Multicultural Resources on the Internet: The United States and Canada* (Libraries Unlimited, 1999) by Vicki Gregory, Marilyn Stauffer, and Thomas Keene.

Reviews of multicultural media can also be found in journals. Two journals that deal specifically with multicultural materials are *MultiCultural Review: Dedicated to a Better Understanding of Ethnic, Racial, and Religious Diversity* (Greenwood) and *Críticas: An English Speaker's Guide to the Latest Spanish Language Titles* (Cahners). These journals review multicultural items for children, teens, and adults.

PROGRAMMING WITH MULTICULTURAL LITERATURE

Multicultural programming in media centers should reach beyond ethnic foods, festivals, and folktales. Although all of these are important in understanding other cultures, too often librarians center their multicultural programs primarily on crafts. Sometimes media specialists can even reinforce stereotypes or trivialize cultural identity when they include crafts such as making Indian headdresses in their library programming. Multicultural programs should be designed to help students develop the social and cognitive skills they need to communicate in our increasingly diverse world, rather than be based wholly on "cultural tourism" (Harrington, 1994).

Through activities such as booktalking, storytelling, music, puppet shows, book discussions groups, and read-alouds media specialists can use multicultural literature to present multicultural perspectives. Producing booklists of multicultural materials for students, teachers, and parents also promotes multicultural educational goals.

When evaluating multicultural programming, one needs to consider whether the program is accurate and meaningful. A program should promote both interest and respect. The materials used should accurately represent cultural differences, as well as universal similarities.

Multicultural literature needs to be an integral part of all library programming. Although it may be appropriate to celebrate certain ethnic history months by providing displays of multicultural books from a specific culture, media specialists should include multicultural materials in all programs whenever possible. A broad spectrum of ethnic and cultural viewpoints should be represented in the materials, and care should always be taken to select media that avoid ethnic or racial stereotypes.

INTEGRATING MULTICULTURAL LITERATURE INTO THE CURRICULUM

Probably no writer has been more prolific than James A. Banks in dealing with the integration of multicultural studies and materials into the curriculum. Through his writings (1993, 1996, 2002, 2003) he has taught educators how to design lessons that focus on diversity.

In one of Banks's earlier writings (1989), he described four curricular models to integrate multicultural content into the regular curriculum. The lowest level, the "contributions approach," focuses on including the study of holidays and heroes from various ethnic backgrounds. In the "additive approach" the basic curriculum is not changed, but multicultural materials are added to topical units of study, such as folktales or food. These contributions and additive models seem to be the most common forms of addressing multiculturalism in the curriculum. However, there are two higher, more meaningful levels in Banks's hierarchy: the "transformation approach" and the "decision-making and social action approach." In the transformation approach, students are encouraged to view problems and issues from the perspective of different cultural groups. An example would be to look at the settling of the West from the perspective of the Native American Indians. In the highest level, decision making and social action, students are challenged to identify and help resolve issues and problems. This could include actions such as writing letters of concern to the media or government representatives, participating on a panel discussion dealing with ethnic or racial concerns, or preparing annotated booklists to be distributed to parents or students (Rasinski & Padak, 1990). School media specialists can be active in all of these levels by working collaboratively with teachers and students to provide multicultural materials that meet the objectives of each of the levels.

Multicultural issues are intrinsic to all areas of the curriculum; thus, it behooves school media specialists to plan collaboratively with all teachers to select the materials that support the curriculum and promote cultural consciousness. By providing the resources needed for multicultural educational curricula, media specialists can lead teachers and young people to an understanding and appreciation of cultural differences and to a commitment to diversity.

REFERENCES

American Association of School Librarians/Association for Educational Communications and Technology. (1988). *Information power: Guidelines for school library media programs*. Chicago: American Library Association.

Banks, J. A. (1989). Integrating the curriculum with ethnic content: Approaches and guidelines. In J. A. Banks & C. A. McGee Banks (Eds.), *Multicultural education: Issues and perspectives* (pp. 189–207). Needham Heights, MA: Allyn and Bacon.

Banks, J. A. (1993). *Multiethnic education: Theory and Practice* (3rd ed.). Boston: Allyn & Bacon.

Banks, J. A. (1996). *Teaching strategies for ethnic studies* (6th ed.). Boston: Allyn & Bacon.

Banks, J. A. (2002). *An introduction to multicultural education*. Boston: Allyn & Bacon.

Banks, J. A. (2003). *The handbook on multicultural education*. Somerset, NJ: Wiley.

Bishop, K. (2003). Making multicultural literature meaningful. *Knowledge Quest, 32*(1), 27–28.

Harrington, J. N. (1994). *Multiculturalism in library programming for children*. Chicago: American Library Association.

Huck, C. S., Hepler, S., Hickman, J., & Kiefer, B.Z. (2002). *Children's literature in the elementary school: With database, CD-ROM and litlinks activity book*. Blacklick, OH: McGraw Hill Higher Education.

Lukens, R. J. (2002). *A critical handbook of children's literature* (7th ed.). Old Tappan, NJ: Allyn & Bacon.

Norton, D. E., & Norton, S. (2002). *Through the eyes of a child* (6th ed.). Old Tappan, NJ: Prentice Hall.

Rasinski, T. V., & Padak, N. D. (1990). Multicultural learning through children's literature. *Language Arts, 67,* 576–580.

Rochman, H. (1993). *Promoting books for a multicultural world.* Chicago: American Library Association.

Sharp, P. T. (1992). Collection development in a multicultural world. In K. H. Howard and M. K. Laughlin (Eds.), *Multicultural aspects of library media programs* (pp. 165-192). Englewood, CO: Libraries Unlimited.

Sutherland, Z. (1997). *Children and books* (9th ed.). Reading, MA: Addison-Wesley.

Tomlinson, C. M., & Lynch-Brown, C. (2002). *The essentials of children's literature* (4th ed.). Boston: Allyn and Bacon.

Yokota, J. (1993). Issues in selecting multicultural children's literature. *Language Arts, 70,* 156–167.

Intellectual Freedom and the
Federal Government after 9/11

Rebecca P. Butler
Educational Technology, Research and Assessment,
Northern Illinois University, DeKalb

Traditionally, times of external pressure on the United States are often characterized by reactionary cries for measures that increase secrecy and security at the price of open access. (Task Force on Restrictions on Access to Government Information, 2003a, 4)

It was a sunny fall morning in DeKalb, Illinois. I had just stopped off at the local coffee shop for a cup before going off to work at Northern Illinois University (NIU). Instead of the cheery greeting I usually got from the woman working behind the counter, I heard, "Have you been listening to the radio? Did you hear about the bombing at the World Trade Center in New York?" The world, as we knew it, had changed. We were at war—a war with a frightening enemy called terrorism. It was September 11, 2001.

Since that date, the U.S. government has expanded its emphasis on keeping selected government documents from the public eye. Types and amounts of federal information no longer available to the general populace have multiplied. The primary reason, we are told, is that if we don't have access to this information, then terrorists also will not be able to access it. In a very real way, many U.S. national offices are censoring, perhaps now more than ever. Additionally, we now live with the thought that the FBI can order libraries and bookstores to turn over records of books we borrow or purchase, without our ever knowing that such a violation to our privacy has occurred. How does this affect those of us in libraries, schools, and technology centers, given the escalating world of information access? The following chapter addresses the federal government and information access in the twentieth and twenty-first centuries; the Bill of Rights; the USA Patriot Act, Homeland Security Act, Freedom of Information Act, and Ashcroft Memorandum, as well as other related acts and bills; the American Library Association's (ALA) stance on the issue; and where this leaves us as information professionals, as we attempt to balance safety with our freedoms.

A SELECTED HISTORY OF THE FEDERAL GOVERNMENT AND SECRECY IN THE TWENTIETH CENTURY

The purpose of this chapter is not to trace the history of the federal government in times of conflict. However, some background on where we have been is necessary to comprehend why we are where we are at the present. Therefore, this section looks briefly at the United States government and selected laws regarding information access and related issues in the twentieth century. The twentieth century is chosen because it was in 1917 that an influential law focusing on governmental secrecy, the Espionage Act, was passed.

The Espionage Act of 1917 was passed by Congress and signed into law by President Woodrow Wilson soon after the United States ended its neutrality and entered World War I on the side of the Allies. Two important provisions to come out of this act were the following:

1. "It became a crime to unlawfully obtain information pertaining to the national defense."

2. "It became a crime to unlawfully disclose such information to a foreign government or its agents." (Task Force on Restrictions on Access to Government Information [Task Force], 2003b, 7)

A year later (1918), Congress passed the Sedition Act. Basically, this act made speech abusive to the U.S. government and constitution illegal and curtailed language that might negatively influence our country's outcome in time of war. It was repealed in 1921 (Task Force, 2003b).

Since its inception, there have been several amendments to the Espionage Act, all of which address the prohibition of passing on government information in formats varying from print to photographs.

Other acts over the years have focused on public access to governmental information as well and, in some cases, have added statutory exemptions for the president, Congress, and selected governmental agencies. This means that although the public might not have all government information available to it, especially in times of war or conflict, its leaders could have such access. Certainly, after World War II, the notion of information that was classified as top secret from its inception became a reality with the Atomic Energy Act. At this same point in time (late 1940s–early 1950s), there existed a "counter-tendency preserving the older principle that democratic government rested upon the people's right to know what actions the government was taking" (Task Force, 2003b, p. 9). What this means is that, at the same time, two groups were in direct conflict—those approving a type of censorship to the public of selected government information (especially that considered "classified, top secret, secret, or confidential") and those promoting the rights of intellectual freedom to the same public and information. One result of this ongoing discord was the 1966 passage of the Freedom of Information Act (FOIA).

The FOIA gives the American public access to many federal documents, except those that fall under the categories of "Internal agency rules, Internal agency memoranda, Trade secrets, Bank reports, Oil and gas well data, Statutory exemptions ... Law enforcement records, National security, [and] privacy" (Task Force, 2003b, p. 10). A 1974 amendment to the FOIA provides the American public with the right to appeal to a court, if a federal agency refuses request for information. Under different presidential administrations, the FOIA's policies have been interpreted in either a more liberal or conservative manner. Both the Jimmy Carter's and Bill Clinton's administrations opened the door to public access of many federal documents; in contrast, the Ronald Reagan and George H. W. Bush administrations leaned more toward keeping such material classified and inaccessible to the public at large. Additionally, in 1996, Congress passed the Electronic Freedom of Information Act. This act means that information in digital and other electronically created formats is accessible to the public in the same manner as all other formats of information available under the FOIA.

Another act of importance to the subject of intellectual freedom and the federal government is the 1974 Privacy Act. The Privacy Act is intended to protect American citizens from law enforcement and other agencies which might, by collecting information about them, violate citizens' First Amendment rights (see Bill of Rights later in the chapter).

It is important at this point to also recognize a program instituted in 1973 by the Federal Bureau of Investigation (FBI). Called the Library Awareness Program, or LAP, the idea behind this plan was that the FBI could go into American libraries and obtain information on what materials "suspicious" people were using or checking out. ("Suspicious" individuals at that time, because it was during the Cold War, were often considered to be foreign nationals from Eastern-block countries; LaFeber, 1985.)

This program ended in the later part of the 1980s when it came under fire from the American Library Association, Congress, and other concerned organizations. As a result, all states except two (Kentucky and Hawaii) have made library records confidential. The USA Patriot Act (see below) supersedes this however. (This is able to happen because federal law supersedes state law.)

Now that we have briefly covered some of those laws of importance to us in the matter of intellectual freedom and the federal government, let us turn to those amendments to the U.S. Constitution of chief importance to us as we deal with information access and intellectual freedom.

THE BILL OF RIGHTS AND OTHER AMENDMENTS TO THE U.S. CONSTITUTION

The Bill of Rights is composed of the first ten amendments to the U.S. Constitution. In addition, there are seventeen more amendments. All constitutional amendments are significant to us as United States citizens. However, for the purposes of intellectual freedom, amendments I, IV, and XIV are listed and considered here.

Article [I.]

Congress shall make no law respecting an establishment of religion, or prohibiting the free exercise thereof; or abridging the freedom of speech, or of the press; or the right of the people peaceably to assemble, and to petition the Government for a redress of grievances. (Amendments to the Constitution, 2004, p. 1)

In terms of intellectual freedom, this amendment stresses the freedoms of speech and press. As American citizens, the First Amendment gives us the right to speak freely, to read freely, and for the press to publish information freely.

Article [IV.]

The right of the people to be secure in their persons, houses, papers, and effects, against unreasonable searches and seizures, shall not be violated, and no Warrants shall issue, but upon probable cause, supported by Oath or affirmation, and particularly describing the place to be searched, and the persons or things to be seized. (Amendments to the Constitution, 2004, p. 1)

Article IV (the Fourth Amendment) affirms intellectual freedom by promoting our rights to be safe in our own homes. It means that no one should be able to enter our homes or work places and do such things as remove our personal papers, read our private emails, listen to our phone conversations, or (in terms of libraries) access our checkout records without "probable cause" and a search warrant.

Article XIV. Section 1.

All persons born or naturalized in the United States, and subject to the jurisdiction thereof, are citizens of the United States and of the State wherein they reside. No State shall make or enforce any law which shall abridge the privileges or immunities of citizens of the United States; nor shall any State deprive any person of life, liberty, or property, without due process of law; nor deny to any person within its jurisdiction the equal protection of the laws. (Amendments to the Constitution, 2004, p. 4)

The Fourteenth Amendment informs the states that they cannot take away the federal rights of their citizens. Simply stated, in regard to intellectual freedom, this means that the states must abide by the First and Fourth Amendments. How has 9/11 changed things? Next, we discuss federal acts and bills and state activities since 9/11.

SINCE 9/11

Federal Responses to 9/11

One of the strongest federal responses to terrorism and increased national security was the passage of the USA Patriot Act (USA Patriot Act, 2001) soon after 9/11. This act was passed at a time when our country was in a turmoil, and "Congress clearly felt that the consequences of inaction outweighed the dangers of a bad law" (Campaign for Reader Privacy, n.d., p. 1). The USA Patriot Act is designed to make terrorist activities against the United States difficult. Additionally, this act facilitates communications among law enforcement organizations. One concern of special note for us as educators and librarians is found in Section 215. Section 215 gives the Federal Bureau of Investigation (FBI) the ability to apply for a secret court order to access any individual's purchasing or borrowing records from bookstores and libraries. "The government does not have to produce any evidence that you are a terrorist—or even that you are suspected of any crime! The order also gags bookstores and librarians, making it illegal to reveal that your records have been searched" (Campaign for Reader Privacy, 2004, p. 1). This means, any time we or our students check out materials, that the records of such activities could be accessed without our knowledge or consent. (It is important to be aware here, however, that some portions of the USA Patriot Act are set to expire on December 31, 2005, unless renewed by Congress. These portions are related to the disclosure of information and surveillance [Butler, 2003].) There is also yet another antiterrorism act on the horizon. Officially titled the Domestic Security Enhancement Act of 2003, this act is also known as "Patriot II." Although it has not officially been released, drafts of it are available on the Internet. According to Dr. David Cole, a Georgetown University law professor, Patriot II "would radically expand law enforcement and intelligence gathering authorities, reduce or eliminate judicial oversight over surveillance, authorize secret arrests, create a DNA database based on unchecked executive 'suspicion,' create new death penalties, and even seek to take American citizenship away from persons who belong to or support disfavored political groups" (Lewis & Mayle, 2003, 2). Given the earlier Bill of Rights discussion, it appears that there is a discrepancy between it and the USA Patriot Act.

Another Act of importance here is the Homeland Security Act of 2002. The nine main divisions or titles of this act are as follows: Department of Homeland Security; Information Analysis and Infrastructure Protection; Chemical, Biological, Radiological, and Nuclear Countermeasures; Border and Transportation Security; Emergency Preparedness and Response; Management; Coordination with Non-Federal Entities, Inspector General, United States Secret Service, General Provisions; Transition; and Conforming and Technical Amendments (Homeland Security Act, 2002). There are three areas of emphasis in this act threatening U.S. civil rights: "reduced privacy, increased government secrecy, (and) strengthened government protection of special interests" (Talanian, 2003, 1). The emphasis on "reduced privacy" is in direct contrast to the Fourth Amendment which protects U.S. citizens from "unreasonable searches and seizures." "Increased government secrecy" contrasts with the 1966 Freedom of Information Act, which was passed to ensure that the general public would have access to unclassified governmental information. The third area, "strengthened government protection of special interests," limits the public's ability to see how the government makes its decisions. In addition, it is also contrary to the Federal Advisory Committee Act of 1972.

In October of 2001, Attorney General John Ashcroft issued a memorandum on the Freedom of Information Act (Ashcroft, 2001). This memo focuses on another aspect of importance to students and faculty, researchers, librarians and others: the ability to access materials. In the Ashcroft Memorandum, the government agencies are informed that they will be protected if they decide to withhold information. What this means is that government information formerly available to us might not be so in the future, and that decisions to withhold such information will be supported by the federal government (Task Force on Restrictions on Access to Government Information, 2003a).

Another memo of importance to us is the Card Memo (Card, 2002). In this memo, the White House chief of staff, Andrew Card, instructs federal agencies to "be diligent in screening from public access information that might pertain to weapons of mass destruction or otherwise be of use to terrorists" (Task Force on Restrictions on Access to Government Information, 2003a, p. 3). In this way, the Card Memo may reclassify "sensitive" information so that it is not accessible to the public. Although in light of the terrorist attacks of September 11, 2001, this may make sense; this memo also thus removes such information from scientists and other researchers who may be able to use such materials for positive purposes.

It is also important to mention Executive Orders 13233 and 13292 here. The first order, issued by President George W. Bush, modifies the Presidential Records Act of 1978, giving the current president more leeway over what presidential documents can be released. The second executive order proposes reclassifying documents formerly declassified (Task Force on Restrictions on Access to Government Information, 2003a). Again, for those of us in education or libraries, this means that library professionals and patrons and students will have reduced ability to obtain information for research and study purposes.

Let's now look at the information "reclassified" or removed from the public eye by actions such as those just cited. Few published examples of what nonclassified materials have been denied to the American public are available. Most articles focus instead on explaining the law and possible abuses. Nonetheless, some examples of information access limitations include removing reports from several agency Web sites and reading rooms, deletion from public access of a number of Defense Technical Information Center records and reports, and elimination from public access of material on chemical terrorism (Centers for Disease Control). Other federal agencies that have removed information from the Web include the Environmental Protection Agency, the Agency for Toxic Substances and Disease Registry, the U.S. Geological Survey, the U.S. Office of Pipeline Safety, the Bureau of Transportation Statistics, the Fish and Wildlife Service, the Federal Aviation Administration, the Food and Drug Administration, National Aeronautics and Space Administration, and the Department of Defense (Butler, 2003; Electronic Frontier Foundation, 2004). The Department of Education also chose to redesign their Web site to "make it easier to use and to remove outdated data—and ensure that material on the site meshes with the Bush administration's political philosophy" (Davis, 2002, 1).

In the last two years, legislation has been introduced to amend the USA Patriot Act and protect our civil liberties. Such legislation includes the Library and Bookseller Protection Act, the Freedom to Read Protection Act, the Surveillance Oversight and Disclosure Act, the Library, Bookseller, and Personal Records Privacy Act, and the Protecting the Rights of Individuals Act. A recent piece, introduced on May 20, 2004, is the Strengthening Homeland Innovation to Emphasize Liberty, Democracy and Privacy Act (H.R. 4414; Strengthening Homeland Innovation to Emphasize Liberty, Democracy and Privacy Act, 2004). If passed, this act would require that all federal agencies appoint chief privacy officers. It would also allow for the creation of the "Commission on Privacy, Freedom and Homeland Security" in order that this group might review agencies' policies and protect our civil liberties (Strohm, 2004). Additionally, there is another piece of legislation waiting to be introduced: the Civil Liberties Restoration Act (CLRA; Bill of Rights Defense Committee, 2004a). CLRA also seeks to amend previous acts eroding our civil liberties.

State Responses to 9/11

States, too, have responded to the threat of terrorism. At least twenty-three states have either proposed or passed antiterrorist legislation. Much of this legislation restricts disclosure of specific state information to the public. Examples of the type of information restricted include: water supply documents, lists of laboratories in possession of biological agents, or state security plans (Task Force on Restrictions on Access to Government Information, 2003a). As the conflict between safety concerns and the public's right to know continues, states are also responding. Alaska, Hawaii, Maine, and Vermont have already passed statewide resolutions toward ensuring that federal anti-terrorism legislation does not erode civil liberties. Several other states are also looking into this, with a number of resolutions waiting to be addressed in their legislative bodies (Bill of Rights Defense Committee, 2004b).

Questions for educators and librarians include the following: Do students and patrons need access to the materials from these Web sites, library reading rooms, and more? Is this material available in another place or in another format (e.g., if not available on the Internet, can it be found in a government document depository)? Could such information be used to support possible terrorist activities? Should this material be public knowledge? Does such removal or lack of access stand in opposition to the Bill of Rights? Now let's take a look at one of the ways that the American Library Association is addressing this issue.

THE AMERICAN LIBRARY ASSOCIATION'S AD HOC TASK FORCE ON RESTRICTIONS ON ACCESS TO GOVERNMENT INFORMATION

How the Task Force Came into Being

Soon after the events of 9/11, the American Library Association's Government Documents Round Table (GODORT), the Legislation Committee, and Government Information Subcommittee (GIS) requested that the ALA president appoint an ad hoc committee to gather information and respond to federal government actions in light of recent terrorist activities. Thus, the "Task Force on Restrictions on Access to Government Information" came into being. It was concerned with the removal from public access of a wide variety of governmental documents, and its affect on libraries, librarians, and the patrons (including researchers, scientists, educators, students, and others) they serve. The makeup of the committee included representatives from a number of groups under the ALA umbrella, such as GODORT and GIS; the ALA Committee on Legislation; the Association for College and Research Libraries; the Young Adult Library Services Association; the Intellectual Freedom Committee; the Federal and Armed Forces Libraries Round Table; the Gay, Lesbian, Bisexual, Transgender Round Table; the Reference and User Services; the Chief Officers of State Library Agencies; and the American Association of School Librarians (AASL). In addition, there were also several ex officio and at large members, as well as two representatives from ALA's Washington, D.C., office.

In essence, ALA asked the task force to

> identify post 9/11 actions that government has taken limiting public access to government information, to review how these government responses to security threats might detrimentally impact the open flow of information necessary to our democratic society, and to recommend to ALA action and policy items in response to the government response. (Task Force on Restrictions on Access to Government Information, 2003a)

It was determined that within the scope of the ad hoc committee, given federal and some state government materials, certain issues needed to be addressed. Among them were the following:

- to maintain in a manner available to the public, records of all federal publications and web sites removed from public access;
- to obtain legal advice regarding the federal government's authority to withdraw or restrict access to government materials, given the conflict between safety concerns and the public's right to know;
- to preserve and archive information removed from public access;
- to locate options for accessing materials;
- to determine if statutes were being violated; and
- to determine what limitations, if any, should be on access. (Butler, 2003; Butler & Bull, 2002)

For the next few national ALA conferences, this task force met to discuss the issues and draft their response which was to be presented to ALA at the 2003 national summer convention.

Conclusions of the ALA Task Force

Conclusions of the task force included the following:

- that our current administration favors security over public access;
- that the ALA and other organizations which advocate open access to government information should be concerned not only about information currently being withheld, but also information that might be withheld from the general public in the future;
- that ALA should continue its lobbying of all governmental branches to communicate concern that information access policy decisions taken by the government in times of national security also take into account public access to this information;
- that ALA work with the government to make changes to some of the more stringent information access policies resulting from 9/11;
- that ALA maintain and expand its collaboration with organizations whose concerns on governmental information policy decisions are similar to their own;
- that ALA "press policy makers work with public stakeholders to implement clear, published procedures and criteria for decisions to withdraw information from public access, and those for reinstating that access" (Task Force on Restrictions on Access to Government Information, 2003a, 4); and
- that ALA work to find ways to maintain present or future access to those materials governmental agencies are removing from public view, or at least maintain a listing of all such materials removed. (Task Force on Restrictions on Access to Government Information, 2003a)

Recommendations of the ALA Task Force

Recommendations were extensive. The June 9, 2003, Report of the Task Force on Restrictions on Access to Government Information suggested that ALA:

- monitor the implementation of the Homeland Security Act for its impact on public access to government information and take timely action;
- oppose changes to the Freedom of Information Act or its implementation that would restrict access to government information;
- identify and evaluate criteria and procedures used by federal agencies to remove or restrict access to information previously available to the public based on assertions of national security concern, and take timely action;
- monitor the implementation of the current Executive Order (which give current and future U.S. presidents more control over what presidential documents can be released to the public) on classification of national security information ... and issues of classification and take appropriate action;
- advocate for preservation of public access to government information in coalition with other organizations ... with interest in public access to government information ...;
- collaborate with state and local organizations concerned with government information policy developments at the state and local levels pertaining to restrictions on access to government information;

- advise and assist state library associations and others in their advocacy efforts (as appropriate);

- monitor the restrictions of access to and removals of government information based on assertions of national security and communicate the library community's concerns with the appropriate policy makers;

- alert (ALA) members to policy developments that would restrict access to government information and encourage members to contact appropriate federal officials expressing their concerns;

- work with the Freedom to Read Foundation and other appropriate organizations toward obtaining a legal opinion providing libraries and librarians guidance on their liability as it relates to providing access to government information that has been withdrawn or withheld based on assertions of national security concern; and

- investigate various library-based models for distributed long-term access to government information as a mechanism for assuring that information withdrawn from public access by the government is not forever lost. (Task Force on Restrictions on Access to Government Information, 2003a, pp. 4–5)

Additionally, the task force recommended that future revisions of the ALA publication, Principles for the Networked World, also consider national security issues.

ALA listened to the task force and its concerned member organizations. For example, the American Library Association's Office of Intellectual Freedom is currently sponsoring a project entitled the Campaign for Reader Privacy (www.readerprivacy.org). The charge of this campaign is to encourage Congress to amend Section 215 of the USA Patriot Act to protect the privacy of library and bookstore records. Through its many divisions, round tables, and affiliates, ALA is working diligently to protect those rights of American citizens which it has determined are threatened by the USA Patriot Act and other federal and state actions.

WHAT DOES THIS MEAN TO EDUCATORS, LIBRARIANS, AND U.S. CITIZENS?

The government's responses to terrorism may have an impact on library professionals as well as students and patrons. It may mean that less information is available to researchers, journalists, and others. If so, this will limit what we teach and what we and our students learn. It may mean less privacy in our online activities, as well as checkout records of school library media centers and public libraries. Questions to ask regarding issues of information access and privacy are the following: Who defines what is sensitive information? Who should be empowered to decide what to do with such information? Can freedom of speech and national security coexist in our country? And what can library professionals do about this?

REFERENCES

Amendments to the Constitution. (2004). Retrieved January 26, 2005, from http://www.house.gov/Constitution/Amend.html

Ashcroft, John. (2001) *Memorandum for Heads of All Federal Departments and Agencies. Subject: The Freedom of Information Act.* (October 12, 2001). Retrieved January 26, 2005, from http://www.usdoj.gov/04foia/011012.htm

Bill of Rights Defense Committee. (2004a). *323 Civil liberties safe zones!* Retrieved January 26, 2005, from http://www.bordc.org/

Bill of Rights Defense Committee. (2004b). *Progress on statewide civil liberties resolutions.* Retrieved January 26, 2005, from http://www.bordc.org/states.htm

Butler, R.P. (2003, October). *Intellectual freedom and the federal government: An update on ALA's ad hoc task force on restrictions on access to government information: ALA's response to USA patriot act and other government restrictions to information access.* Paper presented at the meeting of the American Association of School Librarians National Conference, Chicago, IL.

Butler, R.P., & Bull, B. (2002). *An update on ALA's ad hoc task force on restrictions on access to government information.* Unpublished manuscript, Northern Illinois University at DeKalb, Illinois.

Campaign for Reader Privacy. (2004). *USA Patriot Act vs. your freedom: Tell Congress to restore reader privacy today!* (Available from the Office of Intellectual Freedom, American Library Association, 50 E. Huron St., Chicago, Illinois 60611)

Campaign for Reader Privacy. (n.d.). *What is Section 215?* Retrieved January 26, 2005, from http://www.readerprivacy.com?mod[type]=learn_more

Card, Andrew H., Jr. (2002) *Memorandum for Heads of Executive Departments and Agencies. Subject: Action to Safeguard Information Regarding Weapons of Mass Destruction and Other Sensitive Documents Related to Homeland Security.* [On-line]. Retrieved January 26, 2005, from http://www.usdoj.gov/oip/foiapost/2002foiapost10.htm

Davis, M. R. (2002). No URL left behind? Web scrub raises concerns. *Education Week.* Retrieved January 26, 2005, from http://www.edweek.org/ew/ewstory.cfm?slup=03web.h22

Electronic Frontier Foundation. (2004). *Chilling effects of anti-terrorism: "National security" toll on freedom of expression.* Retrieved January 26, 2005, from http://www.eff.org/Privacy/Surveillance/Terrorism/antiterrorism_chill.html

Freedom of Information Act of 1966. 5 U.S.C. 552 *et seq.*

Homeland Security Act of 2002. 6 U.S.C. 112 *et seq.*

LaFeber, W. (1985). *America, Russia, and the cold war: 1945–1984* (5th ed.). New York: Knopf.

Lewis, C., & Mayle, A. (2003). *Justice Dept. drafts sweeping expansion of anti-terrorism act.* Retrieved January 26, 2005, from http://www.publicintegrity.org/dtaweb/report.asp?ReportID =502&L1...

National Archives and Records Administration. (n.d.). *Clinton presidential materials project.* Retrieved January 26, 2005, from http://clinton.archives.gov/

Strengthening Homeland Innovation to Emphasize Liberty, Democracy and Privacy Act of 2004. H.R. 4414, 108th Congress, 2nd session. Retrieved January 26, 2005, from http://www.house.gov/hsc/democrats/pdf/press/040520_SHIELDPRIVACY2004L.PDF

Strohm, C. (2004). *House Democrats seek to beef up federal privacy protections.* Retrieved January 26, 2005, from http://www.govexec.com/dailyfed/0504/052004c1.htm

Talanian, N. (2003). *The Homeland Security Act: The Decline of privacy; the rise of government secrecy* [brochure]. Florence, MA: Bill of Rights Defense Committee.

Task Force on Restrictions on Access to Government Information. (2003a). *Report of the task force on restrictions on access to government information* (June 9, 2003). Washington, DC: American Library Association.

Task Force on Restrictions on Access to Government Information. (2003b). *Report of the task force on restrictions on access to government information.* (March 24, 2003). Washington, DC: American Library Association.

Uniting and Strengthening America by Providing Appropriate Tools Required to Intercept and Obstruct Terrorism (USA Patriot Act). Pub. Law 107-56. (2001).

USA Patriot Act. Retrieved January 26, 2005, from http://frwebgate.access.gpo.gov/cgi-bin/getdoc.cgi?dbname=107_cong_public_laws&docid=f:publ056.107

Educational Digital Libraries and School Media Programs: Opportunities, Challenges, and Visions

Marcia A. Mardis
Merit Network/University of Michigan

Ellen S. Hoffman
Eastern Michigan University

Throughout the world, digital libraries have proven themselves to be an important technology in promoting human development by providing information about health, agriculture, nutrition, and governmental policy and by cultural expression and preservation (Witten, Loots, Trujillo, & Bainbridge, 2002). This powerful technology has made its impact on higher education as well because of the increasing digitization of rare and special applications and the pervasive use of electronic repositories (Falk, 2003). Educators can greatly benefit from the ease of access to and variety of materials found in digital libraries. This chapter explores some of the implications of digital library use in elementary and secondary education.

A digital library is a computer-based system for acquiring, storing, organizing, searching, and distributing digital materials for end user access (Sharma & Vishwanathan, 2001). Gunn (2002) uses the term *virtual libraries* as an equivalent for the term digital libraries and emphasizes that these collections are different from information located through search engines like Google because they include a variety of formats and are designed with tools and scaffolds that serve a specific user community. Educational digital libraries are a subset of this group and focus on providing materials and services to instructors and students. K–12 users are an even more distinct subgroup because, as we explain later, they have unique and challenging requirements for content, description, and user assistance.

Digital libraries have the potential to set a broad mandate for reshaping the way school media is practiced in contemporary learning environments. This article explores the unique offerings and challenges that digital libraries bring to the K–12 environment in the context of competing legislative, organizational, social, economic, and educational demands. Educational systems, especially school libraries, can embrace digital library innovations as tools that can enhance their missions rather than as competitors that threaten their existence. There remain, however, a set of challenges representing a divide in vision, technologies, and organization that will establish the basis for such collaborative efforts.

In the next section, several examples of existing digital libraries are described to illustrate the state of the art, and the remainder focuses on recurring challenges and possibilities.

PROMISING PRACTICES: THREE EXEMPLARY DIGITAL LIBRARIES FOR STUDENTS AND TEACHERS

Digital libraries for education typically contain a range of media types, such as images, video, audio, text, and applets, that can support K–12 teaching and learning. In many instances, these media types are or can be combined to create powerful learning materials to use by teachers in instruction, as is most common today, or, potentially, by students who use it to enhance their own understanding of materials and concepts. One of the most commonly cited new capabilities of digital libraries is the ability for educators and students to also be contributors, so that there is a blurring of the "user" role not typical of brick-and-mortar libraries.

Digital libraries for education encompass both freely available and commercial offerings, many still in various stages of development with promises of new technologies and content as these become technically and economically feasible. Because of the complexities of the technologies and the less developed reading levels of young children, most digital libraries have been developed for older users and for adults both within and beyond education. Few developers have tackled the many challenges in creating a digital library that is readily usable by young children. The first example shows how digital libraries can support literacy and have a global impact.

THE INTERNATIONAL CHILDREN'S DIGITAL LIBRARY (ICDL)

In response to research-based evidence that suggests that children's use of books promotes development and that children's access to culturally diverse resources increases their sense to relatedness to the world, the International Children's Digital Library (http://icdlbooks.org) provides school media specialists, teachers, and children with an expansive collection of often difficult-to-locate multicultural literature. The University of Maryland College Park and the Internet Archive seeded the online collection with free access to 10,000 complete children's books in more than one hundred languages.

In addition to the size and breadth of the collection, the developers of the ICDL used their extensive experience with children as users and design partners to develop immediately usable interfaces. The technology to view the text and images from these books is designed to enable children to independently find books, read books, and communicate about books. Users can access the collection by geographic area and browse through icons or perform a visual search, thus eliminating the need for language sophistication that is often a barrier to children's information seeking (Cooper, 2002; Weeks et al., 2003). Once a book is located, users may choose from four reader types to view its content. The standard and plus reader tools allow the user to navigate through the books sequentially by using simple forward and back arrows or by clicking on a page image. The comic-strip book reader tool presents the pages in horizontal rows; users can zoom in on a desired page. The spiral reader presents users with the all the pages of the book in a single view, with the ability to zoom in by clicking on the desired page. Reader type preference seems to be linked to user age, so the ICDL developers have ensured that their collection will serve a diverse group of users.

ICDL is a unique digital library in many ways: it serves underserved user groups globally in terms of age, language, and culture, and provides materials that are beyond the capability of any physical school library to provide. In addition to giving children access to books from across the world, ICDL will eventually allow children to participate in a global community of readers. Planned structures for the digital library will allow children to share stories and illustrations as well as participate in discussions. ICDL is designed to be integrated into a public or school library collection so as the project evolves, librarians are included in its development.

Teachers' Domain

Studies of the influence of electronic resources on higher education have shown that the availability digital media types like images and data sets impacts curriculum content (Friedlander, 2003). Digital libraries, then, can affect the direction of curriculum reform in K–12 education to promote inquiry-based learning, increased visualization of concepts, and real-world application. Leading this transformation for teachers and secondary students is Teachers' Domain (http://teachersdomain.org). Part of the National Science Foundation's National Science Digital Library (http://www.nsdl.org), Teachers' Domain is an effort by the WGBH Education Foundation to deliver their broadcast programming linked to supporting educational content to increase its value and usability for teachers and students. This ever-expanding multimedia digital library includes high-quality video digitalized from NOVA, American Experience, and other public television productions and partners in the content areas of Life Science, Physical Science, and Engineering, with more recent additions representing the social sciences including the Civil Rights Movement and *Brown v. Board of Education.*

In each subject area, teachers and students can access online clips from broadcast programs, extended interview segments, interactive Web-based activities, photographs, animations, still images, text translations of original source documents, graphic representations, audio interviews, and outtake footage from WGBH programs. Each resource also includes explanatory background articles.

While Teachers' Domain provides diverse, rich, and high-quality resources for learning, it also employs many features that enable teachers to quickly and effectively integrate the digital library resources into their classrooms. The collection is accessed via a log-in that enables resources to be automatically correlated to national and state curriculum standards. Resources are accompanied by media-rich lesson plans created by curriculum experts that undergo an extensive peer-review process by content experts and teachers. Management tools allow users to create a My Resources list of items from the collection that can be organized into units, lessons, or student assignments. The Custom Resource folder feature allows users to gather resources to a particular folder along with submitted student work and notes on the resources. This feature enables exchange of annotated and compiled content from teacher to student, student to student, or student to teacher.

Teachers' Domain is an important digital library for educators in a number of ways. First, it couples widely recognized and validated content seamlessly with state and national curriculum standards. Second, its ancillary content is generated and reviewed by experts and practitioners (Blumenthal, 2003).The quality and diversity of the resources and rigorous vetting process combined with a small level of granularity ensure that teachers are delivered instructional materials that will help them immediately target curriculum objectives. Third, and most important, Teachers' Domain is a learning environment that couples its repository with workspace and tools that allow teachers to contextualize and customize resources.

The Digital Library for Earth System Education (DLESE)

The Digital Library for Earth System Education (DLESE), founded in 1998, is a mature but extremely progressive educational digital library that was initially aimed at higher education but has increasingly expanded and prioritized its mission to encompass K–12 needs. DLESE involves educators, students, and scientists working together to improve the quality, quantity, and efficiency of teaching and learning about earth systems at all levels, engaging digital library developers, educators, and students. Collection activities include identification of electronic materials for both teachers and learners such as lesson plans, maps, images, data sets, visualizations, assessment activities, curriculum, and online courses. DLESE provides access to data sets and imagery in the earth sciences, including the tools, interfaces, and user documentation that enable their effective use in educational settings. This combination of resources and supportive structures for teachers and learners is complemented by its evaluation activities that inform its own and other digital library developers about the behaviors and needs of users. Evaluation activities encourage a dynamic, iterative approach to operation of DLESE to continually improve quality and usability.

DLESE's vitality as a digital library is not only due to the variety of resources and user services it provides. This digital library intentionally cultivates community involvement by the recognition of user-as-contributor. Digital libraries enable an environment where users can share materials that they create for their own classroom environments; DLESE has fostered this sharing and gathered these resources. This blurring of the line between reader and author allows the dissemination of practitioner-generated activities that previously has not been possible beyond buildings or geographic locations (Gunn, 2002). The project is also sustained by the tireless work of the DLESE organization that is always engaging new user groups, undertaking technological improvements, and scanning the environment for educational changes. The power of this digital library is that it respects and encourages a strong human component in its activities. Rather than viewing the digital library as a one-direction location for information retrieval, DLESE can credit its ongoing success to the community of interactive users it has built and serves as a model for other developing digital library efforts because of its success.

BUILDING A LIBRARY OUT OF THE OPEN WEB: DIGITAL LIBRARY USER SERVICES

Although a number of fully functioning libraries are already making an impact on teaching and learning, the power of the digital world resides in the possibility of creating new structures and functions that will enhance what is possible in the digital library realm. Beyond established discrete collections, a number of digital library services exist to help users locate, organize, and present information on the open Web. Such services may be a way to accomplish tasks already present in school media centers more efficiently and effectively, or they may be an innovation that opens new opportunities to meet user needs. Two example areas are virtual reference services that represent enhancements to traditional user services, while pedagogical tools represent an emerging area to more powerfully support the use of digital libraries for instruction.

The Virtual Reference Desk

Building on the power and user familiarity with human-mediated information-seeking assistance, Digital reference, or "AskA," services are Internet-based question-and-answer services that connect users with experts and subject expertise, thus enhancing traditional reference services by expanding the range of expertise. Digital reference services use the Internet to connect people with people who can answer questions and support the development of skills, particularly by providing knowledgeable support that can add capabilities to a school. Access to human expertise in a range of topics is beyond what a traditional school library can offer (Gunn, 2002).

Query formation is often the most challenging part of students' information seeking process (Bilal, 2002; Fidel, 1999), and projects like the Virtual Reference Desk (http://www.vrd.org) help users negotiate their questions. The Virtual Reference Desk (VRD) Project coordinates a collaborative Internet-based question-and-answer service. The VRD project provides support to Ask-an-Expert (or AskA) services by accepting out-of-scope and overflow questions. When a subject specific AskA service receives questions beyond its scope, it can forward those questions to the VRD Network for assistance. If a question cannot be addressed by another participating service, it will be handled by one of the VRD Network Information Specialists, a librarian volunteering to respond with suggestions or an answer.

Although virtual reference services are widely available and many of them are for children, Silverstein (2003) points out that these services are built on structures designed for adults and often cannot meet the unique information needs and query difficulties of children. As a result, these services are still evolving to fully meet K–12 needs. Silverstein calls for custom-designed architecture with developmentally appropriate question negotiation methods, adapted and facilitated interactions with experts, and increased use of images in navigation and communication as steps in this emerging area. Until these "next-generation" reference services are deployed, current virtual reference services have the best impact when they are used by children and adults together. Nonetheless, projects like VRD enable users to create their own collections of authoritative information through interactions with experts and the review of previously asked questions and responses.

The Instructional Architect

Another promising digital library technology assists users, particularly teachers, with the presentation and contextualization of information. The Instructional Architect (http://ia.usu.edu), a project of Utah State University and funded by the National Science Foundation as part of the National Science Digital Library, allows the dynamic location and combination of learning objects from different digital library collections into personalized collections for learning and instruction. The software is open source and free to download. The Instructional Architect allows users to discover learning objects through its search and retrieval function and create immediately published Web pages that sequence and display learning objects (e.g., activities, simulations, or virtual manipulatives) along with user-generated narrative text. The Web pages structure the materials selected by an individual teacher who can then use them in the classroom or as student tutorials. Case studies of mathematics teachers who used the Instructional Architect revealed that the tool aided their classroom practice and encouraged the use of dynamically generated collections of learning objects in the classroom (Recker, Dorward, & Reinke, 2003). Scaffolding tools like Instructional Architect may allow school library media specialists to partner with teachers in the provision of instructional resources and enable teachers to take an active role in the combination and implementation of digital library resources.

TRENDS AND CHALLENGES

Digital libraries are already having an impact on school media practices as students increasingly favor online over traditional print materials (BellSouth Foundation, 2003; Corporation for Public Broadcasting, 2003; Levin & Arafeh, 2002; NetDay, 2004). Most schools have used CD-ROM or Web-based subscription services for enhancing their print collections for many years. As the Web became an increasingly rich source of freely available content, school media centers were often the first place in schools with computers connected to the Internet and remain one of the higher technology instructional areas in many school buildings (Lance, 2001). As a result, the school media center is increasingly not just a discrete and organized collection of information resource materials physically located in space, but the framework for a collection of "digital libraries." These newly added digital libraries dramatically increase the richness of the information sources by expanding the knowledge base beyond the school walls. At the same time, the expansion increases the complexity of managing the multiple information resources now part of the school media center collection, as well as the need to manage the physical and technology environment to serve a school's population (Gunn, 2002).

In the DL examples provided here, the potential is clearly visible that had been predicted for digital library applications within K–12 settings as the as early 1990s. Although the early forecasts of possibilities were often defined as much by the limitations of the visionaries and shaped by their backgrounds (Kling & Lamb, 1996), many of the promises are slowly being realized. Media specialists dreamed of larger collections readily available locally that would provide rapid access to rich content to support student learning without straining school budgets (Bennett, 2003; O'Connell, 2002). Technologists envisioned infrastructure that would support fast searching and retrieval of large quantities of relevant information, multimedia formats that were accessible to desktop systems, and distributed storage and integrated systems for information that would make the other side of the globe as accessible as the classroom (Brown, 2000). Educators saw digital libraries as increasing the possibilities for personalized delivery to meet the needs of each child and the support systems that would promote new and more powerful teaching and learning strategies (Bennett, 2003; Wallace, Krajcik, & Soloway, 1996). Policy makers are particularly supportive of digital libraries as a means to increase accountability and produce a generation of children who are technically and information literate to power the future economy (U.S. Department of Education, 2000).

At the same time, these future visions remain less than fully realized so that the emergence of digital library technologies has yet to be fully implemented and understood, particularly in terms of impact on school media centers directly and teaching and learning more broadly. Teaching has not changed substantially, users still have great difficulty in locating and retrieving quality information effectively, wonderful collections disappear for lack of social and economic models to support them, huge questions remain about the impact of educational technologies to significantly impact student learning, and children are increasingly finding that the richest sources of knowledge are outside the school building.

The Implications of New Technologies

Educational digital libraries face all the challenges of new technologies in terms of adoption of innovations, with the positive, negative, and unintended consequences on socioeconomic systems (Rogers, 1995). The challenges faced in implementing any new technology are then compounded by issues that are specific to information production, management, and distribution within a technical infrastructure that are specific to digital library technologies. The number of digital libraries may make more information available but most certainly has not made it easier to find or use. For example, the proliferation of digital libraries that use discrete interfaces, lack interoperability, and are intended to operate as stand-alone units do not work from a user perspective as these simply increase information glut—the user is required to "know" which library to choose and how to use its particular tools and services. The task of search and retrieval that was once hard enough in the school card catalog becomes a nightmare of different spaces, search techniques, metadata schemes, and information formats (Fitzgerald, 2001). Too much or inappropriate information is no more helpful than the limited sources that might have been found previously in the school's encyclopedias or outdated nonfiction collections.

Furthermore, as a subset of educational technologies, K–12 digital libraries have the additional challenges of adoption and sustainability within school systems. Widespread adoption of digital libraries faces similar challenges inherent in technology integration generally in schools, such as the need for leadership, planning, professional development, support, and improved infrastructure (Cuban, 2001; Jukes & McCain, 2000). Digital library challenges include systemic implementation, sustainable inclusion in classroom teaching, methods of resource discovery, and adequate levels of user support (Mardis, 2003).

These challenges of innovation and adoption have been well documented in other publications, and thus the focus for the rest of this chapter is on an emerging digital library theme that may have significant implications for school media centers and media specialists.

The Media Center as a Crucial Learning Hub

In the physical media center world, the focus of customer service has traditionally been on students. Although teachers were given support for their instruction in terms of understanding what was available for student use, collections were designed with a focus on the subjects children needed for school assignments and life skills. Media centers might have a few subscriptions and books on teacher professional topics, but this was rarely a central activity.

In the new world of education digital libraries, however, a new focus has emerged that is quite divergent from the traditional role of information access for students. Rather than simply building research subject area collections, educational digital libraries are putting a renewed emphasis on learning and teaching. As with schools more generally, the new emphasis is related to student achievement and an increased understanding of how children learn (Bransford, Brown, & Cocking, 2000).

In this vision of the future, education libraries are composed of learning objects which can be used and repurposed to support teaching and learning (Masullo & Mack, 1996). Although books and periodicals were fuel for papers and oral presentations, the new world of digital libraries views content as the discrete pieces that can be manipulated in multiple formats to create powerful learning tools that are customized by teachers to support classroom instruction and allow students to explore a subject in constructivist terms, accessing and combining learning objects to show the results not only of the product of their learning but also the process, thus supporting deeper content learning and critical thinking skills. Furthermore, users are expected to have the ability to contribute their products back to the library to be shared with other users, along with sharing ideas and commentary (Bruce & Leander, 1997; Wallace et al., 1996). Examples of these capabilities was outlined in the digital library examples provided earlier.

A result of this shift is also a change in user focus. Although school media centers have traditionally served students, digital libraries are increasingly including pedagogical components designed to serve instructional needs that have not been a part of any libraries in the past. These materials, specifically designed for teachers, may range from the high-quality, professionally produced and vetted materials in Teachers Domain to simple lesson plans or WebQuests created by individual teachers to use for a particular class on a particular subject.

This shift has multiple underlying causes, not the least being the difficulties cited earlier in producing digital infrastructure that is easily accessible by children. Furthermore, teachers are seen as the gatekeepers to technology use in schools, so that digital library success is seen as heavily dependant on the adoption by teachers (Mardis, 2003). At the same time, educators and librarians involved with digital libraries have a deep commitment to student learning and student achievement. As a result, the "education" in educational libraries is seen as key component that differentiates these from other digital libraries and from the Internet more generally.

Digital libraries are being designed in new ways to support teachers, teacher readiness to apply these features of digital libraries remains low. Studies show that teachers use the Internet primarily for professional tasks related to instruction rather than in the classroom and to support student learning, as, for example, seeking lesson plans or a handout to be printed (Levin & Arafeh, 2002; National School Boards Foundation, 2001). Where teachers are most likely to see a use for technology in classroom instruction is for research by students rather than the use of interactive or newly constructed Web lessons (NetDay, 2001). Even within the more limited domain of using technology as a research support tool, teachers are not well versed in the ability to find and evaluate materials. Teachers express concerns that digital information is not high quality, is too easily plagiarized, allows students to find inappropriate content, and that students are more concerned with quantity than quality (NetDay, 2001; Zhao, Tan, & Mishra, 2000/2001). Multiple studies of teacher searching behavior have shown that teachers use the Internet for small amounts of time, are frustrated by not being able to find appropriate content, have limited skills for searching, and often do not adequately evaluate information (Norris, Sullivan, Poirot, & Soloway, 2003).

CONCLUSION

As students' technological savvy increases, schools promote to one-to-one computing (Levin & Arafeh, 2002; NetDay, 2004) and media center budgets decline (Miller & Shontz, 2003). School library media specialists are struggling to retain relevance in school environments. Digital libraries stand to transform teaching and learning in ways that will actually increase the need for the media specialist and the school library media program, albeit with new professional and programmatic roles.

On a programmatic level, the school library media programs will need to expose students to information in many contexts and formats. As Friedlander (2003) points out, "The challenge of librarians in this highly heterogeneous information environment will be to recognize the needs of their immediate contexts and to combine a mix of resources in appropriate formats." Because most digital libraries provide a range of resources beyond what school library media specialists would be able to collect, organize, and present in their own collections, and because many digital libraries provide resources at little or no cost, the integration of digital libraries into school library media centers' offerings is an innovative and affordable addition to a collection development strategy.

The use of digital libraries in school library media programs also has the potential to help media specialists further the roles of teacher, instructional partner, information specialist, and program administrator as outlined in *Information Power* (American Association of School Librarians/Association for Educational Communications and Technology, 1998). When this seminal guide for media specialists was released in 1998, digital libraries for K–12 education were nascent. Since then, digital libraries have developed to the point that their focus on collecting, describing, and delivering high-quality educational resources in the context of a learning environment, has the potential to combine and transcend *Information Power*'s roles for working with educators and students.

For school library media specialists, the provision of these unique resources that can be accessed from the classroom, media center, or home can be an important lever to enhanced teacher collaboration and increased student service. The media center can, with the use of digital libraries, evolve from a repository of static material for direct student use to a facilitated learning environment that allows the dynamic combination of media types in various contexts inside and outside of the physical confines of the media center space. The need to support teachers and instruction in ways that have not been the traditional role of media specialists will require "time to nurture an environment that fosters knowledge creation and sharing. It also takes strong leadership and active promotion of successes" (O'Connell, 2002).

Media specialists, when conversant with easily accessible digital library resources, have the opportunity to work more closely with students by adapting to students' information seeking behaviors. Given that students primarily undertake their information seeking in informal contexts like home and public libraries (Levin & Arafeh, 2002; NetDay, 2004), media specialists can shift the focus of their work with students from information retrieval to resource evaluation. It will only become important in an increasingly information-rich environment that students be able to differentiate the information quality and resource appropriateness. The role of teaching these media-specific skills is not in the purview of any person in the school but is an ideal role for the media specialist.

Perhaps the most transcendent role that digital libraries offer school library media specialists is as content contributors. The power of educational digital library collections is that they allow users to contribute their own created and recombined classroom resources for others to use and adapt. Media specialists can embrace a dual role as a conduit for this material to digital library communities and contributors of resources that they create in collaboration with teachers or in their own instruction. Media specialists can also help teachers reuse and repackage their own creations to enable sharing.

Digital libraries are not repositories, nor are they another way in which Web-accessible information makes human mediators of information obsolete. They are pedagogical structures that permit media specialists to expand and enrich their roles as teachers, instructional partners, information specialists, and program administrators. Media specialists have a tremendous opportunity to situate themselves in the center of school activity as the gateways to cutting-edge resources, instead of as the gatekeepers to traditional materials.

REFERENCES

American Association of School Librarians/Association for Educational Communications and Technology. (1998). *Information power: Building partnerships for learning*. Chicago: American Library Association.

BellSouth Foundation. (2003). *The growing technology gap between schools and students: Findings from the BellSouth Power to Teach program*. Retrieved February 20, 2004, from http://www.bellsouthfoundation.org/pdfs/pttreport03.pdf

Bennett, S. (2003). *Redesigning libraries for learning*, Retrieved May 10, 2004, from http://www.clir/org/pubs/abstracts/pub122abst.html

Bilal, D. (2002). Children's use of the Yahoologans! Web search engine. III. Cognitive and physical behaviors on fully-self generated search tasks. *Journal of the American Society for Information Science and Technology, 53*, 1170–1183.

Blumenthal, D. (2003). Teacher's domain: Classroom media resources from public television's WGBH. *Knowledge Quest, 31*(3), 30–32.

Bransford, J., Brown, A. L., & Cocking, R. R. (Eds.). (2000). *How people learn: Brain, mind, experience, and school*. Washington, DC: National Academy Press.

Brown, J. S. (2000). Growing up digital: How the web changes work, education, and the ways people learn. *Change, 32*(2), 11–20.

Bruce, B. C., & Leander, K. M. (1997). Searching for digital libraries in education: Why computers cannot tell the story. *Library Trends, 45*(4), 746–770.

Cooper, L. Z. (2002). A case study of information-seeking behavior in 7-year-old children in a semistructured situation. *Journal of the American Society for Information Science and Technology, 53*(11), 904–922.

Corporation for Public Broadcasting. (2003). *Connected to the future: A report on children's Internet use from the Corporation for Public Broadcasting*. Retrieved May 30, 2003, from http://www.cpb.org/ed/resources/connected/

Cuban, L. (2001). *Oversold and underused: Computers in the classroom*. Cambridge, MA: Harvard University Press.

Falk, H. (2003). Developing digital libraries. *The Electronic Library, 21*(3), 258–261.

Fidel, R. (1999). A visit to the information mall: Web searching behavior of high school students. *Journal of the American Society for Information Science, 50*(1), 24–37.

Fitzgerald, M. (2001). Helping students use virtual libraries effectively. *Teacher Librarian, 29*(1), 8–15.

Friedlander, A. (2003). The Internet and Harry Potter. *Information Outlook, 7*(12), 18–25.

Gunn, H. (2002). Virtual libraries supporting student learning. *School Libraries Worldwide, 8*(2), 27–37.

Jukes, I., & McCain, T. (2000). *Windows on the future: Education in the age of technology*. Thousand Oaks, CA: Corwin Press.

Kling, R., & Lamb, R. (1996). Envisioning electronic publishing and digital libraries: How genres of analysis shape the characteristics of alternative visions. In R. P. Peek, G. Newby & L. Lunin (Eds.), *Scholarly publishing: The electronic frontier*. Cambridge, MA: MIT Press.

Lance, K. C. (2001). *Proof of the power: Recent research on the impact of school library media programs on the academic achievement of U.S. public school students* (Digest No. EDO-IR-2001-05). Syracuse, NY: ERIC Clearinghouse on Information & Technology.

Levin, D., & Arafeh, S. (2002). *The digital disconnect: The widening gap between Internet-savvy students and their schools*. Retrieved Sept. 23, 2002, from http://www.pewinternet.org/reports/

Mardis, M. (2003). If we build it, will they come? An overview of the issues in K–12 digital libraries. In M. Mardis (Ed.), *Developing digital libraries for K–12 education.* Syracuse, NY: ERIC Information Technology Clearinghouse.

Masullo, M., & Mack, R. (1996). Digital libraries in the science classroom. *D-Lib Magazine,* September. Retrieved May 10, 2004, from http://www.dlib.org/dlib/september96/eduport/09masullo.html

Miller, M. L., & Shontz, M. L. (2003, October 1). *The SLJ spending survey.* Retrieved May 10, 2004, from http://www.schoollibraryjournal.com/article/CA326338

National School Boards Foundation. (2001). *Are we there yet: Research and guidelines on schools use of the Internet.* Retrieved December 1, 2002, from http://www.nsbf.org/thereyet/fulltext.htm

NetDay. (2001). *The Internet, technology and teachers.* Retrieved Jan. 29, 2003, from http://www.netday.org/anniversary_survey.htm

NetDay. (2004). *Voices and views of today's tech-savvy students: National report on NetDay Speak Up for Students 2003.* Retrieved Apr. 15, 2004, from http://www.netday.org/speakupday2003_report.htm

Norris, C., Sullivan, T., Poirot, J., & Soloway, E. (2003). No access, no use, no impact: Snapshot surveys of educational technology in K–12. *Journal of Research on Technology in Education, 36*(1), 15–27.

O'Connell, J. (2002). Extending the reach of the school library. *School Libraries Worldwide, 8*(2), 21–26.

Recker, M., Dorward, J., & Reinke, D. (2003). The Instructional Architect: Theory and practice in the development and evaluation of digital library services. In M. Mardis (Ed.), Developing digital libraries for K–12 Education (pp. 107–117). Syracuse, NY: ERIC Clearinghouse of Information and Technology.

Rogers, E. M. (1995). *Diffusion of innovations* (4th ed.). New York: The Free Press.

Sharma, R. K., & Vishwanathan, K. R. (2001). Digital libraries: Development and challenges. *Library Review, 50*(1), 10–15.

Silverstein, J. (2003). Next-generation children's digital reference services: A research agenda. In M. Mardis (Ed.), *Developing digital libraries in K–12 education* (pp. 141–158). Syracuse, NY: ERIC Information & Technology Clearinghouse.

U.S. Department of Education. (2000, December). *The power of the Internet for learning: Moving from promise to practice. Report of the Web Based Education Commission to the President and the Congress of the United States. Washington, DC.,* Retrieved May 20, 2004, from http://www.ed.gov/offices/AC/WBEC/FinalReport/index.html

Wallace, R., Krajcik, J., & Soloway, E. (1996). Digital libraries in the science classroom. *D-Lib Magazine,* September. Retrieved May 10, 2004, from http://www.dlib.org/dlib/september96/umdl/09wallace.html

Weeks, A. C., Druin, A., Bederson, B. B., Hourcade, J. P., Rose, A., Farber, A., et al. (2003). Creating an international digital library for children. In M. Mardis (Ed.), *Developing digital libraries for K–12 education* (pp. 13–28). Syracuse, NY: ERIC Clearinghouse of Information & Technology.

Witten, I. H., Loots, M., Trujillo, M., & Bainbridge, D. (2002). The promise of digital libraries in developing countries. *The Electronic Library, 20*(1), 7–13.

Zhao, Y., Tan, S., & Mishra, P. (2000/2001). Teaching and learning: Whose computer is it? *Journal of Adolescent and Adult Literacy, 44*(4), 348–354.

Electronic Reference Services:
A Teen's-Eye View

Lesley Farmer
California State University Long Beach

Particularly in this digital age, school library media specialists need to meet teens on their ground: cyberspace. A mainstay of library media programs is reference service, which can be of real value to teens—once they understand its dimensions. Of course, to take optimum advantage of reference sources and services, teens need to be information literate. This chapter looks at reference services from a teen's perspective and offers school library media specialists ways to address adolescents' needs. It should be noted from the start that perceptions by both teenagers and by teacher librarians *about* teenagers can be equally simplistic. Thus, the behaviors and attitudes shared below represent the views of *some* teens, but not all. In the final analysis, each person has a unique perspective. Nonetheless, much of the discussion in this chapter reflects "normal" expected developmental issues of adolescents.

TEENAGERS AS INFORMATION SEEKERS

Why do teenagers look for information? Mainly for schoolwork. Sometimes for personal problems or consumer needs. Sometimes just out of curiosity. Often teenagers do not realize that they are doing research, per se. Their focus is on the bottom line, not the process to get there.

Where do teenagers go for information? Not unlike adults, they ask someone, and they go on the Internet. Typically, teens start where they were successful before, staying within their information literacy comfort zone, be it a favorite general encyclopedia or Google. Often they are unaware of online subscription article databases, either because they have not been given associated instruction by the school library media specialist or public librarian or they do not have access to such databases because of a library's financial constraints.

In terms of their searching strategy, teens tend to use unsophisticated methods. If they need just a little information, they are most likely to consult a general encyclopedia by pulling out the likely volume; going first to the index volume is not the usual pattern. If they need more in-depth information, they will typically search the OPAC (online public access catalog) for a book on the subject; looking for a chapter within a book is less common, and they may walk away from the catalog if there's not a whole book on their topic (e.g., praying mantis) rather than search under a more general subject heading (e.g., insects) and then looking in the book's index.

Indeed, the notion of keywords eludes some teenagers. They might not know the term but get the idea if the librarian teacher refers to the use of synonyms. Surprisingly, many teens do not understand—or choose not to use—Boolean operators. In fairness, Boolean AND and OR "behave" differently in formal logic situations than in everyday English. If Joe likes carrots and peas, it means he likes both: together or apart. But if Joe wanted to find out about carrots and about peas, he would need to input "carrots OR peas." Search engines might not provide that option except for advanced searching, which teens do not instantly see and so might ignore. If anything, teens are more likely to type in whole phrases in natural language rather than input "staccato"-like terms: "What are the breeding habits of elephants?" rather than "elephant and reproduction." Likewise, teens seldom use wildcard characters or make good use of "clustering" phrase symbols such as quotation marks, parentheses, or plus signs.

Teenagers' research strategy is goal centered; the process is not the main focus. If there's an easy way to get the answer, teens gravitate to that approach. The context for the research also might not be important to them. Additionally, they may follow a sequential research process in which the evaluation comes *only* at the end, and revisiting the search question or strategy might not occur to teens. This attitude really undermines teens who are not clear about their original task; they may soon become confused. On one hand, if they are easily frustrated, they may simply walk away from the whole project (or borrow other people's work); however, they may also doggedly persist in a fruitless direction, seemingly unable to change tactics halfway through. In either case, they are not successful. When such experiences occur at the last minute, because the teen did not plan ahead or miscalculated the amount of time needed to conduct the research process, success again evades this student.

REFERENCE SERVICE FROM A TEEN'S VIEWPOINT

What is reference service to a teen? Often it serves as a safety net or last resort when other avenues meet a dead end. Usually teens think of reference service relative to schoolwork; it does not occur to them that their search for a job or their need to find a way to cope when their parents divorce is an aspect of reference service. Frankly, teens may fail to see the difference between the terms reference *source* and reference *service*. Reference itself is often equated with facts. Period.

The process of asking the teacher librarian for reference or fact help may be uncomfortable. "I don't know what to ask." "I don't want to bother the librarian." "The librarian is always busy." "I'm not supposed to let other people do my work." Some teenagers don't want to admit ignorance in public. They may feel like Oliver Twist asking the headmaster, "Please, sir, I want some more," afraid that they will be chastised or, worse, ignored. Teen egos can be fragile, and a puzzled look from an authority may be perceived by a teen as an unfriendly rebuke.

What do teens want in terms of reference service? They want a friendly atmosphere, be it face-to-face or online. They assume that close collaboration occurs between classroom teacher and librarian and are disappointed when such teamwork does not exist. Although they might not admit it, teens do want guidance, be it bookmarked sites or a reserve cart; when they do get up the nerve to ask for help, they hope that the teacher librarian will provide just-in-time information that instantly and easily solves the problem. For teens, reference service should be easy to use and to the point: "Just the facts, ma'am."

A WORD ABOUT ELECTRONIC RESOURCES

Although this chapter focuses on electronic reference *service,* some aspects of electronic reference sources needs to be articulated because service can only be implemented in light of available resources. Furthermore, unlike print resources, which may require some instruction on their use, electronic resources may require additional training on the mechanical aspects of locating and navigating through them. Teacher librarians need to consider additional features of electronic reference sources. Issues arise in the areas of selection, storage and retrieval, access, and staffing. The following questions represent a few of the typical concerns.

- Is a print guide sheet needed to help students use a complex online database?
- Should earphones be provided to students so they can hear national anthems, for example, on the electronic encyclopedia?
- How much can students print out or download?

- How do Internet acceptable-use or filtering policies affect access and use of electronic reference sources?

- Can several students use the same electronic resource simultaneously?

- Should access to electronic resources be available from the classroom and from home?

- Should students and faculty be able to check out reference CD-ROMs?

- How are students with special needs accommodated relative to electronic resources?

- How much time is spent on technical troubleshooting rather than on instructional guidance? Who should do this?

STATIC ELECTRONIC REFERENCE SERVICES

Most school libraries that incorporate electronic reference resources begin with in-house electronic resources, such as CD-ROMs or library access to Internet sources. As holdings or access increases, teacher librarians see the need to organize these resources through Web pages or portals that act as a gatekeeper to information. Interestingly, this approach resembles the more traditional warehouse model of librarianship.

Web portals can assume a number of "configurations." Some libraries merely link to a district, library system, or commercial Web portal. Some sites address a number of objectives (e.g., library service, facilities, reference, reading, curriculum support, technology literacy), providing a few links in each area. Some Web portals have a very specific objective, such as a research shop, and may even focus on a few targeted subjects, such as science or social studies; this approach works best for magnet schools that can link to each other, thus providing an overall treatment across the curriculum. A few hardy souls try to accomplish many goals and do each in depth. The problem with this approach is that it requires substantial time to maintain all the links. For that reason, library Web portals often include a few significant library-friendly meta-sites (e.g., http://www.ipl.org, http://www.KidsClick.org, http://www.lii.org) and access to their own subscription databases.

A more substantive electronic reference "system" resembles a virtual library, which "provides remote access to library catalogs and databases, links to Internet resources, Internet-based tutorials, document delivery, and the provision of reference service over the phone or by email" (D'Angelo and Maid, 2000). In this scenario, the school community has physical and intellectual connection to information and information literacy experts. Usually, virtual libraries provide 24/7 (i.e., ongoing) service through a Web interface. Although few school libraries use this model, its existence provides an interesting model—and could well serve as a way for remote schools or districts to share resources and services. Also, virtual libraries reflect a dynamic model of librarianship rather than a passive offering of resources. There is an assumption that virtual libraries include an instructional function, with Web tutorials as well as online reference service that may be conducted in real time.

24/7 REFERENCE SERVICE: ALIGNMENT WITH TEENAGERS

Basically, 24/7 reference service implies that the user can get help from a librarian anytime, anywhere. In its infancy, 24/7 reference service meant leaving the librarian a telephone or e-mail message, with the expectation that the user would get an answer the next day. Nowadays, 24/7 reference service frequently exists in real time, with the user and the librarian chatting in a textual cyberspace (e.g., instant messaging model) or within a Web graphical user interface (GUI) interface where both parties can look at and navigate through shared documents.

Typical 24/7 reference service users may differ from face-to-face inquirers. They tend to be independent and self-motivated, preferring anonymity. Often they work outside the 9 A.M. to 5 P.M. timeframe, yet want convenient, just-in-time service. They are usually technologically comfortable. They have "traditional" language or physical barriers, such as being wheelchair bound or visually impaired. Some are just shy about asking for help in person. Several of these characteristics reflect typical teenager mind-sets.

For this reason alone, teacher librarians should consider providing 24/7 reference service because they may attract current nonusers of library services. Additionally, 24/7 reference service expands physical access to information beyond school hours and facilitates more school and community involvement. It demonstrates value-added service and thus serves as good public relations. Most important, though, 24/7 reference service helps students succeed.

As with electronic reference sources, decisions about 24/7 reference service require addressing several issues.

- Should the service be controlled in-house or outsourced? What staffing and server access are available? Usually the best solution is to join a consortium to share human and material resources.

- What kind of interface should be used? E-mail is the easiest; it is usually a good idea to have a separate e-mail address just for 24/7 service. Instant messaging provides real-time interaction. A common gateway interface (CGI) dialog box can facilitate e-mailing protocols and archiving but requires more technical expertise. A real-time chat that includes a "whiteboard" or other shared visual space to examine documents jointly provides the richest experience but usually entails buying special software programs and getting training to use the product effectively; additionally, some older computer systems might not be able to handle the interface.

- What is acceptable turnaround time? In the e-mail environment, 24 hours is usually considered satisfactory. Even real-time chats often require further research and a follow-up contact, so the 24 hours applies in that situation as well. Teenagers can be impatient with 24/7 service, so it can be better to e-mail them back rather than have them wait in cyberspace while the librarian is trying offline to find an obscure reference source. Whenever possible, the online librarian should tell the user explicitly what process is being done while the blank screen seems to be staring them in the face.

- What kinds of queries should be handled: ready reference, general homework, research projects? To what extent might the librarian unknowingly being doing the students' work? In that respect, having local teacher librarians staffing the service helps mitigate that possibility. However, the issue begs the question: to what extent should the librarian help: giving answers, providing citations, suggesting referrals? Some questions are asked all the time, so FAQ sheets or "scripts" can be developed for those queries, serving as a way to filter questions. For regular, anticipated assignments, librarians might create pathfinders with online links to aid students. Sophistical research projects provide a natural opportunity to teach information literacy skills and processes. Because online reference service is able to archive the "discussion," librarians can view those transcripts later on to develop guidelines for future service.

- What staffing is appropriate? Real-time interaction, in particular with sophisticated software programs, requires facility with online communication practice as well as good reference interviewing and searching skills. Moreover, the reference librarian should know the students' curriculum in order to make sense of the query. In that respect, public librarians might not be as effective as teacher librarians in providing 24/7 reference service to teens. Again, as young people tend to equate reference service with school work, they expect that the librarian will know about school assignments.

- What kind of access should be provided? Because these services are Web-based, they are broadcast publicly. A password might be appropriate to screen users. Sometimes a library card number is a means to authenticate users, although such mechanisms require further programming. Will the service be linked from the library Web portal or the school Web page? Should public libraries have a link to the school service? Having multiple ports of entry maximizes access, but it can also open the way for "outsiders" to monopolize the librarian's reference time.

- What funding factors need to be considered? Staffing, technical help, Web design, Web server hosting, Internet connectivity, software—all of these cost money.

- What legal and ethical issues need to be addressed: filtering, confidentiality and privacy, security, copyright, to name a few? One reason that schools are reluctant to provide access to 24/7 reference service is that the students may be guided to inappropriate web sites. Frankly, many schools do not permit telecommunications—e-mail or chat—because of safety concerns. In that respect, if districts or consortia can provide a K–12 service, some of the fears can be addressed more successfully.

DIGITAL REFERENCE INTERVIEWING WITH TEENS

As hinted earlier, online reference interviewing requires additional skills beyond traditional reference interaction. Although the same respect must be observed with relationships with users, librarians need to be mindful that online communication is much more abstract because it cannot transmit visual or aural cues. Explanations need to be made more explicit and clear. Jargon needs to be avoided. Online users may have difficulty explaining their informational needs both because of information literacy limitations and because of language limitations. It should be noted that e-mail questions are usually longer than "real-time" ones because there is less opportunity to fine-tune the query. Machine delays and crashes can be frustrating for both parties, and even a blank screen while either person is typing or searching can be confused with logging off. Indeed, librarians must be careful not to make assumptions about their online users, be it in terms of age, ability, knowledge, or behavior. Because teens can be sensitive and self-conscious, textual communication can be a delicate negotiation. Furthermore, in this abstract environment, librarians need to go the extra mile to demonstrate their responsiveness to their sometimes restless teens. Straw (2000), Kasowitz, Bennett, and Lankes (2000) offer the following tips to help optimize the interview.

- Determine the type of question (e.g., fact, source, research strategy) and context (school assignment, personal need, etc.).

- Use a mix of closed and open-ended questions; restate the question to make sure that it is understood by both parties. Break down complex queries into discreet steps.

- Know when to stop or contact later.

- Use a "letter correspondence" mind-set.

GETTING THE WORD OUT

As they contemplate 24/7 reference service, teacher librarians tend to worry that they will be overwhelmed with queries. In actuality, 24/7 service tends to be underutilized, and questions are often mundane—just as in face-to-face interactions (e.g., "When is the library open?" "How can I print out an article?" "How do I write a bibliography?"). Focus should be on good reference service, since users who have poor online experiences tend not to try the service again. Frankly, first-time users may try the service just out of curiosity rather than specific information need.

When 24/7 reference service begins, it might not get much use until the community learns about it. In some cases, librarians may wish to keep it low profile until they feel comfortable with the media. However, once they feel confident, they should market the service actively through school communication channels (e.g., announcements, signs, bookmarks, newsletters, newspapers, Web sites, e-mail, visits to the library during class time); telecommunications are especially important and relevant because they model the ultimate service. Teacher librarians should take advantage of available teen help to publicize the service and to provide input on what kind of reference help is needed. They should also consider partnering with public libraries and youth-serving agencies as they develop their online service. In short, teacher librarians should take risks, be flexible, be responsive, and do a good job! Efforts to provide high-quality electronic reference service adds value to the library and helps teens become more information literate.

REFERENCES AND FURTHER READING

Sample 24/7 Reference Services

http://www.247ref.org Metropolitan Cooperative Library System

http://www.pls.lib.ca.us/pls/vrd Peninsula Library System Q&A Café

http://www.ipl.org/ref/QUE Internet Public Library

http://www.askusquestions.com Northeastern Ohio Library Assn. Regl. Library System

http://www.loc.gov/cdrs Library of Congress Collaborative Digital Reference Service

Web Readings

California State University Information Competency Initiative. (2001). Retrieved from http://www.csupomona.edu/~kkdunn/Icassess/ictaskforce.html

Building and maintaining Internet information services: K–12 digital reference services Retrieved from http://ericir/syr.edu/ithome/monographs.html#Building

Interactive reference service at UC Irvine. Retrieved from http://www.ala.org/ acrl/paperhtm/a10.html

Reference and User Services Association. Retrieved from http://www.ala.org/rusa

Tenopir, C. (2001, July). Reference services in the new millennium. *Online, 22,* 40–45. Retrieved from http://www.ala.org/rusa/stnd_consumer.html

Wasik, J. (1999) Building and maintaining digital reference services. Syracuse, NY: ERIC. Retrieved from http://www.askeric.org/ithome/digests/digiref.html

Supporting Studies

Bilal, D. (2001, January 15). Children's use of the "Yahooligans!" Web search engine: II. Cognitive and physical behaviors on research tasks. *Journal of the American Society for Information Science and Technology, 52,* 118–136.

Branch, J. (2001, January) Information-seeking processes of junior high school students. *School Libraries Worldwide, 7,* 11–27.

Callison, D. (1997). Evolution of methods to measure student information use. *Library & Information Science Research, 19,* 347–357.

D'Angelo, B., & Maid, B. (2000, Spring), Virtual classroom, virtual library. *Reference & User Services Quarterly, 39,* 278–283.

Gross, M. (1999). Imposed queries in the school library media center. *Library & Information Science Research, 21,* 501–521.

Julien, H. (1999, January). Barriers to adolescents' information seeking for career decision making. *Journal of the American Society for Information Science, 50,* 38–48.

Kasowitz, A., Bennett, B., & Lankes, D. (2000, summer). Quality standards for digital reference consortia. *Reference & User Services Quarterly, 39,* 355–361.

Latrobe, K., & Havener, W.(1997, winter). The information-seeking behavior of high school honors students. *Journal of Youth Services in Libraries, 10,* 188–200.

Lien, C. (2000, summer). Approaches to Internet searching: An analysis of student in grades 2 to 12. *Journal of Instruction Delivery Systems, 14,* 3, 6–13.

Lubans, J. (1999, September). When students hit the surf: What kids really do on the Internet, and what they want from librarians. *School Library Journal, 45,* 144–147.

Montgomery, P., & Nancy Pickering (Eds.). (1999). *Information literacy and information skills instruction.* Englewood, CO: Libraries Unlimited.

Straw, J. (2000, summer). A virtual understanding. *Reference & User Services Quarterly, 39,* 376–378.

Vansickle, S. (2002, March) Tenth graders' search knowledge and use of the Web. *Knowledge Quest, 30,* 33–37.

Kindergarten Teacher:
A Comprehensive Internet Portal

Mike Tillman
California State University, Fresno, CA
Kindergarten Teacher

Kindergarten Teacher (http://www.lib.csufresno.edu/subjectresources/curriculumjuvenile/kindergarten/) was created during the spring of 2002. The main purpose of the Web site is to provide an extensive and organized collection of substantial educational content available via the Internet and of value to those who teach kindergarten. It is also intended to be of use to other early childhood and primary educators. The site contains original content including Web site descriptions, general Internet information, bibliographies, search terms, and database specific search strategies.

Teachers are very busy. A study conducted by Nelson and O'Brien (1993) found that American primary teachers spend more than thirty hours per week instructing students. They do not have a lot of time to sift through ungraded curriculum materials. Given these time restraints, a grade-specific collection of Internet resources has value.

Since Kindergarten Teacher's release to the public, it has been continuously publicized, updated, and upgraded. During the past two years, a significant amount of user feedback has been received and compiled. Kindergarten teachers and other education professionals have praised the Web site for being content rich, straightforward, user-friendly, extensive, and well chosen.

A permanent online repository of kindergarten bulletin boards, learning and literacy centers, art projects, worksheets, newsletters, communications to parents, lesson plans, and so on will facilitate improved accessibility to kindergarten-related content available on the Internet. Kindergarten Teacher may be an appropriate repository for these types of materials. A centralized online repository will only work if practicing kindergarten teachers are willing to donate curricular and organizational content.

Kindergarten Teacher can benefit from outreach efforts of school librarians. They have cultivated personal relationships with teachers who look to them for advice concerning curriculum materials and technology resources. School librarians can benefit from continuing development of a highly focused Web resource delivered by others within the profession.

DEVELOPMENT

Web site development for Kindergarten Teacher was initiated based on the premise that there was high-quality, kindergarten-appropriate content available. For example, the PBS series Between the Lions targets early educators, including kindergarten teachers. The program's curriculum goals include understanding the alphabetic principle, gaining knowledge of a substantial number of high-frequency words, and understanding key concepts and conventions of print (Strickland & Rath, 2000). Because all of these skill sets are easily adaptable to online presentation, an in-depth Web site was incorporated. All of the activities on the Web site are interactive and include detailed teaching strategies; many of the activities on the site are of value whether or not one has viewed the corresponding television episode. Lineberger (2000) concluded kindergartners who had used the program outperformed other kindergartners on a wide variety of reading achievement outcome measures.

However, even if one presumes there is significant content available, teachers may not be willing to invest the time required to harvest the resource. Coulson (1971) found teacher enthusiasm for computer use was directly proportional to the amount of work it did for them and inversely proportional to the amount of time they were expected to invest. Teachers may also resist the latest technology (the Internet) because they have already experienced excessive hype associated with numerous other types of technology. Hannifin and Savenye (1993, p. 13) concluded that "each technological breakthrough in the past resulted in disappointment followed by disillusionment and eventually abandonment." Furthermore, research conducted in the early 1980s indicated that teachers limit their search for curriculum materials to those that are immediately available. The research also revealed they spend relatively little time engaged in the process of materials selection. One would probably discover similar findings today. If such behaviors persist, it isn't hard to understand why teachers resist the most selection- and evaluation-intensive curriculum resources available to them: Internet curriculum materials.

A search for the word *kindergarten* on Google retrieves more than five million hits. Even searches for kindergarten curriculum and kindergarten lesson plans retrieve so many hits that this methodology is essentially unusable for the average time-stressed kindergarten teacher. Based on a preliminary survey conducted by several practicing kindergarten teachers and myself, a high percentage of kindergarten Internet sites are essentially useless. The vast majority of sites with usable content are limited in scope, often with just a handful of links. Most sites represent an individual kindergarten teacher's effort to organize a small number of links and activities for use in their classroom. Others are sites promoting teaching materials for sale or higher education programs. However, based on our survey, there is a tremendous amount of useful kindergarten content available on the Internet. If the materials are to be of use to the average preservice or inservice kindergarten teacher, they must be compiled in a comprehensive and organized manner.

During the collection development process thousands of Web sites were examined. Many selected sites include practical curriculum (e.g., lesson plans, thematic units, and learning centers). Others provide general information covering topics such as technology integration, classroom management and organization procedures, assessment, conferences, employment, grants, professional associations, and so on. Sites containing full text education research, theory, and practice; booklists; professional development resources; standards; pictures of bulletin boards, word walls, and literacy centers; worksheets; and teacher tools were also selected.

After the selection process was completed, original content that added value to selected links was incorporated. Part of the original content explains how to extract useful information from Internet databases. Lessons learned during the process were summarized, and useful kindergarten content not available on the Internet was identified.

DEVELOPMENT: LESSONS LEARNED

During the four months spent creating Kindergarten Teacher, many preconceived notions regarding the Internet were reinforced. There were also some pleasant surprises. For example, there are numerous alphabet-related activities. Most of them are interactive and engaging. Alphabet activities providing a wide array of practice opportunities as well as appealing graphics, animation, gamelike conditions, and audio are plentiful. These features will motivate many kindergartners (Duffelmeyer, 2002). Additionally, the Internet, in its entirety, contains a significant amount of content that kindergarten teachers have created. The vast majority of this content, however, cannot be accessed efficiently. The most significant lessons learned were the following:

1. Links can and do change. A link that used to lead to a collection of lesson plans or a student activity may now lead to pornography. One way this happens is when an individual or organization registers a domain, creates useful educational content, and places the content on the Internet. Many people link to and enter the site. Time passes and the original owner of the site forgets or declines

to renew the domain. The domain becomes available and is purchased by some-one else, who is free to post whatever type of content they like (Minkel, 2001). A link that led to chemistry teacher resources or primary undersea activities yesterday could lead to pornography today. This process is sometimes called "porn-napping" (Trotter, 2002).

2. The best original content for kindergarten teachers can be found on practicing kindergarten teacher's Web pages. According to Smolin and Lawless (2003) several organizations such as Homestead and Teacherweb allow teachers to create and post Web pages free of charge. Scholastic and Geocities provide sim-ilar services. However, most practicing kindergarten teacher's Web pages do not include a large amount of original content. Many sites with significant origi-nal content are hosted by providers who set limits on the number of visitors, provide relatively slow connections, and insert pop-up ads. If a site includes a lot of pictures it loads at an even slower pace. Despite these minor inconve-niences, practicing kindergarten teacher's Web pages are a primary resource for kindergarten teachers because of the quality and relevance of content found on the sites.

3. Kindergarten teachers can retrieve practical curricula such as lesson plans, the-matic units, and literacy centers on the Internet. They can also retrieve many other types of useful content via the Internet, including full-text education re-search, theory, and practice; classroom management and organization guide-lines; booklists; professional development resources; standards; teacher tools; pictures of bulletin boards, word walls, and literacy centers; technology integra-tion ideas; worksheets; assessment devices; and so on. For instance, ERIC in-cludes three thousand full-text digests covering a wide variety of topics of interest to kindergarten teachers.

4. Kindergarten-related listservs are an important source of practical ideas and curriculum. Many commercial and noncommercial sites facilitate this type of information exchange. Even if one doesn't participate, the archives of various listservs may prove invaluable because topics covered are selected by people in the field and content provided is (in general) created by people in the field. One should try to find listservs that specifically address their interests. As with any-thing else on the Internet, one should use caution when providing personal in-formation. Listservs and chat rooms are often under-monitored or unmonitored and inappropriate messages are sometimes posted.

5. The most efficient path to Internet content is through sites specifically devel-oped for kindergarten teachers. Other efficient paths include sites developed for preschool, early childhood, and primary teachers. Education sites created for prekindergarten through twelfth-grade teachers, such as Gateway to Educa-tional Materials, and sites created for the general public, such as Google, may (if used correctly) provide a wealth of kindergarten related content including lesson plans.

6. Many kindergarten teachers gain access to Internet content via listings of items, that is, directories. Search engines are an overlooked avenue to Internet content. Search engines generally allow the user to search by entering keywords rather than scanning a list of items. Lesson plans and education research, theory, and practice can sometimes be found most efficiently via search engines if the user has a basic understanding of appropriate search terms and search strategies. Kindergarten Teacher provides an in-depth listing of kindergarten related

search terms. One may have to input several variations of a search term. For instance, if one doesn't find what one is looking for when they use the term "family" they should try "families." Generally it is best to use lowercase letters when using search engines. Kindergarten Teacher also includes step-by-step search strategies for a wide variety of appropriate Internet search engines such as the Library of Congress's online catalog, ERIC, Educator's Reference Desk Lesson Plans, Gateway to Educational Materials, and Google Advanced Search.

7. In almost all cases, kindergarten teachers surf the Internet to access full-text materials. They want the entire unit plan or journal article online rather than a citation for a particular item. Sometimes it might be appropriate to surf the Internet for items not available in full-text online. Access to the Library of Congress's online catalog and ERIC can be gained via the Internet. They provide citations for and descriptions of more than a million education books, journal articles, and reports. If something has been published on an education-related topic, it will probably be included in one of these databases. The databases can be used to access information that can make teaching more fulfilling and productive. The databases are somewhat complex, and even though Kindergarten Teacher provides links to the databases as well as potential search terms and search strategies, individual users will need to spend some time searching them to use them proficiently. Also, users will need to record citations and contact a local university, college, or public library to obtain items directly or via interlibrary loan.

FEEDBACK

During the past two years, many Kindergarten Teacher visitors from all over the world (Israel, Vienna, Germany, Tokyo, etc.) have provided general comments such as "Great job!" or "Outstanding." Other commentary has been more specific. Kathy Schrock, developer of the well-respected Discovery School's Guide for Educators, described the site as "a well-chosen collection of resources and information for the kindergarten and primary teacher." The site was also described as "graphically simple, which means easy loading, and content rich." Other adjectives used to describe the site include straightforward, fresh, user-friendly, extensive, and up-to-date. Many stated the site was very easy to navigate. Numerous users who had created their own Web sites expressed appreciation and in some cases amazement at the amount of work invested in the project. One user remarked, "I am utterly amazed at the work you accomplished in a semester!" Another commented, "It looks like you spent quite a bit of time on the Internet. I envy you."

Beyond just commenting on the Web site, many users made specific requests. Kindergarten teachers have asked to have their classroom Web site listed on Kindergarten Teacher. They have also requested kindergarten-related curriculum information. One teacher asked, "Is there any good information on fine motor development and best practices for creating good pencil grips in 5 year olds?" Another requested a listing of clip-art books sorted by seasons or months. Others made inquiries regarding state and national kindergarten conferences, kindergarten teaching openings, and presentation opportunities at kindergarten conferences. Some teachers provided related information along with their requests. One teacher noted, "A common thread in kindergarten teacher discussions is learning centers and center management. It would be helpful to have ideas and suggestions for rotations, workboards, etc."

Not all requests were submitted by kindergarten teachers. Visitors requested information about kindergarten as an institution and a career. Entrepreneurs sought to have Web sites promoting software, search engines, and diagnostic tests listed on the Web site.

MAINTENANCE: LESSONS LEARNED

The profit motive, disappearing links, and time constraints present challenges to nearly everyone who tries to maintain a large Web site. All of these factors affected Kindergarten Teacher during its first two years of existence. The most significant lessons learned were the following:

1. The intent of most Internet educational content providers is to make money. Over the past two years, a significant portion of free Internet educational content disappeared, began to charge a fee for access, or began to include advertisements. While conducting research on the ephemeral nature of educational links, Markwell and Brooks (2002) noticed a trend whereby commercial content providers initially provided content without cost but then changed their policy and started to charge a fee for access. Even when a provider intends to supply a service free of charge, commercial interests can interfere with their mission. For much of past decade, Internet School Library Media Center, a Web site created by Inez Ramsey, served as a commercial free portal to much of what was on the Internet and of value to school librarians. As of June 6, 2003, her Web site indicated that it would be closing. One reason cited was "others are taking my work for profit" (Ramsey, 2003). What is available today might not be available tomorrow. What is free today might not be free tomorrow. What is ad-free today might not be ad-free tomorrow.

2. Links disappear at an alarming rate. Markwell and Brooks (2003) tracked 515 educational biology links and found that one-third of them disappeared within twenty-seven months. In a less scientific forum, Teachers' Net (2003) kindergarten chatboard participants expressed frustration regarding the large number of "dead" links on the Web sites they visit.

3. Web site maintenance continues to be extremely labor intensive. Falcigno and Green (1995) mention heavy maintenance requirements and the need to continually eliminate links. Not much has changed during the past decade. Available link-checking software is not foolproof. Occasionally, links need to be verified by a human. Kathy Schrock believes links need to be thoroughly checked every semester.

4. New links should be added on a regular basis. Continually finding and adding new, high-quality links is time-consuming and necessary. If a Web site is updated at least three or four times a year, users will be more likely to revisit because they will feel somebody is paying attention to it (Minkel, 2002). This assertion was reinforced by a Teacher Net kindergarten chatboard participant, who stated, "I am frustrated that some people don't update their Web sites very often. Some sites haven't changed in over a year."

5. Location- and subject-specific nuisances provide additional challenges. Shortly after Kindergarten Teacher was released to the public, all Web addresses at the university housing the site were changed. About a year later, ERIC went through a major restructuring. Because of the restructuring, a lot of content to which Kindergarten Teacher linked was altered, renamed, or relocated.

FUTURE POSSIBILITIES AND THE POTENTIAL ROLE
OF SCHOOL LIBRARY MEDIA CENTERS

Kindergarten Teacher intends to facilitate improved access to Internet resources. Teachers are busy. Technology resources are endless and searching for them is time-consuming. Education portals on the Web can help teachers overcome these obstacles (Smolin & Lawless, 2003). There are numerous portals seeking to meet the needs of kindergarten teachers. Many of these sites were created by practicing kindergarten teachers. Most kindergarten teachers do not have access to sophisticated technology or technology-related expertise. Nor do they have a lot of time to devote to Web site development. This lack of time is perhaps best expressed by a remark posted on the Teacher Net kindergarten chatboard: "Of course, I get frustrated when I go to a site and it hasn't been updated for years and the links are no longer valid links. However, I always remember that for the most part these Web sites are some teacher's hobby. They have a full-time job and a family to put before updating their Web site." Development of Kindergarten Teacher was undertaken by the Curriculum/Juvenile Library at California State University, Fresno (CSUF), because it has access to essential technology, labor, and curricular expertise.

In the future, the Web site will continue to grow and be publicized. Links will be checked often. Possible additions include a listserv, annotated bibliographies, and a related online course. Original teaching materials created by traditional CSUF teacher education students or students enrolled in the proposed online course may be added. The most exciting possibility involves the acquisition, organization, and posting of original curricular and organizational content created and used by practicing kindergarten teachers. Many of these initiatives will require supplemental funding. The quest for supplemental funding will be aided by the university's collective grant-seeking expertise.

School library media centers serve as a conduit to both information and technology and are therefore essential to Kindergarten Teacher's continuing growth and development. Yesson and Jones (2001) emphasized the importance of bringing in school librarians whenever K–12 outreach is attempted. They noted that school librarians can publicize a project by working with teachers at their school site. They can also get the word out through interactions with other librarians. Their understanding of the potential of a large, centralized database and relationships they have nurtured with teachers could be drawn on in an effort to convince practicing kindergarten teachers to post their creative works on the Web. In the past, libraries have effectively assisted projects like Kindergarten Teacher. For example, the American Library Association helped the highly successful Between the Lions initiative reach a broad audience (Strickland & Rath 2000). Kindergarten Teacher is certainly not in the same league as Between the Lions, but the same general dynamic is in play: librarians facilitating delivery of curriculum materials to teachers.

School librarians can benefit from Kindergarten Teacher's continuing growth and development. Part of a school library media center's mission is to introduce teachers to potential curriculum resources including those available on the Internet. According to Minkel (2002, p. 32) the average school librarian is "so loaded down with three-dimensional work with real people" that they do not have time to create and maintain substantial, focused Web sites. He suggests school librarians rely on Web sites built by other librarians. Research conducted by Markham and Brooks (2002) quantified the ephemeral nature of educational links. They called for education organizations to start pooling resources. Kindergarten Teacher provides school librarians with efficient access to a large pool of curriculum resources. It also facilitates the delivery of resources to early childhood educators, who may not be fully aware of all the Internet has to offer.

REFERENCES

Coulson, J. M. (1971). Computer-assisted instructional management for teachers. *AV Communications Review, 19,* 161–169.

Duffelmeyer, F. A. (2002). Alphabet activities on the Internet. *The Reading Teacher, 55,* 631–635.

Falcigno, K., & Green, T. (1995). Home page, sweet home page: Creating a Web presence. *Database, 20,* 20–28.

Hannafin, R., & Savenye, W. C. (1993). Technology in the classroom: The teacher's new role and resistance to it. *Educational Technology, 33,* 26–31.

Lineberger, D. (2000). *Summative evaluation of Between the Lions.* Unpublished manuscript, University of Kansas, Kansas City.

Markwell, J., & Brooks, D. W. (2002). Broken links: The ephemeral nature of educational WWW hyperlinks. *Journal of Science Education and Technology, 11,* 105–108.

Markwell, J., & Brooks, D. W. (2003). Link rot limits the usefulness of Web-based educational materials in biochemistry and molecular biology. *Biochemistry and Molecular Biology Education, 31,* 69–72.

Minkel, W. (2001). When good Web sites go bad. *School Library Journal, 47,* 37.

Minkel, W. (2002). Seeing the same old sites. *School Library Journal, 48,* 32–33.

Nelson, F. H., & O'Brien, T. (1993). *How U.S. teachers measure up internationally: A comparative study of teacher pay, training, and conditions of service.* Washington, DC: American Federation of Teachers.

Ramsey, I. L. (2003). *Internet school library media center.* Retrieved June 4, 2003, from http://falcon. jmu.edu/~ramseyil/

Smolin, L. I., & Lawless, K. A. (2003). Becoming literate in the technological age: New responsibilities and tools for teachers. *The Reading Teacher, 56,* 570–577.

Strickland, D. S., & Rath, L. K. (2000). *Between the Lions: Public Television promotes early literacy.* (ERIC Document Reproduction Service No. ED 444118)

Teachers' Net. (2003). *Kindergarten teachers' chatboard.* Retrieved February 24, 2003, from http:// teachers.net/mentors/kindergarten/

Trotter, A. (2002). Too often, educators' online links lead to nowhere. *Education Week 22,* 6–7.

Yesson, L., & Jones, L. (2001). Under construction: The California heritage project's K–12 outreach experience at the University of California, Berkeley. *College and Research Library News, 62,* 296–298.

Examining School Librarians' Engagement in the Practice of Questioning Technology

Karen Ferneding

*Department of Curriculum and Instruction, College of Education,
University of Illinois, Urbana—Champaign*

THE POLICY OF TECHNOCENTRISM

Since the publication of *A Nation at Risk* in 1983, reform efforts have focused on accountability, national and state standards, and the rapid diffusion of electronic technologies. Although accountability and standards-based policies have generated political controversy, the quest to infuse schools with information and computer technologies is generally accepted without debate. Unquestioned support for current technocentric reform policy is clearly evidenced by the fact that billions of dollars have been invested over the last decade in the building and maintenance of information and computer technology (ICT) systems in schools.

The promise of technological innovation as a means to reform schools has a long history. Educational scholar and historian Larry Cuban (1986, 2001) examined the process of the diffusion of various technological innovations into education and discovered the complexity of the adoption process. Although proponents of technology-based reforms are quick to blame educators as "computer phobic" or possessing a general indifference to innovation, Cuban's work indicates that educators' resistance arises from a complex interaction of personal, professional, and structural dynamics, thus exposing the inherent weakness in simplistic top-down, technological-fix approaches to educational reform.

In addition, historically, our culture has constructed technology in a highly simplistic and apolitical fashion. Western industrialized cultures equate technology with the Enlightenment myth of progress and therefore a technocratic ideal emphasizing technological innovation tacitly replaced political aspirations (Marx, 1994). This has been especially evident in the history of educational reform policy (Segal, 1996). The fact that technology has been politicized, as evidenced in our technocentric policy, is ironic given the fact that generally we construct technology as a "mere tool." Because this apolitical position exists as commonsense, it thus engenders what political theorist Langdon Winner (1986) has described as a "language of inevitably" whereby new technologies are infused and adopted without debate or discussion. In fact, the narrowing of current educational reform discourse toward functionalist ends and the fact that policy stands as a fait accompli without political debate has concerned many educational scholars. Even so, few have directly questioned the rapid diffusion of electronic technologies as official reform policy although some concerns have been raised.

For example, Winner (1986) argues that, as a society, we have adopted a sensibility about information technology and easy access to information that is akin to a "religious conviction." Those who defend the narrative of "mythinformation" essentialize access to information and envision that it will somehow "automatically produce a better world for human beings" (p. 105). Also, some critics believe that current reform policy, which focuses on the development of the Information Super Highway (ISH), acts to support a technocentric social vision and functionalist demands of a globalized market economy (Kenway, 1998; Peters, 1996). Indeed, education has been reconfigured as a viable market for electronic technology products, an outcome that reflects a general trend towards the privatization of the public sphere. Also, within the context of a generalized corporatization of the lifeworld, students are positioned as consumers whereas school librarians are no longer professional educators but rather technical experts. Both students and educators act within the context of control technologies in the form of standardized tests, accountability and surveillance systems and thus are positioned to perform in accordance with such systems of control. Whenever the issue of control is at stake, so is the issue of power/knowledge, although such factors are seldom discussed as being related to the adoption process.

More specific to the realm of classroom instruction, questions have arisen regarding the academic efficacy of computer-based instruction (Armstrong & Casement, 2000; Bowers, 2000; Healy, 1998; Oppenheimer, 1997) and the use of the Internet and an emphasis on access to information as a basis for instructional reform (Burniske & Monke, 2001; Morrison & Goldberg, 1996). Indeed, in his most recent book Cuban (2001) has called for a moratorium on a technology-based approach to educational reform. Others have raised concern about the wisdom in furthering a deeper immersion of youth within the realm of virtual space given the fact that psychosociological and physical problems have been related to increased exposure to other visual media such as television and video games (Subrahmanyam, Kraut, Greenfield, & Gross, 2000). Also, one may question the techno-utopian vision of policy makers given the present realities that characterize the life world—a breakdown of social structures, a rising number of children living in poverty and teen suicide, and the cooption of the social sphere by a mediated reality of consumerism and violence.

Given that a technocentric social vision of reform is dependent on the diffusion of computer and information technologies, this factor has directly affected the role of school librarians. Librarianship has become aligned with information science. Within schools, libraries as spaces have been renamed to reflect the centrality of technology and their different function—media labs or information resource centers. As experts in information science, one would assume that librarians would have a positive perspective on a technology-based reform policy. The research reported in this chapter, however, problemitizes this assumption.

DESCRIPTION OF THE RESEARCH PROJECT

In my research, I have examined and questioned the current discourse of educational reform policy through the voice of educators (Ferneding, 2003). In this chapter, I report on K–12 librarians' perceptions about current reform policy and more specifically their understanding about the nature of technology and how this may influence their attitudes toward the dominant technocentric discourse.

My informants were K–12 school librarians (or media specialists) from four schools located within central Texas (Table 1). I had also conducted interviews with several teachers and the school principals, but in this chapter I focus on the librarians' experiences and perceptions. My mode of inquiry is qualitative. I used a naturalistic based approach. The data sources consisted of in-depth, open-ended interviews, observations, and various artifacts from the sites such as a school's technology plan. The data analysis process reflects a contextual approach to technology adoption and features three interrelated levels: (1) the technopolitical realm of current technocentric reform discourse (2) the sociopolitical discourse of an alternative social vision which emphasizes democratic ideals and social justice, and (3) the changing role of school librarians within this dialectic of discourse.

Table 1. Study Participants

Site	Informant	Years of Service
Zepeda Elementary	Shelly	12
Shelton Valley Middle School	Mary Jane	26
Countryside Middle School	Annie	16
Lawrence High School	Barbara	12

The list in Table 1 indicates the pseudonyms of the librarian informants at each of the school sites. The years of service indicates how many years they had been involved in education. Some had been classroom teachers for a few years before becoming school librarians.

All of the schools featured in this study were subject to a state-mandated system of standardized tests (TAAS) that associated students' test scores with teachers' performance evaluations and accountability. Schools were also rated in terms of their level of performance and such ratings were published in local newspapers. Both teachers and students were expected to demonstrate a prescribed level of competency in computer technology skills. The state was moving away from a model that emphasized separate courses in technology skills to integration of computer technology throughout the curriculum. There was also considerable state and federal financial support allocated to the development of wide and local area network systems.

The sites were selected to ensure maximum variability in terms of context (e.g., rural versus suburban), students' socialeconomic status (SES), level of instruction (e.g., elementary, middle school, and high school), access to computer technology, and the degree to which computer and information technology was central to a school's reform program. However, because the state's official reform policy was essentially technocentric, many grant programs were specifically associated with technology-based reforms. Also, state and federal grants encouraged school districts' alignment with corporate interests. Indeed, local high-tech businesses were eager to support and participate in such technology-based grant programs. Thus, most school's official reform policies reflected the state's general technocentric vision. Given this contextual factor, all of the sites, with the exception of Zepeda, had adopted some form of a technology-based program of reform.

The following section offers the reader a snapshot or brief description of each of the site's individual stories of reform and examines the roles that the librarians played within the schools' reform efforts. This section is followed by the reporting of two dominant themes that emerged from the data by using the constant comparative method of analysis of the various data sources.

LIVING THE NARRATIVE OF TECHNOCENTRIC REFORM

Zepeda Elementary: A Social Space for Community Solidarity (A Tale of the Quest for Social Justice)

Zepeda resides in an urban setting that services a poor Hispanic community. Their reform program is affiliated with Texas Industrial Area Foundation (TIAF), a nationally based network of Interfaith Organizations dedicated to building community solidarity through raising the political awareness of poor and socially disenfranchised minority citizens. TIAF, in conjunction with a local community-based program dedicated to social justice, Alliance Schools Project (ASP), formed the basis of Zepeda's reform agenda. In effect, their goal, as a school, was to become not only an effective learning institution but also a public space for the community's social renewal. Thus, Zepeda situates technology at the periphery of its reform program while placing the goals of community solidarity and teachers' engagement in decision making at its center.

Zepeda's academic achievement was realized through reform conceived and developed by the teachers. It featured traditional teaching and instructional practices, although an interdisciplinary curriculum was used in the higher grades. Zepeda had no pullout program and used the state's gifted and talented curriculum for their standard curriculum for all students. At the time in which the interviews were conducted, the reforms had been in place for three years, and in that time Zepeda had moved from a nonperforming school to a high-performing school in all subject areas according to the rating of the state's system of standards.

The teachers had a positive relationship with their administrator and described his leadership style as "inspiring." Some teachers exercised their political agency by working with community and ASP leaders who sought to acquire social justice in terms of the community's struggle for decent housing, medical care, and safe neighborhoods. Shelly, the school librarian, was one such volunteer.

Shelly, formally trained as a librarian, had spent most of her twelve years as a school librarian at Zepeda. She was respected by her colleagues and clearly dedicated to the school's children, the community, and its Hispanic culture. Shelly was instrumental in developing and executing several highly effective reading and literacy programs at the school. Such programs were designed for students, parents, and the general community. In fact, all third-graders were on reading level within the third year of the reform program. The various programs addressed both instructional–curricular matters and sociocultural concerns. Both teachers and the administration gave Shelly extensive support. Parents were also supportive. Shelly was convinced, however, that the success of the literacy campaign, especially the support of parents, would not have been feasible without the assistance of ASP and TIAF.

Shelly, as did all other informants, expressed sensitivity to censorship and in particular supported a multicultural approach to curriculum. She was passionate about literacy as being a right for all poor children. She understood literacy from a contextual perspective, noting how teachers' attitudes toward poor students, SES, and cultural factors, such as the dominance of media in our culture, influenced students' ability and interest in reading. She was not opposed to the use of technology as an alternative instructional tool and in fact believed it could be a positive motivating factor. However, she also explained how the typical Zepeda student was isolated and rarely got out of their neighborhood. Thus, she was more inclined to spend money on field trips than software.

At the time of the interviews, the library's system was still not automated. Older students had access to three IBM computers that featured various CD-ROM resources. Access to the Internet was restricted to teachers (the computer with the modem was located behind Shelly's desk). Lines for the district's WAN (wide-area network) had been laid but Zepeda waited for extra state funding for the internal wiring of the building's LAN (local-area network). It seemed that the 1930s architecture posed a great challenge (and cost) in terms of the installation of the lines. Even so, Shelly and the school community did not seem bothered by the indefinite delay in having access to the state's telecommunications system. Shelly, the teachers, and the principal indicated that access to this technology, indeed computer technology in general, would not act as a "magic bullet" in terms of raising standardized test scores, increasing student engagement in learning, or enhance the schools presence as a public space for the community. In fact, the reform program emphasized the power of face-to-face dialogic-based interaction as a means of establishing community solidarity and thus any technological process that mediated social interaction and the experience of authentic communication was seen as suspect. In effect, the community of Zepeda had adopted a political discourse that served as a basis for questioning technology.

Shelton Valley Middle School:
Virtuality and Denial of the Absence of Lived Community (An Ironic Yarn)

Shelton Valley was a rural school servicing low- to middle-income white students. At the time of the interviews, the rural area it served was becoming a bedroom community of a nearby metropolitan area. This situation had created a drastic change in the sociocultural landscape and thus brought challenges to Shelton Valley in the form of in-creased enrollment, overcrowding, higher student–teacher ratios, and higher incidence of discipline-related problems associated with an obvious economic and cultural disparity be-tween wealthy suburbanites and their values and those of the traditional rural community.

The school culture, unlike Zepeda, was not characterized by solidarity with the local community. In fact, there was often contention between parents and teachers. Mistrust also existed between the teachers and the principal despite the official policy of site-based man-agement. Many teachers reported, especially those involved in the disbanded school tech-nology committee, that although the teachers, in the form of committees, would submit formal recommendations, the principal ignored these. Teachers expressed frustration and apathy in the face of such obvious shadow play and pointless intensification of their roles.

The schools' physical isolation added to the school's general sensibility of social iso-lation. Thus, the school sought to overcome its physical and social isolation through the promise of connectivity and the rhetoric of instantaneous access to the world. The irony is that such an endeavor would mean the substitution of real social interaction within actual physical social space by a *virtual* system of mediated communication that creates a simu-lated social reality. Despite their struggle to maintain the integrity of their rural values and community—an endeavor that would require questioning the assumption that *all* change signifies progress—the school and its community exhibited the typical pattern of technology adoption of the 1990s—acquisition of technology for the sake of technology (Kerr, 1996). Thus, Shelton Valley blindly adopted the dominant technocentric discourse as a guiding framework for the school's reform efforts.

Mary Jane, Shelton Valley's librarian, became the school's technology trailblazer and worked closely with the principal. In effect, the technology committee was a powerless entity that eventually disbanded, leaving Mary Jane and the principal to make all technology-related decisions. Mary Jane, who had received formal training as a librarian and had never been a classroom teacher, complained that the teachers were apathetic about technology is-sues. She seemed to have contempt for their alleged fear of the technical, their "computer phobia." In my interviews with several of the teachers, I did not find evidence of such spe-cific fears. Rather, many teachers experienced confusion over the fact that their desire to be active in decision making about technology-related issues was ignored.

The school struggled with many problems of a technical nature. For example, they at-tempted to upgrade an outdated Jostens Integrated Learning System (ILS) and invested sev-eral thousand dollars in the upgrade, then decided to abandon use of that particular system. In addition, the installation of a LAN connecting two computer labs with the library's bank of computers went on for several months because of a dispute between the contractor and Mary Jane. The extended period of technical problems generated lack of access to the computer labs and thus teacher frustration.

Mary Jane, convinced of the official technocentric reform policy's efficacy, believed that computers and telecommunication technology would save education mainly because it not only would usher in much needed reform, but also engage a radical restructuring that would ultimately lead to educational environments dominated by artificial intelligence-based instructional systems versus teachers. Her "technology fix" position afforded an un-questioning belief in the power of telecommunications and access to information as means of automatically addressing the myriad sociocultural problems facing educators within our complex postmodern society. Mary Jane thus exemplified the condition of mythinformation (Winner, 1986) more so than any other informant.

Mary Jane's unquestioning position, and the fact that she made decisions without input from teachers, had disallowed the discussion of substantive issues such as how electronic technologies would positively engage pedagogical and instructional goals. Thus, the school did not use the adoption process as an opportunity to develop a coherent, much less inspired, vision that aligned their curriculum and instructional endeavors with their choice in technological artifacts. The school was thus destined to repeat its past mistakes, such as exposing its growing population of "at risk" or "learning disabled" students to mind-numbing and repetitive drill and practice edutainment-style computer-based instructional systems. Such ILS systems can act to deskill both teachers and students. Moreover, this decision also reflected a failure to understand how social interaction is central to the development of a school's culture. In effect, this decision indicated a lack of sensitivity to servicing the needs of students whose general experience of alienation and separation within the structure of the educational system can be furthered in their instructional experience via the exposure to electronically automated instructional systems. In other words, Shelton Valley's lack of consciousness regarding its own culture of alienation and isolation seemed to be reflected in its decisions regarding the use of electronic technologies.

Countryside Middle School: Computer Technology as the Shining Crown (An Allegory of the Commodity as Fetish)

Countryside Middle School was located in a wealthy suburban area. When the data were collected, Countryside was the leading school in the metropolitan area in terms of its investment in computer and information technologies. The school's library was automated, and its bank of computers was networked. The school's LAN was connected to the district's WAN, and teachers were held accountable to demonstrate technology skills, as were their students. They had just hired a curriculum development and technology integration specialist who would mentor teachers in their efforts to integrate technology into their practice. Most schools in the metropolitan area could not afford subsidizing this position, although such support was needed in all schools.

Also, many students had access to computers and the Internet at home because several parents worked in the high-tech industry. Therefore, the school enjoyed considerable parental support for its technology-based reform agenda. The students also had access to computers and the Internet at school, although teachers closely monitored their activity. Countryside also had an active technology committee and a student computer club and supported summer computer camps for students and teachers.

The school had thus actualized an idealized techno-utopian vision of schools in the twenty-first century. Even so, the school strived for an even greater level of technology adoption by acquiring a substantial grant from the state in support of their continuing technology-based reform efforts. The school was indeed quite advanced in several ways. For example, courses designed to teach specific computer skills (with the exception of multimedia) had been completely eliminated. Instead, the school adopted a project-based curriculum that required students to demonstrate computer skills; a part of the curriculum for which teachers were responsible. Teachers were also required to engage in cross-disciplinary projects, although Annie, the school librarian, noted that recent budget cuts, an increase in enrollment and class size, and a decrease in teachers' planning time was putting a strain on teachers' collaborative efforts. These contextual factors, in addition to pressure resulting from the state's system of standardized testing, resulted in the intensification (Hargraves, 1994) of teachers' work. Despite this condition, as mentioned earlier, the school had acquired the funding to support the upgrade of their computer and information systems.

Parents and some teachers were proud of the apparent progressive position that the high-tech image afforded them within the general community. Annie had recently received her master's degree in library information science at the local university and was knowledgeable about information systems and management. She was convinced that access to information was imperative to the viability of public education and that the infusion of computer technology into schools and society in general was inevitable. Annie generally perceived the infusion of ICT as signifying progressivism, although she also expressed a disquieting ambivalence.

For example, Annie lamented the fact that she spent more time attending to the technical system rather than engaging in more traditional librarian duties of service—assisting students and teachers. She explained that although teachers needed training and support, her interaction with teachers had largely been reduced to mere e-mail exchanges. Having been a classroom teacher herself, she was sympathetic to those who resisted the use of computers. She did not perceive it as indicating technophobia as much as lack of time, pressure to conform to state standards, and the fact that teachers are sensitive to technical processes that mediate the instructional experience (a factor also noted by Larry Cuban [1986, 2001]). Indeed, Annie was concerned about the possible negative consequences of depending too much on mediated social interaction in educational settings. Even so, there was no doubt that Countryside held out its technology-based achievements as a feather in its cap that signified their having achieved the techno-utopian social vision as conceived by official educational reformers.

Lawrence High School—Erecting the Media Center:
A Chamber of Ambivalent Desire (A Gothic Epic)

Lawrence High School, located in an older suburban area of a sprawling metropolis, serviced the children of working poor Hispanic families. Despite the school's high dropout rate, it had low teacher turnover and was generally free of drug-related violence. The school was built in the late 1950s and had an average enrollment of approximately 2,200 students. The majority of students were of Hispanic and African American descent, and the majority of the teaching staff was white. In an effort to address the high dropout rate and better serve the needs of its students, Lawrence had developed a program for supporting schools within the school. One such school was dedicated to international business and technology while another was associated with the arts.

In general, the teachers expressed respect for the school's administration even while the school struggled with departmental isolation. Barbara, the head librarian, had formal training in library information science and was instrumental in both developing and executing a five-year plan to transition the library into a media center—an endeavor that was central to the school's general reform program. This particular reform effort was in its third year and Barbara believed that the school was making good progress.

The media center featured a multimedia lab, an automated indexing system, Internet access, and a bank of networked computers offering various databases. With extended hours of operation and open access to the Internet, parents and community members began using the Media Center facilities. This was exactly what Barbara had hoped would occur. Also, the school community decided to give the students open access to the computers and, to some degree, the Internet. Barbara believed this signified a major shift in teachers' attitudes toward the students in terms of entrusting them with more autonomy in their learning.

Barbara had worked hard to acquire state and federal funding to support the creation of the media center, but, even so, she reported that the effort was severely underfunded. They lacked funds to hire additional well-trained staff, and this meant that both teachers and students were denied adequate technical training. Fortunately, Barbara had support from a local university that had established a mentoring program for teachers interested in improving both their technology skills and developing means to integrate such skills into their practice.

Barbara perceived that some teachers lived an "8:00 A.M. to 3:30 P.M. mentality" and were thus "resistant to change or anything that placed demands on their time." Having previously taught in the classroom (high school language arts), Barbara was sympathetic to the time factor but was not tolerant of teachers whom she perceived were unwilling to "get out of their zone of comfort" and try new tools and learn new skills that might enhance their teaching. Even so, Barbara was aware that the success of the media lab reform effort rested on effective teacher training. She also explained that most educators did not comprehend the fundamental necessity for the careful planning of a technology-based reform program. Nor did most educators foresee how the necessity for continuous upgrading and maintenance would require escalating long-term financial investment.

Because of the population it served, Lawrence was committed to the fact that its students needed to acquire computer skills to be competitive in the job market—a practical but typically functionalist perspective. Having a background in literature and literacy, Barbara also noted how electronic technologies, although featuring some multimedia elements, were primarily text based. Lawrence had a serious problem with students being below grade level in their reading skills. She witnessed how this impeded students' academic achievement but was convinced that the computer motivated students despite their lack of reading skills. Much like Shelly at Zepeda, Barbara also perceived literacy in a contextual fashion, relating various challenges arising from SES, cultural values, peer pressure, and our highly mediated society (i.e., television and video games). She also, as we shall see, expressed ambivalence about the school's technology-based reform program.

HOW SCHOOL LIBRARIANS NARRATE TECHNOCENTRIC DISCOURSE: TWO GRAND THEMES

The two themes discussed in this section reflect the informants' responses to the following: (1) what defines or characterizes the Information Age, (2) what the "inevitability" of the infusion of electronic technologies into education means, (3) consideration of misgivings, if any, about the infusion of technology into education, and (4) what might be the relationship between society and technology.

Theme One: The Essentialization of Access to Information: "It's the Coming and Going of Data"

Annie at Countryside Middle School believed that access to information was central to educational reform. The fact that one could experience "instantaneous access to information" was in fact "revolutionizing" education. The speed aspect was foundational in that she predicted that literacy would become even more important because the hyper speed of instant access coupled with an increase in the amount of information would "make students *have* to be able to read faster." Because of the sheer amount of information, educators needed to teach how to access information rather than memorization of content. Indeed, the processing of content in the form of sorting had been mechanized. So "we teach them [students] how to find information." Also, she assumed that having students participate in online exchanges with students from other cultures automatically taught appreciation for cultural diversity. However, in their research on the use of online correspondence as an instructional tool, Burniske and Monke (2001) found this was not necessarily so. In fact, they discovered that such virtual based activities could inculcate a rather superficial construction of the Other.

Annie often made reference to the use of Boolean logic literally as a way of knowing and as a way of constructing how the human mind works, a rather technicist perspective. When asked if simply accessing information could be a superficial model of learning, she explained how "we teach them how to think in terms of key words" and proceeded to explain how the search engine software operates (e.g., field and keyword functions). This rather "Google-like" (Google is a popular Internet search engine) mentality toward the act of learning was evident in all informants with the exception of Shelly from Zepeda.

Many of the informants' perceptions about the notion of the Information Age could be characterized as a "seduction by the instantaneous." The conflation of access to information with knowledge building was commonsense. On the other hand, the informants displayed ambivalence about the "dream of access." For example, despite Annie's essentializing of information access, she also sensed that students needed to be engaged in classroom discussion to develop a deeper level of reflection and critical thinking. Even so, one is left with a lingering concern that Annie had been so smitten by the "Shining Crown of Technology" that such lucid moments of questioning might fade away with the next delivery of new software.

Mary Jane also essentialized access to information—it literally signified the processes of knowing and learning. She in fact characterized instruction as the "coming and going of information." Oddly enough, Mary Jane rationalized her position by referencing the phenomenon of information overload. She did not perceive the challenges this condition would likely create, however, especially for educators. In the following statement Mary Jane not only essentialized access to information, she also reduced the act of intellectual discovery to a mere push of a button. "Our knowledge base is expanding so rapidly that there is no way that students can learn even a minute portion of the information that is available, and I think we will go into a *total* idea of learning access rather than learning knowledge. So, if you can put your fingertips on it [the computer keyboard]—that's all you need."

In contrast, Shelly did not reference access to information as being essential to the educational experience or its reform. Rather, she believed the crisis in education arose from broader sociocultural issues such as our violent and media-saturated culture, an expanding division between the poor and wealthy, and a sense of apathy and social isolation evidenced in high rates of teen suicide. Shelly also lamented the "absolute resistance to reading" or "antiliteracy," a cultural condition she perceived to be exacerbated by a general cultural attitude of anti-intellectualism and a functional approach to the purpose of education. Moreover, the paradox that these two simultaneous conditions created—antiliteracy and the hyperproduction of data and information—added another layer of complexity about the Information Age that few educators seemed to acknowledge.

She explained how poverty and SES negatively affected the student's transition from elementary to middle school, especially their self-efficacy, and thus resulted in high dropout rates in middle school. The teachers at Zepeda can help students learn how to read but cannot change the structural reality of their poverty. Shelly had no idea how policy makers could conceive of the fact that access to information or computers in general could address such socioeconomic systemic issues.

Barbara's position regarding access to information was contradictory. She believed that the adoption of technology for the sake of technology posed a danger to education. Even so, she reasoned, students needed to have access to the technology because "it's the future." Barbara noted, "I interchange a lot of the time the word information with the word learning in education because they are one in the same." However, she qualified her position by acknowledging the potential for information overload (and by way of association, the generation of a meaninglessness by virtue of excess). For Barbara, the solution to this phenomenon was "management"—specifically, the management of information:

> The Information Age means that the volume of information is beyond comprehension. To be involved in the Information Age is not to know everything as it once was or to have a good feel for most of the references in the information available. But rather it's an ability to *access* certain information points. It is very different from the kinds of information our forefathers dealt with. I

think today it is incomprehensible and indescribable. It is doubling at an astounding exponential rate. That's why it's important to determine what kinds of information we need and then find a way to access it.

Barbara not only addressed the danger of information overload, but also saw problems related to the process of data management, noting how it can become a senseless recursive and thus a self-referent (and meaningless) act as process supercedes content. She in fact described this possibility in the following quotation:

> Information management opens all kinds of doors that were previously closed to an educator who is willing to look beyond the realm of the classroom. It opens up an entirely new kind of virtual world. But there is a price for such opportunities and thus we have to learn to use the kinds of informational gathering tools and be confident using them, so we are not wasting time just using the tools and not finding the answers to our questions.

Barbara's ambivalence toward the system of information production is reflected by her desire not just to manage but to control it. The fear of being overwhelmed, if not seduced, by a sea of data conjures a resistance that rests on the edge of obsession. One risks becoming engaged in the reductionary act of controlling the process of management itself. What one is *not* doing is creating meaning. Rather, one is immersed within a process of mechanization and operationalization. Not only has the librarian become part of the mechanized system of managing information, the commodification of information indicates the presence of the possible absence of meaning—a subtle but powerful irony.

Theme II: Holding the Tiger's Tail: Questioning Technology

Questioning technology is blasphemy for all educators, but especially for school librarians. Thus, to engage in this act of transgression is likened to the experience of holding on to a tiger's tail. One has grasped it, but is uncertain how or why. The challenge is to live the reality of the experience and not get discovered. There possibly exists some gendered element about this act. The transgression of questioning technology, as do all transgressions, has to do with Voice—the process of self-discovery and self-actualization. The emergence of this theme was both exhilarating and troubling as it signified for the informants a passage to an awakening from the given dream of technocentrism.

Mary Jane was a counterexample to this awakening. She displayed what could be described as contempt for teachers' resistance and reveled in an inside–outside divisiveness around the issue of technology adoption within Shelton Valley, thus assuming a technical elitist position. She advocated the replacement of teachers with computers— the ultimate technicist perspective and technological fix mindset. She embodied a position that signified complete and unquestioning allegiance to the technocentric social vision. Her stance, therefore, was fixed and autocratic. To her, the act of questioning technology was blasphemy, or worse, pointless.

Mary Jane's vision of education was thus: "Education will be totally different. You can have interaction through teleconferencing and you'll have some personnel on duty, but it won't be to the extent that we have personnel now—teachers." She did, however, believe that elementary students would require nurturing of an actual teacher. Mary Jane also stated that "schools won't be like we have today. They'll be totally computerized interaction. Everything will be done through terminals." A strong supporter of corporate sponsorship in educational reform, she envisioned distance education schools set up in shopping malls. Unfortunately, her vision has become a reality.

Mary Jane believed that technology is a "force" that operated as "a tool that brings progress towards more refinement" in society. Technology, therefore, is a positive, albeit inescapable, progressive force. It is important to point out that her generally technocentric position was unique at Shelton Valley. Most teachers and the administration expressed that the real crisis in education arose from systemic sociocultural issues, not the inability of schools to meet the demands of the Information Age. Also, most teachers offered a very complex understanding about the technology and society nexus and focused on the possibility of society's lack of control over its inventions. A typical case-in-point offered by other Shelton Valley informants was the threat of environmental disaster and the production of high tech war machines.

Shelly was by far the most engaged in the process of questioning technology. Her responses indicate an understanding about the nature of technology as being a possible autonomous and social process versus a mere tool. She perceived that the crisis in education reflected a larger social crisis that arose from a complex postmodern condition. In effect, she raised serious questions about the efficacy of a technocentric reform agenda.

Shelly explained, "I'd like to think that technology is an outgrowth of society's ability and knowledge. It's just a tool. Technology is a tool that we use to improve our lives. That is what I hope it is." But she noted how this perspective is naïve and largely inadequate. "To me, when I think in terms of how technology is becoming so powerful in our lives, that *we* have become the tool. That's scary! That's science fiction—computers taking over kind of thing." The issue made her feel uncomfortable, but she also noted how she was typical of society in terms of wanting to construct technology in a simplistic fashion and thus not think about it at all. "I am typical of society to a degree. It is one of those things that you really need to think about [society and technology] but I think I'll go home and read my books. It's just too 1984-ish. It has that quality, and I have no control over it."

Shelly further explained that people do not question current technocentric reform policy because they want to "buy into the idea that if getting information and an education and learning is going to get you a job and get it faster—that's good." It therefore is not culturally acceptable to question our relationship to technology "although it is probably the most important question facing society today." Even though she wanted to maintain the attitude that "technology was just one of the many tools that help us to create a healthier and happier, and more compassionate, society," she concluded that "somehow, technology and compassion just don't match."

Annie's ambivalent position regarding the intersection of technology, society, and education swung from adulation to cautionary tales. Although the use of computers and on-line-based instruction is "the way of the future," she was concerned about the loss of "the human element" in such processes. Annie was concerned about how our experience of "presence" within virtual spaces would diminish or somehow change the nature and meaning of relational knowing. She lamented the loss of meaningful communication in the form of conversation and personal contact due to the use of e-mail but found comfort in the efficient convenience of e-mail.

She explained how the use of computers and LCD panels for projection would be positive thing that would revolutionize teaching, as would laptop computers. She also expressed concern, however, about the development of a surveillance society. She envisioned how "everybody is going to have computers connected to their TV" and how this would allow access to personal information. Referencing George Orwell's dystopian narrative *1984*, she explained how "In the future, I see kind of in the science fiction movie where they have an entire wall as a giant screen in their home, and Big Brother could talk to you and always knew what you were doing. That's frightening to me, but it is the kind of thing we may be looking at."

She also worried about the fact that e-mail correspondence encouraged writing and thinking in a discontinuous and fragmentary manner and wondered whether this might have a possible negative impact on students' way of thinking. She also explained how students with social problems seem to be addicted to using the computer and worried about how this implies an escape from experiencing real human social interaction and the responsibilities that go along with it. This condition was especially problematic for children and adolescents.

Annie was also aware that educators can be "seduced by technology," adopting it into education just for the sake of having the technology. "Right now we are at the point of just feeling overpowered and we just need a 'get with it' kind of attitude and better get the machines and software. We have not sat back and tried to realize what effects it might have. I think it is something we need to be thinking about." She was in fact describing the condition at her school.

Another interesting aspect of Annie's ride on the tiger's tail is how she told her story. When relating to the "Shining Crown of Technology," her voice became rather strong but stilted, as if she were reciting a news report. When she moved into the realm of transgression and engaged in the act of questioning technology, her voice dropped into a whisper. It seemed she feared being overheard by someone (Big Brother?). It was clear that what she was saying arose from the space where secrets reside.

Barbara also exhibited a deep ambivalence. For her, the greatest danger arising from the society and technology nexus was the specter of virtuality. We were, she explained, losing the feel for the natural world as we become more immersed in virtual mediated experiences. This condition is leading to a "sterile emotionalism." But even with this intuitive and sensitive insight, Barbara seemed to need to retreat into an instrumental rationalist engineering-like mind-set. As noted earlier, it appears that humanity can be rescued from the challenges of information overload, through "management" of the information production system. But perhaps even Barbara's reflection on the issue of "management" signified the engagement of a deeper level of self-reflection about society's relationship to technology. The possibility that she was standing in a space of awakening from the techno-utopian dream, I believe, is evidenced in the following quotations. For example, she alludes to the rapid infusion of information and computer technologies into schools as a "cancerous growth."

> I guess I am a crooner for change and technology and yet I feel because its moving in such a rapidly changing world and because we are dealing with *so* much information, whatever information is, we're losing our feel for the world and I hate that. There are times when I have to step back and say—am I really moving in the right direction, because I am losing my feel for the earth and my feel for sunsets and a lot of things because I can access it online. Suddenly, I don't have to experience it. And that, in terms of the way we quote unquote experience time and space, in some senses, is not so good. And I can see it in the generation that is coming through our schools right now. I can see an insensitivity even more pronounced than what I ever noticed as a teenager or an adult, and think part of that insensitivity exists because we are exposed to so much through telecommunications and through visual stimuli seen on a screen and sitting in a chair instead of actually *feeling* the climate change, the wind in your face and all that. I really believe that we are moving ourselves very rapidly to a sterile kind of emotionalism.

> There are artificial forces driving the educational process. Until we take those out from our focal point and begin to look at some of the emotional and social forces that are driving it, we in a sense, are really not maybe doing the best thing for our students. There is an insensitivity that comes with technology and a detachment, so the role of the teacher *has* to be a facilitator. You have to be involved with those students more so than ever before. The educational process is *not* driven by economics, which it is now, and we all know that. The bottom line today is money. But we need to take that out of the center. And

again, that's where we need to consider how quickly we move on technological initiatives. Just having the technology in the schools, that's not what it's
all about. It *should* be something that enhances the educational process. . . .
The students have *got* to have the technology. But the one thing I think we
need to be careful about is that we don't move too rapidly. It *cannot* be this
continual cancerous kind of growth, because that is what it is when it
multiplies as quickly as it has.

REFLECTIONS: WHISPERING INTO THE TIGER'S EAR

The findings of this study indicate that school librarians engage in various levels of
questioning technology, a complex reflective process that is deeply connected to their social vision and professional practice. The "technological pessimism" (Marx, 1994), which
characterizes some aspects of their reflections, illustrates the possibility of an underlying
ambivalence toward a technology-based reform narrative. The presence of such ambivalence thus problemitizes the normative position of current technocentric reform policy and
the techno-utopian social vision it projects. Indeed, Andy Hargraves (1994) indicates that
the traditions of education are being challenged by postmodernity and thus educators must
necessarily "engage effectively with the images and technologies of the postmodern
world" while also maintaining "the cultural analysis, moral judgment and studied reflection
they threaten to supercede." Within this paradox they must "be both competent users and
innovators with technology and moral guardians against its most trivializing effects" (p.
76). This study indicates that school librarians can indeed engage in such thoughtful reflection. The problem is that such questioning of technology and technocentric reform is not a
normative act, and there exists few forums within which school librarians can feel safe to
voice their questioning.

In terms of the process of training educators, it is imperative that we focus not only on
acquiring technology skills but also examine what it means to live in a highly technological
society characterized by a mediated social sphere and commodity culture. Standing in a
place of transgression means holding on to the tail of the tiger and asking questions: What is
the nature of technology? Is it only a tool? How does it shape our way of knowing? What
does it mean if Boolean logic becomes the model and possibly a root metaphor for the way
the mind works? Is this a case where the technology acts to shape and frame a way of knowing and thus steps outside the realm of mere tool into that of a language with which we construct the meaning of our experiences? Mark Poster (1993) refers to how the mode of
information shapes consciousness—a proposal in the tradition of communication scholars
such as Harold Innis, Marshall McLuhan, Walter Ong, and James Carey. Our experiences
of the basic coordinates of time and space are altered with the use of ICT. Existing as both
techne and *politeia* (Winner, 1986) such technological systems exist as physical and social
constituting forces. The adoption process is therefore inherently political.

Burniske and Monke (2001) found that much of student online correspondence, perhaps because it is a disembodied experience of communication, can simply invite youth
who are already highly immersed within a mediated and hyperindividualized culture, to engage in deeper, more profound levels of narcissism. The screen becomes not a *window*
through which we gaze out into the world of virtual possibilities. Rather, it is a *mirror*, a
mirror that embodies the nebulous space of virtual selves (Turkle, 1984) and creates a reflexive experience that signifies the possibility of an awakening or a numbing to our participation in the process of social construction (Ferneding, 2002). Moreover, Habermas (1989)
proposes that the instrumental rationalist way of knowing that guides economic reason has
colonized the realm of the lifeworld. Neal Postman (1993) has described this situation—the
surrender of culture to technology—as "technopoly." Andre Gorz (1989) goes a step further, noting that the colonization of the lifeworld by technique and the creation of technical
culture in fact signifies the absence of culture and that we have lost the ability to notice.

What I am reaching for may seem too subtle. What could be the matter with providing more information, more data, and, ipso facto, more learning opportunities? Perhaps we have lost the art of the appreciation for subtlety in our quest to embrace excess—excess information, to be exact. The crisis in postmodern society that haunts educators is not the fact that schools do not support the economic aspirations of multinational corporate globalization (although this is another significant issue in and of itself). Rather, it is the presence of a crisis in meaning itself. The exponential proliferation of data indicates the absence of meaning, certainly wisdom. The process of meaning-making demands reflection, time spent alone in contemplation, quietude. Our daily hyperreality of virtual perpetual contact and the incessant drive to fill the void of silence and aloneness with media entertainment affords little time to engage such introspection.

Some critics of technocentric reform who also study the effects of technology and media on children, express concern about how constant and extended exposure to the simulacra of virtual reality (computers, online activities, TV, video games) has robbed them of interiority, the interior space of the Self (Healy, 1998). This, of course, is a perfect subjectivity for postmodern commodity culture—all surface, no depth. The act of surfing the Net and gathering data may offer the possibility of knowledge building. It may also inculcate as part of a hidden curriculum a commodity sensibility toward knowledge (Lyotard, 1984), thus furthering a commonsense way of knowing that combines instrumental rationalism with a voyeuristic positionality and a narcissistic subjectivity. The danger here, as noted by educational philosopher Maxine Greene (1988), is that to accept and become immersed within the given is not to engage in questioning, and thus is to become mystified by the given. There exists the creation of a peculiar silence signified by the dance of endless images and data files—a cacophony of information characterized by a denial of powerlessness and loss of voice. This is the irony of our Information Age.

What is the consciousness that we have about our devices, our techniques? What is the social vision that we express through them? I ask these questions as I attempt to make meaning of the informants' ambivalence toward the tools of their trade. What do they do with this ambivalence? How do they live it or not? Is much of it suppressed or denied in their everyday lives? What do they experience and what do they feel when, for example, they witness an incidence of "sterile emotionalism" in students? What does this mean to them in terms of their professional standpoint?

Reflecting on this act of research, I cannot help but wonder: Why must we put such faith in our machines? Why are we so blind to the obvious trade-offs they present? Engaging in questioning technology, riding the tail of the tiger, is not to express phobia of the technical. It is an expression of human inquiry. It is common sense. It is to engage in what Hannah Arendt had asked—What we are doing?

I leave readers one question to ponder as they contemplate a ride on the tiger's tail: Is it in fact a tale of progress that the role of the typical school librarian has possibly shifted from servicing people to servicing the information system itself?

REFERENCES

Armstrong, A., & Casement, C. (2000). *The child and the machine: How computers put our children's education at risk*. Beltsville, MD: Robins Lane Press.

Bowers, C. A. (2000). *Let them eat data*. Athens: University of Georgia Press.

Burniske R. W., & Monke, L. (2001). *Digital walls: Learning to teach in a post-modern world*. Albany, NY: SUNY Press.

Clandinin, D. J., & Connelly, F. M. (1995). *Teachers' professional knowledge landscape*. New York: Teachers College Press.

Cuban, L. (1986). *Teachers and machines: The classroom use of technology since 1920.* New York: Teachers College Press.

Cuban, L. (2001). *Oversold and underused: Computers in the classroom.* Cambridge, MA: Harvard University Press.

Ferneding, K. (2002). Stepping through the looking glass: Education within the space between modernity and postmodernity—the lifeworld, the body and technology, *Journal of Curriculum Theorizing, 18*(3), 53–64.

Ferneding, K. (2003). *Questioning technology: Electronic technologies and educational reform.* NY: Peter Lang.

Gorz, A. (1984). *Critique of economic reason.* New York: Verso.

Greene, M. (1988). *The dialectic of freedom.* New York: Teachers College Press.

Habermas, J. (1989). Technology and science as "ideology." In S. Seidman (Ed.), *Jurgen Habermas on society and politics: A reader.* Boston: Beacon Press.

Hargraves, A. (1994). *Changing teachers, changing times.* London: Cassell.

Healy, J. (1998). *Failure to connect: How computers affect our children's minds—for better and worse.* New York: Simon & Schuster.

Kenway, J. (1998). Pulp fictions? Education, markets and the Information Superhighway. In D. Carlson & M. W. Apple (Eds.), *Power/knowledge/pedagogy: The meaning of democratic education in unsettling times.* Boulder, CO: Westview Press.

Kerr, S. (1996). Visions of sugarplums: The future of technology, education and the schools. In Stephen T. Kerr (Ed.), *Technology and the future of schooling* (pp. 1-25). Chicago: University of Chicago Press.

Lyotard, J. (1984). *The postmodern condition.* Minneapolis: University of Minnesota Press.

Marx, L. (1994). The idea of "technology" and postmodern pessimism. In Y. Ezrahi, E. Mendelsohn, & H. Segal (Eds.), *Technology, pessimism and postmodernism* (pp. 11–28). Amherst: University of Massachusetts Press.

Morrison, D., & Goldberg, B. (1996). New actors, new connections: The role of local information infrastructures in school reform. In T. Kosman (Ed.), *CSCL: Theory and practice of an emerging paradigm* (pp. 125–145). Mahwah, NJ: Erlbaum.

Oppenheimer, T. (1997, July). The computer delusion. *The Atlantic Monthly,* pp. 45–62.

Peters, M. (1996). *Poststructuralism, politics and education.* Westport, CT: Bergin & Garvey.

Poster, M. (1993). *Politics, theory and contemporary culture.* New York: Columbia University Press.

Postman, N. (1993). *Technopoly: The surrender of culture to technology.* New York: Vintage.

Segal, H. P. (1996). The American ideology of technological progress: Historical perspectives. In S. Kerr (Ed.), *Technology and the future of schooling* (pp. 24–48). Chicago: University of Chicago Press.

Subrahmanyam, K., Kraut, R., Greenfield P., & Gross, E. (2000). The impact of home computer use on children's activities and development. In R. E. Behrman (Ed.), *The future of children: Children and computer technology, 10*(2), 123–144. Los Altos, CA: The David and Lucile Packard Foundation.

Turkle, S. (1984). *The second self: Computers and the human spirit.* New York: Simon & Schuster.

Winner, L. (1986). *The whale and the reactor.* Chicago: University of Chicago Press.

Perceptions of the Role and Functions of the School Library Professional in K–12 Education by School Principals

Betty Marcoux

The Information School of The University of Washington

When asking educators the question about what would be missed most if the school library were to close, the answer can be telling. It correlates significantly with the issue of budgetary constraints and learning priorities that principals face each year. It also correlates significantly with the issue of the perception of the school library media program, its professional(s), and the value they offer to overall student learning (Hartzell, 2003b; Haycock, 1999; Oberg, 1995, 1997; Oberg, Hay, & Henri, 2000; Wilson & Blake, 1993). Recently various teachers, students, and administrators associated with finalists for the School Library Media Program of the Year (SLMPY) 2004 award were asked this question. The most telling response was usually from the principals or associated administrators. It varied from a shrug to absolute panic at the thought. The evidence of value of school library professionals and their program to the overall learning at a school was dramatically distinct, and principals seemed to articulate this in various ways. Some spoke about the person, some spoke about the resources, but few spoke about the connection between these professionals and learning. When administrators did talk about learning and the school library, regardless of budget resources available to them, the library and its professional(s) were highly valued as integral to the learning process and student success. Clearly, the administrators who spoke about the integral nature of the school library and its professional(s) in their buildings got it and could articulate it. They understood the connection between teaching and learning and the school library professional (Campbell & Cordiero, 1996; Wilson & Lyders, 2001). They understood the value of this professional as a full and important member of the teaching and learning team and believed that this important role could not be filled by any other professional within the building. They had the information that mattered.

In 2003, *School Library Journal* began awarding the Administrator of the Year Award to administrators who were nominated and showed evidence of contributing to the long-term success of the school library (Whelan, 2003b). The top candidates focused not only on the attitude and welcoming nature of the library, but also on the connectedness of the school library and its professional to the issues of student achievement success, articulating an integral role of the school library in student learning. So convinced were these administrators that the school library was a place to manifest this and that the school librarian was the professional who could make it happen, they individually prioritized budget and curriculum concerns in ways that supported and even increased the library program during hard financial times (Whelan, 2003a). They understood and acted on the information that mattered about their programs and professionals, making the connection between student learning and the school library program.

Principals are a strategic target of significant influential interest to the teacher-librarian (Allen, 2004; Hartzell, 2003a). Perceptions of the principals regarding the roles and functions of the professional in the school library are also linked to the budgetary priorities that principals consider when decisions about budget cuts and staff eliminations have to be made (Oberg et al., 2000). The case to retain a professional in the school library may rest with their perceptions about whether the teacher-librarian is a vital and integral contributor to student achievement. In certain elements of educational reform and federal mandates such as the entitled No Child Left Behind (NCLB) legislation, the professional in the school library is often not factored into the equation of improved student achievement (Paige, 2003). NCLB requires a reading program connection that is approved by the state but does not include any language regarding the school library program facilitating or supporting this mandate. NCLB does not recognize the teacher-librarian as a vital component to improve school status, contrary to studies done by Lance (2001) and Krashen (1993). It does, however, recognize test scores as an indicator of student learning and therefore as an indicator of a school that qualifies as performing well under its guidelines (Paige, 2003, p. 13). Through NCLB, principals are encouraged to implement decisions that may diminish the value of the school library program and professional role in improving student learning to comply with the other mandates of the legislation. The mainstreaming of information literacy instruction into content is neither well understood nor articulated as a component through which the teacher-librarian can participate in and make a difference in student learning. This information did not make it through to those writing NCLB.

In a 1998 Delphi study of the national information literacy standards for student learning, as outlined in *Information Power: Building Partnerships for Learning* (American Association of School Librarians/Association for Education Communication & Technology [ALA/AECT], 1998), practicing principals and administrators were the group least likely to understand the connection between certain roles of the professional in the school library and student learning (Marcoux, 1999). Specifically, of all groups surveyed, they were most likely not to understand the connection between the school library's role in facilitating independent learning and student achievement, especially the connection between information literacy and information related to personal interests. This finding suggested a need to develop a plan that would allow administrators to accept more fully the function of the school library professional in facilitating and supporting this type of work. Ironically, it was the practicing school library professionals who seemed not only to understand these standards and what they meant to their work, but also to recognize their importance to holistic student learning. The disconnect between what was perceived as important student learning components and responsibility for working toward these goals as being in the realm of the school library professional world was significantly different between practicing admini- strators and practicing teacher-librarians.

Several authors have recently addressed the concerns of image and the integral role of the school library professional in student learning. Dr. Nancy Everhart (2003), in her recent work on controversial issues in school librarianship, devoted an entire section to the issue of image. Everhart cited image concerns in the media, in education, and within the profession itself. Hartzell (1997) also wrote regarding the invisible image concern of the school library professional, mainly attributable to a principal's lack of understanding of this position and its relationship to student learning. Lance (2000) indicated a corollary improvement in student achievement when there is a library media program that not only houses adequate resources but is also staffed by adequate personnel, including a full-time, certified/endorsed professional (qualified as a school library media specialist) in the school library/media center. Lance and Loertscher (2001) also found a positive effect to student achievement when school library programs have enhanced role understandings for school library professionals, including their integral involvement in all aspects of student learning and instruction. Lance (2001) discussed the evidence that a strong school library program with a full-time professional positively affects student learning. Todd (2003) talked about local accountability of the teacher-librarian as defined through impact on student achievement. A study done recently for the American Association for School Librarians (AASL) addressed the need to create an identity for the school library professional that fits with the roles and functions to be undertaken (AASL, 2003).

A strong concern for the profession would be to dispel a principal current perception of the school library professional from the more traditional predisposed image to one that matches with the various integral roles and functions the professional is charged to perform as outlined in *Information Power,* also known as *IP2* (ALA/AECT, 1998). Kachel (2003) spoke about how to translate school library and curriculum activities into information that allowed the administrator to more clearly understand these connections. She advocated for an organized system that presented an advocacy training program for school principals and included tying the school library and school librarian to the school goals of academic achievement and standards. She suggested financial incentives to capture the interest of the administrator in learning more about the school library and the school librarian with the hoped-for outcome being to have them use this knowledge to promote a stronger school library program in their schools. Jones (2003) suggested a management tool to better communicate these links to the administration, using both written and oral communications to develop greater administrative understanding of the links the school library and school librarian bring to student learning and achievement. Johnson (2003) and Hartzell (2003a) both suggested that the form of communication and the language used for communication influence principal perception. Remembering the role of the administrator as the school instructional leader, teachers also can influence this understanding if they believe in the value it adds to their teaching and advocate for this connection to better serve the learning needs of their students.

Principals encourage the connections of the school library professional with the rest of the teaching staff in a building when they felt a connection between that program and professional and the goals of student achievement (Haycock, 1999; McGregor, 2000; Oberg, 1997). What teachers considered important to retain and even enhance student learning in the face of budgetary constraints seemed to influence administration decisions on future library program and professional support, which was evident as principals determined the value of an enhanced school library program/professional involvement (Oberg et al., 2000). How the school library professional was perceived and utilized rested not only with the teacher-librarian and teachers, but also with the principal understanding of this person roles and utilization of the talents and services of this individual (Hartzell, 2003b). It appeared to be the willingness of the teacher-librarian to become involved and participate in the school's overall goals that most profoundly influenced administrative support of the school library and school library professional (Oberg et al., 2000).

CHANGE INITIATIVE

With these concerns in mind, Washington state began an initiative to develop a program to create a clearer understanding for K–12 principals about the essential links and value of a strong school library program with a professional for improved student learning and achievement. Designed to provide school librarians with information and tools to have a positive impact on student achievement, this initiative worked to align the goals of *IP2* with the actions and work of the building level professional in the school library. A summit was held in spring 2000 to identify these challenges and move forward with actions to improve school library work. Current data, similar to that of the Lance studies, was called for to be used to design curriculum for approximately 1,500 school librarians across the state. Mixed data appeared.

The data were best characterized by their inconsistency across the state, with differences showing up according to local conditions and decisions. What was certain was the need for school librarians to update their training and actions in their schools and make a strong case for integration of information literacy process with students and staff alike. A revised study to investigate these findings further is currently underway throughout the state.

A national survey was undertaken to determine the use of various terms by school-library and education-related agencies, associations, and publications about the school library professional (Marcoux, 2004). The confusion evidenced by this work to develop a common language about the library professional within education seemed to relate significantly to a principal's understanding of the roles and functions of the school library media specialist. Even within the profession itself, much variation in language was discovered. Several researchers (Schon, Helmstadter & Robinson [1991]; Wilson & Lyders [2001]) have indicated that the amount of time an administrator spent in the library seemed to significantly influence his or her understanding of the school library program and therefore understanding of the role and functions of the professional in the school library. Hartzell (2003b) talked about the need to have the principal onboard to effectively affect student achievement. Another study (Alexander, 2003) indicated that the perception of the principal regarding the school library program was low in the four areas of information literacy: collaboration/leadership/technology, learning/teaching, information access/delivery, and program administration. Alexander also indicated that school principals in Kentucky generally regarded the teacher-librarian as only somewhat important to the overall school curriculum and goals. With this evidence in mind, the Washington initiative began.

METHODOLOGY

An initiative in Washington was undertaken to influence the perceptions of the principal about the work of school library professionals regarding their involvement as resources for improving student learning and therefore student achievement. The action for doing this was through the development of the K–12 Library Initiative (www.k12library. info), developed in Washington to improve and update the skills and understanding of practicing state school library media specialists. Funded by state and national funds, (http://www.k12library.info/about/funding.html), this project involved gathering school library professionals from around the state and working on their skill levels as teachers and instructional partners, reading advocates, information specialists, and program managers such that they had a value added status in their own buildings. They received professional development to improve their identity within their schools as well as their integrity or accountability toward their roles in improving student learning and achievement (Allen, 2004). They also received information about strategies for broadcasting messages about their value to those of influence, including their principals (Hartzell, 2003a).

The methodology of the K–12 Library Initiative was to build a curriculum that would positively serve the interests of K–12 school library professionals across the state of Washington. The basis for this work was to develop a sense of empowerment among practicing school library professionals such that they could work on influencing the use and value of their program in their school.

Unable to present this curriculum to all 1,500 professionals at once, a design utilizing the model of trainers and dispersing them throughout the state was developed, with a three-year window of opportunity to take this training offered to practitioners in the state. A curriculum consultant was hired to develop this workshop and train the trainers who would subsequently tailor the curriculum according to their assigned areas and participants. Each trainer was supplied with the curriculum in print and on CD, a set of PowerPoint slides to use for the training sessions, and all handouts. They were asked to customize all materials according to the interests and needs of their specific location. A subsequent follow-up training was held one-year later to facilitate marketing and advocacy strategies for the trainers, which they then took back to their participants for use in finishing the year and completing their annual report.

The K–12 Library Initiative sought to bring these ideas forward and create an understanding among participants of the value of each role for their program and their school. Understanding the identity of the school librarian regarding each of these roles seemed to be the first hurdle; the priority and time emphasis placed on each of these roles seemed second to the functions that were outlined as responsibilities to be undertaken by each building level practitioner.

The first area, *Identity,* was discussed in terms of the *IP2* (ALA/AECT, 1998) four roles of teacher, instructional partner, information specialist, and program manager. These were matched to three major areas of concern as defined by Eisenberg (2002): teaching, reading advocacy, and assuming the role of chief information officer. Relationally, these represented the most important concepts that a principal might desire in his or her school librarian: teacher, reading advocate, and manager of information (both product and process) for the students. Studies indicated that principals seemed to understand more readily the roles associated with being a reading advocate, that is, promoting reading, facilitating reading, and inspiring reading among students but seemed to have little understanding of the teaching role of a school librarian unless related to isolated skill building about the research process or tools of information literacy (Marcoux, 2003). There seemed to be little connection of this work with the content or curriculum of the school, and the research indicated a sense of ancillary importance to the content rather than a full embedding of these processes within the content (Marcoux, 2004). It was also noteworthy that school librarians themselves preferentially recognized their information specialist role more than their instructional partnership role and did not equally embrace both (Marcoux, 1999).

The second area of concern was to develop a sense of *Integrity,* involving the school library program and professional in all aspects of student learning accountability. Washington school librarians were apprised of how to utilize high-stakes testing results to articulate and develop a process plan that would cover these achievement issues within the curriculum and not as ancillary learning. Developing a curriculum map and collaborative plan with site building teachers would result in being able to present this type of information in a cogent and articulate manner to the principal and other decision makers about student learning. This helped to clarify to the teacher-librarians why it was important to have a school library program and professional at every level and in every building and give them information for the third category, one of advocacy.

The third area dealt with *Inspiration,* or advocacy and marketing concerns. Washington school librarians were given tools to develop messages and articulate what it was they could do to improve student learning as well as how they could do it. Techniques for sharing the message as well as sharing the decisions were discussed and outlined. The follow-up training one year later focused mainly on this part of the triad taking what had been done, known, and understood within the framework of the curriculum and student learning and achievement. Great emphasis was placed on reviewing and sharing student test score information that related to information literacy processes potentially influenced by the school library program and professional.

Two research studies were done to ascertain the perceptions of the participants principals regarding their work as the professional in the school library at their site. The methodology used was to create a pre- and post survey instrument that outlined the various roles and functions of the professional in the school library as identified in *IP2*. Test sites were defined by participation of the school librarian in the initial training. There were more than 430 school library personnel attending the August 2003 training; of these, 372 were identified as having contact with the principal. In September 2003, principals in the state of Washington, whose professional in the school library attended the initial K–12 Library Initiative training in August, were polled about the roles and functions of the school library media specialist in their school and the identity of this professional in their building regarding roles and functions. The language used for this survey originated from the current national guidelines for school library media specialist work as defined in *IP2* (ALA/AECT, 1998). The methodology used was a solicitation of 372 public school, K–12, principals for this information via a mailed survey form. Of those sent the survey, 148 responded.

A subsequent survey was sent at the end of this school year to those 148 principals who responded to the first survey to determine whether there had been changes in any of their perceptions as to the work their school library professional engaged in within the site school.

The study was also set up to determine whether the workshop approach of the K–12 Library Initiative influenced perceptions of principals toward their school library program and professional after a year of implementation.

RESULTS

The initial results of the principal study indicated a need to strengthen an understanding of the roles the professional in the school library regarding curriculum development and evaluation of student work. The survey indicated that Washington principals consider the four roles of reading advocate, information specialist, information manager, and instructional partner as part of the work of the school library professional. Conversely, they considered the roles of educational leader, technology manager, technology teacher, and literacy manager as less a part of their work. No attempt was made to define these roles and their functions for the principals, but simply to gain information about their perception of this professional regarding what they perceived this role to be. As shown in Figure 1, there appeared a stronger understanding of the need to be a reading advocate and foster an appreciation of literature, but little understanding of the role of reading advocacy as it related to curriculum. As shown in Figure 2, there appeared to be a strong understanding of the integration of instructional technologies as part of the information specialist role but little understanding in terms of curriculum development or evaluation. Figure 3 shows that principals perceived the information manager as managing the collection but less important regarding curriculum integration and even less influential for curriculum development. Figure 4 indicates that the professional in the school library was perceived as having much to do with teaching but less with curriculum development and even less with assessment of student achievement. Although Washington principals seemed to understand the role of the professional in the school library as being associated with reading advocacy, being an information specialist, and program management, they did not seem to perceive as strong a connection of this work with curriculum or evaluation. Principals seemed not fully to recognize the teacher-librarians as partnering instructionally with teachers for curriculum development or evaluation of student work.

The most interesting message this survey sent was the need to better identify the work of the middle school library professional to the principal. In Figures 1 through 4, the middle school category scored significantly lower in perception than others, yet they represented a significant respondent category to the survey (25 of 141), comprising 35 percent of the total sample. Various theories about why middle schools were particularly misunderstood have been considered, but all point to the need to improve this image even more than at other levels.

Figure 1. The school library professional as reading advocate.

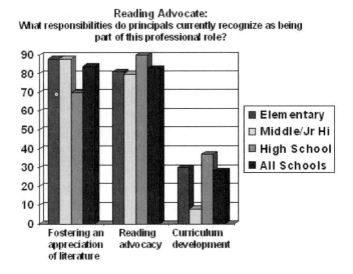

Reading Advocate:
What responsibilities do principals currently recognize as being part of this professional role?

Figure 2. The school library professional as information specialist.

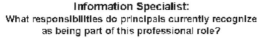
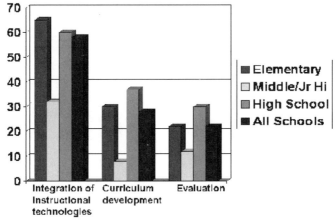

Figure 3. The school library professional as information manager.

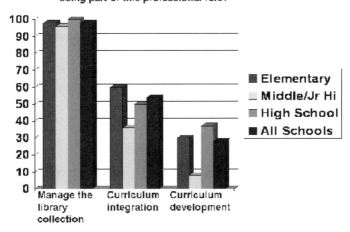

Figure 4. The school library professional as instructional partner.

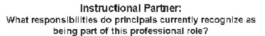

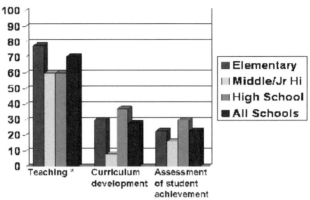

Another interesting finding was the principals' strong interest in retaining this professional in the building (see Figure 5). Although they were not asked to articulate their reasons for this, it is noteworthy that, regardless of reason, there seemed to be a particular desire to maintain the position, considering it essential to the school. This indicated that although principals may not completely understand the role of school library/media center professionals, they value their presence. Todd (Whelan, 2004) also spoke to this in his work in Ohio regarding students interest in using the library to improve their achievement.

Figure 5. How integral are school library professionals?

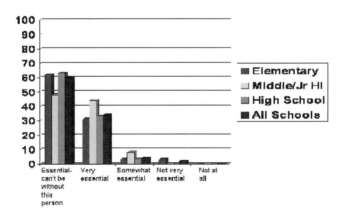

Findings from both the study reported here and the Delphi study (Marcoux, 1999) point to a need to improve principals' perceptions of school library professionals by creating interventions that offer opportunities for better understanding and communication by the professional to the principal. There is strong information for developing continuing education opportunities for practicing school librarians to develop their skills and connections in these areas. A weakness of this study was to develop the curriculum presented to these professionals before ascertaining principal perceptions; however, it was already known from other research that the areas covered stood out as not only underrecognized and misunderstood, but also underperformed.

Concurrent with the K–12 Library Initiative work have been several major attempts to eliminate Washington state language about school library media programs and their staffing. Because of state practitioner interest in updating and devising new and creative ways to encourage principals to remain interested in school library programs, work is underway to develop a definition of what constitutes a school library facility versus what constitutes a school library program. The key to this work continues to be influencing the building level principal as to the value and contributions this program and professional bring to site student learning and achievement.

The K–12 Library Initiative has served as an intervention to offer opportunity for better understanding and communication between the professional and the principal. It has been dependent on each professional in the school library implementing aspects of this intervention such that change would occur. Although not fail-safe, it seemed a start to better understanding and communication between school library professionals and school principals. Its success as an initiative for this purpose will be understood shortly when the post-survey results are analyzed.

A subsequent initiative to the K–12 Library Initiative is to connect school and public libraries through information literacy needs of K–12 students (http://www.secstate.wa.gov/library/libraries/projects/connecting/). This initiative is called Connecting Learners to Libraries and involves the collaboration of school and public libraries to develop plans for improving the information literacy competencies of Washington students, whether in school or at public libraries. The project goals are as follows:

- increase awareness in public library and school communities of K–12 students information literacy behaviors;

- improve public libraries staff members' knowledge of Washington State Essential Academic Learning Requirements (EALR), especially as assessed in the Washington Assessment of Student Learning (WASL), and research models as they relate to K–12 students' information literacy skills;

- improve school communities' knowledge of public library programs and services as they relate to K–12 students information literacy skills; and

- provide funding for collaborative projects between public libraries and schools focused on improving students' information literacy skills.

The Connecting Learners to Libraries Initiative is centering at present on the state requirement of a successful culminating project for all high school seniors by 2008 as the mechanism to use for indication of a successful initiative.

CONCLUSION

If principals are to perceive school library professionals as a vital and integral component for the improvement of student learning and achievement at their schools, and if in difficult budgetary times, principals are going to give priority status to retaining school library professionals and a resource budget that includes not only classroom but also school library resources, there is a need to update and upgrade the skills and roles of school library professionals and to create a perception among principals regarding the value and worth of these professionals for improving student learning as evidenced by improved student achievement. Although there are certain expectations of the school library professional, much work needs to be done to integrate the expectations of student learning and achievement through curriculum development and evaluation as a part of these professionals' work. The quest to make this a priority is elusive, and one that, although understood by some within the profession, is not well understood as a long-range influence on student learning and achievement.

Administrators making decisions about budgetary and staffing matters must understand more comprehensively the roles of the school library professional. Strategic reinforcement of these roles and functions can be done by ensuring that what takes place in the school library program is essential to student learning. The K–12 Library Initiative is one suggestion for examining ways to make the school library an integral component in the educational health and success of K–12 students.

REFERENCES

Alexander, L. B., Smith, R. C., & Carey, J. O. (2003). Education reform and the school library media specialist: Perceptions of principals. *Knowledge Quest, 32*(2), 10–13.

Allen, R. (2004). Sustaining professional development: Collaboration and technology reshape training. *Education Update, 46*(2), 1, 6–8.

American Association of School Librarians. (2003, January). *KRC Research: A report of findings from six focus groups with K–12 parents, teachers, and principals, as well as middle and high school students.* Agenda Exploration Items #30. Presented at the AASL Board of Directors meeting.

American Association of School Librarians/Association for Education Communication & Technology. (1998). *Information Power: Building partnerships for learning.* Chicago: American Library Association.

Campbell, B., & Cordiero, P. (1996). *High school principal roles and implementation themes for mainstreaming information literacy instruction.* Paper presented at the American Educational Research Association Annual Meeting, New York.

Eisenberg, M. E., & Miller, D. B. (2002). This man wants to change your job. *School Library Journal, 48*(9), 46–50.

Everhart, N. (2003). *Controversial issues in school librarianship: Divergent perspectives.* Worthington, OH: Linworth.

Hartzell, G. (1997). The invisible librarian. *School Library Journal, 43*(11), 24–29.

Hartzell, G. (2003a). The power of audience: effective communication with your principal. *Library Media Connection, 22*(2), 20–22.

Hartzell, G. (2003b). Why should principals support school libraries? *Library Reference: http://libraryreference.com/school-libraries.html*

Haycock, K. (1999). Fostering collaboration, leadership, and information literacy: common behaviors of uncommon principals and faculties. *NAASP Bulletin, 83*(605), 82–87.

Hoy, W. K., & Miskel, C. G. (2001). *Educational administration: Theory, research, and practice* (6th ed.). New York: McGraw-Hill.

Johnson, D. (2003). No principal left behind. *Library Media Connection, 21*(6), 110, 108.

Jones, P. A., Jr. (2003). The executive briefing: A management tool for improving communication between school library media specialists and their principals. *Knowledge Quest, 32*(2), 30–34.

Kachel, D. E. (2003). Partners for success: A school library advocacy training program for principals. *Knowledge Quest, 32*(2), 17–19.

Krashen, S. (1993). *The power of reading.* Englewood, CO: Libraries Unlimited.

Lance, K. C. (2000). Dick and Jane go to the head of the class. *School Library Journal, 46*(4), 44.

Lance, K. C. (2001). *Proof of the power: recent research on the impact of school library media programs on the academic achievement of US public school students.* Retrieved May 12, 2004, from http://ericit.org.edu/ithome

Lance, K. C., & Loertscher, D. V. (2001). *Powering achievement: School library media programs make a difference. The evidence mounts* (2nd ed.). San Jose, CA: Hi Willow Research.

Marcoux, E. (1999). *Information literacy standards for student learning: A modified Delphi study of their acceptance by the educational community.* Unpublished doctoral dissertation, University of Arizona, Tucson.

Marcoux, E. (2003). *K–12 Library Initiative Research Study.* Retrieved May 12, 2004, from http://www.k12library.info/evaluations/librarytctraining_eval.html.

Marcoux, E. (2004). The confusion of terminology for the professional of the school library media program: Its impact on roles and functions of this professional in the K–12 education arena. Unpublished manuscript.

McGregor, J. (2002). Flexible scheduling: How does a principal facilitate implementation? *School Libraries Worldwide, 8*(1), 71–84.

Oberg, D. (1995). *Principal support: What does it mean to teacher-librarians?* Paper presented at the International Association of School Librarianship, Worcester, England.

Oberg, D. (1997). The principals role in empowering collaborations between teacher-librarians and teachers: Research findings. *Scan, 16*(3), 6–8.

Oberg, D., Hay, L., & Henri, J. (2000). The role of the principal in an information literate school community: cross country comparisons from an international research project. *School Library Media Research.* (ERIC Document Reproduction Service No. EJ 618 497). Available online at: http://www.ala.org/aasl/SLMR/vol3/principal2/principal2.html

Paige, R. (2003). *No child left behind: A parent's guide.* Washington, DC: US Department of Education.

Schon, I., Helmstadter, G.C., and Robinson, D. (1991). The role of school library media specialists. *School Library Media Quarterly,* 19 (4), 228–233.

St. Lifer, E. (2003). An advocate worth celebrating. *School Library Journal, 49*(11), 13.

Todd, R. (2003). School libraries and evidence: Seize the day, begin the future. *Library Media Connection, 22*(1), 12–18.

Whelan, D. L. (2003a). SC librarians laud top administrator. *School Library Journal, 49*(4), 19.

Whelan, D. L. (2003b). Ultimate advocate. *School Library Journal, 49*(11), 44–46

Whelan, D. L. (2004). 13,000 kids can't be wrong: A new Ohio study shows how school libraries help students learn. *School Library Journal, 46.*

Wilson, P. J., & Blake, M. (1993). The missing piece: A school library media center component in principal preparation programs. *Educational Leadership, 12*(2), 65–68.

Wilson, P. P., & Lyders, J. A. (2001). *Leadership for today's school library: A handbook for the library media specialist and the school principal.* Westport, CT: Greenwood Press.

Inquiry Groups Focusing on Information Literacy:
A Place at Our Table

Gail Bush

Graduate School of Library and Information Science, Dominican University

Educators agree that our shared goals are to improve student learning and in doing so to create lifelong learners who will be responsible citizens of the world. Our role in the library media center is to ensure that students have both a firm grasp of information literacy and an appreciation of literature. That we are passionate about enculturating our future leaders with a joy of reading is an important subject but one for another time. Here we will focus on how we can best serve our young scholars by continuing to strive for more meaningful information literacy instruction.

Our best efforts to achieve our goals with students rely on effective instruction in information literacy. What is it that makes us deem the instruction to be effective? How do we imbue our piece of the teaching and learning domain with educational best practices? One approach is to join together in inquiry groups for purposeful exploration of information literacy instruction. The lessons, units, projects, assignments, and evidence supporting teacher-guided instruction are discussed in relation to the standards that are being met both in discipline(s), process, and assessment. Protocols are used as tools to facilitate discussion and move educator conversation toward an assessment of effective teaching. This established strategy of directed collaborative exploration allows group members to focus on a specific assignment or observable instructional experience and to feel the momentum of informing and improving practice. This chapter gives the reader an overview of inquiry groups; the use of protocols; the role of facilitators; what constitutes evidence; inquiry group meetings in action; information literacy as an integral part of curriculum and instructional strategies conducive to integrating information literacy; and finally offers a representative protocol and suggestions for sources of protocols available for use and/or adaptation.[1]

A PLACE AT OUR TABLE

Too often the only mention of the school library is a recommendation to use a library table as a meeting place for classroom teachers and department chairpersons who gather together to discuss curricular issues. It is time for there to be a place at our table for a discussion relating to information literacy and how we can infuse our standards into the curricular goals of the school. This discussion presumes a broad definition of the educator constituency of the school learning community. We invite all educators who are interested in moving inquiry to action—school library media specialists, instructional technologists, computer teachers, reading specialists, classroom teachers, administrators, and paraprofessional support personnel. Inquiry groups, study groups, critical friends groups, teacher development groups, professional development, staff development, and all other group discussions share a goal of educator development based on collaborative inquiry. The predominant distinction from traditional forms of professional development is where the expertise resides. The days of the professional development expert coming to pontificate at a one-time event and ride out of town never to be seen again are coming to an end (Bush, 2003).

---

1. The inspiration for this discussion comes directly from participation in a facilitation mini-course titled Facilitating Teacher Inquiry Groups taught by Tina Blythe and David Allen at the 2002 Project Zero Summer Institute, Harvard Graduate School of Education (Allen & Blythe, 2004; Evidence Project Staff, 2001; *Looking at Student Work*, 2004).

INQUIRY GROUPS

In our constructivist approach to instruction, we understand that our students are individual learners who are constructing meaning that builds into their own knowledge schema. Likewise, our teachers are responding to who their students are and how best to deliver content, support the learning process, and develop educative assessments that are embedded in instruction. It is therefore reasonable to consider each school setting as a unique learning environment. The expertise that resides firmly in each school's educators is coming to the foreground. These expert-in-residence participants in professional development are deciding just what it is that needs the most attention in their school setting. The clear benefits of the participants directing the focus of professional development efforts include a deeper understanding of learning, more movement toward improved instruction, and shared ownership in the process itself. A focused inquiry group with a proven strategy and evidence to explore is a powerful agency for change.

Regardless of their originating organizations, commonalities among inquiry group behavior include careful listening, questions that clarify and probe thinking, and thoughtful response. Some groups, such as Critical Friends Groups (a component of Coalition of Essential Schools), observe colleagues teaching, schedule conferences to provide feedback, and raise questions. These groups train educators for one-on-one professional relationships. Other collaborative groups and networks move into deeper territory regarding specific lessons. Lesson study groups in Japan base their inquiry on national curriculum lessons (Stigler & Hiebert, 1999); their in-depth study dissects lessons, clarifies approaches used, and informs their practice.

Inquiry groups as they are discussed in this chapter tend to have the following components at each meeting:

- Educators for grades 8–12

- An overarching (school year) question, a (meeting) subquestion

- Evidence—a sample information literacy lesson, unit, project, or assignment

- One member (usually on rotating basis) who acts as a facilitator

- Protocol selected to facilitate discussion

- Consciousness of time and process

THE USE OF PROTOCOLS

The word *protocol* has many meanings; various disciplines define protocol as standard procedure, etiquette, plan, table of contents, code of correct conduct, to name a few recurring themes. Use of the word protocol provokes some reaction from educators who resist the formality that it implies (McDonald, Mohr, Dichter, & McDonald, 2003). Why do we need a tool that will facilitate discussion and force us to focus on specific elements of lesson design? Unlike the myriad accountability measures we have for student achievement, much of what we do in schools is difficult capture. Any attempt to distill a scientific rendering out of the art of teaching invites reflexive resistance from educators. Tacit knowledge is indefinable, and that is just how many educators like it. Old habits of isolation, autonomy, and ownership over work product die hard. Those inquiry groups that focus on student work are one iteration removed from closely inspecting "teacher work." To move forward, however, we need to be prepared for the realities that protocols force on group discussion.

The protocols that are used as guidelines for structured conversations in educator inquiry groups provide a set of steps through which the group moves as guided by a facilitator. The effectiveness of using protocols comes from the trust on which the process is based.

Trust is built because everyone in the group agrees to use the protocol and everyone shares the same understanding of the protocol and how it will work. The culture that results from the use of the protocols promotes trust because it allows for collaborative relationships that result in improved professional practice. Furthermore, the use of protocols fosters trust because substantive work is accomplished, time is used well, the environment is safe for challenging questions, equity and parity are group norms, and there is a feeling of permission whereby we are given a license to listen and space to reflect. The point of using the protocol is not to "do the protocol well" but to use it as a catalyst to explore and discover and inform (Evidence Project Staff, 2001).

The protocols that serve us best in the information literacy curricular areas come primarily from the Evidence Project at Project Zero, Harvard Graduate School of Education; Coalition of Essential Schools; and the National School Reform Faculty. The distinction that we are making, however, is that the protocols traditionally look at student work as evidence. At this point in time, we are beginning our exploration into effective information literacy instruction by using assignments as evidence. As inquiry groups focusing on information literacy become more facile with their processes, we may progress into an exploration of the student-generated end products. Indeed, there are instances in which information literacy advocates believe that the weakest part of the process of learning is its representation. The protocols that are readily available for educators are also designed for adaptation according to a given inquiry group's needs. There has to be consensus that the protocols used in the group are adequate; any adaptations the facilitator makes must be agreed on as well. Do not hesitate to blaze trails with your collaborative partners; just be sure that no participant is left behind in the dust.

THE ROLE OF FACILITATORS

Who facilitates and why? One might suggest that anyone in a leadership role does not belong in a shared inquiry method group. Contrary to common belief, a balance of leadership is an important element within collaborative partnerships. Leadership is flexible and malleable and is shared by various partners at different times. This role of facilitator of an inquiry group studying information literacy instruction requires just such a flexible leader. When the inquiry group is formed, it is understood that the use of protocols assumes someone partaking in the group as the facilitator. Groups may have different ways of approaching this responsibility. One group may decide to change facilitators with each meeting; another group may keep a facilitator for the semester or for the school year. It is recommended that the facilitator be a member of the group, if possible; this configuration goes a long way toward acceptance of the resulting outcomes and increases the shared ownership of the learning process. There is also empathy for the group member in the facilitator's role when and if there are challenges to the safety of the environment.

All facilitators are not created equal. Some group members may take to the role more naturally than others; some might avoid the role completely. This is not to say that rotation won't be the best approach within a particular group. Oftentimes, hidden leadership skills emerge within the safety of such a learning environment. As a facilitator of a protocol in an inquiry group one:

- Is explicit about his or her role as facilitator
- Listens without judging
- Clarifies terminology
- Tunes into differences in perspectives
- Alerts members to awkward points in the protocol
- Focuses on patience and persistence

- Stays focused on the evidence available
- Physically sits back from the discussion as needed
- Debriefs without adding editorial comments
- Asks questions that focus on

> CLARIFYING—What does this assignment tell us about how well the educator understands information literacy? What initial understandings do we see emerging in this assignment?
>
> PROBING—What would it look like if ...? What is another way one might ...?
>
> REFLECTING—What worked well within this process? What are we learning from this experience?

- Directs the pace of a typical meeting as follows:

> *10 minutes—"Hi, everyone. Well, you have looked at the agenda. Let's get started by clarifying what we want to use as a framing question for our meeting today."*
>
> *5 minutes—"OK, I am handing out the protocol that we are going to use today. This is a new one for me. I've never done this before so please bear with me ..."*
>
> 10 minutes—*"Here we go. _____, please present your evidence. Everyone keep in mind our question, '[Repeat the framing question]'."*
>
> *40–60 minutes—*Facilitate the protocol. Mark the end of each part of the protocol and the beginning of the next: *"There may be more to say, but let's move on to the next step...."*
>
> 10 minutes—Wrap up by saying *"That's the end of the protocol. I know we could keep talking about our framing question and _____'s evidence much longer, but let's spend a couple of minutes reflecting on the protocol and our framing question."*
>
> 5 minutes—*"We have a few minutes left. Who else wants to comment on the evidence? Anything else about the framing question and how the evidence led us to our new understanding ... or not?" "Great. Let's talk about what we are going to do between now and the next meeting."*

WHAT CONSTITUTES EVIDENCE FOR STUDYING INFORMATION LITERACY INSTRUCTION

Thus far, the discussion has been fairly generic; the study of inquiry groups and protocols could fit any educational setting. It is time now to invest in the particular study of information literacy instruction and see what distinctions need to be made to accommodate this exploration. In our context, evidence is anything that participants might bring 'to the table' that may help them explore their question or better understand it. In that vein, evidence may not be tangible. It might be a description of a collaborative conversation between a school library media specialist and a classroom teacher. It may involve outside partners such as the public library. For one group, evidence might look like a grant; for another, all evidence will be library- or instructional-technology-oriented assignments.

Evidence most commonly includes artifacts such as assignments, lesson plans, documented observations or conversations, samples of student (or teacher) work, video or audiotapes of students working, and curriculum webs or maps. Generally, when we look at teacher work, it is considered to be *input*. Student work is considered to be *output*. Because we are focusing on our education of the educators regarding information literacy instruction, teacher work, for our purposes, is output.

INQUIRY GROUP MEETINGS IN ACTION

The inquiry group meetings where the focus is on information literacy will, on the surface, look like any other inquiry group meetings. One will find a volunteer facilitator and group members and a presenter; room on tables for evidence to be spread out; comfortable seating; evidence including the types of artifacts described earlier; copies of the agenda for the meeting; copies of the protocol to be used for the meeting; facilitator's notebook (and optional recording device); any necessary technology including computers, projection screen, whiteboard, flipboard; and refreshments. The approximate meeting time may be one and a half hours once a week, every two weeks, or once a month.

Activities may include the following:

1. Discussion of the overarching question and the relevance of the question for this meeting. Revision of the overarching question is a natural result of in-depth study as the school year progresses. Does the question still reflect the intent of the group's shared goals? Framing questions regarding information literacy might be the following: How can I deepen my teachers' understanding of information literacy? How can I help students understand that the information search process is an integral part of learning and not something "extra" that is added on to their studies? How can I most effectively collaboratively plan with my teachers to ensure that information literacy is embedded into their research assignments?

2. What kinds of evidence would best allow the group to explore specific aspects of the question? Brainstorm kinds of relevant evidence and discuss various methods for gathering such evidence. In addition to information literacy assignments, evidence for exploring information literacy instruction might include information literacy models (published or school initiated), instructional technology software, online databases, pathfinders, and school library Web sites.

3. The chosen facilitator will use protocol suited to the type of evidence and purpose of the exploration; the presenter who brought the evidence will follow the facilitator's instructions for presenting the evidence. More than one protocol may be used in one meeting. With experience, groups become comfortable with protocols that are particularly effective with the group dynamics and the overarching question.

4. Reflect on the meeting specifically regarding both the learning that was shared and the process that brought the group to that understanding.

5. Discuss what will happen between meetings and any plans for new information literacy instructional strategies to try that have emerged from the meeting. This is a critically important step in the group process and requires mindful reflection.

6. Plan for the next meeting by deciding on a question to be answered; decide what type of evidence to bring to the meeting, who might choose to present evidence, and who will serve as the facilitator for the next meeting.

7. Document group progress and plans for the next meeting in the facilitator's notebook (print or online).

8. Options include (a) inviting someone from outside the group or school to lead a discussion or make a presentation or (b) discussion of an article or book relevant to the overarching question (Evidence Project Staff, 2001).

INFORMATION LITERACY INSTRUCTION

A thorough study of the information literacy standards in *Information Power: Building Partnerships for Learning (IP2)* guides the educator through potential points of integration into any school's curriculum (1998). Those states where state educational agencies have information literacy standards will likely use their standards; the rest of us are well served by our national standards *(IP2)*. The notion of integrating an information-searching process into curriculum sounds redundant to true believers. We cannot quite grasp a better way to prepare our students for lifelong learning. The reality is, however, that many classroom teachers do not have the same worldview that we share. It is wholly within our responsibility to our students to ensure that our teachers are effective users of information and ideas so that they understand the importance of embedding information searching skills into their curricular units.

Best practices that prevail in classrooms find equal success in the school library. An emphasis on the ill-defined messiness of problem-based learning matched with authentic and engaged learning, differentiating instruction ensuring that all students are appropriately challenged, accommodating for multiple intelligences and learning styles by providing choice in learning and representation of learning, creating collaborative learners through cooperative groups and workshops, and using educative assessments including portfolios and student-generated rubrics all blend well with higher-order thinking skills essential in developing a well-defined information literacy thread throughout a school's curriculum.

Every instructional strategy that challenges students in a constructivist learning environment is equally suitable when considering information literacy. For students to become independent learners who are competent in activating their own prior knowledge and constructing meaning and who are able to apply their new knowledge in novel situations, they need also to understand how to proceed when confronted with an information need. Learning to learn has a trite ring to it. But in fact, isn't that what we need for our future citizens of the world to be competent to lead full and meaningful lives? Educators cannot teach students all that they will ever need to know. Of this much we are certain. Let us focus on teaching our students how they could best use information searching skills to gain a literacy that will serve them as time goes on.

Take a fresh view of the Information Literacy Standards for Student Learning: consider that you are a member of an inquiry group focusing on information literacy. Assume any grade level, integrate into any curricular discipline, and select any aspect of the information literacy standards. What needs to be explicit in the evidence to demonstrate that the presenter has created an exemplary information literacy lesson?

INFORMATION LITERACY STANDARDS FOR STUDENT LEARNING

Information Literacy

> Standard 1: The student who is information literate accesses information efficiently and effectively.

> Standard 2: The student who is information literate evaluates information critically and competently.

> Standard 3: The student who is information literate uses information accurately and creatively.

Independent Learning

> Standard 4: The student who is an independent learner is information literate and pursues information related to personal interests.

> Standard 5: The student who is an independent learner is information literate and appreciates literature and other creative expressions of information.

> Standard 6: The student who is an independent learner is information literate and strives for excellence in information seeking and knowledge generation.

Social Responsibility

> Standard 7: The student who contributes positively to the learning community and to society is information literate and recognizes the importance of information to a democratic society.

> Standard 8: The student who contributes positively to the learning community and to society is information literate and practices ethical behavior in regard to information and information technology.

> Standard 9: The student who contributes positively to the learning community and to society is information literate and participates effectively in groups to pursue and generate information.

Source: American Association of School Librarians and Association for Educational Communications and Technology. (1998). *Information power: Building partnerships for learning*. Chicago: American Library Association. Used with permission.

PROTOCOL ADAPTED FOR INFORMATION LITERACY INSTRUCTION

The protocol used as an example is adapted from the work of the *Looking at Student Work* and the Evidence Project group. There are many other protocols that have much more abbreviated formats and are available for facilitators of inquiry groups to add or subtract steps and questions (Allen & Blythe, 2004; Looking at Student Work, 2004; McDonald et al., 2003). An adaptation of this protocol is useful as a learning tool for all of us to understand effective information literacy instruction. This example is provided to illuminate the possibilities of adapting protocols for focusing on information literacy instruction. Because we base our instruction on our national standards, an exercise evaluating the effectiveness of the standards within a particular assignment seems like a fair place to begin serious inquiry. This adaptation can be altered to suit the particular inquiry from a group as needed.

INFORMATION LITERACY
STANDARDS IN PRACTICE PROTOCOL*

Time: 60 minutes (*plus* the time it takes to complete the assignment). Times are approximate.

Roles:

- Facilitator
- Presenter
- Recorder

1. **All group members complete the assignment (this could be done before the meeting).**

Complete the assignment. This is important: if you don't complete the assignment yourselves, you won't know whether it truly asks for the knowledge and skills you want students to have.

Consider how you would complete the assignment yourselves.

- Take **5 minutes** and jot down some notes.

2. **(10 minutes) The group identifies the information literacy standards that apply to this assignment.**

Take the information literacy standards and find the standards to which this assignment might be directed. In other words, if the students do the assignment, what standards would they be moving toward? (If the answer is "none," then what would be the consequences?) Which information search process model is used, and where does this assignment fit (predominantly) into the model?

- Don't make long lists of standards. Most assignments don't address more than two or three standards. Look at the assignment and **figure out the central learning that it embodies.**

3. **(10 minutes) The group generates a rough scoring guide from the standards and the assignment.** Using the standards and the assignment, develop a scoring guide for this problem by following these steps:

- **(4)** is the highest score. Write the features of an excellent answer/end product to this problem. Discuss with group members and agree on the main points.

- **(3)** is the next highest score. Write the features of an answer/project clearly based on understanding of the concept with perhaps some minor errors that could be simple mistakes or typographical errors. Understanding of the concept and ability to apply it are obvious. A solid job, but not brilliant.

- **(2)** is the next to the lowest score. Write the features of an answer/project that hasn't quite got it, that needs additional teaching.

- **(1)** is the lowest score. Write the feature of an answer/project that hasn't a clue.

4. **(10 minutes) The group asks:** *Will this assignment/lesson meet the standards? If not, what are we going to do about it?* **THIS STEP AND THE FOLLOWING ARE THE MOST IMPORTANT STEPS IN THE**

PROCESS. People tend to think they're done when they've got the assignment scored, but in fact all that was just preparation for answering the most important questions.

What do educators understand about information literacy standards?

- The recorder writes the group's answers to the following questions:

    1. What does this assignment tell us about the teacher's understanding of information literacy standards?

    2. Was the assignment well designed to help students acquire knowledge and exercise information search process skills?

5. (15 minutes) Implications for change: What are we going to do about it? What are we going to do next week, next semester, next year?

What should happen at the library media program, classroom, school, district, and state levels to ensure that all educators could achieve a score of 4 or 3 on assignments clearly aligned with the information literacy standards?

Let's do something about it. What needs to change so that all educators can reach this understanding of information literacy standards?

The following are examples of actions that might be taken to improve learning:

- Examining assignments to make sure that they are all aligned with information literacy standards

- Reorganizing curriculum and instruction using curriculum maps/plans/guides

- Helping parents understand how curriculum has changed, the need for teaching information literacy skills, and what they can do to prepare students for success

- Time and professional development for educators for collaborative inquiry professional development

- Rethinking the use of federal, state, and other funds and grant seeking for supplemental funds

The recorder writes the group's answer to the following question:

What can group members add to this list?

6. **Develop and carry out an action plan.** The group plans and carries out action to improve educators' understanding of information literacy standards and thereby improve student learning. This is a goal that can be achieved by making methodical steps as outlined in an action plan.

*Source: Mitchell, R. (1997). Standards in Practice. *Looking at Student Work.* Retrieved May 13, 2004, from http://www.lasw.org. Adapted by the author with permission.

FORM AN INQUIRY GROUP FOCUSING ON INFORMATION LITERACY

The reader is encouraged to form a group from within the school by including various educators; a group of school library media specialists from the same local area from the same grade levels; a group of school library media specialists from a consolidated district P–12; or any variation of these groups. It would be difficult to take dedicated educators who share a vision of information literate students and the resources provided for inquiry group activities and not have an effective outcome that is rewarding as a professional development experience. The proof of the experience comes in the action that comes of the inquiry process. Yes, the process in itself is of value to the educators. But it is in the action that our students will ultimately benefit. If we choose not to explore seriously the value of information literacy instruction, we have no hope of improving instruction and student learning. Inquiry groups effect change within a school learning community, and the elements that make it work are promising to all educators who dwell in a universe of inquiry.

REFERENCES

Allen, D., & Blythe, T. (2004). *The facilitator's book of questions: Tools for looking together at student and teacher work*. New York: Teachers College Press.

American Association of School Librarians and Association for Educational Communications and Technology. (1998). *Information power: Building partnerships for learning*. Chicago: American Library Association.

Burnaford, G., Fischer, J., & Hobson, D. (Eds.). (2001). *Teachers doing research: The power of action through inquiry*. Mahwah, NJ: Erlbaum.

Bush, G. (2003). *The school buddy system: The practice of collaboration*. Chicago: American Library Association.

Critical friends groups. (2004). Coalition of Essential Schools Northwest. Retrieved May 12, 2004, from: http://www.cesnorthwest.org/critical_friends_groups.htm

Evidence Project Staff. (2001). *The evidence process: A collaborative approach to understanding and improving teaching and learning*. Cambridge, MA: Harvard Project Zero.

Looking at Student Work. (2004). Retrieved May 12, 2004, from http://www.lasw.org

McDonald, J. P., Mohr, N., Dichter, A., & McDonald, E. C. (2003). *The power of protocols: An educator's guide to better practice*. New York: Teachers College Press.

Mitchell, R. (1997). Standards in Practice. *Looking at Student Work*. Retrieved May 13, 2004, from: http://www.lasw.org

National School Reform Faculty. (2004). Retrieved May 12, 2004, from http://www.nsrfharmony.org

Stigler, J. W., & Hiebert, J. (1999). *The teaching gap: Best ideas from the world's teachers for improving education in the classroom*. New York: Free Press.

Part Three
Leadership Profiles

Introduction

The purpose of this section is to profile individuals who have made significant contributions to the field of instructional technology. There is no formal survey or popularity contest to determine the persons for whom the profiles are written, but those selected are usually emeritus faculty who may or may not be active in the field.

Leaders profiled in the *Yearbook* have either held prominent offices, written important works, or made significant contributions that have in some way influenced the contemporary vision of the field. They have often been directly responsible for mentoring individuals who have themselves become recognized for their contributions. The following are those previously profiled in earlier volumes of the *Yearbook*:

James D. Finn	Thomas F. Gilbert
James W. Brown	Wesley Joseph McJulien
Wilbur Schramm	Stanley A. Huffman
Robert E. De Kieffer	John C. Belland
Jean E. Lowrie	Robert M. Diamond
Robert Morris	Paul Robert Wendt
William Travers	Don Carl Smellie
Robert Mills Gagné	Bob Casey
Robert Heinich	Kent Gustafson
Charles Francis Schuller	Tjeerd Plomp
Harry Alleyn Johnson	Walter Dick
Robert M. Morgan	Frank Dwyer
Paul Saettler	John Hedberg
Donald P. Ely	Robert K. Branson
James Okey	Roger Kaufman
Constance Dorothea Weinman	Rita C. Richey
Castelle (Cass) G. Gentry	Howard Sullivan
	Paul Welliver

There are special reasons to feature people of national and international renown, and the editors of this volume of the *Educational Media and Technology Yearbook* believe we have selected two outstanding leaders in our field for this issue: Betty Collis and M. David Merrill.

You are welcome to nominate individuals to be featured in this section. Your nomination of someone to be profiled in this section must also be accompanied by the name of the person who would agree to compose the leadership profile. Please direct any comments, questions, and suggestions about the selection process to the Senior Editor.

Michael Orey

Betty Collis

Shell Professor of Networked Learning, University of Twente

Thomas C. Reeves
The University of Georgia

If I have seen further it is by standing on the shoulders of giants.

—Sir Isaac Newton

If asked to use only three words to describe Professor Betty Collis, my choices would be *pioneer, international,* and *partner.* As a *pioneer,* Betty began using computers in education a quarter century ago, at the dawn of the microcomputer age; five years later, she was one of the first people anywhere to utilize early versions of the Internet for teaching and learning. She has been on the cutting edge of new telecommunications and educational technology research and development ever since, as a visit to her impressive Web site (http://users.edte.utwente.nl/collis/) will reveal to anyone unfamiliar with her numerous contributions to the field of educational communications and technology.

With respect to *international,* few scholars in our field are more widely known around the globe than Betty Collis. Part of her strong international reputation derives from the five hundred presentations she has given at various professional conferences, with nearly fifty of those being invited keynotes. Perhaps more of her renown derives from the nearly six hundred scholarly publications she has to her credit, including a dozen books, fifty-plus book chapters, and more than 120 refereed journal articles. In addition to spending significant parts of her education and professional career in the United States, Canada, and The Netherlands, Betty has visited more than thirty countries as a consultant, speaker, researcher, and teacher. Holding dual U.S. and Canadian citizenship and maintaining residences in The Netherlands and the United States, she is a true global citizen.

Finally, as a *partner,* Betty exemplifies authentic collaboration. Although many in the fields of educational media, telecommunications, and technology have benefited from working with Betty, her professional and personal soulmate is Jef Moonen, who recently retired as a professor and former dean at the University of Twente. Their collaboration is actually detailed in a recent article published in the *Educational Technology Research and Development* journal that provides fascinating details of what they describe as their "Core Connections" (Moonen & Collis, 2003). It is a unique and special partnership that began as a professional one in 1987 and rapidly blossomed into a relationship and marriage that someday deserves to be made into a grand romantic film akin to *Out of Africa* or *The English Patient.*

But of course, I am allowed more than three words in this chapter; indeed, the editor has allocated 1,200. It is hardly enough, but let me start again at the beginning. Born in 1944 in Detroit, Michigan, Betty Collis spent her childhood there before going off to college to earn an honors degree in mathematics (magna cum laude) at the University of Michigan. Subsequently, she earned a master's degree with honors in mathematics education at Stanford University, one of the top ten universities in the United States. Interestingly, her master's thesis was funded by Shell through the Paul deHart Hurt Award for Mathematics. Little did Shell know that it was helping to prepare its future Shell Professor of Networked Learning!

Betty began her professional career teaching mathematics as a high school teacher, a challenging roles she undertook in California and British Columbia from 1967 to 1974. In 1974, she shifted from teaching high school students to teaching future teachers at the University of Victoria while also pursuing a Ph.D. focused on the measurement and evaluation of computer applications in education. When she completed her doctorate in 1983, it was surely one of the first of its kind. After earning her Ph.D., once again with honors, she remained a member of the faculty at Victoria for five more years before joining the Faculty of Educational Science and Technology at the University of Twente in 1988. (In 2002, the faculty changed its name to Behavioural Sciences.) Today the University of Twente enjoys a strong reputation as one of the foremost institutions of higher learning in the areas of educational telecommunications and technology, in no small part thanks to the leadership of Betty Collis and Jef Moonen.

Today, Betty keeps one foot in academe at the University of Twente and another in the business world as the Shell Professor of Networked Learning. Wearing her academic robes, she supervises doctoral students, teaches graduate courses, conducts funded research, and provides an amazing amount of professional service. Wearing her business suit, she is helping Shell, one of the largest corporations in the world, identify better models of e-learning while providing a real-world context for her and her graduate students to conduct research and development in innovative areas such as blended learning, learning objects, and technology-supported organizational learning. With all this, she still manages to have "a life," and she is cherished as a wife, mother, and grandmother.

With respect to scholarship, summarizing Betty's contributions in the few remaining words is quite a challenge. Certainly among the highlights is her leadership in developing the 4-E Model that identifies environment, (perception or expectation of) educational effectiveness, ease of use, and personal engagement as four key factors in predicting use of educational computing in practice. Another highlight is her leadership of the team that created TeleTOP, one of the first robust Web-based course management systems to be used in both higher education and industry. She has performed advanced research on many other topics including the pedagogical underpinnings of using computers and telecommunications technology for education and training, the adoption of information and communications technology for higher education around the world, and organization learning. As a methodologist, she has created improved approaches to evaluation research and the scholarship of teaching.

With respect to teaching, Betty has an outstanding reputation as a teacher, including being chosen as the Instructor of the Year by her students and colleagues at the University of Twente. She has been a true pioneer in the application of technologies such as teleconferencing systems and Web-based Instruction to support flexible learning. She has guided numerous doctoral and master's students and provided superior mentoring for young scholars from around the world. She frequently provides tutorials and workshops at international conferences on topics such as Web-based instruction, educational telecommunications, evaluation research, and flexible learning.

With respect to service, Betty's noteworthy contributions include multiple roles in a score of international professional associations, most notably the Association for the Advancement of Computers in Education (AACE) and the International Society for Technology in Education (ISTE), of which she is a lifetime honorary member. She has been a significant contributor to many IFIP (International Federation for Information Processing) Working Groups and a member of the Editorial Boards for numerous refereed journals, including *International Journal on E-Learning, The Internet in Higher Education, Interactive Learning Environments, Journal of Interactive Learning Research, Journal of Computer Assisted Learning, Computers & Education,* the *International Journal for Educational Telecommunications,* and *Journal of Research on Computing in Education.*

On a personal note, I have known Betty Collis for at least fifteen years, and I value our friendship dearly. My colleagues and I have had the good fortune to have Betty visit our Instructional Technology program at the University of Georgia, and we all sincerely hope she will "come on down" to UGA again soon. In addition to being a world-class scholar, Betty is a fun person, as is her life partner, Jef, whether it involves trying out exotic ethnic restaurants, bumping along in a thrill ride at Disneyland, or walking awestruck through amazing art galleries in The Netherlands.

Everyone has faults, of course, and I am forced to admit that Betty is not perfect. Her major failing is that as a professional role model, her amazing productivity has probably set the bar far too high for the rest of us. But then, as even Sir Isaac Newton noted, we all stand on the shoulders of giants. Betty Collis is definitely someone on whose shoulders many a career has been, is being, and will be launched. As a result, her enormous contributions to our field will go on and on.

REFERENCE

Moonen, J., & Collis, B. (2002). Core connections. *Education and Training Research and Development* (ETRD), *50*(3), 112–118.

M. David Merrill

Department of Instructional Technology, Utah State University

Byron R. Burnham
Utah State University

Andrew Gibbons
Brigham Young University

Dr. M. David Merrill is one of those rare individuals who has touched the intellectual heart of a field of study and practice. Dave—he would prefer the more familiar reference —has been involved in research, teaching, outreach, and international activities.

His teaching has inspired a considerable following. In classes Dave relies upon real-world problems presented by real clients. He brings clients to campus (Motorola, IBM, and others) to present problems to students, which they solve and present back to the client. His student following is not limited to the few that are privileged to attend his courses. Dave is an outstanding conference presenter and is in demand as a keynote speaker around the globe. He has made friends for our department, university, and field of practice in Asia, Europe, the Middle East, and the Pacific Rim through his constant effort to bring a systematic approach to the field of instructional technology.

His teaching has affected individuals in the annual Summer Instructional Technology Institute held in Logan, Utah. Dave has been the inspiration and moving force in bringing professionals and students together for the week just before Labor Day to share the latest in advances in the field and practice of IT. Again the scope of this activity has been international in nature with attendees and speakers from Europe, New Zealand, and Asia as well as from across the United States and Canada. Dave has turned this conference into a learning experience for IT graduate students by allowing them to meet and mingle with persons they would otherwise only read about in the important journals of the field: Alan Lesgold, Beverly Woolf, Alan Collins, Jeroen von Merrinboer, Dexter Fletcher, and a long list of others—scholars, publishers, and business leaders.

David is an outstanding mentor. Over the course of thirty years, seventeen of them at Utah State University, he has chaired the committees of a singularly distinguished and accomplished generation of students. An unusually large number of these have gone on to make major contributions of their own to the field of instructional technology. Dave's list of graduates reads like a "Who's Who" for the field. These graduate students have made outstanding contributions to the field of academic study and practice. It is unusual to pick up a publication in our field without finding an article, a chapter, or a reference to the work of Dave or one of his students. Most of Dave's long list of publications are jointly authored, and virtually all of the joint-authored publications are with his students. Dave uses publication deadlines in his mentoring role to structure writing assignments. Students are challenged to write drafts and work through (what to them seem alike endless) review meetings until the article or chapter is of publication quality. As a consequence, Dave's students are not afraid of publication and actively seek it as a routine activity.

Dave has sufficient contact with the world of commerce that his students have little to worry about in terms of placement. Students are often spoken for before they graduate. His former students represent both academic and corporate employment. The University of Minnesota, University of Colorado (Denver), San Diego State University, and Indiana University are a few of the higher education institutions benefiting from Dave's former students. Many students have started their own successful corporations. These organizations are cutting-edge businesses engaged in research and development of new technologies.

Dave's contributions to the technical side of distance education will be felt worldwide for a long time to come. Some version of his principle of Knowledge Objects has been adopted by all of the major toolmakers (Macromedia, Oracle, NetG, Microsoft, and others) and incorporated into their training design and, in some cases, into their commercial products. The intense international standard-setting activity now underway in the Instructional Management System (IMS) project and the IEEE Learning Technology Systems Architecture (LTSA) project, as well as European efforts with the same goal, are attempts to regularize the notion of interchangeable, interoperable objects and their properties. Dave's work has been a major contribution to the initial structuring of the industry that will undergird Web-based education and educational commerce for the next several decades.

Few writers in the field of instructional technology are cited more often than Dave Merrill. Moreover, of the other top five cited, at least two (Charles Reigeluth and Brent Wilson) are Dave's students. Over the course of his career, Dave's work has become a standard for comparison, referred to by both those who agree and disagree. In about 1973, Dave published a revolutionary Component Display Theory (CDT). Since then his theory has changed the way technology-based instruction is designed, structured, and manufactured. CDT, viewed at first with skepticism, has had the effect over time of redefining the way most designers think of and execute their designs. Years later, Dave broadened his scope by publishing Instructional Transaction Theory (ITT), which he feels is a key to allowing computers to generate instructional interactions in real time from primitive components. Dave's publication record underlies his worldwide contributions to the field: 12 books, 16 chapters in edited books, 65 journal articles, 123 technical reports, 18 instructional computer products, and 5 expert system prototypes. Dave was listed among the most productive educational psychologists (Gordon et al., *Educational Researcher*, August-September, 1984), among the most frequently cited authors in the computer-based instruction literature (Wedman, *Journal of Computer-Based Instruction,* Summer, 1987), and ranked among the most influential people in the field of instructional technology (Moore & Braden, *Performance Instruction*, March, 1988).

Dave's professional contributions go beyond his publication and consulting practices, affecting the way professional organizations go about their work. He has been a leading member of professional organizations, including the American Educational Research Association (AERA); the Association for Educational Research and Technology (AECT) on which he has had major influence, particularly in the area of publications; the American Psychological Association (APA); the Association for Computer-Based Instructional Systems (ADCIS) of which he is a past president; and the National Society for Performance and Instruction (NSPE, now the International Society, ISPI).

Dave's influence, as already noted, has been worldwide. He has actively sought the best international students to mentor. He has chaired doctoral committees for students from Iran, Kuwait, Lebanon, Ireland, and China.

Dave's passion for quality "training" is also exemplified in his personal life by his dedication to model railroading. He has built and operated the Ascape Tennsion & Sulphur Gulch Railroad, which has grown to fill several rooms in his home. He loves to share his passion for model trains and can often be found on his hands and knees tracing some malfunction so that his trains, like his training, operate on time and effectively.

As Dave retires from the university, he is not retiring from the field. Through service to his church, he is currently using his considerable skill and worldwide reputation to assist young learners in the geographically vast and culturally diverse Pacific Basin to use distance education in preparation for university-level study.

Part Four
Organizations and Associations

Introduction

Part Four includes annotated entries for associations and organizations, most of which are headquartered in North America (one organization based in Cape Town, South Africa, is cited), whose interests are in some manner significant to the fields of instructional technology and educational media. This part begins with a classified list designed to facilitate location of organizations by their specialized interests or services, followed by an alphabetical list with more information on the organizations. For the most part, these organizations are associations of professionals in the field or agencies that offer services to the educational media community.

Information for this section was obtained through e-mails directing each organization to an individual Web form through which the updated information could be submitted electronically into a database created by Dr. Mike Orey. Although the section editor made every effort to contact and follow up with organization representatives, responding to the annual request for an update was left up to the organization representatives. The editing team would like to thank those respondents who helped ensure the currency and accuracy of this section by responding to the request for an update. So that readers can judge the accuracy of information provided by each entry, a "last updated" date has been provided. Readers are encouraged to contact the editors with names of unlisted media-related organizations for investigation and possible inclusion in the 2006 edition.

Figures quoted as dues refer to annual amounts unless stated otherwise. Where dues, membership, and meeting information is not applicable such information is omitted.

Jo McClendon

Organizations and Associations

CLASSIFIED LIST

Adult and Continuing Education

(ALA Round Table) Continuing Library Education Network and Exchange (CLENERT)
Association for Continuing Higher Education (ACHE)
Association for Educational Communications and Technology (AECT)
ERIC Clearinghouse on Adult, Career, and Vocational Education (CE)
National Education Telecommunications Organization & Education Satellite Company
    (NETO/EDSAT)
National University Continuing Education Association (NUCEA)
Network for Continuing Medical Education (NCME)
PBS Adult Learning Service (ALS)
University Continuing Education Association (UCEA)

Children- and Youth-Related Organizations

Adjunct ERIC Clearinghouse for Child Care (ADJ/CC)
American Montessori Society
Association for Childhood Education International (ACEI)
Association for Library Service to Children (ALSC)
(CEC) Technology and Media Division (TAM)
Children's Television International, Inc.
Close Up Foundation
Computer Learning Foundation
Council for Exceptional Children (CEC)
National Association for the Education of Young Children (NAEYC)
National PTA
Young Adult Library Services Association (YALSA)

Communication

Association for Educational Communications and Technology (AECT)
Health Science Communications Association (HeSCA)
International Association of Business Communicators (IABC)
Lister Hill National Center for Biomedical Communications of the National Library of
    Medicine
National Communication Association (NCA)
National Council of the Churches of Christ

Computers

(AECT) Division of Interactive Systems and Computers (DISC)
Association for Computers and the Humanities (ACH)
Association for the Advancement of Computing in Education (AACE)
Computer Learning Foundation

Computer-Using Educators, Inc. (CUE)
International Society for Technology in Education (ISTE)
Online Computer Library Center (OCLC)
Society for Computer Simulation (SCS)

Copyright

Association of American Publishers (AAP)
Association of College and Research Libraries (ACRL)
Copyright Clearance Center (CCC)
Hollywood Film Archive
International Copyright Information Center (INCINC)
Library of Congress
Multimedia Education Group, University of Cape Town (MEG)

Distance Education

Community College Satellite Network (CCSN)
Instructional Telecommunications Council (ITC)
International Society for Technology in Education (ISTE)
International Telecommunications Satellite Organization (INTELSAT)
National Education Telecommunications Organization & EDSAT Institute
(NETO/EDSAT)

Education—General

American Society of Educators (ASE)
Association for Childhood Education International (ACEI)
Association for Experiential Education (AEE)
Council for Basic Education
Education Development Center, Inc.
Institute for Development of Educational Activities, Inc. (I|ID|E|A|)
Minorities in Media (MIM)
National Association of State Textbook Administrators (NASTA)
National Clearinghouse for Bilingual Education
National Council for Accreditation of Teacher Education (NCATE)
National School Boards Association (NSBA) Institute for the Transfer of Technology to
Education (ITTE)
The Learning Team (TLT)

Education—Higher

American Association of Community Colleges (AACC)
American Association of State Colleges and Universities
Association for Continuing Higher Education (ACHE)
Association for Library and Information Science Education (ALISE)
Community College Association for Instruction and Technology (CCAIT)
Consortium of College and University Media Centers (CCUMC)
Multimedia Education Group (MEG)

Northwest College and University Council for the Management of Educational Technology
PBS Adult Learning Service
University Continuing Education Association (UCEA)

Equipment

Association for Childhood Education International (ACEI)
Educational Products Information Exchange (EPIE Institute)
ITA
Library and Information Technology Association (LITA)
National School Supply and Equipment Association (NSSEA)
Society of Cable Telecommunications Engineers (SCTE)

ERIC

ERIC Document Reproduction Service (EDRS)

Film and Video

Academy of Motion Picture Arts and Sciences (AMPAS)
(AECT) Division of Telecommunications (DOT)
(AECT) Industrial Training and Education Division (ITED)
Agency for Instructional Technology (AIT)
American Society of Cinematographers
Anthropology Film Center (AFC)
Association for Educational Communications and Technology (AECT)
Association of Independent Video and Filmmakers/Foundation for Independent Video and
    Film (AIVF/FIVF)
Cable in the Classroom
Central Educational Network (CEN)
Children's Television International, Inc.
Close Up Foundation
Community College Satellite Network
Council on International Non-theatrical Events (CINE)
Film Advisory Board
Film Arts Foundation (FAF)
Film/Video Arts, Inc.
Great Plains National ITV Library (GPN)
Hollywood Film Archive
International Teleconferencing Association (ITCA)
International Television Association (ITVA)
ITA
National Aeronautics and Space Administration (NASA)
National Alliance for Media Arts and Culture (NAMAC)
National Association of Broadcasters (NAB)
National Education Telecommunications Organization & Education Satellite Company
    (NETO/EDSAT)
National Endowment for the Humanities (NEH)
National Film Board of Canada (NFBC)

National Film Information Service (offered by AMPAS)
National Information Center for Educational Media (NICEM)
National ITFS Association (NIA/ITFS)
National Telemedia Council, Inc. (NTC)
The New York Festivals
Pacific Film Archive (PFA)
PBS Adult Learning Service (ALS)
PBS VIDEO
Public Broadcasting Service (PBS)
Society of Cable Telecommunications Engineers (SCTE)

Games, Toys, Play, Simulation, Puppetry

Puppeteers of America, Inc. (POA)
Society for Computer Simulation (SCS)
USA-Toy Library Association (USA-TLA)

Health-Related Organizations

Health Science Communications Association (HeSCA)
Lister Hill National Center for Biomedical Communications
Medical Library Association (MLA)
National Association for Visually Handicapped (NAVH)
Network for Continuing Medical Education (NCME)

Information Science

Association for Library and Information Science Education (ALISE)
Freedom of Information Center
International Information Management Congress (IMC)
Library and Information Technology Association (LITA)
Lister Hill National Center for Biomedical Communications
National Commission on Libraries and Information Science (NCLIS)

Innovation

Institute for Development of Educational Activities, Inc. (I|I|D|E|A|)
Institute for the Future (IFTF)
World Future Society (WFS)

Instructional Technology, Design, and Development

(AECT) Division of Educational Media Management (DEMM)
(AECT) Division of Instructional Development (DID)
Agency for Instructional Technology (AIT)
Association for Educational Communications and Technology (AECT)
Community College Association for Instruction and Technology (CCAIT)
International Society for Performance and Instruction (ISPI)
Multimedia Education Group, University of Cape Town (MEG)
Professors of Instructional Design and Technology (PIDT)

Society for Applied Learning Technology (SALT)
The Learning Team (TLT)

International Education

(AECT) International Division (INTL)
East-West Center
International Association for Learning Laboratories, Inc. (IALL)
International Visual Literacy Association, Inc. (IVLA)
National Clearinghouse for Bilingual Education (NCBE)

Language

International Association for Learning Laboratories, Inc. (IALL)
National Clearinghouse for Bilingual Education (NCBE)

Libraries—Academic, Research

American Library Association (ALA)
Association of College and Research Libraries (ACRL)

Libraries—Public

American Library Association (ALA)
Association for Library Service to Children (ALSC)
Library Administration and Management Association (LAMA)
Library and Information Technology Association (LITA)
Public Library Association (PLA)
Young Adult Library Services Association (YALSA)

Libraries and Media Centers—School

(AECT) Division of School Media Specialists (DSMS)
(ALA Round Table) Continuing Library Education Network and Exchange (CLENERT)
American Association of School Librarians (AASL)
American Library Association (ALA)
American Library Trustee Association (ALTA)
Association for Educational Communications and Technology (AECT)
Association for Library Collections and Technical Services (ALCTS)
Association for Library Service to Children (ALSC)
Catholic Library Association (CLA)
Consortium of College and University Media Centers
International Association of School Librarianship (IASL)
Library of Congress
National Alliance for Media Arts and Culture (NAMAC)
National Association of Regional Media Centers (NARMC)
National Commission on Libraries and Information Science (NCLIS)
National Council of Teachers of English (NCTE), Commission on Media
On-Line Audiovisual Catalogers (OLAC)

Southeastern Regional Media Leadership Council (SRMLC)

Libraries—Special

American Library Association (ALA)
Association for Library Service to Children (ALSC)
Association of Specialized and Cooperative Library Agencies (ASCLA)
Medical Library Association (MLA)
Special Libraries Association
Theater Library Association
USA Toy Library Association (USA-TLA)

Media Production

(AECT) Media Design and Production Division (MDPD)
American Society of Cinematographers (ASC)
Association for Educational Communications and Technology (AECT)
Association of Independent Video and Filmmakers/Foundation for Independent Video and
      Film (AIVF/FIVF)
Film Arts Foundation (FAF)
International Graphics Arts Education Association (IGAEA)

Museums and Archives

(AECT) Archives
Association of Systematics Collections
George Eastman House
Hollywood Film Archive
Library of Congress
Museum Computer Network (MCN)
Museum of Modern Art
National Gallery of Art (NGA)
National Public Broadcasting Archives (NPBA)
Pacific Film Archive (PFA)
Smithsonian Institution

Photography

Electronic Camera Repair, C&C Associates
George Eastman House
International Center of Photography (ICP)
National Press Photographers Association, Inc. (NPPA)
Photographic Society of America (PSA)
Society for Photographic Education (SPE)
Society of Photo Technologists (SPT)

Publishing

Graphic Arts Technical Foundation (GATF)
International Graphics Arts Education Association (IGAEA)

Magazine Publishers of America (MPA)
National Association of State Textbook Administrators (NASTA)

Radio

(AECT) Division of Telecommunications (DOT)
American Women in Radio and Television (AWRT)
Corporation for Public Broadcasting (CPB)
National Endowment for the Humanities (NEH)
National Federation of Community Broadcasters (NFCB)
National Public Broadcasting Archives (NPBA)
National Religious Broadcasters (NRB)
Western Public Radio (WPR)

Religious Education

Catholic Library Association (CLA)
National Council of the Churches of Christ in the USA
National Religious Broadcasters (NRB)

Research

(AECT) Research and Theory Division (RTD)
American Educational Research Association (AERA)
Appalachia Educational Laboratory, Inc. (AEL)
ECT Foundation
Education Development Center, Inc.
Mid-continent Regional Educational Laboratory (McREL)
Multimedia Education Group, University of Cape Town (MEG)
National Center for Improving Science Education
National Education Knowledge Industry Association (NEKIA)
National Endowment for the Humanities (NEH)
National Science Foundation (NSF)
The NETWORK
North Central Regional Educational Laboratory (NCREL)
Northwest Regional Educational Laboratory (NWREL)
Pacific Regional Educational Laboratory (PREL)
Research for Better Schools, Inc. (RBS)
SouthEastern Regional Vision for Education (SERVE)
Southwest Educational Development Laboratory (SEDL)
WestEd

Special Education

Adaptech Research Project
American Foundation for the Blind (AFB)
Association for Experiential Education (AEE)

Association of Specialized and Cooperative Library Agencies (ASCLA)
Council for Exceptional Children (CEC)
National Association for Visually Handicapped (NAVH)
National Center to Improve Practice (NCIP)
Recording for the Blind and Dyslexic (RFB&D)

Telecommunications

(AECT) Division of Telecommunications (DOT)
Association for the Advancement of Computing in Education (AACE)
Association of Independent Video and Filmmakers/Foundation for Independent Video and Film (AIVF/FIVF)
Community College Satellite Network (CCSN)
Instructional Telecommunications Council (ITC)
International Telecommunications Satellite Organization (INTELSAT)
International Teleconferencing Association (ITCA)
Library and Information Technology Association (LITA)
National Education Telecommunications Organization & Education Satellite Company (NETO/EDSAT)
Research for Better Schools, Inc. (RBS)
Teachers and Writers Collaborative (T&W)

Television

American Women in Radio and Television (AWRT)
Central Educational Network (CEN)
Children's Television International, Inc. (CTI)
Corporation for Public Broadcasting (CPB)
International Television Association (ITVA)
National Cable Television Institute (NCTI)
National Federation of Community Broadcasters (NFCB)
Society of Cable Telecommunications Engineers (SCTE)

Training

(AECT) Industrial Training and Education Division (ITED)
American Management Association (AMA)
American Society for Training and Development (ASTD)
Association for Educational Communications and Technology (AECT)
Federal Educational Technology Association (FETA)
International Society for Performance Improvement (ISPI)

ALPHABETICAL LIST

Academy of Motion Picture Arts and Sciences (AMPAS). 8949 Wilshire Blvd, Beverly Hills, CA 90211-1972. (310) 247-3000. Fax (310) 859-9351. E-mail: answers@oscars.org. Web site: http://www.oscars.org. Bruce Davis, Exec. Dir. An honorary organization composed of outstanding individuals in all phases of motion pictures. Seeks to advance the arts and sciences of motion picture technology and artistry. Presents annual film awards; offers artist-in-residence programs; operates reference library and National Film Information Service. *Membership:* 6,000. *Publications: Annual Index to Motion Picture Credits; Academy Players Directory.*

ACCESS Network. 3720 76 Ave., Edmonton, AB T6B 2N9 Canada. (403) 440-7777. Fax (403) 440-8899. E-mail: promo@ccinet.ab.ca. Dr. Ronald Keast, Pres.; John Verburgt, Creative Services Manager. The ACCESS Network (Alberta Educational Communications Corporation) was purchased by Learning and Skills Television of Alberta in 1995. The newly privatized network works with Alberta's educators to provide all Albertans with a progressive and diverse television-based educational and training resource to support their learning and skills development needs using cost-effective methods and innovative techniques, and to introduce a new private sector model for financing and efficient operation of educational television in the province.

Adaptech Research Network. Dawson College, 3040 Sherbrooke St. West, Montreal, QC H3Z 1A4. (514) 931-8731 #1546. Fax (514) 931-3567, attn: Catherine Fichten. E-mail: catherine.fichten@mcgill.ca. Web site: http://www.adaptech.org. Catherine Fichten, Ph.D., Co-director; Jennison V. Asuncion, M.A., Co-Director; Maria Barile, M.S.W., Co-Director. Based at Dawson College (Montreal), we are a Canada-wide, grant-funded team, conducting bilingual empirical research into the use of computer, learning, and adaptive technologies by postsecondary students with disabilities. One of our primary interests lies in issues around ensuring that newly emerging instructional technologies are accessible to learners with disabilities. *Membership:* Our research team is composed of academics, practitioners, students, consumers, and others interested in the issues of access to technology by students with disabilities in higher education. *Dues:* n/a. *Meetings:* n/a. *Publications:* Fichten, C. S., Asuncion, J. V., Robillard, C., Fossey, M. E., & Barile, M. (2003). Are you considering all students, including those with disabilities, when planning for technology integration? *Canadian Journal of Learning and Technology, 29*(2), 5–34. Retrieved November 20, 2003, from http://www.cjlt.ca/content/vol29.2/cjlt29-2_art-1.html. Fichten, C.S., Barile, M., & Asuncion, J. V. (2003). Computer technologies that level the playing field for people with disabilities: Implications for rehabilitation psychologists. *Rehabilitation Psychology, 48*(3), 207–214. Asuncion, J., Fichten, C. S., Fossey, M., & Barile, M. (2002). Dialoguing with developers and suppliers of adaptive computer technologies: Data and recommendations. *Universal Access in the Information Society, 1*(3), 177–196.

AEL, Inc. (AEL). P.O. Box 1348, Charleston, WV 25325-1348. (304) 347-0400, (800) 624-9120. Fax (304) 347-0487. E-mail: aelinfo@ael.org. Web site: http://www.ael.org. Dr. Doris L. Redfield, President and CEO. AEL is a catalyst for schools and communities to build lifelong learning systems that harness resources, research, and practical wisdom. To contribute knowledge that assists low-performing schools to move toward continuous improvement, AEL conducts research, development, evaluation, and dissemination activities that inform policy, affect educational practice, and contribute to the theoretical and procedural knowledge bases on effective teaching, learning, and schooling. Strategies build on research and reflect a commitment to empowering individuals and building local capacity. AEL serves Kentucky, Tennessee, Virginia, and West Virginia. *Publications:* The AEL

Electronic Library contains links to free online tools and information created by staff on a wide array of education-related topics. In addition, there are the online versions of AELs newsletters. *The Link* is a free quarterly publication that provides helpful information to practitioners about trends in education, and *TransFormation* is written for those interested in policy related to education.

Agency for Instructional Technology (AIT). Box A, Bloomington, IN 47402-0120. (812) 339-2203. Fax (812) 333-4218. info@ait.net. Web site: http://www.ait.net. Charles E. Wilson, Executive Director. The Agency for Instructional Technology has been a leader in educational technology since 1962. A nonprofit organization, AIT is one of the largest providers of instructional TV programs in North America. AIT is also a leading developer of other educational media, including online instruction, CDs, videodiscs, and instructional software. AIT learning resources are used on six continents and reach nearly 34 million students in North America each year. AIT products have received many national and international honors, including an Emmy and Peabody award. Since 1970, AIT has developed thirty-nine major curriculum packages through the consortium process it pioneered. American state and Canadian provincial agencies have cooperatively funded and widely used these learning resources. Funding for other product development comes from state, provincial, and local departments of education; federal and private institutions; corporations and private sponsors; and AITs own resources.

American Association of Colleges for Teacher Education (AACTE). 1307 New York Ave., NW, Suite 300, Washington, DC 20005-4701. (202) 293-2450. Fax (202) 457-8095. Web site: http://www.aacte.org/. David G. Imig, President and Chief Executive Officer. Adjunct to the ERIC Clearinghouse on Teaching and Teacher Education. The American Association of Colleges for Teacher Education (AACTE) provides leadership for the continuing transformation of professional preparation programs to ensure competent and caring educators for all Americas children and youth. It is the principal professional association for college and university leaders with responsibility for educator preparation. It is the major voice, nationally and internationally, for American colleges, schools, and departments of education, and is a locus for discussion and decision-making on professional issues of institutional, state, national and international significance. *Membership:* more than 2,400 members; Membership in AACTE is institutional and there are three categories: regular, affiliate, and candidate. Regular membership is available to four-year degree-granting colleges and universities with significant commitment to the preparation of education personnel, which meet all the criteria for regular or candidate membership. Affiliate membership is available to not-for-profit two-year or four-year degree-granting foreign institutions of higher education; not-for-profit two-year domestic degree-granting institutions of higher education; and not-for-profit organizations, state education associations, regional education laboratories, university-based research or policy centers, and other not-for-profit education associations as identified by the AACTE Board of Directors. *Meetings:* Many meetings including the New Deans Institute. See: http://www.aacte.org/Events/default.htm. *Publications:* AACTE publishes books and other publications in a range of areas that address key issues related to teacher education. We have more than seventy titles available in a variety of subject areas.

American Association of Community Colleges (AACC). One Dupont Circle, NW, Suite 410, Washington, DC 20036-1176. (202) 728-0200. Fax (202) 833-9390. E-mail: nkent@aacc.nche.edu. Web site: http://www.aacc.nche.edu. George R. Boggs, President and CEO. AACC is a national organization representing the nations more than 1,100 community, junior, and technical colleges. Headquartered in Washington, D.C., AACC serves as a national voice for the colleges and provides key services in the areas of advocacy, research, information, and professional development. The nations community colleges serve more than 10 million students annually, almost half (44%) of all U.S. undergraduates. *Membership:* 1,151 institutions, 31 corporations, 15 international associates, 79 educational associates, 4 foundations. *Dues:* vary by category. *Meetings:* Annual Convention,

April of each year. *Publications:* Community College Journal (bi-monthly); Community College Times (bi-weekly newspaper); College Times; Community College Press (books, research and program briefs, and monographs).

(AACC) Community College Satellite Network (CCSN). One Dupont Cir. NW, Suite 410, Washington, DC 20036. (202) 728-0200. Fax (202) 833-2467. E-mail: CCSN@AACC.NCHE.EDU. Web site: http://www.aacc.nche.edu. Monica W. Pilkey, Dir. An office of the American Association of Community Colleges (AACC), CCSN provides leadership and facilitates distance education, teleconferencing, and satellite training to the nation's community colleges. CCSN offers satellite training, discounted teleconferences, free program resources, and general informational assistance in telecommunications to the nation's community colleges. CCSN meets with its members at various industry trade shows and is very active in the AACC annual convention held each spring. CCSN produces a directory of community college satellite downlink and videoconference facilities. *Membership:* 150. *Dues:* $400 for AACC members; $800 for non-AACC members. *Publications: Schedule of Programming* (2/yr.; contains listings of live and taped teleconferences for training and staff development); *CCSN Fall & Spring Program Schedule* (listing of live and taped teleconferences for training, community and staff development, business and industry training, and more); *Teleconferencing at U.S. Community Colleges* (directory of contacts for community college satellite downlink facilities and videoconference capabilities). A free catalog is available.

American Association of School Librarians (AASL). 50 E. Huron St., Chicago, IL 60611-2795. (312) 280-4386. (800) 545-2433, ext. 4386. Fax (312) 664-7459. E-mail: aasl@ala.org. Web site: http://www.ala.org/aasl. Julie A. Walker, Exec. Dir. A division of the American Library Association, AASL is interested in the general improvement and extension of school library media services for children and youth. Activities and projects of the association are divided among thirty committees and three sections. *Membership:* 9,500. *Dues:* Personal membership in ALA (1st yr., $50; 2nd yr., $75; 3rd and subsequent yrs., $100) plus $40 for personal membership in AASL. Inactive, student, retired, unemployed, and reduced-salary memberships are available. *Meetings:* National conference every two years; next national conference to be held in October 2005. *Publications: School Library Media Research* (electronic research journal, http://www.ala.org/aasl/SLMR/); *Knowledge Quest* (print journal; online companion at http://www.ala.org/aasl/kqWeb/), *AASL Hotlinks* (e-mail newsletter), nonserial publications (http://www.ala.org/aasl/pubs_menu.html).

American Association of State Colleges and Universities (AASCU). One Dupont Cir. NW, Suite 700, Washington, DC 20036-1192. (202) 293-7070. Fax (202) 296-5819. E-mail: currisc.aascu.org. James B. Appleberry, Pres. Membership is open to regionally accredited institutions of higher education (and those in the process of securing accreditation) that offer programs leading to the degree of bachelor, master, or doctor, and that are wholly or partially state supported and controlled. Organized and operated exclusively for educational, scientific, and literary purposes, its particular purposes are to improve higher education within its member institutions through cooperative planning, studies, and research on common educational problems and the development of a more unified program of action among its members; and to provide other needed and worthwhile educational services to the colleges and universities it may represent. *Membership:* 393 institutions (university), twenty-eight systems, and ten associates. *Dues:* based on current student enrollment at institution. *Publications: MEMO: To the President; The Center Associate; Office of Federal Program Reports; Office of Federal Program Deadlines.* (Catalogs of books and other publications available upon request.)

American Educational Research Association (AERA). 1230 17th St. NW, Washington, DC 20036-3078. (202) 223-9485. Fax (202) 775-1824. E-mail: outreach@aera.net. Web site: http://www.aera.net. Marilyn Cochran-Smith, President of the Board, 2004–2005, cochrans@bc.edu. AERA is an international professional organization with the primary goal of advancing educational research and its practical application. Its members include educators and administrators; directors of research, testing, or evaluation in federal, state, and local agencies; counselors; evaluators; graduate students; and behavioral scientists. The broad range of disciplines represented includes education, psychology, statistics, sociology, history, economics, philosophy, anthropology, and political science. AERA has more than 145 Special Interest Groups, including Advanced Technologies for Learning, Computer Applications in Education, Electronic Networking, Instructional Systems and Intelligent Tutors, Instructional Technology, and Text, Technology and Learning Strategies. *Membership:* 23,000. *Dues:* vary by category, ranging from $20 for students to $45 for voting members, for one year. See AERA Web site for complete details: www.aera.net. *Meetings:* 2005 Annual Meeting, April 11–15, Montreal, Canada. *Publications: Educational Researcher; American Educational Research Journal; Journal of Educational and Behavioral Statistics; Educational Evaluation and Policy Analysis; Review of Research in Education; Review of Educational Research.* Books: *Handbook of Research on Teaching, 2001* (revised, 4th edition), *Ethical Standards of AERA, Cases and Commentary, 2002 Standards for Educational and Psychological Testing* (revised and expanded, 1999), co-published by AERA, American Psychological Association, and the National Council on Measurement in Education.

American Foundation for the Blind (AFB). 11 Penn Plaza, Suite 300, New York, NY 10001. (212) 502-7600, (800) AFB-LINE (232-5463). Fax (212) 502-7777. E-mail: afbinfo@afb.net. Web site: http://www.afb.org/default.asp. Carl R. Augusto, Pres.; Kelly Parisi, Vice Pres. of Communications. AFB is a leading national resource for people who are blind or visually impaired, the organizations that serve them, and the general public. A nonprofit organization founded in 1921 and recognized as Helen Keller's cause in the United States, AFBs mission is to enable people who are blind or visually impaired to achieve equality of access and opportunity that will ensure freedom of choice in their lives. AFB is headquartered in New York City with offices in Atlanta, Chicago, Dallas, and San Francisco. A governmental relations office in AFB is headquartered in New York City with offices in Atlanta, Chicago, Dallas, San Francisco, and Washington, DC. *Publications: AFB News* (free); *Journal of Visual Impairment & Blindness; AFB Press Catalog of Publications* (free). *AccessWorld*™; Subscriptions Tel: (800) 232-3044 or (412) 741-1398 afbsub@abdintl.com.

American Library Association (ALA). 50 E. Huron St., Chicago, IL 60611. (800) 545-2433. Fax (312) 440-9374. E-mail: ala@ala.org. Web site: http://www.ala.org. Keith Michael Fields, Exec. Dir. The ALA is the oldest and largest national library association. Its 64,200 members represent all types of libraries: state, public, school, and academic, as well as special libraries serving persons in government, commerce, the armed services, hospitals, prisons, and other institutions. The ALA is the chief advocate of achievement and maintenance of high-quality library information services through protection of the right to read, educating librarians, improving services, and making information widely accessible. See separate entries for the following affiliated and subordinate organizations: American Association of School Librarians, American Library Trustee Association, Association for Library Collections and Technical Services, Association for Library Service to Children, Association of College and Research Libraries, Association of Specialized and Cooperative Library Agencies, Library Administration and Management Association, Library and Information Technology Association, Public Library Association, Reference and User Services Association, Young Adult Library Services Association, and Continuing Library Education Network and Exchange Round Table. *Membership:* 64,200 members at present; everyone who cares about libraries is allowed to join the American Library Association. *Dues:* Professional rate: $50, first year; $75, second year; third year & renewing, $100;

Student members: $25; Retirees: $35 International librarians: $50, first year; $60, second year; Trustees: $45; Associate members (those not in the library field): $45. *Meetings:* Annual Conference: June 23–June 29, 2005, Chicago; January 20–25, 2006, San Antonio. *Publications: American Libraries; Booklist; Choice; Book Links.*

American Library Trustee Association (ALTA). 50 E. Huron St., Chicago, IL 60611. (312) 280-2161. Fax (312) 280-3257. E-mail: kward@ala.org. http://www.ala.org/alta. Susan Roman, Exec. Dir. A division of the American Library Association, ALTA is interested in the development of effective library service for people in all types of communities and libraries. Members, as policymakers, are concerned with organizational patterns of service, the development of competent personnel, the provision of adequate financing, the passage of suitable legislation, and the encouragement of citizen support for libraries. *Membership:* 1,710. *Dues:* $50 plus membership in ALA. *Meetings:* Held in conjunction with ALA. *Publications: Trustee Voice* (q. newsletter); professional monographs and pamphlets.

American Management Association International (AMA). 1601 Broadway, New York, NY 10019-7420. (212) 586-8100. Fax (212) 903-8168. E-mail: cust_serv@amanet.org. Web site: http://www.amanet.org. Barbara M. Barrett, Pres. and CEO. Founded in 1923, AMA provides educational forums worldwide where members and their colleagues learn superior, practical business skills and explore best practices of world-class organizations through interaction with each other and expert faculty practitioners. AMA's publishing program provides tools individuals use to extend learning beyond the classroom in a process of life-long professional growth and development through education. AMA operates management centers and offices in Atlanta, Boston (Watertown), Chicago, Hamilton (NY), Kansas City (Leawood), New York, San Francisco, Saranac Lake (NY), and Washington, DC, and through AMA/International, in Brussels, Tokyo, Shanghai, Islamabad, and Buenos Aires. In addition, it has affiliated centers in Toronto, Mexico City, Sao Paulo, Taipei, Istanbul, Singapore, Jakarta, and Dubai. AMA offers conferences, seminars, and membership briefings where there is an interchange of information, ideas, and experience in a wide variety of management topics. *Membership:* over 75,000. *Dues:* corporate, $595–$1,645; growing company, $525–$1,845; indiv., $165 plus $40 per additional newsletter. *Publications: Management Review* (membership); *Compensation & Benefits Review; Organizational Dynamics; HR Focus; President; Getting Results;* and *The Take-Charge Assistant.* Also 70 business-related books per year, as well as numerous surveys and management briefings. Other services offered by AMA include FYI Video; Extension Institute (self-study programs in both print and audio formats); AMA Interactive Series (self-paced learning on CD-ROM); Operation Enterprise (young adult program); AMA On-Site (videoconferences); the Information Resource Center (for AMA members only), a management information and library service; and six bookstores.

American Montessori Society (AMS). 281 Park Ave. S, New York, NY 10010. (212) 358-1250. Fax (212) 358-1256. E-mail: mimi@amshq.org. Web site: http://www.amshq.org. Eileen Roper Ast, Executive Director. Dedicated to promoting better education for all children through teaching strategies consistent with the Montessori system. Membership is composed of schools in the private and public sectors, teacher education programs, Montessori-credentialed teachers, parents, and other individuals. It serves as a resource center and clearinghouse for information and data on Montessori education, prepares teachers in different parts of the country, and conducts a consultation service and accreditation program for school members.

The mission of the American Montessori Society is to promote high-quality Montessori education for all children by providing service to parents, teachers and schools. *Membership:* Membership includes schools, teachers, parents, school heads, and friends of Montessori. This total is approximately 11,000. *Dues:* Due vary based on membership. Membership is available for Certified Montessori Teachers, Montessori School and General Members (includes those who are not Certified Montessori Teachers, parents, friends of AMS). *Meetings:* three regional and four professional development symposia under the auspices of the AMS Teachers. *Publications: AMS Montessori LIFE* (q); *Schoolheads* (newsletter); *Montessori in Contemporary American Culture,* Margaret Loeffler, Editor; *Authentic American Montessori School; AMS The Montessori School Management Guide;* AMS position papers; and the following AMS Publications: *Montessori Teaching: A Growth Profession; The Elementary School Years 6–12; Your Child Is in an Accredited School; Some Considerations in Starting a Montessori School; Montessori Education Q&A; The Early Childhood Years, 3–6; Attracting and Preparing Montessori Teacher for the 21st Century; Adolescent Programs; The Kindergarten Experience; Some Comparisons of Montessori Education with Traditional Education; Helping Children Become All They Can Become; The Montessori Family: A Parent Brochure; Tuition and Salary Surveys.*

American Society for Training and Development (ASTD). 1640 King St., Box 1443, Alexandria, VA 22313. (703) 683-8100. Fax (703) 683-1523. E-mail: customercare @astd.org. Web site: http://www.astd.org. Tony Bingham, President and CEO. Founded in 1944, ASTD is the world's premiere professional association in the field of workplace learning and performance. ASTDs membership includes more than 70,000 people in organizations from every level of the field of workplace performance in more than 100 countries. Its leadership and members work in more than 15,000 multinational corporations, small and medium-sized businesses, government agencies, colleges, and universities. ASTD is the leading resource on workplace learning and performance issues, providing information, research, analysis, and practical information derived from its own research, the knowledge and experience of its members, its conferences and publications, and the coalitions and partnerships it has built through research and policy work. ASTD has a board membership of 16 and staff of 90 to serve member needs. *Membership:* 70,000 National and Chapter members. *Dues:* The Classic Membership ($150.00) is the foundation of ASTD member benefits. Publications, newsletters, research reports, discounts and services, and much more, are all designed to help you do your job better. Here's what you have to look forward to when you join:

- *Training and Development*—Monthly publication of the Industry. Stay informed on trends, successful practices, public policy, ASTD news, case studies and more.

- *Performance in Practice*—Quarterly newsletter offers articles written by members for members.

- *Hot Topics*—ASTDs online reading list gets you up to speed on leading edge issues in the training and performance industry.

- Database and Archive Access—free online access to *Trainlit,* ASTD's searchable database featuring products reviews, book and article summaries and archived articles.

- *Learning Circuits*—Monthly Webzine features articles, departments, and columns that examine new technologies and how they're being applied to workplace learning.

- *Human Resource Development Quarterly*—In-depth studies and reports on human resource theory and practice give you a scholarly look at the training profession. HRDQ is available only online with archives dating back to 1998.

- *ASTD News Briefs*—Weekly news briefs relating to the training and performance industry.

- Special Reports and Research—*Trends Report, State of the Industry, Learning Outcomes and International Comparison Report.*

- *Training Data Book*—An annual publication, now online, draws on ASTD research and highlights the nature and magnitude of corporate investment in employer-provided training.

- Research Assistance—ASTD provides an Information Center that can provide you with the research you're looking for while you're on the phone. You can also send your research request through the Web site. Just provide your member number! Membership Directory—Online directory and searchable by a variety of criteria. Access to the Membership Directory is for members only and is being enhanced for future networking capabilities.

- *Buyers Guide & Consultants Directory*—A one-stop resource for information on over 600 suppliers of training and performance products and services.

We also have several segments that you can add on to your Classic Membership:

- Membership Plus: Your choice of 12 info lines or four prechosen ASTD books. $79.00.

- Training Professionals: Includes an annual subscription to *Info-lines, Pfeiffer's Best of Training,* and the *ASTD Training and Performance Yearbook.* $130.00.

- Organizational Development/Leadership Professionals: Includes *Pfeiffers Consulting Annual, Leader to Leader,* and *Leadership in Action.* $200.00

- Consulting: Includes annual subscription to *C2M* (quarterly journal), and *Pfeiffer's Consulting Annual.* $75.00.

- E-Learning: Includes *Training Media Review Online* (Database and newsletter that evaluates audio, video, software, and online products 6/year e-mail newsletters yr.) and *ASTD Distance Learning Yearbook.* $175.00.

Publications: Training & Development Magazine; Info-Line; The American Mosaic: An In-depth Report of Diversity on the Future of Diversity at Work; ASTD Directory of Academic Programs in T&D/HRD; Training and Development Handbook; Quarterly publications: Performance in Practice; National Report on Human Resources; Washington Policy Report. ASTD also has recognized professional forums, most of which produce newsletters.

American Society of Cinematographers (ASC). 1782 N. Orange Dr., Hollywood, CA 90028. (213) 969-4333. Fax (213) 876-4973, (213) 882-6391. E-mail: suzanne.lezotte @creativeplanet.com. Victor Kemper, Pres. ASC is an educational, cultural, and professional organization. *Membership:* 336. Membership is by invitation to those who are actively engaged as directors of photography and have demonstrated outstanding ability. Classifications are Active, Active Retired, Associates, and Honorary. *Meetings:* Book Bazaar (Open House); Awards Open House; Annual ASC Awards. *Publications: American Cinematographer Video Manual; Light on Her Face;* and *American Cinematographers Magazine.*

American Society of Educators (ASE). 1429 Walnut St., Philadelphia, PA 19102. (215) 563-6005. Fax (215) 587-9706. E-mail: tatjana@media-methods.com. Web site: http://www.media-methods.com. Michele Sokolof, Publisher & Editorial Director. American Society of Educators publishes Media & Methods Magazine, the recognized authoritative publication dedicated to exemplary teaching practices and resource materials for K–12 educators. Full of pragmatic articles on how to use todays instructional technologies and teaching tools, *Media & Methods* is the flagship magazine of practical educational applications specifically for school district technology coordinators, media specialists, school librarians, administrators, and teachers. A long-respected and treasured magazine focusing on how to integrate today's tools for teaching as well as for administrative and library management in K–12 schools. *Membership:* Individuals subscribe to *Media & Methods* magazine. *Dues:* None. *Meetings:* Meetings occur at national education conferences. *Publications: Media & Methods* magazine is published 7 times a year. Cost: $33.50 per year.

American Telecommunications Group (ATG). 1400 E. Touhy, Suite 260, Des Plaines, IL 60018-3305. (847) 390-8700. Fax (847) 390-9435. E-mail: gerie@atgonline.org. Web site: http://www.itmonline.com/Marketplace/atg.htm. James A. Fellows, President. The American Telecommunications Group serves as an umbrella framework for six entities that are organized to provide and support educational and programming services, professional development and policy development for public broadcasting, educational telecommunications and related public service media: American Center for Children and Media—a professional development and resource center for people who create, commission, distribute and study children's TV and digital media; Center for Education Initiatives—supports distance learning, adult training, and evaluation of new technology initiatives in education; Central Educational Network a nonprofit, executive-level association of public broadcasting licensees that undertakes joint activities and services, administers program funds and awards, and conducts leadership exchanges; Continental Program Marketing—distributes quality programming to U.S. public television stations; The Hartford Gunn Institute—assists in developing fundamental plans for building the second generation of public telecommunications; the Higher Education Telecommunications Consortium—assists colleges and universities in managing telecommunications operations and advances the expansion and development of higher education-based telecommunication services. *Membership:* Membership in the CEN component of ATG is available to public television and telecommunications organizations and agencies. Membership in the Higher Education Telecommunications Consortia is available to public television stations that are licensed to colleges and universities. *Publications:* "Close Up Online" is a periodic briefing that keeps readers informed about the various services and activities of the organizations that are a part of the ATG. "Close Up Online" also reports on noteworthy people and activities throughout our nationwide constituency.

American Women in Radio and Television (AWRT). 8405 Greensboro Drive, Suite 800, McLean, VA 22102. (703) 506-3290. Fax (703) 506-3266. E-mail: info@awrt.org. Web site: http://www.awrt.org. Maria E. Brennan. American Women in Radio and Television is a national, nonprofit organization that extends membership to qualified professionals in the electronic media and allied fields. AWRT's mission is to advance the impact of women in the electronic media and allied fields by educating, advocating and acting as a resource to its members and the industry. Founded in 1951, AWRT has worked to improve the quality of broadcast programming and the image of women as depicted in radio and television. *Membership:* 40 chapters. Student memberships available. *Dues:* $125. *Meetings:* Annual Leadership Summit, Annual Gracie Allen Awards. *Publications: News and Views; Resource Directory; Careers in the Electronic Media; Sexual Harassment;* mentoring brochure (pamphlet).

Anthropology Film Center (AFC). #5 Paseo Sin Nombre, Valencia, NM 87535-9635. (505) 757-2219. E-mail: info@anthrofilm.org. Web site: http://www.anthrofilm.org. Carroll Williams, Dir. Offers the Ethnographic/Documentary Film Program, a 32-week full-time course for 16mm film, CD, and DVD production and theory. Workshops are offered as well. AFC also provides consultation, research facilities, and a specialized library. Workshops in Visual Anthropology are offered. September and June starts. Mailing address is HC70 Box 3209, Glorieta, NM 87535-9635. *Membership:* n/a *Meetings:* None scheduled. *Publications:* A filmography for American Indian Education.

Association for Childhood Education International (ACEI). 17904 Georgia Ave., Suite 215, Olney, MD 20832. (301) 570-2111. Fax (301) 570-2212. E-mail: ACEIHQ@aol.com. Web site: http://www.udel.edu/bateman/acei/. Anne W. Bauer, Ed. and Dir. ACEI publications reflect careful research, broad-based views, and consideration of a wide range of issues affecting children from infancy through early adolescence. Many are media-related in nature. The journal (*Childhood Education*) is essential for teachers, teachers-in-training, teacher educators, day-care workers, administrators, and parents. Articles focus on child development and emphasize practical application. Regular departments include book reviews (child and adult); film reviews, pamphlets, software, research, and classroom idea-sparkers. Six issues are published yearly, including a theme issue devoted to critical concerns. *Membership:* 12,000. *Dues:* $45, professional; $26, student; $23, retired; $80, institutional. *Publications: Childhood Education* (official journal) with *ACEI Exchange* (insert newsletter); *Journal of Research in Childhood Education;* professional division newsletters (*Focus on Infants and Toddlers, Focus on Pre-K and K, Focus on Elementary,* and *Focus on Middle School*); *Celebrating Family Literacy Through Intergenerational Programming; Selecting Educational Equipment for School and Home; Developmental Continuity Across Preschool and Primary Grades; Implications for Teachers; Developmentally Appropriate Middle Level Schools; Common Bonds: Antibias Teaching in a Diverse Society; Childhood 1892–1992; Infants and Toddlers with Special Needs and Their Families* (position paper); and pamphlets.

Association for Computers and the Humanities (ACH). c/o Ray Siemens, Exec. Secretary, Dept. of English, Malaspina University College, Nanaimo, BC V9R 5S5. (250) 753-2345 ext. 2046. Fax (250) 740-6459. E-mail: siemensr@mala.bc.ca. Web site: http:// www.ach.org. Ray Siemens, Exec. Secretary. The Association for Computers and the Humanities is an international professional organization. Since its establishment, it has been the major professional society for people working in computer-aided research in literature and language studies, history, philosophy, and other humanities disciplines, and especially research involving the manipulation and analysis of textual materials. The ACH is devoted to disseminating information among its members about work in the field of humanities computing, as well as encouraging the development and dissemination of significant textual and linguistic resources and software for scholarly research. *Membership:* 300. *Dues:* Individual regular member, US $65 Student or Emeritus Faculty member, US $55. Joint membership (for couples), Add US $7. *Meetings:* Annual meetings held with the Association for Literary and Linguistic Computing. *Publications: Computers and the Humanities; Humanist.*

Association for Continuing Higher Education (ACHE). Trident Technical College, P.O. Box 118067, CE-M, Charleston, SC 29423-8067. (803) 574-6658. Fax (803) 574-6470. E-mail: irene.barrineau@tridenttech.edu. Web site: http://www.acheinc.org/. Dr. Jerry Hickerson, President; Dr. Pamela R. Murray, President Elect. ACHE is an institution-based organization of colleges, universities, and individuals dedicated to the promotion of lifelong learning and excellence in continuing higher education. ACHE encourages professional networks, research, and exchange of information for its members and advocates continuing higher education as a means of enhancing and improving society. *Membership:* 1,622 individuals in 674 institutions. *Dues:* $60, professional; $240, institutional. *Meetings:* For a list of Annual and Regional Meetings, see http://www.acheinc.org/calendar_of_events.html. *Publications: Journal of Continuing Higher Education* (3/yr.); *Five Minutes with ACHE* (newsletter, 10/yr.); *Proceedings* (annual).

Association for Educational Communications and Technology (AECT). 1800 N Stonelake Dr., Suite 2, Bloomington, IN 47404. (812) 335-7675. Fax (812) 335-7678. E-mail: aect@aect.org. Web site: http://www.aect.org. Phillip Harris, Executive Director; Ed Caffarella, President. AECT is an international professional association concerned with the improvement of learning and instruction through media and technology. It serves as a central clearinghouse and communications center for its members, who include instructional technologists, library media specialists, religious educators, government media personnel, school administrators and specialists, and training media producers. AECT members also work in the armed forces, public libraries, museums, and other information agencies of many different kinds, including those related to the emerging fields of computer technology. Affiliated organizations include the Association for Media and Technology in Education in Canada (AMTEC), Community College Association for Instructional and Technology (CCAIT), Consortium of College and University Media Centers (CCUMC), International Association for Learning Laboratories (IALL), International Visual Literacy Association (IVLA), Minorities in Media (MIM), National Association of Regional Media Centers (NARMC), New England Educational Media Association (NEEMA), and the Southeastern Regional Media Leadership Council (SRMLC). Each of these affiliated organizations has its own listing in the Yearbook. The ECT Foundation is also related to the Association for Educational Communications and Technology and has an independent listings. Divisions are listed below. *Membership:* 3,000 members in good standing from K–12, college and university and private sector/government training. Anyone interested can join. There are different memberships available for students, retirees, corporations, and international parties. We also have a new option for electronic membership for international affiliates. *Dues:* $95.00 standard membership discounts are available for students and retirees. Additional fees apply to corporate memberships or international memberships. *Meetings:* Summer Leadership Institute held each July. Annual Conference each year in conjunction with the NSBA Technology Conference in early November. *Publications: TechTrends* (6/yr., free with membership; $55 nonmembers); *Educational Technology Research and Development* (q., $35 members; $75 nonmembers); *Quarterly Review of Distance Education* (q., $55 members); many books; videotapes.

AECT Archives (AECT). University of Maryland, Hornbake Library, College Park, MD 20742. (301) 405-9255. Fax (301) 314-2634. E-mail: tc65@umail.umd.edu. Web site: http://www.library.umd.edu/UMCP/NPBA/npba.html. Thomas Connors, Archivist, National Public Broadcasting Archives. A collection of media, manuscripts, and related materials representing important developments in visual and audiovisual education and in instructional technology. The collection is housed as part of the National Public Broadcasting Archives. Maintained by the University of Maryland in cooperation with AECT. Open to researchers and scholars.

AECT Training & Performance (T&P). 1800 North Stonelake Drive, Suite 2, Bloomington, IN 47408. (812) 335-7675. Fax (812) 335-7678. E-mail: sschaff@purdue.edu. Web site: http://www.aect.org/T&P/. Scott Schaffer, President; Pam Loughner, President-Elect; Sheila Christy, Past-President; Nada Dabbagh, Board Representative; Cynthia Conn, VP-Communications; Jim Ellsworth, Brice Jewell, and Angela Benson, Members-at-Large. AECTs Training & Performance (T&P) Division serves members from government, business and industry, and academic communities. Its members are training, performance, and education professionals interested in applying current theory and research to training and performance improvement initiatives. Topics of interest to T&P Division members are real world solutions that intersect the use of hard technologies (e.g., computers, the Internet), soft technologies (e.g., instructional design and performance technology processes and models), and current learning and instructional theories (e.g., Constructivism, Problem based learning). The Training & Performance Division resulted from the 2000 merger of the former Industrial Training and Education Division (ITED) and the Division for Learning and Performance Environments (DLPE). *Membership:* If you're a training, performance, or education professional who values the application of theory and research to practice, join Association for Educational Communications and Technology (http://www.aect.org/Membership/) and be sure to specify Training & Performance as one of the divisions you'd like to join. *Dues:* Training & Performance Division membership is free with your AECT membership. *Meetings:* Meetings are held in conjunction with the annual AECT Conference.

(AECT) Division of Design and Development (D&D). 1800 N. Stonelake Dr. Suite 2, Bloomington, IN 47408. (315) 443-1362. Fax (315) 443-1218. E-mail: martindalee@mail.ecu.edu. Web site: http://reusability.org/blogs/dd/. Trey Martindale, President. D&D is composed of individuals from business, government, and academic settings concerned with the systematic design of instruction and the development of solutions to performance problems. Members interests include the study, evaluation, and refinement of design processes; the creation of new models of instructional development; the invention and improvement of techniques for managing the development of instruction; the development and application of professional ID competencies; the promotion of academic programs for preparation of ID professionals; and the dissemination of research and development work in ID. *Membership:* Approximately 750; membership is open to any AECT member. *Dues:* Division membership can be indicated when joining or renewing AECT membership or any time thereafter and has no additional cost associated. *Meetings:* held in conjunction with the annual AECT Convention. *Publications:* D&D listserv with an occasional D&D newsletter and papers; members regularly contribute to and read Educational Technology Research & Development and TechTrends. Division news can be found at: http://reusability.org/blogs/dd/.

(AECT) Division of Learning and Performance Environments (DLPE). 1025 Vermont Ave. NW, Suite 820, Washington, DC 20005. (202) 347-7834. Fax (928) 523-7624. E-mail: sschaff@purdue.edu. Web site: http://www.aect.org/T&P/index.htm. Scott Schaffer, President; Pam Loughner, President-Elect. Supports human learning and performance through the use of computer-based technology; design, development, evaluation, assessment, and implementation of learning environments and performance systems for adults. *Membership:* A Division of AECT. See www.aect.org for membership information. *Dues:* One division membership included in the basic AECT membership; additional division memberships $10. *Meetings:* Held in conjunction with the annual AECT Convention. *Publications: TechTrends* in coordination with AECT.

(AECT) Division of School Media and Technology (DSMT). 1800 N. Stonelake Dr., Suite #2, Bloomington, IN 47404. (812) 335-7675. Fax (812) 335-7678. E-mail: aect@aect.org. Web site: http://www.aect.org/Divisions/mt.asp and http://www.coe.ecu.edu/aect/dsmt/Default.htm. Lois Wilkins, Pres., lwilkins@tapnet.net, and Nancy Reicher, Sec., nreichkc@pei.edu. The School Media and Technology (K–12) Division provides leadership in educational communications and technology by linking professionals holding a common interest in the use of instructional technology and its applicaton to the learning process in the school environment. *Membership:* This division of AECT is of special interest to School Library Media Specialists and others who work with technology in a K–12 environment. *Dues:* One division membership included in the basic AECT membership which is $95 for regular status and $130 for comprehensive status; additional division memberships $10. *Meetings:* DSMT meets in conjunction with the annual AECT National Convention. *Publications: DSMT Update* is now published in electronic format. The *Update* editors are Mary Alice Anderson and Mary Ann Fitzgerald. Please direct all content questions and comments to them. E-mail to: mfitzger@coe.uga.edu or maryalic@wms.luminet. net. In addition, *TechTrends* is published six times annually.

(AECT) International Division (INTL). 1025 Vermont Ave. NW, Suite 820, Washington, DC 20005. (202) 347-7834. E-mail: khanb@gwis2.circ.gwu.edu. Badrul Khan, President. INTL encourages practice and research in educational communication and distance education for social and economic development across national and cultural lines, promotes international exchange and sharing of information, and enhances relationships among international leaders. *Membership:* 295. *Dues:* one division membership included in the basic AECT membership; additional division memberships $10. *Meetings:* held in conjunction with the annual AECT Convention. *Publications:* Newsletter.

(AECT) Media Design and Production Division (MDPD). 1025 Vermont Ave. NW, Suite 820, Washington, DC 20005. (202) 347-7834. E-mail: chuck@cc.usu.edu. Chuck Stoddard, Pres. MDPD provides an international network that focuses on enhancing the quality and effectiveness of mediated communication, in all media formats, in educational, governmental, hospital, and corporate settings through the interaction of instructional designers, trainers, researchers, and evaluators with media designers and production team specialists who utilize state-of-the-art production skills. *Membership:* 318. *Dues:* one division membership included in the basic AECT membership; additional division memberships $10. *Meetings:* held in conjunction with annual AECT Convention. *Publications:* Newsletter.

(AECT) Research and Theory Division (RTD). 1800 N. Stonelake Dr., Suite 2, Bloomington, IN 47404. (812) 335-7675. Fax 812-335-7678. E-mail: aect@aect.org. Web site: www.aect.org. Phil Harris, AECT Executive Director. Seeks to improve the design, execution, utilization, and evaluation of educational technology research; to improve the qualifications and effectiveness of personnel engaged in educational technology research; to advise the educational practitioner as to the use of the research results; to improve research design, techniques, evaluation, and dissemination; to promote both applied and theoretical research on the systematic use of educational technology in the improvement of instruction; and to encourage the use of multiple research paradigms in examining issues related to technology in education. *Membership:* 452. *Dues:* one division membership included in the basic AECT membership; additional division memberships $10. *Meetings:* held in conjunction with annual AECT Convention. *Publications:* Newsletter.

(AECT) Systemic Change in Education Division (CHANGE). 1800 N. Stonelake Dr., Suite 2, Bloomington, IN 47408. (877) 677-AECT. Fax (812) 335-7675. E-mail: frick@indiana.edu. Web site: http://ide.ed.psu.edu/change/. Roberto Joseph, President. CHANGE advocates fundamental changes in educational settings to dramatically improve the quality of education and to enable technology to achieve its potential. *Membership:* Members of the Association for Educational Communications and Technology (AECT) are welcome to join the CHANGE Division. In March, 2004, there are approximately 2,500 members of AECT and of those about 150 are members of CHANGE. *Dues:* Membership in AECT (the Association for Educational Communications and Technology) is required. Once an AECT member, one can join the CHANGE Division at no extra cost. *Meetings:* held in conjunction with annual AECT Convention. *Publications:* See the Web site: http://ide.ed.psu.edu/change/.

Association for Experiential Education (AEE). 2305 Canyon Blvd., Suite 100, Boulder, CO 80302-5651. (303) 440-8844. Fax (303) 440-9581. E-mail: info@aee.org. Web site: http://www.aee.org. Kristin E. Von Wald, Ph.D., Executive Director. AEE is a nonprofit, international, professional organization committed to the development, practice, and evaluation of experiential education in all settings. AEE's vision is to be a leading international organization for the development and application of experiential education principles and methodologies with the intent to create a just and compassionate world by transforming education and promoting positive social change. *Membership:* More than 1,500 members in over 30 countries including individuals and organizations with affiliations in education, recreation, outdoor adventure programming, mental health, youth service, physical education, management development training, corrections, programming for people with disabilities, and environmental education. *Dues:* $55–$95, individual; $125, family; $240, organizational. *Meetings:* AEE Annual Conference in November. Regional Conferences in the Spring. *Publications: The Journal of Experiential Education* (3/yr.); *Experience and the Curriculum; Adventure Education; Adventure Therapy; Therapeutic Applications of Adventure Programming; Manual of Accreditation Standards for Adventure Programs; The Theory of Experiential Education, Third Edition; Experiential Learning in Schools and Higher Education; Ethical Issues in Experiential Education, Second Edition; The K.E.Y. (Keep Exploring Yourself) Group: An Experiential Personal Growth Group Manual; Book of Metaphors, Volume II; Women's Voices in Experiential Education;* bibliographies, directories of programs, and membership directory. New publications since last year: *Exploring the Boundaries of Adventure Therapy; A Guide to Women's Studies in the Outdoors; Administrative Practices of Accredited Adventure Programs; Fundamentals of Experience-Based Training; Wild Adventures: A Guidebook of Activities for Building Connections with Others and the Earth; Truth Zone: An Experimental Approach to Organizational Development.*

The Association for Information and Image Management (AIIM International). 1100 Wayne Avenue, Suite 1100, Silver Spring, MD 20910. (301) 587-8202. Fax (301) 587-2711. E-mail: pwinton@aiim.org. Web site: http://www.aiim.org/. John Mancini, President. AIIM International is the industry's leading global organization. We believe that at the center of an effective business infrastructure in the digital age is the ability to capture, manage, store, preserve, and deliver enterprise content to support business processes. The requisite technologies to establish this infrastructure are an extension of AIIM's core document and content technologies. These Enterprise Content Management (ECM) technologies are key enablers of e-Business and include Content/Document Management, Business Process Management, Enterprise Portals, Knowledge Management, Image Management, Data Warehousing, and Data Mining. AIIM is a neutral and unbiased source of information. We produce educational, solution-oriented events and conferences, provide up-to-the-minute industry information through publications and our online ECM Resource Center, and are an ANSI/ISO-accredited standards developer. *Membership:* Trade Membership; Professional Membership. *Dues:* Trade Membership: $1,000/yr; New Professional Membership: $62.50; Renewal Professional Membership: $125. *Meetings:* AIIM Content Management Solutions Seminars, AIIM Service Company Executive Forum. *Publications: AIM E-DOC Magazine; DOC.1 e-Newsletter.*

Association for Library and Information Science Education (ALISE). 11250 Roger Bacon Drive, Suite 8, Reston, VA 20190-5202. (703) 234-4146. Fax (703) 435-4390. E-mail: alise@drohanmgmt.com. Web site: http://www.alise.org. Louise Robbins, Professor and Director. Seeks to advance education for library and information science and produces annual Library and Information Science Education Statistical Report. Open to professional schools offering graduate programs in library and information science; personal memberships open to educators employed in such institutions; other memberships available to interested individuals. *Membership:* 500 individuals, 73 institutions. *Dues:* institutional, sliding scale, $325–600; $200 associate; $125 international; personal, $90 full-time; $50 part-time, $40 student, $50 retired. *Publications: Journal of Education for Library and Information Science; ALISE Directory and Handbook; Library and Information Science Education Statistical Report.*

Association for Library Collections & Technical Services (ALCTS). 50 E. Huron St., Chicago, IL 60611. (312) 280-5038. Fax (312) 280-5033. E-mail: alcts@ala.org. Web site: www.ala.org/alcts. Charles Wilt, Executive Director; Carol Pitts Diedrichs, President (2004-2005); Brian E.C. Schottlaender, Past-President (2004-2005). A division of the American Library Association, ALCTS is dedicated to acquisition, identification, cataloging, classification, and preservation of library materials; the development and coordination of the country's library resources; and aspects of selection and evaluation involved in acquiring and developing library materials and resources. Sections include Acquisitions, Cataloging and Classification, Collection Management and Development, Preservation and Reformatting, and Serials. *Membership:* 5,091. Membership is open to anyone who has an interest in areas covered by ALCTS. *Dues:* $45 plus membership in ALA. *Publications: Library Resources & Technical Services* (q.); *ALCTS Newsletter Online* (6/yr.).

Association for Library Service to Children (ALSC). 50 E. Huron St., Chicago, IL 60611. (312) 280-2163. Fax (312) 944-7671. E-mail: alsc@ala.org. Web site: http://www.ala.org/alsc. Malore I. Brown. ALSC: Who We Are—The Association for Library Service to Children develops and supports the profession of children's librarianship by enabling and encouraging its practitioners to provide the best library service to our nations children. The Association for Library Service to Children is interested in the improvement and extension of library services to children in all types of libraries. It is responsible for the evaluation and selection of book and nonbook library materials and for the improvement of techniques of library service to children from preschool through the eighth grade or junior high school age, when such materials and techniques are intended for use in more than one type of library. Committee membership is open to ALSC members. *Membership:* 3,600. *Dues:* $45 plus membership in ALA. *Meetings:* Annual Conference and Midwinter Meeting with ALA National Institutes. *Publications: Children and Libraries: The Journal of the Association for Library Service to Children* (3 times per year); *ALSConnect* (quarterly newsletter).

Association for Media and Technology in Education in Canada (AMTEC). 3-1750 The Queensway, Suite 1318, Etobicoke, ON M9C 5H5. (403) 220-3721. Fax (403) 282-4497. E-mail: wstephen@ucalgary.ca. Web site: http://www.amtec.ca. Bob Brandes: Past President; Christine Shelton, Pres. ; Wendy Stephens, Sec./Treas. AMTEC is Canada's national association for educational media and technology professionals. The organization provides national leadership through annual conferences, publications, workshops, media festivals, and awards. It responds to media and technology issues at the international, national, provincial, and local levels, and maintains linkages with other organizations with similar interests. *Membership:* AMTEC members represent all sectors of the educational media and technology fields. *Dues:* $101.65, Canadian regular; $53.50, student and retiree. *Meetings:* Annual Conferences take place in late May or early June. 1999, Ottawa; 2000, Vancouver. *Publications: Canadian Journal of Learning and Technology* (a scholarly journal published 3 times a year); *Media News* (3/yr.); *Membership Directory* (with membership).

Association for the Advancement of Computing in Education (AACE). P.O. Box 2966, Charlottesville, VA 22902. (804) 973-3987. Fax (804) 978-7449. aace@virginia.edu. Web site: http://www.aace.org. Gary Marks, Exec. Dir.; April Ballard, contact person. AACE is an international, educational, and professional organization dedicated to the advancement of learning and teaching at all levels with information technology. AACE publishes major journals, books, and CD-ROMs on the subject and organizes major conferences. AACE's membership includes researchers, developers, and practitioners in schools, colleges, and universities; administrators, policy decision makers, trainers, adult educators, and other specialists in education, industry, and the government with an interest in advancing knowledge and learning with information technology in education. *Membership:* 6,500. *Dues:* basic membership of $75 includes one journal subscription and Educational Technology Review subscription. *Publications:* Educational Technology Review (ED-TECH Review) (2 or 3 times yearly); *Journal of Computers in Mathematics and Science Teaching*

(JCMST); Journal of Computing in Childhood Education (JCCE); Journal of Educational Multimedia and Hypermedia (JEMH); Journal of Interactive Learning Research (JILR) (formerly Journal of Artificial Intelligence in Education); Journal of Technology and Teacher Education (JTATE); International Journal of Educational Telecommunications (IJET). A catalog of books and CD-ROMs is available upon request or by visiting http://www.aace.organize/conf/pubs.

Association of American Publishers (AAP). 50 F Street, NW, Suite 400, Washington, DC 20001. (202) 347-3375. Fax (202) 347-3690. E-mail: kblough@publishers.org. Web site: http://www.publishers.org. Patricia S. Schroeder, Pres. and CEO (DC); Judith Platt, Dir. of Communications/Public Affairs. The Association of American Publishers is the national trade association of the U.S. book publishing industry. AAP was created in 1970 through the merger of the American Book Publishers Council, a trade publishing group, and the American Textbook Publishers Institute, a group of educational publishers. AAP's approximately 300 members include most of the major commercial book publishers in the United States, as well as smaller and nonprofit publishers, university presses, and scholarly societies. AAP members publish hardcover and paperback books in every field and a range of educational materials for the elementary, secondary, postsecondary, and professional markets. Members of the Association also produce computer software and electronic products and services, such as online databases and CD-ROMs. AAP's primary concerns are the protection of intellectual property rights in all media, the defense of free expression and freedom to publish at home and abroad, the management of new technologies, development of education markets and funding for instructional materials, and the development of national and global markets for its members products. *Membership:* Regular Membership in the Association is open to all U.S. companies actively engaged in the publication of books, journals, looseleaf services, computer software, audiovisual materials, databases and other electronic products such as CD-ROM and CD-I, and similar products for educational, business and personal use. This includes producers, packagers, and co-publishers who coordinate or manage most of the publishing process involved in creating copyrightable educational materials for distribution by another organization. "Actively engaged" means that the candidate must give evidence of conducting an ongoing publishing business with a significant investment in the business. Each Regular Member firm has one vote, which is cast by an official representative or alternate designated by the member company. Associate Membership (nonvoting) is available to U.S. not-for-profit organizations that otherwise meet the qualifications for regular membership. A special category of associate membership is open to nonprofit university presses. Affiliate Membership is a nonvoting membership open to paper manufacturers, suppliers, consultants, and other nonpublishers directly involved in the industry. *Dues:* Dues are assessed on the basis of annual sales revenue from the print and electronic products listed above (under Regular Membership), but not from services or equipment. To maintain confidentiality, data is reported to an independent agent. *Meetings:* Annual Meeting (February), Small and Independent Publishers Meeting (February), School Division Annual Meeting (January), PSP Annual Meeting (February). *Publications: AAP Monthly Report.*

Association of College and Research Libraries (ACRL). 50 E. Huron St., Chicago, IL 60611-2795. (312) 280-2523. Fax (312) 280-2520. E-mail: dconnolly@ala.org. Web site: http://www.ala.org/acrl.html. Frances Maloy, President, libfm@emory.edu. An affiliate of the American Library Association, ACRL provides leadership for development, promotion, and improvement of academic and research library resources and services to facilitate learning, research, and the scholarly communications process. It provides access to library standards for colleges, universities, and two-year institutions, and publishes statistics on academic libraries. Committees include Academic/Research Librarian of the Year Award, Appointments, Hugh C. Atkinson Memorial Award, Budget and Finance, Colleagues, Committee on the Status of Academic Librarians, Bylaws, Copyright, Council of Liaisons, Doctoral Dissertation Fellowship, Government Relations, Intellectual Freedom, International Relations, Samuel Lazerow Fellowship, Media Resources, Membership,

Nominations, New Leader Orientation, Professional Development, Publications, Racial and Ethnic Diversity, Research, K. G. Saur Award for the Best C&RL Article, Scholarly Communication, Standards and Accreditation, Statistics. The association administers 15 different awards in three categories: Achievement and Distinguished Service Awards, Research Awards/Grants, and Publications. *Membership:* over 11,000. *Dues:* $35 (in addition to ALA membership). *Meetings:* 2003 ACRL National Conference, Apr 10-13, Charlotte. *Publications: College & Research Libraries* (6/yr.); *College & Research Libraries News* (11/yr.); *RBM: A Journal of Rare Books, Manuscripts, and Cultural Heritage* (2/yr); *CHOICE Magazine: Current Review for Academic Libraries* (11/yr.). *CLIP Notes* (current issues are nos. 16, 17, 20–26). Recent titles include *Making the Grade; Literature in English; The Collaborative Imperative; Assessing Information Literacy Programs* (CLIP Note 32); *Library Web Site Policies* (CLIP Note 29); *Academic Library Trends and Statistics;* and *Proceedings of the 10th ACRL National Conference.* A free list of materials is available. ACRL also sponsors an open discussion listserv, ACRL-FRM@ALA.ORG.

Association of Independent Video and Filmmakers/Foundation for Independent Video and Film (AIVF/FIVF). 304 Hudson St., 6th Floor, New York, NY 10013. (212) 807-1400. Fax (212) 463-8519. E-mail: info@aivf.org. Web site: http://www.aivf.org. Beni Matias, Interim Executive Director, AIVF. AIVF is the national trade association for independent video and filmmakers, representing their needs and goals to industry, government, and the public. Programs include screenings and seminars, insurance for members and groups, and information and referral services. Recent activities include seminars in filmmaking technology, meets with distributors, and regular programs on related topics. AIVF also advocates public funding of the arts, public access to new telecommunications systems, and monitoring censorship issues. *Membership:* Membership includes: annual subscription to the Independent magazine; AIVF trade discounts; online and phone information service; Web members-only area; discounted admission to events, etc. *Dues:* $55, indiv.; $75, library; $100, nonprofit organization; $150, business/industry; $35, student. *Meetings:* annual membership meeting. *Publications: The Independent Film and Video Monthly; The AIVF Guide to International Film and Video Festivals; The AIVF Guide to Film and Video Distributors; The Next Step: Distributing Independent Films and Videos; the AIVF Self Distribution Toolkit & the AIVF Film & Video Exhibitors Guide.*

Association of Specialized and Cooperative Library Agencies (ASCLA). 50 E. Huron St., Chicago, IL 60611. (800) 545-2433, ext. 4398. Fax (312)944-8085. E-mail: ascla@ala.org. Web site: http://www.ala.org/ascla. Cathleen Bourdon, Exec. Dir. A division of the American Library Association, ASCLA represents state library agencies, multitype library organizations, independent libraries and libraries serving special populations to promote the development of coordinated library services with equal access to information and material for all persons. The activities and programs of the association are carried out by 21 committees, 4 sections, and various discussion groups. *Membership:* 917. *Dues:* Join ALA and ASCLA new member $90; student member $40 ($25 for ALA plus $15 for ASCLA); trustee and associate member $85 ($45 for ALA plus $40 for ASCLA); add ASCLA to current ALA membership $40; renew ALA and ASCLA membership $140 ($100 for ALA plus $40 for ASCLA). *Meetings:* ASCLA meets in conjunction with the American Library Association. *Publications: Interface* (q); see Web site (http://www.ala.org/ascla) for list of other publications.

Audiovisual Committee (of the Public Library Association). 50 E. Huron St., Chicago, IL 60611. (312) 280-5752. James E. Massey, Chair. Promotes use of audiovisual materials in public libraries.

C&C Associates. 11112 S. Spotted Rd, Cheney, WA 99004. (888) 662-7678 or (509) 624-9621. Fax (509) 323-4811 or (509) 624-5320. E-mail: cc@iea.com. C&C Associates has the only Electronic Camera Repair Home Study course in the world. It has more than two centuries' experience with educating camera repair technicians. The only college certified camera repair instructor in the world teaches the 18-lesson course. C&C also publishes repair guides for cameras and also writes technical repair guides for several manufactures.

Cable in the Classroom (CIC). 1724 Massachusetts Avenue, NW, Washington, DC 20036. (202) 775-1040. Fax (202) 775-1047. E-mail: cic@ciconline.org. Web site: http://www.ciconline.org. Peggy O'Brien, Ph.D., Executive Director. Cable in the Classroom represents the cable telecommunications industry's effort to use cable content and new technologies to improve teaching and learning for children in schools, at home, and in their communities. By focusing on five essential elements of a good education in the 21st century—visionary and sensible use of technologies, engagement with rich content, community with other learners, excellent teaching, and the support of parents and other adults—the cable industry works for positive change in education locally and nationally. *Membership:* Cable in the Classroom is a consortium of more than 8,500 local cable companies and 40 national cable programming networks. Local cable companies provide free basic cable service to all accredited K–12 schools passed by cable. Cable networks offer free educational programming with no commercials or viewing requirements and with extended copyright clearances so teachers can tape for classroom use. In addition, cable companies and networks create print and online resources to help teachers use the resources effectively in the classroom. *Publications*: Cable in the Classroom Magazine (mo.).

Canadian Broadcasting Corporation/Société Radio-Canada (CBC/SRC). P.O. Box 500, Station A, Toronto, ON. E-mail: fortinj@toronto.cbc.ca. Web site: http://www.cbc.ca. The CBC is a publicly owned corporation established in 1936 by an Act of the Canadian Parliament to provide a national broadcasting service in Canada in the two official languages. CBC services include English and French television networks; English and French AM mono and FM stereo radio networks virtually free of commercial advertising; CBC North, which serves Canada's North by providing radio and television programs in English, French, and eight native languages; *Newsworld* and its French counterpart, *Le Réseau de l'information* (RDI), 24-hour national satellites to cable English-language and French-language news and information service respectively, both funded entirely by cable subscription and commercial advertising revenues; and Radio Canada International, a shortwave radio service that broadcasts in seven languages and is managed by CBC and financed by External Affairs. The CBC is financed mainly by public funds voted annually by Parliament.

Canadian Education Association/Association canadienne déducation (CEA). 317 Adelaide Street West, suite 300, Toronto, ON M5V 1P9. (416) 591-6300. Fax (416) 591-5345. E-mail: cea-ace@acea.ca. Web site: http://www.acea.ca. Penny Milton, Executive Director, Valérie Pierre-Pierre, Research Officer. CEA is a national, bilingual, charitable organization that advances public commitment to education by engaging diverse perspectives in finding common ground on issues that affect the learning of all children and youth in our society. Current issues include ICT and learning; social equity; school improvement. *Membership:* Sustaining Members—provincial, territorial departments of education, and federal government. Organization Members—Nonprofit: educational institutions, research organizations, stakeholder associations. For profit: firms with interests in the education sector. Individuals—educators, researchers. *Dues:* $120, indiv.; $360, not-for-profit organizations; $500, for profit organizations; school boards, based on enrollment. *Meetings:* Technology Summit, National Education Forum, Superintendents Forum. *Publications: CEA Handbook; Education Canada* (q.); *CEA Newsletter* (8/yr.); *Connections Series.*

Canadian Library Association (CLA). 328 Frank Street, Ottawa, ON K2P 0X8. (613) 232-9625. Fax (613) 563-9895. E-mail: info@cla.ca. Web site: http://www.cla.ca. Linda Sawden Harris, Manager of Financial Services. The mission of the Canadian Library Association is to provide leadership in the promotion, development, and support of library and information services in Canada for the benefit of Association members, the profession, and Canadian society. In the spirit of this mission, CLA aims to engage the active, creative participation of library staff, trustees, and governing bodies in the development and management of high quality Canadian library service; to assert and support the right of all Canadians to the freedom to read and to free universal access to a wide variety of library materials and services; to promote librarianship and to enlighten all levels of government as to the significant role that libraries play in educating and socializing the Canadian people; and to link libraries, librarians, trustees, and others across the country for the purpose of providing a unified nationwide voice in matters of critical concern. *Membership:* 2,300 individuals, 700 institutions, 100 Associates and Trustees. *Dues:* $50-$300. *Meetings:* Annual Conference (with ALA). *Publications: Feliciter* (membership magazine, 6/yr.).

Canadian Museums Association/Association des musées canadiens (CMA/AMC). 280 Metcalfe St., Suite 400, Ottawa, ON K2P 1R7. (613) 567-0099. Fax (613) 233-5438. E-mail: info@museums.ca. Web site: http://www.museums.ca. John G. McAvity, Exec. Dir. The Canadian Museums Association is a nonprofit corporation and registered charity dedicated to advancing public museums and museum works in Canada, promoting the welfare and better administration of museums, and fostering a continuing improvement in the qualifications and practices of museum professionals. *Membership:* 2,000 museums and individuals, including art galleries, zoos, aquariums, historic parks, etc. *Dues:* Individual ($75: For those who are or have been associated with a recognized museum in Canada.Affiliate ($100):For those outside the museum community who wish to support the aims and programs of the Assocation. Foreign ($100): For individuals and institutions, residing or based outside Canada. Institutional/Association: For all recognized Canadian museums that are nonprofit, have a collection and are open to the public. Fee is 0.001 (one tenth of one percent) of operating budget (i.e., if your budget is $150,000, you would pay $150). The minimum fee payable is $100, and the maximum, $2,500. Corporate ($250): For corporations wishing to support the aims and programs of the Association while developing opportunities within the museum community. Student ($50): Special rate for students. Please enclose a photocopy of your student ID; Senior ($50): For those who are retired and have been associated with a recognized museum in Canada. *Meetings:* CMA Annual Conference, spring. *Publications: Muse* (bi-monthly magazine, colour, Canada's only national, bilingual, magazine devoted to museums, it contains museum-based photography, feature articles, commentary, and practical information); *The Official Directory of Canadian Museums and Related Institutions* (online directory) lists all museums in Canada plus information on government departments, agencies, and provincial and regional museum associations.

Canadian Publishers Council (CPC). 250 Merton St., Suite 203, Toronto, ON M4S 1B1. (416) 322-7011. Fax (416) 322-6999. E-mail: pubadmin@pubcouncil.ca. Web site: http://www.pubcouncil.ca. Jacqueline Hushion, Exec. Dir. CPC members publish and distribute an extensive list of Canadian and imported learning materials in a complete range of formats from traditional textbook and ancillary materials to CDs and interactive video. The primary markets for CPC members are schools, universities and colleges, bookstores, and libraries. CPC also provides exhibits throughout the year and works through a number of subcommittees and groups within the organization to promote effective book publishing. CPC was founded in 1910. *Membership:* 27 companies, educational institutions, or government agencies that publish books as an important facet of their work. *Dues:* To be assessed when a membership application form is submitted for consideration. *Meetings:* TBA. *Publications:* Please visit the CPC Web site at www.pubcouncil.ca for various publications.

Catholic Library Association (CLA). 100 North Street, Suite 224, Pittsfield, MA 01201-5109. (413) 443-2CLA. Fax (413) 442-2CLA. E-mail: cla@vgernet.net. Jean R. Bostley, SSJ, Exec. Dir. Provides educational programs, services, and publications for Catholic libraries and librarians. *Membership:* approx. 1,000. Dues: $45, indiv.; special rates for students and retirees. *Meetings:* Meetings are held in conjunction with the National Catholic Educational Association annually. *Publications: Catholic Library World* (q.); *Catholic Periodical and Literature Index* (q. with annual cumulations).

Childrens Television International (CTI)/GLAD Productions, Inc. (CTI/GLAD). PO Box 87723, San Diego, CA 92138. (619) 445-4647. Fax (619) 445-2813. E-mail: cti-gladprod@worldnet.att.net. Tim Gladfelter, Pres. and Dir. of Customer Services. An educational organization that develops, produces, and distributes a wide variety of color television and video programming and related publications as a resource to aid the social, cultural, and intellectual development of children and young adults. Programs cover language arts, science, social studies, history, and art for home, school, and college viewing. *Publications:* Teacher guides for instructional series; *The History Game: A Teachers Guide;* complementary catalog for educational videos.

Close Up Foundation (CUF). 44 Canal Center Plaza, Alexandria, VA 22314. (703) 706-3300. Fax (703) 706-0000. E-mail: alumni@closeup.org. Web site: http://www. closeup.org. Stephen A. Janger, CEO. A nonprofit, nonpartisan civic education organization promoting informed citizen participation in public policy and community service. Programs reach more than a million participants each year. Close Up brings 25,000 secondary and middle school students and teachers and older Americans each year to Washington for week-long government studies programs and produces television programs on the C-SPAN cable network for secondary school and home audiences. *Membership:* Any motivated 10th- to 12th-grade or 6th- to 8th-grade student who wants to learn about government and American history is eligible to come on the program. There are no "dues." *Dues:* Tuition is required to participate on Close Up educational travel programs. A limited amount of tuition assistance is available to qualified students through the Close Up Fellowship program. With a designated number of students, teachers receive a fellowship that covers the adult tuition and transportation price. Please contact (800) CLOSE UP (256-7387), ext. 606, for more information. *Meetings:* Meetings are scheduled most weeks during the academic year in Washington, DC, all with a government, history, or current issues focus. *Publications: Current Issues; The Bill of Rights: A Users Guide; Perspectives; International Relations; The American Economy;* documentary videotapes on domestic and foreign policy issues.

Community College Association for Instruction and Technology (CCAIT). New Mexico Military Institute, 101 W. College Blvd., Roswell, NM 88201-5173. (505) 624-8382. Fax (505) 624-8390. E-mail: klopfer@yogi.nmmi.cc.nm.us. Jerry Klopfer, Pres. A national association of community and junior college educators interested in the discovery and dissemination of information relevant to instruction and media technology in the community environment. Facilitates member exchange of data, reports, proceedings, and other information pertinent to instructional technology and the teaching-learning process; sponsors AECT convention sessions, an annual video competition, and social activities. *Membership:* 250. *Dues:* $20. *Meetings:* AECT National Convention. *Publications:* Regular newsletter; irregular topical papers.

Computer Assisted Language Instruction Consortium (CALICO). 214 Centennial Hall, Texas State University, 601 University Dr., San Marcos, TX 78666. (512) 245-1417. Fax (512) 245-9089. E-mail: info@calico.org. Web site: http://calico.org. Robert Fischer, Exec. Dir. CALICO is devoted to the dissemination of information on the application of technology to language teaching and language learning. *Membership:* 1,000 members from United States and 20 foreign countries. Anyone interested in the development and use of technology in the teaching/learning of foreign languages are invited to join. *Dues:* $50 annual/individual. *Meetings:* annually. *Publications: CALICO Journal* (three times a year), CALICO Monograph Series.

Computer-Using Educators, Inc. (CUE). 1210 Marina Village Parkway, Suite 100, Alameda, CA 94501. (510) 814-6630. Fax (510) 814-0195. E-mail: cueinc@cue.org. Web site: http://www.cue.org. Bob Walczak, Exec, Dir. CUE, a California nonprofit corporation, was founded in 1976 by a group of teachers interested in exploring the use of technology to improve learning in their classrooms. The organization has never lost sight of this mission. Today, CUE has an active membership of 11,000 professionals worldwide in schools, community colleges, and universities. CUE's 23 affiliates in California provide members with local year-round support through meetings, grants, events, and mini-conferences. Special Interest Groups (SIGs) support members interested in a variety of special topics. CUE's annual conferences, newsletter, advocacy, Web site, and other programs help the technology-using educator connect with other professionals. *Membership:* 11,000 individual, corporate, and institutional members. *Dues:* $30. *Publications: CUE NewsLetter.*

Consortium for Computers in the Humanities/Consortium pour Ordinateurs en Sciences Humaines (COCH/COSH). Arts 200, UofA, Edmonton, AB T6G 2E6. (780) 492-6768. Fax (780) 492-9106. E-mail: ss@huco.ualberta.ca. Web site: http://coch-coch. ca/. Ray Siemens (President-English), Jean-Claude Guédon (President-French), Geoffrey Rockwell (Vice President), Stéfan Sinclair (Secretary). The Consortium for Computers in the Humanities is a Canada-wide association of representatives from Canadian colleges and universities that began in 1986. Our objective is to foster communications about, and sharing of, information technology developed by Canadian institutions for the betterment of postsecondary education across Canada. Le Consortium pour ordinateurs en sciences humaines, fondé en 1986, est une association constituée de représentants de collèges et duniversités du Canada. Notre but est dencourager la dissemination dinformation sur les technologies nouvelles développées par les organisations canadiennes et ainsi de contribuer à lavancement des études supérieures partout au Canada. *Membership:* 120. *Dues:* Annual, $65 CDN. *Meetings:* May, annually, with the HSSFC Congress. *Publications:* COCH/COSH has formal affiliation with the journals: *Text Technology, Computing in the Humanities Working Papers,* and *Surfaces,* and is pleased to have also enjoyed publications relationships with Early Modern Literary Studies.

Consortium of College and University Media Centers (CCUMC). 1200 Communications Bldg.-ITC, Iowa State University, Ames, IA 50011-3243. (515) 294-1811. Fax (515) 294-8089. E-mail: ccumc@ccumc.org. Web site: www.ccumc.org. Donald A. Rieck, Exec. Dir. CCUMC is a professional group of higher education media personnel whose purpose is to improve education and training through the effective use of educational media. Assists educational and training users in making films, video, and educational media more accessible. Fosters cooperative planning among university media centers. Gathers and disseminates information on improved procedures and new developments in instructional technology and media center management. *Membership:* 750 individuals at 325 institutions/corporations. Institutional Memberships: Individuals within an institution of higher education who are associated with the support of instruction and presentation technologies in a media center and/or technology support service. Corporate Memberships— Individuals within a corporation, firm, foundation or other commercial or philanthropic whose business or activity is in support of the purposes and objectives of CCUMC. Associate Membershsips—Individuals from a public library, religious, governmental or other organization not otherwise eligible for other categories of membership. Student Memberships—Any student in an institution of higher education who is not eligible for an institutional membership. *Dues:* $295 institutional; $295, corporate; $50, student; $295, associate. *Meetings:* 2005, Portland, OR   Oct. 6 10. *Publications: College & University Media Review* (journal—semiannual). *Leader* (newsletter—3 issues annually in electronic format).

Continuing Library Education Network and Exchange Round Table (CLENERT). 50 E. Huron St., Chicago, IL 60611. (800) 545-2433. E-mail: wramsey@cml.lib.oh.us. Web site: http://www.ala.org. Wendy Ramsey. An affiliate of the American Library Association, CLENERT seeks to provide access to quality continuing education opportunities for librarians and information scientists and to create an awareness of the need for such education in helping individuals in the field to respond to societal and technological changes. *Membership:* $350. *Dues:* open to all ALA members; $15, indiv.; $50, organization. *Publications*: CLENExchange (q.), available to nonmembers by subscription at $20.

Copyright Clearance Center, Inc. (CCC). 222 Rosewood Drive, Danvers, MA 01923. (978) 750-8400. Fax (978) 750-0347. E-mail: marketing@copyright.com. Web site: http://www.copyright.com. Joseph S. Alen, Pres. Copyright Clearance Center, Inc. (CCC) is the world's largest licenser of text reproduction rights and provider of many licensing services for the reproduction of copyrighted materials in print and electronic formats. Formed in 1978 to facilitate compliance with U.S. copyright law, CCC manages the rights relating to more than 1.75 million textbooks, newspapers, magazines, and other copyrighted works. CCC-licensed customers in the U.S. number over 10,000 corporations and subsidiaries (including most of the Fortune 100 companies), as well as thousands of government agencies, law firms, document suppliers, libraries, academic institutions, copy shops and bookstores. CCC's licensing services include:Annual Authorizations Service (AAS)—a blanket annual photocopy license for companies with more than 750 employees, as well as law firms of any size. Their employees can photocopy content for distribution in-house; Photocopy Authorizations License (PAL)—the same as the AAS license, but for companies with fewer than 750 employees; Digital Repertory Amendment—a blanket annual license that provides companies with the rights to copy copyrighted content for distribution in-house via e-mail, intranet sites, and other digital formats; Multinational Repertory License—a blanket annual photocopy license that covers U.S. companies' employees working in other countries; Multinational Digital Repertory Amendment—a similar license to the Digital Repertory Amendment, but for U.S. companies with employees working outside of the U.S.; Transactional Reporting Service (TRS)—an online "pay as you go" service that enables customers to acquire photocopy permissions on an as-needed basis for library reserves, inter-library loans, as well as general photocopy needs. Customers also use TRS to report their photocopying activity; Republication Licensing Service (RLS)—an online service that provides customers with permissions to reproduce copyrighted materials for the purpose of republishing that content into a variety of formats, such as Web sites, brochures, books, ads, etc.; Academic Permissions Service (APS)—an online permissions service that colleges and universities can use to get the rights to photocopy copyrighted content for use in coursepacks; Electronic Course Content Service (ECCS)—an online service that colleges and universities can use to acquire permissions to reproduce copyrighted content for use in electronic coursepacks and reserves, as well as for distance learning; Digital Permissions Service (DPS)—a transactional service that customers can use to order permissions to reproduce and distribute copyrighted content electronically either in-house or outside of their organizations; Rightslink—a digital rights management service that licenses, packages and delivers digital content from publishers' Web sites; Foreign Authorizations Service (FAS)—authorizes photocopying of U.S. copyrighted materials in foreign countries and distributes royalties collected by foreign reproduction rights organizations to U.S. publishers, authors and other rightsholders; Federal Government Photocopy Licensing Service—a blanket annual license that provides rights for federal government employees to photocopy content for in-house use.

Corporation for Public Broadcasting (CPB). 401 9th St., NW, Washington, DC 20004-2037. (202) 879-9600. Fax (202) 879-9700. E-mail: info@cpb.org. Web site: http://www.cpb.org. Robert T. Coonrod, Pres. and CEO. A private, nonprofit corporation created by Congress in 1967 to develop noncommercial television, radio, and online services for the American people. CPB created the Public Broadcasting Service (PBS) in 1969 and National Public Radio (NPR) in 1970. CPB distributes grants to over 1,000 local public television and radio stations that reach virtually every household in the country. The Corporation is the industry's largest single source of funds for national public television and radio program development and production. In addition to quality educational and informational programming, CPB and local public stations make important contributions in the areas of education, training, community service, and application of emerging technologies. *Membership:* CPB has over 100 employees. *Publications: Annual Report; CPB Public Broadcasting Directory.*

Council for Basic Education (CBE). 1319 F St. NW, Suite 900, Washington, DC 20004-1152. (202) 347-4171. Fax (202) 347-5047. E-mail: jkeiser@c-b-e.org. Web site: http://www.c-b-e.org. A. Graham Down, Acting CEO, gdown@c-b-e.org. CBEs mission is to strengthen teaching and learning of the core subjects (mathematics, English, language arts, history, government, geography, the sciences, foreign languages, and the arts) in order to develop the capacity for lifelong learning and foster responsible citizenship. As an independent, critical voice for education reform, CBE champions the philosophy that all children can learn, and that the job of schools is to achieve this goal. CBE advocates this goal by publishing analytical periodicals and administering practical programs as examples to strengthen content in curriculum and teaching. CBE is completing a kit of Standards for Excellence in Education, which includes a CD-ROM; guides for teachers, parents, and principals, and a book of standards in the core subjects. *Publications: Basic Education: A Journal of Teaching and the Liberal Arts.* The publication of *Basic Education* was suspended as of September 2003. Copies of past issues are still available for ordering. (Single copy $10 which includes shipping and handling; contact CBE for bulk orders; issues of BE before September 2002 are $4 a copy; change price on order form.) Each issue contains analyses, opinions, and reviews of the key issues in K–12 education.

Council for Exceptional Children (CEC). 1110 N. Glebe Rd. #300, Arlington, VA 22201. (703) 620-3660. TTY: (703) 264-9446. Fax (703) 264-9494. E-mail: cec@cec.sped.org. Web site: http://www.cec.sped.org. Nancy Safer, Exec. Dir. CEC is the largest international organization dedicated to improving the educational success of students with disabilities and/or gifts and talents. CEC advocates for governmental policies supporting special education, sets professional standards, provides professional development, and helps professionals obtain conditions and resources necessary for high quality educational services for their students. *Membership:* Teachers, administrators, professors, related services providers (occupational therapists, school psychologists), and parents. CEC has approximately 50,000 members. *Dues:* $89 a year. *Meetings:* Annual Convention and Expo attracting approximately 6,000 special educators. *Publications:* Journals, newsletters, books, and videos with information on new research findings, classroom practices that work, and special education publications. (See also the ERIC Clearinghouse on Disabilities and Gifted Education.)

> **(CEC) Technology and Media Division (TAM).** 1920 Association Dr., Reston, VA 20191-1589. (703) 620-3660. TTY: (703) 264-9446. Fax (703) 264-9494. E-mail: cec@cec.sped.org. Web site: http://www.cec.sped.org. Council for Exceptional Children. The Technology and Media Division (TAM) of The Council for Exceptional Children (CEC) encourages the development of new applications, technologies, and media for use as daily living tools by special populations. This information is disseminated through professional meetings, training programs, and publications. TAM members receive four issues annually of the *Journal of Special Education Technology* containing articles on specific technology programs and applications, and five issues of the TAM newsletter, providing news of current research, developments, products, conferences, and special programs information. *Membership:* 1,700. *Dues:* $10 in addition to CEC membership.

Council on International Non-Theatrical Events (CINE). 1112 16th Street, N.W., Suite 510, Washington, DC 20036. (202) 785-1136. Fax (202) 785-4114. info@cine.org. Web site: http://www.cine.org. Carole L. Feld, President. CINEs mission is to discover, reward, educate and support professional and new emerging talent in the film and video fields. It accomplishes its mission through major film and video competitions that recognize and celebrate excellence, and through various educational programs. CINE is best known for its prestigious CINE Golden Eagle competitions, culminating annually in a gala Awards Ceremony in Washington, D.C. Awards are given in 20 major categories, encompassing all genres of professional and pre-professional film and video production. CINE also facilitates Alphalist into worldwide film festivals for its own competition winners; at the same time, it has reciprocal arrangements whereby distinguished works from outside the United States achieve CINE recognition and viewership in the U.S. *Meetings:* CINE Showcase and Awards held annually in Washington, DC. *Publications*: *CINE Annual Yearbook of Film and Video Awards; Worldwide Directory of Film and Video Festivals and Events.*

East-West Center. 1601 East-West Rd., Honolulu, HI 96848-1601. (808) 944-7111. Fax (808) 944-7376. E-mail: ewcinfo@EastWestCenter.org. Web site: http://www. eastwestcenter.org/. Dr. Charles E. Morrison, Pres. The U.S. Congress established the East-West Center in 1960 with a mandate to foster mutual understanding and cooperation among the governments and peoples of Asia, the Pacific, and the United States. Officially known as the Center for Cultural and Technical Interchange Between East and West, it is a public, nonprofit institution with an international board of governors. Funding for the center comes from the U.S. government, with additional support provided by private agencies, individuals, and corporations, and several Asian and Pacific governments, private agencies, individuals, and corporations. The center, through research, education, dialog, and outreach, provides a neutral meeting ground where people with a wide range of perspectives exchange views on topics of regional concern. Scholars, government and business leaders, educators, journalists, and other professionals from throughout the region annually work with center staff to address issues of contemporary significance in such areas as international economics and politics, the environment, population, energy, the media, and Pacific islands development.

ECT Foundation (ECT). c/o AECT, 1800 N. Stonelake Drive, Suite 2, Bloomington, IN 47404. (812) 335-7675. Fax (812) 335-7678. E-mail: aect@aect.org. Web site: http://www.aect.org. Hans-Erik Wennberg, Pres. The ECT Foundation is a nonprofit organization whose purposes are charitable and educational in nature. Its operation is based on the conviction that improvement of instruction can be accomplished, in part, by the continued investigation and application of new systems for learning and by periodic assessment of current techniques for the communication of information. In addition to awarding scholarships, internships, and fellowships, the foundation develops and conducts leadership training programs for emerging professional leaders. Its operations are closely allied to AECT program goals, and the two organizations operate in close conjunction with each other.

Education Development Center, Inc. 55 Chapel St., Newton, MA 02458-1060. (617) 969-7100. Fax (617) 969-5979. E-mail: comment@edc.org. Web site: http://www.edc.org. Janet Whitla, Pres., Jwhitla@edc.org. EDC is a not-for profit organization that works in the United States and worldwide in the fields of education, health, and human development. Active projects include curriculum development, teacher and administrator professional development, materials development, research and evaluation. EDC seeks to bridge research and practice in order to improve education at all levels by providing services to the school and the community. EDC produces interactive Web sites, CD-ROMs, DVDs and videocassettes, primarily in connection with curriculum development and teacher training. *Publications: Annual Report;* Detailed Web site with vast archive of publications, technical reports, and evaluation studies.

Educational Communications, Inc., Environmental and Media Projects of. P.O. Box 351419, Los Angeles, CA 90035. (310) 559-9160. Fax (310) 559-9160. E-mail: ECNP@aol.com. Web site: http://www.ecoprojects.org. Nancy Perlman, Executive Director and Producer. Educational Communications is dedicated to enhancing the quality of life on this planet and provides radio and television programs about the environment. Serves as a clearinghouse on ecological issues. Programming is available on 100 stations in 25 states. These include: ECONEWS television series and Environmental Direction radio series. Services provided include a speakers bureau, award-winning public service announcements, radio and television documentaries, volunteer and intern opportunities, and input into the decision-making process. Its mission is to educate the public about both the problems and the solutions in the environment. Other projects include the Ecology Center of Southern California(a regional conservation group), Project Ecotourism, Take-to-the-Hills, and Earth Cultures (providing ethnic dance performances). *Membership:* Non-membership except for the Ecology Center of Southern California. *Dues:* $20 for regular. All donations accepted. *Publications: Compendium Newsletter* (bi-monthly); *Directory of Environmental Organizations. ECOVIEW* newspaper articles.

Educational Products Information Exchange (EPIE Institute). 103 W. Montauk Highway, Hampton Bays, NY 11946. (516) 728-9100. Fax (516) 728-9228. E-mail: kkomoski@optonline.net. Web site: http://www.epie.org. P. Kenneth Komoski, Exec. Dir. Assesses educational materials and provides consumer information, product descriptions, and citations for virtually all educational software and curriculum-related Web sites. All of EPIEs services are available to schools and state agencies as well as parents and individuals. Online access is restricted to states with membership in the States Consortium for Improving Software Selection (SCISS). *Publications: The Educational Software Selector Database* (TESS), available to anyone. All publication material now available on CD-ROM.

Eisenhower National Clearinghouse for Mathematics and Science Education (ENC). 1929 Kenny Road, Columbus, OH 43210-1079. (800) 621-5785, (614) 292-7784. Fax (614) 292-2066. E-mail: info@enc.org. Web site: http://www.enc.org. Dr. Len Simutis, Director. The Eisenhower National Clearinghouse for Mathematics and Science Education (ENC) is located at The Ohio State University and funded by the U.S. Department of Educations Office of Elementary and Secondary Education (OESE). ENC provides K–12 teachers and other educators with a central source of information on mathematics and science curriculum materials, particularly those that support education reform. Among ENCs products and services are ENC Online; 12 demonstration sites located throughout the nation; and a variety of publications, including the Guidebook of Federal Resources for K–12 Mathematics and Science, a listing of federal resources in mathematics and science education, ENC Focus, a free online and print magazine on topics of interest to math and science educators, and professional development CD-ROMs. Users include K–12 teachers, other educators, policymakers, and parents. *Membership:* Magazine subscriptions are free and there are no fees for any ENC services. ENC Focus magazine has more than 130,000 subscribers, mostly K–12 math and science teachers. *Publications: ENC Focus* (an online and print magazine on selected topics); *Guidebook of Federal Resources for K–12 Mathematics and Science* (federal programs in mathematics and science education); CD-ROMs on professional development topics. *ENC Online* is available online (http://www.enc.org).

ERIC Document Reproduction Service (EDRS). 7420 Fullerton Rd., Suite 110, Springfield, VA 22153-2852. (800) 443-ERIC (3742). Fax (703) 440-1408. E-mail: service@edrs.com. Web site: http://www.edrs.com. Peter M. Dagutis, Dir. Provides subscription services for ERIC document collections in electronic format (from 1993 forward) and on microfiche (from 1966 forward). Links to the full text at EDRS are incorporated into a number of ERIC search products. On-demand delivery of ERIC documents is also available in formats including paper, electronic PDF image, fax, and microfiche. Delivery methods include shipment of hardcopy documents and microfiche, document fax-back, and online delivery. Back collections of ERIC documents, annual subscriptions, and other ERIC-related materials are also available. ERIC documents can be ordered by toll-free phone call, fax, mail, or online through the EDRS Web site. Document ordering also available from EBSCO, OVID, DIALOG and OCLC.

Federal Communications Commission (FCC). 445 12th St. SW, Washington, DC 20554. (888) 225-5322. Fax (202) 418-1232. E-mail: fccinfo@fcc.gov. Web site: http://www.fcc.gov. Michael Powell, Chairman. The Federal Communications Commission (FCC) is an independent United States government agency, directly responsible to Congress. The FCC was established by the Communications Act of 1934 and is charged with regulating interstate and international communications by radio, television, wire, satellite and cable. The FCC's jurisdiction covers the 50 states, the District of Columbia, and U.S. possessions.

Film Arts Foundation (Film Arts). 145 9th St. #101, San Francisco, CA 94103. (415) 552-8760. Fax (415) 552-0882. E-mail: info@filmarts.org. Web site: http://www. filmarts.org. n/a. Service organization that supports and promotes independent film and video production. Services include low-cost 16mm, Super-8, and dV equipment rental; on and off-line editing including AVID, Final Cut, 16mm flatbeds, VHS & S-VHS, as well as a Pro Tools sound room and Optical Printer; resource library; group legal and production insurance plans; monthly magazine; seminars; grants program; annual film and video festival; nonprofit sponsorship; exhibition program; and advocacy and significant discounts on film- and video-related products and services. *Membership:* 3,500+. *Dues:* $45 for "supporter" level benefits including monthly magazine, and access to libraries and on-line databases. $65 for full "filmmaker" benefits including above plus: access to equipment and post production facilities, discounts on seminars, nonprofit fiscal sponsorship, group legal and Delta Dental plans. *Meetings:* Annual Festival, annual membership meeting, and network events. *Publications: Release Print* (magazine).

Film/Video Arts (F/VA). 462 Broadway, suite 520, New York, NY 10013. (212) 941-8787. Fax (212) 219-8924. E-mail: education@fva.com. Web site: http://www. fva.com. Eileen Newman, Exec. Dir. Film/Video Arts has come a long way since its founding in 1968 when educators Rodger Larson and Lynne Hofer in collaboration with filmmaker Jaime Barrios introduced 16mm motion picture equipment to Latino youth on the Lower East Side. Operating out of a storefront just off the Bowery, the teenagers were soon making highly personal films, mostly concerned with growing up in the neighborhood. In 1968, the organization was officially incorporated as the Young Filmakers Foundation, to encourage filmmaking as an artistic, educational and vocational experience for young people. A major grant in 1970 made it possible for Young Filmakers to stabilize and expand its programs citywide. In 1971, in collaboration with the New York State Council on the Arts, Young Filmakers established the first public media equipment access center in a basement on West 53rd Street. Known as Media Equipment Resource Center (MERC), this program served film and video makers of all ages with production and postproduction services free of charge. In 1973, the activities of the organization were consolidated in a loft building at 4 Rivington Street. By 1978, Young Filmakers had introduced modest fees and redirected its focus to adults. In 1985, Young Filmakers changed its name to Film/Video Arts and relocated to 817 Broadway. The new location and major equipment upgrades enabled the organization to evolve from a set of experimental programs to an established service institution. In 1997, Film/Video Arts built the Digital Studio and initiated the Digital Arts Certificate Program. Consequently, a new generation of digital media producers were emerging from Film/Video Arts with the benefit of having equal access to necessary resources. In 2001, Film/Video Arts relocated to its present address at 462 Broadway (corner of Grand Street). The future of the Film/Video Arts at its new location holds forth many possibilities as the organization continues to grow with the emergence of newer technologies. Drawing from its rich history Film/Video Arts has steadily evolved, all the time maintaining its staunch commitment to supporting the needs of independent film, video and digital media producers. The founders mission, to make the tools and skills of the media arts available to those who might otherwise not have access to them, remains the guiding force behind all Film/Video Arts activities and programs. *Membership:* Join Film/Video Arts today and become a part of a thriving community of independent film, video and multimedia producers. A Film/Video Arts membership allows one to take courses, receive fiscal sponsorship and mentorship and receive access to the postproduction facilities for affordable rates. Membership contributions help support Film/Video Arts equipment purchases and low service fees. Memberships are valid for one year from the date of issue. Contributions are tax-deductible to the full extent of the law. To become a member fill out the Membership Application and submit it to Film/Video Arts (with membership payment) via email or regular mail. Individual $75/Organization $95. Access to Film/Video Arts courses, production equipment rentals and postproduction services at affordable rates.

Fiscal Sponsorship Referrals for affordable premiums on General Liability and Production Insurance.

Opportunities to exhibit work in Members Screenings. A subscription to Film/Video Arts Email Newsletter. Enrollment in Film/Video ARts Membership Discount Program which entitles F/VA members to savings at several film and video service providers. Note: Individual membership is for one person only. An organizational membership is for two authorized individuals. Fiscal sponsorship program: This program serves the independent producer who is seeking funding for projects. Film/Video Arts will act as a fiscal sponsor for independent producers in cases where a donor (such as a governmental body, nonprofit organization, an individual or other entity) stipulates in their funding guidelines that the recipient have nonprofit status under 501(c)3 of the Internal Revenue Code. In such cases Film/Video Arts can use its nonprofit status to receive and administer grants, gifts or donations that are made in the name of the producers project. As a Fiscal Sponsor, Film/Video Arts does not supervise the actual production of projects, but is responsible for monitoring their progress. In order to apply to the program, individuals must complete and send in the Fiscal Sponsor Application accompanied by a project proposal which includes a detailed description/treatment of the project, fundraising and distribution plan, résumés of key personnel, a list of project advisors (as applies), a budget and a sample reel. A non-refundable membership fee of $75 is required for review of the project proposal. The proposal will be reviewed by a Film/Video Arts screening committee. The review process takes approximately two weeks. Once a project is accepted into Film/Video Arts Fiscal Sponsor Program, Film/Video Arts will then administer and turn over all funding raised by the producer after deducting a 6% administrative fee. *Dues:* $75, indiv., $95, organization.

Freedom of Information Center (FOI Center). 127 Neff Annex, University of Missouri, Columbia, MO 65211-0012. (573) 882-4856. Fax (573) 882-9002. E-mail: FOI@missouri.edu. Web site: http://www.missouri.edu/~foiwww. Dr. Charles N. Davis, Director; Kathleen Edwards, Manager; Robert W. Anderson, Web Manager. Located in the Missouri School of Journalism, the Freedom of Information Center is an academic research facility specializing in educational advocacy. The collection focuses on the centrality of open government to its role in fostering democracy. The Center staff assists the public with requests or questions about freedom of information with the help of an extensive archive of materials dating from the FOI movements inception. The Centers operating hours are Monday through Friday, 8:00 A.M. to 5:00 P.M., excluding University holidays. *Membership:* The FOI Center does not offer memberships. The Center serves approximately 23,000 researchers annually through its Web page and through individual contacts. *Dues:* No dues charged. Minimal fees may be charged for research. *Meetings:* The FOI Center meets annually with the National Freedom of Information Coalition. *Publications*: Access to Public Information: A Resource Guide to Government in Columbia and Boone County, Missouri, a directory of public records, and the *FOI Advocate,* a periodic electronic newsletter. Both publications are linked to the center's Web page. Some older publications are available for sale by contacting the Center.

George Eastman House International Museum of Photography and Film (GEH). 900 East Ave., Rochester, NY 14607. (585) 271-3361. Fax (585) 271-3970. E-mail: tbannon@geh.org. Web site: http://www.eastman.org. Anthony Bannon, Dir. World-renowned museum of photography and cinematography established to preserve, collect, and exhibit photographic art and technology, film materials, and related literature, and to serve as a memorial to George Eastman. Services include archives, traveling exhibitions, research library, school of film preservation, center for the conservation of photographic materials, and photographic print service. Educational programs, exhibitions, films, symposia, music events, tours, and internship stipends offered. Eastman's turn-of-the-century mansion and gardens have been restored to their original grandeur. *Membership:* 13,000. *Dues:* $40, library; $50, family; $40, indiv.; $36, student; $30, senior citizen; $75, Contributor; $125, Sustainer; $250, Patron; $500, Benefactor; $1,000, George Eastman Society. *Publications:* Newsletter; *Annual Report: The George Eastman House and Gardens; Masterpieces of Photography from the George Eastman House Collections; Index to American Photographic Collections;* and exhibition catalogs.

The George Lucas Educational Foundation (GLEF). P.O. Box 3494, San Rafael, CA 94912. (415) 507-0399. Fax (415) 507-0499. E-mail: edutopia@glef.org. Web site: http://glef.org. Milton Chen, PhD., Exec. Dir. Mission: The George Lucas Educational Foundation (GLEF) is a nonprofit operating foundation that documents and disseminates models of the most innovative practices in our nation's K–12 schools. We serve this mission through the creation of media—from films, books, and newsletters to CD-ROMS. GLEF works to provide its products as tools for discussion and action in conferences, workshops, and professional development settings. Audience: A successful educational system requires the collaborative efforts of many different stakeholders. Our audience includes teachers, administrators, school board members, parents, researchers, and business and community leaders who are actively working to improve teaching and learning. Vision: The Edutopian vision is thriving today in our country's best schools: places where students are engaged and achieving at the highest levels, where skillful educators are energized by the excitement of teaching, where technology brings outside resources and expertise into the classroom, and where parents and community members are partners in educating our youth. *Meetings:* Annual Advisory meeting. *Publications: Edutopia Online:* The Foundation's Web site, Edutopia Online (www.glef.org) celebrates the unsung heroes who are making Edutopia a reality. All of GLEF's multimedia content dating back to 1997 is available on its Web site. A special feature, the Video Gallery, is an archive of short documentaries and expert interviews that allow visitors to see these innovations in action and hear about them from teachers and students. Detailed articles, research summaries, and links to hundreds of relevant Web sites, books, organizations, and publications are also available to help schools and communities build on successes in education. *Edutopia: Success Stories for Learning in the Digital Age:* This book and CD-ROM include numerous stories of innovative educators who are using technology to connect with students, colleagues, the local community, and the world beyond. The CD-ROM contains more than an hour of video footage. Published by Jossey-Bass. *Teaching in the Digital Age* (TDA) Videocassettes. This video series explores elements of successful teaching in the Digital Age. The project grows out of GLEFs belief that an expanded view is needed of all our roles in educating children and supporting teachers. The series explores School Leadership, Emotional Intelligence, Teacher Preparation, and Project-Based Learning and Assessment. Learn & Live: This documentary film and 300-page companion resource book showcases innovative schools across the country. The film, hosted by Robin Williams, aired on public television stations nationwide in 1999 and 2000. The Learn & Live CD-ROM includes digital versions of the film and book in a portable, easy-to-use format. *Edutopia Newsletter:* This free, semiannual print newsletter includes school profiles, summaries of recent research, and resources and tips for getting involved in public education.

Graphic Arts Technical Foundation (GATF). 200 Deer Run Road, Sewickley, PA 15143-2600. (412) 741-6860. Fax (412) 741-2311. E-mail: info@gatf.org. Web site:

http://www.gain.net. George Ryan, Executive Vice President and Chief Operating Officer. GATF is a member-supported, nonprofit, scientific, technical, and educational organization dedicated to the advancement of graphic communications industries worldwide. For 77 years GATF has developed leading-edge technologies and practices for printing, and each year the Foundation develops new products, services, and training programs to meet the evolving needs of the industry. GATF consolidated its operations with the Printing Industries of America (PIA) in 1999. *Membership:* 13,000 corporate members, 520 teachers, 100 students. *Dues:* $45, teachers; $30, students; corporations pay dues to regional printing organizations affiliated with GATF/PIA. *Meetings:* see www.gain.net. *Publications:* GATF publishes books relating to graphic communications. GATF's Publications Catalogs promotes 320 books, 100 of which are published by GATF. Recent publications include: *Customer Service in the Printing Industry, What the Printer Should Know About Ink, Total Production Maintenance, Managing Mavericks: The Official Printing Industry Guide to Effective Sales Management, Print Production Scheduling Primer, Paper Buying Primer,* and *Print Production Management Primer.*

Great Plains National ITV Library (GPN). P.O. Box 80669, Lincoln, NE 68501-0669. (402) 472-2007, (800) 228-4630. Fax (800) 306-2330. E-mail: gpn@unl.edu. Web site: http://gpn.unl.edu. Stephen C. Lenzen, Executive Director. Produces and distributes educational media, video, CD-ROMs and DVDs, prints and Internet courses. Available for purchase for audiovisual or lease for broadcast use. *Publications:* GPN Educational Video Catalogs by curriculum areas; periodic brochures. Complete listing of GPN's product line is available via the Internet along with online purchasing. Free previews available.

Health Sciences Communications Association (HeSCA). One Wedgewood Dr., Suite 27, Jewett City, CT 06351-2428. (203) 376-5915. Fax (203) 376-6621. E-mail: keven@hesca.org. Web site: http://www.hesca.org/. Ronald Sokolowski, Exec. Dir. An affiliate of AECT, HeSCA is a nonprofit organization dedicated to the sharing of ideas, skills, resources, and techniques to enhance communications and educational technology in the health sciences. It seeks to nurture the professional growth of its members; serve as a professional focal point for those engaged in health sciences communications; and convey the concerns, issues, and concepts of health sciences communications to other organizations which influence and are affected by the profession. International in scope and diverse in membership, HeSCA is supported by medical and veterinary schools, hospitals, medical associations, and businesses where media are used to create and disseminate health information. *Membership:* 150. *Dues:* $150, indiv.; $195, institutional ($150 additional institutional dues); $60, retiree; $75, student; $1,000, sustaining. All include subscriptions to the journal and newsletter. *Meetings:* Annual meetings, May-June. *Publications*: Journal of Biocommunications; Feedback (newsletter).

Hollywood Film Archive (HFA). 8391 Beverly Blvd., #321, Hollywood, CA 90048. (323) 655-4968. Fax (323) 555-4321. E-mail: info@hfa.com. Web site: http://.hfa.com. D. Richard Baer, Dir. Archival organization for information about feature films produced worldwide, from the early silents to the present. *Dues:* Inquire. *Meetings:* As scheduled. *Publications:* Comprehensive movie reference works for sale, including *Variety Film Reviews* (1907–1996) and the *American Film Institute Catalogs* (1893–1910,1911–20, 1921–30, 1931–40, 1941–50, 1961–70), as well as the *Film Superlist* (1894–1939, 1940–1949, 1950–1959) volumes, which provide information both on copyrights and on motion pictures in the public domain; *Harrisons Reports and Film Reviews* (1919–1962).

The Institute for the Advancement of Emerging Technologies in Education at AEL (IAETE). PO Box 1348, Charleston, WV 25325-1348. (304) 347-1848. Fax (304) 347-1847. E-mail: info@iaete.org. Website: www.iaete.org. Dr. John D. Ross, Associate Director. The mission of the Institute for the Advancement of Emerging Technologies in Education (IAETE) is to support the purposeful use of new and emerging technologies to improve teaching, learning, and school management. IAETE is committed to providing unbiased, research-based information to the education community as well as to product developers. *Membership:* Not applicable. *Dues:* Not applicable. *Meetings:* Annual National Conference. *Publications:* IAETE publishes several white papers, briefs, and reports annually in both print and electronic format. All address new and emerging technologies and their impact on teaching, learning, and school management. For more information, please visit www.iaete.org.

Institute for Development of Educational Activities, Inc. (|I|D|E|A|). 259 Regency Ridge, Dayton, OH 45459. (937) 434-6969. Fax (937) 434-5203. E-mail: IDEADayton@aol.com. Web site: http://www.idea.org. Dr. Steven R. Thompson, Pres. I|D|E|A| is an action-oriented research and development organization originating from the Charles F. Kettering Foundation. It was established in 1965 to assist the educational community in bridging the gap that separates research and innovation from actual practice in the schools. Its goal is to design and test new responses to improve education and to create arrangements that support local application. Activities include developing new and improved processes, systems, and materials; training local facilitators to use the change processes; and providing information and services about improved methods and materials. |I|D|E|A| sponsors an annual fellowship program for administrators and conducts seminars for school administrators and teachers.

Institute for the Future (IFTF). 2744 Sand Hill Rd., Menlo Park, CA 94025-7020. (650) 854-6322. Fax (650) 854-7850. E-mail: info@iftf.org. Web site: http://www.iftf.org. Robert Johansen, Pres. The cross-disciplinary professionals at IFTF have been providing global and domestic businesses and organizations with research-based forecasts and action-oriented tools for strategic decision making since 1968. IFTF is a nonprofit, applied research and consulting firm dedicated to understanding technological, economic, and societal changes and their long-range domestic and global consequences. Its work falls into four main areas: Strategic Planning, Emerging Technologies, Health Care Horizons, and Public Sector Initiatives. IFTF works with clients to think systematically about the future, identify socioeconomic trends and evaluate their long-term implications, identify potential leading-edge markets around the world, understand the global marketplace, track the implications of emerging technologies for business and society, leverage expert judgment and data resources, offer an independent view of the big picture, and facilitate strategic planning processes.

Instructional Technology Council (ITC). One Dupont Cir., NW, Suite 410, Washington, DC 20036-1176. (202) 293-3110. Fax (202) 833-2467. E-mail: cdalziel@aacc.nche.edu. Web site: http://www.itcnetwork.org. Christine Dalziel, Executive Director. An affiliated council of the American Association of Community Colleges established in 1977, the Instructional Technology Council (ITC) provides leadership, information and resources to expand access to, and enhance learning through, the effective use of technology. lTC represents higher education institutions in the United States and Canada that use distance learning technologies. ITC members receive a subscription to the ITC News and ITC list serv with information on whats happening in distance education, participation in ITC's professional development audioconference series, distance learning grants information, updates on distance learning legislation, discounts to attend the annual Telelearning Conference which features more than 80 workshops and seminars, discounts to downlink PBS/ALS videoconferences, and a free copy of ITC publications and research. *Membership:* Members include single institutions and multi-campus districts; regional and statewide systems of community, technical and two-year colleges; for-profit organizations; four-year institutions; and nonprofit organizations that are interested or involved in instructional telecommunications. Members use a vast array of ever-changing technologies for distance learning. They often combine different systems according to students needs. The technologies they use and methods of teaching include: audio and video conferences, cable television, compressed and full-motion video, computer networks, fiber optics, interactive videodisc, ITFS, microwave, multimedia, public television, satellites, teleclasses, and telecourses. *Dues:* $450, Institutional; $750, Corporate. *Meetings:* Annual Telelearning Conference. *Publications: Quality Enhancing Practices in Distance Education: Vol. 2 Student Services; Quality Enhancing Practices in Distance Education: Vol. 1 Teaching and Learning; New Connections: A Guide to Distance Education* (2nd ed.); *New Connections: A College President's Guide to Distance Education; Digital Video: A Handbook for Educators; Faculty Compensation and Support Issues in Distance Education; ITC News* (monthly publication/newsletter); ITC Listserv.

International Association for Language Learning Technology (IALLT). Instr. Media Svcs, Concordia Coll., Moorhead, MN 56562. (218) 299-3464. Fax (218) 299-3246. E-mail: business@iallt.org. Web site: http://iallt.org. Peter Liddell President; Ron Balko, Business Manager. IALLT is a professional organization whose members provide leadership in the development, integration, evaluation and management of instructional technology for the teaching and learning of language, literature and culture. *Membership:* 500 members.

Membership/Subscription Categories:

- Educational Member: for people working in an academic setting such as a school, college or university. These members have voting rights.

- Full-time Student Member: for full-time students interested in membership. Requires a signature of a voting member to verify student status. These members have voting rights.

- Commercial Member: for those working for corporations interested in language learning and technology. This category includes for example language laboratory vendors, software and textbook companies.

- Library Subscriber: receive our journals for placement in libraries.

Dues: 1 year: $50, voting member; $25, student; $60, library subscription; $75 commercial. 2 year: $90, voting member; $140 commercial. *Meetings:* Biennial IALLT conferences treat the entire range of topics related to technology in language learning as well as management and planning. IALLT also sponsors sessions at conferences of organizations with related interests, including CALICO and ACTFL. *Publications: IALLT Journal of Language Learning Technologies* (2 times annually); materials for language lab management and design, language teaching and technology. Visit our Web site for details. Web site: http://iallt.org.

International Association of Business Communicators (IABC). One Hallidie Plaza, Suite 600, San Francisco, CA 94102. (415) 544-4700. Fax (415) 544-4747. E-mail: service_centre@iabc.com. Web site: http://www.iabc.com. Elizabeth Allan, Pres. and CEO. IABC is the worldwide association for the communication and public relations profession. It is founded on the principle that the better an organization communicates with all its audiences, the more successful and effective it will be in meeting its objectives. IABC is dedicated to fostering communication excellence, contributing more effectively to organizations' goals worldwide, and being a model of communication effectiveness. *Membership:* 13,500 plus. *Dues:* $175 in addition to local and regional dues. *Meetings:* Annually. *Publications:* Communication World.

International Association of School Librarianship (IASL). Box 34069, Dept. 962, Seattle, WA 98124-1069. (604) 925-0266. Fax (604) 925-0566. E-mail: iasl@rockland.com. Web site: http://.iasl-slo.org/. Dr. Penny Moore, Exec. Dir. Seeks to encourage development of school libraries and library programs throughout the world; promote professional preparation and continuing education of school librarians; achieve collaboration among school libraries of the world; foster relationships between school librarians and other professionals connected with children and youth and to coordinate activities, conferences, and other projects in the field of school librarianship. *Membership:* 900 plus. *Dues:* $50 Zone A (e.g., United States, Canada, Western Europe, Japan); $35 Zone B (e.g. Eastern Europe, Latin America, Middle East); $20 Zone C (e.g. Angola, India, Bulgaria, China) Based on GNP. *Meetings:* Annual Conference, Hong Kong, China, from 8–12 July. *Publications: IASL Newsletter* (3/yr.); *School Libraries Worldwide* (semiannual); *Conference Professionals and Research Papers* (annual); *Connections: School Library Associations and Contact People Worldwide; Sustaining the Vision: A Collection of Articles and Papers on Research in School Librarianship; School Librarianship: International Issues and Perspectives; Information Rich but Knowledge Poor? Issues for Schools and Libraries Worldwide: Selected Papers from the Annual Conferences of the IASL.*

International Center of Photography (ICP). 1114 Avenue of the Americas, New York, NY 10036. (212) 857-0001. Fax (212) 857-0091. E-mail: info@icp.org. Web site: http://www.icp.org. Willis Hartshorn, Dir.; Phyllis Levine, Dir. of Public Information. A comprehensive photographic institution whose exhibitions, publications, collections, and educational programs embrace all aspects of photography from aesthetics to technique; from the 19th century to the present; from master photographers to newly emerging talents; from photojournalism to the avant garde. Changing exhibitions, lectures, seminars, workshops, museum shops, and screening rooms make ICP a complete photographic resource. ICP offers two options of Graduate Study in conjunction with New York University: 1. a Master of Fine Arts in Studio Art with a concentration in Media Studies (1yr, 60-point program) 2. a Master in Studio Art with a concentration in Photography (36-point program)and one-year certificate programs in Documentary Photography and Photojournalism and General Studies in Photography. *Membership:* 6,000. *Dues:* $60, indiv.; $75, double; $150, Supporting Patron; $300, Photography Circle; $600, Silver Card Patron; $1,200, Gold Card Patron;$3,000 Benefactor; corporate memberships available. *Meetings:* The Annual ICP Infinity Awards. *Publications: Telling Tales, Kiki Smith, Reflections in a Glass Eye; Images from the Machine Age: Selections from the Daniel Cowin Collection; Library of Photography; A Singular Elegance: The Photographs of Baron Adolph de Meyer; Talking Pictures: People Speak about the Photographs That Speak to Them; Encyclopedia of Photography: Master Photographs from PFA Collection; Man Ray in Fashion; Quarterly Program Guide; Quarterly Exhibition Schedule.*

International Council for Educational Media (ICEM). Hanns-Fay Strasse 1, Frankenthal, N/A D67227. 49 6233 46051. Fax 49 6233 46355. E-mail: secretariat@icem-cime.com. Web site: http://www.icem-cime.com. Dr. Marina McIsaac, Pres. and U.S. member, Margo Van Sluizer, Secretary General. The objectives of ICEM are to provide a channel for the international exchange of information and experience in the field of educational technology, with particular reference to preschool, primary, and secondary education, technical and vocational training, and teacher and continuing education; encourage organizations with a professional responsibility for the design, production, promotion, distribution, and use of educational media in member countries; promote an understanding of the concept of educational technology on the part of both educators and those involved in their training; contribute to the pool of countries by the sponsorship of practical projects involving international cooperation and co-production; advise manufacturers of hardware and software on the needs of an information service on developments in educational technology; provide consultancy for the benefit of member countries; and cooperate with other international organizations in promoting the concept of educational technology. ICEM has established operational relations with UNESCO. *Membership:* There are national memberships as well as those for individuals, students, academic institutions and corporate entities. Membership is open those who work in the area of educational and instructional media, Grades 12-Adult. There are presently 30 member nations in ICEM and 195 individual members. *Dues:* Dues for National Members are 2,500 Swiss francs (SF) per year and may be paid in either Swiss francs or US Dollars. Individual dues are $85 or 125 SF. Students and retired individual dues are $40 or 58 SF. Primary and Secondary School dues are $135 or 200 SF. Public and nonprofit organization dues are $205 or 300 SF (includes government departments, foundations, associations, universities, etc.). Commercial organization dues are $275 or 400 SF (producers, distributors, manufacturers, etc.). *Meetings:* Annually. *Publications: Educational Media International,* a quarterly refereed journal. The Editor-in-Chief is Dr. John Hedberg, Faculty of Education, University of Wollongong, Wollongong, NSW 2522 AUSTRALIA. john_hedberg@uow.edu.au.

International Graphics Arts Education Association (IGAEA). 1899 Preston White Drive, Reston, VA 20191-4367. (703) 758-0595. Fax none. E-mail: gcc@teched.vt.edu. Web site: http://www.igaea.org. Mark Sanders, gcc@teched.vt.edu. IGAEA is an association of educators in partnership with industry, dedicated to sharing theories, principles, techniques, and processes relating to graphic communications and imaging technology. Teachers network to share and improve teaching and learning opportunities in fields related to graphic arts, imaging technology, graphic design, graphic communications, journalism, photography, and other areas related to the large and rapidly changing fields in the printing, publishing, packaging, and allied industries. *Membership:* Approx. 600 members. Open to educators, middle school through college and university, who teach graphic arts, graphic communications, printing and publishing, desktop publishing, multimedia, and photography. *Dues:* $20, regular; $12, associate (retired); $5, student; $10, library; $50-$200, sustaining membership based on number of employees. *Meetings:* See Web site for info: Web site: http://www.igaea.org. *Publications: The Communicator; Visual Communications Journal* (annual).

International Recording Media Association (IRMA). 182 Nassau St., Princeton, NJ 08542-7005. (609) 279-1700. Fax (609) 279-1999. E-mail: info@recordingmedia.org. Web site: http://www.recordingmedia.org. Charles Van Horn, President.; Phil Russo, Exec. Director. IRMA is the advocate for the growth and development of all recording media and is the industry forum for the exchange of information regarding global trends and innovations. Members include recording media manufacturers, rights holders to video programs, recording and playback equipment manufacturers, and audio and video replicators. For more than 30 years, the Association has provided vital information and educational services throughout the magnetic and optical recording media industries. By promoting a greater awareness of marketing, merchandising, and technical developments, the association serves all areas of the entertainment, information, and delivery systems industries. *Membership:* 450 corporations. Corporate membership includes benefits to all employees. *Dues:* Corporate membership dues based on sales volume. *Meetings:* IRMA Executive Forum; IRMA Marketing Summit; DVD Entertainment. *Publications: Membership Quarterly Magazine; Seminar Proceedings; International Source Directory, Marketing Statistics.*

International Society for Performance Improvement (ISPI). 1400 Spring Street, Suite 260, Silver Spring, MD 20910. (301) 587-8570. Fax (301) 587-8573. E-mail: info@ispi.org. Web site: http://www.ispi.org. Richard D. Battaglia, Exec. Dir. Founded in 1962, the International Society for Performance Improvement (ISPI) is the leading international association dedicated to improving productivity and performance in the workplace. ISPI represents more than 10,000 international and chapter members throughout the United States, Canada, and 40 other countries. ISPI's mission is to develop and recognize the proficiency of our members and advocate the use of Human Performance Technology. Assembling an Annual Conference & Expo and other educational events like the Institute, publishing books and periodicals, and supporting research are some of the ways ISPI works toward achieving this mission. *Membership:* 10,000. Performance technologists, training directors, human resources managers, instructional technologists, human factors practitioners, and organizational consultants are members of ISPI. They work in a variety of settings including business, academia, government, health services, banking, and the armed forces. *Dues:* Membership Categories: Active Membership ($145 annually). This is an individual membership receiving full benefits and voting rights in the Society. Student Membership ($60 annually). This is a discounted individual full membership for full-time students. Proof of full-time enrollment must accompany the application. Retired Membership ($60 annually). This is a discounted individual full membership for individuals who are retired from full-time employment. Special Organizational Membership Categories: These groups support the Society at the top level. Sustaining Membership ($950 annually). This is an organizational membership and includes five active memberships and several additional value-added services and discounts. Details available upon request. Patron Membership ($1400 annually). This is an organizational membership and includes five active memberships and several additional value-added services and discounts. Details available upon request. *Meetings:* Annual International Performance Improvement Conference & Exposition each April, Performance-Based Instructional Systems Design Conference each September, various Human Performance Technology Institutes throughout the year. *Publications: Performance Improvement Journal* (10/yr). The common theme is performance improvement practice or technique that is supported by research or germane theory. P*erformanceXpress* (12/yr): Monthly newsletter published on-line. *Performance Improvement Quarterly:* PIQ is a peer-reviewed journal created to stimulate professional discussion in the field and to advance the discipline of HPT through publishing scholarly works. *ISPI Bookstore:* The ISPI online publications and book catalog.

International Society for Technology in Education (ISTE). 480 Charnelton Street, Eugene, OR 97401. (800) 336-5191 (U.S. & Canada) (541) 302-3777 (Intl.). Fax (541) 302-3780. E-mail: iste@iste.org. Web site: http://www.iste.org. Don Knezek, CEO; Cheryl Williams, Co-President; Cathie Norris, Co-President. As the leading organization for educational technology professionals, the International Society for Technology in Education is a professional organization that supports a community of members through research, publications, workshops, symposia, and inclusion in national policy making through ISTE-DC. Home of the National Center for Preparing Tomorrows Teachers to Use Technology (NCPT3), ISTE works in conjunction with the U.S. Department of Education and various private entities to create and distribute solutions for technology integration. ISTE's National Educational Technology Standards (NETS) for students and teachers have been adopted by hundreds of districts nationwide. ISTE is also the home of NECC, the premier U.S. educational technology conference, is a forum for advancing educational philosophies, practices, policies, and research that focus on the appropriate use of current and emerging technologies to improve teaching and learning in K–12 and teacher education. *Membership:* ISTE members are leaders. ISTE members contribute to the field of educational technology as classroom teachers, lab teachers, technology coordinators, school administrators, teacher educators, and consultants.

ISTE provides leadership and professional development opportunities for its members. In addition to other benefits, ISTE members can participate in ISTE-sponsored invitational events at the National Educational Computer Conference (NECC), join one of ISTE's many Special Interest Groups (SIGs), and test and evaluate the latest in educational technology products and services through the ISTE Advocate Network. ISTE Members also enjoy subscriptions to ISTE Update and "Learning & Leading with Technology" or the "Journal for Research on Technology in Education." In the member's areas of the ISTE Web site, ISTE members can join discussion lists and other online forums for participation, review a database of educational technology resources, network with a cadre of education professionals, and review online editions of ISTE publications. *Dues:* Annual dues for individual ISTE members are $58. Membership to SIG communities are $20 for ISTE members. Contact iste@iste.org to become a member. Contact iste100@iste.org for more information. Group discounts are available. To see if you qualify, contact groupdiscounts @iste.org. *Meetings:* National Educational Computing Conference (NECC). *Publications:* ISTE's publications include *ISTE Update* (online member newsletter); *Learning & Leading with Technology*; the *Journal of Research on Technology in Education* (q.; formerly

Journal of Research on Computing in Education); and books about incorporating technology in the K–16 classroom.

International Telecommunications Satellite Organization (INTELSAT). 3400 International Dr. NW, Washington, DC 20008. (202) 944-7500. Fax (202) 944-7890. Web site: http://www.intelsat.int. Conng L. Kullman, Dir. Gen. and CEO; Tony A. Trujillo, Dir., Corporate Communications. INTELSAT owns and operates a global communications satellite system providing capacity for voice, video, corporate/private networks, and Internet in more than 200 countries and territories. In addition, the INTELSAT system provides educational and medical programming via satellite for selected participants around the world.

International Teleconferencing Association (ITCA). 100 Four Falls Corporate Center, Suite 105, West Conshohocken, PA 19428. (610) 941-2015. Fax (610) 941-2015. E-mail: staff@itca.org and president@itca.org. Web site: http://www.itca.org. Henry S. Grove III, Pres.; Eileen Hering, Manager, Member Services; Rosalie DiStasio, Asst. Manager, Member Services. ITCA, an international nonprofit association, is dedicated to the growth and development of teleconferencing as a profession and an industry. ITCA provides programs and services that foster the professional development of its members, champions teleconferencing and related technology as communications tools, recognizes and promotes broader applications and the development of teleconferencing and related technologies, and serves as the authoritative resource for information and research on teleconferencing and related technologies. *Membership:* ITCA represents over 1,000 teleconferencing professionals throughout the world. ITCA members use teleconferencing services to advise customers and vendors, conduct research, teach courses via teleconference, and teach about teleconferencing. They represent such diverse industry segments as health care, aerospace, government, pharmaceutical, education, insurance, finance and banking, telecommunications, and manufacturing. *Dues:* 6,250, Platinum Sustaining, $2,500, Gold Sustaining; $1,250, Sustaining; $625, Organizational; $325, small business; $125, indiv.; and $35, student. *Meetings:* spring and fall MultimediaCom Shows; spring show in San Jose, fall show in Boston, August 30-September 2. *Publications:* Forum newsletter; member directories; white paper; *Teleconferencing Success Stories.*

International Visual Literacy Association, Inc. (IVLA). Darrell Beauchamp, IVLA Treasurer, Navarro College, 3200 W. 7th Ave., Corsicana, TX 75110. (903) 875-7441. Fax (903) 874-4636. E-mail: darrell.beauchamp@navarrocollege.edu. Web site: http://www.ivla.org. Darrell Beauchamp. IVLA provides a multidisciplinary forum for the exploration, presentation, and discussion of all aspects of visual learning, thinking, communication, and expression. It also serves as a communication link bonding professionals from many disciplines who are creating and sustaining the study of the nature of visual experiences and literacy. It promotes and evaluates research, programs, and projects intended to increase effective use of visual communication in education, business, the arts, and commerce. IVLA was founded in 1968 to promote the concept of visual literacy and is an affiliate of AECT. *Membership:* Membership of 500 people, mostly from academia and from many disciplines. We are an international organization and have conferences abroad once every third year. Anyone interested in any visual-verbal area should try our organization: architecture, engineering, dance, the arts, computers, video, design, graphics, photography, visual languages, mathematics, acoustics, physics, chemistry, optometry, sciences, literature, library, training, education, etc. *Dues:* $40 regular; $20 student and retired; $45 outside United States; corporate memberships available; $500 lifetime membership. *Meetings:* Yearly conference usually Oct./Nov. in selected locations. *Publications: The Journal of Visual Literacy* (biannual—juried research papers); *Selected Readings from the Annual Conference;* and *The Visual Literacy ReView* (newsletter—4 times per year).

The Learning Team (TLT). Suite 204 84 Business Park Drive, Armonk, NY 10504. (914) 273-2226. Fax (914) 273-0936. E-mail: NMcLaren@LearningTeam.org. Web site: http://www.

learningteam.org. Executive Director—Tom Laster. The Learning Team is a not-for-profit company that is focused on publishing inquiry-based, supplementary, technology resources for science education. The multimedia resources include: Science, mathematics and utilities software and videos. Science subjects include: physics, physical sciences, biology, earth sciences (geosciences), environmental sciences, general science, chemistry, energy use, and culture and technology. Software includes inquiry-based student resources, teacher resources and professional development. Resources available include High School Geography Product (HSGP), Intermediate Science Curriculum Study (ISCS), Man: A Course of Study (MACOS) and Human Sciences Project (HSP). Most of the resources come from National Science Foundation (NSF)funding and have been done in conjunction with institutions such as the American Association of Physics Teachers (AAPT), the American Institute of Physics (AIP), American Geological Institute (AGI). *Membership:* Although the term membership does not apply specifically to our organization, it loosely applies to the range of licensors, collaborators and colleagues that cooperate with us and are active in the area of science education. *Dues:* NIL. *Meetings:* as appropriate. *Publications: Physics InfoMall, CPU—Constructing Physics Understanding, Exploring the Nardoo, Investigating Lake Iluka, The Dynamic Rainforests, Insects—Little Creatures in a Big World, Culture & Technology, Enhanced Science Helper, Enhanced Science Helper Videos, The Green Home, The Sun's Joules, Whelmers, EarthView Explorer, GETIT—Geosciences Education through Interactive Technology, Crossword Wizard, Cloze word Wizard Maths Worksheet Wizard.*

Library Administration and Management Association (LAMA). 50 E. Huron St., Chicago, IL 60611. (312) 280-5032. Fax (312) 280-5033. E-mail: lama@ala.org. Web site: http://www.ala.org/lama. Lorraine Olley, Executive Director; Paul Anderson, President. A division of the American Library Association, LAMA provides an organizational framework for encouraging the study of administrative theory, improving the practice of administration in libraries, and identifying and fostering administrative skills. Toward these ends, the association is responsible for all elements of general administration that are common to more than one type of library. Sections include Buildings and Equipment Section (BES); Fundraising & Financial Development Section (FRFDS); Library Organization & Management Section (LOMS); Human Resources Section (HRS); Public Relation and Marketing Section (PRMS); Systems & Services Section (SASS); and Measurement, Assessment and Evaluation Section (MAES). *Membership:* 4,800. *Dues:* $50 regular(in addition to ALA membership); $65 organizations and corporations; $15, library school students. *Meetings:* 2005, Chicago, June 23–29; 2005, Boston, Jan 14–19; 2006, New Orleans, June 22–28. *Publications: Library Administration & Management* (q); *LEADS from LAMA* (electronic newsletter, irregular).

Library and Information Technology Association (LITA). 50 E. Huron St, Chicago, IL 60611. (312) 280-4270, (800) 545-2433, ext. 4270. Fax (312) 280-3257. E-mail: lita@ala.org. Web site: http://www.lita.org. Mary C. Taylor, Exec. Dir., mtaylor@ala.org. An affiliate of the American Library Association, LITA is concerned with library automation; the information sciences; and the design, development, and implementation of automated systems in those fields, including systems development, electronic data processing, mechanized information retrieval, operations research, standards development, telecommunications, video communications, networks and collaborative efforts, management techniques, information technology, optical technology, artificial intelligence and expert systems, and other related aspects of audiovisual activities and hardware applications. *Membership:* LITA's members come from all types of libraries and institutions focusing on information technology in libraries. They include library decision-makers, practitioners, information professionals and vendors. Approximately 5,400 members. *Dues:* $35 (first time) plus membership in ALA; $25, library school students; $35, first year; renewal memberships $45 plus ALA cost. *Meetings:* National Forum, fall. *Publications: LITA Newsletter* (electronic only; see Web site). *Information Technology and Libraries* (ITAL: Contains the table of contents, abstracts and some full-text of *ITAL,* a refereed journal published quarterly by the Library and Information Technology Association.) *Technology Electronic Reviews* (TER): TER is an irregular electronic serial publication that provides reviews and pointers to a variety of print and electronic resources about information technology. LITA Publications List: Check for information on LITA Guides and Monographs.

Library of Congress (LOC). James Madison Bldg., 101 Independence Ave. SE, Washington, DC 20540. (202) 707-5000. Fax (202) 707-1389. E-mail: pao@loc.gov. Web site: http://www.loc.gov. Dr. James Billington, Librarian of Congress. The Library of Congress is the major source of research and information for the Congress. In its role as the national library, it catalogs and classifies library materials in some 460 languages, distributes the data in both printed and electronic form, and makes its vast collections available through interlibrary loan, on-site to anyone over high school age, and through its award-winning Web site at www.loc.gov. The Library is the largest library in the world, with more than 126 million items on 532 miles of bookshelves. The collections include nearly 19 million cataloged books, 2.6 million recordings, 12 million photographs, 4.8 million maps, and 56 million manuscripts. It contains the world's largest television and film archive, acquiring materials through gift, purchase, and copyright deposit. In 2002, some 23 million items (discs, cassettes, Braille materials) produced by the Library in Braille and recorded formats for persons who are blind or physically challenged were circulated to a readership of more than 500,000. The collections of the Motion Picture, Broadcasting and Recorded Sound Division include nearly 900,000 moving images. The Library's public catalog, as well as other files containing copyright and legislative information, are available on the Librarys Web site. In 2000, the Library launched the Americas Library Web site for children and families. This easy-to-use, interactive site www.americaslibrary.gov) allows children to "have fun with history." The site receives more than 150 million hits annually. *Publications:* See list on library's Web site.

Lister Hill National Center for Biomedical Communications (LHNCBC). National Library of Medicine, 8600 Rockville Pike, Bethesda, MD 20894. (301) 496-4441. Fax (301) 402-0118. E-mail: publicinfo@nlm.nih.gov. Web site: http://www.nlm.nih.gov. Robert Mehnert, Director, mehnert@nlm.nih.gov. The Lister Hill National Center for Biomedical Communications is a research and development division of the National Library of Medicine (NLM). The Center conducts and supports research and development in the dissemination of high quality imagery, medical language processing, high-speed access to biomedical information, intelligent database systems development, multimedia visualization, knowledge management, data mining and machine-assisted indexing. The Lister Hill Center also conducts and supports research and development projects focusing on educational applications of state-of-the-art technologies including the use of microcomputer technology incorporating stereoscopic imagery and haptics, the Internet, and videoconferencing technologies for training health care professionals and disseminating consumer health information. The Centers Collaboratory for High Performance Computing and Communication serves as a focus for collaborative research and development in those areas, cooperating with faculties and staff of health sciences educational institutions. Health profession educators are assisted in the use and application of these technologies through periodic training, demonstrations and consultations. High Definition (HD) video is a technology area that has been explored and developed within the Center, and is now used as the NLM standard for all motion imaging projects considered to be of archival value. Advanced three dimensional animation and photorealistic rendering techniques have also become required tools for use in visual projects within the Center. *Publications:* fact sheet at Web site: http://www.nlm.nih.gov/pubs/factsheets/lister_hill.html.

Magazine Publishers of America (MPA). 919 Third Ave., 22nd Floor, New York, NY 10022. (212) 872-3700. Fax (212) 888-4217. E-mail: infocenter@magazine.org. Web site: http://www.magazine.org. Nina Link, Pres. MPA is the trade association of the consumer magazine industry. MPA promotes the greater and more effective use of magazine advertising, with ad campaigns in the trade press and in member magazines, presentations to advertisers and their ad agencies, and magazine days in cities around the United States. MPA runs educational seminars, conducts surveys of its members on a variety of topics, represents the magazine industry in Washington, DC, and maintains an extensive library on magazine publishing. *Membership:* 230 publishers representing more than 1,200 magazines. *Meetings:* Annually in Oct. *Publications: Newsletter of Consumer Marketing; Sales Edge; Newsletter of International Publishing; Magazine; Washington Newsletter.*

Media Communications Association—International (MCA-I). 7600 Terrace Avenue, Suite 203, Middleton, WI 53562. (608) 827-5034. Fax (608) 831-5122. E-mail: info@mca-i.org. Web site: http://www.mca-i.org. Susan Rees, Executive Director—The Rees Group. Formerly the International Television Association. Founded in 1968, MCA-Is mission is to provide media communications professionals opportunities for networking, forums for education and resources for information. MCA-I also offers business services, such as low-cost insurance, buying programs, etc., to reduce operating costs. MCA-I also confers the highly acclaimed Media Festival awards(The Golden Reel is back!)on outstanding multimedia productions. Visit MCA-Is Web site for full details. *Membership:* Over 3,000 individual and corporate members. Membership programs also are available to vendors for relationship and business development. *Dues:* $160, individual.; $455, organizational; PLATINUM—$7,500; GOLD—$5,500; SILVER—$2,500; BRONZE—$1250. *Meetings:* Various Partnerships with Association Conferences. *Publications: MCA-I News* (quarterly newsletter); *MCA-I Member2Member E-News* (6/yr.); *Membership Directory* (annual).

Medical Library Association (MLA). 65 E. Wacker Pl., Ste. 1900, Chicago, IL 60601-7298. (312) 419-9094. Fax (312) 419-8950. E-mail: info@mlahq.org. Web site: http://www.mlanet.org. Carla J. Funk, MLS, MBA, CAE, Executive Director. MLA is an educational organization of more than 1,000 institutions and 3,800 individual members in the health sciences information field. MLA members serve society by developing new health information delivery systems, fostering educational and research programs for health sciences information professionals, and encouraging an enhanced public awareness of health care issues. *Membership:* MLA is an educational organization of more than 1,000 institutions and 3,800 individual members in the health sciences information field. MLA fosters excellence in the professional achievement and leadership of health sciences library and information professionals to enhance the quality of health care, education, and research. Membership categories: Regular Membership, Institutional Membership, International Membership, Affiliate Membership, Student Membership. *Dues:* $135, regular; $90, introductory; $210-$495, institutional, based on total library expenditures, including salaries, but excluding grants and contracts; $90, international; $80, affiliate; $30, student. *Meetings:* National annual meeting held every May; most chapter meetings are held in the fall. *Publications: MLA News* (newsletter, 10/yr.); *Journal of the Medical Library Association* (quarterly scholarly publication.); MLA DocKit series, collections of representative, unedited library documents from a variety of institutions that illustrate the range of approaches to health sciences library management topics); MLA BibKits, selective, annotated bibliographies of discrete subject areas in the health sciences literature; standards; surveys; and copublished monographs.

Mid-continent Research for Education and Learning (McREL). 2550 S. Parker Rd., Suite 500, Aurora, CO 80014. (303) 337-0990. Fax (303) 337-3005. E-mail: info@mcrel.org. Web site: http://www.mcrel.org. J. Timothy Waters, Exec. Dir. McREL is a private, nonprofit organization whose purpose is to improve education through applied research and development. McREL provides products and services, primarily for K–12 educators, to promote the best instructional practices in the classroom. McREL houses one of 10 regional educational laboratories funded by the U.S. Department of Education, Institute for Educational Science. The regional laboratory helps educators and policymakers work toward excellence in education for all students. It also houses one of 10 Eisenhower Regional Consortia for Mathematics and Science Education. McREL has particular expertise in standards-based education systems, leadership for school improvement, effective instructional practices, teacher quality, mathematics and science education improvement, early literacy development, and education outreach programs. *Meetings:* annual conference. *Publications: Changing Schools* (q. newsletter); *Noteworthy* (annual monograph on topics of current interest in education reform). Numerous technical reports and other publications. Check Web site for current listings.

Minorities in Media (MIM). 1800 N. Stonelake Dr. Suite 2, Bloomington, IN 47408. (703) 993-3669. Fax (313) 577-1693. E-mail: moorejoi@missouri.edu. Joi Moore, President. MIM is a special interest group of AECT that responds to the challenge of preparing students of color for an ever-changing international marketplace and recognizes the unique educational needs of today's diverse learners. It promotes the effective use of educational communications and technology in the learning process. MIM seeks to facilitate changes in instructional design and development, traditional pedagogy, and instructional delivery systems by responding to and meeting the significant challenge of educating diverse individuals to take their place in an ever-changing international marketplace. MIM encourages all of AECT's body of members to creatively develop curricula, instructional treatments, instructional strategies, and instructional materials that promote an acceptance and appreciation of racial and cultural diversity. Doing so will make learning for all more effective, relevant, meaningful, motivating, and enjoyable. MIM actively supports the Wes McJulien Minority Scholarship, and selects the winner. *Membership:* contact MIM president. *Dues:* $20, student; $30, nonstudent. *Publications:* Newsletter is forthcoming online. The MIM listserv is a membership benefit.

Multimedia Education Group, University of Cape Town (MEG). Hlanganani Building, Upper Campus University of Cape Town, Rondebosch, Cape Town, South Africa 7700. 27 21 650 3841. Fax 27 21 650 3841. E-mail: lcz@its.uct.ac.za. Web site: http://.meg.uct. ac.za. Director Laura Czerniewicz. MEG aims to research and harness the potential of interactive computer based technologies and approaches (ICBTA) to support effective learning and teaching. Our work focuses on meeting the needs of South African students from diverse backgrounds, particularly those at the University of Cape Town. *Membership:* We employ multimedia researchers and developers with strong educational interests in diversity, redress and access. *Publications:* See our Web site www.meg.uct.ac.za.

Museum Computer Network (MCN). 65 Enterprise, Aliso Viejo, CA 92656. (877) 626-3800. Fax (949) 330-7621. E-mail: membership@mcn.edu. Web site: http://www. mcn.edu. Leonard Steinbach, Pres 2001-2002; Fred Droz, Admin. MCN is a nonprofit organization of professionals dedicated to fostering the cultural aims of museums through the use of computer technologies. We serve individuals and institutions wishing to improve their means of developing, managing and conveying museum information through the use of automation. We support cooperative efforts that enable museums to be more efficient at creating and disseminating cultural and scientific knowledge as represented by their collections and related documentation. MCN members are interested in building databases complete with images and multimedia components for their collections, in using automated systems to tract membership, manage events and design exhibits, in discovering how multimedia systems can increase the effectiveness of educational programs, and in developing professional standards to ensure the investment that information represents. *Membership:* MCNs membership includes a wide range of museum professionals representing more than 600 major cultural institutions throughout the world. The primary job duties of our membership include 33% Registrar/Collection Managers; 33% IT professionals; and the remaining third comprised of administrator, curators, and education professionals. Our membership comes from all sorts of cultural heritage organizations, including art, historical and natural history museums and academia. Each member receives a complimentary issue of Spectra (published three times a year), a discount on conference fees, can subscribe to MCN-L, the online discussion list, and can join, at no additional cost, any of our Special

Interest Groups which focus on such topics as intellectual property, controlled vocabulary, digital imaging, IT managers, and data standards. *Dues:* $300, corporate; $200, institution; $60, individual. *Meetings:* Annual Conference, held in the fall; educational workshops. *Publications:* Spectra (newsletter), published three times a year. Subscription to Spectra is available to libraries only for $75 plus $10 surcharge for delivery. eSpectra is a monthly electronic magazine featuring online links to information of interest to the museum computing community, job openings, and a calendar of museum-related events, such as workshops, conferences, or seminars.

Museum of Modern Art, Circulating Film and Video Library (MoMA). 11 W. 53rd St., New York, NY 10019. (212) 708-9530. Fax (212) 708-9531. E-mail: circfilm@ moma.org. Web site: http://www.moma.org. William Sloan, Libr. Provides film and video rentals and sales of over 1,300 titles covering the history of film from the 1890s to the present. It also includes an important collection of work by leading video artists and is the sole distributor of the films of Andy Warhol. The Circulating Film and Video Library continues to add to its holdings of early silents, contemporary documentaries, animation, avant-garde, independents and video and to make these available to viewers who otherwise would not have the opportunity to see them. The Circulating Film and Video Library has 16mm prints available for rental, sale, and lease. Some of the 16mm titles are available on videocassette. The classic film collection is not. The video collection is available in all formats for rental and sale. The Library also has available a limited number of titles on 35mm, including rare early titles preserved by the Library of Congress. They also now distribute some films on art and artists formally handled by the American Federation of the Arts as well as the film work of contemporary artists such as Richard Serra and Yoko Ono. *Publications:* Information on titles may be found in the free Price List, the Documentaries on the Arts brochure and the Films of Andy Warhol brochure, all available from the Library. Circulating Film and Video Catalog Vols. 1 and 2, a major source book on film and history, is available from the Museum's Mail Order Dept. (To purchase by mail order, a form is included in the Price List.)

National Aeronautics and Space Administration (NASA). NASA Headquarters, Code N, Washington, DC 20546. (202) 358-0103. Fax (202) 358-3032. E-mail: shelley.canright@nasa.gov. Web site: http://education.nasa.gov. Dr. Adena Williams Loston, Associate Administrator for Education, Dr. Clifford Huston, Deputy Associate Administrator for Education Programs. From elementary through postgraduate school, NASAs educational programs are designed to inspire the next generation of explorers by capturing students interest in science, mathematics, and technology at an early age; to channel more students into science, engineering, and technology career paths; and to enhance the knowledge, skills, and experiences of teachers and university faculty. NASAs educational programs include NASA Spacelink (an electronic information system); videoconferences (60-minute interactive staff development videoconferences to be delivered to schools via satellite); and NASA Television (informational and educational television programming). Additional information is available from the Office of Education at NASA Headquarters and counterpart offices at the nine NASA field centers. Over 200,000 educators make copies of Teacher Resource Center Network materials each year, and thousands of teachers participate in interactive video teleconferencing, use Spacelink, and watch NASA Television. Additional information may be obtained from the NASA Education Homepage www.education.nasa.gov and also accessible from the NASA Public Portal at www.nasa.gov. See learning in a whole new light! *Publications:* see http://spacelink. nasa.gov.

National Alliance for Media Arts and Culture (NAMAC). 346 9th St., San Francisco, CA 94103. (415) 431-1391. Fax (415) 431-1392. E-mail: namac@namac.org. Web site: http://www.namac.org. Helen DeMichel, National Dir. NAMAC is a nonprofit organization dedicated to increasing public understanding of and support for the field of media arts in the United States. Members include media centers, cable access centers, universities, and media artists, as well as other individuals and organizations providing services for production, education, exhibition, distribution, and preservation of video, film, audio, and intermedia. NAMAC's information services are available to the general public, arts and non-arts organizations, businesses, corporations, foundations, government agencies, schools, and universities. *Membership:* 200 organizations, 150 individuals. *Dues:* $75-$450, institutional (depending on annual budget); $75, indiv. *Meetings:* Biennial Conference. *Publications: Media Arts Information Network; The National Media Education Directory,* annual anthology of case-studies "A Closer Look," periodic white paper reports, *Digital Directions: Convergence Planning for the Media Arts.*

National Association for the Education of Young Children (NAEYC). 1509 16th St., Washington, DC 20036-1426. (202) 232-8777. Fax (202) 328-1846. E-mail: naeyc@naeyc.org. Web site: http://www.naeyc.org. Mark R. Ginsberg, Ph.D., Exec. Dir.; Alan Simpson, Communications. Dedicated to improving the quality of care and education provided to young children (birth–8 years). *Membership:* NAEYC has over 100,000 members, including teachers and directors in child care, preschool and Head Start programs and in classrooms from kindergarten through third grade. Other members include researchers, professional development experts and parents. Anyone who is interested in improving early childhood education is welcome to join NAEYC. *Dues:* Most members join NAEYC as well as state and local Affiliates in their area, and the dues vary according to which Affiliates you join. Generally, dues range between $45 and $75 annually, with lower rates for full-time students. *Meetings:* Annually. *Publications:* Young Children (journal); more than 100 books, posters, videos, and brochures.

National Association for Visually Handicapped (NAVH). 22 West 21st St., 6th Floor, New York, NY 10010. (212) 889-3142. Fax (212) 727-2931. E-mail: staff@navh.org. Web site: http://www.navn.org. Dr. Lorraine H. Marchi, Founder/CEO; Cesar Gomez, COO. Making the difference in the lives of people with low vision, the HARD OF SEEING® —that's been NAVHs Mission for almost 50 years!! Serves the partially sighted (not totally blind). Offers all type of optical aids, to writing aids, personal items, and more we've got the things to make your life a lot easier and informational literature for the layperson and the professional, most in large print. Maintains a loan library of large-print books. A resource for visual aids counseling, use and distribution. Provides emotional support and guidance, advocacy, and referrals for the visually impaired and their families, and the professionals and paraprofessionals who work with them. *Membership:* 15,000 Members, but it is not mandatory to became a member in order to receive our services. *Dues:* $50 indiv.; sliding scale or no fee for those unable to afford membership. *Meetings:* Seniors support group 2 times at month; Yearly Medical Advisory Board meetings at the Amer. Acad. of Ophth. Annual Meetings. *Publications:* Newsletter updated quarterly, distributed free throughout the English-speaking world; "navhUPDATE" (quarterly); Visual Aids magnifiers to writing aids, personal items, and more weve got the things to make your life a lot easier and Informational Material Catalog; Large Print Loan Library catalog; informational pamphlets on topics ranging from Diseases of the Macula to knitting and crochet instructions.

National Association of Media and Technology Centers (NAMTC). NAMTC, 7105 First Ave. SW, Cedar Rapids, IA 52405. (319) 654-0608. Fax (319) 654-0609. E-mail: bettyge@mchsi.com. Web site: http://.namtc.org. Betty Gorsegner Ehlinger, Executive Director. NAMTC is committed to promoting leadership among its membership through networking, advocacy, and support activities that will enhance the equitable access to media, technology, and information services to educational communities. Membership is open to regional, K–12, and higher education media centers which serve K–12 students as well as commercial media and technology centers. *Membership:* Institutional and corporate members numbering approximately 225. *Dues:* $75, institutions; $300, corporations. *Meetings:* Regional meetings are held throughout the United States annually. A national Leadership

Summit is held in the fall. *Publications:* Membership newsletter is *ETIN*, a quarterly publication.

National Association of State Textbook Administrators (NASTA). 120 S. Federal Place, Room 206, Santa Fe, NM 87501. (505) 827-1801. Fax (505) 827-1826. E-mail: president@nasta.org. Web site: http://www.nasta.org. David P. Martinez, President. NASTAs purposes are to (1) foster a spirit of mutual helpfulness in adoption, purchase, and distribution of instructional materials; (2) arrange for study and review of textbook specifications; (3) authorize special surveys, tests, and studies; and (4) initiate action leading to better quality instructional materials. Services provided include a working knowledge of text construction, monitoring lowest prices, sharing adoption information, identifying trouble spots, and discussions in the industry. The members of NASTA meet to discuss the textbook adoption process and to improve the quality of the instructional materials used in the elementary, middle, and high schools. NASTA is not affiliated with any parent organization and has no permanent address. *Membership:* Textbook administrators from each of the 21 states that adopt instructional material at the state level on an annual basis. *Dues:* $25 annually per individual. *Meetings:* NASTA meets annually during the month of July. *Publications: Manufacturing Standards and Specifications for Textbooks* (MSST).

National Center to Improve Practice (NCIP). Education Development Center, Inc., 55 Chapel St., Newton, MA 02458-1060. (617) 969-7100 ext. 2387 TTY (617) 969-4529. Fax (617) 969-3440. E-mail: jzorfass@edc.org. Web site: http://www.edc.org/FSC/NCIP. Judith Zorfass, Project Dir.; NCIP, a project funded by the U.S. Department of Educations Office for Special Education Programs (OSEP), promoted the effective use of technology to enhance educational outcomes for students (preschool to grade 12) with sensory, cognitive, physical, social, and emotional disabilities. NCIP's award-winning Web site offers users online discussions (topical discussions and special events) about technology and students with disabilities, an expansive library of resources (text, pictures, and video clips), online workshops; guided tours; of exemplary classrooms; spotlights; on new technology, and links to more than 100 sites dealing with technology and/or students with disabilities. NCIP also produces a series of videos illustrating how students with disabilities use a range of assistive and instructional technologies to improve their learning. *Meetings:* NCIP presented sessions at various educational conferences around the country. *Publications:* Video Profile Series: Multimedia and More: Help for Students with Learning Disabilities; Jeff with Expression: Writing in the Word Prediction Software; Write; Tools for Angie: Technology for Students Who Are Visually Impaired; Telling Tales in ASL and English: Reading, Writing and Videotapes; Welcome to My Preschool: Communicating with Technology. Excellent for use in training, workshops, and courses, videos may be purchased individually or as a set of five by calling (800) 793-5076. A new video to be released this year focuses on standards, curriculum, and assessment in science.

National Clearinghouse for Bilingual Education (NCBE). The George Washington University, 2011 Street NW, Suite 200, Washington, DC 20006. (202) 467-0867. Fax (800) 531-9347, (202) 467-4283. E-mail: askncbe@ncbe.gwu.edu. Web site: http://www. ncbe.gwu.edu. Dr. Minerva Gorena, Interim Dir. NCBE is funded by the U.S. Department of Educations Office of Bilingual Education and Minority Languages Affairs (OBEMLA) to collect, analyze, synthesize, and disseminate information relating to the education of linguistically and culturally diverse students in the United States. NCBE is operated by The George Washington University Graduate School of Education and Human Development, Center for the Study of Language and Education in Washington, DC. Online services include the NCBE Web site containing an online library of hundreds of cover-to-cover documents, resources for teachers and administrators, and library of links to related Internet sites; an e-mail-based, bi-weekly news bulletin, Newsline; an electronic discussion group, NCBE Roundtable; and an e-mail-based question answering service, AskNCBE. Publications: short monographs, syntheses, and reports. Request a publications catalog for prices.

The catalog and some publications are available at no cost from the NCBE and other Web sites.

The National Center for Improving Science Education. 1726 M Street, NW, #704, Washington, DC 20036. (202) 467-0652. Fax (202) 467-0659. E-mail: info@ncise.org. Web site: http://.wested.org. Senta A. Raizen, Dir. A division of WestEd (see separate listing) that works to promote changes in state and local policies and practices in science curriculum, teaching, and assessment through research and development, evaluation, technical assistance, and dissemination. *Publications: Science and Technology Education for the Elementary Years: Frameworks for Curriculum and Instruction; Developing and Supporting Teachers for Elementary School Science Education; Assessment in Elementary School Science Education; Getting Started in Science: A Blueprint for Elementary School Science Education; Elementary School Science for the 90s; Building Scientific Literacy: Blueprint for the Middle Years; Science and Technology Education for the Middle Years: Frameworks for Curriculum and Instruction; Assessment in Science Education: The Middle Years; Developing and Supporting Teachers for Science Education in the Middle Years; The High Stakes of High School Science; Future of Science in Elementary Schools: Educating Prospective Teachers; Technology Education in the Classroom: Understanding the Designed World; What College-Bound Students Abroad Are Expected to Know About Biology (with AFT); Examining the Examinations: A Comparison of Science and Mathematics Examinations for College-Bound Students in Seven Countries. Bold Ventures series: Vol. 1: Patterns of U.S. Innovations in Science and Mathematics Education; Vol. 2: Case Studies of U.S. Innovations in Science Education; Vol. 3: Case Studies of U.S. Innovations in Mathematics.* A publications catalog and project summaries are available on request.

National Clearinghouse for English Language Acquisition and Language Instruction Educational Programs (National Clearinghouse). The George Washington University, 2121 K Street NW, Suite 260, Washington, DC 20037. (800) 321-6223, (202) 467-0867. Fax (800) 531-9347, (202) 467-4283. E-mail: askncbe@ncbe.gwu.edu. Web site: http://www.ncbe.gwu.edu. Dr. Minerva Gorena, Director. The National Clearinghouse for English Language Acquisition and Language Instruction Educational Programs is funded by the U.S. Department of Education's Office of English Language Acquisition, Language Enhancement and Academic Achievement for Limited English Proficient Students (OELA) to collect, analyze, synthesize, and disseminate information relating to the education of linguistically and culturally diverse students in the United States. Online services include a Web site containing an online library of hundreds of cover-to-cover publications, resources for teachers and administrators; links to related Web sites; a weekly email news bulletin, Newsline; a monthly email magazine, Outlook; and an email question answering service. The National Clearinghouse is operated by The George Washington University Graduate School of Education and Human Development, Center for the Study of Language and Education in Washington, DC. *Membership:* The National Clearinghouse is funded by the U.S. Department of Education. There is no membership, and services are provided no cost. *Publications:* Short monographs, syntheses, and reports. Request a publications catalog for prices. The catalog and most publications are available at no cost from the National Clearinghouse Web site.

National Clearinghouse for United States-Japan Studies (NCUSJS). 2805 E. 10th St., Suite 120, Bloomington, IN 47408-2698. (812) 855-3838, (800) 266-3815. Fax (812) 855-0455. E-mail: japan@indiana.edu. Web site: http://www.indiana.edu/~japan. Roger Sensenbaugh, Assoc. Dir. Provides educational information on topics concerning Japan and U.S.-Japan relations. *Membership:* Anybody interested in teaching or learning about Japan may contact the Clearinghouse for information. *Publications: Guide to Teaching Materials on Japan; Teaching about Japan: Lessons and Resources; The Constitution and Individual Rights in Japan: Lessons for Middle and High School Students; Internationalizing the U.S. Classroom: Japan as a Model; Tora no Maki II: Lessons for Teaching about*

Contemporary Japan; The Japan Digest Series (complementary, concise discussions of various Japan-related topics): *Fiction about Japan in the Elementary Curriculum; Daily Life in Japanese High Schools; Rice: It's More Than Food in Japan; Ideas for Integrating Japan into the Curriculum; Japanese Popular Culture in the Classroom; An Introduction to Kabuki; Building a Japanese Language Program from the Bottom Up; Teaching Primary Children about Japan through Art; The History and Artistry of Haiku; Learning from the Japanese Economy; Teaching about Japanese-American Internment; Using Museums to Teach about Japan; Lessons on the Japanese Constitution; Using Film to Explore History; Shinbun* (project newsletter).

National Commission on Libraries and Information Science (NCLIS). 1110 Vermont Ave. NW, Suite 820, Washington, DC 20005-3552. (202) 606-9200. Fax (202) 606-9203. E-mail: info@nclis.gov. Web site: http://www.nclis.gov. Robert S. Willard, Exec. Dir. A permanent independent agency of the U.S. government charged with advising the executive and legislative branches on national library and information policies and plans. The Commission reports directly to the president and Congress on the implementation of national policy; conducts studies, surveys, and analyses of the nation's library and information needs; appraises the inadequacies of current resources and services; promotes research and development activities; conducts hearings and issues publications as appropriate; and develops overall plans for meeting national library and information needs and for the coordination of activities at the federal, state, and local levels. The Commission provides general policy advice to the Institute of Museum and Library Services (IMLS) director relating to library services included in the Library Services and Technology Act (LSTA). *Membership:* 16 commissioners (14 appointed by the president and confirmed by the Senate, the Librarian of Congress, and the Director of the IMLS). *Meetings:* Average 3 meetings a year with a combined meeting of NCLIS/IMLS. *Publications:* Annual Report.

National Communication Association (NCA). 1765 N Street, NW, Washington,, DC 22003. (202) 464-4622. Fax (202) 464-4600. E-mail: dwallick@natcom.org. Web site: http://www.natcom.org. James L. Gaudino, Exec. Dir. A voluntary society organized to promote study, criticism, research, teaching, and application of principles of communication, particularly of speech communication. Founded in 1914, NCA is a nonprofit organization of researchers, educators, students, and practitioners, whose academic interests span all forms of human communication. NCA is the oldest and largest national organization serving the academic discipline of Communication. Through its services, scholarly publications, resources, conferences and conventions, NCA works with its members to strengthen the profession and contribute to the greater good of the educational enterprise and society. Research and instruction in the discipline focus on the study of how messages in various media are produced, used, and interpreted within and across different contexts, channels, and cultures. *Membership:* 7,000. *Meetings:* Four regional conferences (ECA, ESCA, SSCA, WSCA) and 1 Annual National Conference. *Publications: Spectra Newsletter* (mo.); *Quarterly Journal of Speech; Communication Monographs; Communication Education; Critical Studies in Mass Communication; Journal of Applied Communication Research; Text and Performance Quarterly; Communication Teacher; Index to Journals in Communication Studies* through 1995; *National Communication Directory of NCA and the Regional Speech Communication Organizations* (CSSA, ECA, SSCA, WSCA). For additional publications, request brochure.

National Council for Accreditation of Teacher Education (NCATE). 2010 Massachusetts Ave. NW, Suite 500, Washington, DC 20036. (202) 466-7496. Fax (202) 296-6620. E-mail: ncate@ncate.org. Web site: http://www.ncate.org. Arthur E. Wise, Pres. NCATE is a consortium of professional organizations that establishes standards of quality for and accredits professional education units in schools, colleges, and departments of education. *Membership:* Members include 34 National Professional organizations. NCATE accredits colleges of education in over 550 higher education institutions and over 100 institutions are in candidacy. *Dues:* see http://www.ncate.org/accred/fees.htm. *Meetings:* see http://www.

ncate.org/partners/meetings.htm. *Publications: Standards; Quality Teaching* (newsletter, twice yearly); online resources for institutions and the public; *NCATE Speakers Guide; Handbook for Accreditation Visits.* Check our Web site for the complete publications list.

National Council of Teachers of English: Commission on Media, Committee on Instructional Technology, Assembly on Media Arts (NCTE). 1111 W. Kenyon Rd., Urbana, IL 61801-1096. (217) 328-3870. Fax (217) 328-0977. E-mail: public_info@ncte.org. Web site: http://www.ncte.org. Kent Williamson, NCTE Executive Director; Mary T. Christel, Commission Director; Trevor Owen, Committee Chair; Alan Teasley, Assembly Chair. The NCTE Commission on Media is a deliberative and advisory body which each year identifies and reports to the NCTE Executive Committee on key issues in the teaching of media; reviews what the Council has done concerning media during the year; recommends new projects and persons who might undertake them. The commission monitors current and projected NCTE publications (other than journals), suggests topics for future NCTE publications on media, and performs a similar role of review and recommendation for the NCTE Annual Convention program. Occasionally, the commission undertakes further tasks and projects as approved by the Executive Committee. The NCTE Committee on Instructional Technology studies emerging technologies and their integration into English and language arts curricula and teacher education programs; identifies the effects of such technologies on teachers, students, and educational settings, with attention to people of color, handicapped, and other students not well served in current programs; explores means of disseminating information about such technologies to the NCTE membership; serves as liaison between NCTE and other groups interested in computer-based education in English and language arts; and maintains liaison with the NCTE Commission on Media and other Council groups concerned with instructional technology. The NCTE Assembly on Media Arts promotes communication and cooperation among all individuals who have a special interest in media in the English language arts; presents programs and special projects on this subject; encourages the development of research, experimentation, and investigation in the judicious uses of media in the teaching of English; promotes the extensive writing of articles and publications devoted to this subject; and integrates the efforts of those with an interest in this subject. *Membership:* The National Council of Teachers of English, with 75,000 individual and institutional members worldwide, is dedicated to improving the teaching and learning of English and the language arts at all levels of education. Members include elementary, middle, and high school teachers; supervisors of English programs; college and university faculty; teacher educators; local and state agency English specialists; and professionals in related fields. The members of the NCTE Commission on Media and Committee on Instructional Technology are NCTE members appointed by the director and chair of the groups. Membership in the Assembly on Media Arts is open to members and nonmembers of NCTE. *Dues:* Membership in NCTE is $40 a year; adding subscriptions to its various journals adds additional fees. Membership in the Assembly on Media Arts is $10 a year. *Meetings:* http://www.ncte.org/conventions/. Annual Meetings. *Publications:* NCTE publishes about 20 books a year. Visit http://www.ncte.org/books/ and http://bookstore.ncte.org. NCTEs journals include *Language Arts, English Journal, College English, College Composition and Communication, English Education, Research in the Teaching of English, Teaching English in the Two-Year College, Voices from the Middle Primary Voices, K–6 Talking Points, Classroom Notes Plus English Leadership Quarterly, The Council Chronicle* (included in NCTE membership). Journal information is available at http://www.ncte.org/journals/. The Commission on Media and Committee on Instructional Technology do not have their own publications. The Assembly on Media Arts publishes *Media Matters,* a newsletter highlighting issues, viewpoints, materials, and events related to the study of media. Assembly members receive this publication.

National Council of the Churches of Christ in the USA (NCC). Communication Commission, 475 Riverside Dr., New York, NY 10115. (212) 870-2574. Fax (212) 870-2030. E-mail: dpomeroy@ncccusa.org. Web site: http://www.ncccusa.org. Wesley M. "Pat" Pattillo, Director of Communication. Ecumenical arena for cooperative work of Protestant and Orthodox denominations and agencies in broadcasting, film, cable, and print media. Offers advocacy to government and industry structures on media services. Services provided include liaison to network television and radio programming; film sales and rentals; information about telecommunications; and news and information regarding work of the National Council of Churches, related denominations, and agencies. Works closely with other faith groups in the Interfaith Broadcasting Commission. Online communication Web site: www.ncccusa.org. *Membership:* 36 denominations. *Meetings:* Twice a year. *Publications: EcuLink.*

National Education Knowledge Industry Association (NEKIA). 1718 Connecticut Avenue, NW, Suite 700, Washington, DC 20009-1162. (202) 518-0847. Fax (202) 785-3849. E-mail: info@nekia.org. Web site: http://www.nekia.org. James W. Kohlmoos, Pres. Founded in 1997, NEKIA is a nonpartisan, nonprofit trade association representing the emerging knowledge industry. In the same way that research and development are crucial to the sciences, manufacturing and agriculture, research and development is vital to the field of education. In recent years, a new field; the education knowledge industry; has emerged to provide structure, quality and coherence to education practices, policies and products. The members of this industry include researchers, educational developers, service providers, and a rapidly increasing number of entrepreneurs. Together, they work across the education spectrum from research to development to dissemination to practice. NEKIA brings educational innovation and expertise to all communities while providing its members with leadership, policy development, advocacy, professional development, and the promotion of quality products and services. NEKIA's mission is to advance the development and use of research based knowledge for the improvement of the academic performance of all children. The association's members are committed to finding new and better ways to support and expand high-quality education research, development, dissemination, technical assistance, and evaluation at the federal, regional, state, tribal, and local levels. *Membership:* 28. *Meetings:* Annual Legislative and Policy Conference; Annual Meeting. *Publications: Plugging In: Choosing and Using Educational Technology; Probe: Designing School Facilities for Learning; Education Productivity; Technology Infrastructure in Schools.*

National Education Telecommunications Organization & EDSAT Institute (NETO/EDSAT). 1899 "L" Street NW, Suite 600, Washington, DC 20036. (202) 293-4211. Fax (202) 293-4210. E-mail: neto-edsat@mindspring.com. Web site: http://www.netoedsat.org. Shelly Weinstein, Pres. and CEO. NETO/EDSAT is a nonprofit organization bringing together U.S. and non-U.S. users and providers of telecommunications to deliver education, instruction, health care, and training in classrooms, colleges, workplaces, health centers, and other distance education centers. NETO/EDSAT facilitates and collaborates with key stakeholders in the education and telecommunications fields. Programs and services include research and education, outreach, seminars and conferences, and newsletters. The NETO/EDSAT mission is to help create an integrated multitechnology infrastructure, a dedicated satellite that links space and existing secondary access roads (telephone and cable) over which teaching and education resources are delivered and shared in a user-friendly format with students, teachers, workers, and individuals. NETO/EDSAT seeks to create a modern-day "learning place" for rural, urban, migrant, suburban, disadvantaged, and at-risk students that provides equal and affordable access to and utilization of educational resources. *Membership:* Members include more than 60 U.S. and non-U.S. school districts, colleges, universities, state agencies, public and private educational consortia, libraries, and other distance education providers. *Publications: NETO/EDSAT UPDATE* (newsletter, q.); *Analysis of a Proposal for an Education Satellite,* EDSAT Institute, 1991; *Global Summit on Distance Education Final Report,* Oct 1996; *International Report of the NETO/EDSAT Working Group on the Education and Health Care Requirements for Global/Regional Dedicated Networks,* June 1998.

National Endowment for the Humanities (NEH). Division of Public Programs, Media Program, 1100 Pennsylvania Ave., NW, Room 426, Washington, DC 20506. (202) 606-8269. Fax (202) 606-8557. E-mail: publicpgms@neh.gov. Web site: http://www. neh.gov. Nancy Rogers, Director, Division of Public Programs. The NEH is an independent federal grant-making agency that supports research, educational, and public programs grounded in the disciplines of the humanities. The Media Program supports film and radio programs in the humanities for public audiences, including children and adults. *Membership:* Nonprofit institutions and organizations including public television and radio stations. *Publications:* Visit the Web site (http://www.neh.gov) for application forms and guidelines as well as the Media Log, a cumulative listing of projects funded through the Media Program.

National Federation of Community Broadcasters (NFCB). 1970 Broadway, Ste. 1000`, Oakland, CA 94612. (510) 451-8200. Fax (510) 451-8208. E-mail: nfcb@aol.com. Web site: http://www.nfcb.org. Carol Pierson, President and CEO. NFCB represents non-commercial, community-based radio stations in public policy development at the national level and provides a wide range of practical services, including technical assistance. *Membership:* 200. Noncommercial community radio stations, related organizations, and individuals. *Dues:* range from $200 to $3,000 for participant and associate members. *Meetings:* 2005 Baltimore. *Publications: Public Radio Legal Handbook; AudioCraft; Community Radio News; Let a Thousand Voices Speak: A Guide to Youth in Radio Projects.*

National Film Board of Canada (NFBC). 350 Fifth Ave., Suite 4820, New York, NY 10118. (212) 629-8890. Fax (212) 629-8502. E-mail: j.sirabella@nfb.ca. Web site: http://.nfb.ca. John Sirabella, U.S. Marketing Mgr./Nontheatrical Rep. The National Film Board of Canada has been producing and distributing films for over sixty years, and has become particularly well known for its insightful point of view documentaries and creative amateur animation. The NFBC has made more than 10,000 original films, which have won more than 4,000 prizes including ten Academy Awards.

National Film Information Service (NFIS). Center for Motion Picture Study, 333 So. La Cienega Blvd., Beverly Hills, CA 90211. (310) 247-3000. Fax (310) 657-5597. E-mail: nfis@oscars.org. Web site: http://www.oscars.org/mhl/nfis.html. The fee-based National Film Information Service of the Margaret Herrick Library can answer queries from patrons outside of a 150-mile radius from the Fairbanks Center for Motion Picture Study. NFIS can accept inquiries via email, fax or letter but all work undertaken by NFIS requires payment in advance. Requests for information should be as specific as possible.

National Gallery of Art (NGA). Department of Education Resources, 2000B South Club Drive, Landover, MD 20785. (202) 842-6273. Fax (202) 842-6935. EdResources @nga.gov. Web site: http://www.nga.gov/education/classroom/loanfinder/. Leo J. Kasun, Education Resources Supervisory Specialist. This department of NGA is responsible for the production and distribution of 120+ educational audiovisual programs, including interactive technologies. Materials available (all loaned free to individuals, schools, colleges and universities, community organizations, and noncommercial television stations) range from videocassettes and color slide programs to videodiscs, CD-ROMs, and DVDs. A free catalog of programs is available on request. All videodiscs, CD-ROMS, DVDs, utilizing digitized images on the gallerys collection are available for long-term loan. *Membership:* We have no members. However, last year we provided programs to over 1million borrowers. Our programs are available to anyone who requests them. *Publications:* Extension Programs Catalogue.

National Information Center for Educational Media (NICEM). P.O. Box 8640, Albuquerque, NM 87198-8640. (505) 265-3591, (800) 926-8328. Fax (505)256-1080. E-mail: nicem@nicem.com. Web site: http://www.nicem.com. Roy Morgan, Exec. Dir.; Marjorie M. K. Hlava, Pres., Access Innovations, Inc. The National Information Center for Educational Media maintains an international database of information about educational nonprint materials for all age levels and subject areas in all media types. NICEM editors collect, catalog, and index information about media that is provided by producers and distributors. This information is entered into an electronic masterfile. Anyone who is looking for information about educational media materials can search the database by a wide variety of criteria to locate existing and archival materials. Producer and distributor information in each record then leads the searcher to the source of the educational media materials needed. NICEM makes the information from the database available in several forms and through several vendors. CD-ROM editions are available from NICEM, SilverPlatter, and BiblioFile. Online access to the database is available through NICEM, EBSCO, SilverPlatter, and The Library Corporation. NICEM also conducts custom searches and prepares custom catalogs. NICEM is used by college and university media centers, public school libraries and media centers, public libraries, corporate training centers, students, media producers and distributors, and researchers. *Membership:* NICEM is a nonmembership organization. There is no charge for submitting information to be entered into the database. Corporate member of AECT, AIME, NAMTC, CCUMC. *Publications:* A-*V Online on SilverPlatter; NICEM A-V MARC by BiblioFile; NICEM Reference CD-ROM; NICEM MARC CD-ROM; NICEM Producer & CD-ROM.*

National ITFS Association (NIA). 77 W. Canfield, Detroit, MI 48201. (313) 577-2085. Fax (313) 577-5577. E-mail: p.gossman@wayne.edu. Web site: http://www.itfs.org. Patrick Gossman, Chair, Bd. of Dirs.; Don MacCullough, Exec. Dir. Established in 1978, NIA is a nonprofit, professional organization of Instructional Television Fixed Service (ITFS) licensees, applicants, and others interested in ITFS broadcasting. ITFS is a very high frequency television broadcast service that is used to broadcast distance learning classes, two way internet service and data service to schools and other locations where education can take place. The goals of the association are to gather and exchange information about ITFS, gather data on utilization of ITFS, act as a conduit for those seeking ITFS information, and assist migration from video broadcast to wireless, broadband Internet services using ITFS channels. The NIA represents ITFS interests to the FCC, technical consultants, and equipment manufacturers. The association uses its Web site and Listserv list to provide information to its members in areas such as technology, programming content, FCC regulations, excess capacity leasing and license and application data. *Membership:* The current membership consists of Educational Institutions and nonprofit organizations that hold licenses issued by the Federal Communications Commission for Instructional Television Fixed Service (ITFS). We also have members that have an interest in ITFS and members such as manufacturers of ITFS related equipment and Law firms that represent Licensees. *Dues:* We have two main types of memberships: Voting memberships for ITFS licensees only, and non-voting memberships for other educational institutions and sponsors. See the Web site http://www.itfs.org for details. *Meetings:* Annual Member Conference, January/February. *Publications:* http://www.itfs.org.

National Press Photographers Association, Inc. (NPPA). 3200 Croasdaile Dr., Suite 306, Durham, NC 27705. (919) 383-7246. Fax (919) 383-7261. E-mail: president@nppa.org. Web site: http://www.nppa.org. Todd Stricker, President. An organization of professional news photographers who participate in and promote photojournalism in publications and through television and film. Sponsors workshops, seminars, and contests; maintains an audiovisual library of subjects of media interest. *Membership:* 9,000. *Dues:*

$90, domestic; $120, international; $55, student. *Meetings:* An extensive array of conferences, seminars, and workshops are held throughout the year. *Publications: News Photographer* (magazine, mo.); *The Best of Photojournalism* (annual book).

National PTA (National PTA). 330 N. Wabash, Suite 2100, Chicago, IL 60611. (312) 670-6782. Fax (312) 670-6783. E-mail: info@pta.org. Web site: http://www.pta.org. Linda Hodge (July 2003–June 2005); Anna Weselak, President-Elect (2005–2007); Warlene Gary, Chief Executive Officer. Advocates the education, health, safety, and well-being of children and teens. Provides parenting education and leadership training to PTA volunteers. National PTA partners with the National Cable & Telecommunications Association on the "Taking Charge of Your TV" project by training PTA and cable representatives to present media literacy workshops. The workshops teach parents and educators how to evaluate programming so they can make informed decisions about what to allow their children to see. The National PTA in 1997 convinced the television industry to add content information to the TV rating system. *Membership:* 6.2 million Membership open to all interested in the health, welfare, and education of children and support the PTA mission—http://www.pta.org/aboutpta/mission_en.asp. *Dues:* vary by local unit—national dues portion is $1.75 per member annually. *Meetings:* National convention, held annually in June in different regions of the country, is open to PTA members; convention information available on the Web site. *Publications: Our Children* (magazine) plus electronic newsletters and other Web-based information for members and general public.

National Public Broadcasting Archives (NPBA). Hornbake Library, University of Maryland, College Park, MD 20742. (301) 405-9255. Fax (301) 314-2634. E-mail: tc65@umail.umd.edu. Web site: http://www.library.umd.edu/UMCP/NPBA/npba.html. Thomas Connors, Archivist. NPBA brings together the archival record of the major entities of noncommercial broadcasting in the United States. NPBAs collections include the archives of the Corporation for Public Broadcasting (CPB), the Public Broadcasting Service (PBS), and National Public Radio (NPR). Other organizations represented include the Midwest Program for Airborne Television Instruction (MPATI), the Public Service Satellite Consortium (PSSC), Americas Public Television Stations (APTS), Children's Television Workshop (CTW), and the Joint Council for Educational Telecommunications (JCET). NPBA also makes available the personal papers of many individuals who have made significant contributions to public broadcasting, and its reference library contains basic studies of the broadcasting industry, rare pamphlets, and journals on relevant topics. NPBA also collects and maintains a selected audio and video program record of public broadcastings national production and support centers and of local stations. Oral history tapes and transcripts from the NPR Oral History Project and the Televisionaries Oral History Project are also available at the archives. The archives are open to the public from 9 A.M. to 5 P.M., Monday through Friday. Research in NPBA collections should be arranged by prior appointment. For further information, call (301) 405-9988.

National Religious Broadcasters (NRB). 9510 Technology Dr., Manassas, VA 20110. (703) 330-7000. Fax (703) 330-7100. E-mail: atower@nrb.org. Web site: http://www. nrb.org. Dr. Frank Wright, President, E-mail: fwright@nrb.org. National Religious Broadcasters is a Christian international association of radio and TV stations, Webcasters, program producers, consultants, attorneys, agencies and churches. NRB maintains rapport with the FCC, the broadcasting industry and government bodies. NRB encourages growth of Christian communications through education, professional training, publications and networking opportunities. The association maintains relationships with other media associations to promote cutting-edge technology and practice. NRB fosters high professional standards through its Code of Ethics and Statement of Faith. *Membership:* 1,500 members who are organizations and individuals representing Christian TV, radio and Internet stations and broadcasters, program producers, churches, agencies, consultants, attorneys and companies who are directly or indirectly related to Christian broadcasting. Intercollegiate Religious Broadcasters (IRB) is a chapter of NRB for colleges and universities who have a student run broadcast. Membership is open for both faculty and students. *Dues:* based on broadcast related expenses—associate members have fixed rates. *Meetings:* Annual NRB Convention and Exhibition, 5 regional conventions held during summer and fall. *Publications: NRB* magazine 10 issues a year; *Directory of Religious Media and CD ROM; Inside NRB* for members only, an e-mail broadcast, *Convention News,* a daily newspaper at national convention.

National School Boards Association/ITTE: Education Technology Programs (NSBA/ITTE). 1680 Duke St, Alexandria, VA 22314. (703) 838-6722. Fax (703) 548-5516. E-mail: itte@nsba.org. Web site: http://www.nsba.org/itte. Ann Lee Flynn, Director, Education Technology. ITTE was created to help advance the wise uses of technology in public education. ITTE renders several services to state school boards associations, sponsors conferences, publishes, and engages in special projects. The Technology Leadership Network, the membership component of ITTE, is designed to engage school districts nationwide in a dialogue about technology in education. This dialogue is carried out via newsletters, meetings, special reports, projects, and online communications. The experience of the Network is shared more broadly through the state associations' communications with all school districts. *Membership:* Approximately 400 school districts in 47 states and Canada. Membership includes mostly public school districts, though private schools are eligible as well. Contacts include technology directors, superintendents, board members, curriculum directors, library/media specialists, teachers. *Dues:* Based upon the school district's student enrollment. *Meetings:* Annually. *Publications: Virtual Realities: A School Leaders Guide to Online Education; Connecting Schools and Communities through Technology; Technology Professional Development for P–12 Educators; Legal Issues and Education Technology: A School Leader's Guide,* 2nd edition; *Education Leadership Toolkit: A Desktop Companion; Plans and Policies for Technology in Education: A Compendium,* 2nd edition; *Models of Success: Case Study of Technology in Schools; Investing in School Technology: Strategies to Meet the Funding Challenge/School Leader's Version; Leadership and Technology: What School Board Members Need to Know; Technology Leadership Newsletter; Technology & School Design: Creating Spaces for Learning.*

National School Supply and Equipment Association (NSSEA). 8300 Colesville Rd., Suite 250, Silver Spring, MD 20910. (301) 495-0240. Fax (301) 495-3330. E-mail: nssea@aol.com. Web site: http://www.nssea.org. Tim Holt, Pres. A service organization of more than 1,600 manufacturers, distributors, retailers, and independent manufacturers' representatives of school supplies, equipment, and instructional materials. Seeks to maintain open communications between manufacturers and dealers in the school market and to encourage the development of new ideas and products for educational progress. *Meetings:* Annually. *Publications:* Tidings; Annual Membership Directory.

National Science Foundation (NSF). 4201 Wilson Blvd., Arlington, VA 22230. (703) 292-5111. E-mail: lboutchy@nsf.gov. Web site: http://www.nsf.gov/start.htm. Mary Hanson, Chief, Media Relations and Public Affairs. Linda Boutchyard, Contact Person. NSF, an independent federal agency, funds research and education in all fields of science, mathematics and engineering. With an annual budget of about $5 billion, NSF funds reach all 50 states, through grants, contracts, and cooperative agreements to more than 2,000 colleges, universities and other institutions nationwide. NSF receives more than 50,000 requests for funding annually, including at least 30,000 new proposals. Applicants should refer to the NSF Guide to Programs. Scientific material and media reviews are available to help the public learn about NSF-supported programs. NSF news releases and tipsheets are available electronically via NSFnews. To subscribe, send an e-mail message to listmanager@nsf.gov; in the body of the message, type "subscribe nsfnews" and then type your name. Also see NSF news products at http://www.nsf.gov/od/lpa/news/start.htm, http://www.eurekalert.org/, and http://www.ari.net/newswise. In addition, NSF has developed a Web site that offers information about NSF directorates, offices, programs, and publications at http://nsf.gov.

National Telemedia Council Inc. (NTC). 1922 University Ave., Madison, WI 53705. (608) 218-1182. Fax (608) 218-1183. E-mail: NTelemedia@aol.com. Web site: http://www.nationaltelemediacouncil.org. Dr. Martin Rayala, President; Marieli Rowe, Exec. Dir. The NTC is a national, nonprofit professional organization dedicated to promoting media literacy, or critical media viewing skills. This is done primarily through work with teachers, parents, and caregivers. NTC activities include publishing Telemedium: The Journal of Media Literacy, the Teacher Idea Exchange (T.I.E.), the Jessie McCanse Award for individual contribution to media literacy, assistance to media literacy educators and professionals. *Membership:* Our membership is open to all those interested in media literacy. *Dues:* $30, basic; $50, contributing; $100, patron. *Publications: Telemedium; The Journal of Media Literacy* (q. newsletter).

Native American Public Telecommunications (NAPT). 1800 North 33rd St., P.O. Box 83111, Lincoln, NE 68501-3111. (402) 472-3522. Fax (402) 472-8675. E-mail: native@unl.edu. Web site: http://nativetelecom.org. Frank Blythe, Exec. Dir. The mission of NAPT is to inform, educate, and encourage the awareness of tribal histories, cultures, languages, opportunities, and aspirations through the fullest participation of America Indians and Alaska Natives in creating and employing all forms of educational and public telecommunications programs and services, thereby supporting tribal sovereignty. *Publications: The Vision Maker* (newsletter).

Natural Science Collections Alliance (NSC Alliance). 1725 K St. NW, Suite 601, Washington, DC 20006. (202) 835-9050. Fax (202) 835-7334. E-mail: general@nscalliance.org. Web site: http://www.nscalliance.org. Executive Director. Fosters the care, management, and improvement of biological collections and promotes their utilization. Institutional members include free-standing museums, botanical gardens, college and university museums, and public institutions, including state biological surveys and agricultural research centers. The NSC Alliance also represents affiliate societies, and keeps members informed about funding and legislative issues. *Membership:* 85 institutions, 31 affiliates, 120 individual and patron members. *Dues:* depend on the size of collections. *Meetings:* Annual Meeting (June). *Publications: Alliance Gazette* (newsletter for members and nonmember subscribers, quarterly); *Guidelines for Institutional Policies and Planning in Natural History Collections; Global Genetic Resources; A Guide to Museum Pest Control.*

NCTI (NCTI). 8022 Southpark Circle, Suite 100, Littleton, CO 80120. (303) 797-9393. Fax (303) 797-9394. E-mail: info@ncti.com. Web site: http://www.ncti.com. Tom Brooksher, President and CEO ; Alan Babcock, Chief Learning Officer. Located in the Denver area, NCTI provides workforce performance products, services, and education to the cable and broadband industry. NCTI offers extensive and up-to-date training in electronic, instructor-led, paper-based and Web-delivery formats; services such as customized curriculum development, performance assessment and testing; and professional development through college credit and industry certification. Since 1968, system operators, contractors, and industry vendors have turned to NCTI to train more than 250,000 industry professionals. By creating innovative products that develop and improve skills; services that evaluate, identify, and improve workforce competencies; and education that advances careers; NCTI remains committed to providing individuals and their employers the knowledge they need to succeed in the broadband industry. For more information, please visit www.ncti.com.

The NETWORK, Inc. (NETWORK). 136 Fenno Drive, Rowley, MA 01969-1004. (800) 877-5400, (978) 948-7764. Fax (978) 948-7836. E-mail: davidc@thenetworkinc.org. Web site: http://.thenetworkinc.org. David Crandall, President. A nonprofit research and service organization providing training, research and evaluation, technical assistance, and materials for a fee to schools, educational organizations, and private sector firms with educational interests. The NETWORK has been helping professionals manage and learn about change since 1969. Our Leadership Skills series of computer-based simulations extends the widely used board game versions of Making Change (tm) and Systems Thinking/Systems Changing(tm)with the addition of Improving Student Success: Teachers,Schools and Parents to offer educators a range of proven professional development tools. *Membership:* none required. *Dues:* no dues, fee for service. *Meetings:* call. *Publications: Making Change: A Simulation Game* [board and computer versions]; *Systems Thinking/Systems Changing: A Simulation Game* [board and computer versions]; *Improving Student Success: Teachers, Schools and Parents* [computer based simulation]; *Systemic Thinking: Solving Complex Problems; Benchmarking: A Guide for Educators.*

Network for Continuing Medical Education (NCME). One Harmon Plaza, 6th Floor, Secaucus, NJ 07094. (201) 867-3550. Produces and distributes videocassettes, CD-ROMs & Web-Based Programs to hospitals for physicians' continuing education. Programs are developed for physicians in the practice of General Medicine, Anesthesiology, Emergency Medicine, Gastroenterology, and Surgery. Physicians who view all the programs can earn up to 25 hours of Category 1 (AMA) credit and up to 10 hours of Prescribed (AAFP) credit each year. *Membership:* More than 1,000 hospitals provide NCME programs to their physicians. *Dues:* subscription fees: VHS-$2,160/yr. Sixty-minute videocassettes & CD-ROMs are distributed to hospital subscribers every 18 days.

New England Educational Media Association (NEEMA). c/o Charles White, Executive Director, 307 Cumberland Terrace, 5C, Myrtle Beach, SC 29572. (843) 497-4630. Fax (617) 559-6191. E-mail: nadeau@ccsu.edu. Website: http://www.neema.org. Charles White, Executive Director. An affiliate of AECT, NEEMA is a regional professional association dedicated to the improvement of instruction through the effective utilization of school library media services, media, and technology applications. For over 75 years, it has represented school library media professionals through activities and networking efforts to develop and polish the leadership skills, professional representation, and informational awareness of the membership. The Board of Directors consists of departments of education as well as professional leaders of the region. An annual conference program and a Leadership Program are offered in conjunction with the various regional state association conferences. *Membership:* NEEMA focuses on school library media issues among the six New England states, consequently, membership is encouraged for school library media specialists in this region. *Dues:* Regular membership $20. Student /retired membership $10. *Meetings:* Annual Leadership Conference and Business Meeting. *Publications: NEEMS Views.*

The New York Festivals (NYF). 7 West 36th Street, 14th Fl., New York, NY 10018. (212) 643-4800. Fax (212) 643-0170. E-mail: info@newyorkfestivals.com. http://www. newyorkfestivals.com. Tara Dawn, Director, Creative Services. The New York Festivals sponsors the International Non-Broadcast Awards, which are annual competitive festivals for industrial and educational film and video productions, filmstrips and slide programs, multi-image business theater and interactive multimedia presentations, and television programs. Alphalist fees begin at $125. First Alphalist deadline is Aug 3 for U.S. entrants and Sept 15 for overseas entrants. The Non-Broadcast competition honors a wide variety of categories, including Education Media. As one of the largest competitions in the world, achieving finalist status is a notable credit to any company's awards roster. Winners are announced each year at a gala awards show in New York City and published on the World Wide Web. *Membership:* No membership feature. The competition is open to any one who produces, Industrials, Educational & Informational Programs, Home Videos, Short Films, Multi-Image, Business Theatre. *Publications:* Winners are posted on our Web site at www.newyorkfestivals.com.

North Central Regional Educational Laboratory (NCREL). 1120 E. Diehl Road Suite 200, Naperville, IL 60563-1486. (630) 649-6500, (800) 356-2735. Fax (630) 649-6700. E-mail: info@ncrel.org. Web site: http://www.ncrel.org. Gina Burkhardt, Executive Director. NCRELs work is guided by a focus on comprehensive and systemic school restructuring that is research-based and learner-centered. One of 10 Office of Educational Research and Improvement (OERI) regional educational laboratories, NCREL disseminates information about effective programs, develops educational products, holds conferences, provides technical assistance, and conducts research and evaluation. A special focus is on technology and learning. In addition to conventional print publications, NCREL uses computer networks, videoconferencing via satellite, and video and audio formats to reach its diverse audiences. NCREL's Web site includes the acclaimed Pathways to School Improvement. NCREL operates the Midwest Consortium for Mathematics and Science Education, which works to advance systemic change in mathematics and science education. Persons living in Illinois, Indiana, Iowa, Michigan, Minnesota, Ohio, and Wisconsin are encouraged to call the NCREL Resource Center with any education-related questions. NCREL also hosts the North Central Regional Technology in Education Consortium which helps states and local educational agencies successfully integrate advanced technologies into K–12 classrooms, library media centers, and other educational settings. *Membership:* Staff of 100, region covers Michigan, Minnesota, Wisconsin, Illinois, Ohio, Indiana and Iowa. *Meetings:* Annual conference. *Publications: Learning Point* (three times a year).

Northwest College and University Council for the Management of Educational Technology (NW/MET). c/o WITS, Willamette University, 900 State St., Salem, OR 97301. (503) 370-6650. Fax (503) 375-5456. E-mail: mmorandi@willamette.edu. Web site: http://www.nw-met.org. Tom Matney, Director.; Marti Morandi, Membership Chair. NW/MET is a group of media professionals responsible for campuswide media services. Founded in 1976, NW/MET is comprised of members from three provinces of Canada and 4 northwestern states. *Membership:* is restricted to information technology managers with campuswide responsibilities for information technology services in the membership region. Corresponding membership is available to those who work outside the membership region. Current issues under consideration include managing emerging technologies, distance education, adaptive technologies, staff evaluation, course management, faculty development, copyright, and other management/administration issues. Organizational goals include identifying the unique status problems of media managers in higher education. Membership: approx. 75. *Dues:* $35. *Meetings:* An annual conference and business meeting are held each year, rotating through the region. *Publications:* An annual newsletter and *NW/MET Journal.*

Northwest Regional Educational Laboratory (NWREL). 101 SW Main St., Suite 500, Portland, OR 97204. (503) 275-9500. Fax (503) 275-0448. E-mail: info@nwrel.org. Web site: http://www.nwrel.org. Dr. Carol Thomas, Exec. Dir. One of 10 Office of Educational Research and Improvement (OERI) regional educational laboratories, NWREL works with schools and communities to improve educational outcomes for children, youth, and adults. NWREL provides leadership, expertise, and services based on the results of research and development. The specialty area of NWREL is school change processes. It serves Alaska, Idaho, Oregon, Montana, and Washington. *Membership:* 856 organizations. *Dues:* None. *Meetings:* Education Now and in The Future Conference. *Publications: Northwest Report* (newsletter). *Northwest Education* (quarterly journal).

Online Audiovisual Catalogers, Inc. (OLAC). E-mail: neumeist@buffalo.edu. Web site: http://www.olacinc.org/. n/a. In 1980, OLAC was founded to establish and maintain a group that could speak for catalogers of audiovisual materials. OLAC provides a means for exchange of information, continuing education, and communication among catalogers of audiovisual materials and with the Library of Congress. While maintaining a voice with the bibliographic utilities that speak for catalogers of audiovisual materials, OLAC works toward common understanding of AV cataloging practices and standards. *Membership:* 700. *Dues:* United States and Canada: Personal Memberships: One year $12.00, Two years $22.00, Three years $30.00; Institutional Memberships: One year $18.00, Two years $34.00, Three years $48.00. Other Countries: All Memberships: One year $20.00, Two years $38.00, Three years $54.00. *Meetings:* bi-annual. *Publications:* OLAC Newsletter.

Online Computer Library Center, Inc. (OCLC). 6565 Frantz Rd., Dublin, OH 43017-3395. (614) 764-6000. Fax (614) 764-6096. E-mail: oclc@oclc.org. Web site: http://www.oclc.org. Jay Jordan, President and CEO. Founded in 1967, OCLC Online Computer Library Center is a nonprofit, membership, computer library service and research organization dedicated to the public purposes of furthering access to the world's information and reducing information costs. More than 45,000 libraries in 84 countries and territories around the world use OCLC services to locate, acquire, catalog, lend and preserve library materials. Researchers, students, faculty, scholars, professional librarians and other information seekers use OCLC services to obtain bibliographic, abstract and full-text information. OCLC and its member libraries cooperatively produce and maintain WorldCat—the OCLC Online Union Catalog. OCLC FOREST PRESS, a division of OCLC since 1988, publishes the Dewey Decimal Classification. Digital Collection and Preservation Services, a division of OCLC since 1994, provides digitizing, microfilming and archiving services worldwide. OCLCs netLibrary provides libraries with eContent solutions that support Web-based research, reference and learning. *Membership:* OCLC welcomes information organizations around the world to be a part of our unique cooperative. A variety of participation levels are available to libraries, museums, archives, historical societies and professional associations. OCLC membership represents more than 45,000 libraries in 84 countries and territories around the world. OCLC also has 60 Members Council delegates who are elected by and represent the OCLC member libraries in their respective regions. *Meetings:* OCLC Members Council (3/yr.) Held in Dublin, Ohio. *Publications:* *Annual Report* (1/yr.); *OCLC Newsletter* (4/yr.); *OCLC Abstracts* (1/week, electronic version only).

Ontario Film Association, Inc. (also known as the Association for the Advancement of Visual Media/L'association pour l'avancement des médias visuels). 100 Lombard St. 303, Toronto, ON M5C 1M3. (416) 363-3388. Fax (800) 387-1181. E-mail: info@accessola.com. Web site: http://.accessola.org. Lawrence A. Moore, Exec. Dir. A membership organization of buyers, and users of media whose objectives are to promote the sharing of ideas and information about visual media through education, publications, and advocacy. *Membership:* 112. *Dues:* $120, personal membership; $215, associate membership. *Meetings: OFA Media Showcase,* spring.

Pacific Film Archive (PFA). University of California, Berkeley Art Museum, 2625 Durant Ave., Berkeley, CA 94720-2250. (510) 642-1437 (library); (510) 642-1412 (general). Fax (510) 642-4889. E-mail: pfalibrary@uclink.berkeley.edu. Web site: http://www.bampfa.berkeley.edu. Edith Kramer, Dir. and Curator of Film; Nancy Goldman, Head, PFA Library and Film Study Center. Sponsors the exhibition, study, and preservation of classic, international, documentary, animated, and avant-garde films. Provides on-site research screenings of films in its collection of over 7,000 titles. Provides access to its collections of books, periodicals, stills, and posters (all materials are noncirculating). Offers BAM/PFA members and University of California, Berkeley, affiliates reference and research services to locate film and video distributors, credits, stock footage, etc. Library hours are 1 P.M.–5 P.M. Mon.–Thurs. *Membership:* Membership is through our parent organization, the UC Berkeley Art Museum and Pacific Film Archive, and is open to anyone. The BAM/PFA currently has over 3,000 members. Members receive free admission to the Museum; reduced-price tickets to films showing at PFA; access to the

PFA Library & Film Study Center; and many other benefits. Applications and more information is available at http://www.bampfa.berkeley.edu/membership/index.html. *Dues:* $40 indiv. and nonprofit departments of institutions. *Publications: BAM/PFA Calendar* (6/yr).

Pacific Resources for Education and Learning (PREL). 900 Fort Street Mall, Suite 1300, Honolulu, HI 96813. (808) 441-1300. Fax (808) 441-1385. E-mail: askprel@prel. org. Web site: http://www.prel.org/. Tom Barlow, President and Chief Executive Officer. PREL is a nonprofit 501(c)(3) corporation dedicated to helping educators and policymakers solve educational problems in their schools. Using the best available research and the expertise of professionals, PREL helps to implement new approaches in education and provides training to teachers and administrators. The PRELStar program utilizes telecommunications technology to provide distance learning opportunities to the Pacific region. The Pacific Regional Technology in Education Consortium program builds local school and community capacity to acquire and utilize technology to improve teaching and learning. NEARStar provides an interactive, Web-based supplemental early reading program for English language learners. The Ethnomathematics Digital Library provides high quality educational resources online about ethnomathematics worldwide, with emphasis on the Pacific. The first three projects are funded by the US Department of Education, and the latter by the National Science Foundation. *Membership:* PREL serves teachers and departments and ministries of education in American Samoa, Commonwealth of the Northern Mariana Islands, Federated States of Micronesia (Chuuk, Kosrae, Pohnpei, and Yap) Guam, Hawaii, the Republic of the Marshall Islands, and the Republic of Palau. *Dues: -. Meetings:* PREL supports the annual Pacific Educational Conference, held each July. *Publications:* Publications are listed on the PREL Web site at http://ppo.prel.org/. Most are available in both PDF and HTML format.

PBS Adult Learning Service (ALS). 1320 Braddock Place, Alexandria, VA 22314-1698. (800) 257-2578. Fax (703) 739-8471. E-mail: als@pbs.org. Web site: http://www.pbs. org/als/. Clinton OBrien, Senior Director. The PBS Adult Learning Service is a provider of course content to colleges and universities nationwide. Offerings include Web-based online courses and video-based telecourses. Content is developed by prominent educators and producers and designed for college-credit use. Public television stations nationwide cooperate with colleges that offer PBS courses to reach local populations of adult learners. A pioneer in the widespread use of video in college-credit learning, PBS first began distributing telecourses in 1981. Since that time, more than 3 million students have earned college credit through telecourses from PBS. *Membership:* Nearly 500 institutions are PBS Associate Colleges. These members save on licensing and acquisition fees for PBS courses and are entitled to discounts on related services such as Web-based scheduling, master broadcast tape duplication, and educational videotape purchase. Nonmembers still have access to the same content and services; they simply pay higher fees. *Dues:* $1,500. Multicollege and consortium rates are available. *Publications: PBS Adult Learning Service Course Catalog. PBS Course Bulletin* (monthly e-mail update for course faculty and administrators).

PBS VIDEO (PBS VIDEO). 1320 Braddock Pl., Alexandria, VA 22314. (703) 739-5380; (800) 344-3337. Fax (703) 739-5269. E-mail: jcecil@pbs.org. Web site: http://shop2. org/pbsvideo/. Jon Cecil, Dir. PBS VIDEO Marketing. Markets and distributes PBS television programs for sale on videocassette and DVD to colleges, public libraries, schools, governments, and other organizations and institutions. *Membership:* N/A. *Dues:* N/A. *Meetings:* N/A. *Publications*: PBS VIDEO Catalogs of New and Popular Video (4/yrs). Web site: *PBS VIDEO Online Catalog* at http://shopPBS.com/teachers.

Penn State Media Sales (PSMS). 118 Wagner Building, University Park, PA 16802. (800) 770-2111, (814) 863-3102. Fax (814) 865-3172. E-mail: MediaSales@outreach.psu.edu. Web site: http://www.MediaSales.psu.edu. Robin P. Guillard, Coordinator.

Distributor of educational video with a primary audience of post secondary education. One of America's largest collections on historic psychology, including Stanley Milgram's experiments, psychosurgery, and early mental illness treatments. Other catogories are anthropology, including the Mead/Bateson studies, primatology, sciences, agriculture, and training. Closed circuit television, broadcast and footage use available on many titles. Call for more information. *Publications:* Product catalog.

Photographic Society of America (PSA). 3000 United Founders Blvd., Suite 103, Oklahoma City, OK 73112. (405) 843-1437. Fax (405) 843-1438. E-mail: hq@psa-photo. org. Web site: http://www.psa-photo.org. Linda Lowery, operations manager. A nonprofit organization for the development of the arts and sciences of photography and for the furtherance of public appreciation of photographic skills. Its members, largely advanced amateurs, consist of individuals, camera clubs, and other photographic organizations. Divisions include electronic imaging, color slide, video motion picture, nature, photojournalism, travel, pictorial print, stereo, and techniques. Sponsors national, regional, and local meetings, clinics, and contests. *Membership:* 5500. *Dues:* $42, North America; $48 elsewhere.

Professors of Instructional Design and Technology (PIDT). Instructional Technology Dept., 220 War Memorial Hall, Virginia Tech, Blacksburg, VA 24061-0341. (540) 231-5587. Fax (540) 231-9075. E-mail: moorem@VT.EDU. Web site: https://www. conted.vt.edu/ssl/pidt-reg.htm. Dr. Mike Moore, or Dr. Ed Caffarella, contact persons. An informal organization designed to encourage and facilitate the exchange of information among members of the instructional design and technology academic and corporate communities. Also serves to promote excellence in academic programs in instructional design and technology and to encourage research and inquiry that will benefit the field while providing leadership in the public and private sectors in its application and practice. *Membership:* Faculty employed in higher education institutions whose primary responsibilities are teaching and research in instructional technology, their corporate counterparts, and other persons interested in the goals and activities of the PIDT. No formal membership. Contact either Dr. Mike Moore (moorem@vt.edu), or Dr. Ed Caffarella (CAFFAREL@unco.edu) to be added to listserv for announcements of meeting times, location and conference registration. Cohosts alternate between Virginia Tech and University of Northern Colorado and meetings alternate annually between Virginia and Colorado. Meeting usually is around the middle of May and usually runs from Friday P.M. to Monday A.M. Contact Dr. Mike Moore (moorem@vt.edu), or Dr. Ed Caffarella (CAFFAREL@unco.edu) for information. *Meetings:* Annual conference alternates between Virginia and Colorado; see above e-mail address for information and registration. *Publications:* none.

Public Broadcasting Service (PBS). 1320 Braddock Pl., Alexandria, VA 22314. Web site: http://www.pbs.org. Ervin S. Duggan, CEO and Pres. National distributor of public television programming, obtaining all programs from member stations, independent producers, and sources around the world. PBS services include program acquisition, distribution, and scheduling; development and fundraising support; engineering and technical development; and educational resources and services. Through the PBS National Program Service, PBS uses the power of noncommercial television, the Internet, and other media to enrich the lives of all Americans through quality programs and education services that inform and inspire. Subsidiaries of PBS include PBS Adult Learning Service, and PBS Video, which are described below. PBS is owned and operated by local public television organizations through annual membership fees and governed by a board of directors elected by PBS members for three-year terms.

Public Library Association (PLA). 50 E. Huron St., Chicago, IL 60611. (312) 280-5PLA. Fax (312) 280-5029. E-mail: pla@ala.org. Web site: http://.pla.org. Greta Southard, Exec. Dir. A division of the American Library Association, PLA is concerned with the development, effectiveness, and financial support of public libraries. It speaks for the profession and seeks to enrich the professional competence and opportunities of public librarians. *Membership:* PLA has 9,940 members as of 2/2002. Any member of the American Library Association is eligible to join PLA. *Dues:* $50, open to all ALA members. *Meetings:* Annually. *Publications: Public Libraries* (bi-monthly); electronic newsletter sent to members.

Puppeteers of America, Inc. (POA). PO Box 29417, Parma, OH 44129-0417. (888) 568-6235. Fax (440) 843-7867. E-mail: PofAjoin@aol.com. Web site: http://www.puppeteers.org. Joyce and Chuck Berty , Membership Officers. Formed in 1937, POA holds festivals for puppetry across the country, supports local guilds, presents awards, sponsors innovative puppetry works, provides consulting, and provides research materials through the Audio-Visual Library. A National Festival is held in the odd number years and Regional Festivals are held in the even number years at various locations around the United States. The group supports a National Day of Puppetry the last Saturday in April. Local celebrations of the Art of Puppetry are held throughout the United States. The Puppetry Store is an invaluable source of books and miscellaneous printed materials for Puppeteers or anyone interested in Puppetry. The Puppetry Journal is the magazine published quarterly for the members of the organization and Playboard is the Bi-Monthly newsletter. *Membership:* Our current membership is over 2,200 memberships from people around the world interested in the art of puppetry. Our Membership consists of Performing Professionals to librarians, storytellers or someone just interested in the art of puppetry. We offer subscription memberships to Libraries and discounted memberships to Seniors and Youths. *Dues:* $40, Single Adult; $50, couple; $20, youth (17—6); $25 Full-time Student; $25 Senior (65 and over); $60, family; $70 Company or Business; $35, Journal subscription available to libraries. *Meetings:* Regional Annual Meetings. *Publications: The Puppetry Journal* (q) A quarterly magazine published only for our membership. It is the only publication in the United States dedicated to Puppetry in America. Playboard bi-monthly newsletter published to update the voting membership on the business of the organization.

Recording for the Blind and Dyslexic (RFB&D). 20 Roszel Road, Princeton, NJ 08540. (609)452-0606. Customer Service (800) 221-4792. Fax (609) 987-8116. E-mail: information @rfbd.org. Web site: http://www.rfbd.org. Richard Scribner, Pres. Recording for the Blind & Dyslexic (RFB&D), a national nonprofit volunteer organization founded in 1948, is the nation's educational library serving people who cannot read standard print effectively because of a learning disability, visual impairment or other physical disability. RFB&D operates 32 recording studios and offices across the country. Our more than 90,000 volume library contains a broad selection of titles, from literature & history to math and the sciences, at all academic levels, from kindergarten through postgraduate and professional. RFB&D offers individual and institutional Learning Through Listening memberships, scholarship programs, a reference service and a custom recording service. RFB&D also offers for nonprofit sale a variety of playback devices and accessories. *Membership:* RFB&DS materials are for people who cannot read standard print because of visual impairment, learning disability or physical disability. Potential individual members must complete an application form, which contains a "disability verification"; There are 102,000 Individuals Members and 4200 Institutions Members. *Dues:* The cost of an individual membership is $25 per year, plus a one time $50 registration fee for qualified individuals. Fees for institutional membership vary based on level of membership chosen. (Contact Customer Service). *Publications: RFB&D Learning through Listening Impact Newsletter.*

Recording Industry Association of America, Inc. (RIAA). 1330 Connecticut Ave. NW #300, Washington, DC 20036. (202) 775-0101. Fax (202) 775-7253. E-mail: aweiss@riaa.com. Web site: http://www.riaa.com/. Hilary Rosen, Chairman and CEO.

Founded in 1952, RIAA's mission is to promote the mutual interests of recording companies, as well as the betterment of the industry overall through successful government relations (both federal and state), intellectual property protection, and international activities; evaluating all aspects of emerging technologies and technology-related issues; and promoting an innovative and secure online marketplace. RIAA represents the recording industry, whose members create and/or distribute approximately 90 percent of all legitimate sound recordings produced and sold in the United States. RIAA is the official certification agency for gold, platinum, and multiplatinum record awards. *Membership:* Over 250 recording companies. *Publications: Consumer Profile.*

Reference and User Services Association (RUSA). 50 E. Huron St., Chicago, IL 60611. (800) 545-2433, ext. 4398. Fax (312) 944-8085. E-mail: cbourdon@ala.org. Web site: http://www.ala.org/rusa. Cathleen Bourdon, Exec. Dir. A division of the American Library Association, RUSA is responsible for stimulating and supporting in every type of library the delivery of reference information services to all groups and of general library services and materials to adults. *Membership:* 4,900. *Dues:* Join ALA and RUSA $95; RUSA membership $45(added to current ALA membership); student member $45 ($25 for ALA and $20 for RUSA). *Meetings:* Meetings are held in conjunction with the American Library Association. *Publications:* RUSQ (q.), information provided on RUSA Web site at www.ala.org/rusa, select publications.

Research for Better Schools, Inc. (RBS). 112 North Broad Street, Philadelphia, PA 19102-1510. (215)568-6150. Fax (215)568-7260. E-mail: info@rbs.org. Web site: http://www.rbs.org/. Keith M. Kershner & Louis Maguire, Co-Executive Directors. Research for Better Schools is a nonprofit education organization that has been providing services to teachers, administrators, and policy makers since 1966. Our mission is to help students achieve high learning standards by supporting improvement efforts in schools and other education environments. The staff are dedicated to and well experienced in providing the array of services that schools, districts, and states need to help their students reach proficient or higher learning standards: 1) technical assistance in improvement efforts; 2) professional development that is required for the successful implementation of more effective curricula, technologies, or instruction; 3) application of research in the design of specific improvement efforts; 4) evaluation of improvement efforts; 5) curriculum implementation and assessment; and 6) effective communication with all members of the school community. RBS has worked with a wide range of clients over the years, representing all levels of the education system, as well as business and community groups. *Membership:* There is no membership in Research for Better Schools. The Mid-Atlantic Eisenhower Consortium for Mathematics and Science Education, which RBS operates, does encourage regional educators to become members. Information is available online at http://www.rbs.org/eisenhower/membership.shtml. The Mid-Atlantic Eisenhower Consortium currently has over 18,000 members, who include teachers, school administrators, representatives from higher education, state department of education staff, professional association representatives, business persons, and other community members interested in mathematics and science education. *Dues:* N/A. *Meetings:* The Mid-Atlantic Eisenhower Consortium sponsors an annual regional conference and state team meetings throughout the year. *Publications:* RBS publishes the *Currents* newsletter, available in print, online, and delivered via e-mail (http://www.rbs.org/currents/index.shtml). The Consortium also publishes the electronic newsletter, Riptides (http://www.rbs.org/archives/riptides.html). The catalog for RBS Publications is online (visit our homepage at http://www.rbs.org).

School Media and Technology Division, Association for Educational Communications and Technology (SMT). 1800 N. Stonelake Dr. Suite 2, Bloomington, IN 47408. (877) 677-AECT. Fax (912) 267-4234. E-mail: ctibbits@mindspring.com. Web site: http://.soe.ecu.edu/aect/dsmt. Neal Bachman, President; Dr. Carol Brown, President-elect; Connie Tibbitts, Board representative. SMT strives to improve instruction and promotes excellence in student learning in the K–12 setting by developing, implementing, and evaluating media programs and by planning and integrating technology in the classroom. *Membership:* Members of this division are primarily School Library Media Specialists, Instructional Technology Coordinators in K-12 school districts, and Higher Ed Teachers preparing people to work in Library Media programs. *Dues:* Division membership included in the basic AECT membership. *Meetings:* Held in conjunction with the annual AECT Convention.

Smithsonian Institution. 1000 Jefferson Drive SW, Washington, DC 20560. (202) 357-2700. Fax (202) 786-2515. E-mail: info@info.si.edu. Web site: http://www.si.edu. I. Michael Heyman, Sec. An independent trust instrumentality of the United States that conducts scientific, cultural, and scholarly research; administers the national collections; and performs other educational public service functions, all supported by Congress, trusts, gifts, and grants. Includes 16 museums, including the National Museum of Natural History, the National Museum of American History, the National Air and Space Museum, and the National Zoological Park. Museums are free and open daily except December 25. The Smithsonian Institution Traveling Exhibition Service (SITES) organizes exhibitions on art, history, and science and circulates them across the country and abroad. *Membership:* Smithsonian Associates. *Dues:* $24-$45. *Publications: Smithsonian; Air & Space/Smithsonian; The Torch* (staff newsletter, mo.); *Research Reports* (semi-technical, q.); Smithsonian Institution Press Publications, 470 L'Enfant Plaza, Suite 7100, Washington, DC 20560.

Society for Applied Learning Technology (SALT). 50 Culpeper St., Warrenton, VA 20186. (540) 347-0055. Fax (540) 349-3169. E-mail: info@lti.org. Web site: http://www.salt.org. Raymond G. Fox, Pres. The society is a nonprofit, professional membership organization that was founded in 1972. Membership in the society is oriented to professionals whose work requires knowledge and communication in the field of instructional technology. The society provides members with a means to enhance their knowledge and job performance by participation in society-sponsored meetings, subscription to society-sponsored publications, association with other professionals at conferences sponsored by the society, and membership in special interest groups and special society-sponsored initiatives. In addition, the society offers member discounts on society-sponsored journals, conferences, and publications. *Membership:* 350. *Dues:* $55. *Meetings:* Bi-Annually. *Publications: Journal of Educational Technology Systems; Journal of Instruction Delivery Systems; Journal of Interactive Instruction Development.* Send for list of available publications.

Society for Computer Simulation (SCS). P.O. Box 17900, San Diego, CA 92177-7900. (619) 277-3888. Fax (619) 277-3930. E-mail: info@scs.org. Web site: http://www.scs.org. Bill Gallagher, Exec. Dir. Founded in 1952, SCS is a professional-level technical society devoted to the art and science of modeling and simulation. Its purpose is to advance the understanding, appreciation, and use of all types of computer models for studying the behavior of actual or hypothesized systems of all kinds and to sponsor standards. Additional office in Ghent, Belgium. *Membership:* 1,900. *Dues:* $75 (includes journal subscription). *Meetings:* Local, regional, and national technical meetings and conferences. *Publications: Simulation* (mo.); Simulation series (q.); *Transactions of SCS* (q.).

Society for Photographic Education (SPE). 110 Art Building, Miami University, Oxford, OH 45056. (513) 529-8328. Fax (513) 529-1532. E-mail: speoffice@spenational.org. Web site: http://www.spenational.org. Jennifer P. Yamashiro, Executive Director. An association of college and university teachers of photography, museum photographic curators, writers, publishers and students. Promotes discourse in photography education, culture, and art. *Membership:* 1,800. Membership dues are for the calendar year, January through December. *Dues:* 2005 Membership Dues: $90, Regular Membership; $50, Student Membership; $600, Corporate Member; $380, Collector Member (with print); $150,

Sustaining Member; $65, Senior Member. *Meetings:* Portland, Oregon, March 17–20, 2005. *Publications: Exposure* (photographic journal), biannual; quarterly newsletter.

Society of Cable Telecommunications Engineers (SCTE). 140 Philips Rd. Exton, PA 19341-1318. (610) 363-6888. Fax (610) 363-5898. E-mail: info@scte.org. Web site: http://www.scte.org. John Clark, Pres. & CEO. The Society of Cable Telecommunications Engineers is a nonprofit professional organization committed to advancing the careers of cable telecommunications professionals and serving their industry through excellence in professional development, information and standards. SCTE currently has approximately 14,000 members from the U.S. and 70 countries worldwide and offers a variety of programs and services for the industry's educational benefit. SCTE has more than 70 chapters and meeting groups and has technically certified more than 3,000 employees of the cable telecommunications industry. Visit www.scte.org. *Membership:* 14,000 worldwide. *Dues:* $58 Individual, $350 Sustaining Members, $29 Full-time Student, Unemployed or Retired (one-year). *Meetings:* Conference on Emerging Technologies: Cable-Tec Expo, San Antonio, TX, June 14–17, 2005. *Publications: Interval Membership Directory SCTE Monthly, Credentials, Standards Bulletin, Leadership Forum.*

Society of Photo Technologists (SPT). 11112 S. Spotted Rd., Cheney, WA 99004. (888)662-7678 or (509) 624-9621. Fax (509) 624-5320. E-mail: cc5@earthlink.net. Web site: http://www.spt.info/. Chuck Bertone, Executive Director. An organization of photographic equipment repair technicians, which improves and maintains communications between manufacturers and repair shops and technicians. We publish Repair Journals, Newsletters, Parts & Service Directory and Industry Newsletters. We also sponsor SPTNET (a technical email group), Remanufactured parts and residence workshops. *Membership:* 1,000 shops and manufacturers worldwide, eligible people or businesses are any who are involved full or part time in the camera repair field. *Dues:* $97.50–$370. Membership depends on the size/volume of the business. Most one man shops are Class A/$170 dues. Those not involved full time in the field is $95.50/Associate Class. *Publications: SPT Journal; SPT Parts and Services Directory; SPT Newsletter; SPT Manuals—Training and Manufacturer's Tours.*

Southeastern Regional Media Leadership Council (SRMLC). Dr. Vykuntapathi Thota, Director, Virginia State University, P.O. Box 9198, Petersburg, VA 23806. (804) 524-5937. Fax (804) 524-5757. An affiliate of AECT, the purpose of the SRMLC is to strengthen the role of the individual state AECT affiliates within the Southeastern region; to seek positive change in the nature and status of instructional technology as it exists within the Southeast; to provide opportunities for the training and development of leadership for both the region and the individual affiliates; and to provide opportunities for the exchange of information and experience among those who attend the annual conference.

SouthEastern Regional Vision for Education (SERVE). SERVE Tallahassee Office, 1203 Governor's Square Blvd., Suite 400, Tallahassee, FL 32301. (800) 352-6001, (904) 671-6000. Fax (904) 671-6020. E-mail: wmccolsk@serve.org. Web site: http://www. serve.org/. Wendy McColskey, Program Director. SERVE is a regional educational research and development laboratory funded by the U.S. Department of Education to help educators, policymakers, and communities improve schools so that all students achieve their full potential. The laboratory offers the following services: field-based models and strategies for comprehensive school improvement; publications on hot topics in education, successful implementation efforts, applied research projects, and policy issues; database searches and information search training; a regional bulletin board service that provides educators electronic communication and Internet access; information and assistance for state and local policy development; and services to support the coordination and improvement of assistance for young children and their families. The Eisenhower Mathematics and Science Consortium at SERVE promotes improvement of education in these targeted areas by coordinating regional resources, disseminating exemplary instructional materials, and offering technical assistance for implementation of effective teaching methods and assessment tools. *Meetings:* For dates and topics of conferences and workshops, contact Gladys Jackson, (800) 755-3277. *Publications: Reengineering High Schools for Student Success; Schools for the 21st Century: New Roles for Teachers and Principals* (rev. ed.); *Designing Teacher Evaluation Systems That Promote Professional Growth; Learning by Serving: 2,000 Ideas for Service-Learning Projects; Sharing Success: Promising Service-Learning Programs; Future Plans* (videotape, discussion guide, and pamphlet); *Future Plans Planning Guides.*

Southwest Educational Development Laboratory (SEDL). 211 East Seventh St., Austin, TX 78701. (512) 476-6861. Fax (512) 476-2286. E-mail: info@sedl.org. Web site: http://www.sedl.org. Dr. Wesley A. Hoover, Pres. and CEO. The Southwest Educational Development Laboratory (SEDL) is a private, not-for-profit education research and development corporation based in Austin, Texas. SEDL has worked in schools to investigate the conditions under which teachers can provide student-centered instruction supported by technology, particularly computers alone with other software. From that field-based research with teachers, SEDL has developed a professional development model and modules, which resulted in the production of Active Learning with Technology. Active Learning is a multimedia training program for teachers. Using the modules, videotapes, and CD, teachers can learn how to apply student-centered, problem-based learning theory to their instructional strategies that are supported by technologies. Copies of Active Learning can be ordered from SEDL's Office of Institutional Communications. SEDL also operates the SouthCentral Regional Technology in Education Consortium (SouthCentral RTEC), which seeks to support educational systems in Arkansas, Louisiana, New Mexico, Oklahoma and Texas in the use of technology to foster student success in achieving state content standards. A particular focus is on schools serving high populations of disadvantaged students. The RTEC delivers research-based professional development and information resources to teachers, college faculty, district and state level staff developers, as well as local and state decision makers. *Publications: SEDL LETTER* and other newsletters and documents are available for free general distribution in print and online. Topic-specific publications related to educational change, education policy, mathematics, language arts, science, and disability research. Publications catalog available on the SEDL Web site at http://www.sedl.org/pubs.

Special Libraries Association. 1700 Eighteenth St., NW, Washington, DC 20009-2514. (202) 234-4700. Fax (202) 265-9317. E-mail: sla@sla.org. Web site: http://www.sla.org. Dr. David R. Bender, Exec. Dir. The Special Libraries Association is an international association representing the interests of nearly 15,000 information professionals in 60 countries. Special librarians are information and resource experts who collect, analyze, evaluate, package, and disseminate information to facilitate accurate decision making in corporate, academic, and government settings. The association offers myriad programs and services designed to help its members serve their customers more effectively and succeed in an increasingly challenging environment of information management and technology. These services include career and employment services, and professional development opportunities. *Membership:* 14,500. *Dues:* $105, indiv.; $25, student. *Meetings:* Bi-annually. *Publications: Information Outlook* (monthly glossy magazine that accepts advertising). Special Libraries Association also has an active book publishing program.

Teachers and Writers Collaborative (T&W). 5 Union Square W., New York, NY 10003-3306. (212) 691-6590, (888) 266-5789. Fax (212) 675-0171. E-mail: info@twc.org. http://www.twc.org and http://www.writenet.org. Nancy Larson Shapiro, Dir. Teachers & Writers Collaborative (T&W) provides a link between New York City's rich literary community and the public schools, where the needs for effective ways to teach writing and for programs that support innovative teaching are greater than ever. T&W not only places professional writers and artists into schools and other community settings, but also publishes books on teaching writing—books that provide sound theory and practical curriculum ideas for the classroom. In our welcoming Center for Imaginative Writing on Union Square, writers and educators come together for workshops, readings, and seminars, and through our Youth Speaks program we hold free after-school writing workshops for students. The National Endowment for the Arts has called T&W the nation's group that is "most familiar with creative writing/literature in primary and secondary schools." *Membership:* T&W has over 1,000 members across the country. The basic membership is $35; patron membership is $75; and benefactor membership is $150 or more. Members receive a free book or T-shirt; discounts on publications; and a free one-year subscription to Teachers & Writers magazine. (Please see http://www.twc.org/member.htm.) *Dues:* T&W is seeking general operating support for all of our programs and program support for specific projects, including: 1) T&W writing residencies in New York City area schools; 2) T&W publications, books and a bimonthly magazine, which we distribute across the country; 3) Youth Speaks, T&Ws free after-school writing and performance workshops for teens; and 4) WriteNet, T&Ws Internet programs for teachers, writers, and students. Grants to T&Ws Endowment support the stability of the organization and help to guarantee the continuation of specific programs. *Meetings:* T&W offers year-round public events in our Center for Imaginative Writing in New York City. For a list of events, please see http://www.twc.org/events.htm. *Publications:* T&W has published over 60 books on the teaching of imaginative writing, including *The T&W Handbook of Poetic Forms; The Dictonary of Wordplay; The Story in History; Personal Fiction Writing; Luna, Luna: Creative Writing from Spanish and Latino Literature; The Nearness of You: Students and Teachers Writing On-Line.* To request a free publications catalog, please send e-mail to info@twc.org or call 888-BOOKS-TW. (Please see http://www.twc.org/tpubs.htm.)

Technology in Public Libraries Committee. 50 E. Huron St., Chicago, IL 60611. (312) 280-5752. William Ptacek, Chair. Collects and disseminates information on technology applications in public libraries.

Theatre Library Association (TLA). 149 W. 45th St., New York, NY 10036. (212) 944-3895. Fax (212) 944-4139. E-mail: kwinkler@nypl.org. Web site: http://www.brown.edu/Facilities/University_Library/beyond/TLA/TLA.html. Maryann Chach, Exec. Sec. Seeks to further the interests of collecting, preserving, and using theater, cinema, and performing arts materials in libraries, museums, and private collections. *Membership:* 500. *Dues:* $30, indiv.; $30, institutional; $20, students and retirees. *Publications: Performing Arts Resources* (membership annual, Vol. 20, Denishawn Collections).

University Continuing Education Association (UCEA). One Dupont Cir. NW, Suite 615, Washington, DC 20036. (202) 659-3130. Fax (202) 785-0374. E-mail: shirley@ucea.edu. Web site: http://www.ucea.edu/. Kay J. Kohl, Executive Director, kjkohl@ucea.edu. UCEA is an association of public and private higher education institutions concerned with making continuing education available to all population segments and to promoting excellence in continuing higher education. Many institutional members offer university and college courses via electronic instruction. *Membership:* 425 institutions, 2,000 professionals. *Dues:* vary according to membership category; see: http://www. ucea.edu/membership.htm. *Meetings:* UCEA has an annual national conference and several professional development seminars throughout the year. See: http://www.ucea. edu/page02.htm. *Publications:* monthly newsletter; quarterly; occasional papers; scholarly journal, *Continuing Higher Education Review; Independent Study Catalog;* with Peterson's, *The Guide to Distance Learning; Guide to Certificate Programs at American Colleges and Universities;* UCEA-ACE/Oryx Continuing Higher Education book series; *Lifelong Learning Trends* (a statistical factbook on continuing higher education); organizational issues series; membership directory.

USA Toy Library Association (USA-TLA). 1326 Wilmette Ave., Ste. 201, Wilmette, IL 60091. (847) 920-9030. Fax (847) 920-9032. E-mail: usatla@aol.com. Web site: http://usatla.deltacollege.org. Judith Q. Iacuzzi, Exec. Dir. The mission of the USA-TLA is to provide a networking system answering to all those interested in play and play materials to provide a national resource to toy libraries, family centers, resource and referrals, public libraries, schools, institutions serving families of special need, and other groups and individuals involved with children; to support and expand the number of toy libraries; and to advocate for children and the importance of their play in healthy development. Individuals can find closest toy libraries by sending an e-mail or written inquiry in a self-addressed stamped envelope. *Membership:* 80 institutions, 150 individuals. Members receive a subscription to the quarterly newsletter *Child's Play*, reduced fees on conferences, workshops, books, videos and other publications and products sold by the USA Toy Library Association. Comprehensive members receive a bonus gift each year. *Dues:* $165, comprehensive; $55, basic; $15, student. *Meetings:* Regional workshops in the spring and fall. *Publications: Child's Play* (q. newsletter); *How to Start and Operate a Toy Library; Play Is a Child's Work* (videotape); other books on quality toys and play.

WestEd (None). 730 Harrison St., San Francisco, CA 94107-1242. (415) 565-3000. Fax (415) 565-3012. E-mail: lcardin@wested.org. http://www.WestEd.org. Glen Harvey, CEO; Richard Whitmore, Chief Financial Officer; Sri Ananda, Chief Development Officer. WestEd is a nonprofit research, development, and service agency dedicated to improving education and other opportunities for children, youth, and adults. Drawing on the best from research and practice, WestEd works with practitioners and policymakers to address critical issues in education and other related areas, including accountability and assessment; early childhood intervention; curriculum, instruction, and assessment; the use of technology; career and technical preparation; teacher and administrator professional development; science and mathematics education; safe schools and communities. WestEd was created in 1995 to unite and enhance the capacity of Far West Laboratory and Southwest Regional Laboratory, two of the nation's original education laboratories. In addition to its work across the nation, WestEd serves as the regional education laboratory for Arizona, California, Nevada, and Utah. A publications catalog is available and WestEd.org has a comprehensive listing of services offered. *Meetings:* Various, relating to our work, plus quarterly Board meetings. *Publications:* See Resources at www.WestEd.org.

Western Public Radio (WPR). Ft. Mason Center, Bldg. D, San Francisco, CA 94123. (415) 771-1160. Fax (415) 771-4343. E-mail: wprsf@aol.com. Karolyn van Putten, Ph.D., Pres./CEO; Lynn Chadwick, Vice Pres./COO. WPR provides analog and digital audio production training, public radio program proposal consultation, and studio facilities for rent. WPR also sponsors a continuing education resource for audio producers, www. radiocollege.org.

World Future Society (WFS). 7910 Woodmont Ave., Suite 450, Bethesda, MD 20814. (301) 656-8274. Fax (301) 951-0394. E-mail: wfsinfo@wfs.org. Web site: http://www.wfs.org. Edward Cornish, Pres. Organization of individuals interested in the study of future trends and possibilities. Its purpose is to provide information on trends and scenarios so that individuals and organizations can better plan their future. *Membership:* 30,000. *Dues:* $39, general; $95, professional; call Society for details on all membership levels and benefits. *Meetings:* Annually. *Publications: The Futurist: A Journal of Forecasts, Trends and Ideas about the Future; Futures Research Quarterly; Future Survey.* The society's bookstore offers audiotapes and videotapes, books, and other items.

Young Adult Library Services Association (YALSA). 50 E. Huron St., Chicago, IL 60611. (312) 280-4390. Fax (312) 664-7459. E-mail: yalsa@ala.org. Web site: http://www.ala.org/yalsa. Julie A. Walker, Exec. Dir.; Cindy C. Welch, Deputy Exec. Dir.; Audra Caplan, Pres. A division of the American Library Association, YALSA seeks to advocate, promote, and strengthen service to young adults as part of the continuum of total library services, and assumes responsibility within the ALA to evaluate and select books and nonbook media and to interpret and make recommendations regarding their use with young adults. Committees include Best Books for Young Adults, Popular Paperbacks, Quick Picks for Reluctant Young Adults, Intellectual Freedom, Outreach to Young Adults with Special Needs, Outstanding Books for the College Bound, Youth Participation, Media Selection and Usage, Publishers Liaison, and Selected Films for Young Adults. *Membership:* 4,100. YALSA members may be young adult librarians, library directors, childrens librarians, publishers, or anyone for whom library service to young adults is important. *Dues:* $40 (in addition to ALA membership); $15, students. *Meetings:* two conferences yearly, Midwinter (January or February) and Annual (June or July). *Publications: Young Adult Library Services: A Journal* (twice a year). *YAttitudes:* a quarterly electronic newsletter.

Part Five
Graduate Programs

Introduction

This directory describes graduate programs in Instructional Technology, Educational Media and Communications, School Library Media, and closely allied programs in the United States. One institution indicated that their program had been discontinued, and that program was deleted from the listings. Masters, specialist, and doctoral degrees are combined into one unified list.

Entries provide as much of the following information as furnished by respondents: (1) name and address of the institution; (2) chairperson or other individual in charge of the program; (3) types of degrees offered and specialization, emphases, or tracks, including information on careers for which candidates are prepared; (4) special features of the degree program; (5) admission requirements; (6) degree requirements; (7) number of full-time and part-time faculty; (8) number of full-time and part-time students; (9) types of financial assistance available; and (10) the number of degrees awarded by type in 2004. All grade-point averages (GPAs), test scores, and degree requirements are minimums unless stated otherwise. The Graduate Record Examination, Miller Analogies Test, National Teacher's Examination, and other standardized tests are referred to by their acronyms. The Test of English as a Foreign Language (TOEFL) appears in many of the *Admission Requirements,* and in most cases this test is required only for international students. Although some entries explicitly state application fees, most do not. Prospective students should assume that most institutions require a completed application, transcripts of all previous collegiate work, and a nonrefundable application fee.

Directors of advanced professional programs for instructional technology or media specialists should find this degree program information useful as a means of comparing their own offerings and requirements with those of institutions offering comparable programs. This listing, along with the Classified List, should also assist individuals in locating institutions that best suit their interests and requirements. In addition, a comparison of degree programs across several years may help scholars with historical interests trace trends and issues in the field over time.

Information in this section can be considered current as of early 2004 for most programs. Information for this section was obtained by e-mail directing each organization to an individual Web form through which the updated information could be submitted electronically. Although the section editor made every effort to contact and follow up with program representatives, it is up to the program representatives to respond to the annual request for an update. The editing team would like to thank those respondents who helped ensure the currency and accuracy of this section by responding to the request for an update.

Additional information on the programs listed, including admission procedure instructions, may be obtained by contacting individual program coordinators. General or graduate catalogs and specific program information usually are furnished for a minimal charge. In addition, most graduate programs now have e-mail contact addresses and Web sites that provide a wealth of descriptive information.

Again, we are indebted to those individuals who responded to our requests for information. Although the editors expended considerable effort to ensure currency and completeness of the listings, there may be institutions within the United States that now have programs of which we are unaware. Readers are encouraged to furnish new information to the publisher who, in turn, will contact the program for inclusion in the next edition of *EMTY.*

Jo McClendon

329

Graduate Programs in Instructional Technology (IT)

CLASSIFIED LIST

Computer Applications

California State University-San Bernardino [M.A.]
State University of New York at Stony Brook [Master's: Technological Systems Management/ Educational Computing]
Temple University. Instructional and Learning Technology (ILT)/ Educational Psychology Program [Ed.M., Ph.D.]
University of Iowa [M.A.]
Valdosta State University [M.Ed. in IT/Technology Applications]

Computer Education

Appalachian State University [M.A.: Educational Media and Technology/Computers]
Arkansas Tech University [Master's]
Buffalo State College [M.S.: Education/Educational Computing]
California State University-Dominguez Hills [M.A., Certificate: Computer-Based Education]
California State University-Los Angeles [M.A. in Education/Computer Education]
California State University-San Bernardino [Advanced Certificate Program: Educational Computing]
Central Connecticut State University [M.S.: Educational Technology/Computer Technologies]
Concordia University [M.A.: Computer Science Education]
East Carolina University [M.A.: Education/IT Computers]
Eastern Washington University [M.Ed.: Computer Education]
Emporia State University. School of Library and Information Management Fairfield University [M.A.: Media/Educational Technology with Computers in Education]
Florida Institute of Technology [Master's, Ph.D.: Computer Education]
Fontbonne College [M.S.]
George Mason University [M.Ed.: Special Education Technology, Computer Science Educator]
Iowa State University [M.S., M.Ed., Ph.D.: Curriculum and IT/Instructional Computing]
Jacksonville University [Master's: Computer Education]
Kansas State University [M.S. in Secondary Education/Educational Computing; Ed.D., Ph.D.: Curriculum and Instruction/Educational Computing]
Kent State University [M.A., M.Ed.: Instructional Computing]
Minot State University [M.Ed., M.S.: Math and Computer Science]
New York Institute of Technology [Specialist Certificate: Computers in Education]
North Carolina State University [M.S., M.Ed.: IT-Computers]
Northern Illinois University [M.S.Ed., Ed.D.: IT/Educational Computing]
Northwest Missouri State University [M.S.: School Computer Studies; M.S.Ed.: Educational Uses of Computers]
Nova Southeastern University [M.S., Ed.S.: Computer Science Education]
Ohio University [M.Ed.: Computer Education and Technology]
Pace University [M.S.E.: Curriculum and Instruction/Computers]

San Diego State University [Master's in Educational Technology/Computers in Education]
San Francisco State University [Master's: Instructional Computing]
San Jose State University [Master's: Computers and Interactive Technologies]
State University College of Arts and Sciences at Potsdam [M.S.Ed.: IT and Media Management/Educational Computing]
State University of New York at Stony Brook [Master's: Technological Systems Management/Educational Computing]
Syracuse University [M.S., Ed.D., Ph.D., Advanced Certificate: Media Production]
Texas A&M University-Commerce [Master's: Learning Technology and Information Systems/Educational Micro Computing]
Texas Tech University [M.Ed.: IT/Educational Computing]
University of Georgia [M.Ed., Ed.S.: Computer-Based Education]
University of Illinois at Urbana-Champaign [M.A., M.S., Ed.M.: Educational Computing; Ph.D.: Education Psychology/Educational Computing]
University of Memphis. Instruction and Curriculum Leadership/Instructional Design & Technology [M. S., Ed.D]
University of North Texas [M.S.: Computer Education and Instructional Systems]
The University of Oklahoma [Master's: Computer Applications]
University of Toledo [Master's, Ed.S., D.Ed.: Instructional Computing]
University of Washington [Master's, Ed.D., Ph.D.]
Virginia Polytechnic Institute and State University [M.A., Ed.D., Ph.D.: IT]
Wright State University [M.Ed.: Computer Education; M.A.: Computer Education]

Distance Education

Emporia State University. School of Library and Information Management [Ph.D.: Library and Information Management]
Fairfield University [M.A.: Media/Educational Technology with Satellite Communications]
Iowa State University [M.S., M.Ed., Ph.D.: Curriculum and IT]
New York Institute of Technology [Specialist certificate]
Nova Southeastern University [M.S., Ed.D.: IT]
San Jose State University [Master's: Telecommunications & online courses via Internet]
Texas A&M University [Ph.D.: EDCI]
Texas Tech University [M.Ed.: IT]
University of Missouri-Columbia. College of Education [Masters: Technology in Schools, Networked Learning Systems, or Training and Development]
University of Northern Colorado [Ph.D.: Educational Technology]
Western Illinois University [Master's]

Educational Leadership

Auburn University [Ed.D.]
Barry University [Ph.D.: Educational Technology Leadership]
George Washington University [M.A.: Education and Human Development/Educational Technology Leadership]
United States International University [Master's, Ed.D.: Technology Leadership for Learning]
University of Colorado at Denver [Ph.D.: Educational Leadership and Innovation/Curriculum, Learning, and Technology]
Valdosta State University [M.Ed., Ed.S.: IT/Technology Leadership]

Human Performance

Boise State University [M.S.: IT and Performance Technology]
Governors State University [M.A.: Communication with Human Performance and Technology]
Temple University. Instructional and Learning Technology (ILT)/ Educational Psychology
        Program [Ed.M., Ph.D.]
University of Southern California [Ed.D.: Human Performance Technology]
University of Toledo [Master's, Ed.S., Ed.D.: Human Resources Development]

Information Studies

Drexel University [M.S., M.S.I.S.]
Emporia State University [Ph.D.: Library and Information Management]
Rutgers [M.L.S.: Information Retrieval; Ph.D.: Communication (Information Systems)]
Simmons College [M.S.: Information Science/Systems]
Southern Connecticut State University [Sixth Year Professional Diploma: Library-Information
        Studies/IT]
St. Cloud State University [Master's, Ed.S.: Information Technologies]
Texas A&M-Commerce [Master's: Learning Technology and Information Systems/Library
        and Information Science]
University of Alabama [Ph.D.]
University of Arizona [M.A.: Information Resources and Library Science]
University of Central Arkansas [M.S.: Information Science/Media Information Studies]
University of Florida. School of Teaching and Learning. [M.S., Ed.S., Ed.D., Ph.D.]
University of Maryland [Doctorate: Library and Information Services]
University of Missouri-Columbia [Ph.D.: Information and Learning Technologies]
The University of Oklahoma [Dual Master's: Educational Technology and Library and In-
        formation Systems]
The University of Rhode Island [M.L.I.S.]
University of Washington [Master's, Ed.D., Ph.D.]
Western Oregon State College [MS: Information Technology]

Innovation

Pennsylvania State University [M.Ed., M.S., Ed.D., Ph.D.: Instructional Systems/Emerging
        Technologies]
University of Colorado at Denver [Ph.D.: Educational Leadership and Innovation]
Walden University [M.S., Ph.D.: Educational Change and Technology Innovation]

Instructional Design and Development

Arizona State University, Educational Technology [M.A., Ph.D.]
Auburn University [M.Ed., M.S.]
Bloomsburg University [M.S.: IT]
Brigham Young University [M.S., Ph.D.]
Clarion University of Pennsylvania [M.S.: Communication/Training and Development]
Fairfield University [Certificate of Advanced Studies: Media/Educational Technology: In-
        structional Development]
George Mason University [M.Ed.: IT/Instructional Design and Development]

Governors State University [M.A.: Communication with Human Performance and Training/
   Instructional Design]
Indiana University [Ph.D., Ed.D.: Instructional Analysis, Design, and Development]
Iowa State University [M.S., M.Ed., Ph.D.: Curriculum and IT/Instruction Design]
Ithaca College [M.S.: Corporate Communications]
Lehigh University [Master's]
Michigan State University [M.A.: Educational Technology and Instructional Design]
North Carolina Central University [M.S.: Instructional Development/Design]
Northern Illinois University [M.S.Ed., Ed.D.: IT/Instructional Design]
Pennsylvania State University [M.Ed., M.S., D.Ed., Ph.D.: Instructional Systems/Systems
   Design]
Purdue University [Master's, Specialist, Ph.D.: Instructional Development]
San Francisco State University [Master's/Training and Designing Development]
San Jose State University [M.S.: Instructional Design and Development]
Southern Illinois University at Carbondale [M.S.: Education/Instructional Design]
State University of New York at Albany [M.Ed., Ph.D.: Curriculum and Instruction/In-
   structional Design and Technology]
State University of New York at Stony Brook [Master's: Technological Systems Manage-
   ment/Educational Computing]
Syracuse University [M.S., Ed.D., Ph.D., Advanced Certificate: Instructional Design; Edu-
   cational Evaluation; Instructional Development]
Temple University. Instructional and Learning Technology (ILT)/ Educational Psychology
   Program [Ed.M., Ph.D.]
Towson State University [M.S.: Instructional Development]
University of Cincinnati [M.A., Ed.D.: Curriculum and Instruction/Instructional Design
   and Technology]
University of Colorado at Denver [Master's, Ph.D.: Instructional Design]
University of Florida. School of Teaching and Learning. [M.S., Ed.S., Ed.D., Ph.D.]
University of Houston at Clear Lake [Instructional Design]
University of Illinois at Urbana-Champaign [M.A., M.S., Ed.M.; Ph.D. in Educational
   Psychology/Instructional Design]
University of Iowa [M.A., Ph.D.: Training and Human Resources Development]
University of Massachusetts-Boston [M.Ed.]
University of Memphis. Instruction and Curriculum Leadership/Instructional Design &
   Technology [M. S., Ed.D]
University of Missouri-Columbia [Master's, Ed.S., Ph.D.]
University of Northern Colorado [Ph.D. in Educational Technology/Instructional Develop-
   ment and Design]
The University of Oklahoma [Master's]
University of Toledo [Master's, Specialist, doctorate: Instructional Development]
University of Washington [Master's, Ed.D., Ph.D.]
Utah State University [M.S., Ed.S.: Instructional Development]
Virginia Polytechnic Institute and State University [Master's, Ed.D., Ph.D.: IT]

Instructional Technology [IT]

Appalachian State University [M.A.: Educational Media and Technology]
Arizona State University, Educational Technology program. [M.Ed., Ph.D.]
Azusa Pacific University [M.Ed.]

Barry University [M.S., Ed.S.: Educational Technology]

Bloomsburg University [M.S.: IT]

Boise State University [M.S.]

Boston University [Ed.M., Certificate of Advanced Graduate Study: Educational Media &
Technology; Ed.D.: Curriculum and Teaching/Educational Media and Technology]

California State University-Los Angeles [M.A.: Education/IT]

California State University-San Bernardino [Advanced Certificate in Educational Technology]

Central Connecticut State University [M.S.: Educational Technology]

Clarke College [M.A.: Technology and Education]

East Carolina University [M.A.: Education/IT Computers]

East Tennessee State [M.Ed.]

Eastern Michigan University [M.A.: Educational Psychology/Educational Technology]

Edgewood College [M.A.: Education/IT]

Fairfield University [M.A., Certificate of Advanced Study: Media/Educational Technology]

Fitchburg State College [M.S.: Communications Media/IT]

Florida Institute of Technology [Master's, Ph.D.]

George Mason University [M.Ed., Ph.D.]

George Washington University [M.A.: Education and Human Development/Educational
Technology Leadership]

Georgia Southern University [M.Ed., Ed.S.: IT; Ed.D.: Curriculum Studies/IT]

Georgia State University [M.S., Ph.D.]

Harvard University [M.Ed.: Technology in Education]

Indiana State University [Master's, Ed.S.]

Indiana University [M.S., Ed.S., Ed.D., Ph.D.]

Iowa State University [M.S., M.Ed., Ph.D.: Curriculum and IT]

Jacksonville University [Master's: Educational Technology and Integrated Learning]

Johns Hopkins University [M.S. in Educational Technology for Educators]

Kent State University [M.Ed., M.A; Ph.D.: Educational Psychology/IT]

Lehigh University [Master's; Ed.D.: Educational Technology]

Lesley College [M.Ed., Certificate of Advanced Graduate Study: Technology Education;
Ph.D.: Education/Technology Education]

Mankato State University [M.S.: Educational Technology]

Michigan State University [M.A.: Educational Technology]

Montclair State College [certification]

New York Institute of Technology [Master's]

New York University [M.A., Certificate of Advanced Study in Education, Ed.D., Ph.D.]

North Carolina Central University [M.A.: Educational Technology]

North Carolina State University [M.Ed., M.S.: IT—Computers; Ph.D.: Curriculum and
Instruction/IT]

Northern Illinois University [M.S.Ed., Ed.D.]

Nova Southeastern University [Ed.S., M.S.: Educational Technology; M.S., Ed.D.: IT]

Ohio University [M.Ed.: Computer Education and Technology]

Purdue University [Master's, Specialist, Ph.D.: Educational Technology]

Radford University [M.S.: Education/Educational Media/Technology]

Rosemont College [M.Ed.: Technology in Education; Certificate in Professional Study in
Technology in Education]

San Diego State University [Master's: Educational Technology]

Southern Connecticut State University [M.S.]

Southern Illinois University at Carbondale [M.S.: Education; Ph.D.: Education/IT]

State University College of Arts and Sciences at Potsdam [M.S.: Education/IT]

State University of New York at Albany [M.Ed., Ph.D.: Curriculum and Instruction/Instructional Theory, Design, and Technology]

State University of West Georgia [M.Ed., Ed.S.]

Temple University. Instructional and Learning Technology (ILT)/ Educational Psychology Program [Ed.M., Ph.D.]

Texas A&M University [M.Ed.: Educational Technology; Ph.D.: EDCI/Educational Technology; Ph.D.: Educational Psychology Foundations/Learning and Technology]

Texas A&M University-Commerce [Master's: Learning Technology and Information Systems/Educational Media and Technology]

Texas Tech University [M.Ed.; Ed.D.]

United States International University [Ed.D.: Technology and Learning]

University of Central Florida [M.A.: IT/Instructional Systems, IT/Educational Media; doctorate: Curriculum and Instruction/IT]

University of Cincinnati [M.A., Ed.D.: Curriculum and Instruction/Instructional Design and Technology]

University of Colorado at Denver [Master's, Ph.D.: Learning Technologies]

University of Connecticut [Master's, Ph.D.: Educational Technology]

University of Florida. School of Teaching and Learning. [M.S., Ed.S., Ed.D., Ph.D.]

University of Georgia [M.Ed., Ed.S., Ph.D.]

University of Hawaii-Manoa [M.Ed.: Educational Technology]

University of Houston. Department of Curriculum and Instruction. [M.Ed.]

University of Louisville [M.Ed.: Occupational Education/IT]

University of Maryland [Ph.D.: Library Science and Educational Technology/Instructional Communication]

University of Massachusetts-Lowell [M.Ed., Ed.D., Certificate of Advanced Graduate Study: Educational Technology]

University of Michigan [Master's, Ph.D.: IT]

University of Missouri-Columbia [Master's, Ed.S., Ph.D.]

University of Nebraska at Kearney [M.S.]

University of Nevada [M.S., Ph.D.]

University of Northern Colorado [M.A., Ph.D.: Educational Technology]

University of Northern Iowa [M.A.: Educational Technology]

The University of Oklahoma [Master's: Educational Technology Generalist; Educational Technology; Teaching with Technology; dual Master's: Educational Technology and Library and Information Systems; doctorate: Instructional Psychology and Technology]

University of South Alabama [M.S., Ph.D.]

University of South Carolina [Master's]

University of Southern California [M.A., Ed.D., Ph.D.]

University of Tennessee-Knoxville [M.S.: Education, Ed.S., Ed.D., Ph.D.]

The University of Texas [Master's, Ph.D.]

University of Toledo [Master's, Specialist, doctorate]

University of Virginia [M.Ed., Ed.S., Ed.D., Ph.D.]

University of Washington [Master's, Ed.D., Ph.D.]

University of Wisconsin-Madison [M.S., Ph.D.]

Universiti Sains Malaysia. Centre for Instructional Technology and Multimedia Centre for Instructional Tech and Multimedia [M.Ed. Instructional Technology, Ph.D. Instructional Technology]

Utah State University [M.S., Ed.S., Ph.D.]

Virginia Polytechnic Institute and State University [M.A., Ed.D., Ph.D.: IT]

Virginia State University [M.S., M.Ed.: Educational Technology]

Wayne State University [Master's, Ed.D., Ph.D., Ed.S.]

Webster University [Master's]

Western Illinois University [Master's]

Western Washington University [M.Ed.: IT in Adult Education; Elementary Education; IT in Secondary Education]

Wright State University [Specialist: Curriculum and Instruction/Educational Technology; Higher Education/Educational Technology]

Integration

Bloomsburg University [M.S.: IT]

George Mason University [M.Ed.: IT/Integration of Technology in Schools]

Jacksonville University [Master's: Educational Technology and Integrated Learning]

University of Northern Colorado [Ph.D.: Educational Technology/Technology Integration]

Management

Bloomsburg University [M.S.: IT]

Central Connecticut State University [M.S.: Educational Technology/Media Management]

Drexel University [M.S., M.S.I.S.]

Emporia State University [Ph.D.: Library and Information Management]

Fairfield University [Certificate of Advanced Studies: Media/Educational Technology with Media Management]

Fitchburg State College [M.S.: Communications Media/Management]

Indiana University [Ed.D., Ph.D.: Implementation and Management]

Northern Illinois University [M.S.Ed., Ed.D.: IT/Media Administration]

Rutgers [M.L.S.: Management and Policy Issues]

Simmons College [M.L.S.: History (Archives Management); Doctor of Arts: Administration; Media Management]

State University College of Arts and Science [M.S.: Education/IT and Media Management]

State University of New York at Stony Brook [Master's: Technological Systems Management]

Syracuse University [M.S., Ed.D., Ph.D., Advanced Certificate]

Temple University. Instructional and Learning Technology (ILT)/ Educational Psychology Program [Ed.M., Ph.D.]

University of Tennessee-Knoxville [Certification: Instructional Media Supervisor]

Virginia Polytechnic Institute and State University [M.A., Ed.D., Ph.D.: IT]

Wright State University [M.Ed.: Media Supervisor; Computer Coord.]

Media

Appalachian State University [M.A.: Educational Media and Technology/Media Management]

Boston University [Ed.M., Certificate of Advanced Graduate Study: Educational Media and Technology; Ed.D.: Curriculum and Teaching/Educational Media and Technology]

Central Connecticut State University [M.S.: Educational Technology/Materials Production]

Fitchburg State College [M.S.: Communications Media]

Indiana State University [Ph.D.: Curriculum and Instruction/Media Technology]
Indiana University [Ed.D., Ph.D.: Instructional Development and Production]
Jacksonville State University [M.S.: Education/Instructional Media]
Montclair State College [certification]
Radford University [M.S.: Education/Educational Media/Technology]
San Jose State University [Master's.: Media Design and Development/Media Services
    Management]
Simmons College [Master's: Media Management]
St. Cloud State University [Master's, Ed.S.: Educational Media]
State University College of Arts and Science at Potsdam [M.S.: Education/IT and Media
    Management]
Syracuse University [M.S., Ed.D., Ph.D., Advanced Certificate: Media Production]
Texas A&M University-Commerce [Master's: Learning Technology and Information Systems/
    Educational Media and Technology]
University of Central Florida [M.Ed.: IT/Educational Media]
University of Florida. School of Teaching and Learning. [M.S., Ed.S., Ed.D., Ph.D.]
University of Iowa [M.A.: Media Design and Production]
University of Memphis. Instruction and Curriculum Leadership/Instructional Design &
    Technology [M. S. and Ed. D]
University of Nebraska at Kearney [M.S., Ed.S.: Educational Media]
University of Nebraska-Omaha [M.S.: Education/Educational Media; M.A.: Education/
    Educational Media]
University of South Alabama [M.A., Ed.S.]
University of Tennessee-Knoxville [Ph.D.: Instructional Media and Technology; Ed.D.:
    Curriculum and Instruction/Instructional Media and Technology]
University of Virginia [M.Ed., Ed.S., Ed.D., Ph.D.: Media Production]
Virginia Polytechnic Institute and State University [M.A., Ed.D., Ph.D.: IT]
Wright State University [M.Ed.: Educational Media; Media Supervision; M.A.: Educa-
    tional Media]

Multimedia

Bloomsburg University [M.S.: IT]
Brigham Young University [M.S.: Multimedia Production]
Fairfield University [M.A.: Media/Educational Technology with Multimedia]
Ithaca College [M.S.: Corporate Communications]
Jacksonville University [Master's: Educational Technology and Integration Learning]
Johns Hopkins University [Graduate Certificate]
Lehigh University [Master's]
New York Institute of Technology [Specialist Certificate]
San Francisco State University [Master's: Instructional Multimedia Design]
State University of New York at Stony Brook [Master's: Technological Systems Management/
    Educational Computing]
Syracuse University [M.S., Ed.D., Ph.D., Advanced Certificate: Media Production]
Temple University. Instructional and Learning Technology (ILT)/ Educational Psychology
    Program [Ed.M., Ph.D.]
Texas A&M University [M.Ed.: Educational Technology]
University of Northern Colorado [Ph.D.: Educational Technology/Interactive Technology]
University of Virginia [M.Ed., Ed.S., Ed.D., Ph.D.: Interactive Multimedia]

University of Washington [Master's, Ed.D., Ph.D.]
University of Memphis. Instruction and Curriculum Leadership/Instructional Design & Technology [M. S. and Ed. D]
Utah State University [M.S., Ed.S.]
Wayne State University [Master's: Interactive Technologies]
Western Illinois University [Master's: Interactive Technologies]

Research

Brigham Young University [M.S., Ph.D.: Research and Evaluation]
Drexel University [M.S., M.S.I.S.]
Iowa State University [Ph.D.: Educational/Technology Research]
Syracuse University [M.S., Ed.D., Ph.D., Advanced Certificate: Educational Research and Theory]
University of Washington [Master's, Ed.D., Ph.D.]

School Library Media

Alabama State University [Master's, Ed.S., Ph.D.]
Arkansas Tech University [Master's]
Auburn University [M.ED., Ed.S.]
Bloomsburg University [M.S.]
Boston University [Massachusetts certification]
Bridgewater State College [M.Ed.]
Central Connecticut State University [M.S.: Educational Technology/Librarianship]
Chicago State University [Master's]
East Carolina University [M.L.S., Certificate of Advanced Study]
East Tennessee State [M.Ed.: Instructional Media]
Emporia State University [Ph.D.: Library and Information Management; M.L.S.; School Library certification]
Kent State University
Louisiana State University [M.L.I.S., C.L.I.S. (post-Master's certificate), Louisiana School Library certification]
Mankato State University [M.S.]
Northern Illinois University [M.S.Ed. Instructional Technology with Illinois state certification]
Nova Southeastern University [Ed.S, M.S.: Educational Media]
Radford University [M.S.: Education/Educational Media; licensure]
Rutgers [M.L.S., Ed.S.]
Simmons College [M.L.S.: Education]
Southern Illinois University at Edwardsville [M.S. in Education: Library/Media]
St. Cloud State University [Master's, Ed.S.]
St. John's University [M.L.S.]
State University of West Georgia [M.Ed., Ed.S.: Media]
Towson State University [M.S.]
University of Alabama [Master's, Ed.S.]
University of Central Arkansas [M.S.]
University of Florida. School of Teaching and Learning. [M.S., Ed.S., Ed.D., Ph.D.]
University of Georgia [M.Ed., Ed.S]
University of Maryland [M.L.S.]

University of Montana [Master's, Ed.S.]
University of North Carolina [M.S.]
University of Northern Colorado [M.A.: Educational Media]
University of South Florida [Master's]
University of Toledo
University of Wisconsin-La Crosse [M.S.: Professional Development/Initial Instructional
    Library Specialist; Instructional Library Media Specialist]
Utah State University [M.S., Ed.S.]
Valdosta State University [M.Ed., Ed.S.: Instructional Technology/Library/Media]
Webster University
Western Maryland College [M.S.]
William Paterson College [M.Ed., Ed.S., Associate]

Special Education

George Mason University [M.Ed.: IT/Assistive/Special Education Technology; M.Ed.:
    Special Education Technology; Ph.D.: Special Education Technology]
Johns Hopkins University [M.S. in Special Education/Technology in Special Education]
Western Washington University [M.Ed.: IT in Special Education]

Systems

Bloomsburg University [M.S.: IT]
Drexel University [M.S., M.S.I.S.]
Florida State University [M.S., Ed.S., Ph.D.: Instructional Systems]
Pennsylvania State University [M.Ed., M.S., D.Ed., Ph.D.: Instructional Systems]
Simmons College [Master's: Information Science/Systems]
Southern Illinois University at Edwardsville [M.S.: Education/Instructional Systems Design]
State University of New York at Stony Brook [Master's: Technological Systems Management]
Texas A&M University-Commerce [Master's: Learning Technology and Information Systems]
University of Central Florida [M.A.: IT/Instructional Systems]
University of Maryland, Baltimore County [Master's: School Instructional Systems]
University of North Texas [M.S.: Computer Education and Instructional Systems]
The University of Oklahoma [Dual Master's: Educational Technology and Library and In-
    formation Systems]

Technology Design

Governors State University [M.A.: Design Logistics]
Kansas State University [Ed.D., Ph.D.: Curriculum and Instruction/Educational Comput-
    ing, Design, and Telecommunications]
United States International University [Master's, Ed.D.: Designing Technology for Learning]
University of Colorado at Denver [Master's, Ph.D.: Design of Learning Technologies]

Telecommunications

Appalachian State University [M.A.: Educational Media and Technology/Telecommunications]
Johns Hopkins University [Graduate Certificate]
Kansas State University [Ed.D., Ph.D.: Curriculum and Instruction/Educational Comput-
    ing, Design, and Telecommunications]

San Jose State University [Telecommunications and Distance Learning]
Western Illinois University [Masters: Telecommunications]

Training

Clarion University of Pennsylvania [M.S.: Communication/Training and Development]
Pennsylvania State University [M.Ed., M.S., D.Ed., Ph.D.: Instructional Systems/Corporate Training]
St. Cloud State University [Master's, Ed.S.: Human Resources Development/Training]
Syracuse University [M.S., Ed.D., Ph.D., Advanced Certificate]
University of Maryland, Baltimore County [Master's: Training in Business and Industry]
University of Northern Iowa [M.A.: Communications and Training Technology]
Wayne State University [Master's: Business and Human Services Training]

Video Production

California State University-San Bernardino [M.A.]
Fairfield University [Certificate of Advanced Study: Media/Educational Technology with TV Production]

ALPHABETICAL LIST

Alabama

Alabama State University. Department of Instructional Support Programs. 915 South Jackson Street, Montgomery, AL 36101-0271. (334) 229-6829. Fax (334) 229-6904. http://www.alasu.edu. Dr. Agnes Bellel, Coord. Instructional Technology and Media. abellel@asunet.alasu.edu. *Specializations:* School media specialist preparation (K–12) only; master's and specialist degrees. *Features:* N/A. *Admission Requirements:* The applicant must hold a bachelor's degree from an accredited institution. All admission requirements for graduate programs in education should be completed prior to registration for courses. Application forms should be secured from and returned to the School of Graduate Studies. Full admission status should be granted to persons who meet all applicable admission requirements prior to enrollment. Under extraordinary circumstances, a student may be considered as conditionally admitted, but in all circumstances, the requirements for admission to graduate program in education must be met during the *first enrollment period.* When such requirements are met, the student's status will be changed from conditional to full admission, retroactive to the beginning of the enrollment period. A special status may be granted to those persons who do not wish to pursue a degree program but who wish to enroll in a limited number of graduate classes. Admission to a master's degree program requires that the applicant:

1. hold a Class B Certificate (General Counseling does not require a teachers certificate);

2. take and attain satisfactory scores on specified national tests (Graduate Record Examination [GRE] or Miller Analogy Test [MAT];

3. for all graduate programs, the applicant must submit two letters of recommendation from persons who are qualified to evaluate an applicants ability to do graduate work;

4. hold a Class A Certificate in a teaching field (for admission to a certification program in Administration and Supervision only).

Admission to an Education Specialist degree program requires that the applicant:

1. hold professional certification and a master's degree in the area they want to pursue an Education Specialist degree in;

2. have at least two years of successful work experience;

3. must have a 3.25 G.P.A. on master's degree;

4. make a satisfactory score on the Graduate Record Examination (GRE) or Miller Analogy Test (MAT);

5. AA Certification Programs require a 3.25 graduate G.P.A., appropriate Class A Certification, and approval of the major department.

Degree Requirements: master's: 33 semester hours with 300 clock-hour internship. specialist: 36 semester hours in 600-level courses. *Faculty:* 13. *Students:* master's, 50 part-time; specialist, 8 part-time. *Financial Assistance:* student loans and scholarships. *De-*

grees Awarded 2003: 15 M.Ed., 1 Ed.S.

Auburn University. Educational Foundations, Leadership, and Technology. 3402 Haley Center, Auburn, AL 36849-5216. (334) 844-4291. Fax (334) 844-4292. http://www.auburn.edu/academic/college_of_education/academics/departments/eflt.html. Susan H. Bannon, Associate Professor & Program Coordinator. bannosh@auburn.edu. *Specializations:* M.Ed. (nonthesis) and Ed.S. for school library media certification. *Features:* The Department of Educational Foundations, Leadership & Technology (EFLT) prepares exemplary educational practitioners and develops cooperative partnerships with university departments, schools, community agencies, and business and industry to provide high-quality educators, trainers and leaders. Faculty are committed to guiding students toward becoming competent and professional educational leaders. This department ensures that students will participate in theoretical, applied and practitioner-based research enhancing the fields of Adult Education, Educational Leadership, Educational Media/Technology and Educational Psychology. Outreach partnerships are continually established in these respective fields to provide students with an informative and experiential curriculum. All programs emphasize interactive technologies and computers. *Admission Requirements:* All programs: graduate school admission; GRE test scores less than 5 years old; three letters of recommendation; bachelor's degree from accredited institution; and teacher certification at least at bachelor's level. *Degree Requirements:* Library Media Master's: 33 semester hours. Specialist: 30 semester hours. *Faculty:* 3 full-time. *Students:* 2 full-time, 15 part-time. *Financial Assistance:* graduate assistantships. *Degrees Awarded 2003:* 2.

Jacksonville State University. Educational Resources. 700 Pelham Road N., Jacksonville, AL 36265. (256) 782-5096. Fax (256) 782-5872. http://www.jsu.edu. Dr. Martha Merrill, Coord., Instructional Media Program. mmerrill@jsucc.jsu.edu. *Specializations:* M.S. in Education with emphasis in Library Media. Add-on Certification in Library Media. *Features:* Technology, Management, Literature, Reference. *Admission Requirements:* bachelor's degree in Education. *Degree Requirements:* 36-39 semester hours including 24 hours in library media. *Faculty:* 2 full-time. *Students:* 30 full- and part-time. *Financial Assistance:* Yes. *Degrees Awarded 2003:* 10.

University of Alabama. School of Library and Information Studies. Box 870252, Tuscaloosa, AL 35487-0252. (205) 348-4610. Fax (205) 348-3746. http://www.slis.ua.edu. Joan Atkinson, Director; Gordy Coleman, Coordinator of School Media Program. jatkinso@slis.ua.edu; gcoleman@slis.ua.edu. *Specializations:* M.L.I.S. degrees in a varied program including school, public, academic, and special libraries. Ph.D. in the larger College of Communication and Information Sciences; flexibility in creating individual programs of study. Also a Master of Fine Arts Program in Book Arts (including history of the book). *Features:* M.L.I.S. is one of 56 accredited programs in the United States and Canada. *Admission Requirements:* M.L.I.S.: 3.0 GPA; 50 MAT or 1000 GRE and an acceptable score on Analytical Writing. Doctoral: 3.0 GPA; 60 MAT or 1200 GRE and acceptable score on Analytical Writing. *Degree Requirements:* master's: 36 semester hours. Doctoral: 48–60 semester hours plus 24 hours dissertation research. *Faculty:* 10 full-time; five part-time. *Students:* master's, 45 full-time, 140 part-time; doctoral, 1 full-time, 3 part-time. *Financial Assistance:* assistantships, grants, student loans, scholarships, work assistance, campus work. *Degrees Awarded 2003:* 88 M.L.I.S; 4 educational specialist; 3 MFA in Book Arts.

University of South Alabama. Department of Behavioral Studies and Educational Technology, College of Education. University Commons 3700, Mobile, AL 36688. (251) 380-2861. Fax (251) 380-2713. http://www.southalabama.edu/coe/bset/. Daniel W. Surry, IDD Program Coor.; Mary Ann Robinson, Ed Media Program Coor. dsurry@usouthal.edu. *Specializations:* M.S. and Ph.D. in Instructional Design and Development. M.Ed. in Educational Media (Ed Media). Online master's degrees in ED Media and IDD are available for qualified students. For information about online master's degree programs, http://usaonline.southalabama.edu. *Features:* The IDD master's and doctoral programs emphasize extensive education and training in the instructional design process, human performance technology and multimedia- and online-based training. The IDD doctoral program has an additional emphasis in research design and statistical analysis. The Ed Media master's program prepares students in planning, designing, and administering library/media centers at most levels of education, including higher education. *Admission Requirements:* For the ED Media & IDD master's: undergraduate degree in appropriate academic field from an accredited university or college; admission to graduate school; satisfactory score on the GRE. ED Media students must have completed requirements for a certificate at the baccalaureate or master's level in a teaching field. For IDD Ph.D.: master's degree, all undergraduate and graduate transcripts, three letters of recommendation, written statement of purpose for pursuing Ph.D. in IDD, satisfactory score on GRE. *Degree Requirements:* Ed Media master's: satisfactorily complete program requirements (minimum 33 semester hours), 3.0 or better GPA, satisfactory score on comprehensive exam. IDD master's: satisfactorily complete program requirements (minimum 40 semester hours), 3.0 or better GPA; satisfactory complete comprehensive exam. Ph.D.: satisfactory complete program requirements (minimum 82 semester hours of approved graduate courses), one-year residency, satisfactory score on examinations (research and statistical exam and comprehensive exam), approved dissertation completed. Any additional requirements will be determined by students doctoral advisory committee. *Faculty:* 17 full-time in department; 8 part-time faculty. *Students:* 68 IDD master's, 100 Ph.D., 44 Ed Media master's, 26 Ed Media certificate. *Financial Assistance:* 10 graduate assistantships. *Degrees Awarded 2003:* 12 Ed Media master's; 10 IDD master's; 5 IDD doctoral.

Arizona

Arizona State University; Educational Technology program. Division of Psychology in Education. Box 870611, Tempe, AZ 85287-0611. (480) 965-3384. Fax (480) 965-0300. http://coe.asu.edu/psyched. James D. Klein, Professor; Nancy Archer, Admissions Secretary. dpe@asu.edu. *Specializations:* The Educational Technology program at Arizona State University offers an M.Ed. degree and a Ph.D. degree that focus on the design, development, and evaluation of instructional systems and educational technology applications to support learning. *Features:* The program offers courses in a variety of areas such as instructional design technology, media development, technology integration, performance improvement, evaluation, and distance education. The doctoral program emphasizes research using educational technology in applied settings. *Admission Requirements:* Requirements for admission to the M.Ed. program include a 4-year undergraduate GPA of 3.0 or above and a score of either 500 or above on verbal section of the GRE or 50 or above on the MAT. A score of 550 or above on the paper-based TOEFL (or 213 on the computer-based test) is also required for students who do not speak English as their first language. Requirements for admission to the Ph.D. program include a 4-year undergraduate GPA of 3.20 or above and a combined score of 1200 or above on the verbal and quantitative sections of the GRE. A score of 600 or above on the paper-based TOEFL (or 250 on the computer-based test) is also required for students who do not speak English as their first language. *Degree Requirements:* The M.Ed. degree requires completion of a minimum of 30 credit hours including 18 credit hours of required coursework and a minimum of 12 credit hours of electives. M.Ed. students also must complete an internship and a comprehensive examination. The Ph.D. degree requires a minimum of 84 semester hours beyond the bachelor's degree. At least 54 of these hours must be taken at ASU after admission to the program. Ph.D. students must fulfill a residence requirement and are required to be continuously enrolled in the program. Students also take a comprehensive examination and must satisfy a publication requirement prior to beginning work on their dissertation. *Faculty:* The Educational Technology program at ASU has 6 full-time faculty. *Students:* 40 M.Ed. and 30 Ph.D. students are currently enrolled in the program. *Financial Assistance:* Financial assistance such as scholarships, fellowships, graduate assistantships, loans, and professional work opportunities are available to qualified applicants. *Degrees Awarded 2003:* 16 M.Ed. degrees and 3 Ph.D. degrees were awarded in 2003.

University of Arizona. School of Information Resources and Library Science. 1515 E. First St, Tucson, AZ 85719. (520) 621-3565. Fax (520) 621-3279. http://www.sir.arizona.edu. Susan Irwin. sirwin@u.arizona.edu. *Specializations:* The School of Information Resources and Library Science offers courses focusing on the study of information and its impact as a social phenomenon. *Features:* The School offers a virtual education program via the Internet. Between two and three courses are offered per semester. *Admission Requirements:* Very competitive for both degrees. Minimum criteria include undergraduate GPA of 3.0 or better; competitive GRE scores; two letters of recommendation reflecting the writer's opinion of the applicants potential as a graduate student; a resume of work and educational experience; written statement of intent. The school receives a large number of applications and accepts the best-qualified students. Admission to the doctoral program may require a personal interview and a faculty member must indicate willingness to work with the student. *Degree Requirements:* M.A.: a minimum of 36 units of graduate credit. Students may elect the thesis option replacing 6 units of coursework. Ph.D.: at least 48 hours of coursework in the major, a substantial number of hours in a minor subject supporting the major, dissertation. The university has a 6-unit residency requirement that may be completed in the summer or in a regular semester. More detailed descriptions of the program are available at the school's Web site. *Faculty:* 8 full-time. *Students:* 220 total; M.A.: 51 full-time; Ph.D.: 12 full-time. *Financial Assistance:* scholarships, teaching assistantships, tuition fee waivers. *Degrees Awarded 2003:* 75.

Arkansas

Arkansas Tech University. Curriculum and Instruction. 308 Crabaugh, Russellville, AR 72801-2222. (501) 968-0434. Fax (501) 964-0811. http://education.atu.edu/. Connie Zimmer, Assoc. Professor of Secondary Education, Coord. Connie.Zimmer@mail.atu.edu. *Specializations:* Master of Education in Instructional Technology with specializations in library media education, instructional design, and instructional technology. NCATE accredited institution. *Features:* A standards-based program meeting the requirements of the Arkansas State Department of Education's licensure requirements for school library media specialist. Classrooms have the latest technology available. *Admission Requirements:* GRE or MAT, 2.5 undergraduate GPA, bachelor's degree. Teaching licensure required for the school library media specialization. *Degree Requirements:* 36 semester hours, B average in major hours, action research project. *Faculty:* 2 full-time. *Students:* 5 full-time, 72 part-time. *Financial Assistance:* graduate assistantships, work-study, student loans. *Degrees Awarded 2003:* 45.

University of Central Arkansas. Middle/Secondary Education and Instructional Technologies. Campus Box 4918, Conway, AR 72035. (501) 450-5463. Fax (501) 450-5680. http://www.coe.uca.edu/. Stephanie Huffman, Program Director of the Library Media and Information Technologies Program. steph@mail.uca.edu. *Specializations:* M.S. in Library Media and Information Technologies Tracks: School Library Media and Public Information Agencies. *Features:* Specialization in school library media. *Admission Requirements:* transcripts, GRE scores, and a copy of the candidates teaching certificate (if enrolled in School Library Media Track). *Degree Requirements:* 36 semester hours, practicum (for School Library Media), and a professional portfolio. *Faculty:* 3 full-time, 3 part-time. *Students:* 6 full-time, 51 part-time. *Financial Assistance:* 3 to 4 graduate assistantships each year. *Degrees Awarded 2003:* 30.

California

Alliant University. School of Education. 10455 Pomerado Rd., San Diego, CA 92131-1799. (619) 635-4715. Fax (619) 635-4714. http://www.alliant.edu/gsoe/. Karen Schuster Webb, Systemwide Dean for the Graduate School of Education. lbanerjee @alliant.edu. *Specializations:* master's in Designing Technology for Learning, Planning Technology for Learning, and Technology Leadership for Learning. Ed.D. in Technology and Learning offers three specializations: Designing Technology for Learning, Planning Technology for Learning, and Technology Leadership for Learning. *Features:* interactive multimedia, cognitive approach to integrating technology and learning. *Admission Requirements:* master's, English proficiency, interview, 3.0 GPA with 1900 GRE or 2.0 GPA with satisfactory MAT score. *Degree Requirements:* Ed.D.: 88 graduate quarter units, dissertation. *Faculty:* 2 full-time, 4 part-time. *Students:* master's, 32 full-time, 12 part-time; doctoral, 6 full-time, 1 part-time. *Financial Assistance:* internships, graduate assistantships, grants, student loans, scholarships.

Azusa Pacific University. EDUCABS—Advanced Studies. 901 E. Alosta, Azusa, CA 91702. (626) 815-5355. Fax (626) 815-5416. http://www.apu.edu. Kathleen Bacer, Online program. kbacer@apu.edu. Joanne Gilbreath, site-based program. *Specializations:* Educational Technology, site-based and online program. *Features:* Master of Arts in Educational Technology and Learning Program offered at five locations (Azusa, Inland, Menifee, Orange, Ventura). Online Master of Arts in Educational Technology program. *Admission Requirements:* undergraduate degree from accredited institution with at least 12 units in education, 3.0 GPA, ownership of a designated laptop computer and software. *Degree Requirements:* 36 unit program. *Faculty:* 2 full-time, 16 part-time. *Students:* 180 part-time. *Financial Assistance:* student loans. *Degrees Awarded 2003:* 89.

California State University—Dominguez Hills. Graduate Education. 1000 E. Victoria St., Carson, CA 90747. (310) 243-3524. Fax (310) 243-3518. http://www.csudh.soe.edu. Peter Desberg, Prof., Coord., Technology-Based Education Program. pdesberg@ csudh.edu. *Specializations:* M.A. and Certificate in Technology-Based Education. *Features:* M.A. and Certificate in Technology-Based Education. *Admission Requirements:* 2.75 GPA. *Degree Requirements:* M.A.: 30 semester hours including project. Certificate: 15 hours. *Faculty:* 2 full-time, 2 part-time. *Students:* 60 full-time, 40 part-time. *Financial Assistance:* Available. *Degrees Awarded 2003:* 30.

California State University—Los Angeles. Division of Educational Foundations and Interdivisional Studies. 5151 State University Drive, Los Angeles, CA 90032. (323) 343-4330. Fax (323) 343-5336. http://www.calstatela.edu/dept/efis/. Dr. Fernando A. Hernandez, Division Chairperson. efis@calstatela.edu. *Specializations:* Our four major programmatic areas include Educational Foundations, which offers a graduate degree in Educational Foundations focusing on Educational Sociology, Educational Psychology, Urban Education, or the Philosophy of Education; Instructional Technology and Computer Education, which offers graduate degrees in Instructional Technology and Computer Education; TESOL, which offers a graduate degree in Teaching as a Secondary Language (for more information see the TESOL homepage); and Educational Research, Evaluation, and Statistics, which offers service courses to other Education degree programs in statistics, educational research, and evaluation. *Features:* M.A. degree in Education, option in New Media Design and Production; Computer Education and Leadership; Joint Ph.D. in Special Education with UCLA. *Degree Requirements:* 2.75 GPA in last 90 quarter units, 45 quarter units, comprehensive written exam or thesis or project. Must also pass Writing Proficiency Examination (WPE), a California State University—Los Angeles requirement. *Faculty:* 7 full-time.

California State University—San Bernardino. Department of Science, Mathematics, and Technology Education. 5500 University Parkway, San Bernardino, CA 92407. (909) 880-5290, (909) 880-5688. Fax (909) 880-7040. http://soe.csusb.edu/etec/index.html. Olga E. Cordero, Administrative Support Coordinator. ocordero@csusb.edu. *Specializa-*

tions: Technology integration, online instruction, instructional design. *Features:* Preparing educators in K–12, corporate, and higher education. *Admission Requirements:* bachelor's degree, appropriate work experience, 3.0 GPA, completion of introductory computer course and expository writing course. *Degree Requirements:* 48 units including a master's project (33 units completed in residence); 3.0 GPA; grades of "C" or better in all courses. *Faculty:* 6 full-time, 9 part-time. *Students:* 106. *Financial Assistance:* Contact Office of Graduate Studies. *Degrees Awarded 2003:* M.A.

San Diego State University. Educational Technology. 5500 Campanile Dr., San Diego, CA 92182-1182. (619) 594-6718. Fax (619) 594-6376. http://edtec.sdsu.edu/. Dr. Donn Ritchie, Prof., Chair. dritchie@mail.sdsu.edu. *Specializations:* Certificate in Instructional Technology. Advanced Certificate in Distance Learning. Master's in Education with an emphasis in Educational Technology. Doctorate in Education with an emphasis in Educational Technology (a joint program with the University of San Diego). *Features:* Combining theory and practice in relevant, real-world experiences. Both campus and online programs. *Admission Requirements:* Please refer to SDSU Graduate bulletin at http://libWeb.sdsu.edu/bulletin/. Requirements include 950 GRE (verbal + quantitative) and GRE Writing Assessment Exam with score of 4.5 or better. Grades of B+ or better in EDTEC 540 and EDTEC 541. *Degree Requirements:* 36 semester hours for the master's (including 6 prerequisite hours). 15 semester hours for the certificates. *Faculty:* 9 full-time, 5 part-time. *Students:* 120 in campus program; 100 in online program. *Financial Assistance:* graduate assistantships. *Degrees Awarded 2003:* 40.

San Francisco State University. College of Education, Department of Instructional Technology. 1600 Holloway Ave., San Francisco, CA 94132. (415) 338-1509. Fax (415) 338-0510. www.itec.sfsu.edu. Dr. Kim Foreman, Chair; Anna Kozubek, Office Coord. kforeman@sfsu.edu. *Specializations:* master's degree with emphasis on Instructional Multimedia Design, Training and Designing Development, and Instructional Computing. The school also offers an 18-unit Graduate Certificate in Training Systems Development, which can be incorporated into the master's degree. *Features:* This program emphasizes the instructional systems approach, cognitivist principles of learning design, practical design experience, and project-based courses. *Admission Requirements:* bachelor's degree, appropriate work experience, 2.5 GPA, purpose statement, 2 letters of recommendation, interview with the department chair. *Degree Requirements:* 30 semester hours, field study project, or thesis. Three to nine units of prerequisites, assessed at entrance to the program/. *Faculty:* 4 full-time, 16 part-time. *Students:* 250-300. *Financial Assistance:* Contact Office of Financial Aid. *Degrees Awarded 2003:* 60.

San Jose State University. Instructional Technology. One Washington Square, San Jose, CA 95192-0076. (408) 924-3620. Fax (408) 924-3713. http://sweeneyhall.sjsu.edu/depts/it. Dr. Roberta Barba, Program Chair. rbarba@email.sjsu.edu. *Specializations:* master's degree. *Features:* MA in Education with an emphasis on Instructional Technology. *Admission Requirements:* Baccalaureate degree from approved university, appropriate work experience, minimum GPA of 2.5, and minimum score of 550 on TOEFL(Test of English as a Foreign Language). Thirty-six semester hours (which includes 6 prerequisite hours). *Degree Requirements:* 30 units of approved graduate studies. *Faculty:* 4 full-time, 12 part-time. *Students:* 50 full-time master's students, 260 part-time. *Financial Assistance:* Assistantships, grants, student loans and scholarships. *Degrees Awarded 2003:* 42.

University of Southern California. Instructional Technology, Division of Learning and Instruction. 502C W.P.H., Rossier School of Education, Los Angeles, CA 90089-0031. (213) 740-3288. Fax (213) 740-3889. http://www.usc.edu/dept/education/index2.html. Dr. Richard Clark, Prof., doctoral programs; Dr. Edward J. Kazlauskas, Prof., Program Chair, master's programs in Instructional Technology. kazlausk@usc.edu. *Specializations:* M.A., Ed.D., Ph.D. to prepare individuals to teach instructional technology; manage educational media and training programs in business, industry, research and development organizations, schools, and higher education institutions; perform research in instructional technology and media; and deal with computer-driven technology. *Features:* Special emphasis on instructional design, human performance at work, systems analysis, and computer-based training. *Admission Requirements:* bachelor's degree, 1000 GRE. *Degree Requirements:* M.A.: 28 semester hours, thesis optional. Doctoral: 67 units, 20 of which can be transferred from a previous master's degree. Requirements for degree completion vary according to type of degree and individual interest. Ph.D. requires an outside field in addition to coursework in instructional technology and education, more methodology and statistics work, and coursework in an outside field. *Faculty:* 3 full-time, 2 part-time. *Students:* M.A., 5 full-time, 15 part-time; doctoral, 5 full-time, 20 part-time. *Financial Assistance:* Part-time, instructional technology-related work available in the Los Angeles area and on campus, some scholarship monies available. Full support for Ph.D. students. *Degrees Awarded 2003:* 28.

Colorado

University of Colorado at Denver. School of Education. Campus Box 106, P.O. Box 173364, Denver, CO 80217-3364. (303) 556-4478. Fax (303) 556-4479. http://www.cudenver.edu/ilt. Brent Wilson, Program Coordinator, Information and Learning Technologies, Division of Technology and Special Services. brent.wilson@cudenver. edu. *Specializations:* M.A. in Information and Learning Technologies; Ph.D. in Educational Leadership and Innovation with emphasis in Learning Technologies. *Features:* design and use of learning technologies; instructional design. Ph.D. students complete 12 semester hours of doctoral labs (small groups collaborating with faculty on difficult problems of practice). Throughout the program, students complete a product portfolio of research, design, teaching, and applied projects. The program is cross-disciplinary, drawing on expertise in technology, adult learning, systemic change, research methods, reflective practice, and cultural studies. *Admission Requirements:* M.A. and Ph.D.: satisfactory GPA, GRE (for low GPA), writing sample, letters of recommendation, transcripts. See Web site for more detail. *Degree Requirements:* M.A.: 36 semester hours including 28 hours of core coursework; professional portfolio; field experience. Ph.D.: 50 semester hours of coursework and labs, plus 20 dissertation hours; portfolio; dissertation. *Faculty:* 5 full-time, several part-time (see Web). *Students:* M.A., 15 full-time, 80 part-time; Ph.D., 3 full-time, 8 part-time. *Financial Assistance:* assistantships, internships. *Degrees Awarded* 2003: 45.

University of Northern Colorado. Educational Technology. College of Education, Greeley, CO 80639. (970) 351-2816. Fax (970) 351-1622. http://www.coe.unco. edu/edtech/. Kay Persichitte, Professor, Department Chair, Educational Technology. kay.persichitte@unco.edu. *Specializations:* M.A. in Educational Technology; M.A. in Educational Media; Nondegree endorsement for school library media specialists; Ph.D. in Educational Technology with emphases in Distance Education, Instructional Development/ Design, Interactive Technology, and Technology Integration. *Features:* Graduates are prepared for careers as instructional technologists, course designers, trainers, instructional developers, media specialists, and human resource managers. Graduates typically follow employment paths into K–12 education, higher education, business, industry, and, occasionally the military. *Admission Requirements:* M.A.: bachelor's degree, 3.0 undergraduate GPA, 1000 GRE verbal and quantitative and 3.5 on the written/analytical, 3 letters of recommendation, statement of career goals. Endorsement: Same as MA but no GRE. Ph.D.: 3.2 GPA in last 60 hours of coursework, three letters of recommendation, congruency between applicants statement of career goals and program goals, 1100 GRE verbal and quantitative and 3.5 on the written/analytical, interview with faculty. *Degree Requirements:* MA-Ed Tech: 30 semester hours (min), MA-Ed Media: 36–39 semester hours (min) Endorsement: 30–33 semester hours (min), Ph.D.: 67 semester hours (min). *Faculty:* 6

full-time. *Students:* M.A., 20 full-time, 130 part-time; Ph.D., 20 full-time, 25 part-time. *Financial Assistance:* Assistantships, grant development, student loans, fellowships, scholarships through the Graduate School. Very competitive with first consideration to full-time doctoral students. *Degrees Awarded 2003:* >30 MA; 3 Ph.D.

Connecticut

Central Connecticut State University. Educational Technology. 1615 Stanley St., New Britain, CT 06050. (860) 832-2139. Fax (860) 832-2109. http://www.ccsu.edu. Farough Abed, Director., Educational Technology Program. abedf@ccsu.ctstateu.edu. *Specializations:* M.S. in Educational Technology. Curriculum emphases include instructional technology, instructional design, message design, and computer technologies. Degree applies to Public School, Business-Training and Development, and College teaching position. *Features:* The program supports the Center for Innovation in Teaching and Technology to link students with client-based projects. Hands-on experience with emphasis on design, production, and evaluation. Students work as teams in their second year. *Admission Requirements:* bachelor's degree, 2.7 undergraduate GPA. *Degree Requirements:* 36 semester hours, optional thesis or master's final project (3 credits). Bachelor, two letters of reference, and goal statement. *Faculty:* 2 full-time, 4 part-time. *Students:* Full 3, Part time 45. *Financial Assistance:* graduate assistant position. *Degrees Awarded 2003:* 28.

Fairfield University. Educational Technology, N. Benson Road, Fairfield, CT 06824. (203) 254-4000. Fax (203) 254-4047. http://www.fairfield.edu. Dr. Ibrahim M. Hefzallah, Prof., Chair., Educational Technology Department; Dr. Justin Ahn, Assistant Professor of Educational Technology. ihefzallah@mail.fairfield.edu, jahn@mail.fairfield.edu. *Specializations:* M.A. and a certificate of Advanced Studies in Educational Technology in one of five areas of concentrations: Computers-in-Education, Instructional Development, School Media Specialist, Applied Educational Technology in Content Areas, and Television Production; customized course of study also available. *Features:* emphasis on theory, practice, and new instructional developments in computers in education, multimedia, school/media, and applied technology in education. *Admission Requirements:* bachelor's degree from accredited institution with 2.67 GPA. *Degree Requirements:* 33 credits. *Faculty:* 2 full-time, 8 part-time. *Students:* 4 full-time, 74 part-time. *Financial Assistance:* assistantships, student loans. *Degrees Awarded 2003:* 12.

Southern Connecticut State University. Information and Library Science. 501 Crescent St., New Haven, CT 06515. (203) 392-5781. Fax (203) 392-5780. http://www.southernct.edu/. Arlene Bielefield, JD, Chairperson; Edward Harris, PhD, Dean. mckayl1@southernct.edu. *Specializations:* M.S. in Instructional Technology; Sixth-Year Professional Diploma Library—Information Studies (student may select area of specialization in Instructional Technology). *Features:* Courses in instructional design and technology and in corporate training and development. *Admission Requirements:* bachelor's degree from an institution accredited by a recognized regional accrediting agency in the United States. Degrees from outside the U.S. must be evaluated by an accredited evaluating agency. Undergraduate cumulative average of at least 2.5 on a scale of A = 4. Initial teacher certification programs require a minimum of 2.7. Recommendation of the graduate program coordinator. *Degree Requirements:* for Instructional Technology only, 36 semester hours. For sixth-year degree: 30 credit hours with 6 credit hours of core requirements, 9–15 credit hours in specialization. *Faculty:* 1 full-time; 4 part-time. *Students:* 3 full-time and 38 part-time in M.S./IT program. *Financial Assistance:* graduate assistantship (salary $1,800 per semester; assistants pay tuition and a general university fee sufficient to defray cost of student accident insurance).

University of Connecticut. Educational Psychology. 249 Glenbrook Rd, Unit 2064, Storrs, CT 06269-2064. (860) 486-0182. Fax (860) 486-0180. http://www.epsy.uconn. edu/. Michael Young, program coordinator. myoung@UConnvm.UConn.edu. *Specializations:* M.A. in Educational Technology (portfolio or thesis options), one-year partially on-line master's (summer, fall, spring, summer), 6th Year certificate in Educational Technology and Ph.D. in Learning Technology. *Features:* MA can be on-campus or two Summers (on campus) and Fall–Spring (Online) that can be completed in a year. The Ph.D. emphasis in Learning Technology is a unique program at UConn. It strongly emphasizes Cognitive Science and how technology can be used to enhance the way people think and learn. The Program seeks to provide students with knowledge of theory and applications regarding the use of advanced technology to enhance learning and thinking. Campus facilities include $2 billion 21st-Century UConn enhancement to campus infrastructure, including a new wing to the Neag School of Education. Faculty research interests include interactive video for anchored instruction and situated learning, telecommunications for cognitive apprenticeship, technology-mediated interactivity for learning by design activities, and in cooperation with the National Research Center for Gifted and Talented, research on the use of technology to enhance cooperative learning and the development of gifted performance in all students. *Admission Requirements:* admission to the graduate school at UConn, GRE scores (or other evidence of success at the graduate level). Previous experience in a related area of technology, education, or experience in education or training. *Degree Requirements:* completion of plan of study coursework, comprehensive exam (portfolio-based with multiple requirements), and completion of an approved dissertation. *Faculty:* The program in Cognition and Instruction has 7 full-time faculty; 3 full-time faculty administer the emphasis in Educational Technology. *Students:* 8 M.A., 10 Ph.D.. *Financial Assistance:* graduate assistantships, research fellowships, teaching assistantships, and federal and minority scholarships are available competitively. *Degrees Awarded 2003:* 4 MA, 2 PhD.

District of Columbia

George Washington University. School of Education and Human Development. Washington, DC 20052. (202) 994-1701. Fax (202) 994-2145. http://www.gwu.edu/~etl. Dr. William Lynch, Educational Technology Leadership Program. Program is offered through Jones Education Company (JEC). Contact student advisors at (800) 777-MIND. unirel@www.gwu.edu. *Specializations:* M.A. in Education and Human Development with a major in Educational Technology Leadership. *Admission Requirements:* application fee, transcripts, GRE or MAT scores (50th percentile), two letters of recommendation from academic professionals, computer access, undergraduate degree with 2.75 GPA. *Degree Requirements:* 36 credit hours (including 24 required hours). Required courses include computer application management, media and technology application, software implementation and design, public education policy, and quantitative research methods. *Faculty:* Courses are taught by GWU faculty. *Financial Assistance:* For information, contact the Office of Student Financial Assistance, GWU. Some cable systems that carry JEC offer local scholarships.

Florida

Barry University. Department of Educational Computing and Technology, School of Education. 11300 N.E. Second Ave., Miami Shores, FL 33161. (305) 899-3608. Fax (305) 899-3718. http://www.barry.edu/ed/programs/master's/ect/default.htm. Donna Lenaghan, Dir. dlenaghan@bu4090.barry.edu. *Specializations:* M.S. and Ed.S. in Educational Technology Applications and Ph.D. degree in Educational Technology Leadership. *Features:* These programs and courses prepares educators to integrate computer/technologies in their disciplines and/or train individuals to use computers/technologies. The focus is on improving the teaching and learning process through integration of technologies into curricula and learning activities. *Admission Requirements:* GRE scores, letters of recommendation, GPA, interview, achievements. *Degree Requirements:* M.S. or Ed. S.: 36 semester credit hours. Ph.D.: 54 credits beyond the master's including dissertation credits. *Faculty:* 5 full-time, 10 part-time. *Students:* M.S., 8 full-time, 181 part-time; Ed.S., 5 full-time, 44 part-time; Ph.D., 3 full-time, 15 part-time. *Financial Assistance:* assistantships, student loans. *Degrees Awarded 2003:* 75.

Florida Institute of Technology. Science Education Department, 150 University Blvd., Melbourne, FL 32901-6975. (321) 674-8126. Fax (321) 674-7598. http://www.fit.edu/cat-alog/sci-lib/comp-edu.html#master-info. Dr. David Cook, Dept. Head. dcook@fit.edu. *Specializations:* master's degree options in Computer Education and Instructional Technology; Ph.D. degree options in Computer Education and Instructional Technology. *Features:* Flexible program depending on student experience. *Admission Requirements:* master's: 3.0 GPA for regular admission; 2.75 for provisional admission. Ph.D.: master's degree and 3.2 GPA. *Degree Requirements:* master's: 33 semester hours (15 in computer or and technology education, 9 in education, 9 electives); practicum; no thesis or internship required. Ph.D.: 48 semester hours (12 in computer and technology education, 12 in education, 24 dissertation and research). *Faculty:* 4 full-time. *Students:* 11 full-time, 10 part-time. *Financial Assistance:* loans, limited graduate student assistantships (full tuition plus stipend) available. *Degrees Awarded 2003:* 5.

Florida State University. Educational Psychology and Learning Systems. 305 Stone Bldg., Tallahassee, FL 32306. (850) 644-4592. Fax (850) 644-8776. http://www.epls.fsu. edu/is/index.htm. Mary Kate McKee, Program Coordinator. MMcKee@oddl.fsu.edu. *Specializations:* M.S., Ed.S, Ph.D. in Instructional Systems with specializations for persons planning to work in academia, business, industry, government, or military, both in the United States and in International settings. *Features:* Core courses include systems and materials development, development of multimedia, project management, psychological foundations, current trends in instructional design, and research and statistics. Internships are recommended. *Admission Requirements:* M.S.: 3.0 GPA in last two years of undergraduate program, 1000 GRE (verbal plus quantitative), 550 TOEFL (for international applicants). Ph.D.: 1100 GRE (V+Q), 3.5 GPA in last two years; international students, 550 TOEFL. *Degree Requirements:* M.S.: 36 semester hours, 2-4 hour internship, comprehensive exam preparation of professional portfolio. *Faculty:* 7 full-time, 4 part-time. *Students:* M.S., 50; Ph.D., 50. *Financial Assistance:* Graduate research and teaching assistantships on faculty grants and contracts; Program, college, and university fellowships.

Jacksonville University. Division of Education. 2800 University Boulevard North, Jacksonville, FL 32211. (904) 745-7132. Fax (904) 745-7159. Dr. Margaret Janz, Interim Dir., School of Education, or Dr. June Main, Coordinator of MAT in Integrated Learning with Educational Technology. mjanz@mail.ju.edu. *Specializations:* The Master's in Educational Technology and Integrated Learning is an innovative program designed to guide certified teachers in the use and application of educational technologies in the classroom. It is based on emerging views of how we learn, of our growing understanding of multiple intelligences, and of the many ways to incorporate technology in teaching and learning. Activity-based classes emphasize instructional design for a multimedia environment to reach all students. M.A.T. degrees in Computer Education and in Integrated Learning with Educational Technology. *Features:* The M.A.T. in Computer Education is for teachers who are already certified in an area of education, for those who wish to be certified in Computer Education, kindergarten through community college level. *Degree Requirements:* M.A.T. in Computer Education and in Integrated Learning with Educational Technology: 36 semester hours, including 9–12 hours in core education graduate courses and the rest in computer education with comprehensive exam in last semester of program. Master's in Educational Technology and Integrated Learning: 36 semester hours, including 9 in core graduate education courses, 6 in integrated learning, and the rest in educational technology. Comprehensive exam is to develop a practical group of multimedia applications. *Financial Assistance:* student loans and discounts to graduate education *students.* Students: Computer Education, 8; Integrated Learning with Educational Technology, 20.

Nova Southeastern University—Fischler Graduate School of Education and Human Services. Programs in Instructional Technology and Distance Education (ITDE). 1750 NE 167th Street, North Miami Beach, FL 33162. (954) 262-8572. (800) 986-3223, ext. 8572. Fax (954) 262-3905. itde.nova.edu. Marsha L. Burmeister, Recruitment Coordinator and Program Professor ITDE. itdeinfo@nova.edu. *Specializations:* M.S. and Ed.D in Instructional Technology and Distance Education. *Features:* M.S. 21 months (M.S. ITDE program graduates may continue with the Ed.D. program as second year students). Ed.D. 36 months, M.S. and Ed.D. combined: 4+ years, Blended/hybrid delivery model with limited face-to-face and via instruction at-a-distance using Web-based technologies. *Admission Requirements:*

- Active employment in the field of instructional technology/distance education.
- Completion of bachelor's degree for M.S. program (2.5 minimum GPA); master's degree required for admission to Ed.D. program (3.0 minimum GPA).
- Miller Analogies Test (MAT) score (test taken within last 5 years)
- Submission of application/supplementary materials
- Approval of Skills Checklist (application)
- Three letters of recommendation
- Official copies of transcripts for all graduate work
- Resume
- Oral interview (via telephone)
- Demonstrated potential for successful completion of the program via acceptance of application
- Internet service provider; laptop computer

Degree Requirements: 21 months and 30 semester credits. Ed.D. 3 years and 65 semester credits. M.S. program: 3 "extended weekends": one extended weekend in the fall (5 days), one extended weekend in the spring (4 days), one summer instructional session (4–5 days; July), final term online delivery. Ed.D. program: same as above, continues throughout the 3 years (3 sessions in first year, 2 sessions in the second year, and one instructional session in the third year for a total of six face-to-face sessions). *Faculty:* 6 full-time and 20 adjuncts. *Students:* 300 full-time. *Financial Assistance:* Student loans; apply to Nova Southeastern University Office of Student Financial Assistance: http://www.nova.edu/cwis/finaid/index.html. All ITDE students are considered full-time students for the purposes of financial aid. *Degrees Awarded 2003:* 100.

University of Central Florida. College of Education—ERTL. 4000 Central Florida Blvd., Orlando, FL 32816-1250. (407) 823-4835. Fax (407) 823-4880. http://pegasus.cc.ucf. edu/~instsys/, http://pegasus.cc.ucf.edu/~edmedia, http://pegasus.cc.ucf.edu/~ edtech. Gary Orwig, Instructional Systems Judy Lee, Educational Media Glenda Gunter, Educational Technology. orwig@mail.ucf.edu; jlee@pegasus.cc.ucf.edu; ggunter@pegasus. cc.ucf.edu. *Specializations:* M.A. in Instructional Technology/Instructional Systems, http://pegasus.cc.ucf.edu/~instsys/; M.Ed. in Instructional Technology/Educational Media —entirely Web-based, http://pegasus.cc.ucf.edu/~edmedia/; M.A. in Instructional Technology/Educational Technology, http://pegasus.cc.ucf.edu/~edtech . Ph.D. and Ed.D. with specialization in Instructional Technology. http://www.graduate.ucf.edu. There are approximately 18 Ed.D. students and 22 Ph.D. students in the doctoral programs. *Features:* All programs rely heavily on understanding of fundamental competencies as reflected by ASTD, AECT, AASL, and ISTE. There is an emphasis on the practical application of theory through intensive hands-on experiences. Orlando and the surrounding area is home to a plethora of high-tech companies, military training and simulation organizations, and tourist attractions. UCF, established in 1963, now has in excess of 36,000 students, representing more than 90 countries. It has been ranked as one of the leading "most-wired" universities in North America. *Admission Requirements:* Interviews (either in person or via e-mail); GRE score of 840 if last 60 hours of undergraduate degree is 3.0 or above, 1000 if less; TOEFL of 550 (270 computer-based version) if English is not first language; three letters of recommendation; resume, statement of goals; residency statement, and health record. Financial statement if coming from overseas. *Degree Requirements:* M.A. in Instructional Technology/Instructional Systems, 39–42 semester hours; M.Ed. in Instructional Technology/Educational Media, 39-45 semester hours; M.A. in Instructional Technology/Educational Technology, 36–45 semester hours. Practicum required in all three programs; thesis, research project, or substitute additional coursework. Ph.D. and Ed.D. require between 58–69 hours beyond the master's for completion. *Faculty:* 4 full-time, 12 part-time. *Students:* Inst Sys, 70; Ed Media, 35; Ed Technology, 50. Full-time, 120; part-time, 35. *Financial Assistance:* Competitive graduate assistantships in department and college, numerous paid internships, limited number of doctoral fellowships. *Degrees Awarded 2003:* 65.

University of Florida. School of Teaching and Learning. 2403 Norman Hall, Gainesville, FL 32611-7048. (352) 392-9191 ext. X261. Fax (352) 392-9193. http://www.coe.ufl.edu/Courses/EdTech/index.html. Kara Dawson. dawson@coe.ufl.edu. *Specializations:* Educational technology students may earn M.S., Ed.S., Ed.D. or Ph.D. degrees and have an opportunity to specialize in one of three tracks: (1) teaching and teacher education, (2) production, or (3) instructional design. Teacher education students and students in other degree programs may also elect to specialize in Educational Technology. *Features:* Students take core courses listed on our Educational Technology Web site and then select an area of specialization. *Admission Requirements:* Please see the Educational Technology Web site for the most up-to-date information. Current admission requirements are as follows: Obtain a GRE score of 1000 or more on the verbal and quantitative components of the GRE. Applicants must have a score of 450 or higher for each component (verbal and quantitative). Submit a written document outlining (1) your career goals and (2) the track you wish to specialize in the Educational Technology program. *Degree Requirements:* Please see the Educational Technology Web site for the most up-to-date information. Program and college requirements must be met but there is considerable flexibility for doctoral students to plan an appropriate program with their advisors. *Faculty:* 3 full-time faculty members; 2 faculty members teach part-time within the program. *Students:* approximately 50 students are enrolled in our Educational Technology. *Financial Assistance:* A limited number of graduate assistantships are available. Interested students should submit an assistantship application with their admissions application. Students should also check the Web site for information about available assistantships.

University of South Florida. Instructional Technology Program, Secondary Education Department, College of Education. 4202 E. Fowler Avenue, EDU162,, Tampa, FL 33620-5650. (813) 974-3533. Fax (813) 974-3837. http://www.coedu.usf.edu/it. Dr. William Kealy, Graduate Certificates; Dr. Frank Breit, master's program; Dr. Ann Barron, Education Specialist program; Dr. James White, Doctoral program. See@http://www.coedu.usf.edu/it. *Specializations:* Graduate Certificates in Web Design, Instructional Design, Multimedia Design, School Networks, and Distance Education M.Ed., Ed.S., and

Ph.D. in Curriculum and Instruction with emphasis in Instructional Technology. *Features:* Many students gain practical experience in the Florida Center for Instructional Technology (FCIT), which provides services to the Department of Education and other grants and contracts; the Virtual Instructional Team for the Advancement of Learning (VITAL), which provides USF faculty with course development services; and Educational Outreach. The College of Education is one of the largest in the United States in terms of enrollment and facilities. As of Fall 1997, a new, technically state-of-the-art building was put into service. The University of South Florida has been classified by the Carnegie Foundation as a Doctoral/Research University—Extensive. *Admission Requirements:* See http://www.coedu. usf.edu/it. *Degree Requirements:* See http://www.coedu.usf.edu/it. *Faculty:* 4 full-time, 6 part-time. *Students:* 120 full-time, 255 part-time. *Financial Assistance:* some assistantships, grants, loans, scholarships, and fellowships. *Degrees Awarded 2003:* 60+.

Georgia

Georgia Southern University. College of Education. Box 8131, Statesboro, GA 30460-8131. (912) 681-5307. Fax (912) 486-7104. http://coe. georgiasouthern. edu/eltr/tech/inst_tech/index.htm. Judi Repman. Professor, Dept. of Leadership, Technology, and Human Development. jrepman@georgiasouthern.edu. *Specializations:* M.Ed. and GA certification for School Library Media Specialist. An Instructional Technology strand is available in the Ed.S. in Teaching and Learning Program and in the Ed.D. program in Curriculum Studies. *Features:* GA Special Technology Certification course available strong emphasis on technology. *Admission Requirements:* BS (teacher certification not required), MAT score of 44 or GRE score of 450 verbal and 450 quantitative for Regular admission. Provisional admission requires lower scores but also requires letters of intent/reference. *Degree Requirements:* 36 semester hours, including a varying number of hours of media for individual students. *Faculty:* 3 full-time. *Students:* 100 part-time. *Financial Assistance:* See graduate catalog for general financial aid information. *Degrees Awarded 2003:* 20.

Georgia State University. Middle-Secondary Education and Instructional Technology. University Plaza, Atlanta, GA 30303. (404) 651-2510. Fax (404) 651-2546. http://www. gsu.edu/~wwwmst/. Dr. Stephen W. Harmon, contact person. swharmon@gsu.edu. *Specializations:* M.S., Ed.S., and Ph.D. in Instructional Technology or Library Media. *Features:* focus on research and practical application of instructional technology in educational and corporate settings. *Admission Requirements:* M.S.: bachelor's degree, 2.5 undergraduate GPA, 800 GRE, 550 TOEFL. Ed.S.: master's degree, teaching certificate, 3.25 graduate GPA, 48 MAT or 900 GRE. Ph.D.: master's degree, 3.30 graduate GPA, 53 MAT or 500 verbal plus 500 quantitative GRE or 500 analytical GRE. *Degree Requirements:* M.S.: 36 semester hours, internship, portfolio, comprehensive examination. Ed.S.: 30 semester hours, internship, and scholarly project. Ph.D.: 66 semester hours, internship, comprehensive examination, dissertation. *Faculty:* 8 full-time, 3 part-time. *Students:* 200 M.S., 40 Ph.D. *Financial Assistance:* assistantships, grants, student loans. *Degrees Awarded 2003:* 44 M.S., 6 Ed.S., 5 Ph.D.

State University of West Georgia. Department of Media and Instructional Technology. 138 Education Annex, Carrollton, GA 30118. (770) 836-6558 or 836-4442. Fax (770) 838-3088. http://coe.westga.edu/mit/index.html. Dr. Barbara K. McKenzie, Professor and Chair. bmckenzi@westga.edu. *Specializations:* M.Ed. with specializations in Media and Instructional Technology and Add-On certification for students with master's degrees in other disciplines. The Department also offers an Ed.S. program in Media with two options, Media Specialist or Instructional Technology. The program strongly emphasizes technology integration in the schools. *Features:* master's degree students and initial certification students are required to complete a practicum. *Admission Requirements:* M.Ed.: 800 GRE, 44 MAT, 550 NTE Core, 2.5 undergraduate GPA. Ed.S.: 900 GRE, 48 MAT, or 575 NTE and 3.25 graduate GPA. *Degree Requirements:* 36 semester hours for Med 27 semester hours for EdS. *Faculty:* 6 full-time in Media/Technology; 1 full-time instructor in Instructional Technology; 2 part-time in Media/Instructional Technology. *Students:* Approximately 450, part-time. *Financial Assistance:* two graduate research assistantships for the department. *Degrees Awarded 2003:* Approximately 60 across both levels.

University of Georgia. Department of Instructional Technology, College of Education. 604 Aderhold Hall, Athens, GA 30602-7144. (706) 542-3810. Fax (706) 542-4032. http://it.coe.uga.edu. Dr. Janette Hill, Graduate Coordinator. janette@coe.uga.edu. *Specializations:* M.Ed. and Ed.S. in Instructional Technology; Ph.D. for leadership positions as specialists in instructional design and development and university faculty. The program offers advanced study for individuals with previous preparation in instructional media and technology, as well as a preparation for personnel in other professional fields requiring a specialty in instructional systems or instructional technology. Representative career fields for graduates include designing new courses, tutorial programs, and instructional materials in state and local school systems, higher education, business and industry, research and nonprofit settings, and in instructional products development. *Features:* Minor areas of study available in a variety of other departments. Personalized programs are planned around a common core of courses and include practica, internships, or clinical experiences. Research activities include grant-related activities and applied projects, as well as dissertation studies. *Admission Requirements,* all degrees: application to graduate school, satisfactory GRE score, other criteria as outlined in Graduate School Bulletin and on the program Web site. *Degree Requirements:* M.Ed.: 36 semester hours with 3.0 GPA, portfolio with oral exam. Ed.S.: 30 semester hours with 3.0 GPA and project exam. Ph.D.: three full years of study beyond the master's degree, two consecutive semesters full-time residency, comprehensive exam with oral defense, internship, dissertation with oral defense. *Faculty:* 13 full-time, 1 part-time. *Students:* M.Ed 158; Ed.S. 72; Ph.D. 52. *Financial Assistance:* Graduate assistantships available. *Degrees Awarded 2003:* 60.

Valdosta State University. Curriculum and Instructional Technology. 1500 N. Patterson St., Valdosta, GA 31698. (229) 333-5927. Fax (229) 333-7167. http://education.valdosta.edu/info/cait/. Gayle Brooks. gbrooks@valdosta.edu. *Specializations:* M.Ed. in Instructional Technology with two tracks: Library/Media or Technology Applications; Online Ed.S. in Instructional Technology; Ed.D. in Curriculum and Instruction. *Features:* The program has a strong emphasis on systematic design and technology in M.Ed., Ed.S., and Ed.D. Strong emphasis on change leadership, reflective practice, applied research in Ed.S and Ed.D. *Admission Requirements:* M.Ed.: 2.5 GPA, 800 GRE. Ed.S.: master's degree, 3 years of experience, 3.0 GPA, 850 GRE, MAT 36 and less than 5 years old. Ed.D.: master's degree, 3 years of experience, 3.50 GPA, 1000 GRE. *Degree Requirements:* M.Ed.: 33 semester hours. Ed.S.: 27 semester hours. Ed.D.: 54 semester hours. *Faculty:* 6 full-time, 4 part-time. *Students:* 119 master's, 109 Specialist, 31 doctoral students. *Financial Assistance:* graduate assistantships, student loans, scholarships. *Degrees Awarded 2003:* M.Ed., Ed.S., Ed.D.

Hawaii

University of Hawaii—Manoa. Department of Educational Technology. 1776 University Ave, Honolulu, HI 96822-2463. (808) 956-7671. Fax (808) 956-3905. http://www .hawaii.edu/edtech. Geoffrey Z. Kucera, Prof., Chair. edtech-dept@hawaii.edu-. *Specializations:* M.Ed. in Educational Technology. *Features:* min. 39 semester hours, including 3 in practicum, 3 in internship; thesis and nonthesis available. *Admission Requirements:* bachelor's degree in any field, B average (3.0 GPA) *Degree Requirements:* 39 semester hours (plus 6 semester hrs of prerequisites if needed). *Faculty:* 6 full-time, 1 part-time. *Students:* 13 full-time, 35 part-time students. *Financial Assistance:* Consideration given to meritorious second-year students for tuition waivers and scholarship applications. *Degrees Awarded 2003:* 12 (2003), 16 (2002), 11 (2001).

Idaho

Boise State University. Instructional and Performance Technology. 1910 University Drive, ET-338, Boise, ID 83725. (208) 424-5135;(800) 824-7017 ext. 4457. Fax (208) 426-1970. http://ipt.boisestate.edu/. Dr. David Cox, IPT Program Dir.; Jo Ann Fenner, IPT Program Developer and distance program contact person. bsuipt@boisestate.edu. *Specializations:* M.S. in Instructional and Performance Technology is available in a traditional campus setting or via asynchronus computer conferencing to students located anywhere there is access to the Internet. The program is fully accredited by the Northwest Commission of Colleges and Universities and is the recipient of an NUCEA award for Outstanding Credit Program offered by distance education methods. *Features:* Leading experts in learning styles, evaluation, and leadership principles serve as adjunct faculty in the program via computer and modem from their various remote locations. For details, visit our faculty Web page at http://ipt.boisestate.edu/faculty.htm. *Admission Requirements:* undergraduate degree with 3.0 GPA, one-to-two page essay describing why the applicant wants to pursue this program and how it will contribute to his or her personal and professional development, and a resume of personal qualifications and work experience. For more information, visit http://ipt.boisestate.edu/application_admission.htm. *Degree Requirements:* 36 semester hours in instructional and performance technology and related coursework; project or thesis available for on-campus program and an oral comprehensive exam required for distance program (included in 36 credit hours). *Faculty:* 5 full-time, 10 part-time. *Students:* 190 part-time. *Financial Assistance:* DANTES funding for some military personnel, low-interest loans to eligible students, graduate assistantships for on-campus enrollees. *Degrees Awarded 2003:* 47.

Illinois

Chicago State University. Department of Library Science and Communications Media, Chicago, IL 60628. (312) 995-2278;(312) 995-2503. Fax (312) 995-2473. Janice Bolt, Prof., Chair, Dept. of Library Science and Communications Media. l-robinson@csu.edu. *Specializations:* master's degree in School Media. Program has been approved by NCATE: AECT/AASL through accreditation of University College of Education; State of Illinois Entitlement Program. *Admission Requirements:* teacher's certification or bachelor's in education; any B.A. or B.S. *Degree Requirements:* 36 semester hours; thesis optional. *Faculty:* 2 full-time, 5 part-time. *Students:* 88 part-time. *Financial Assistance:* assistantships, grants, student loans.

Governors State University. College of Arts and Sciences. University Drive, University Park, IL 60466. (708) 534-4082. Fax (708) 534-7895. m-stelnicki@govst.edu. Michael Stelnicki, Prof., Human Performance and Training. m-stelni@govst.edu. *Specializations:* M.A. in Communication and Training with Human Performance and Training major. Program concentrates on building instructional design skills. *Features:* Emphasizes three professional areas: Instructional Design, Performance Analysis, and Design Logistics. *Admission Requirements:* Undergraduate degree in any field. *Degree Requirements:* 36 credit hours (trimester), all in instructional and performance technology; internship or advanced field project required. Metropolitan Chicago–area based. *Faculty:* 2 full-time. *Students:* 30 part-time. *Financial Assistance:* Contact Student Assistance. *Degrees Awarded 2003:* 10.

Northern Illinois University. Educational Technology, Research and Assessment. 208 Gabel Hall, DeKalb, IL 60115. (815) 753-9339. Fax (815) 753-9388. http://www.cedu.niu.edu/etra. Dr. Jeffrey B. Hecht, Department Chair. etra@niu.edu. *Specializations:*

M.S.Ed. in Instructional Technology with concentrations in Instructional Design, Distance Education, Educational Computing, and Media Administration; Ed.D. in Instructional Technology, emphasizing instructional design and development, computer education, media administration, and preparation for careers in business, industry, and higher education. In addition, Illinois state certification in school library media is offered in conjunction with either degree or alone. *Features:* Program is highly individualized. All facilities remodeled and modernized in 2002–2003 featuring five smart classrooms and over 110 student use desktop and laptop computers. Specialized equipment for digital audio and video editing, Web site and CD creation, and presentations. All students are encouraged to create portfolios highlighting personal accomplishments and works (required at master's). Master's program started in 1968, doctorate in 1970. *Admission Requirements:* M.S.Ed.: 2.75 undergraduate GPA, GRE verbal and quantitative scores, two references. Ed.D.: 3.25 M.S. GPA, writing sample, three references, interview. *Degree Requirements:* M.S.Ed.: 39 hours, including 30 in instructional technology; portfolio. Ed.D.: 63 hours beyond master's, including 15 hours for dissertation. *Faculty:* 8 full-time, 18 part-time. *Students:* M.S., 185 part-time; Ed.D., 135 part-time. *Financial Assistance:* Assistantships available at times in various departments, scholarships, and minority assistance. *Degrees Awarded 2003:* 2001 degrees awarded: 93 M.S.Ed. in IT; 11 Ed.D. in IT.

Southern Illinois University at Carbondale. Department of Curriculum and Instruction, Carbondale, IL 62901-4610. (618) 536-2441. Fax (618) 453-4244. http://www.siu.edu/~currinst/index.html. Sharon Shrock, Coord., Instructional Technology/Development. sashrock@siu.edu. *Specializations:* M.S. in Education with specializations in Instructional Development and Instructional Technology; Ph.D. in Education including specialization in Instructional Technology. *Features:* All specializations are oriented to multiple education settings. The ID program emphasizes nonschool (primarily corporate) learning environments. *Admission Requirements:* M.S.: bachelor's degree, 2.7 undergraduate GPA, transcripts. Ph.D.: master's degree, 3.25 GPA, MAT or GRE scores, letters of recommendation, transcripts, writing sample. *Degree Requirements:* M.S., 32 credit hours with thesis; 36 credit hours without thesis; Ph.D., 40 credit hours beyond the master's degree in courses, 24 credit hours for the dissertation. *Faculty:* 5 full-time, 2 part-time. *Students:* M.S., 35 full-time, 45 part-time; Ph.D., 8 full-time, 19 part-time. *Financial Assistance:* some graduate assistantships and scholarships available to qualified students.

Southern Illinois University at Edwardsville. Instructional Technology Program. School of Education, Edwardsville, IL 62026-1125. (618) 692-3277. Fax (618) 692-3359. http://www.siue.edu. Dr. Charles E. Nelson, Dir., Dept. of Educational Leadership. cnelson@siue.edu. *Specializations:* M.S. in Education with concentrations in (1) Instructional Design and (2) Teaching, Learning, and Technology. *Features:* evening classes only. *Admission Requirements: Degree Requirements:* 36 semester hours; thesis optional. *Faculty:* 6 part-time. *Students:* 125.

University of Illinois at Urbana-Champaign. Department of Educational Psychology. 210 Education Bldg.1310 S. 6th St., Champaign, IL 61820. (217) 333-2245. Fax (217) 244-7620. Charles K. West, Prof., Div. of Learning and Instruction, Dept. of Educational Psychology. c-west@uiuc.edu. *Specializations:* M.A., M.S., and Ed.M. with emphasis in Instructional Design and Educational Computing. Ph.D. in Educational Psychology with emphasis in Instructional Design and Educational Computing. *Features:* Ph.D. program is individually tailored and strongly research-oriented with emphasis on applications of cognitive science to instruction. *Admission Requirements:* excellent academic record, high GRE scores, and strong letters of recommendation. *Degree Requirements:* 8 units for Ed.M., 6 units and thesis for M.A. or M.S. Ph.D.: 8 units coursework, approx. 4 units of research methods courses, minimum 8 hours of written qualifying exams, 8 units Thesis credits. *Faculty:* 8 full-time, 5 part-time. *Students:* 31 full-time, 7 part-time. *Financial Assistance:* scholarships, research assistantships, and teaching assistantships available; fellowships for very highly academically talented; some tuition waivers.

Western Illinois University. Instructional Technology and Telecommunications. 37 Harrabin Hall, Macomb, IL 61455. (309) 298-1952. Fax (309) 298-2978. http://www. wiu.edu/users/miitt/. M.H. Hassan, Chair. Specialization: master's degree. mh-hassan@ wiu.edu. *Features:* New program approved by Illinois Board of Higher Education in January 1996 with emphases in Instructional Technology, Telecommunications, Interactive Technologies, and Distance Education. Selected courses delivered via satellite TV and compressed video. *Admission Requirements:* bachelor's degree 3.0/4.0 GRE score. *Degree Requirements:* 32 semester hours, thesis or applied project, or 35 semester hours with portfolio. Certificate Program in Instructional Technology Specialization. Graphic applications, training development, video production. Each track option is made of 5 courses or a total of 15 semester hours. *Faculty:* 8 full-time. *Students:* 35 full-time, 150 part-time. *Financial Assistance:* graduate and research assistantships, internships, residence hall assistants, veterans' benefits, loans, and part-time employment.

Indiana

Indiana State University. Dept. of Curriculum, Instruction, and Media Technology, Terre Haute, IN 47809. (812) 237-2937. Fax (812) 237-4348. Dr. James E. Thompson, Program Coord. efthomp@befac.indstate.edu. *Specializations:* master's degree in Instructional Technology with education focus or with non-education focus; Specialist Degree program in Instructional Technology; Ph.D. in Curriculum, Instruction with specialization in Media Technology. *Degree Requirements:* master's: 32 semester hours, including 18 in media; thesis optional; Ed.S.: 60 semester hours beyond bachelor's degree; Ph.D., approximately 100 hours beyond bachelor's degree. *Faculty:* 5 full-time. *Students:* 17 full-time, 13 part-time. *Financial Assistance:* 7 assistantships.

Indiana University. School of Education. W. W. Wright Education Bldg., Rm. 2276, 201 N. Rose Ave., Bloomington, IN 47405-1006. (812) 856-8451. Fax (812) 856-8239. http://education.indiana.edu/~ist/. Elizabeth Boling, Chair, Dept. of Instructional Systems Technology. istdept@indiana.edu. *Specializations:* M.S. and Ed.S. degrees designed for individuals seeking to be practitioners in the field of Instructional Technology. M.S. degree also offered in Web-based format with instructional product and portfolio requirements. Offers Ph.D. degree with four program focus areas: Foundations; Instructional Analysis, Design, and Development; Instructional Development and Production; and Implementation and Management. *Features:* Requires computer skills as a prerequisite and makes technology utilization an integral part of the curriculum; eliminates separation of various media formats; and establishes a series of courses of increasing complexity integrating production and development. The latest in technical capabilities have been incorporated, including teaching, computer, and laptop-ready laboratories, a multimedia laboratory, and video and audio production studios. *Admission Requirements:* M.S.: bachelor's degree from an accredited institution, 1350 GRE (3 tests required) or 900 plus 3.5 analytical writing (new format), 2.75 undergraduate GPA. Ed.S. and Ph.D.: 1650 GRE (3 tests required) or 1100 plus 4.5 analytical writing (new format), 3.5 graduate GPA. *Degree Requirements:* M.S.: 36 credit hours (including 15 credits in required courses); colloquia; an instructional product; and 9 credits in outside electives, and portfolio. Ed.S.: 65 hours, capstone project with written report and a portfolio. Ph.D.: 90 hours, portfolio, and thesis. *Faculty:* 11 full-time, 2 part-time. *Students:* 240 (includes full-time, part-time, and ABDs). *Financial Assistance:* assistantships, fellowships. *Degrees Awarded 2003:* 48 M.S.; 2 Ed.S.; 10 Ph.D. (2002).

Purdue University. School of Education, Department of Curriculum and Instruction. 100 N. University St., W. Lafayette, IN 47907-2098. (765) 494-5669. Fax (765) 496-1622. http://www.edci.purdue.edu/et/. Dr. Tim Newby, Prof. of Educational Technology. edtech@soe.purdue.edu. *Specializations:* master's degree and Ph.D. in Educational Technology. Master's program started in 1982, Ph.D. in 1985. *Features:* Vision Statement

—The Educational Technology Program at Purdue University nurtures graduates who are effective designers of learning experiences and environments that incorporate technology to engage learners and improve learning. *Admission Requirements:* master's and Ph.D.: 3.0 GPA, three letters of recommendation, statement of personal goals. A score of 550 (paper-based) or 213 (computer-based) or above on the Test of English as a Foreign Language (TOEFL) for individuals whose first language is not English. Ph.D. Additional Requirement: 1000 GRE (verbal + quantitative); verbal score of at least 500 preferred. *Degree Requirements:* master's: minimum of 32 semester hours (17 in educational technology, 6–9 in research, development, and exit requirements, 6–9 electives); thesis optional. Ph.D.: 60 semester hours beyond the master's degree (15–18 in educational technology, 27–30 in education and supporting areas; 15 dissertation research hours). *Faculty:* 6 full-time; 1 part-time. *Students:* 22 M.S.; 34 Ph.D.. *Financial Assistance:* assistantships and fellowships. *Degrees Awarded 2003:* 10.

Iowa

Clarke College. Graduate Studies. 1550 Clarke Drive, Dubuque, IA 52001. (563) 588-8180. Fax (563) 584-8604. http://www.clarke.edu. Margaret Lynn Lester. llester@clarke.edu. *Specializations:* M.A. in Technology and Education. *Features:* This program offers hybrid courses in educational technology. Courses are offered through WebCT and face-to-face. Course objectives are aligned with the National Educational Technology Standards. *Admission Requirements:* 2.5 GPA, GRE (verbal + quantitative) or MAT, $25 application fee, two letters of recommendation. *Degree Requirements:* 12 hours of core courses and 18–21 hours in technology courses for teachers. *Faculty:* 1 full-time, 1–2 part-time. *Students:* 10 part-time. *Financial Assistance:* scholarships, student loans. *Degrees Awarded 2003:* 3.

Iowa State University. College of Education. E262 Lagomarcino Hall, Ames, IA 50011. (515) 294-7021. Fax (515) 294-6260. http://www.educ.iastate.edu/. Niki Davis, Director, Center for Technology in Learning and Teaching. nedavis@iastate.edu. *Specializations:* M.Ed., M.S., and Ph.D. in Curriculum and Instructional Technology. *Features:* Prepares candidates as practitioners and researchers in the field of curriculum and instructional technology. All areas of specialization emphasize appropriate and effective applications of technology in teacher education. M.Ed. program also offered at a distance (online and face-to-face learning experiences). Practicum experiences related to professional objectives, supervised study and research projects tied to long-term studies within the program, development and implementation of new techniques, teaching strategies, and operational procedures in instructional resources centers and computer labs, program emphasis on technologies for teachers. *Admission Requirements:* M.Ed. and M.S.: bachelor's degree, top half of undergraduate class, official transcripts, three letters, autobiography. Ph.D.: top half of undergraduate class, official transcripts, three letters, autobiography, GRE scores, scholarly writing sample. *Degree Requirements:* M.Ed. 32 credit hours (7 research, 12 foundations, 13 applications and leadership in instructional technology); and action research project. M.S. 36 credit hours (16 research, 12 foundations, 8 applications and leadership in instructional technology); and thesis. Ph.D. 78 credit hours (minimum of 12 research, minimum of 15 foundations, additional core credits in conceptual, technical and advanced specialization areas, minimum of 12 dissertation);portfolio, and dissertation. *Faculty:* 5 full-time, 2 part-time. *Students:* M.Ed. and M.S.: 80. Ph.D.: 45. *Financial Assistance:* Assistantships and fellowships.

University of Iowa. Division of Psychological and Quantitative Foundations. College of Education, Iowa City, IA 52242. (319) 335-5519. Fax (319) 335-5386. http://www. uiowa.edu/~coe2/facstaff/salessi.htm. Stephen Alessi, 361 Lindquist Center. provost-office@uiowa.edu. *Specializations:* M.A. and Ph.D. with specializations in Training and Human Resources Development, Computer Applications, and Media Design and Production

(MA only). *Features:* flexibility in planning to fit individual needs, backgrounds, and career goals. The program is interdisciplinary, involving courses within divisions of the College of Education, as well as in the schools of Business, Library Science, Radio and Television, Linguistics, and Psychology. *Admission Requirements:* MA: 2.8 undergraduate GPA, 500 GRE (verbal + quantitative), personal letter of interest. Ph.D.: master's degree, 1000 GRE (verbal + quantitative), 3.2 GPA on all previous graduate work for regular admission. Conditional admission may be granted. Teaching or relevant experience may be helpful. *Degree Requirements:* MA: 35 semester hours, 3.0 GPA, final project or thesis, comprehensive exam. Ph.D.: 90 semester hours, comprehensive exams, dissertation. *Faculty:* 4 full-time, 3 part-time. *Financial Assistance:* assistantships, grants, student loans, and scholarships.

University of Northern Iowa. Educational Technology Program. 618 Schinder Education Center, Cedar Falls, IA 50614-0606. (319) 273-3250. Fax (319) 273-5886. http://ci.coe. uni.edu/edtech/index.html. Sharon E. Smaldino. Sharon.Smaldino@UNI.edu. *Specializations:* M.A. in Curriculum and Instruction: Educational Technology, M.A. in Performance and Training Technology. *Features:* The master's degrees are designed to meet the AECT/ECIT standards and are focused on addressing specific career choices. The Educational Technology master's is designed to prepare educators for a variety of professional positions in educational settings, including: school building level, school district level, vocational-technical school, community college, and university. The Performance and Training Technology master's is designed for persons planning to work in nonschool settings. Majors in this area will complete a basic core of coursework applicable to all preparing for work as media specialists, trainers in industry and business, or communications designers. Specific areas of interest will determine the supporting electives. Licensure as a teacher is not required for admission to either master's in Iowa. The bachelor's degree may be in any field. *Admission Requirements:* bachelor's degree, 3.0 undergraduate GPA, 500 TOEFL. *Degree Requirements:* 38 semester credits, optional thesis worth 6 credits or alternative research paper of project, comprehensive exam. *Faculty:* 4 full-time, 6 part-time. *Students:* 120. *Financial Assistance:* assistantships, grants, student loans, scholarships, student employment. *Degrees Awarded 2003:* 32.

Kansas

Emporia State University. Instructional Design and Technology (IDT). 1200 Commercial St., Campus Box 4037, Emporia, KS 66801. (620) 341-5829. Fax (620) 341-5785. http://idt.emporia.edu. Dr. Marcus D. Childress, Chair. marcus.childress@emporia.edu. *Specializations:* distance education, Web-based education, corporate education. *Features:* All required courses available via the Internet. All forms and application materials available at the Web site: http://idt.emporia.edu. *Admission Requirements:* 2.75 undergrad. GPA; resume; two recommendations; writing competency. Two admission approval dates each year: September 15 (for spring semester admission) and February 15 (for fall semester admission). Only applicants with completed admission packets will be considered. An IDT admission committee will meet to review admission materials. Applicants will be admitted to the IDT graduate program based on the selection process. Those applicants who are not admitted may request that their names be placed on a waiting list for the next semester. *Degree Requirements:* 36 semester hours: 19 credits core, 6 credits research, 11 credits electives. *Faculty:* 5.5 full-time. *Students:* 10 full-time; 140 part-time. *Financial Assistance:* 4 GTA positions per year. *Degrees Awarded 2003:* 28 awarded in 2003–2004.

Emporia State University. School of Library and Information Management. 1200 Commercial, P.O. Box 4025, Emporia, KS 66801. (800) 552-4770. Fax (620) 341-5233. http://slim.emporia.edu. Daniel Roland, Director of Communications. sliminfo@emporia.edu. *Specializations:* Master's of Library Science (ALA accredited program); Master's in Legal Information Management, in partnership with the University of Kansas School of

Law, 50 semester hours or 15-hour certificate. School Library Certification program, which includes 27 hours of the M.L.S. program; Ph.D. in Library and Information Management; B.S. in Information Resource Studies; Information Management Certificate: 18 hours of MLS curriculum; Library Services Certificates: 6 separate 12-hour programs of undergraduate work available for credit or noncredit. Areas include Information Sources and Services; Collection Management; Technology; Administration; Youth Services; and Generalist. *Features:* The Master of Library Science program is also delivered to satellite campus sites in Denver, Salt Lake City, Portland, Oregon. New programs tend to start every three years in each location. New programs include Denver, Summer 2004; Portland, Spring 2005, Salt Lake City, Fall 2005. *Admission Requirements:* Undergrad GPA of 3.0 or better for master's degrees, 3.5 or better for PhD. GRE score of 1,000 points combined in Verbal and Analytical sections for master's degrees, 1,100 for PhD. GRE can be waived for students already holding a graduate degree in which they earned a 3.75 GPA or better. Admission interview. *Degree Requirements:* M.L.S.: 42 semester hours. Ph.D.: total of 55-59 semester hours beyond the master's. *Faculty:* 10 full-time, 25 part-time. *Students:* 71 full-time, 297 part-time. *Financial Assistance:* assistantships, grants, student loans, scholarships, doctoral fellowships. *Degrees Awarded 2003:* 127 master's degrees, 2 doctoral degrees.

Kansas State University. Educational Computing, Design, and Online Learning. 363 Bluemont Hall, Manhattan, KS 66506. (785) 532-7686. Fax (785) 532-7304. http://coe.ksu.edu/ecdol. Dr. Diane McGrath. dmcgrath@ksu.edu. *Specializations:* M.S. in Curriculum and Instruction with a specialization in Educational Computing, Design, and Online Learning; Ph.D. and Ed.D. in Curriculum & Instruction with a specialization in Educational Computing, Design, and Online Learning. Master's program started in 1982; doctoral in 1987. *Features:* Coursework focuses on research, theory, practice, ethics, and design of learning environments. Students work in a project-based learning environment much of the time but also read, discuss, and write and present papers. The program does not focus on how to do particular applications, but rather on how and why one might use technology to improve the learning environment. Some courses focus on the K–12 learning environment (generally MS coursework) and others on lifelong learning. *Admission Requirements:* M.S.: B average in undergraduate work, one programming language, 590 TOEFL. Ed.D. and Ph.D.: B average in undergraduate and graduate work, one programming language, GRE or MAT, three letters of recommendation, experience or course in educational computing. *Degree Requirements:* M.S.: 33 semester hours (minimum of 15 in Educational Computing); thesis, internship, or practicum not required, but all three are possible. Capstone project or research is required. Ed.D.: 94 semester hours (minimum of 18 hours in Educational Computing or related area approved by committee, 16 hours dissertation research, 12 hours internship); thesis. Ph.D.: 90 semester hours (minimum of 21 hours in Educational Computing, Design, and Online Learning or related area approved by committee, 30 hours for dissertation research); thesis; internship or practicum not required but available. *Faculty:* 1 full-time, 2 part-time, other faculty available to serve on committees. *Students:* M.S., 0 full-time, est. 30 part-time; doctoral, 20 full-time, 10 part-time. *Financial Assistance:* 2–3 assistantships typically go to people associated with the program; 3 assistantships on a related grant project; other assistantships sometimes available in other departments. *Degrees Awarded 2003:* 2002: 1 MS degree and 1 EdD. 2003: 1 MS degree and 5 PhDs.

Kentucky

University of Louisville. College of Education and Human Development. Belknap Campus, Louisville, KY 40292. (502) 852-6667. Fax (502) 852-4563. http://www.louisville.edu/edu. Carolyn Rude-Parkins, Chair of Leadership, Foundations, Human Resource

Education. cparkins@louisville.edu. *Specializations:* Master's in Instructional Technology (appropriate for K–12 teacher and for trainers / adult educators), post-master's/Rank 1 in Instructional Technology (K–12 teachers). Doctoral strand in Instructional Technology Leadership. Technology Leadership Institute Cohort for Jefferson County Schools offered onsite. *Features:* Appropriate for business or school audiences. Program is based on ISTE and ASTD standards, as well as Kentucky Experienced Teacher Standards. *Admission Requirements:* 2.75 GPA, 800 GRE, 2 letters of recommendation, application fee. *Degree Requirements:* 30 semester hours, internship. *Faculty:* 2 full-time, 6 part-time. *Students:* 75 part-time students. *Financial Assistance:* graduate assistantships. *Degrees Awarded 2003:* 20 M.Ed.

Louisiana

Louisiana State University. School of Library and Information Science. 267 Coates Hall, Baton Rouge, LA 70803. (225) 578-3158. Fax (225) 578-4581. http://slis.lsu.edu. Beth Paskoff, Dean, Assoc. Prof., School of Library and Information Science. bpaskoff@lsu.edu. *Specializations:* M.L.I.S., C.L.I.S. (post-master's certificate), Louisiana School Library Certification. An advanced certificate program is available. *Features:* none. *Admission Requirements:* bachelor's degree, with 3.00 average. *Degree Requirements:* M.L.I.S.: 40 hours, comprehensive exam, one semester full-time residence, completion of degree program in five years. *Faculty:* 10 full-time. *Students:* 84 full-time, 86 part-time. *Financial Assistance:* A large number of graduate assistantships are available to qualified students. *Degrees Awarded 2003:* 90.

Maryland

McDaniel College (formerly Western Maryland College). Department of Education,. 2 College Hill, Westminster, MD 21157. (410) 857-2507. Fax (410) 857-2515. http://www.mcdaniel.edu. Dr. Ramona N. Kerby, Coord., School Library Media Program, Dept. of Education. rkerby@mcdaniel.edu. *Specializations:* M.S. in Education with an emphasis in School Library Media. *Features:* School librarianship. *Admission Requirements:* 3.0 Undergraduate GPA, 3 reference checklist forms from principal and other school personnel, acceptable application essay, acceptable Praxis test scores. *Degree Requirements:* 34 credit hours, including professional digital portfolio. *Faculty:* 1 full-time, 7 part-time. *Students:* 140, most part-time.

The Johns Hopkins University. Graduate Division of Education, Technology for Educators Program. Columbia Gateway Park, 6740 Alexander Bell Drive, Columbia, MD 21046. (410) 309-9537. Fax (410) 312-3868. http://www.spsbe.jhu.edu. Dr. Linda Tsantis, Program Coordinator; Dr. John Castellani, Program Coordinator. tsantis@jhu.edu. *Specializations:* The Department of Technology for Education offers programs leading to the M.S. degree in Education, the M.S. in Special Education, and four specialized advanced Graduate Certificates: Technology for Multimedia and Internet-Based Instruction; Instructional Technology for Online Professional Development and Training; Data-Driven Decision-Making; and Assistive Technology for Communication and Social Interaction. *Features:* Focuses on training educators to become decision makers and leaders in the use of technology, with competencies in the design, development, and application of emerging technologies for teaching and learning. Incorporates basic elements that take into account the needs of adult learners, the constantly changing nature of technology, and the need for schools and universities to work together for schoolwide change. The Center for Technology in Education works in partnership with the graduate program linking research and teaching of the University with the leadership and policy direction of the Maryland State Department of Education. *Admission Requirements:* bachelor's degree with strong background in teaching, curriculum and instruction, special education, or a related service field.

Degree Requirements: 36 Credit hour part-time program, Electronic Portfolio in place of comprehensive exams. *Faculty:* 2 full-time, 30 part-time. *Students:* 300 part-time. *Financial Assistance:* grants, student loans, scholarships. *Degrees Awarded 2003:* 48.

Towson University. College of Education. Hawkins Hall, Towson, MD 21252. (410) 704-6268. Fax (410) 704-4227. http://wwwnew.towson.edu/coe/rset/insttech/. Dr. David R. Wizer, Associate Professor. Dept.: Reading, Special Education, and Instructional Technology. wizer@towson.edu. *Specializations:* M.S. degrees in Instructional Development, Educational Technology and School Library Media. Ed.D. degrees in Instructional Technology. *Features:* Excellent labs. Strong practical hands-on classes. Focus of MS program: Students produce useful multimedia projects for use in their teaching and training. Many group activities within courses. Innovative Ed.D. program with online hybrid courses and strong mix of theory and practical discussions. *Admission Requirements:* bachelor's degree from accredited institution with 3.0 GPA. (Conditional admission granted for many applicants with a GPA over 2.75.) *Degree Requirements:* MS degree is 36 graduate semester hours without thesis. Ed. D. is 63 hours beyond the MS degree. *Faculty:* Faculty: 10 full-time, 5 adjunct. *Students:* 20 full-time, 190 part-time [approximately]. *Financial Assistance:* graduate assistantships, work study, scholarships, loans. *Degrees Awarded 2003:* ~25 in master's degree program.

University of Maryland. College of Library and Information Services. 4105 Hornbake Library Bldg., South Wing, College Park, MD 20742-4345. (301) 405-2038. Fax (301) 314-9145. Ann Prentice, Dean and Program Chair. ap57@umail.umd.edu. *Specializations:* Master's of Library Science, including specialization in School Library Media; doctorate in Library and Information Services including specialization in Educational Technology/Instructional Communication. *Features:* Program is broadly conceived and interdisciplinary in nature, using the resources of the entire campus. The student and the advisor design a program of study and research to fit the student's background, interests, and professional objectives. Students prepare for careers in teaching and research in information science and librarianship and elect concentrations including Educational Technology and Instructional Communication. *Admission Requirements:* doctoral: bachelor's degree (the majority of doctoral students enter with master's degrees in Library Science, Educational Technology, or other relevant disciplines), GRE general tests, three letters of recommendation, statement of purpose. Interviews required when feasible for doctoral applicants. *Degree Requirements:* M.L.S.: 36 semester hours; thesis optional. *Faculty:* 15 full-time, 8 part-time. *Students:* master's, 106 full-time, 149 part-time; doctoral, 5 full-time, 11 part-time. *Financial Assistance:* assistantships, grants, student loans, scholarships, fellowships.

University of Maryland Baltimore County (UMBC). Department of Education. 1000 Hilltop Circle, Baltimore, MD 21250. (410) 455-2310. Fax (410) 455-3986. http://www.research.umbc.edu/~eholly/ceduc/isd/. Greg Williams, Ed.D, Program Director. isd-td@umbc.edu. *Specializations:* M.A. degrees in School Instructional Systems, Post-Baccalaureate Teacher Certification, Training in Business and Industry, Experienced Teacher—Advanced Degree, ESOL/Bilingual. *Features:* Programs are configured with evening courses to accommodate students who are changing careers. Maryland teacher certification is earned two-thirds of the way through the postbaccalaureate program. *Admission Requirements:* 3.0 undergraduate GPA, GRE scores. *Degree Requirements:* 36 semester hours (including 18 in systems development for each program); internship. *Faculty:* 18 full-time, 25 part-time. *Students:* 59 full-time, 254 part-time. *Financial Assistance:* assistantships, scholarships. *Degrees Awarded 2003:* 75.

Massachusetts

Boston University. School of Education. Two Sherborn St., Boston, MA 02215-1605. (617) 353-3181. Fax (617) 353-3924. http://Web.bu.edu/EDUCATION. David B.

Whittier, Asst. Professor and Coord., Program in Educational Media and Technology. whittier@bu.edu. *Specializations:* Ed.M., CAGS (Certificate of Advanced Graduate Study) in Educational Media and Technology; Ed.D. in Curriculum and Teaching, Specializing in Educational Media and Technology; preparation for Massachusetts public school certificates as Instructional Technology Specialist. *Features:* The master's program prepares graduates for professional careers as educators, instructional designers, developers of educational materials, and managers of the human and technology-based resources necessary to support education and training with technology. Graduates are employed in K–12 schools, higher education, industry, medicine, government, and publishing. Students come to the program from many backgrounds and with a wide range of professional goals. The doctoral program sets the study of Educational Media and Technology within the context of education and educational research in general, and curriculum and teaching in particular. In addition to advanced work in the field of Educational Media and Technology, students examine and conduct research and study the history of educational thought and practice relating to teaching and learning. Graduates make careers in education as professors and researchers, technology directors and managers, and as developers of technology-based materials and systems. Graduates also make careers in medicine, government, business, and industry as instructional designers, program developers, project managers, and training directors. Graduates who work in both educational and noneducational organizations are often responsible for managing the human and technological resources required to create learning experiences that include the development and delivery of technology-based materials and distance education. *Admission Requirements:* Ed.M.: recommendations, minimum 2.7 undergraduate GPA, graduate test scores are required and either the GRE or MAT must be completed within past five years. CAGs: Ed.M., recommendations, 2.7 undergraduate GPA, graduate test scores are required and either the GRE or MAT must be completed within past five years. Ed.D.: 3 letters of recommendation, MAT or GRE scores, transcripts, writing samples, statement of goals and qualifications, analytical essay, minimum 2.7 GPA. *Degree Requirements:* Ed.M.: 36 credit hours (including 24 hours from required core curriculum, 12 from electives). CAGs: 32 credits beyond Ed.M., one of which must be a curriculum and teaching course and a mini-comprehensive exam. Ed.D.: 60 credit hours of courses in Educational Media and Technology, curriculum and teaching, and educational thought and practice with comprehensive exams; coursework and apprenticeship in research; dissertation. *Faculty:* 1 full-time, 1 half-time, 10 part-time. *Students:* 20 full-time, 25 part-time. *Financial Assistance:* U.S. Government sponsored work study, assistantships, grants, student loans, scholarships. *Degrees Awarded 2003:* EdM = 17; Ed D = 2.

Bridgewater State College. Library Media Program. Hart Hall, Rm. 219, Bridgewater, MA 02325. (508) 697-1320. Fax (508) 697-1771. http://www.bridgew.edu. Mary Frances Zilonis, Coord., Library Media Program. *Specialization:* M.Ed. in Library Media Studies. fzilonis@bridgew.edu. *Features:* This program heavily emphasizes teaching and technology. *Degree Requirements:* 39 semester hours; comprehensive exam. *Faculty:* 2 full-time, 6 part-time. *Students:* 58 in degree program, 30 nondegree. *Financial Assistance:* Graduate assistantships, graduate internships.

Fitchburg State College. Division of Graduate and Continuing Education. 160 Pearl Street, Fitchburg, MA 01420. (978) 665-3544. Fax (978) 665-3055. http://www.fsc.edu. Dr. Randy Howe, Chair. rhowe@fsc.edu. *Specializations:* M.S. in Communications Media with specializations in Applied Communication, Instructional Technology, and Library Media. *Features:* Collaborating with professionals working in the field both for organizations and as independent producers, Fitchburg offers a unique M.S. program. The objective of the Master of Science in Communications/Media Degree Programs is to develop in candidates the knowledge and skills for the effective implementation of communication within business, industry, government, not-for-profit agencies, health services, and education. *Admission Requirements:* MAT or GRE scores, official transcript(s) of a baccalaureate degree, two or more years of experience in communications or media, department interview and portfolio presentation, three letters of recommendation. *Degree Requirements:* 36 semester credit hours. *Faculty:* 1 full-time, 7 part-time. *Students:* 48 part-time. *Financial Assistance:* assistantships, student loans, scholarships. *Degrees Awarded 2003:* 7 MS in Communications/Media.

Harvard University. Graduate School of Education. Appian Way, Cambridge, MA 02138. (617) 495-3541. Fax (617) 495-3626. http://www.gse.harvard.edu/tie. Joseph Blatt, director, Technology in Education Program; Kristen DeAmicis, program coordinator, Technology in Education Program. deamickr@gse.harvard.edu. *Specializations:* Available degrees: Ed.M. in Technology in Education; Certificate of Advanced Study in Technology in Education; Ed.D. in Learning and Teaching, with research focus in technology in education. *Features:* Courses in design, technology policy and leadership, research and evaluation. Access to other courses throughout Harvard University, and at MIT. Internship opportunities. *Admission Requirements:* bachelor's degree, MAT or GRE scores, 600 TOEFL, 3 recommendations. Students interested in further information about the TIE Program should visit the Web site (URL above), which includes a link to the Harvard Graduate School of Education online application. *Degree Requirements:* 32 semester credits. *Faculty:* 5 full-time, 4 part-time. *Students:* approx. 55: 45 full-time, 10 part-time. *Financial Assistance:* Determined by Harvard policies. *Degrees Awarded 2003:* 45.

Lesley University. Technology In Education. 29 Everett St., Cambridge, MA 02138-2790. (617) 349-8419. Fax (617) 349-8169. http://www.lesley.edu/soe/111tech.html. Dr. Isa Kaftal Zimmerman, Division Director. ikzimmer@lesley.edu. *Specializations:* M.Ed. in Technology in Education GAGS in Technology in Education. PhD in Educational Studies with specialization in Technology in Education. *Features:* M.Ed. program is offered off-campus at 70+ sites in 21 states; contact (617) 349-8311 for information. The degree is also offered completely online. Contact Maureen Yoder, myoder@lesley.edu, or (617) 348-8421 for information. Or check our Web site (URL above). *Admission Requirements:* Completed bachelor's degree. *Degree Requirements:* M.Ed.: 33 semester hours in technology, integrative final project in lieu of thesis, no internship or practicum. C.A.G.S.: 36 semester hours. Ph.D. requirements available on request. *Faculty:* 12 full-time and 1 part-time core, approximately 200 part-time adjuncts on the master's and doctorate levels. *Students:* 1500+ part-time. *Financial Assistance:* Information available from Admissions Office. *Degrees Awarded 2003:* Approximately 375.

Simmons College. Graduate School of Library and Information Science. 300 The Fenway, Boston, MA 02115-5898. (617) 521-2800. Fax (617) 521-3192. http://www.simmons.edu/gslis/. Dr. James C. Baughman, Prof. jbaughman@simmons.edu. *Specializations:* M.S. Dual degrees: M.L.S./M.A. in Education (for School Library Media Specialists); M.L.S./M.A. in History (Archives Management Program). A Doctor of Arts in Administration is also offered. *Features:* The program prepares individuals for a variety of careers, media technology emphasis being only one. There are special programs for School Library Media Specialist and Archives Management with strengths in Information Science/Systems, Media Management. *Admission Requirements:* B.A. or B.S. degree with 3.0 GPA, statement, three letters of reference. *Degree Requirements:* 36 semester hours. *Faculty:* 14 full-time. *Students:* 75 full-time, 415 part-time. *Financial Assistance:* assistantships, grants, student loans, scholarships.

University of Massachusetts—Boston. Graduate College of Education. 100 Morrissey Blvd, Boston, MA 02125. (617) 287-5980. Fax (617) 287-7664. http://www.umb.edu. Donald D. Babcock, Graduate Program Dir. babcock@umbsky.cc.umb.edu. *Specializations:* M.Ed. in Instructional Design. *Admission Requirements:* MAT or previous master's degree, goal statement, three letters of recommendation, resume, interview. *Degree Requirements:* 36 semester hours, thesis or project. *Faculty:* 1 full-time, 9 part-time. *Students:* 8 full-time, 102 part-time. *Financial Assistance:* graduate assistantships providing tuition plus stipend.

University of Massachusetts—Lowell. Graduate School of Education. 255 Princeton Street, North Chelmsford, MA 01863. (508) 934-4601. Fax (508) 934-3005. http://gse. uml.edu/. Vera Ossen, Coordinator, Graduate Program in Teaching. vera_ossen@uml.edu. *Specializations:* M.Ed., CAGS, and Ed.D. concentrations in Educational Technology may be pursued in the context of any degree program area (Leadership, Administration and Policy; Curriculum and Instruction; Math and Science Education; Reading, Language Arts and Literacy). The M.Ed. program in Curriculum and Instruction has a specialization strand in educational technology. The Certificate of Advanced Graduate Study (CAGS), equivalent to 30 credits beyond a M.Ed., is also offered. *Features:* As part of the U Mass Lowell "CyberEd" online learning initiative, a new Web-based M.Ed./state certification program in educational administration was launched in 2001 and is now in full swing. The school also manages an extensive video network that links the university with other campuses in the state higher education system and with area public schools. Technology is heavily infused into the teacher preparation and school support programs, where new initiatives have been supported by grants from several federal and nonfederal sources. *Admission Requirements:* For admission at the master's level, a bachelor's degree from an accredited institution in an academic discipline is required, along with a completed application form, recent GRE scores, a narrative statement of purpose, and three written recommendations. Additional admission requirements and conditions are described in the UMass Lowell Graduate Catalog. *Degree Requirements:* M.Ed. 30 credits beyond bachelor's; Ed.D. 60 credits beyond master's plus dissertation based on original research and demonstration of comprehensive mastery in relevant fields of inquiry. *Faculty:* Various full-time and part-time faculty members teach educational technology courses in the school. *Students:* FTE approximately 500. *Financial Assistance:* Assistantships; work-study; student loans; occasional scholarships. *Degrees Awarded 2003:* Approximately 75.

Michigan

Eastern Michigan University. Teacher Education. 313 John W. Porter Building, Ypsilanti, MI 48197. (734) 487-3260. Fax (734) 487-2101. http://www.emich.edu. Toni Stokes Jones, Ph.D., Assistant Professor/Graduate Coordinator. tsjones@online.emich.edu. *Specializations:* M.A. in Educational Psychology with concentration in Educational Technology. The mission of this program is to prepare professionals who are capable of facilitating student learning in a variety of settings. The program is designed to provide students with both the knowledge base and the application skills that are required to use technology effectively in education. Focusing on the design, development, utilization, management and evaluation of instructional systems moves us toward achieving this mission. Students who complete the educational technology concentration will be able to (a) provide a rationale for using technology in the educational process; (b) identify contributions of major leaders in the field of educational media technology and instructional theory, and the impact that each leader has had on the field; (c) assess current trends in the area of educational media technology and relate the trends to past events and future implications; (d) integrate technology into instructional programs; (e) teach the operation and various uses of educational technology in instruction; (f) act as consultants/facilitators in educational media technology; (g) design and develop instructional products to meet specified needs; and (h) evaluate the effectiveness of instructional materials and systems. *Features:* Courses in our 30 credit hour Educational Media and Technology (EDMT) program include technology and the reflective teacher, technology and student-centered learning, technology enhanced learning environments, issues and emerging technologies, instructional design, internet for educators, advanced technologies, psychology of the adult learning, principles of classroom learning, curriculum foundations, research seminar and seminar in educational technology. Effective Spring 2003, all of the EDMT courses will be taught online. In some EDMT courses, students may be asked to come to campus only 3 times during the semester. Students who do not want to receive a master's degree can apply for admission to our 18-credit-hour Educational Media and Technology certificate. The

EDMT courses for the certificate are also offered online. *Admission Requirements:* Individuals seeking admission to this program must:

1. comply with the Graduates School admission requirements

2. score 550 or better on the TOEFL and 5 or better on TWE, if a nonnative speaker of English

3. have a 2.75 undergraduate grade point average, or a 3.30 grade point average in 12 hours or more of work in a master's program

4. solicit three letters of reference

5. submit a statement of professional goals

Degree Requirements: To graduate, each student is expected to:

1. complete all work on an approved program of study (30 semester hours)

2. maintain a B (3.0 GPA) average or better on coursework taken within the program

3. get a recommendation from the faculty adviser

4. fill out an application for graduation and obtain the advisers recommendation

5. meet all other requirements for a master's degree adopted by the Graduate School of Eastern Michigan University

6. complete a culminating experience (research, instructional development or evaluation project) as determined by the student and faculty adviser

Faculty: 5 full-time; 3 part-time. *Students:* 75. *Financial Assistance:* graduate assistantship. *Degrees Awarded 2003:* 10.

Michigan State University. College of Education. 513E Erickson, East Lansing, MI 48824. (517) 353-0637. Fax (517) 353-6393. http://edutech.educ.msu.edu/master's/ TLTEL.htm. Susan Way. ways@msu.edu. *Specializations:* M.A. in Educational Technology with Learning, Design and Technology specialization. *Features:* Extensive opportunities to work with faculty in designing online courses and online learning environments. Several courses available online. *Admission Requirements:* bachelor's degree, two letters of recommendation, goal statement *Degree Requirements:* 30 semester hours, Web-based portfolio. *Faculty:* 14 full-time. *Students:* approximately 60. *Financial Assistance:* some assistantships for highly qualified students. *Degrees Awarded 2003:* 6.

University of Michigan. Department of Educational Studies. 610 East University, Ann Arbor, MI 48109-1259. (734) 763-7500. Fax (734) 615-1290. http://www.soe.umich.edu/learningtechnologies/. Barry J. Fishman. fishman@umich.edu. *Specializations:* M.A., M.S., Ph.D. in Learning Technologies. *Features:* The Learning Technologies Program at the University of Michigan integrates the study of technology with a focus in a substantive content area. A unique aspect of the program is that your learning and research will engage you in real-world educational contexts. You will find that understanding issues related to a specific content area provides an essential context for meaningful research in learning. Your understanding of technology, school contexts, and a content area will place you among the leaders who design and conduct research on advanced technological systems that change education and schooling. The doctoral specialization in Learning Technologies must be taken in conjunction with a substantive concentration designed in consultation with your advisor. Current active concentrations include: Science, Literacy, Culture and

Gender, Teacher Education, Design and Human-Computer Interaction, Policy, and Social Studies. Other areas are possible. The Master's Degree in Learning Technologies at the University of Michigan prepares professionals for leadership roles in the design, development, implementation, and research of powerful technologies to enhance learning. Our approach to design links current knowledge and research about how people learn with technological tools that enable new means of organizing and evaluating learning environments. Course and project work reflects the latest knowledge and practice in learning, teaching, and technology. Core courses prepare students to use current understandings about learning theory, design principles, research methodologies, and evaluation strategies in educational settings ranging from classrooms to Web-based and distributed learning environments. Faculty work with students to shape programs that meet individual interests. Practical experience is offered through internships with area educational institutions. *Admission Requirements:* GRE, B.A. for M.A., M.S., or Ph.D.; TOEFL for students from countries where English is not the primary language. *Degree Requirements:* M.A. and M.S.: 30 hours beyond B.A. Ph.D.: 60 hours beyond B.A. or 30 hours beyond master's plus research paper/qualifying examination, and dissertation. *Faculty:* 3 full-time, 6 part-time. *Students:* 35 full-time, 1 part-time. *Financial Assistance:* assistantships, grants, student loans, scholarships, internships. *Degrees Awarded 2003:* 10.

Wayne State University. 381 Education, Detroit, MI 48202. (313) 577-1728. Fax (313) 577-1693. http://www.coe.wayne.edu/InstructionalTechnology. Rita C. Richey, Prof., Program Coord., Instructional Technology Programs, Div. of Administrative and Organizational Studies, College of Education. rrichey@coe.wayne.edu. *Specializations:* M.Ed. degrees in Performance Improvement and Training, K–12 Educational Technology, and Interactive Technologies. Ed.D. and Ph.D. programs to prepare individuals for leadership in business, industry, health care, and the K–12 school setting as instructional design and development specialists; media or learning resources managers or consultants; specialists in instructional video; and computer-assisted instruction and multimedia specialists. The school also offers a six-year specialist degree program in Instructional Technology. *Features:* Guided experiences in instructional design and development activities in business and industry are available. *Admission Requirements:* Ph.D.: master's degree, 3.5 GPA, GRE, MAT, strong professional recommendations, interview. *Degree Requirements:* M.Ed.: 36 semester hours, including required project; internship recommended. *Faculty:* 6 full-time, 5 part-time. *Students:* 525 M.Ed.; 95 doctoral, most part-time. *Financial Assistance:* student loans, scholarships, and paid internships.

Minnesota

Minnesota State University. Educational Leadership, College of Education. MSU 313 Armstrong Hall, Mankato, MN 56001. (507) 389-1965. Fax (507) 389-5751. http://www.coled.mnsu.edu/coled_new_home/coe_new.htm. Dr. P. Gushwa. prudence. gushwa@mnsu.edu. *Specializations:* M.S. in Educational Technology with three tracks; M.S. in Library Media Specialist; SP in Library Media Education. *Features:* Educational Technology certificates, Licensure program in Library Media. *Admission Requirements:* bachelor's degree, 2.75/4.0 for last 2 years of undergraduate work. *Degree Requirements:* 32 semester hour credits, comprehensive exam. *Faculty:* 4 full-time. *Students:* About 75. *Financial Assistance:* Contact Financial Aid Office.

St. Cloud State University. College of Education, St. Cloud, MN 56301-4498. (612) 255-2022. Fax (612) 255-4778. John G. Berling, Prof., Dir., Center for Information Media. jberling@tigger.stcloud.msus.edu. *Specializations:* master's degrees in Information Technologies, Educational Media, and Human Resources Development/Training. A Specialist degree is also offered. *Admission Requirements:* acceptance to Graduate School, written preliminary examination, interview *Degree Requirements:* master's: 51 quarter hours with thesis; 54 quarter hours, Plan B; 57 quarter hours, portfolio; 200-hour practicum is required for media generalist licensure. Coursework applies to Educational Media Master's program. *Faculty:* 7 full-time. *Students:* 15 full-time, 150 part-time. *Financial Assistance:* assistantships and scholarships.

Walden University. 155 5th Avenue South, Minneapolis, MN 55401. (800) 444-6795. http://www.waldenu.edu; http://www.waldenu.edu/ecti/ecti.html. Dr. Gwen Hillesheim, Chair. www@waldenu.edu or info@waldenu.edu. *Specializations:* M.S. in Educational Change and Technology Innovation. Ph.D. in Education in Learning and Teaching with specialization in Educational Technology. In 1998, a specialization in Distance Learning will be added. In addition, there is a generalist Ph.D. in Education in which students may choose and design their own areas of specialization. *Features:* delivered primarily online. *Admission Requirements:* accredited bachelor's. Ph.D.: accredited master's, goal statement, letters of recommendation. *Degree Requirements:* master's: 45 credit curriculum, 2 brief residencies, master's project. *Faculty:* 18 part-time. *Students:* 50 full-time, 53 part-time in master's program. *Financial Assistance:* student loans, 3 fellowships with annual review.

Missouri

Fontbonne College. 6800 Wydown Blvd., St. Louis, MO 63105. (314) 889-1497. Fax (314) 889-1451. Dr. Mary K. Abkemeier, Chair. mabkemei@fontbonne.edu. *Specializations:* M.S. in Computer Education. Features: small classes and coursework immediately applicable to the classroom. *Admission Requirements:* 2.5 undergraduate GPA, 3 letters of recommendation. *Degree Requirements:* 33 semester hours, 3.0 GPA. *Faculty:* 2 full-time, 12 part-time. *Students:* 4 full-time, 90 part-time. *Financial Assistance:* grants.

Northwest Missouri State University. Department of Computer Science/Information Systems. 800 University Ave., Maryville, MO 64468. (660) 562-1600. Fax 660-562-1963. http://www.nwmissouri.edu/~csis. Dr. Phillip Heeler, Chairperson. pheeler@mail.nwmissouri.edu. *Specializations:* M.S.Ed. in Instructional Technology. Certificate program in Instructional Technology. *Features:* These degrees are designed for industry trainers and computer educators at the elementary, middle school, high school, and junior college level. *Admission Requirements:* 3.0 undergraduate GPA, 700 GRE (V+Q). *Degree Requirements:* 32 semester hours of graduate courses in computer science education and instructional technology courses. Fifteen hours of computer education and instructional technology courses for the Certificate. *Faculty:* 12 full-time. *Students:* 5 full-time, 20 part-time. *Financial Assistance:* assistantships, grants, student loans, and scholarships. *Degrees Awarded 2003:* 10.

Southwest Missouri State University. School of Teacher Education. 901 S. National, Springfield, MO 65804. (417) 836-5280. Fax (417) 836-6252. http://www.smsu.edu/. Dr. Roger Tipling. RogerTipling@smsu.edu. *Specializations:* M.S. in Education. Emphasis areas: Technology Coordinator strand; Building Level Technology Specialist strand; School Library Media Specialist strand; Business/Industrial/Medical strand. *Features:* Production, Administration, Instructional Design, Selection and Utilization, Networking, Web Based Education, Hardware and Software Troubleshooting, Library Certification Courses, Building Level Technology Specialist Certificate Research Practicum. *Admission Requirements:* Graduate College Admission Standards, Three letters of reference, Autobiography, *Degree Requirements:* Minimum of 33 hrs. in Instructional Design and Technology, Major research paper or project, Comprehensive Exam, Practicum (dependent on emphasis). *Faculty:* Three full-time faculty, two part-time faculty. *Students:* Five to ten full-time students, more than 50 part-time students. *Financial Assistance:* Graduate Assistantships. *Degrees Awarded 2003:* 6.

University of Missouri—Columbia. School of Information Science & Learning Technologies. 303 Townsend Hall, Columbia, MO 65211. 573-882-4546. Fax 573-884-2917. www.coe.missouri.edu/~sislt. John Wedman. wedmanj@missouri.edu. *Specializations:* The Educational Technology emphasis area prepares educators and technologists for excellence and leadership in the design, development, and implementation of technology in education, training, and performance support. The program offers three focus areas: Technology in Schools, Networked Learning Systems, Training Design and Development Each focus area has its own set of competencies, coursework, and processes. *Features:* All three focus areas are available online via the Internet or on the MU campus. The Technology in Schools focus area is based on the ISTE competencies and culminates in an online portfolio based on these competencies. Several courses are augmented by technical resources developed at MU, including a technology integration knowledge repository and online collaboration tools. The Networked Learning Systems focus area offers a truly challenging and innovative set of technical learning experiences. Students have opportunities to work on large-scale software development projects, acquiring valuable experience and broadening their skill-set. The Digital Media ZONE supports anytime/anywhere technical skill development.

The Training and Development focus area links to business, military, and government contexts. The curriculum is offered by faculty with extensive experience in these contexts and is grounded in the problems and processes of today's workplace. EdS and PhD programs are also available. *Admission Requirements:* bachelor's degree with 3.0 in last 60 credit hours of coursework. GRE (V>500; A>500; W>3.5); TOEFL of 540 (207 computer-based test) (if native language is not English); letters of reference. *Degree Requirements:* master's: 30–34 credit hours; 15 hours at 400 level. Specific course requirements vary by focus area. *Faculty:* 8 full-time; 20 part-time. *Students:* 30 full-time; 210 part-time. *Financial Assistance:* Numerous graduate assistantships are available. Assistantships include stipend and tuition waiver. *Degrees Awarded 2003:* 72.

University of Missouri—Columbia. College of Education. 303 Townsend Hall, Columbia, MO 65211. (573) 882-4546. Fax (573) 884-2917. http://sislt.missouri.edu. John Wedman. wedmanj@missouri.edu. *Specializations:* The Educational Technology program takes a theory-based approach to designing, developing, implementing, and researching computer-mediated environments to support human activity. We seek individuals who are committed to life-long learning and who aspire to use advanced technology to improve human learning and performance. Graduates of the program will find opportunities to use their knowledge and competencies as classroom teachers, media specialists, district technology specialists and coordinators, designers and developers of technology-based learning and information systems, training specialists for businesses, medical settings, and public institutions, as well as other creative positions.

The curriculum has three focus areas: Technology in Schools; Network Learning Systems; Designing and Developing Learning Systems; with coursework tailored to each focus area. *Features:* Entire master's program is available online. Visit our Web site at: MUEdTech.Missouri.edu. *Admission Requirements:* master's: bachelor's degree, 1500 GRE score. Ph.D.: 3.2 graduate GPA, 1500 GRE, letter of recommendation, statement of purpose. *Degree Requirements:* Minimum of 30–35 graduate credit hours required for the degree. Minimum of 15 credit hours of upper division (400/9000) coursework.

Maximum of 6 hours of transfer credit. *Faculty:* 9 Full time; ~10 part-time. *Students:* master's ~200; Ph.D. 55. *Financial Assistance:* master's: assistantships, grants, student loans, scholarships. Ph.D.: graduate assistantships with tuition waivers; numerous academic scholarships ranging from $200 to $18,000. *Degrees Awarded 2003:* 55.

Webster University. Learning and Communication Arts, College of Education, St. Louis, MO 63119. (314) 968-7490. Fax (314) 968-7118. http://www.Webster.edu/gradcatalog/ed_tech.html. Dr. Phyllis Wilkinson. wilkinsp@Webster.edu. *Specializations:* master's degree (M.A.T.); State Certification in Media Technology is a program option. *Features:* -. *Admission Requirements:* bachelor's degree with 2.5 GPA *Degree Requirements:* 33 semester hours (including 24 in media); internship required. *Faculty:* 5. *Students:* 7 full-time, 28 part-time. *Financial Assistance:* partial scholarships, minority scholarships, government loans, and limited state aid.

Montana

University of Montana. School of Education. 32 Campus Drive, Missoula, MT 59812. (406) 243-5785. Fax (406) 243-4908. http://www.umt.edu. Dr. Carolyn Lott, Professor of Library/Media. carolyn.lott@mso.umt.edu. *Specializations:* M.Ed. and Specialist degrees; K–12 School Library Media specialization with School Library Media Certification endorsement. *Features:* 22 of 25 credits online. Combined program with University of Montana-Western in Dilon, MT. *Admission Requirements:* (both degrees): GRE, letters of recommendation, 2.5 GPA *Degree Requirements:* M.Ed.: 37 semester credit hours (18 overlap with library media endorsement). Specialist: 28 semester hours (18 overlap). *Faculty:* 2 full-time. *Students:* 5 full-time, 20 part-time. *Financial Assistance:* assistantships; contact the University of Montana Financial Aid Office. *Degrees Awarded 2003:* 1.

Nebraska

University of Nebraska—Kearney. Teacher Education. 905 West 25th Street, Kearney, NE 68849-5540. (308) 865-8833. Fax (308) 865-8097. http://www.unk.edu/departments/pte. Dr. Scott Fredrickson, Professor and Chair of the Instructional Technology Graduate Program. fredricksons@unk.edu. *Specializations:* M.S.ED in Instructional Technology, M.S.ED in Educational Media. *Features:* Four emphasis areas—Instructional Technology; Multimedia Development; Educational Media; Assistive Technology. *Admission Requirements:* M.S. GRE (or electronic portfolio meeting dept. requirements), acceptance into graduate school, approval of Instructional Technology Committee *Degree Requirements:* M.S.: 36 credit hours, Instructional technology project or field study. *Faculty:* 5 full-time, 10 part-time. *Students:* 120 full-time equivalent. *Financial Assistance:* assistantships, grants, student loans. *Degrees Awarded 2003:* 30.

University of Nebraska—Omaha. Department of Teacher Education. College of Education, Kayser Hall 208D, Omaha, NE 68182. (402) 554-2119. Fax (402) 554-2125. www.unomaha.edu/~edmedia. Dr. R. J. Pasco. rpasco@mail.unomaha.edu. *Specializations:* Library Media Endorsement (undergraduate and Graduate); M.S. in Secondary and Elementary Education, M.A. in Secondary and Elementary Education, both with Library Media concentration; M.S. in Reading with Library Media concentration; M.S. in Educational Administration, with Library Media concentration; Master's in Library Science Program (cooperative program with University of Missouri at Columbia); Instructional Technology Certificate—Graduate program only. *Features:* Library Media Endorsement (Undergraduate and Graduate); M.S. in Secondary and Elementary Education, M.A. in Secondary and Elementary Education, both with Library Media concentration; M.S. in Reading with Library Media concentration; M.S. in Educational Administration, with Educational Media concentration; Master's in Library Science Program (Cooperative program with University of Missouri at Columbia); Instructional Technology Certificate—Graduate program only. *Admission Requirements:* As per University of Nebraska at Omaha undergraduate and graduate requirements. *Degree Requirements:* Library Media Endorsement (Undergraduate and Graduate)—33 hours M.S. in Secondary and Elementary Education, M.A. in Secondary and Elementary Education, both with Library Media concentration—36 hours; M.S. in Reading with Library Media concentration—45 hours; M.S. in Educational Administration, with Educational Media concentration; Master's in Library Science Program (cooperative program with University of Missouri at Columbia)—42 hours. *Faculty:* 1 full-time, 4 part-time (adjunct). *Students:* 21 undergraduates; 157 graduate students (mix of part-time and full-time). *Financial Assistance:* Contact Financial Aid Office. *Degrees Awarded 2003:* 23.

Nevada

University of Nevada. Counseling and Educational Psychology Dept. College of Education, Reno, NV 89557. (702) 784-6327. Fax (702) 784-1990. http://www.unr.edu/unr/colleges/educ/cep/cepindex.html. Dr. LaMont Johnson, Program Coord., Information Technology in Education. Marlowe Smaby, Dept. Chair. ljohnson@unr.edu. *Specializations:* M.S. and Ph.D. *Admission Requirements:* bachelor's degree, 2.75 undergraduate GPA, 750 GRE (V+Q). *Degree Requirements:* 36 semester credits, optional thesis worth 6 credits, comprehensive exam. *Faculty:* 2 full-time, 1 part-time. *Students:* M.S., 15; Ph.D., 10.

New Jersey

Montclair State University. Department of Curriculum & Teaching. 1 Normal Avenue, Montclair, NJ 07043. (973) 655-5187. Fax (973) 655-7084. http://www.monclair.edu/pages/edmedia. Dr. Vanessa Domine, Professor of Educational Technology. dominev@mail.montclair.edu. *Specializations:* MSU offers two post-baccalaureate certification programs for Associate Educational Media Specialist Certification and (advanced) Educational Media Specialist Certification. A new master of education degree program in Educational Technology will take effect Fall 2005. Educational Technology courses will be offered beginning Fall 2004. *Features:* The Media Specialist programs provide instruction for persons preparing to function as directors of school media centers and programs at three levels: district, secondary and elementary. The curriculum focuses on the role of instructional context and the necessity to recognize and respect perceptions and views of the individual learner. Theory and practice are combined in the curriculum to afford students opportunities for productive roles in various educational and multicultural contexts. *Admission Requirements:* The advanced program provides certification (endorsement) as a Media Specialist for certified teachers who possess a master's degree in a related educational field. The Associate Educational Media Specialists certificate requires a bachelor's degree and a standard New Jersey teaching certificate. Potential candidates submit applications to the Graduate School office for review and evaluation. Approved applications will be forwarded to the Department of Curriculum and Teaching for review and the scheduling of interviews. *Degree Requirements:* Certification Requirements:18–21 semester hours of media and technology are required for the AEMS program and 30–33 hours for the EDMS program. *Faculty:* 3 full-time, 5 part-time. *Students:* 220. *Financial Assistance:* n/a. *Degrees Awarded 2003:* n/a.

Rutgers—The State University of New Jersey. Ph.D. Program in Communication, Information, and Library Studies, The Graduate School, New Brunswick, NJ 08901-1071. (732) 932-7447. Fax (732) 932-6916. http://www.scils.rutgers.edu/. Dr. Lea P. Stewart, Director, Master's Program, Dept. of Library and Information Studies, School of Communication, Information and Library Studies. (732) 932-9717. Fax (732) 932-2644. Dr. Carol Kuhlthan, Chair. lstewart@scils.rutgers.edu. *Specializations:* M.L.S. degree with specializations in Information Retrieval, Technical and Automated Services, Reference, School Media Services, Youth Services, Management and Policy Issues, and Generalist Studies. Ph.D. programs in Communication; Media Studies; Information Systems, Structures, and Users; Information and Communication Policy and Technology; and Library and Information Services. The school also offers a six-year specialist certificate program. *Features:* Ph.D. Program provides doctoral-level coursework for students seeking theoretical and research skills for scholarly and professional leadership in the information and communication fields. A course on multimedia structure, organization, access, and production is offered. *Admission Requirements:* Ph.D.: master's degree in Information Studies, Communication, Library Science, or related field; 3.0 undergraduate GPA; GRE scores; TOEFL (for applicants whose native language is not English). *Degree Requirements:* M.L.S.: 36 semester hours, in which the hours for media vary for individual students; practicum of 150 hours. *Faculty:* M.L.S., 15 full-time, 12 adjunct; Ph.D., 43. *Students:* M.L.S., 97 full-time, 199 part-time; Ph.D., 104. *Financial Assistance:* M.L.S.: scholarships, fellowships, and graduate assistantships. Ph.D.: assistantships.

William Paterson University. College of Education. 300 Pompton Rd., Wayne, NJ 07470. (973) 720-2140. Fax (973) 720-2585. http://pwcWeb.wilpaterson.edu/wpcpages/library/default.htp. Dr. Amy G. Job, Librarian, Assoc. Prof., Coord., Program in Library/Media, Elementary and Early Childhood Dept. joba@wpunj.edu. *Specializations:* M.Ed. for Educational Media Specialist, Associate Media Specialist, Ed.S. *Features:* Provides training for New Jersey certified Educational Media Specialists and Associate Media Specialists. *Admission Requirements:* teaching certificate, 2.75 GPA, MAT or GRE scores, 1 year teaching experience. Assoc.Ed.S.: certificate, 2.75 GPA *Degree Requirements:* M.Ed.: 33 semester hours, including research projects and practicum. Assoc.Ed.S.: 18 semester hours. *Faculty:* 6 full-time, 2 part-time. *Students:* 30 part-time. *Financial Assistance:* limited. *Degrees Awarded 2003:* 6.

New York

Buffalo State College. CIS Department. 1300 Elmwood Ave., Buffalo, NY 14222-1095. (716) 878-4923. Fax (716) 878-6677. http://www.buffalostate.edu/depts/edcomputing/. Dr. Anthony J. Nowakowski, Program Coordinator. nowakoaj@buffalostate.edu. *Specializations:* M.S. in Education in Educational Computing. *Features:* This program is designed for educators who wish to develop and expand their skills in the educational application of computers. Emphasis is given to the use of computers in the instructional process. *Admission Requirements:* bachelor's degree from accredited institution, 3.0 GPA in last 60 hours, 3 letters of recommendation. *Degree Requirements:* 33 semester hours (15 hours in computers, 12–15 hours in education, 3-6 electives); thesis or project (see: www.buffalostate.edu/edc). *Faculty:* 5 part-time. *Students:* 3 full-time, 98 part-time.

Fordham University. Department of Communication and Media Studies. Rose Hill Campus, 441 E. Fordham Rd., Bronx, NY 10458. (718) 817-4860. Fax (718) 817-4868. http://www.fordham.edu. Robin Andersen, Department Chair; James Capo, Director of Graduate Studies. andersen@fordham.edu. *Specializations:* MA in Communications. *Features:* Internship or thesis option; full-time students can complete program in 12 months. *Admission Requirements:* 3.0 undergraduate GPA. *Degree Requirements:* 10 courses plus internship or thesis. *Faculty:* 8 full-time, 2 part-time. *Students:* 8 full-time, 22 part-time. *Financial Assistance:* assistantships, student loans, scholarships.

Ithaca College. School of Communications. Park Hall, Ithaca, NY 14850. (607) 274-1025. Fax (607) 274-7076. http://www.ithaca.edu/ocld. Sandra L. Herndon, Professor, Chair, Graduate Program in Communications; Roy H. Park, School of Communications. herndon@ithaca.edu. *Specializations:* M.S. in Communications. Students in this program find employment in such areas as instructional design/training, multimedia/Web development, corporate/community/public relations and marketing, and employee communication. The program can be tailored to individual career goals. *Features:* Program is interdisciplinary, incorporating organizational communication, instructional design, management, and technology. *Admission Requirements:* 3.0 GPA, recommendations, statement of purpose, resume, application forms and transcripts, TOEFL 550 (or 213 computer-scored) where applicable. *Degree Requirements:* 36 semester hours including capstone seminar. *Faculty:* 8 full-time. *Students:* approx. 20 full-time, 10 part-time. *Financial Assistance:* graduate assistantships, research fellowships (for continuing students). *Degrees Awarded 2003:* 15.

New York Institute of Technology. Dept. of Instructional Technology. Tower House, Old Westbury, NY 11568. (516) 686-7777. Fax (516) 686-7655. http://www.nyit.edu. Davenport Plumer, Chair, Depts. of Instructional Technology and Elementary Education—preservice and inservice. dplumer460@aol.com. *Specializations:* M.S. in Instructional Technology; M.S. in Elementary Education; Specialist Certificates in Computers in Education, Distance Learning, and Multimedia (not degrees, but are earned after the first 18 credits of the master's degree). *Features:* computer integration in virtually all courses; online courses; evening, weekend, and summer courses. *Admission Requirements:* bachelor's degree from accredited college with 3.0 cumulative average. *Degree Requirements:* 36 credits with 3.0 GPA for M.S., 18 credits with 3.0 GPA for certificates. *Faculty:* 11 full-time, 42 part-time. *Students:* 112 full-time, 720 part-time. *Financial Assistance:* graduate assistantships, institutional and alumni scholarships, student loans.

New York University. Educational Communication and Technology Program, Steinhardt School of Education. 239 Greene St., Suite 300, New York, NY 10003. (212) 998-5520. Fax (212) 995-4041. http://www.nyu.edu/education/alt/ectprogram. Francine Shuchat-Shaw, Assoc. Prof. (MA Advisor), Dir.; W. Michael Reed, Prof. (Doctoral Advisor). sm24@nyu.edu. *Specializations:* M.A., Ed.D., and Ph.D. in Education—for the preparation of individuals as instructional media designers, developers, media producers, and/or researchers in education, business and industry, health and medicine, community services, government, museums and other cultural institutions; and to teach or become involved in administration in educational communications and instructional technology programs in higher education, including instructional television, microcomputers, multi-media, Internet and telecommunications. The program also offers a post-M.A. 30-point Certificate of Advanced Study in Education. *Features:* emphasizes theoretical foundations, especially a cognitive science perspective of learning and instruction, and their implications for designing media-based learning environments and materials. All efforts focus on video, multimedia, instructional television, Web-based technology and telecommunications; participation in special research and production projects and field internships. http://create.alt.ed.nyu.edu. Consortium for Research and Evaluation of Advanced Technologies in Education—uses an apprenticeship model to provide doctoral students and advanced MA students with research opportunities in collaboration with faculty. *Admission Requirements:* M.A.: 3.0 undergraduate GPA, responses to essay questions, interview related to academic and professional goals. Ph.D.: 3.0 GPA, 1000 GRE, responses to essay questions, interview related to academic or professional preparation and career goals. For international students, 600 TOEFL and TWE. *Degree Requirements:* M.A.: 36 semester hours including specialization, elective courses, thesis, English Essay Examination. Ph.D.: 57 semester hours beyond MA, including specialization, foundations, research, content seminar, and elective coursework; candidacy papers; dissertation; English Essay Examination. *Faculty:* 4 full-time, 6 part-time. *Students:* M.A.: 40 full-time, 35 part-time. Ph.D.: 14 full-time, 20 part-time. *Financial Assistance:* graduate and research assistantships, student loans, fellowships, scholarships, and work assistance programs.

Pace University. School of Education. 861 Bedford Road, Pleasantville, NY 10570. (914) 773-3200, (914) 773-3870. Fax (915) 773-3871. http://www.pace.edu. Janet McDonald, Dean and Professor of Education. jmcdonald@pace.edu. *Specializations:* M.Ed. in Educational Technology (leads to New York State Certification as an Educational Technology Specialist.) Advanced Certificate in Educational Technology leads to New York State Certification as an Educational Technology Specialist.) Pace certificate in Computing for Teachers. *Features:* Results in New York State Educational Technology Specialist Certification (2/2004). Program is individualized to meet the needs of two distinct populations: those with an education background or those with a technology background. Some courses are delivered through a distance learning platform. *Admission Requirements:* bachelor's degree or higher from an accredited institution; Minimum GPA of at least 3.0 (upon the recommendation of the Dean, Graduate Faculty Admissions Committee or the Director of Student Support Services, candidates whose GPA is less than 3.0 may be admitted on a conditional basis, provided that it is determined that the candidate has the necessary knowledge and skills to complete the program successfully.) A transcript review is required of all candidates to determine if any Arts and Sciences content knowledge required for certification are unmet. If unmet requirements exist, they must be met during the course of the program; however, the credit hours earned completing them may not be counted toward the graduate degree. Transcript review demonstrating Arts and Sciences and Content Area background comparable to New York State requirements including preparation to teach to the New York State Learning Standards. Completion of the application process, including an essay, two letters of recommendation, personal statement and, in some cases, an interview. *Degree Requirements:* 36–39 semester hours. *Faculty:* 8 full-time, 50 part-time. *Students:* 60–70 part-time. *Financial Assistance:* assistantships, internships, scholarships. *Degrees Awarded 2003:* Program was implemented as of September 2001.

St. Johns University. Division of Library and Information Science. 8000 Utopia Parkway, Jamaica, NY 11439. (718) 990-6200. Fax (718) 990-2071. http://www.stjohns.edu/libraryscience. Elizabeth B. Pollicino, Associate Director. libis@stjohns.edu. *Specializations:* M.L.S. with specialization in School Media. The school also offers a 24-credit Advanced Certificate program in which students may also take School Media and Technology courses. *Features:* small class size, personal advisement, student lounge and computer lab, high-tech classrooms. *Admission Requirements:* 3.0 GPA, 2 letters of reference, statement of professional goals. GRE (General) required for assistantships. *Degree Requirements:* 36 semester hours, comprehensive exam, practicum. *Faculty:* 6 full-time, 10 part-time. *Students:* 30 full-time, 77 part-time. *Financial Assistance:* 4 assistantships in DLIS; others available in University Library. Rev. Brian J. O'Connell, CM Library Studies Scholarships (for incoming students with superior academic records). *Degrees Awarded 2003:* 29.

State University College of Arts and Science at Potsdam. Information and Communication Technology. 302 Satterlee Hall, Potsdam, NY 13676. (315) 267-2525. Fax (315) 267-2987. http://www.potsdam.edu/EDUC/gradpages/MSEdPrograms/ICTHome.html. Dr. Anthony Betrus, Chair, Information and Communications Technology. betrusak@potsdam.edu. *Specializations:* M.S. in Education in Instructional Technology with concentrations in: Educational Technology Specialist, Human Performance Technology, Information Technology, and Organizational Leadership. *Features:* A progressive, forward looking program with a balance of theoretical and hands-on practical coursework. *Admission Requirements:* (1) Submission of an official transcript of an earned baccalaureate degree from an accredited institution. (2) A minimum GPA of 2.75 (4.0 scale) in the most recent 60 credit hours of coursework. (3) Submission of the Application for Graduate Study (w/ $50 nonrefundable fee). (4) For students seeking the Educational Technology Specialist Certification, a valid NYS Teaching Certificate is required. *Degree Requirements:* 36–39 semester hours, including internship or practicum; culminating project required. *Faculty:* 3 full-time, 3 part-time. *Students:* 33 full-time, 92 part-time. *Financial Assistance:* student loans, student work study, graduate assistantship. *Degrees Awarded 2003:* 28.

State University of New York at Albany. School of Education. 1400 Washington Ave., Albany, NY 12222. (518) 442-5032. Fax (518) 442-5008. Karen Swan (ED114A), contact person. swan@cnsunix.albany.edu. *Specializations:* M.Ed. and Ph.D. in Curriculum and Instruction with specializations in Instructional Theory, Design, and Technology. Med offered entirely online over the World Wide Web. *Admission Requirements:* bachelor's degree, GPA close to 3.0; transcript, three letters of recommendation. Students desiring New York State permanent teaching certification should possess preliminary certification. *Degree Requirements:* M.Ed.: 30 semester hours with 15-18 credits in specialization. Ph.D.: 78 semester hours, internship, portfolio certification, thesis. *Faculty:* 13 full-time, 7 part-time. *Students:* 100 full-time, 350 part-time. *Financial Assistance:* fellowships, assistantships, grant, student loans, minority fellowships.

State University of New York at Stony Brook. Technology and Society. College of Engineering and Applied Sciences, SUNY at Stony Brook, Stony Brook, NY 11794-3760. Carole (631) 632-8765,(631) 632-8770, (631) 632-8765 Rita (631) 632-1057. Fax (631) 632-7809. http://www.stonybrook.edu/est/. Carole Rose. Carole.Rose@stonybrook.edu. *Specializations:* master's Degree in Technological Systems Management with concentration in Educational Computing (30 credits. Students may simultaneously earn an Advanced Graduate Certificate (ACG) in Educational Computing (18 credits). *Features:* Students develop the skills to be effective educational leaders and decision-makers. Graduates manage technology-based learning environments and integrate technology into education in meaningful and innovative ways. Our program emphasizes the (a) design of standard-based learning modules, (b) research, and evaluation of educational technologies, and (c) development of prototype learning technologies and learning activities. *Admission Requirements:* bachelor's degree in engineering, natural sciences, social sciences, mathematics, or closely related area; 3.0 undergraduate GPA, have taken the GRE, experience with computer applications or computer applications or use of computers in teaching. *Degree Requirements:* 30 semester credits, including two general technology core courses, 5 required educational computing courses, and 3 eligible electives. *Faculty:* 5 full-time, 8 part-time. *Students:* 15 full-time, 30 part-time. *Financial Assistance:* assistantships, grants, student loans. *Degrees Awarded 2003:* 14.

Syracuse University. Instructional Design, Development, and Evaluation Program, School of Education. 330 Huntington Hall, Syracuse, NY 13244-2340. (315) 443-3703. Fax (315) 443-1218. http://idde.syr.edu. J. Michael Spector, Professor and Chair. lltucker@syr.edu. *Specializations:* Certificates in Educational Technology and Adult Lifelong Learning and M.S., C.A.S., and Ph.D. degree programs for Instructional Design, Educational Evaluation, Human Issues in Instructional Development, Technology Integration, and Educational Research and Theory (learning theory, application of theory, and educational media research). Graduates are prepared to serve as curriculum developers, instructional designers, program and product evaluators, researchers, resource center administrators, technology coordinators, distance learning design delivery specialists, trainers and training managers, and higher education faculty. *Features:* The courses are typically project centered. Collaborative project experience, field work and internships are emphasized throughout. There are special issues seminars, as well as student- and faculty-initiated mini-courses, seminars and guest lecturers, faculty-student formulation of department policies, and multiple international perspectives. International collaborations are an ongoing feature of the program in IDD&E. The graduate student population is highly diverse. *Admission Requirements:* M.S.: undergraduate transcripts, recommendations, personal statement, interview recommended; TOEFL for international applicants; GRE recommended. Doctoral: Relevant master's degree from accredited institution or equivalent, GRE scores, recommendations, personal statement, TOEFL for international applicants; interview strongly encouraged. *Degree Requirements:* M.S.: 36 semester hours, comprehensive exam and portfolio required. Ph.D.: 90 semester hours, research apprenticeship, portfolio, qualifying exams and dissertation required. *Faculty:* 5 full-time, 4 part-time. *Students:* master's: 19 full-time, 31 part-time; doctoral: 20 full-time, 30 part-time. *Financial Assistance:* fellowships, scholarships, and graduate assistantships entailing either research or administrative duties in instructional technology. *Degrees Awarded 2003:* 16 MS; 3 PhD.

North Carolina

Appalachian State University. Department of Curriculum and Instruction. College of Education, Boone, NC 28608. 828-262-2277. Fax 828-262-2686. http://edtech.ced.appstate. edu. Robert Muffoletto. muffoletto@appstate.edu. *Specializations:* M.A. in Educational Media and Technology with three areas of concentration: Computers, Media Literacy, and Media Production. A plan of study in internet distance teaching is offered online. Two certificate programs: (1) Distance Learning -Internet delivered; (2) Media Literacy. *Features:* Business, university, community college, and public school partnership offers unusual opportunities for learning. The programs are focused on developing learning environments over instructional environments. *Admission Requirements:* Undergraduate degree. *Degree Requirements:* 36 graduate semester hours. We also have certificates in (1) Distance Learning and (2) Media Literacy. *Faculty:* 6 full-time faculty. *Students:* 35. *Financial Assistance:* assistantships, grants, student loans. *Degrees Awarded 2003:* 5.

East Carolina University. Department of Librarianship, Educational Technology, and Distance Instruction. 102 Joyner East, Greenville, NC 27858-4353. (252) 328-4373. Fax (252) 328-4368. ltdi.soe.ecu.edu. Dr. Diane D. Kester, Assoc. Prof., Chair. kesterd@ mail.ecu.edu. *Specializations:* Master of Library Science; Certificate of Advanced Study (Library Science); Master of Arts in Education (North Carolina Instructional Technology Specialist licensure); Master of Science in Instructional Technology; Certificate of Tele-learning; Certificate of Virtual Reality in Education and Training; Certificate for Special Endorsement in Computer Education. *Features:* M.L.S. graduates are eligible for North Carolina School Media Coord. certification and for NC Public Library Certification; C.A.S. graduates are eligible for North Carolina School Media Supervisor certification; M.A.Ed. graduates are eligible for North Carolina Instructional Technology certification; Cert. for Special Endorsement in Computer Education for North Carolina Licensure as Technology Facilitator. All programs available 100% online. *Admission Requirements:* M.S., M.A.ED., and M.L.S.: bachelor's degree; C.A.S.: M.L.S. or equivalent degree. Admission to Graduate School. *Degree Requirements:* M.L.S.: 39 semester hours; M.A.Ed.: 39 semester hours; M.S.: 39 semester hours; C.A.S.: 30 semester hours. *Faculty:* 14 full-time; 3 part-time. *Students:* 7 full-time, 250 part-time. *Financial Assistance:* graduate assistantships. *Degrees Awarded 2003:* 35 MLS; 16 MAED; 15 MS.

North Carolina Central University. School of Education. 1801 Fayetteville St., Durham, NC 27707. (919) 560-6692. Fax (919) 560-5279. Dr. James N. Colt, Assoc. Prof., Coordinator., Graduate Program in Educational Technology. bWebb@nccu.edu. *Specializations:* M.A. with special emphasis on Instructional Development/Design. *Features:* Graduates are prepared to implement and utilize a variety of technologies applicable to many professional ventures, including institutions of higher education (college resource centers), business, industry, and professional schools such as medicine, law, dentistry, and nursing. *Admission Requirements:* undergraduate degree, GRE. Degree Requirements: 33 semester hours (including thesis). *Degree Requirements:* 33 semester hours (including thesis). *Faculty:* 2 full-time, 2 part-time. *Students:* 19 full-time, 18 part-time. *Financial Assistance:* assistantships, grants, student loans.

North Carolina State University. Department of Curriculum and Instruction. P.O. Box 7801, Raleigh, NC 27695-7801. (919) 515-1779. Fax (919) 515-6978. http://www. ncsu.edu/ced/ci/. Dr. Ellen Vasu, Professor. Ellen_Vasu@ncsu.edu. *Specializations:* M.Ed. and M.S. in Instructional Technology-Computers (program track within one master's in Curriculum and Instruction). Ph.D. in Curriculum and Instruction with focus on Instructional Technology as well as other areas. *Admission Requirements:* master's: undergraduate degree from an accredited institution, 3.0 GPA in major or in latest graduate degree program; transcripts; GRE or MAT scores; 3 references; goal statement. Ph.D.: undergraduate degree from accredited institution, 3.0 GPA in major or latest graduate program; transcripts; recent GRE scores, writing sample, interview, three references, vita, goal statement (see http://www2.acs.ncsu.edu/grad/prospect.htm). *Degree Requirements:* master's: 36 semester hours, practicum, thesis optional; Ph.D.: 72 hours beyond bachelor's (minimum 33 in Curriculum and Instruction core, 27 in Research); other information available on request. *Faculty:* 2 full-time, 2 part-time. *Students:* master's, 15 part-time; Ph.D., 6 part-time 1 full-time. *Financial Assistance:* some assistantships available on a limited basis. *Degrees Awarded 2003:* 5 master's degrees.

University of North Carolina. School of Information and Library Science. CB#3360, Chapel Hill, NC 27599-3360. (919) 962-8062, 962-8366. Fax (919) 962-8071. http://www.ils.unc.edu/. Evelyn H. Daniel, Prof., Coord., School Media Program. daniel@ils.unc.edu. *Specializations:* Master of Science Degree in Library Science (M.S.L.S.) with specialization in school library media work. Post-master's certification program. *Features:* Rigorous academic program plus teaching practicum requirement; excellent placement record. Many courses offered online. *Admission Requirements:* Competitive admission based on all three GRE components (quantitative, qualitative, analytical), undergraduate GPA (plus graduate work if any), letters of recommendation, and student statement of career interest and school choice. *Degree Requirements:* 48 semester hours, practicum, comprehensive exam, master's paper. *Faculty:* 22 full-time, 10 part-time. *Students:* 300 full-time, 50 part-time (about 20 students specialize in SLMC). *Financial Assistance:* Grants, assistantships, student loans. *Degrees Awarded 2003:* 130 degrees awarded; 20 for school library media certification.

Ohio

Kent State University. Instructional Technology. 405 White Hall, Kent, OH 44242. (330) 672-2294. Fax (330) 672-2512. http://itec.educ.kent.edu. Dr. David Dalton, Coord., Instructional Technology Program. ddalton@kent.edu. *Specializations:* M.Ed. or M.A. in Instructional Technology, Computing/Technology, and Library/Media Specialist; Ph.D. in Educational Psychology with emphasis in Instructional Technology. *Features:* Programs are planned individually to prepare students for careers in elementary, secondary, or higher education, business, industry, government agencies, or health facilities. Students may take advantage of independent research, individual study, practica, and internships. *Admission Requirements:* master's: bachelor's degree with 2.75 undergraduate GPA. *Degree Requirements:* master's: 37–43 semester hours. *Faculty:* 4 full-time, 7 part-time. *Students:* 75. *Financial Assistance:* 6 graduate assistantships, John Mitchell and Marie McMahan Awards, 5 teaching fellowships. *Degrees Awarded 2003:* 25.

Ohio University. Educational Studies. 250 McCracken Hall, Athens, OH 45701-2979. (740) 593-4561. Fax (740) 593-0477. http://www.ohiou.edu/edstudies/comped.html. Teresa Franklin, Instructional Technology Program Coordinator. franklit@ohio.edu. *Specializations:* M.Ed. in Computer Education and Technology. Ph.D. in Curriculum and Instruction with a specialization in Instructional Technology also available; call for details or visit the Web site: http://www.ohiou.edu/edstudies/tech/DOC.HTM. *Features:* master's program is a blended online and face-to-face delivery. *Admission Requirements:* bachelor's degree, 2.5 undergraduate GPA, 35 MAT, 420 GRE (verbal), 400 GRE (quantitative), 550 TOEFL, three letters of recommendation. *Degree Requirements:* master's: 54 quarter credits, electronic portfolio or optional thesis worth 2–10 credits or alternative seminar and paper. Students may earn two graduate degrees simultaneously in education and in any other field. Ph.D.: 109 hours with 20 hours being dissertation work. *Faculty:* 3 full-time, 1 part-time. *Students:* M.Ed.: 44 Ph.D.: 18. *Financial Assistance:* assistantships. *Degrees Awarded 2003:* 21 MED, 6 PhD.

University of Cincinnati. College of Education. 401 Teachers College, ML002, Cincinnati, OH 45221-0002. (513) 556-3579. Fax (513) 556-1001. http://www.uc.edu/. Richard Kretschmer. richard.kretschmer@uc.edu. *Specializations:* M.Ed. or Ed.D. in Curriculum and Instruction with an emphasis on Instructional Design and Technology; Educational Technology degree programs for current professional, technical, critical, and personal knowledge. *Features:* Contact division for features. *Admission Requirements:* bachelor's degree from accredited institution, 2.8 undergraduate GPA; GRE 1500 or better. *Degree Requirements:* 54 quarter hours, written exam, thesis or research project (12–15 credit hours college core; 12–15 C&I; 18–27 credit hours specialization; 3-6 credit hours thesis or project). *Faculty:* 3 full-time. *Students:* In C&I there are 74 doctoral students and

25 Master students. *Financial Assistance:* scholarships, assistantships, grants. *Degrees Awarded 2003:* C&I Degrees 26 M.Ed., 12 Ed.D.

University of Toledo. Curriculum & Instruction. MS 924, Carver Education Center, Toledo, OH 43606. (419) 530-2837. Fax (419) 530-2466. http://www.utoledo.edu/~rsulliv/. Robert F. Sullivan, Ph.D. Robert.Sullivan@utoledo.edu. *Specializations:* Technology Using Educator/Technology Coordinator, Instructional Designer, and Performance Technologist. *Features:* Graduate students may concentrate in one of the three primary "roles," or may choose a blended program of study. Program was completely redesigned in 2004. *Admission Requirements:* master's: 3.0 undergrad. GPA, GRE (if undergrad. GPA < 2.7), recommendations; doctorate: master's degree, GRE, TOEFL (as necessary), recommendations, entrance writing samples, and interview. *Degree Requirements:* master's: 36 semester hours, culminating project; doctorate: 76 semester hours (after master's), major/minor exams, dissertation. *Faculty:* 4 full-time, 1 part-time (Fall 2004). *Students:* master's, 12 FT, 50 PT; doctoral, 4 FT, 25 PT (approximate). *Financial Assistance:* assistantships, scholarships, fellowships, and fee waivers (extremely competitive); student loans. *Degrees Awarded 2003:* approximately 15 (graduate) awarded in 2003.

Wright State University. College of Education and Human Services, Dept. of Educational Leadership. 421 Allyn Hall, 3640 Colonel Glenn Highway, Dayton, OH 45435. (937) 775-2509 or (937) 775-2821. Fax (937) 775-4485. http:// www.ed.wright.edu. Dr. Bonnie K. Mathies, Associate Dean; Dr. Roger Carlsen, Program Coordinator. bonnie.mathies @wright.edu. *Specializations:* M.Ed. in Computer/Technology, Library Media, or Administrative SpecialistTechnology Leader; M.A. in Educational Media or Computer Education; Specialist degree in Curriculum and Instruction with a focus on Educational Technology; Specialist degree in Higher Education with a focus on Educational Technology. *Features:* Ohio licensure available in Multi-age library media (ages 3–21); Computer/technology endorsement; Administrative Specialist—Curriculum, Instruction, Professional Development—Technology. Above licensure only available on a graduate basis and with teaching credentials. *Admission Requirements:* Completed application with nonrefundable application fee, bachelor's degree from accredited institution, official transcripts, 2.7 overall GPA for regular status (conditional acceptance possible), statement of purpose, satisfactory scores on MAT or GRE. *Degree Requirements:* M.Ed. requires a comprehensive portfolio; M.A. requires a 6-hour thesis. *Faculty:* 2 full-time, 10 part-time, including other university full-time faculty and staff. *Students:* approx. 2 full-time, approx. 180 part-time. *Financial Assistance:* 2 graduate assistantships in the College's Educational Resource Center; plus graduate fellowships for full-time students available; limited number of small graduate scholarships. *Degrees Awarded 2003:* 11; we also work with numerous students who are seeking Ohio licensure.

Oklahoma

Southwestern Oklahoma State University. School of Education. 100 Campus Drive, Weatherford, OK 73096. (405) 774-3140. Fax (405) 774-7043. http://www.swosu.edu. Gregory Moss, Asst. Prof., Chair, Dept of School Service Programs. mossg@swosu.edu. *Specializations:* M.Ed. in Library/Media Education. *Admission Requirements:* 2.5 GPA, GRE or GMAT scores, letter of recommendation, GPA 150 + GRE = 1100. *Degree Requirements:* 32 semester hours (including 24 in library media). *Faculty:* 1 full-time, 4 part-time. *Students:* 17 part-time.

The University of Oklahoma. Instructional Psychology and Technology, Department of Educational Psychology. 321 Collings Hall, Norman, OK 73019. (405) 325-5974. Fax (405) 325-6655. http://www.uoknor.edu/education/iptwww/. Dr. Teresa DeBacker, Area Head. debacker@ou.edu. *Specializations:* master's degree with emphases in Educational Technology Generalist, Educational Technology, Computer Application, Instructional Design, Teaching with Technology; Dual master's Educational Technology and Library and Information Systems. Doctorate in Instructional Psychology and Technology. *Features:* strong interweaving of principles of instructional psychology with design and development of Instructional Technology. Application of IP&T in K–12, vocational education, higher education, business and industry, and governmental agencies. *Admission Requirements:* master's: acceptance by IPT program and Graduate College based on minimum 3.00 GPA for last 60 hours of undergraduate work or last 12 hours of graduate work; written statement that indicates goals and interests compatible with program goals. Doctoral: 3.0 in last 60 hours undergraduate, 3.25 GPA, GRE scores, written statement of background and goals. *Degree Requirements:* master's: approx. 39 hours coursework (specific number of hours dependent upon Emphasis) with 3.0 GPA; successful completion of thesis or comprehensive exam. Doctorate: see program description from institution or http://www.ou.education.iptwww. *Faculty:* 9 full-time. *Students:* master's, 10 full-time, 200 part-time; doctoral, 10 full-time, 50 part-time. *Financial Assistance:* assistantships, grants, student loans, scholarships. *Degrees Awarded 2003:* 14.

Oregon

Western Oregon State College. Teacher Education. 345 N. Monmouth Ave., Monmouth, OR 97361. (503) 838-8471. Fax (503) 838-8228. http://www.wou.edu/education/elms/msed.html. Dr. Dana Ulveland, Coordinator for Information Technology. ulvelad@wou.edu. *Specializations:* M.S. in Information Technology. *Features:* offers advanced courses in library management, instructional development, multimedia, and computer technology. Additional course offerings in distance delivery of instruction and computer-interactive video instruction. *Admission Requirements:* 3.0 GPA, GRE or MAT. *Degree Requirements:* 45 quarter hours; thesis optional. *Faculty:* 3 full-time, 6 part-time. *Students:* 6 full-time, 131 part-time. *Financial Assistance:* assistantships, grants, student loans, scholarship, work assistance.

Pennsylvania

Bloomsburg University. Institute for Interactive Technologies—Instructional Technology. 1210 McCormick Bldg., Bloomsburg, PA 17815. (717) 389-4506. Fax (717) 389-4943. http://iit.bloomu.edu. Dr. Timothy L. Phillips, contact person. tphillip@bloomu.edu. *Specializations:* M.S. in Instructional Technology with emphasis on preparing for careers as interactive media specialists. The program is closely associated with the Institute for Interactive Technologies. *Features:* instructional design, authoring languages and systems, media integration, managing multimedia projects. *Admission Requirements:* bachelor's degree. *Degree Requirements:* 33 semester credits (27 credits + 6 credit thesis, or 30 credits + three credit internship). *Faculty:* 4 full-time. *Students:* 53 full-time, 50 part-time. *Financial Assistance:* assistantships, grants, student loans.

Clarion University of Pennsylvania. Library Science. 209 Carlson Library Building, Clarion, PA 16214. (814) 393-2271. Fax (814) 393-2150. www.clarion.edu/libsci. Dr. Andrea L. Miller, Chair. amiller@clarion.edu. *Specializations:* Master of Science in Library Science; Master of Science in Library Science with Pennsylvania School Library Media Certification; Certificate of Advanced Studies. Students may specialize in various areas of library science as determined by program of study. Clarion has a Rural Libraries program and began an online cohort program with a focus on rural and small libraries in January of 2004. In January of 2005, an online cohort program with a master's of Library Science with Pennsylvania School Library Media Certification will begin. *Features:* The graduate program in library science provides professional study encompassing the principles and techniques common to all types of libraries and information centers with the opportunity for advanced work in areas of special interest. The curriculum reflects today's applications of information technology in libraries and information centers. The master's program at Clarion University was initiated in 1967 and has the distinction of being the first graduate library science program offered within the State System of Higher Education. The program has been accredited by the American Library Association since 1976. As part of its commitment to meeting the needs of all residents of the Commonwealth of Pennsylvania, the Department of Library Science offers a variety of distance education programs. These programs utilize various delivery techniques, including on-site instruction, interactive television (ITV), and Web-based delivery. ITV delivery involves two or more sections of the same course that are taught simultaneously by the same instructor from a central location. Students at remote sites participate in the class via two-way audio and video. Courses offered via the World Wide Web may, at the instructors discretion, require some on-campus meetings. Clarion presently offers the program at the Dixon Center in Harrisburg, PA and at the Free Library in Philadelphia. In January of 2004, Clarion began offering an Web-based online cohort program with a focus on rural and small libraries. In January of 2005, Clarion will offer a Web-based online cohort program, Master of Science in Library Science with Pennsylvania School Library Media Certification. *Admission Requirements:* Applicants for admission to the Master of Science in Library Science degree program must meet Division of Graduate Studies admission requirements with the following additions:

1. an overall quality-point average for the baccalaureate degree of at least 3.00 on a 4.00 scale; or

2. a 3.00 quality-point average for the last 60 credits of the baccalaureate degree with an overall quality-point average of at least 2.75; or

3. a 2.75 to 2.99 overall quality-point average for the baccalaureate degree with a score of at least 50 on the Miller Analogies Test or a combined score of at least 1,000 on the quantitative and verbal sections of the Graduate Record Examination; or

4. a graduate degree in another discipline with an overall quality-point average of at least 3.00 and an overall undergraduate quality-point average of at least 2.75. International students are required to achieve a minimum score of 550 on the TOEFL. M.S.L.S. with Pennsylvania School Library Media Certification.

In addition to the above, students who begin their M.S.L.S. with Pennsylvania School Library Media Certification program in spring 2002 or later must meet the following additional requirements:

1. completion of at least six credits of college-level mathematics; and

2. completion of at least six credits of college-level English composition and literature.

Applicants without valid teacher certification must also pass the Praxis I pre-professional skills tests. State law limits the number of applicants with an overall quality-point average for the baccalaureate degree of less then 3.00 on a 4.00 scale who can be admitted to the School Library Media Certification program. *Degree Requirements:* The degree of Master of Science in Library Science is conferred upon the candidate who has met the following requirements: The completion of 36 hours of approved graduate study, including five required core courses (LS 500, 501, 502, 504, and 550), one management course (LS 530, 531, 532, 533, or 569), and six elective courses. The maintenance of a cumulative average of 3.00 or higher. A student who receives a grade of "C" or lower in two or more courses is disqualified as a candidate in the degree program unless special permission to continue is obtained from the dean of the College of Education and Human Services and the coordinator of Graduate Studies. The completion of all degree requirements within a six-year period. Coursework over six years old may not be applied toward the degree. Master of Science in Library Science Degree with Pennsylvania School Library Media Certification.

A student wishing to obtain Pennsylvania School Library Media Certification, K–12, must hold a valid teaching certificate (or meet the requirements for preliminary certification by taking required undergraduate courses); complete 36 semester hours of an approved curriculum in library science; and complete three semester hours of internship in a school library media center. Students without prior certification will substitute twelve semester hours of student teaching for the internship requirement; students with emergency Pennsylvania School Library Media Certification may petition the department to substitute a site visit and portfolio for the internship requirement. Required courses for the Master of Science in Library Science degree with Pennsylvania School Library Media Certification, K–12, include: LS 459g, 490g, 500, 501, 502, 504, 532, 550, 577, 570, 583, 589, and one elective course. Praxis Series: Professional Assessments for Beginning Teachers®, The Commonwealth of Pennsylvania requires that all candidates for teacher certification take and pass specified tests in the Praxis Series, which is administered by the Educational Testing Service (ETS). Students without prior certification take the Praxis I, Academic Skills Assessments, to qualify for entry into teacher certification programs administered by the College of Education and Human Services. Tests in the Praxis II Series, Subject Assessments, are required of all students for licensure. These include Elementary Education, Content Knowledge (10014) and, for Pennsylvania School Library Media Certification, K–12, Library Media Specialist (10310). Students must pass the latter test with a minimum score of 620. Starting in spring 2004, students without prior certification must pass these tests prior to student teaching. The departments certification curricula are designed to cover topics found on this test. Click on the following link for a list of topics and the courses in which they are covered. Master of Science in Library Science/Juris Doctor Program. The department offers a joint M.S.L.S./J.D. program in cooperation with Widener University School of Laws Harrisburg, Pennsylvania, campus. Students must be admitted to both programs separately. Any six credits of coursework taken as part of a students J.D. program may be applied to that students M.S.L.S. program, and vice versa. These courses will be chosen in consultation with the students faculty advisors. Effective spring 2002. Certificate of Advanced Studies: The Certificate of Advanced Studies program is designed to provide the post-master's student an opportunity to expand and update professional skills and competencies through a structured pattern of continuing education. Study may be either full- or part-time. On a full-time basis, the certificate may be completed in two semesters. Requirements include a written statement of personal/professional goals, completion of a program of 24 graduate credits within a four-year period, and maintenance of a 3.00, (B) quality-point average. *Faculty:* 6 full-time and a large number of professional part-time faculty. *Students:* 45 full-time and 175 part-time. *Financial Assistance:* Assistantships and various scholarships and Awards. *Degrees Awarded 2003:* 55.

Drexel University. College of Information Science and Technology. 3141 Chestnut Street, Philadelphia, PA 19104-2875. (215) 895-2474. Fax (215) 895-2494. http://www.cis. drexel.edu. David E. Fenske, Dean. info@cis.drexel.edu. *Specializations:* M.S. Master of Science (Library and Information Science; M.S.I.S. Master of Science in Information Systems; M.S.S.E. Master of Science in Software Engineering; Ph.D. *Features:* On campus and online degree programs for M.S. and M.S.I.S. *Admission Requirements:* GRE scores; applicants with a minimum 3.2 GPA in last half of undergraduate credits may be eligible for admission without GRE scores. *Degree Requirements:* 60 credits. *Faculty:* 27 full-time, 25-30 active adjuncts per term. *Students:* Graduate, 79 full-time; 458 part-time. *Financial Assistance:* The IST Web site currently lists all IST scholarships available in the academic year. IST offers many different types of scholarships including, graduate assistantships, endowed scholarships, deans and doctoral fellowships, and IST alumni loan funds. *Degrees Awarded 2003:* 186 Graduate degrees (2003).

Lehigh University. College of Education. 111 Research Drive, Bethlehem, PA 18015. (610) 758-4794. Fax (610) 758-3243. http://www.lehigh.edu. Ward Cates, Coord., Educational Technology Program. ward.cates@LEHIGH.EDU. *Specializations:* M.S. in Instructional Design and Development: Emphasizes how to create technology products for teaching and learning in diverse settings. M.S. in Educational Technology: Degree aimed at our international program, emphasizing implementation of technology in International Schools abroad. Ed.D. in Educational Technology: Emphasizes design, development, implementation, and evaluation of technology-based teaching and learning products in a variety of settings. *Features:* Heavy emphasis on instructional design and interface design. Coursework in Web and resource development. Practical, professional-level design and development work. All work cross-platform and cross-browser. Both master's and doctoral students collaborate with faculty on projects and studies (including national presentation and publication). The Educational Technology program has a high level of collaboration with Technology-based Teacher Education. We are working on a new Learning, Sciences, and Technology Ph.D. degree program that will involve university-wide collaboration with departments in all four colleges of the university. This program will ultimately replace our current ed tech doctorate. *Admission Requirements:* M.S. (competitive): 3.0 undergraduate GPA or 3.0 graduate GPA, GREs recommended, transcripts, at least 2 letters of recommendation, statement of personal and professional goals, application fee. Application deadlines: July 15 for fall admission, Dec 1 for spring admission, Apr 30 for summer admission. Ed.D. (highly competitive): 3.5 graduate GPA, GREs required. Copy of two extended pieces of writing (or publications); statement of future professional goals; statement of why Ed Tech at Lehigh best place to meet those goals; identification of which presentations, publications, or research by Lehigh faculty attracted applicant to Lehigh. Application deadline: February 1 (admission only once per year from competitive pool). *Degree Requirements:* M.S.: 30 semester hours; thesis option. Ed.D.: 48 hours past the master's plus dissertation. *Faculty:* 3.5 full-time, 1 part-time. *Students:* M.S.: 8 full-time, 40 part-time; Ed.D.: 4 full-time, 12 part-time. *Financial Assistance:* University graduate and research assistantships, graduate student support as participants in R&D projects, paid internships in local businesses and schools doing design and development. *Degrees Awarded 2003:* 12.

Pennsylvania State University. Instructional Systems. 314 Keller Bldg., University Park, PA 16802. (814) 865-0473. Fax (814) 865-0128. http://www.ed.psu.edu/insys/. Alison Carr-Chellman, Associate Professor of Education, Professor in Charge of Instructional Systems. ali.carr@psu.edu. *Specializations:* M.Ed., M.S., D.Ed, and Ph.D. in Instructional Systems. Current teaching emphases are on Corporate Training, Interactive Learning Technologies, and Educational Systems Design. Research interests include multimedia, visual learning, educational reform, emerging technologies, constructivist learning, open-ended learning environments, scaffolding, technology integration in classrooms, technology in higher education, change and diffusion of innovations. *Features:* A common thread throughout all programs is that candidates have basic competencies in the understanding of human learning; instructional design, development, and evaluation; and research procedures. Practical experience is available in mediated independent learning, research, instructional development, computer-based education, and dissemination projects. Exceptional opportunities for collaboration with faculty (30%+ of publications and presentations are collaborative between faculty and students). *Admission Requirements:* D.Ed., Ph.D.: GRE (including written GRE), TOEFL, transcript, three letters of recommendation, writing sample, vita or resume, and letter of application detailing rationale for interest in the degree, match with interests of faculty. *Degree Requirements:* M.Ed.: 33 semester hours; M.S.: 36 hours, including either a thesis or project paper; doctoral: candidacy exam, courses, residency, comprehensives, dissertation. *Faculty:* 9 full-time, 1 joint appointment in Information Sciences, 4 affiliate and 1 adjunct. *Students:* master's, approx. 46; doctoral, 103. *Financial Assistance:* assistantships, graduate fellowships, student aid loans, internships; assistantships on grants, contracts, and projects. *Degrees Awarded 2003:* Ph.D., D.Ed., M.S., M.Ed.

Rosemont College. Graduate Studies in Education. 1400 Montgomery Ave., Rosemont, PA 19010-1699. (610) 526-2982; (800) 531-9431. Fax (610) 526-2964. http://www.rosemont.edu/root/grad_studies/gs_education.html. Dr. Robert Siegfried, Director of Technology and Education. rsiegfried@rosemont.edu. *Specializations:* M.Ed. in Technology in Education, Certificate in Professional Study in Technology in Education. *Admission Requirements:* GRE or MAT scores. *Degree Requirements:* Completion of 12 units (36 credits) and comprehensive exam. *Faculty:* 7 full-time, 10 part-time. *Students:* 110 full- and part-time. *Financial Assistance:* graduate student grants, assistantships, Federal Stafford Loan Program.

Temple University. Department of Curriculum, Instruction and Technology in Education. 1301 Cecil B. Moore Avenue, Philadelphia, PA 19122. (215) 204-4497. Fax (215) 204-6013. http://www.temple.edu/education/. C. Kent McGuire, Dean, College of Education. kent.mcguire@temple.edu. *Specializations:* Instructional and Learning Technology (ILT) is a new master's program within the Educational Psychology Program in the Department of Psychological Studies in Education. As such, ILT is designed to address conceptual as well as technical issues in using technology for teaching and learning. Program areas include(a) instructional theory and design issues, (b) application of technology, and (c) management issues. *Features:* Instructional Theory and Design topics includes psychology of the learner, cognitive processes, instructional theories, human development, and individual differences as well as psychological and educational characteristics of technology resources, and identification of strengths and weaknesses of instructional technology resources. The Application of Technology area focuses on clarification of instructional objectives, identification of resources to facilitate learning, operation and application of current and emergent technologies, facility using graphic design, multimedia, video, distributed learning resources, WWW and print publishing. Management and Consultation is structured around defining instructional needs, monitoring progress, and evaluating outcomes, designing technology delivery systems, preparing policy statements, budgets, and facility design criteria, managing skill assessment and training, understanding legal and ethical issues, and managing and maintaining facilities. *Admission Requirements:* bachelor's degree from an accredited institution, GRE (MAT) scores, 3 letters of recommendation, transcripts from each institution of higher learning attended (undergraduate and graduate), goal statement. *Degree Requirements:* Coursework (33 hours: 5 core courses, 3 technology electives, 3 cognate area courses). Practicum in students area of interest, Comprehensive Exam, Portfolio of Certification Competencies (for students interested in PA Dept. of Ed Certification as Instructional Technology Specialist). *Faculty:* 2 full-time, 1 part- time (plus educational psychology faculty). *Financial Assistance:* Presidential, Russell Conwell, and University Fellowships, Graduate School Tuition and Fellowship Funds, Graduate Teaching Assistantships and Assistantships in Administrative Offices, CASHE (College Aid Sources for Higher Education).

Universiti Sains Malaysia. Centre for Instructional Technology and Multimedia. Centre for Instructional Tech and Multimedia, Universiti Sains Malaysia, Minden, PA 11800. (604) 653-3222. Fax (604) 6576749. http://www.ptpm.usm.my. Zarina Samsudin, Director. ina@usm.my. *Specializations:* Instructional Design, Web/Internet Instruction and learning, Educational Training/Resource Management, Instructional Training, Technology/Evaluation, Instructional System Development, Design and Development of Multimedia/Video/Training materials, Instructional and Training Technology Constructivism in Instructional Technology. *Features:* A new program—Master's in Instructional Technology—started in academic year 2004–2005, full-time—1–2 years, part-time—2–4 years. Teaching Programs—Postgraduate programs and research; consultancy—services on the application of educational technology in teaching learning; training and diffusion— Diploma in Multimedia, Certificate in Training Technology and Continuing Education; Academic Support Services—services to support research, teaching and learning activities and centers within the University. *Admission Requirements:* bachelor's and master's degree from accredited institution. *Faculty:* 13 full-time. *Students:* Postgraduate students 30 full-time, 60 part-time. *Financial Assistance:* None.

Rhode Island

The University of Rhode Island. Graduate School of Library and Information Studies. Rodman Hall, 94 W. Alumni Ave., Kingston, RI 02881-0815. (401) 874-2947. Fax (401) 874-4964. http://www.uri.edu/artsci/lsc. W. Michael Havener, Ph.D., Director. mhavener@uri.edu. *Specializations:* M.L.I.S. degree with specialties in School Library Media Services, Youth Services Librarianship, Public Librarianship, Academic Librarianship, and Special Library Services. *Admission Requirements:* undergraduate GPA of 3.0, score in 50th percentile or higher on SAT or MAT, statement of purpose, current resume, letters of reference. *Degree Requirements:* 42 semester-credit program offered in Rhode Island and regionally in Amherst and Worcester, MA, and Durham, NH. *Faculty:* 8 full-time, 30 part-time. *Students:* 247. *Financial Assistance:* graduate assistantships, some scholarship aid, student loans. *Degrees Awarded 2003:* 80.

South Carolina

University of South Carolina Aiken and University of South Carolina Columbia. Aiken: School of Education, Columbia: Department of Educational Psychology. 471 University Parkway, Aiken, SC 29801. 803.641.3489. Fax 803.641.3720. http://edtech. usca.edu. Dr. Thomas Smyth, Professor, Program Director. smyth@usca.edu. *Specializations:* Master of Education in Educational Technology (A Joint Program of The University of South Carolina, Aiken and Columbia). *Features:* The master's degree in Educational Technology is designed to provide advanced professional studies in graduate level coursework to develop capabilities essential to the effective design, evaluation, and delivery of technology-based instruction and training (e.g., software development, multimedia development, assistive technology modifications, Web-based development, and distance learning). The program is intended (1) to prepare educators to assume leadership roles in the integration of educational technology into the school curriculum, and (2) to provide graduate-level instructional opportunities for several populations (e.g., classroom teachers, corporate trainers, educational software developers) that need to acquire both technological competencies and understanding of sound instructional design principles and techniques.

Several course offerings will be delivered from only one campus, though students on both campuses will enroll in the courses. These will include Web-based courses, two-way video courses, and courses that include a combination of Web-based, two-way video, and face-to-face meetings. *Admission Requirements:* Application to the Educational Technology Program can be made after completion of at least the bachelor's degree from a college or university accredited by a regional accrediting agency. The standard for admission will be based on a total profile for the applicant. The successful applicant should have an undergraduate grade point average of at least 3.0, a score of 45 on the Miller's Analogies Test or scores of 450 on both the verbal and quantitative portions of the Graduate Record Exam, a well-written letter of intent that matches the objectives of the program and includes a description of previous technology experience, and positive letters of recommendation from individuals who know the professional characteristics of the applicant. Any exceptions for students failing to meet these standards shall be referred to the Admissions Committee for review and final decision. *Degree Requirements:* 36 semester hours, including instructional theory, computer design, and integrated media. *Faculty:* 4 FT, 11 PT. *Students:* 39.

Financial Assistance: Graduate Assistantships are available. *Degrees Awarded 2003:* This is a new program which began Fall 2002.

Tennessee

East Tennessee State University. College of Education, Dept. of Curriculum and Instruction. Box 70684, Johnson City, TN 37614-0684. (423) 439-7843. Fax (423) 439-8362. http://coe.etsu.edu/department/cuai/meda.htm. Harold Lee Daniels. danielsh@etsu.edu. *Specializations:* 1) M. Ed. in School Library Media; 2) M.Ed. in Educational Technology; 3) 24 hour School Library media specialist add on for those with current teaching license and a master's degree.; 4) M.Ed. in Classroom Technology for those with teaching license. *Features:* Two(MAC &PC) dedicated computer labs (45+ computers) Online and evening course offerings for part-time, commuter, and employed students.

Student pricing/campus licensing on popular software (MS, Adobe, Macromedia, etc.) Off site cohort programs for classroom teachers. Extensive software library (900+ titles) with review/checkout privileges. *Admission Requirements:* bachelor's degree from accredited institution, transcripts, personal essay; in some cases, GRE and/or interview. *Degree Requirements:* 36 semester hours, including 12 hours in common core of instructional technology and media, 18 professional content hours and 5 credit hour practicum (200 field experience hours). *Faculty:* 2 full-time, 4 part-time. *Students:* 15 full-time, 50 part-time. *Financial Assistance:* Scholarships, assistantships, aid for disabled. *Degrees Awarded 2003:* 8.

University of Memphis. Instruction and Curriculum Leadership/Instructional Design & Technology. 406 Ball Hall, Memphis, TN 38152. 901-678-2365. Fax 901-678-3881. http://idt.memphis.edu. Dr. Richard Van Eck. rvaneck@memphis.edu. *Specializations:* Instructional Design, Web-based instruction, Computer-based instruction, Digital Video, K–12 NTeQ technology integration model, Instructional Games, Pedagogical Agents. *Features:* The Advanced Instructional Media (AIM) lab, staffed and run by IDT faculty and students, serves as an R&D space for coursework and research involving technologies such as digital media, WBT/CBT (Dreamweaver, Flash, Authorware, WebCT, DV cameras, DV editing, DVD authoring, etc.), pedagogical agents, gaming and simulation. The AIM lab and IDT program is connected to the Center for Multimedia Arts in the FedEx Institute of Technology. The AIM Lab brings in outside contract work from corporate partners to provide real-world experience to students. We have also partnered with the Institute for Intelligent Systems and the Tutoring Research Group (www.autotutor.org) to work on intelligent agent development and research. *Admission Requirements:* Minimum standards which identify a pool of master's level applicants from which each department selects students to be admitted:

An official transcript showing a bachelor's degree awarded by an accredited college or university with a minimum GPA of 2.0 on a 4.0 scale, competitive MAT or GRE scores, GRE writing test, two letters of recommendation, graduate school and departmental application. Doctoral students must also be interviewed by at least two members of the program. *Degree Requirements:* M.S.: 36 hours, internship, master's project or thesis, 3.0 GPA. Ed.D: 54 hours, 45 in major, 9 in research; residency project; comprehensive exams; dissertation. *Faculty:* 4 full-time, 6 part-time. *Students:* 10 full-time, 50 part-time. *Financial Assistance:* teaching assistantships (two classes, full tuition waiver plus stipend). Graduate assistantships (20 hours per week, full tuition plus stipend). *Degrees Awarded 2003:* 2002/2003: 8 doctoral, 10 master's. 2003/2004: 5 doctoral, 10 master's.

University of Tennessee—Knoxville. Instructional Technology and Educational Studies, College of Education. A535 Claxton Addition, Knoxville, TN 37996-3456. (423) 974-5037. http://Web.utk.edu/~itce/. Dr. Michael L. Waugh. waugh@utk.edu. *Specializations:* M.S. Ed.S. and Ph.D. in Ed. Concentrations in Curriculum/Evaluation/Research and Instructional Technology; M.S. and Ph.D. in Ed. Concentration in Cultural Studies in Education. *Features:* coursework in media production and management, advanced software production, utilization, research, theory, instructional computing, and instructional development. *Admission Requirements:* Send for Graduate Catalog, The University of Tennessee *Degree Requirements:* See Graduate Catalog for current program requirements. *Faculty:* 12 full-time. *Students:* M.S., 80 ; Ed.S., 30 ; Ed.D., 40; PhD, 50. *Degrees Awarded 2003:* approximately 20 across all levels.

Texas

Texas A&M University. Educational Technology Program, Dept. of Educational psychology. College of Education and Human Development, College Station, TX 77843-4225. (979) 845-7276. Fax (979) 862-1256. http://educ.coe.tamu.edu/~edtc. Ronald D. Zellner, Assoc. Prof., Coord. Program information/ Carol Wagner for admissions materials. zellner@tamu.edu/c-wagner@tamu.edu. *Specializations:* M.Ed. in Educational Technology; EDCI Ph.D. program with specializations in Educational Technology and in Distance Education; Ph.D. in Educational Psychology Foundations: Learning and Technology. The purpose of the Educational Technology Program is to prepare educators with the competencies required to improve the quality and effectiveness of instructional programs at all levels. A major emphasis is placed on multimedia instructional materials development and techniques for effective distance education and communication. Teacher preparation with a focus on field-based instruction and school to university collaboration is also a major component. The program goal is to prepare graduates with a wide range of skills to work as professionals and leaders in a variety of settings, including education, business, industry, and the military. *Features:* Program facilities include laboratories for teaching, resource development, and production. Computer, video, and multimedia development are supported in a number of facilities. The college and university also maintain facilities for distance education materials development and fully equipped classrooms for course delivery to nearby collaborative school districts and sites throughout the state. *Admission Requirements:* M.Ed.: bachelor's degree, (range of scores, no specific cutoffs) 400 GRE Verbal, 550 (213 computer version) TOEFL; Ph.D.: 3.0 GPA, 450 GRE Verbal. Composite score from GRE verbal & Quantitative and GPA, letters of recommendation, general background, and student goal statement. *Degree Requirements:* M.Ed.: 39 semester credits, oral exam; Ph.D.: coursework varies with student goals -degree is a Ph.D. in Educational Psychology Foundations with specialization in educational technology. *Faculty:* 4 full-time, 1 lecturer; several associated faculty from related programs in EPSY. *Students:* M.Ed., 25 full-time, 15 part-time; Ph.D., 12 full-time, 10 part-time. *Financial Assistance:* several graduate assistantships and teaching assistantships. *Degrees Awarded 2003:* M.Ed. 20, Ph.D. 3.

Texas A&M University—Commerce. Department of Secondary and Higher Education. PO Box 3011, Commerce, TX 75429-3011. (903) 886-5607. Fax (903) 886-5603. http://www.tamu-commerce.edu/. Dr. Sue Espinoza, Associate Professor, Program Coordinator. Sue_Espinoza@tamu-commerce.edu. *Specializations:* M.S. or M.Ed. degree in Learning Technology and Information Systems with emphases in Educational Computing, Educational Media and Technology, and Library and Information Science. Certifications offered: School Librarian, and Technology Applications, both approved by the Texas State Board for Educator Certification. *Features:* Courses are offered in a variety of formats, including traditional classroom/lab based, and distance ed, via video teleconferencing and/or online. Most courses are taught in only one of these, but some include multiple delivery methods. *Degree Requirements:* 36 hours for each master's degree; Educational Computing includes 30 hours of required courses, and 6 hours of electives; Media & Technology includes 21 hours of required courses, and 15 hours of electives, selected in consultation with advisor; Library includes courses in Library, Educational Technology, and Education. *Faculty:* 3 full-time, 5 part-time. *Students:* 30 full-time, 150 part-time. *Financial Assistance:* graduate assistantships in teaching and research, scholarships, federal aid program. *Degrees Awarded 2003:* 15.

Texas Tech University. College of Education. Box 41071,TTU, Lubbock, TX 79409. (806) 742-1997, ext. 287. Fax (806) 742-2179. http://www.educ.ttu.edu/edit. Dr. Nancy Maushak, Program Coordinator, Instructional Technology. nancy.maushak@ttu.edu. *Specializations:* M.Ed. in Instructional Technology; completely online M.Ed. in Instructional Technology; Ed.D. in Instructional Technology. *Features:* Program is NCATE accredited and follows ISTE and AECT guidelines. *Admission Requirements:* holistic evaluation based on GRE scores, GPA, student goals and writing samples. *Degree Requirements:* M.Ed.: 39 hours (30 hours in educational technology, 6 hours in education, 3 hours electives). Ed.D.: 93 hours (60 hours in educational technology, 21 hours in education or resource area, 12 hours dissertation. *Faculty:* 5 full-time, 1 part-time, 6 Teaching assistants. *Students:* M.Ed.:10 full-time, 30 part-time; Ed.D.:15 full-time, 15 part-time. *Financial Assistance:* teaching and research assistantships available ($9,000 for 9 months); small scholarships. *Degrees Awarded 2003:* 6 M.Ed, 2 Ed.D.

University of Houston. Curriculum & Instruction. 256 Farish, Houston, TX 77204. (713) 743-4950. Fax (713) 743-4990. http://www.it.coe.uh.edu/. Bernard Robin, Program Area Director. brobin@uh.edu. *Specializations:* urban community partnerships enhanced by technology integration of technology in teaching; visual representation of information; collaborative design teams innovative uses of technology in instruction. *Features:* The IT Program at the University of Houston can be distinguished from other IT programs at other institutions through our unique philosophy based on a strong commitment to the broad representations of community, the individual, and the collaboration that strengthens the two. We broadly perceive community to include our college, the university, and the local Houston environment. The community is a rich context and resource from which we can solicit authentic learning tasks and clients, and to which we can contribute new perspectives and meaningful products. Our students graduate with real-world experience that can only be gained by experience with extended and coordinated community-based projects, not by contrived course requirements. Our program actively seeks outside funding to promote and continue such authentic projects because we so strongly believe it is the best context in which our students can develop expertise in the field. We recognize that each student brings to our program a range of formal training, career experience, and future goals. Thus, no longer can we be satisfied with presenting a single, static curriculum and still effectively prepare students for a competitive marketplace. Our beliefs have led us to develop a program that recognizes and celebrates student individuality and diversity. Students work with advisors to develop a degree plan that begins from their existing knowledge and strives toward intended career goals. We aim to teach not specific software or hardware operations, but instead focus on transferable technical skills couched in solid problem-solving experiences, theoretical discussions, and a team-oriented atmosphere. Students work throughout the program to critically evaluate their own work for the purpose of compiling a performance portfolio that will accurately and comprehensively portray their individual abilities to themselves, faculty, and future employers. Completing our philosophical foundation is a continuous goal of collaboration. Our faculty operates from a broad collaborative understanding that recognizes how everyone involved in any process brings unique and valuable experiences and perspectives. Within the IT program, faculty, staff, and students rely on each other to contribute relevant expertise. Faculty members regularly seek collaboration with other faculty in the College of Education, especially those involved with teacher education, as well as with faculty in other schools across campus. Collaboration is a focus that has been infused through the design of our courses and our relationships with students. *Admission Requirements:* Admission information for graduate programs: http://www. it.coe.uh.edu/. Master's program: 3.0 grade point average (GPA) for unconditional admission or a 2.6 GPA or above for conditional admission over the last 60 hours of coursework attempted GRE or MAT scores: The 30 percentile on each section (Verbal, Quantitative, and Analytic) of the GRE serves as the minimum guideline for admission to all master's programs in the College of Education. A score of 35 on the MAT serves as the minimum guideline for admissions to all master's programs in the College of Education. The GRE or the MAT must have been taken within five (5) years of the date of application for admission to any Graduate program in the College of Education.

Doctoral program: Each applicant must normally have earned a master's degree or have completed 36 semester hours of appropriate graduate work with a minimum GPA of 3.0 (A = 4.0). GRE: The 35th percentile on each section (Verbal, Quantitative, and Analytic) of the GRE serves as the minimum guideline for admission to all doctoral programs in the College of Education. The GRE or the MAT must have been taken within five (5) years of the date of application for admission to any Graduate program in the College of Education. *Degree Requirements:* master's: Students with backgrounds in educational technology can complete the master's program with 36 hours of coursework. For the typical student, the M.Ed. in Instructional Technology consists of 9 semester hours of core courses required by the College of Education, and an additional 18 hour core in Instructional Technology as well as 9 hours that are determined by the students career goals (K–12, higher education, business and industry). Students take a written comprehensive examination over the program, coursework, and experiences.

The minimum hours required in the doctoral program is 66. More details about the courses and requirements can be found on the IT Web site: http://www.it.coe.uh.edu/. *Faculty:* 5 full-time, 5 part-time. *Students:* 20 full-time, 120 part-time. *Financial Assistance:* Graduate Assistantships (20 hours week) University and College Scholarships. *Degrees Awarded 2003:* approximately 30.

University of North Texas. Technology & Cognition (College of Education). Box 311337, Denton, TX 76203-1337. (940) 565-2057. Fax (940) 565-2185. http://www. cecs.unt.edu. Dr. Mark Mortensen & Mrs. Donna Walton, Computer Education and Cognitive Systems. Dr. Jon Young, Chair, Dept. of Technology and Cognition. coeinfo@ coefs.coe.unt.edu. *Specializations:* M.S. in Computer Education and Cognitive Systems —two emphasis areas: (1) Instructional Systems Technology and Teaching and (2) Learning with Technology. Ph.D. in Educational Computing. See www.cecs.unt.edu. *Features:* Unique applications of theory through research and practice in curriculum integration of technology, digital media production, and Web development. See www.cecs.unt.edu. *Admission Requirements:* Toulouse Graduate School Requirements, 18 hours in education, acceptable GRE: 405 V,489 A, 3 Analytical Writing for M.S. Degree. Increased requirements for Ph.D. program. *Degree Requirements:* 36 semester hours (12-hour core, 12-hour program course requirement based on M.S. track, 12-hour electives; see www. cecs.unt.edu). *Faculty:* 8 full-time, 1 part-time. *Students:* 300+ actively enrolled students in M.S. Highly selective Ph.D. program. *Financial Assistance:* Please see http://essc. unt.edu/finaid/index.htm. *Degrees Awarded 2003:* 10–30.

The University of Texas at Austin. Curriculum & Instruction. 406 Sanchez Building, Austin, TX 78712-1294. (512) 471-5211. Fax (512) 471-8460. http://jabba.edb. utexas.edu/it/. Min Liu, Ed.D., Associate Professor and IT Program Area Coordinator/ Graduate Advisor. Mliu@mail.utexas.edu. *Specializations:* The Instructional Technology Program at the University of Texas—Austin is a graduate program and offers degrees at the master and doctoral levels. This comprehensive program prepares professionals for various positions in education and industry. Master's degrees (M.A. and M.Ed.) in Instructional

Technology focus on the processes of systematic planning, design and development of instruction. Since IT requires more than skill in the production of instructional materials and use of machines, the instructional technologist emerging from our program uses knowledge of learning theory, curriculum development, instructional systems, communications theory, and evaluation to support appropriate uses of instructional resources.

The doctoral programs in Instructional Technology are comprehensive and research-oriented, providing knowledge and skills in areas such as instructional systems design, learning and instructional theories, instructional materials development and design of learning environments using various technology-based systems and tools. Graduates assume academic, administrative, and other leadership positions such as instructional evaluators, managers of instructional systems, and professors and researchers of instructional design and performance technology. *Features:* The program is interdisciplinary in nature, although certain competencies are required of all students. Programs of study and dissertation research are based on individual needs and career goals. Learning resources include a model Learning Technology Center, computer labs and classrooms, a television studio, and interactive multimedia lab. Students can take courses offered by other departments, including Radio-TV Film, school of information, Computer Science, and Educational Psychology. *Admission Requirements:* 95% of the current students and recent graduates admission materials included the following: master's: 3.5 GPA; 450 GRE Verbal, 1150 GRE Verbal + Quantitative; strong letters of recommendation; statement of study goals that can be satisfied with existing program offerings and resources. Doctoral: 3.5 GPA; 500 GRE Verbal, 1250 GRE Verbal + Quantitative; strong letters of recommendation; statement of study goals that can be satisfied with existing program offerings and resources. *Degree Requirements:* see http://jabba.edb.utexas.edu/it/ for details. *Faculty:* 3 full-time, 1 part-time. *Students:* 14 master's, 32 doctoral. *Financial Assistance:* Different forms of financial aid are often available to develop instructional materials, supervise student teachers in local schools, and assist with research/service projects. *Degrees Awarded 2003:* (in fall 2002–summer 2003) 5 master's; 6 doctoral.

Utah

Brigham Young University. Department of Instructional Psychology and Technology. 150 MCKB, BYU, Provo, UT 84602. (801) 422-5097. Fax (801) 422-0314. http://www.byu.edu/ipt. Russell Osguthorpe, Prof., Chair. russ_osguthorpe@byu.edu. *Specializations:* M.S. degrees in Instructional Design, Research and Evaluation, and Multimedia Production. Ph.D. degrees in Instructional Design, and Research and Evaluation. *Features:* Course offerings include principles of learning, instructional design, assessing learning outcomes, evaluation in education, empirical inquiry in education, project management, quantitative reasoning, microcomputer materials production, multimedia production, naturalistic inquiry, and more. Students participate in internships and projects related to development, evaluation, measurement, and research. *Admission Requirements:* both degrees: transcript, 3 letters of recommendation, letter of intent, GRE scores. Apply by Feb 1. Students agree to live by the BYU Honor Code as a condition for admission. *Degree Requirements:* master's: 38 semester hours, including prerequisite (3 hours), core courses (14 hours), specialization (12 hours), internship (3 hours), thesis or project (6 hours) with oral defense. Ph.D.: 94 semester hours beyond the bachelor's degree, including: prerequisite and skill requirements (21 hours), core course (16 hours), specialization (18 hours), internship (12 hours), projects (9 hours), and dissertation (18 hours). The dissertation must be orally defended. Also, at least two consecutive 6-hour semesters must be completed in residence. *Faculty:* 10 full-time, 1 half-time. *Students:* master's, 25 full-time, 2 part-time; Ph.D., 47 full-time, 3 part-time. *Financial Assistance:* internships, tuition scholarships, loans, and travel to present papers. *Degrees Awarded 2003:* 18.

Utah State University. Department of Instructional Technology, College of Education. 2830 Old Main Hill, Logan, UT 84322-2830. (435) 797-2694. Fax (435) 797-2693. http://www.coe.usu:edu/it/. Dr. Byron R. Burnham, Prof., Chair. byron.burnham@ usu.edu. *Specializations:* M.S. and Ed.S. with concentrations in the areas of Instructional Development, Multimedia, Educational Technology, and Information Technology/School Library Media Administration. Ph.D. in Instructional Technology is offered for individuals seeking to become professionally involved in instructional development in corporate education, public schools, community colleges, and universities. Teaching and research in higher education is another career avenue for graduates of the program. *Features:* M.S. and Ed.S. programs in Information Technology/School Library Media Administration and Educational Technology are also delivered via an electronic distance education system. The doctoral program is built on a strong master's and Specialists program in Instructional Technology. All doctoral students complete a core with the remainder of the course selection individualized, based upon career goals. *Admission Requirements:* M.S. and Ed.S.: 3.0 GPA, a verbal and quantitative score at the 40th percentile on the GRE or 43 MAT, three written recommendations. Ph.D.: master's degree in Instructional Technology, 3.0 GPA, verbal and quantitative score at the 40th percentile on the GRE, three written recommendations. *Degree Requirements:* M.S.: 39 semester hours; thesis or project option. Ed.S.: 30 semester hours if M.S. is in the field, 40 hours if not. Ph.D.: 62 total hours, dissertation, 3-semester residency, and comprehensive examination. *Faculty:* 11 full-time, 7 part-time. *Students:* M.S., 70 FT, 119 PT; Ed.S., 6 full-time, 9 part-time; Ph.D., 50. *Financial Assistance:* approx. 18 to 26 assistantships (apply by April 1). *Degrees Awarded 2003:* 36 M.S.; 42 Med; 4 PhD.

Virginia

George Mason University. Instructional Technology Programs. Mail Stop 5D6, 4400 University Dr., Fairfax, VA 22030-4444. (703) 993-3798. Fax (703) 993-2722. http://it.gse.gmu.edu/. Dr. Eamonn Kelly, Coord. of Instructional Technology Academic Programs. akelly1@gmu.edu. *Specializations:* PhD specializations in Instructional Design and Development; Integration of Technology in Schools; Assistive Technology; master's degrees in Curriculum and Instruction with emphasis in Instructional Technology: Track I—Instructional Design and Development; Track II—Integration of Technology in Schools; Track III—Assistive Technology; Track IV—Technology Innovations in Education. Graduate Certificates: Multimedia Development; Integration of Technology in Schools; Assistive Technology. *Features:* The Instructional Technology program promotes the theory-based design of learning opportunities that maximize the teaching and learning process using a range of technology applications. Program efforts span a range of audiences, meeting the needs of diverse learners—school-aged, adult learners, and learners with disabilities—in public and private settings. Within this framework, the program emphasizes research, reflection, collaboration, leadership, and implementation and delivery models. The Instructional Technology (IT) program provides professionals with the specialized knowledge and skills needed to apply today's computer and telecommunications technologies to educational goals within school, community and corporate settings. The IT program serves professional educators as well as those involved in instructional design, development and training in government and private sectors. Master degrees and certificates can be earned in each of three program tracks. Refer to the IT Web site (http://it.gse.gmu.edu/) for detailed information on admissions, Track 1—Instructional Design and Development (IDD)—Students are prepared to craft effective solutions within public, private and educational contexts to instructional challenges by using the latest information technologies in the design and development of instructional materials.

Track II: Integration of Technology in Schools (ITS)—Students are prepared to effectively integrate technology in the K–12 learning environment. Graduates frequently become the local expert and change agent for technology in schools.

Track III: Assistive/Special Education Technology (A/SET)—Graduates will use technology to assist individuals to function more effectively in school, home, work and community environments. Graduates are prepared to incorporate technology into the roles of educators, related service providers, Assistive Technology consultants, hardware/software designers and school based technology coordinators.

Track IV: TIE focuses on the following concepts and practical applications of technology in educational environments: Emerging educational trends and innovations in technology and their potential impact on learning, Policy and leadership issues, Creating community partnerships, Distance learning and its present and future impact on education. This program is intended for students who are already familiar with technology and are looking to expand their knowledge and skills. The program will combine instructional design activities with integration in K–12, higher education, and corporate learning environments. Exciting aspects of the program include the building and programming of robots using Lego Mindstorms, designing and creating an innovative project and then evaluating its effectiveness for learning, developing partnerships with the Museum of Art and serving as online mentors for pre-service teachers. *Admission Requirements:* Teaching or training experience, undergrad GPA of 3.0, TOEFL of 575(written) /230(computer), three letters of recommendation, goal statement. *Degree Requirements:* M.Ed. in Curriculum and Instruction: 39 hours; practicum, internship, or project. M.Ed. in Special Education: 36-42 hours. Ph.D.: 56-62 hours beyond master's degree for either specialization. Certificate programs: 12-15 hours. *Faculty:* 8 full-time, 15 part-time. *Students:* MEd full-time 75, MEd part-time 150, certificate programs 300. *Financial Assistance:* Information on assistantships, fellowships, loans and other types of financial aid is available through the Office of Student Financial Aid at 703-993-2353 or at apollo.gmu.edu/finaid. The IDD cohort offers tuition assistance. *Degrees Awarded 2003:* 130.

Radford University. Educational Studies Department, College of Education and Human Development. P.O. Box 6959, Radford,, VA 24142. (540) 831-5302. Fax (540) 831-5059. http://www.radford.edu. Dr. Martin S. Aylesworth, Acting Dept. Chair. mayleswo @radford.edu. *Specializations:* M.S. in Education with Educational Media/Technology emphasis. *Features:* School Library Media Specialist licensure. *Admission Requirements:* bachelor's degree, 2.7 undergraduate GPA *Degree Requirements:* 33 semester hours, practicum; thesis optional. *Faculty:* 2 full-time, 3 part-time. *Students:* 2 full-time, 23 part-time. *Financial Assistance:* assistantships, grants, student loans, scholarships.

University of Virginia. Department of Leadership, Foundations, and Policy, Curry School of Education. Ruffner Hall, Charlottesville, VA 22903. (434) 924-7471. Fax (434) 924-0747. http://curry.edschool.virginia.edu/curry/dept/edlf/instrtech/. John B. Bunch, Assoc. Prof., Coord., Instructional Technology Program, Dept. of Leadership, Foundations and Policy Studies. jbbunch@virginia.edu. *Specializations:* M.Ed., Ed.S., Ed.D, and Ph.D. degrees with focal areas in Media Production, Interactive Multimedia, e-Learning/Distance learning and K–12 Educational Technologies. *Features:* The IT program is situated in a major research university with linkages to multiple disciplines. Graduate Students have the opportunity to work with faculty across the Curry School and the University. *Admission Requirements:* undergraduate degree from accredited institution in any field, undergraduate GPA 3.0, 1000 GRE (V+Q), 600 TOEFL. Financial aid application deadline is March 1st of each year for the fall semester for both master's and doctoral degrees; admission is rolling. *Degree Requirements:* M.Ed.: 36 semester hours, comprehensive examination. Ed.S.: 60 semester hours beyond undergraduate degree. Ed.D.: 54 semester hours, dissertation, at least one conference presentation or juried publication, comprehensive examination, residency; Ph.D.: same as Ed.S. with the addition of 18 semester hours. For specific degree requirements, see Web site, write to the address above, or refer to the UVA. *Faculty:* 5 full-time, 2 part-time. *Students:* M.Ed. 7/11 Ed.D, 2/6; Ph.D., 12/18. *Financial Assistance:* Graduate assistantships and scholarships are available on a competitive basis. *Degrees Awarded 2003:* 5 MEd, 3 PhD EdD.

Virginia Polytechnic Institute and State University. College of Liberal Arts and Human Sciences. 220 War Memorial Hall, Blacksburg, VA 24061-0341. (540) 231-5587. Fax (540) 231-9075. http://www.tandl.vt.edu/it/default.htm. Katherine Cennamo, Program Area Leader, Instructional Technology, Dept. of Teaching and Learning. cennamo@vt.edu. *Specializations:* M.A., Ed.S. Ed.D., and Ph.D. in Instructional Technology. Preparation for education, higher education, faculty development, business, and industry. *Features:* Areas of emphasis are Instructional Design, Distance Education, and Multimedia Development. Facilities include two computer labs, extensive digital video and audio equipment, distance education classroom, and computer graphics production areas. *Admission Requirements:* Ed.D. and Ph.D.: 3.3 GPA from master's degree, GRE scores, writing sample, three letters of recommendation, transcripts. MA.: 3.0 GPA Undergraduate. *Degree Requirements:* Ph.D.: 96 hrs above B.S., 2-year residency, 12 hrs. research classes, 30 hrs. dissertation; Ed.D.: 90 hrs. above B.S., 1 year residency, 12 hrs. research classes; MA.: 30 hrs. above B.S. *Faculty:* 4 full-time, 3 part-time. *Students:* 35 FT and 10 PT, doctoral level. 15 FT and 150PT (online) master's. *Financial Assistance:* 10 assistantships, limited tuition scholarships. *Degrees Awarded 2003:* 9 PhD and 50 MS.

Virginia State University. School of Graduate Studies, Research and Outreach. 1 Hayden Drive, Box 9402, Petersburg, VA 23806. (804) 524-5377. Fax (804) 524-5104. http://www.vsu.edu. Vykuntapathi Thota, Chair, Dept. of Education. *Specializations:* M.S., M.Ed. in Educational Technology. *Features:* Video Conferencing Center and PLATO Laboratory, internship in ABC and NBC channels. *Admission Requirements:* See http://www.vsu.edu/catalogweb/graduate/admission/requirement.htm. *Degree Requirements:* 30 semester hours plus thesis for M.S.; 33 semester hours plus project for M.Ed.; comprehensive exam. *Faculty:* 1 full-time, 2 part-time. *Students:* 8 full-time, 50 part-time. *Financial Assistance:* Scholarships through the School of Graduate Studies.

Washington

Eastern Washington University. Department of Computer Science. 202 Computer Science Building, Cheney, WA 99004-2412. (509) 359-6260. Fax (509) 359-2215. http://acm.ewu.edu/csd/. Ray O. Hamel, PhD, Linda Kieffer, PhD. compsci@ mailserver.ewu.edu. *Specializations:* M.Ed. in Computer and Technology Supported Education; M.S. Interdisciplinary. Master's program started in 1983. *Features:* Many projects involve the use of high-level authoring systems to develop educational products, technology driven curriculum, and Web projects. *Admission Requirements:* 3.0 GPA for last 90 graded undergraduate quarter Credits *Degree Requirements:* M.S Interdisciplinary.: 52 quarter hours (30 hours in computers, 15 hours outside education; the hours do not total to 52 because of freedom to choose where Methods of Research is taken, where 12 credits of supporting courses are taken, and where additional electives are taken); research project with formal report. M.Ed.: 52 quarter hours (28 hours in computer education, 16 hours in education, 8 hours outside education). *Faculty:* 1 full-time. *Students:* approx. 25. *Financial Assistance:* some research and teaching fellowships.

University of Washington. College of Education. 115 Miller Hall, Box 353600, Seattle, WA 98195-3600. (206) 543-1847. Fax (206) 543-8439. http://www.educ.washington.edu/ COE/c-and-i/c_and_i_med_ed_tech.htm. William Winn, Prof. of Education. billwinn@u. washington.edu. *Specializations:* M.Ed., Ed.D, and Ph.D. for individuals in business, industry, higher education, public schools, and organizations concerned with education or communication (broadly defined). *Features:* Emphasis on design of materials and programs to encourage learning and development in school and non-school settings; research and related activity in such areas as interactive instruction, Web-based learning, virtual environments, use of video as a tool for design and development. Close collaboration with program in Cognitive Studies. *Admission Requirements:* M.Ed.: goal statement (2-3pp.), writing sample, 1000 GRE (verbal plus quantitative), undergraduate GPA indicating po-

tential to successfully accomplish graduate work. Doctoral: GRE scores, letters of reference, transcripts, personal statement, master's degree or equivalent in field appropriate to
the specialization with 3.5 GPA, two years of successful professional experience and/or experience related to program goals. *Degree Requirements:* M.Ed.: 45 quarter hours (including 24 in technology); thesis or project recommended, exam optional. Ed.D.: see
http://www.educ.washington.edu/COEWeb   site/programs/ci/EdD.html.   Ph.D.:   http://
www.educ.washington.edu/COEWeb   site/students/prospective/phdDescrip.html.   *Faculty:* 4 full-time, 3 part-time. *Students:* 12 full-time, 32 part-time; 26 M.Ed., 18 doctoral.
Financial Assistance: assistantships awarded competitively and on basis of program needs;
other assistantships available depending on grant activity in any given year. *Degrees
Awarded 2003:* 5.

Western Washington University. Woodring College of Education, Instructional Technology. MS 9087, Bellingham, WA 98225-9087. 360) 650-3387. Fax (360) 650-6526.
http://www.wce.wwu.edu/depts/IT.   Dr.   Les   Blackwell,   Prof.,   Department   Chair.
Les.Blackwell@wwu.edu. *Specializations:* M.Ed. with emphasis in Instructional Technology in Adult Education, Special Education, Elementary Education, and Secondary Education. *Admission Requirements:* 3.0 GPA in last 45 quarter credit hours, GRE or MAT
scores, 3 letters of recommendation, and, in some cases, 3 years of teaching experience.
Degree Requirements: 48–52 quarter hours (24–28 hours in instructional technology; 24
hours in education-related courses, thesis required; internship and practicum possible).
Faculty: 6 full-time, 8 part-time. *Students:* 5 full-time, 10 part-time. *Financial Assistance:*
assistantships, student loans, scholarships.

Wisconsin

Edgewood College. Department of Education. 1000 Edgewood College Drive, Madison,
WI 53711-1997. (608) 663-2293. Fax (608) 663-6727. http://www.edgewood.edu. Dr. Joseph E. Schmiedicke, Chair, Dept. of Education. schmied@edgewood.edu. *Specializations:* M.A. in Education with emphasis on Instructional Technology. Master's program
started in 1987. *Features:* classes conducted in laboratory setting with emphasis on applications and software. *Admission Requirements:* 2.75 GPA. *Degree Requirements:* 36 semester hours. *Faculty:* 2 full-time, 3 part-time. *Students:* 5 full-time, 150 part-time.
Financial Assistance: grants, student loans. *Degrees Awarded 2003:* 8.

University of Wisconsin—La Crosse. Educational Media Program. Rm. 235C, Morris
Hall, La Crosse, WI 54601. (608) 785-8121. Fax (608) 785-8128. http://www.uwlax.
edu/mediaservices/soe/html/soe-about.htm. Ronald Rochon, Ph. D., Interim Associate
Dean, Director of School of Education. rochon.rona@uwlax.edu. *Specializations:* M.S. in
Professional Development with specializations in Initial Instructional Library Specialist,
License 901; Instructional Library Media Specialist, License 902 (39 credits). *Degree Requirements:* 30 semester hours, including 15 in media; no thesis. *Faculty:* 2 full-time, 4
part-time. *Students:* 21. *Financial Assistance:* guaranteed student loans, graduate
assistantships.

University of Wisconsin—Madison. Curriculum and Instruction, School of Education.
225 North Mills Street, Madison, WI 53706. 608) 263-4670. Fax (608) 263-9992.
http://www.education.wisc.edu/ci/. Michael J. Streibel. streibel@education.wisc.edu. *Specializations:* M.S. and Ph.D. degree programs to prepare college and university faculty.
On-going research in photography and visual culture in education as well as educational
game design and design experiments in education. *Features:* Traditional instructional technology courses are processed through social, cultural, and historical frames of reference.
Current curriculum emphasizes new media theories, critical cultural and visual culture theories, and constructivist theories of instructional design and development. Many courses
offered in the evening. *Admission Requirements:* Master's and Ph.D.: previous experience

in Instructional Technology preferred, previous teaching experience, 3.0 GPA on last 60 undergraduate credits, acceptable scores on GRE, 3.0 GPA on all graduate work. *Degree Requirements:* M.S.: 24 credits plus thesis and exam (an additional 12 credits of Educational Foundations if no previous educational background); Ph.D.: 1 year of residency beyond the bachelor's, major, minor, and research requirements, preliminary exam, dissertation, and oral exam. *Faculty:* 2 full-time, 1 part-time. *Students:* M.S., 14; Ph.D., 10. *Financial Assistance:* TA and PA positions are available. *Degrees Awarded 2003:* 2 Ph.D., 4 M.S.

Part Six
Mediagraphy

Introduction

CONTENTS

This resource lists media-related journals, books, ERIC documents, journal articles, and nonprint media resources of interest to practitioners, researchers, students, and others concerned with educational technology and educational media. The primary goal of this section is to list current publications in the field. The majority of materials cited here were published in 2003 or mid-2004. Media-related journals include those listed in past issues of *EMTY* and new entries in the field. A thorough list of journals in the educational technology field has been updated for the 2005 edition using Ulrich's Periodical Index Online and journal Web sites. This chapter is not intended to serve as a specific resource location tool, although it may be used for that purpose in the absence of database access. Rather, readers are encouraged to peruse the categories of interest in this chapter to gain an idea of recent developments within the field. For archival purposes, this chapter serves as a snapshot of the field in 2005. Readers must bear in mind that technological developments occur well in advance of publication and should take that fact into consideration when judging the timeliness of resources listed in this chapter.

SELECTION

Items were selected for the Mediagraphy in several ways. The EBSCO Host Databases were used to locate most of the journal citations. Others were reviewed directly by the editors. Items were chosen for this list when they met one or more of the following criteria: reputable publisher, broad circulation, coverage by indexing services, peer review, and coverage of a gap in the literature. The editors chose items on subjects that seem to reflect the instructional technology field as it is today. Because of the increasing tendency for media producers to package their products in more than one format and for single titles to contain mixed media, titles are no longer separated by media type. The editors make no claims as to the comprehensiveness of this list. It is, instead, intended to be representative.

OBTAINING RESOURCES

Media-Related Periodicals and Books: Publisher, price, and ordering/subscription address are listed wherever available.

ERIC Documents: As of December 31, 2003, ERIC was no longer funded. However, ERIC documents can still be read and copied from their microfiche form at any library holding an ERIC microfiche collection. The identification number beginning with ED (for example, ED 332 677) locates the document in the collection. Document delivery services and copies of most ERIC documents can also continue to be available from the ERIC Document Reproduction Service. Prices charged depend on format chosen (microfiche or paper copy), length of the document, and method of shipping. Online orders, fax orders, and expedited delivery are available.

To find the closest library with an ERIC microfiche collection, contact: ACCESS ERIC, 1600 Research Blvd., Rockville, MD 20850-3172; (800) LET-ERIC (538-3742); e-mail: acceric@inet.ed.gov

To order ERIC documents, contact:

ERIC Document Reproduction Service (EDRS)
7420 Fullerton Rd., Suite 110, Springfield, VA 22153-2852
(800) 443-ERIC (443-3742); (703) 440-1400
fax: (703) 440-1408
e-mail: service@edrs.com.

Journal articles: Photocopies of journal articles can be obtained in one of the following ways: (1) from a library subscribing to the title, (2) through interlibrary loan, (3) through the purchase of a back issue from the journal publisher, or (4) from an article reprint service such as UMI.

UMI Information Store, 500 Sansome Street, Suite 400
San Francisco, CA 94111
(800) 248-0360 (toll-free in U.S. and Canada); (415) 433-5500
(outside U.S. and Canada)
E-mail: orders@infostore.com

Journal articles can also be obtained through the Institute for Scientific Information (ISI).

ISI Document Solution
P.O. Box 7649
Philadelphia, PA 19104-3389
(215) 386-4399
Fax (215) 222-0840 or (215)386-4343
E-mail: ids@isinet.com

ARRANGEMENT

Mediagraphy entries are classified according to major subject emphasis under the following headings:

- Artificial Intelligence, Robotics, and Electronic Performance Support Systems
- Computer-Assisted Instruction
- Distance Education
- Educational Research
- Educational Technology
- Information Science and Technology
- Innovation
- Instructional Design and Development
- Interactive Multimedia
- Libraries and Media Centers
- Media Technologies
- Professional Development
- Simulation, Gaming, and Virtual Reality
- Special Education and Disabilities
- Telecommunications and Networking

Jo McClendon

Mediagraphy

ARTIFICIAL INTELLIGENCE, ROBOTICS,
AND ELECTRONIC PERFORMANCE SUPPORT SYSTEMS

Artificial Intelligence Review. Kluwer Academic Publishers, 101 Philip Drive, Norwell, MA 02061, kluweronline@wkap.com, www.wkap.nl/journalhome.htm/0269-2821 [6 issues/yr, $187 indiv., $483 inst.]. Publishes commentary on issues and development in artificial intelligence foundations and current research.

AI Magazine (Online). AAAI Press, American Association for Artificial Intelligence, 445 Burgess Drive, Menlo Park, California 94025-3442, http://www.aaai.org, http://www.aaai.org/Magazine/magazine.html, [4 issues/yr, free with membership]. Proclaimed "journal of record for the AI community," AI magazine provides full-length articles on research, new literature but is written to allow access to those reading outside their area of expertise.

Chou, C., et al. (2003). Redefining the learning companion: The past, present, and future of educational agents. **Computers & Education, 40**(3), 255–270. Learning companion systems (LCS) go beyond intelligent tutoring systems (ITS) by assuming dual roles of intelligent tutor as well as learning companion. Additional discussion on educational agents in networked learning environments.

Connell, James E., & Witt, Joseph C. (2004, Spring). Applications of computer-based instruction: Using specialized software to aid letter–name and letter–sound recognition. **Journal of Applied Behavior Analysis, 37**(1), 67–71. This study evaluated equivalence based software tutorials written with educational authoring software. The study used children with pre-reading learning difficulties.

Henzinger, M., & Leonardi, S. (2003). Scheduling multicasts on unit-capacity trees and meshes. **Journal of Computer and System Sciences, 66**(3), 567–605. Discusses admission and routing control problems in multicasting initiatives. Offers solutions to problems.

International Journal of Robotics Research. Sage Science, (805) 499-0721. [Mo., indiv., $150, $995 inst., available online]. Interdisciplinary approach to the study of robotics for researchers, scientists, and students. The first scholarly publication on robotics research.

Journal of Interactive Learning Research. Association for Advancement of Computing in Education, Box 2966, Charlottesville, VA 22902-2966, aace@virginia.edu, www.aace.org [Q.; $95 indiv., $55 student]. International journal publishes articles on how intelligent computer technologies can be used in education to enhance learning and teaching. Reports on research and developments, integration, and applications of artificial intelligence in education.

Journal of Intelligent and Robotic Systems. Kluwer Academic/Plenum Publishers, PO Box 358, Accord Station, Hingham MA 02018-0358, kluweronline@wkap.com, www.wkap.nl/journalhome.htm/0921-0296 [Mo., $1059 inst., $629.00 indiv., for print OR online format]. The main objective is to provide a forum for the fruitful interaction of ideas and techniques that combine systems and control science with artificial intelligence—and other related computer science—concepts. It bridges the gap between theory and practice.

Knowledge-Based Systems. Elsevier Science Inc., P.O. Box 945, New York, NY 10159-0945, www.elsevier.com/locate/knosys [8 issues/yr, $892 inst., except in Europe and Japan]. Interdisciplinary applications-oriented journal on fifth-generation computing, expert systems, and knowledge-based methods in system design.

Moreno, R., & Mayer, R. (2004, Mar.). Personalized messages that promote science learning in virtual environments. **Journal of Educational Psychology, 96** (1), 165–173. This article discusses a novel use of virtual reality technologies used to teach plant biology. Research found enhanced student performance when the program used a personalized styled voice rather than a nonpersonalized style when providing automated feedback.

Minds and Machines: Journal for Artificial Intelligence, Philosophy and Cognitive Science. Kluwer Academic Publishers, 101 Philip Drive, Norwell, MA 02061. [Q., $205 indiv., $459 inst.]. Discusses issues concerning machines and mentality, artificial intelligence, epistemology, simulation, and modeling.

Tseng, Y., et al. (2003). A stop-or-move mobility model for PCS networks and its location-tracking strategies. **Computer Communications, 26**(12), 1288–1302. A new Stop-or-Move Mobility (SMM) model is proposed. Features include: "transition between stop and move," "infrequent transition," "memory of roaming direction," and "oblivious in different moves." As a result, an adaptive location-tracking scheme is developed. These minimize the information needed for individual users. Suggestions for further development and research are included.

COMPUTER-ASSISTED INSTRUCTION

Australian Educational Computing. Australian Council for Computers in Education. P.O. Box 1255, Belconnen, ACT 2616, Australia. Available online at www.acce.edu.au, journaleditor@acce.edu.au [irregular publishing, online]. Educational computer issues forum.

Barron, A., et al. (2003). Large-scale research study on technology in K–12 school: Technology as it relates to the national technology standards. **Journal of Research on Technology in Education, 35**(4), 489–508. Examines the findings of a survey of more than 2000 teachers. Over 50 percent reported integrating technology as a classroom communication and teaching tool. Suggestions from findings are reported as relate to national standards for technology in the classroom.

CALICO Journal. Computer Assisted Language Instruction Consortium, Southwest Texas State University, 116 Centennial Hall, San Marcos, TX 78666, info@calico.org, www.calico.org [Q., $50 indiv., $90 inst., $140 corporations]. Provides information on the applications of technology in teaching and learning languages.

Children's Software & New Media Revue. CSR, 120 Main Street, Flemington, NJ 08822; www.childrenssoftware.com. [online $19, Paper 6/Yr., $26]. Provides reviews and other information about software to help parents and educators more effectively use computers with children.

Chung, S., Severance, C., & Chung, M. (2003). Design of support tools for knowledge building in a virtual university course. **Interactive Learning Environments, 11**(1), 41–68. Support tools have been created that prompt students to engage in inquiry on their own to enhance quality learning online. Argues that interaction alone is not sufficient for critical thinking among students. Implications for theory are included.

Computer Assisted Composition Journal. Human Technology Interface, Inc. Press 163 Wood Wedge Way, Sandford, NC 27330. Tel: (919) 499-9216. Ed. Lynn Veach Sadler. [3/yr., $15]. Publishes essays pertaining to computer applications in writing.

Computers and Composition. Elsevier Science, Inc., P.O. Box 945, New York, NY 10159-0945 [4/yr., $62 indiv., $245 inst.]. International journal for teachers of writing focuses on the use of computers in writing instruction and related research and dialogue.

Computers & Education. Elsevier, Regional Sales Office, Customer Support Department, P.O. Box 945, New York, NY 10159-0945. [8/Yr., indiv., $169, inst., $1,078]. Presents technical papers covering a broad range of subjects for users of analog, digital, and hybrid computers in all aspects of higher education.

Computer Education. Staffordshire University, Computer Education Group, c/o CEG Treasurer, Beaconside, Staffs, ST18 0AD, United Kingdom, Ed. S. Kennewell. [3/yr., 25 GBP to US]. Covers Educational Computer application for students 11–18 years of age.

Computers and the Humanities. Kluwer Academic Publishers, Order Department, P.O. Box 358, Accord Station, Hingham, MA 02018-0358. [Q., indiv., $167, inst. $444, print or online format, add 20% for both formats]. Contains papers on computer-aided studies, applications, automation, and computer-assisted instruction.

Computers in Human Behavior. Elsevier, Regional Sales Office, Customer Support Department, P.O. Box 945, New York, NY 10159-0945. [6/yr., $233 indiv., $1033 inst.]. Scholarly journal dedicated to examining the use of computers from a psychological perspective.

Computers in the Schools. Haworth Press, 10 Alice St., Binghamton, NY 13904-1580, (800) HAWORTH, Fax (800) 895-0582, getinfo@haworthpressinc.com, www.haworthpress.com [Q., $60 indiv., $90 inst., $300 libraries]. Features articles that combine theory and practical applications of small computers in schools for educators and school administrators.

Computer Education. K.K. Roy, Ltd., 55 Gariahat Rd., P.O. Box 10210, Calcutta, West Bengal 700 019, India. Ed. K.K. Roy. Tel. (+91) 33-475-4872. [Bi, $35 US]. Discusses how schools and universities are using educational software. Profiles and reviews new educational software in the market in content areas such as science, social science, and the humanities.

Computer Learning. Computer Learning Foundation, P.O. Box 60007, Palo Alto, CA 94306-0007, clf@computerlearning.org, http://www.computerlearning.org. Focuses people's attention on the importance of technology in children's learning. Includes tips for parents and teachers.

Computer Studies: Computers in Education. Dushkin-McGraw-Hill, Sluice Dock, Gyulliford, CT 06437-9989. Ed. John Hirschbuhl. [Annual, $12.25]. Features articles on computer-based education applications, specifically logistics surrounding the use of computers in education.

Computers in Education Journal. American Society for Engineering Education, Computers in Education Decision, P.O. Box 68, Port Royal Sq, Port Royal. VA 22535, Ed. W. W. Everett, Jr. [Q., $45 US, $65 foreign]. Covers transactions, scholarly research papers, application notes, and teaching methods.

Computers in the Schools. Haworth Press, Inc., 10 Alice St., Binghamton, NY 13904-6362. getinfo@haworthpressinc.com, http://www.haworthpressinc.com. Ed. D

Lamont Johnson. [Q., $60 indiv., $90 inst., $300 to libraries]. Features articles related to small personal computer use in schools.

Converge. Imagine Media, Inc., 100 Blue Ravine, Folsom, CA 95630, toll-free (877) 487-7377. cz@convergemag.com, http://www.convergemag.com [Mo., $ US, $267 International] Pub. Marina Leight. Explores the revolution of technology in education.

Coppola, N. W., Hiltz, Starr R., & Rotter, N. G. (2004, June). Building Trust in Virtual Teams. **IEEE Transactions on Professional Communication, 47**(2), 95–105. Study examined team taught courses and ratings. Findings suggest swift and immediate development of trust among the team results in improved course ratings.

Curriculum-Technology Quarterly. Association for Supervision and Curriculum Development, Education & Technology Resource Center, 1703 N Beauregard St., Alexandria, VA 22314, (800) 933-2723, member@ascd.org, http://www.ascd.org. Ed. Larry Mann. [Q.]. Explores strategies for using technology for enhancing classroom instruction. Includes pull-out sections on curriculum content areas. For K–12 teachers and curriculum developers.

Dr. Dobb's Journal. Miller Freeman Inc., 600 Harrison St., San Francisco, CA 94107, (800) 456-1215. www.djj.com/djj [Mo., $34.95 US, $45 Mexico and Canada, $70 elsewhere]. Articles on the latest in operating systems, programming languages, algorithms, hardware design and architecture, data structures, and telecommunications; in-depth hardware and software reviews.

DeBord, Kurt A., Aruguete, Mara S., & Muhlig, Jeannette. (2004, Winter). Are computer-assisted teaching methods effective? **Teaching of Psychology, 31**(1), 65–68. Two groups of psychology students were studied for preferences for computer-assisted instruction tools and techniques. Students preferred CAI supported learning methods.

Education Technology News. Business Publishers, Inc., 8737 Colesville Rd., 11th Floor, Silver Spring, MD 20910-3928, (800) 274-6737, bpinews@bpinews.com, http://www. bpinews.com. Ed. Rasheda Childress, [Bi-w., $337 domestic, 356 out of North America]. For teachers and other persons interested in the educational uses of computers in the classroom. Includes future articles on application, educational software, and pertinent programs.

Educational Software Review. Growth Systems, Inc. 855 Normandy Rd., Encinitas, CA 92024, Ed. Stewart Walton. [M., $33.75].

Educational Technology and Society. International Forum of Educational Technology and Society. IEEE Computer Society, Learning Technology Task Force, kinshuk@ieee.org, http://ifets.gmd.de/periodical. Ed., Dr. Kinshuk. [Q., no cost]. Explores issues concerning educational software developers and educators.

Educational Technology Review. Association for the Advancement of Computing in Education, P.O. Box 2966, Charlottesville, VA 22902-2966, info@aace.org, http://www. aace.org. Ed. Gary H Marks. [Q., $40 domestic to nonmembers, $50 to nonmembers]. Publishes articles dealing with the issues in instructional technology application.

Edwards, M. (2003). The lap of learning. **School Administrator, 60**(4), 6–12. Discusses the use of laptops in education to date, the advantages of wireless technology, and the need for teachers to keep students on task with challenging problem-solving learning objectives.

Electronic Education Report. SIMBA Information, 11 Riverbend Dr S, Box 4234, Stamford, CT 06907-0234, (800) 307-2529, info@simbanet.com, http://www.simbanet.com.

Ed. Kathleen Martucci. [Bi-w., $479 North America, $529 elsewhere]. Newsletter discussing software and multimedia educational technologies.

Electronic School. National School Boards Association, 1680 Duke Street, Alexandria VA 22314, subscriptions@electronic-school.com, http://www.electronic-school.com/ [Q.] Trade publication that discusses trends and strategies for integrating technology into primary and secondary education.

e-WEEK. Ziff-Davis Publishing Co., P.O. Box 3402, Northbrook IL 60065-3402. [W., $195, Canada and Mexico $250, free to qualified personnel]. Provides current information on the IBM PC, including hardware, software, industry news, business strategies, and reviews of hardware and software.

Helic, D., Maurer, H., & Scerbakov, N. (2004, Aug.). Knowledge transfer processes in a modern WBT system. **Journal of Network & *Computer* Applications, 27**(3), 163–191. Study examines the Web as a tool of conveyance connecting knowledge holders with those in search of information. It evaluates the knowledge transfer system and gives suggestions.

Garland, K., & Noyes, J. (2004, June). The effects of mandatory and optional use on students' ratings of a computer-based learning package. **British Journal of Educational Technology, 35**(3), 263–274. As the number of students learning via the Web increases in the UK, a shift has taken place from lecture based instruction to student-driven choices. This article discusses a study of students' perceptions of the usefulness of Web-based learning packages.

Information Technology in Childhood Education. Association for the Advancement for Computing in Education, P.O. Box 3728, Norfolk, VA 22902-2966. infor@aace.org, http://www.aace.org, [Q., $85 domestic, $85 domestic to institutions]. Scholarly trade publication reporting on research and investigations into the applications of instructional technology.

InfoWorld. InfoWorld Publishing, 155 Bovet Rd., Suite 800, San Mateo, CA 94402, (650) 572-7341. [W., $195]. News and reviews of PC hardware, software, peripherals, and networking.

Instructor. Scholastic Inc., 555 Broadway, New York, NY 10012, (212) 505-4900. [8/yr., $24]. Features articles on applications and advances of technology in education for K–12 and college educators and administrators.

INTERACTIVE. Question Publishing Company, Ltd., 27 Frederick St., Hockley, Birmingham, Warks, B1 3HH, United Kingdom, Tel (+44) 121-212-0919, Fax (+44) 121-212-1959. [9/yr., GBP 18 outside Europe, GBP 22 in Europe]. Designed to help all primary and secondary teachers get the most from information technology in the classroom.

Interactive Learning Environments. Swets and Zeitlinger, PO Box 582 Downingtown, PA 19335-998. orders@swets.nl, http://www.swets.nl/sps/journals/ile1.html [3/yr., $79 indiv., $227 inst with online]. Explores the implications of the Internet and multimedia presentation software in education and training environments.

Internet & Personal Computing Abstracts (IPCA). Information Today, 143 Old Marlton Pike, Medford, NJ 08055, (800) 300-9868. [4/yr., $235 US]. Abstracts literature on the use of microcomputers in business, education, and the home, covering over 175 publications.

Journal of Computer Assisted Learning. Blackwell Scientific Ltd., Journal Subscriptions, journals.cs@blacksci.co.uk, www.blackwell-science.com. [Q., $106 indiv., $506 inst.]. Articles and research on the use of computer-assisted learning.

Journal of Educational Computing Research. Baywood Publishing Co., 26 Austin Ave., P.O. Box 337, Amityville, NY 11701. [8/yr. $120 indiv., $313 inst.]. Presents original research papers, critical analyses, reports on research in progress, design and development studies, article reviews, and grant award listings.

Journal of Educational Multimedia and Hypermedia. Association for the Advancement of Computing in Education, Box 2966, Charlottesville, VA 22902-2966, aace@virginia. edu, www.aace.org. [Q., $40 indiv., $50 foreign]. A multidisciplinary information source presenting research about and applications for multimedia and hypermedia tools.

Journal of Hypermedia and Multimedia Studies. ISTE, University of Oregon, 1787 Agate St., Eugene, OR 97403-1923, (800) 336-5191, cust_svc@ccmail.uoregon.edu, www.iste.org [Q., $29; $39 intl., $42 intl. air]. Features articles on projects, lesson plans, and theoretical issues, as well as reviews of products, software, and books.

Journal of Research on Technology in Education. ISTE, University of Oregon, 1787 Agate St., Eugene, OR 97403-1923, (800) 336-5191, cust_svc@ccmail.uoregon.edu, www.iste.org [Q., $38, 1 year; $73, 2 years; $108, 3 years]. Contains articles reporting on the latest research findings related to classroom and administrative uses of technology, including system and project evaluations.

Laffey, J., et al. (2003). Supporting learning and behavior of at-risk young children: Computers in urban education. **Journal of Research in Technology and Education, 35**(4), 423–441. The study used interactive computer technology in an attempt to address behavior problems in at-risk urban youths. A control group was used to verify findings.

Learning and Leading with Technology: Serving Teachers in the Classroom. ISTE, University of Oregon, 1787 Agate St., Eugene, OR 97403-1923, (800) 336-5191, cust_svc@ccmail.uoregon.edu, www.iste.org [8/yr, $38, 1 year; $73, 2 years; $108, 3 years]. Focuses on the use of technology, coordination, and leadership; written by educators for educators. Appropriate for classroom teachers, lab teachers, technology coordinators, and teacher educators.

Logo Exchange. ISTE, University of Oregon, 1787 Agate St., Eugene, OR 97403-1923, (800) 336-5191, cust_svc@ccmail.uoregon.edu, www.iste.org [Q., $29, $44 intl., $34 intl. air]. Brings ideas from Logo educators throughout the world, with current information on Logo research, resources, and methods.

MacWorld. MacWorld Communications, Box 54529, Boulder, CO 80322-4529, www.macworld.com. [Mo., $19.97]. Describes hardware, software, tutorials, and applications for users of the Macintosh microcomputer.

OnCUE. Computer Using Educators, Inc. 1210 Marina Village Parkway, Ste 100, Alameda, CA 94501-0195, cueinc@cue.org, http://www.cue.org. Ed. Maria McDonough. [Bi-m., $40 domestic, $55 foreign]. Contains articles, news items and trade advertisements addressing computer based education.

The One-Computer Classroom. [Video, 36 min., $129]. Films for the Humanities & Sciences, www.films.com. Explores how a single computer in the classroom can be used as a workstation, a presentation device, and a tool used for interactive learning.

PC Magazine: The Independent Guide to IBM-Standard Personal Computing. Ziff-Davis Publishing Co., Box 54093, Boulder, CO 80322. [25 issues., $25 US, $66 foreign]. Comparative reviews of computer hardware and general business software programs.

ReCALL. European Association for Computer Assisted Language Learning. (EUROCALL), Cambridge University Press, Edinburgh Building, Sharftesbury Rd., Cambridge CB2 2RU, United Kingdom, http://www.cup.cam.ac.uk. Ed. June Thompson. [semi-annual, $104 US, $65 Great Britain]. Contains articles on research and development in the area of computer assisted language learning.

Roffe, Ian. (2004). E-learning for SMEs: Competition and dimensions of perceived value. **Journal of European Industrial Training, 28**(5), 440–456. Examines the use of computer aided instruction in a small to medium enterprise environment to enhance perceptions of competitive strategies.

Social Science Computer Review. Sage Publications Inc., 2455 Teller Rd., Thousand Oaks, CA 91320, order@sagepub.com, www.sagepub.com [Q., $68 indiv., $350 inst.]. Features include software reviews, new product announcements, and tutorials for beginners.

Software Magazine. Sentry Publishing Co., Inc., 1 Research Dr., Suite 400B, Westborough, MA 01581-3907. [6 issues/yr., $42 US, $58 Canada, $140 elsewhere, free to qualified personnel]. Provides information on software and industry developments for business and professional users, and announces new software packages.

Technology and Learning. Miller Freeman, Inc., 600 Harrison Street, San Francisco, CA 94107, (415) 905-2200, http://www.techlearning.com [8/yr., $29.95 US, $39.95 Can and Mexico, $69.95 elsewhere]. Features discussions of new innovations in educational hardware and software.

Wagner, G. Dale, & Flannery, Daniele D. (2004). A quantitative study of factors affecting learner acceptance of a computer-based training support tool. **Journal of European Industrial Training, 28** (5), 383–400. Study examines the use of computer training in work environments and examines employee acceptance of technology use for training.

Wegerif, R. (2004, Aug.). The role of educational software as a support for teaching and learning conversations. *Computers & Education*, 43(1/2), 179–192. Research was done to examine how computers can be used as smart tools for framing learning for small children as a "participant" in classroom conversations.

Wireless Networks: The Journal of Mobile Communication, Computation and Information. Kluwer Academic Publishers, 101 Philip Drive, Norwell, MA 02061, (617) 871-6600, fax (617) 871-6528, kluwer@wkap.com [6/yr., $376 Euro, $377 USD institution]. A journal devoted to the technological innovations that result from the mobility allowed by wireless technology. Referred and research-based publication.

Workman, M. (2004, July). Performance and perceived effectiveness in computer-based and computer-aided education: Do cognitive styles make a difference? **Computers in Human Behavior**, 20(4), 517–524. CD Rom and Web-based instruction was studied to determine their performance and perceived effectiveness when examining learning styles and their impacts. Results provide suggestions for instructional designers using CBE and CAE.

Zenios, M., Goodyear, P., Jones, C. (2004, Aug.). Researching the impact of the networked information environment on learning and teaching. **Computers & Education, 43**(1/2), 205–214. Focused around the UK-networked resource called Distributed National Electronic Resource (DNER) and more recently renamed the Information Environment (IE), this paper discussed the impact of networked resources and how such planning can impact teaching and learning as end users.

DISTANCE EDUCATION

American Journal of Distance Education. Lawrence Erlbaum Associates, Inc., Michael G. Moore, Ed., College of Education, The State University of Pennsylvania, 409E Keller Building, University Park, PA 16802-3202, www.ajde.com [3/yr.; $55 indiv.; $120 inst.]. Created to disseminate information and act as a forum for criticism and debate about research in and practice of systems, management, and administration of distance education.

Cameron, B. (2003). Effectiveness of simulation in a hybrid and online networking course. **Quarterly Review of Distance Education, 4**(1), 51–56. Discusses the uses and effectiveness of simulation in distance education courses.

Carnevale, D. (2003). Congress may end distance-education limit. **Chronicle of Higher Education, 49**(22), A43–A45. Describes 2003 bill on education which removes the limit on the number of students enrolled. Also discusses distant education provider requirements.

Carnevale, D. (2003). **The virtual lab experiment**. **Chronicle of Higher Education, 49**(29), A30–A34. Discusses the popularity of online laboratory based courses, gives a list of those universities and schools offering such programs and looks at problems and issues related to online science offerings.

Cheng, L., & Myles, J. (2003). Managing the change from on-site to online: Transforming ESL courses for teachers. **Open Learning, 18**(1), 29–39. Examines the challenges of teaching nonnative speakers in education and the migration of ESL curriculum at Queen's University to an online delivery system.

Chou, C. (2003). Interactivity and interactive functions in web-based learning systems: A technical framework for designers. **British Journal of Educational Technology, 34**(3), 265–280. Paper includes a review of the literature for communication, computer-assisted instruction, distance education, and interactive dimensions and functions for Web systems. A framework is created to incorporate all of these dimensions into an online course. This framework is tested by outside reviewers and feedback is included.

Collins, J., & Pascarella, E. T. (2003). Learning on campus and learning at a distance: A randomized instructional experiment. **Research in Higher Education, 44**(3), 315–327. Randomized true experiment used to assess learning issues by comparing face to face education with the distance experience.

Cornford, J., & Pollock, N. (2003). **Putting the university online: Information, technology, and organizational change.** [Book, 144 p.] Open University Press. This book discusses the instructor, student, and administrative implications of putting courses and programs online.

Curda, S., & Curda, L. (2003). Advanced distributed education. **Quarterly Review of Distance Education, 4**(1), 1–14. Recommends advanced distributed learning (ADL) for military education and considers problems and solutions for military educational training.

DEOS News. (Distance Education Online Symposium). Penn State University, College of Education, American Center for the Study of Distance Education, 110 Rackley Building, University Park, PA 16802-3202. acsde@psuvm.psu.edu, http://www.ed.psu.edu/acsde/

deos/deosnews/deosnews.asp [online]. Posts information on distance education research and practice and is the most widely referenced online journal in the field.

Distance Education Report. Magna Publications, Inc., 2718 Dryden Dr., Madison, WI 53704. [24/yr., $399]. Digests periodical, Internet, and conference information into monthly reports.

Extended Studies E-zine. California State University at San Marcos, (800) 500-9377, jubran@mailhost1.csusm.edu, http://ww2.csusm.edu. Online newsletter dedicated to the topic of distance learning.

Fay, R., & Hill, M. (2003). Educating language teachers through distance learning: The need for culturally appropriate DL methodology. **Open Learning, 18**(1), 9–28. Argues effective distance education must be culturally appropriate to the learners. Examines the sharing of online courseware between British universities and suggests methods for meaning negotiation for new students to make transplanted content meaningful.

Journal of Computing in Teacher Education (SIGTE). International Society for Technology in Education, Special Interest Group for Technology in Education, 1787 Agate St., Eugene, OR 97403-1923. (800) 336-5191. Fax (541) 302-3778, Ed. Ann Thompson and Denise A. Schmidt. [Q., $48 members, $28 students and retirees]. Provides a forum for sharing information on issues effective use of technology in education.

Journal of Distance Education. Canadian Association for Distance Education, Secretariat, One Stewart St., Suite 205, Ottawa, ON K1N 6H7, Canada. (Text in English and French.) [2/yr., $60 indiv., $30 student, $220 organization]. Aims to promote and encourage scholarly work of empirical and theoretical nature relating to distance education in Canada and throughout the world.

Journal of Library and Information Services for Distance Learning. 2710 University Drive, Richland, WA 99352-1671, (509) 372-7204, Haworth Information Press, www.HaworthPress.com [Q., $48 indiv., $150 inst., $150 libraries.] Contains peer-reviewed articles, essays, narratives, current events, and letters from distance learning and information science experts.

Journal of Library Services for Distance Education. Irvine Sullivan Ingram Library State University of West Georgia, Carrollton, GA 30118, http://www.westga.edu/~ library/jlsde/, (706) 836-6500 [Ann., online]. A peer-reviewed e-journal, international in scope, publishing refereed articles focusing on the issues and challenges of providing research/information services to students enrolled in formal postsecondary distance education.

Journal of Research on Technology in Education. International Society for Technology in Education. SIG, 1787 Agate St. Eugene, OR, 97403-1923. (800) 336-5191. Fax (541) 302-3778, Ed. Lynn Schrum. [Q., $48 domestic to members, $28 to students and retired persons.]. This peer-reviewed publication presents communications technology, projects, research findings, publication references, and international contact information in instructional technology.

Kozma, R. (2003). **Technology, Innovation, and Educational Change—A Global Perspective.** (Book, 250 p., $31.95 member, $34.95 nonmember). International Society for Technology in Education (ISTE). This book highlights the scope and variety of curricular change with educational technology. Research teams from 28 countries in North America, Europe, Asia, South America, and Africa developed 174 case reports of innovative classrooms all over the globe.

Lustig, D. (2003). The truth about collaborative e-learning. **Learning & Training Innovations, 4**(3), 33–35. Argues that the most effective learning occurs when there is collaboration among students. Successful collaboration online requires virtual classrooms with a full set of communication tools. Strategies for successful Web-conferencing discussed.

McGorry, S. Y. (2003). Measuring quality in online programs. **Internet & Higher Education, 6**(2), 159–178. Examines the literature in the field of distance education resulting in the development of a model suggesting flexibility, responsiveness, interaction, student learning, technical support, technology, and student satisfaction as critical elements for success. Suggests additional research based on the model and literature.

McPherson, M., & Nunes, M. B. (2004, June). The failure of a virtual social space (VSS) designed to create a learning community: lessons learned. **British Journal of Educational Technology, 35**(3), 305–322. A report on a virtual social space (VSS) built to help distance education students overcome the typical compartmentalized learning management system experience. In particular the scenario was the intended development of a learning community for a continuing professional distance education (CPDE) masters in IT management.

Monolescu, D., Schifter, C. C., & Greenwood, L. (2004). **The Distance Education Evolution: Issues and Case Studies**. Hershey, PA: Information Science Publishing. Discusses the applied and theoretical perspectives of design, implementation, and evaluation of online programs based on experiences at Temple University.

Namin, S., & Chan, J. (2004, June). Direct and indirect effects of online learning on distance education. **British Journal of Educational Technology, 35**(3), 275–289. This study examined 285 students whose distance learning experience was delivered via the Web. It examined the students' achievement, satisfaction, and intent-to-persist as impacted by the Transactional Presence of the delivering institution. Resulting findings about students' perception of the availability and connectedness to the institution are discussed.

New Review of Learning Technologies. Centre for Studies in Advanced Learning Technology, Department of Educational Research, Lancaster University, Lancaster LA1 4YL, UK, Taylor Publishing, www.taylorpublishing.com. Christine Steeples, Ed. [Annual, $75 Eur., $140 USD]. Designed as a medium for communication between researchers and practitioners on the research, issues, developments, and applications of technology-enabled solutions to critical problems in learning.

Nordkvelle, Y. (2004, July/Aug). Technology and didactics: Historical mediations of a relation. **Journal of Curriculum Studies, 36**(4), 427–445. Examines the relationship between didactics and technology in light of the reunion of the two concepts with today's use of educational technology. Based on the writings of John Dewey and Carl Mitcham.

Olsen, F. (2003). Investments in privately held distance education companies dropped in 2002. **Chronicle of Higher Education, 49**(34), A40. Reports on findings of EduVentures, Inc., which found a decline in investments in distance education companies. It also outlines major private companies active in distance education and publishing.

Open Learning. Taylor & Frances Group, Open University, Walton Hall, Milton Keynew, MK7 6AA UK [3/yr., $62 indiv., $190 inst.]. Academic, scholarly publication on aspects of open and distance learning anywhere in the world. Includes issues for debate and research notes.

Panettieri, J. C. (2004, June). Virtually perfect. (Cover story). **University Business, 7**(6), 40–46. Using major online programs from around the US, this articles details the advances made by educational institutions to capture, store and retrieve content for future use.

Price, S., & Rogers, Y. (2004, Aug.). Let's get physical: The learning benefits of interacting in digitally augmented physical spaces. **Computers & Education, 43**(1/2), 137–152. Discusses new ways of creating and using digitally augmented physical spaces to encourage children to "interact" with their world.

Richardson, J., Long, G. L., & Foster, S. B. (2004). Academic Engagement in Students with a Hearing Loss in Distance Education. **Journal of Deaf Studies & Deaf Education, 9**(1), 68–85. A study examining 267 hearing impaired students and 187 nonimpaired students in a distance learning environment. Findings show hearing impaired students' scores were lower but they felt that communication via the Web was an improvement over the normal classroom environment.

Rovai, A. P. (2004, June). A constructivist approach to online college learning. **Internet & Higher Education, 7**(2), 79–94. Takes a look at instructor to student, student to student and authentic learning in online environments. Recognizes the teaching role often taken by students with valuable life experiences.

Rungtusanatham, M., Ellram, L. M., Siferd, S. P., & Salik, S. (2004, Fall). Toward a Typology of Business Education in the Internet Age. **Decision Sciences Journal of Innovative Education, 2**(2), 101–121. Creates a typology of Internet-delivered education: Overview Model, Overview Model with Feedback, Technical-Skills Model, and Managerial Learning Model. Suggests awareness and attendance to these models can provide success and sustainability for programs offered via the Web.

Scanlon, E.; Colwell, C.; Cooper, M., Di Paolo, T. (2004, Aug.). Remote experiments, reversioning and rethinking science learning. **Computers & Education, 43**(1/2), 153–164. Discusses the distance learning initiative called Practical Experimentation by Accessible Remote Learning (PEARL), which is built on the assumption that science and engineering students need experiments to be anchored in work settings. Findings support further use of the remote experiment approach.

Van den Boom, G., Paas, F., van Merriënboer, J. J. G., & van Gog, T. (2004, July). Reflection prompts and tutor feedback in a web-based learning environment: effects on students' self-regulated learning competence. **Computers in Human Behavior, 20**(4), 551–568. A study focused on reflection prompts and tutor feedback results on self-regulation among 42 students.

Worley, R., & Dyrud, M. (2003). Grading and assessment of student writing. **Business Communication Quarterly, 66**(1), 72–74. Discusses the impact of technology in distance education in the submission and grading of student performance. Further examines the performance standards of business communication and the use of rubrics in education.

USDLA Journal. United States Distance Learning Association, Winter Stree, Suite 508, Boston, MA 02108, http://www.usdla.org/html/membership/publications.htm. [Mo., free]. The publication for USDLA publishes articles on research and practice on the many areas related to distance education and online learning. These areas include administrative issues, teaching practices, student concerns, international applications and more.

EDUCATIONAL RESEARCH

American Educational Research Journal. American Educational Research Association, 1230 17th St., NW, Washington, DC 20036-3078. [Q., $41 indiv., $56 inst.]. Reports original research, both empirical and theoretical, and brief synopses of research.

Current Index to Journals in Education (CIJE). Oryx Press, 4041 N. Central at Indian School Rd., Phoenix, AZ 85012-3397. [Mo., $245 ($280 outside North America); semi-ann. cumulations $250 ($285 foreign); combination $475]. A guide to articles published in some 830 education and education-related journals. Includes complete bibliographic information, annotations, and indexes. Semiannual cumulations available. Contents are produced by the ERIC (Educational Resources Information Center) system, Office of Educational Research and Improvement, and the US Department of Education.

Education Index. H. W. Wilson, 950 University Ave., Bronx, NY 10452. [Mo., except July and August; $1,295 for CD-ROM, including accumulations]. Author-subject index to educational publications in the English language. Cumulated quarterly and annually.

Educational Research. Routledge, 11 Fetter Ln., London EC4P 4EE, England. [3/yr., $78 indiv., $231 inst.]. Reports on current educational research, evaluation, and applications.

Educational Researcher. American Educational Research Association, 1230 17th St., NW, Washington, DC 20036-3078. [9/yr., $44 indiv., $61 inst.]. Contains news and features of general significance in educational research.

Journal of Interactive Learning Research. Association for the Advancement of Computing in Education, PO Box 2966, Charlottesville, VA 22902-2966, info@aace.org, http://www.aace.org. Ed. Tom Reeves. [Q., $85 domestic indiv., $120 domestic inst.,]. Publishes articles pertaining to theory, implementation, and overall impact of interactive learning environments in education.

Learning Technology. IEEE Computer Society, Learning Technology Task Force, Private Bag 11-222, Massey University, Palmerston North, New Zealand. http://lttf.ieee.org/learn_tech. [Q., online]. Reports developments, projects, conferences, and findings of the Learning Technology Task Force.

Logo Exchange. International Society for Technology in Education, Special Interest Group for Logo-Using Educators, 1787 Agate St., Eugene, OR 97403-1923. Ed. Gary Stager. [Q., $34 domestic to nonmembers, $44 foreign to members, $24 domestic to members, $34 foreign to members.$14.40 domestic to students, $24.40 foreign to students]. Provides current information on research, lesson plans, and methods related to LOGO.

LTRREPORT. Node Learning Technologies Network, 26 Burdy Drive, St. Catharines, Ontario L2S 3E4 Canada, http://thenode.org/ltreport/. Ed. Erin Bale. [semi-annual, online, $90]. Provides practical information for the use of technology in education and training.

McNiece, R., Bidgood, P., & Soan, P. (2004, Summer). An investigation into using national longitudinal studies to examine trends in educational attainment and development. **Educational Research, 46**(2), 119–137. A look at the trend toward the use of longitudinal studies at comparing the differences in learners and achievement.

MERIDIAN (RALEIGH). C/O Edwin Gerler, College of Education and Psychology, North Carolina State University, Box 7801, Raleigh, NC 27695-7801. meridian@poe. coe.ncsu.edu. http://www.ncsu.edu/meridian. Ed. Cheryl Mason. [Semi-annual, online]. Online journal dedicated to research in middle school educational technology use.

Research in Science & Technological Education. Taylor & Francis Group, 11 New Fetter Lane, London EC4P 4EE, www.tandf.co.uk. [2/yr., $133 indiv., $670 inst.]. Publication of original research in the science and technological fields. Includes articles on psychological, sociological, economic, and organizational aspects of technological education.

Resources in Education (RIE). Superintendent of Documents, US Government Printing Office, P.O. Box 371954, Pittsburgh, PA 15250-7954, www.access.gpo.gov. [Mo., $78 US, $97.50 elsewhere]. Announcement of research reports and other documents in education, including abstracts and indexes by subject, author, and institution. Contents produced by the ERIC (Educational Resources Information Center) system, Office of Educational Research and Improvement, and the U.S. Department of Education.

Software and Networks for Learning. Shrewsbury Publishing, PO Box 3894, Santa Barbara, CA, 93130, Ed. Urban Streitz. [9/yr., $65, online full text]. Newsletter.

TESS (The Educational Software Selector). Educational Products Information Exchange (EPIE) Institute, 103 W. Montauk Hwy. 3, Hampton, NY 11946-4006, Tel. 516-728-9100, Fax 516-728-9228. [Annual, $82.50 base volume (1996), $ 32.50 for update]. A guide listing annotated references to educational software for preschool through postgraduate education.

EDUCATIONAL TECHNOLOGY

Appropriate Technology. Intermediate Technology Publications, Ltd., 103-105 Southampton Row, London, WC1B 4HH, England, www.itdg.org, journals.edit@ itpubs.org.uk. [Q., $28 indiv., $37 inst.]. Articles on less technologically advanced, but more environmentally sustainable, solutions to problems in developing countries.

Brewer, C. (2003). Computers in the classroom: How information technology can improve conservation education. **Biology, 17**(3), 657–661. Conservation teaching and learning can be enhanced by the use of information technology by the Internet, real-time assessment of student learning, and more.

British Journal of Educational Technology. National Council for Educational Technology, Millburn Hill Rd., Science Park, Coventry CV4 7JJ, England. [Q., $99 indiv., $338 inst.]. Published by the National Council for Educational Technology, this journal includes articles on education and training, especially theory, applications, and development of educational technology and communications.

CELL Journal. ISTE, University of Oregon, 1787 Agate St., Eugene, OR 97403-1923, (800) 336-5191, cust_svc@ccmail.uoregon.edu, www.iste.org. [Q., $29; $39 intl., $42 intl. air]. Focuses on current issues facing computer-using language teachers; covers trends, products, applications, research, and program evaluation.

Canadian Journal of Learning and Technology Communication. Association for Media and Technology in Education in Canada, 3-1750 The Queensway, Suite 1318, Etobicoke, ON M9C 5H5, Canada, http://www.cjlt.ca/ [3/yr., no cost]. Concerned with all aspects of educational systems and technology.

Chang, L.-J., Chou, C.-Y., Chen, Z.-H., & Chan, T.-W. (2004, July). An approach to assisting teachers in building physical and network hybrid community-based learning environments: the Taiwanese experience. **International Journal of Educational Development, 24**(4), 383–397. Discusses a program called Educational Applications Providers Platform (EAPP) created to make networking

Educational Technology. Educational Technology Publications, Inc., 700 Palisade Ave., Englewood Cliffs, NJ 07632-0564, (800) 952-BOOK. [Bi-mo., $119 US, $139 elsewhere]. Covers telecommunications, computer-aided instruction, information retrieval, educational television, and electronic media in the classroom.

Educational Technology Abstracts. Taylor & Francis Group, 11 New Fetter Lane, London EC4P 4EE, www.tandf.co.uk. [6/yr., $347 indiv., $940 inst.]. An international publication of abstracts of recently published material in the field of educational and training technology.

Educational Technology Research and Development. AECT, ETR&D Subscription Dept., 1800 N. Stonelake Dr., Suite 2, Bloomington, IN 47404, www. aect.org. [Q., indiv. $55 US, $63 foreign, inst. $150 US, $175 elsewhere]. Focuses on research, instructional development, and applied theory in the field of educational technology; peer-reviewed.

Harlow, G., et al. (2003). Computer-assisted life stories. **Computers in Human Behavior, 19**(4), 391–407. A pilot project tested the use of emergent technology in capturing the life stories of the elderly. Digital recording and voice-to-text software allowed their stories to be made into text and digitized with little effort on their part. Voice and digital sound are mirrored on one site. Broader uses are suggested by the success of this pilot program.

Hasan, B. (2003). The influence of specific computer experiences on computer self-efficacy beliefs. **Computers in Human Behavior, 19**(4), 443–451. Past research has proven computer experience increases self-efficacy among computer users. This research seeks to examine eight specific computer related experiences to determine their impact on self-efficacy. These experiences include programming, graphics applications, spreadsheet and database applications, and more. Results can inform computer instruction and training.

Hazzan, Orit. (2004, June). Mental constructions and constructions of Web sites: learner and teacher points of view. **British Journal of Educational Technology, 35**(3), 323–345. Based on the reflections of 40 preservice and inservice teachers on the building of Web pages for educational uses.

Hoisko, J. (2003). Early experiences of visual memory prosthesis for supporting episodic memory. **International Journal of Human-Computer Interaction, 15**(2), 209–241. Describes the use of a audio-visual recorder which helps support memory of personal events (retrospective episodic memory). These events were collected sporadically using a body-worn camera and DAT-recorder. These files were determined to increase memory of related events which were not recorded. Results suggest personal and business application potential.

International Journal of Educational Technology. University of Western Australia, Department of Education, Nedlands, W.A. 6907 Australia rhacker@ecel.uwa.edu.au, http://www.outreach.uiuc.edu/ijet/ Ed. Roger Hacker. [Semi-annual, online full text]. Posts information about computer-based educational technologies.

International Journal of Technology and Design Education. Kluwer Academic Publishers, 101 Philip Drive, Norwell, MA 02061, (617) 871-6600, fax (617) 871-6528, kluwer@wkap.com. [3/yr., $118 individual, $198 institution]. Publishes research reports and scholarly writing about aspects of technology and design education.

Jenson, J., & Rose, C. (2003). Women@Work: Listening to gendered relations of power in teachers' talk about technologies. **Gender & Education, 15**(2), 169–182. This study illustrates some of the less obvious inequities in school systems regarding computers and technologies. Gender inequities were maintained by experiences and expectations with regards to technology use and access in the school.

Journal of Computing in Higher Education. Norris Publishers, Box 2593, Amherst, MA 01004-2593. cmacknight@oit.umass.edu, www.jchesite.org. Ed. Carol B MacKnight. [Semi-annual, $35 US indiv., $65 foreign indiv., $75 domestic to inst., $80 in Canada to inst., $90 foreign to inst.]. Publishes scholarly essays, case studies, and research that discuss instructional technologies.

Journal of Educational Technology Systems. Society for Applied Learning Technology, Baywood Publishing Co., Inc., 26 Austin Ave, Box 337, Amityville, NY 11701 Baywood@baywood.com, http://baywood.com. [Q., $218 US,]. Discusses educational hardware and software.

Journal of Interactive Media In Education. Open University, Knowledge Media Institute, Milton Keynes, MK7 6AA United Kingdom, Eds. Simon Buckingham Shum, Tamara Sumner. [Online, full text]. A multidisciplinary forum for debate and idea sharing concerning the practical aspects of interactive media and instructional technology.

Journal of Science Education and Technology. Kluwer Academic/Plenum Publishers, 233 Spring Street, New York, NY 10013-1578, (781) 871-6600, info@plenum.com, www.plenum.com [Q., $86 individual, $426 institution]. Publishes studies aimed at improving science education at all levels in the US.

Kozma, R., McGhee, R., Quellmalz, E., & Zalles, D. (2004, July). Closing the digital divide: Evaluation of the World Links program. **International Journal of Educational Development, 24**(4), 361–382. An evaluation of three years of the World Links program which worked to place computers in classrooms in developing countries. Draws implications from the program for policy in developing countries.

Kynigos, C., & Argyris, M. (2004, Aug). Teacher beliefs and practices formed during an innovation with computer-based exploratory mathematics in the classroom. **Teachers & Teaching, 10**(3), 247–274. Discusses beliefs and practices of teachers involved in an innovative "mathematical investigations" school program, as well as teachers' roles and how those may be influenced by larger educational system values.

Multimedia Schools. Information Today, Inc., 213 Danbury Rd., Wilton, CT 06897-4006, custserv@info today.com, http://www.infotoday.com/MMSchools/. Ed. Ferdi Serim [Online, full-text, 6/yr., $39.95 US, $54 Canada & Mexico, $63 other]. Reviews and evaluates hardware and software. Presents information pertaining to basic troubleshooting skills.

Namazi, K., & McClintic, M. (2003). Computer use among elderly persons in long-term care facilities. **Educational Gerontology, 29**(6), 535–551. Residence in care facilities physically removes the elderly from society in many ways. Computers can bring culture, society, and events to those who are place bound. Twenty-four elderly persons were taught several times a week in an effort to give them independence in computer operation. After fifteen months, only five remained but these persisted in using computers for many reasons including email, letters, Internet, games, and special projects. Results discuss possible reasons for discontinuation including: physical, cognitive, personal, technological, organizational, and environmental issues.

Rafaeli, S., Barak, M., Dan-Gur, Y., & Toch, E. (2004, Nov). QSIA–a Web-based environment for learning, assessing and knowledge sharing in communities. **Computers & Education, 43**(3), 273–290. QSIA is an environment designed to enhance learning, collaboration and sharing knowledge. Findings suggest enhanced opportunities for critical thinking and communication between teachers and learners.

Romeo, G., et al. (2003). Touching the screen: Issues related to the use of touch-screen technology in early childhood education. **British Journal of Educational Technology, 34**(3), 329–340. Data was collected in a study of five classrooms by observation, journals, field notes, and interviews. Five themes emerged in relation to children's interaction with touch-screen technology: developmental issues, input preference, technical issues, collaboration tendencies and individual preferences.

Sawchuck, P. (2003). Informal learning as a speech-exchange system: Implications for knowledge production, power and social transformation. **Discourse & Society, 14**(3), 291–308. This study points out informal learning discussions as very specific speech-exchange systems with formal communication and pedagogical implications. Two computer users create a "Zone of Proximal Development" by collaboratively learning computer tasks. This suggests that learning occurs without the power relationship of a "More Knowledgeable Other." Thus informal learning may transform knowledge forms.

Science Communication (formerly **Knowledge: Creation, Diffusion, Utilization**). Sage Publications Inc., 2455 Teller Rd., Thousand Oaks, CA 91320, order@sagepub.com, www.sagepub.com [Q., $94 indiv., $455 inst.]. An international, interdisciplinary journal examining the nature of expertise and the translation of knowledge into practice and policy.

SIGTC Connections. ISTE, University of Oregon, 1787 Agate St., Eugene, OR 97403-1923, (800) 336-5191, cust_svc@ccmail.uoregon.edu, www.iste.org. [Q., $29, $39 intl., $42 intl. air]. Provides forum to identify problems and solutions and share information on issues facing technology coordinators.

Social Science Computer Review. North Carolina State University, Social Science Research and Instructional Computing Lab, Sage Publications, Inc., 2455 Teller Rd., Thousand Oaks, CA, 91320 info@sagepub.com, http:/hcl.chass.ncsu.edu/sscore/sscore.htm. Ed. David Garson. [Q., GBP 58, $84 indiv., GBP 252, $366 inst.,]. Presents research and practical applications of instructional technology in social science.

TECHNOS. Agency for Instructional Technology, Box A, 1800 North Stonelake Drive, Bloomington, IN 47402-0120. [Q., $28 indiv., $24 libr., $32 foreign]. A forum for discussion of ideas about the use of technology in education, with a focus on reform.

TechTrends. AECT, 1800 N Stonelake Dr. Suite 2, Bloomington, IN 47404, www.aect.org. [6/yr., $40 US, $44 elsewhere, $6 single copy]. Targeted at leaders in education and training; features authoritative, practical articles about technology and its integration into the learning environment.

T.H.E. Journal (Technological Horizons in Education). T.H.E., 150 El Camino Real, Suite 112, Tustin, CA 92680-3670. [11/yr., $29 US, $95 elsewhere]. For educators of all levels. Focuses on a specific topic for each issue, as well as technological innovations as they apply to education.

INFORMATION SCIENCE AND TECHNOLOGY

Canadian Journal of Information and Library Science/Revue canadienne des sciences de l'information et de bibliothèconomie. CAIS, University of Toronto Press, Journals Dept., 5201 Dufferin St., Downsview, ON M3H 5T8, Canada. [Q., $65 indiv., $95 inst., orders outside Canada +$15]. Published by the Canadian Association for Information Science to contribute to the advancement of library and information science in Canada.

Case, D. (2003). **Looking for Information: A Survey of Research on Information Seeking, Needs, and Behavior.** [Book, 350 p., $89.95 Hardcover]. Elsevier Science & Technology Books. Based on decades of research on human information seeking behavior, this work seeks to bring consensus to methods and findings. The bibliography of more than seven hundred listings renders this a valuable reference tool for any library.

CD-ROM Databases. Worldwide Videotex, Box 3273, Boynton Beach, FL 33424-3273. [Mo., $150 US, $190 elsewhere]. Descriptive listing of all databases being marketed on CD-ROM with vendor and system information.

Chung, J., & Tan, F. B. (2004, Sep). Antecedents of perceived playfulness: an exploratory study on user acceptance of general information-searching websites. **Information & Management, 41**(7), 869–882. Research conducted on the user's perception of information usefulness that also extends past work by considering the use of perceived playfulness as an element of acceptance of the Internet.

Crudge, S. E., & Johnson, C. (2004).Using the Information Seeker to Elicit Construct Models for Search Engine Evaluation. **Journal of the American Society for Information Science & Technology, 55**(9), 794–807. A research study which examined users' perceptions of search engines as an evaluation tool and also employed repertory grid technique to establish users' models of appropriateness of search engines.

EContent (formerly **Database**). Online, Inc. 462 Danbury Rd., Wilton, CT 06897. [Bi-mo., $55 US, $65 Canada, $90 intl. air mail.]. Features articles on topics of interest to online database users; includes database search aids.

Ford, N., Miller, D., Moss, N. (2003). Web search strategies and approaches to studying. **Journal of the American Society for Information Science & Technology, 54**(6), 473–490. This research examines the correlation between information seeking behavior and study patterns. Web-based searches were Boolean, best-match, and combined. Examining more than 500 queries, the emerging trends showed that Boolean logic was used when searchers experienced anxiety and active interest. Best-match strategies were apparent when there was reduced anxiety. Results indicate that a connection exists between study habits and information seeking behaviors. Further study is warranted.

Gale Directory of Databases (in 2 vols: Vol. 1, **Online Databases**; Vol. 2, **CD-ROM, Diskette, Magnetic Tape Batch Access, and Handheld Database Products**). The Gale Group, P.O. Box 9187, Farmington Hills, MI 48333-9187. [Annual plus semi-annual update $280; Vol. 1, $199; Vol. 2, $119]. Contains information on database selection and database descriptions, including producers and their addresses.

Haas, S. (2003). Improving the search environment: Informed decision making in the search for statistical information. **Journal of the American Society for Information Science & Technology, 54**(8), 782–798. The information retrieval process is seen as a series of decisions made by the researcher. This is impacted by existing knowledge of the searcher and the information retrieval system itself. The United States Bureau of Labor Statistics Web site is used as the information retrieval system for this study. The study revealed that the rich Web site poses some areas of decision points which should provide user assistance. Further tests are needed to determine the form of this user help.

Hawkins, D., Larson, S., & Caton, B. (2003). Information science abstracts: Tracking the literature of information science. Part 2: A new taxonomy for information science. **Journal of the American Society for Information Science & Technology, 54**(8), 771–782. This research is a continuation of earlier attempts to create a taxonomy for information science in order to "map" the field and it related peripheral areas. Two experiments were conducted with information science community members using 3,000 abstracts. Results are discussed.

Hsinchun, C., Lally, A., Bin, Z., & Chau, M. (2003). HelpfulMed: Intelligent searching for medical information over the Internet. **Journal of the American Society for Information Science & Technology, 54**(7), 683–695. This study seeks to create an information retrieval architecture which will result in fine-grained, highly specific information for medical professionals. This interface, called HelpfulMed, was successful in retrieving useful information from the Internet, online databases, thesaurus, and a graphical display of related topics. The spidering algorithm used outperformed other search engines.

Information Processing and Management. Pergamon Press, 660 White Plains Rd., Tarrytown, NY 10591-5153. [Bi-mo., $270 indiv. whose inst. subscribes, $1045 inst.]. International journal covering data processing, database building, and retrieval.

Information Retrieval and Library Automation. Lomond Publications, Inc., Box 88, Mt. Airy, MD 21771. [Mo., $66 US, foreign $79.50]. News, articles, and announcements on new techniques, equipment, and software in information services.

Information Services & Use. I.O.S. Press, Box 10558, Burke, VA 22009-0558. [4/yr., $267]. An international journal for those in the information management field. Includes online and offline systems, library automation, micrographics, videotex, and telecommunications.

The Information Society. Taylor & Francis Group, 11 New Fetter Lane, London EC4P 4EE, www.tandf.co.uk Taylor and Francis, 47 Runway Road, Suite G, Levittown, PA 19057, tisj@indiana.edu. [5/yr, $97 indiv.; $264 inst.]. Provides a forum for discussion of the world of information, including transborder data flow, regulatory issues, and the impact of the information industry.

Information Technology and Libraries. American Library Association, ALA Editions, 50 East Huron St., Chicago, IL 60611-2795, (800) 545-2433, fax (312) 836-9958. [Q., $50 US, $55 Canada, Mexico; $60 elsewhere]. Articles on library automation, communication technology, cable systems, computerized information processing, and video technologies.

Information Today. Information Today, 143 Old Marlton Pike, Medford, NJ 08055, (800) 300-9868. [11/yr., $69.95; Canada and Mexico, $87; outside North America, $96]. Newspaper for users and producers of electronic information services. Articles and news about the industry, calendar of events, and product information.

Information Management. IDEA Group, www.idea-group.com, 1331 E. Chocolate Avenue, Hershey, PA 17033-1117, (800) 345-4332. [Semi-annual., $40 indiv., $65 inst.]. This semi-annual newsletter includes essays on current topics in information science, expert reviews of information management products, and updates on professional conferences and events.

Information Technology Newsletter. IDEA Group, www.idea-group.com, 1331 E. Chocolate Avenue, Hershey, PA 17033-1117, (800) 345-4332. [B., $20 indiv., $35 inst.]. Designed for library information specialists, this bi-annual newsletter presents current issues and trends in information science presented by and for specialists in the field.

Internet Reference Service Quarterly. 223 Capen Hall, University at Buffalo, Buffalo, NY 14260, (716) 645-2756, Haworth Information Press, www.HaworthPress.com. [Q.,

$45 indiv., $75 inst., $75 libraries.] Discusses multidisciplinary aspects of incorporating the Internet as a tool for reference service.

Jewitt, Carey; Adamson, Ross. (2003, Nov). The multimodal construction of rule in computer programing applications. **Education, Communication & Information, 3**(3), 361–383. Computer programming systems, Pathways and ToonTalk, allow children to create and build computer games. Includes discussion of children's modes of communication, such as writing and image making.

Journal of the American Society for Information Science & Technology. American Society for Information Science, 8720 Georgia Avenue, Suite 501, Silver Spring, Maryland 20910-3602, (301) 495-0900, www.asis.org [14/yr., inst. rate: $1259 US, $1399 Canada/ Mexico, $1518 Outside N. America]. Provides an overall forum for new research in information transfer and communication processes, with particular attention paid to the context of recorded knowledge.

Journal of Database Management. Idea Group Publishing, 4811 Jonestown Rd., Suite 230, Harrisburg, PA 17109-1751. [Q., $85 indiv., $245 inst.]. Provides state-of-the-art research to those who design, develop, and administer DBMS-based information systems.

Journal of Documentation. Aslib, The Association for Information Management, Staple Hall, Stone House Court, London EC3A 7PB, +44 (0) 20 7903 0000, aslib@aslib.com. [6/yr.; £176 ($275) members , £220 ($345) nonmembers]. Describes how technical, scientific, and other specialized knowledge is recorded, organized, and disseminated.

Journal of Access Services. SUNY Albany, Science Library, Room 142, 1400 Washington Avenue, Albany, NY 12222, (518) 437-3951, Haworth Information Press, www.HaworthPress.com [Q., $48 indiv., $120 inst., $120 libraries]. Peer-reviewed journal containing feature columns, essays, articles, reviews, and conference reports on a large scope of information resource issues.

Journal of Bibliographic Instruction for Electronic Resources. 207 Hillman Library, Pittsburgh, PA 15260, (412) 648-7732, Haworth Information Press, www. HaworthPress.com [Q., $36 indiv., $48 inst., $48 libraries]. Peer-reviewed journal covering emerging trends in electronic resources.

Journal of Electronic Resources. 128 Owsley Avenue, Lexington, KY 40502-1526, (606) 257-0500, ext. 2120, Haworth Information Press, www.HaworthPress.com [Q., $48 indiv., $150 inst., $150 libraries]. Devoted to issues related to selecting, budgeting, and assessing effectiveness of electronic resources for the academic, special and public library setting.

Journal of Internet Cataloging. Haworth Information Press, 10 Alice Street, Binghamton, NY 13904-1580, (800) 342-9678, www.HaworthPress.com [Q., $40 indiv., $85 inst., $85 libraries]. Gives library cataloging experts a system for managing Internet reference resources in the library catalog.

Pennanen, M., & Vakkari, P. (2003). Students' conceptual structure, search process, and outcome while preparing a research proposal: A longitudinal case study. **Journal of the American Society for Information Science & Technology, 54**(8), 759–771. Focusing on student information needs while conceptualizing research topics, the study hopes to better understand the search process and results. Twenty-two psychology undergraduates were studied in pre- and postsearch interviews. Think-aloud sessions were recorded and transaction logs taken. Students' ability to extract partial information from early searches helped their evolving research topic and process.

Resource Sharing & Information Networks. Haworth Press, 10 Alice St., Binghamton, NY 13904-1580, (800) HAWORTH, fax (800) 895-0582, getinfo@haworth.com, www.haworthpress.com [2/yr., $50 indiv., $225 inst. and libraries]. A forum for ideas on the basic theoretical and practical problems faced by planners, practitioners, and users of network services.

Web Feet. Rock Hill Communications, 14 Rock Hill Road, Bala Cynwyd, PA 19004, (888) ROCK HIL, fax (610) 667-2291, http://www.webfeetguides.com/ [12/yr., $225]. Indexes Web sites for general interest, classroom use, and research; reviews Web sites for quality, curricular relevance, timeliness, and interest.

Wilson, K., Wallin, J., & Reiser, C. (2003). Social stratification and the digital divide. **Social Science Computer Review, 21**(2), 133–144. This article examines the digital divide and seeks to understand if racial, geographical, and gender divides explain or contribute to digital inequities in the United States.

Wishart, J. (2004, Aug.). Internet safety in emerging educational contexts. **Computers & Education, 43**(1/2), 193–205. A report on Internet safety practices designed to protect children employed at over 500 schools in England.

INSTRUCTIONAL DESIGN AND DEVELOPMENT

Ashwin, P. (2003). Peer support: Relations between the context, process and outcomes for the students who are supported. **Instructional Science, 31**(3), 159–173. Discussion of a peer support scheme used in a study showing positive correlation with academic performance for those students in the test group. Control group used to validate findings.

Crowther, M. S., Keller, C. C., & Waddoups, G. L. (2004, June). Improving the quality and effectiveness of computer-mediated instruction through usability evaluations. **British Journal of Educational Technology, 35**(3), 289–304. Based on the instructional design work at Brigham Young University of Utah, this article suggests usability evaluation improves the overall quality and effectiveness of online courses.

Gold, M. (2003). Enterprise e-learning. **T+D, 57**(4), 28–34. Discusses one business example of employee e-learning purchased to train its entire staff online via SkillSoft online course library in areas such as information technology, business skills, and executive education.

Hackman, H. W., & Rausche, L. (2004, June). A pathway to access for all: Exploring the connections between universal instructional design and social justice education. **Equity & Excellence in Education, 37**(2), 114–124. Serving the needs of students with learning and physical disabilities, this article discusses the intersection of universal design and social justice education. Each area can help inform the other and extend accessibility for all.

Human-Computer Interaction. Lawrence Erlbaum Associates, 365 Broadway, Hillsdale, NJ 07642, http://hci-journal.com/ [Q., $55 indiv. US and Canada, $85 elsewhere, $430 inst., $460 elsewhere]. A journal of theoretical, empirical, and methodological issues of user science and of system design.

Instructional Science. Kluwer Academic Publishers, 101 Philip Drive, Norwell, MA 02061, (617) 871-6600, fax (617) 871-6528, kluwer@wkap.com, Eds. Peter Goodyear and Patricia Alexander. [Bi-mo., $190 indiv., $467 inst., Eur. & USD]. Promotes a deeper understanding of the nature, theory, and practice of the instructional process and the learning resulting from this process.

International Journal of Human-Computer Interaction. Lawrence Erlbaum Associates, 365 Broadway, Hillsdale, NJ 07642, http://hci-journal.com/ [Q., $90 indiv. US and Canada, $135 elsewhere, $595 inst., $640 elsewhere]. A journal which addresses the cognitive, social, health, and ergonomic aspects of work with computers. It also emphasizes both the human and computer science aspects of the effective design and use of computer interactive systems.

Ivarsson, J. (2003, Nov). Kids in Zen: Computer-supported learning environments and illusory intersubjectivity. **Education, Communication & Information, 3**(3), 383–403. A study in rich media scaffolding for children involved in complex tasks. Cues are built into the virtual interface anchoring learning to the physical environment.

Journal of Educational Technology Systems. Learning Technology Institute, Society for Applied Learning Technology, 50 Culpepper St., Warrenton, VA 20186. [Q., $60, requires SALT membership to receive]. JETS deals with systems in which technology and education interface and is designed to inform educators who are interested in making optimum use of technology.

Journal of Interactive Instruction Development. Learning Technology Institute, Society for Applied Learning Technology, 50 Culpepper St., Warrenton, VA 20186. [Q., $40 member, $60 nonmember; add $20 postage outside N. America]. A showcase of successful programs that will heighten awareness of innovative, creative, and effective approaches to courseware development for interactive technology.

Journal of Instructional Delivery Systems. Learning Technology Institute, Society for Applied Learning Technology, 50 Culpepper St., Warrenton, VA 20186. [Q., $40 member, $60 nonmember; add $20 postage outside N. America]. JIDS is devoted to the issues, problems, and applications of instructional delivery systems in education, training, and job performance.

Journal of Technical Writing and Communication. Baywood Publishing Co., 26 Austin Ave., Box 337, Amityville, NY 11701. [Q., $60 indiv., $237 inst.]. Essays on oral and written communication, for purposes ranging from pure research to needs of business and industry.

Journal of Visual Literacy. International Visual Literacy Association, c/o John C. Belland, 122 Ramseyer Hall, 29 West Woodruff Ave., Ohio State University, Columbus, OH 43210. [Bi-ann., $40]. Interdisciplinary forum on all aspects of visual/verbal languaging.

Oliver, R., & Herrington, J. (2003). Exploring Technology-mediated learning from a pedagogical perspective. **Interactive Learning Environments, 11**(2), 111–116. Often online educational products fail because of poor planning and targeting of learning outcomes. Presents a framework for supporting the design process. Strategies include the selection of learning tasks, the selection of learning supports, and the selection of learning supports as a strategy for the development of online learning settings that promote knowledge construction.

Performance Improvement Journal. International Society for Performance Improvement, 1300 L St. NW, Suite 1250, Washington, DC 20005. [10/yr., $69 nonmembers, free to members]. Journal of ISPI; promotes performance science and technology. Contains articles, research, and case studies relating to improving human performance.

Performance Improvement Quarterly. International Society for Performance Improvement, 1300 L St. NW, Suite 1250, Washington, DC 20005. [Q., $50 nonmembers, $40 members]. Presents the cutting edge in research and theory in performance technology.

Training. Lakewood Publications, Inc., 50 S. Ninth, Minneapolis, MN 55402. http://www.trainingmag.com/training/index.jsp [Mo., $78 US, $88 Canada, $154 elsewhere]. Covers all aspects of training, management, and organizational development, motivation, and performance improvement.

Willis, L. L., & Lockee, B. B. (2004). A pragmatic instructional design model for distance learning. **International Journal of Instructional Media, 31**(1), 9–18. Based on theoretical models, this article centers around the practical application of instructional design for distance learning with the knowledge that much of online teaching and learning requires flexibility due to technology concerns.

LIBRARIES AND MEDIA CENTERS

Balas, J. (2003). Is the reference librarian real or virtual? **Computers in Libraries, 23**(4), 48–52. Just as customers complain about telephone menus, patrons now chaff against Web form options and drop-down menus. This article argues that reference services should remain a personal service handled person to person to maintain the integrity of the reference interview and therefore the quality of service.

Bell, D., et al. (2004). **Cyberculture: The Key Concepts.** New York: Routledge. Discusses all things cyber including the Internet, digital TV, robots, related movies, and emerging technologies. Serves as a glossary and reference guide to cyberculture at large.

Boone, R., & Higgins, K. (2003). Reading, writing, and publishing digital text. **Remedial & Special Education, 24**(3), 132–141. The digitization of information has implications for all society; specifically, the digitization of texts will have a great impact on teaching and learning. Research, reading, and writing will all change as a result of the Internet. CD-ROMs, electronic books, electronic libraries, and other electronic resources. Therefore, instructional strategies, access issues, and copyright concerns should be revisited. Suggestions on productive uses are included.

Brandt, D. (2003). Whether to wireless. **Computers in Libraries, 23**(3), 37. Argues author's opinion on why libraries should move to wireless technology: cost, convenience, patron requests, and additional services.

Carlson, S. (2004, June 25). To use that library computer, please identify yourself. **Chronicle of Higher Education, 50**(42), A39. Discusses the controversial trend toward libraries requiring patrons to create usernames and passwords making them identifiable. Discusses authentication systems in libraries in general and University of Texas, Austin, specifically.

Collection Building. M.C.B. University Press Ltd., 60-62 Toller Ln., Bradford, W. Yorks. BD8 9BY, England, www.mcb.co.uk [Q., $599]. Focuses on all aspects of collection building, ranging from microcomputers to business collections to popular topics and censorship.

Computers in Libraries. Information Today, 143 Old Marlton Pike, Medford, NJ 08055, (800) 300-9868. [10/yr., $89.95 US; $99.95 Canada, Mexico; $59.95 outside North America]. Covers practical applications of microcomputers to library situations and recent news items.

Dressang, E., Gross, M., & Holt, L. (2003). Project CATE: Using outcome measures to assess school-age children's use of technology in urban public libraries: A collaborative research process. **Library & Information Science Research, 25**(1), 1943. Examines the widespread use of outcome-based assessment in other agencies, use of technology in public libraries, and the definitions and models of outcome-based evaluation. Explores the need for more research on children's use of technology within the context of public libraries.

Discusses Project CATE, a model developed in collaboration between the Saint Louis Public Library and Florida State University School of Information Studies.

The Electronic Library. Emerald, 60-62 Toller Ln., Bradford, W. Yorks. BD8 9BY, UK, http://www. Emeraldinsight.com/journals/ [Bi-mo., $399 U. S.; $466.54 Eur.]. International journal for minicomputer, microcomputer, and software applications in libraries; independently assesses current and forthcoming information technologies.

Ellis-Newman, J. (2003, Winter). Activity-based costing in user services of an academic library. **Library Trends, 51**(3), 333–349. Activity-based costing (ABC) tracks and determines indirect costs to products and services based on the factors that most influence them. This study focuses on costing out user services.

Gibson, M., & Ruotolo, C. (2003). Beyond the Web: TEI, the digital library, and the ebook revolution. **Computers & the Humanities, 37**(1), 57 4. Discusses the efforts of the University of Virginia and the Electronic Text Center to distribute free electronic books, delivery formats, TEI standards, e-book production, and limitations of current technology. Advantages and disadvantages of current classroom application of e-book technology for students and faculty.

Government Information Quarterly. Elsevier Science/Regional Sales Office, Customer Support Department, JAI Books, P.O. Box 945, New York, NY 10159-0945. [Q., $113 indiv., $269 inst.]. International journal of resources, services, policies, and practices.

Hughes-Hassell, S., & Miller, E. (2003). Public library Web sites for young adults: Meeting the needs of today's teens online. **Library & Information Science Research, 25**(2), 143–157. A study conducted to examine the motivations for and obstacles to creating Web pages to meet young adult readers' at public library Web sites. Further discussion relates these issues to Internet use and searching behaviors of teens.

Information Outlook (formerly **Special Libraries**). Special Libraries Association, 1700 18th St., NW, Washington, DC 20009-2508, www.sla.com [Mo., $80 US; $95 elsewhere]. Discusses administration, organization, and operations. Includes reports on research, technology, and professional standards.

Information Services and Use. Elsevier Science Publishers, Box 10558, Burke, VA 22009-0558. [4/yr., $254]. Contains data on international developments in information management and its applications. Articles cover online systems, library automation, word processing, micrographics, videotex, and telecommunications.

Jackson, M., Banwell, L., & Proud, D. (2003). A transformation in further education: Technology, the electronic library and the Cinderella sector. **Journal of Further & Higher Education, 27**(2), 167–175. Reviews the literature in further education and examines the impact of technology changes on students, staff, and library personnel. Significant mention is made of growth of electronic resources and services for teaching and learning.

Journal of Academic Librarianship. Elsevier Science/Regional Sales Office, Customer Support Department, JAI Books, P.O. Box 945, New York, NY 10159-0945. [6/yr., $81 indiv., $195 inst.]. Results of significant research, issues and problems facing academic libraries, book reviews, and innovations in academic libraries.

Journal of Government Information (formerly **Government Publications Review**). Elsevier Science Ltd., Journals Division, 660 White Plains Rd., Tarrytown, NY 10591-5153. [6/yr., $534]. An international journal covering production, distribution, bibliographic control, accessibility, and use of government information in all formats and at all levels.

Journal of Librarianship and Information Science. Worldwide Subscription Service Ltd., Unit 4, Gibbs Reed Farm, Ticehurst, E. Sussex TN5 7HE, England. [Q., $155]. Deals with all aspects of library and information work in the United Kingdom and reviews literature from international sources.

Journal of Library Administration. Haworth Press, 10 Alice St., Binghamton, NY 13904-1580, (800)-HAWORTH, fax (800) 895-0582, getinfo@haworth.com, www.haworthpress.com [8/yr., $45 indiv., $125 inst.] Provides information on all aspects of effective library management, with emphasis on practical applications.

Levy, S., & Pierssens, M. (2003). Of journals and eternity. **Substance: A Review of Theory and Literary Criticism, 32**(1), 11–13. Discusses the publication of journals in electronic formats, conservation of journals, Internet availability, and the agenda of a national library.

Library and Information Science Research. Ablex Publishing Corp., 100 Prospect Street, P.O. Box 811, Stamford, CT 06904-0811, (203) 323-9606, fax (203) 357-8446. www.jaipress.com [Q., $95 indiv., $245 inst.]. Research articles, dissertation reviews, and book reviews on issues concerning information resources management.

Library Computing (formerly **Library Software Review**). Sage Publications, Inc., 2455 Teller Rd., Thousand Oaks, CA 91320, order@sagepub.com, www.sagepub.com [Q., $59 indiv., $252 US inst..]. Emphasizes practical aspects of library computing for libraries of all types, including reviews of automated systems ranging from large-scale mainframe-based systems to microcomputer-based systems, and both library-specific and general-purpose software used in libraries.

Library Hi Tech. Pierian Press, Box 1808, Ann Arbor, MI 48106, (800) 678-2435, www.pierianpress.com. [Q., $169.]. Concentrates on reporting on the selection, installation, maintenance, and integration of systems and hardware.

Library Hi Tech News. Pierian Press, Box 1808, Ann Arbor, MI 48106, (800) 678-2435, www.pierianpress.com [10/yr., $199.]. Supplements *Library Hi Tech* and updates many of the issues addressed in-depth in the journal and keeps you fully informed of the latest developments in library automation, new products, network news, new software and hardware, and people in technology.

Library Journal. 245 West 17th Street, New York, NY 10011, (212) 463-6819. [20/yr., $109 US, $138.50 Canada, $188.50 elsewhere]. A professional periodical for librarians, with current issues and news, professional reading, a lengthy book review section, and classified advertisements.

Library Media Connection (previously **Book Report**). Linworth Publishing, 480 E. Wilson Bridge Rd., Suite L., Worthington, OH 43085-2372, (800) 786-5017, fax (614) 436-9490, orders@linworth.com, linworth.com. [5/school yr., $44 US, $9 single copy]. Journal for junior and senior high school librarians provides articles, tips, and ideas for day-to-day school library management, as well as reviews of audiovisuals and software, all written by school librarians.

Library Quarterly. University of Chicago Press, 5720 S. Woodlawn Ave., Chicago, IL 60637. [Q., $35 indiv., $73 inst.]. Scholarly articles of interest to librarians.

Library Resources and Technical Services. Association for Library Collections and Technical Services, 50 E. Huron St., Chicago, IL 60611-2795. [Q., $55 nonmembers]. Scholarly papers on bibliographic access and control, preservation, conservation, and reproduction of library materials.

Library Trends. University of Illinois Press, Journals Dept., 1325 S. Oak St., Champaign, IL 61820. [Q., $60 indiv.; $85 inst.; add $7 elsewhere]. Each issue is concerned with one aspect of library and information science, analyzing current thought and practice and examining ideas that hold the greatest potential for the field.

LISA: Library and Information Science Abstracts. Bowker-Saur Ltd., Maypole House, Maypole Rd., E. Grinsted, W. Sussex, RH19 1HH, England, www.bowker-saur.com. [Mo., $960 US, £545 elsewhere]. More than 500 abstracts per issue from more than 500 periodicals, reports, books, and conference proceedings.

McGriff, N., Harvey, C., & Preddy, L. (2004, May). Collecting the Data: Collection Development. **School Library Media Activities Monthly, 20**(9), 27–30. Suggests methods for collecting data for media center statistics especially regarding items not actively used in the collection for stack maintenance.

Moyer, M., & Baker, R. (2004, Apr/May). Re-designing a school library media center for the 21st century. **Library Media Connection, 22**(7), 24–26. Discusses a case study of a redesign which focused on specific objectives such as atmosphere, clear visibility, traffic patterns, and more.

The Public-Access Computer Systems Review. An electronic journal published on an irregular basis by the University Libraries, University of Houston, Houston, TX 77204-2091, LThompson@uh.edu. Free to libraries. Contains articles about all types of computer systems that libraries make available to their patrons and technologies to implement these systems.

Public Libraries. Public Library Association, American Library Association, ALA Editions, 50 East Huron St., Chicago, IL 60611-2795; (800) 545-2433; fax (312) 836-9958. [Bi-mo., $50 US nonmembers, $60 elsewhere, $10 single copy]. News and articles of interest to public librarians.

Public Library Quarterly. Haworth Press, 10 Alice St., Binghamton, NY 13904-1580, (800)-HAWORTH, fax (800) 895-0582, getinfo@haworth.com, www.haworthpress.com. [Q., $50 indiv., $165 inst.]. Addresses the major administrative challenges and opportunities that face the nation's public libraries.

Quandt, R. (2003). Scholarly materials: Paper or digital? **Library Trends, 51**(3), 349–375. This article discusses budget cuts in libraries, corporate mergers among publishing conglomerates, and considerations of electronic media on the cost of serials acquisitions. It also suggests that initial estimates of savings from electronic serials were too large, as archiving and indexing costs were not given enough weight. Discussion continues wit pricing structures from major publishers including bundling of journals. Additional concern is give to the impact these publishing decisions will have on teaching, learning, and research.

Reference and User Services Quarterly. (Formerly **RQ**). Reference and Adult Services Association, American Library Association, ALA Editions, 50 East Huron St., Chicago, IL 60611-2795, (800) 545-2433, fax (312) 836-9958. [Q., $50 nonmembers, $55 nonmembers Canada/Mexico, $60 elsewhere, $15 single copy]. Disseminates information of interest to reference librarians, bibliographers, adult services librarians, those in collection development and selection, and others interested in public services; double-blind refereed.

The Reference Librarian. Haworth Press, 10 Alice St., Binghamton, NY 13904-1580, (800)-HAWORTH, fax (800)895-0582, getinfo@haworth.com, www.haworthpress.com. [2/yr.; $60 indiv., $225 inst.]. Each issue focuses on a topic of current concern, interest, or practical value to reference librarians.

Reference Services Review. Pierian Press, Box 1808, Ann Arbor, MI 48106, (800) 678-2435, www.pierianpress.com [Q., $169.]. Dedicated to the enrichment of reference knowledge and the advancement of reference services. It prepares its readers to understand and embrace current and emerging technologies affecting reference functions and information needs of library users.

Richards, J. (2003). What do I see? What do I think? What do I wonder? (STW): A visual literacy strategy to help emergent readers focus on storybook illustrations. **The Reading Teacher, 56**(5), 442–445. These three questions were developed as a method of visual literacy for emergent readers. This method increases the time young readers spend examining illustrations and promotes critical thinking skills.

Ripp Safford, B. (2004, May). Pondering the Virtual School Library Media Center. **School** *Library Media* **Activities Monthly, 20**(9), 32–34. This article supports digital resources but suggests that virtual libraries are not viable for the K–12 environment because basic research skills require traditional face-to-face methods for instruction.

School Library Journal. Box 57559, Boulder, CO 80322-7559, (800) 456-9409, fax (800) 824-4746. [Mo., $97.50 US, $139 Canada, $149 elsewhere]. For school and youth service librarians. Reviews about 4,000 children's books and 1,000 educational media titles annually.

School Library Media Activities Monthly. LMS Associates LLC, 17 E. Henrietta St., Baltimore, MD 21230-3190. [10/yr., $49 US, $54 elsewhere]. A vehicle for distributing ideas for teaching library media skills and for the development and implementation of library media skills programs.

School Library Media Research. American Association of School Librarians, American Library Association. [Available online: www.ala.org/aasl/SLMR/index.html]. For library media specialists, district supervisors, and others concerned with the selection and purchase of print and nonprint media and with the development of programs and services for preschool through high school libraries.

Schank, J., & Dewald, N. (2003). Establishing our presence in courseware: Adding library services to the virtual classroom. **Information Technology & Libraries, 22**(1), 38–43. Discusses the increasing trend for courseware-supplemented college classes and the benefits of adding library elements in the electronic classroom.

Shigo, K. (2003). Research libraries collaborate on DSpace. **Computers in Libraries, 23**(4), 8. MIT Libraries is collaborating with Columbia University, Cornell University, Ohio State University, and the universities of Rochester, Toronto, and Washington in the development of DSpace Federation. DSpace (http://www.dspace.org) began in 2002 as the product of work between MIT Libraries and Hewlett-Packard Labs as an open source system. This is a digital library to "capture, store, index, preserve, and redistribute the intellectual output of a university's research faculty in digital formats." Explores potential for even small institutions to participate.

Shim, W. (2003). Applying DEA technique to library evaluation in academic research libraries. **Library Trends, 51**(3), 312–333. In an effort to document library usefulness in an era of budget cuts, this study used Data Envelopment Analysis (DEA) to calculate efficiency among 95 ARL libraries. This method allows best practices to emerge while giving each institution a performance score. Discussion of the methodology used is included.

Stevenson, J. (2003). Vision 2020: Modernizing the academy with preservation of past prospicience and foresight for the future at a research-intensive university. **Education,**

123(3), 455–459. Vision 2020 is a plan mandating Jackson State to determine its marketplace niche for the future. Determining what any school does best will allow it to focus its energies and funds where it best serves its consumer base and community interests. Some areas of interest at Jackson State are action research, library resources, partnerships with other institutions in the region, technology, and global awareness.

Teacher Librarian. Box 34069, Dept. 284, Seattle, WA 98124-1069, TL@rockland.com. [Bi-mo. except July-August, $49]. "The journal for school library professionals"; previously known as *Emergency Librarian.* Articles, review columns, and critical analyses of management and programming issues for children's and young adult librarians.

The Unabashed Librarian. Box 2631, New York, NY 10116. [Q., $40 US, $48 elsewhere]. Down-to-earth library items: procedures, forms, programs, cataloging, booklists, software reviews.

Xu, Hong. (2003). Information technology courses and their relationship to faculty in different professional ranks in library and information science programs. **Library & Information Science Research, 25**(2), 207–213. This study examines the growing relationship between information technology and library (ALA accredited) programs and courses. Twenty percent are technology-related courses; 57 percent require technology prerequisites. These skills and topics go well beyond the traditional bounds of librarianship, and as such are reflected in the faculty hired to teach these courses, many of whom come from other specialities.

MEDIA TECHNOLOGIES

Broadcasting and Cable. Reed Business Information, (800) 554-5729, broadcastingcable @espcomp.com, http://www.broadcastingcable.com/index.asp?layout=webzine [W., $149/yr. US print and online ($14.95/mo., online only), $219 Canada, $350 elsewhere]. All-inclusive newsweekly for radio, television, cable, and allied business.

Multichannel News. Reed Business Information, (888) 343-5563, multichannelnews @espcomp.com, http://www.multichannel.com/index.asp?layout=webzine [Semi-monthly; $149 US, print and online ($12.95/mo online only), $165 elsewhere]. A newsmagazine for the cable television industry. Covers programming, marketing, advertising, business, and other topics.

Communication Abstracts. Sage Publications, Inc., 2455 Teller Rd., Thousand Oaks, CA 91320, order@sagepub.com, www.sagepub.com [Bi-mo., $244 US indiv., $980 inst.]. Abstracts communication-related articles, reports, and books. Cumulated annually.

Communications News. Nelson Publishing Co., 2504 N. Tamiami Trail, Nokomis, FL 34275, www.comnews.com. [Mo., no cost]. Up-to-date information from around the world regarding voice, video, and data communications.

Downing, K., & Tat, C. (2004, Sept). Reflectors as online extraverts? **Educational Studies, 30**(3), 265–277. Examines personality types in online environments and findings suggest that those considered "reflectors" may seem to be introverts in traditional settings, may also be extroverts in online environments which allow for additional time to reflect and construct answers.

Educational Media International. Routledge, 11 New Fetter Lane, London EC49.4EE, UK, http://www.tandf.co.uk/journals/routledge/09523987.html [Q., $83 indiv., $321 inst.]. The official journal of the International Council for Educational Media.

Federal Communications Commission Reports. Superintendent of Documents, Government Printing Office, Box 371954, Pittsburgh, PA 15250-7954, http://www.fcc.gov/ [Daily Digest, Weekly Update, online, no cost]. Decisions, public notices, and other documents pertaining to FCC activities.

Fryer, W. (2004, May). The Battle for Desktop Control. **Technology & Learning, 24**(10), 27–28. Discusses the struggle instructors have with computer network administration methods which do not allow downloading instructional materials and programs to computer desktops.

Hasseibring, T., & Goin, L. (2004, Apr/June). Literacy instruction for older struggling readers: what is the role of technology? **Reading & Writing Quarterly, 20**(2), 123–145. Based on reading acquisition theory, this article discusses a prototype technology intervention created for use with older teens experiencing reading difficulties.

Historical Journal of Film, Radio, and Television. Carfax Publishing Limited in association with the International Association for Media and History, info@iamhist.org, 875-81 Massachusetts Ave., Cambridge, MA 02139. [Q., $185 indiv., $532 inst.]. Articles by international experts in the field, news and notices, and book reviews concerning the impact of mass communications on political and social history of the 20th century.

International Journal of Instructional Media. Westwood Press, Inc., ll8 Five Mile River Road, Darien, CT 06820. [Q., $148.80 US, $156.80 Can & Eur./per volume]. Focuses on quality research; ongoing programs in instructional media for education, distance learning, computer technology, instructional media and technology, telecommunications, interactive video, management, media research and evaluation, and utilization.

International Digital Media and Arts Association Journal. International Digital Media and Arts Association, Florida State University, PO Box 1150,Tallahassee, FL 32306-1150. [New, publication dates undetermined, $95 US]. For more information, contact Conrad Gleber, Editor; cgleber@mailer.fsu.edu, (850) 766-0188. Focuses on both the use of and the administration of new an emerging technologies such as mobile computing (GPS, personal digital assistants, cell phones), ubiquitous computing ("smart houses," "information appliances"), interactive television, online role-playing games, virtual reality, distributed collaborations.

Journal of Broadcasting and Electronic Media. Broadcast Education Association, (888) 380-7222, beainfo@beaweb.org, 1771 N St., NW, Washington, DC 20036-2891. [Q., $50 indiv., $90 inst. US, $60 indiv., $110 elsewhere]. Includes articles, book reviews, research reports, and analyses. Provides a forum for research relating to telecommunications and related fields.

Journal of Educational Media (formerly **Journal of Educational Television**). Carfax Publishing Co., 875-81 Massachusetts Ave., Cambridge, MA 02139, http://www.tandf.co.uk/journals/carfax/13581651.html [3/yr., $189 indiv., $705 inst.]. This journal of the Educational Television Association serves as an international forum for discussions and reports on developments in the field of television and related media in teaching, learning, and training.

Journal of Educational Multimedia and Hypermedia. Association for the Advancement of Computing In Education, PO Box 3728, Norfolk, VA 23514, info@aace.org, http://www.aace.org. Ed. Gary H. Marks, R&P Sarah D Williams. [Q., $35 indiv. member, $130 domestic to inst., $145 foreign to inst.]. Presents research and applications on multimedia and hypermedia tolls that allow one to integrate images and sound into educational software.

Journal of Popular Film and Television. Heldref Publications, 1319 Eighteenth St., NW, Washington, DC 20036-1802. (800) 365-9753. [Q., $39 indiv., $76 inst.]. Articles on film and television, book reviews, and theory. Dedicated to popular film and television in the broadest sense. Concentrates on commercial cinema and television, film and television theory or criticism, filmographies, and bibliographies. Edited at the College of Arts and Sciences of Northern Michigan University and the Department of Popular Culture, Bowling Green State University.

Library Talk (formerly **Technology Connection**). Linworth Publishing, 480 E. Wilson Bridge Rd., Suite L., Worthington, OH 43085-2372, (800) 786-5017, fax (614) 436-9490, orders@linworth.com, linworth.com. [6/yr., $49 US, $7 single copy]. The only magazine published for the elementary school library media and technology specialist. A forum for K–12 educators who use technology as an educational resource, this journal includes information on what works and what does not, new product reviews, tips and pointers, and emerging technology.

Loh, C. S., Branch, R. M., Shewanown, S., & Ali, R. (2003). The effect of text spacing after the period on time for on-screen reading tasks. **The 2002 International Visual Literacy Association Selected Readings.** Robert E. Griffin (Ed.). Research examining the effect of text spacing between sentences on reading time for computer work. Visual literacy issues are detailed.

Media and Methods; educational products, technologies & programs for schools & universities. American Society of Educators, 1429 Walnut Street, Philadelphia, PA 19102, http://www.media-methods.com. Ed. Christine Weiser [5/yr., $33.50 US]. This educational magazine offers practical information regarding instructional technologies.

Multimedia Schools. Information Today, 143 Old Marlton Pike, Medford, NJ 08055, http://www.infotoday.com/MMSchools/default.shtml, (800) 300-9868. [6/yr., $39.95 US; $54 Canada/Mexico, $63 elsewhere]. Reviews new titles, evaluates hardware and software, offers technical advice and troubleshooting tips, and profiles high-tech installations.

Multimedia Systems. Springer-Verlag New York Inc., Secaucus, NJ 07096-2485, (800) SPRINGER, http://www.bertelsmannspringer.de/, custserv@springer-ny.com [6/yr., $415 US]. Publishes original research articles and serves as a forum for stimulating and disseminating innovative research ideas, emerging technologies, state-of-the-art methods and tools in all aspects of multimedia computing, communication, storage, and applications among researchers, engineers, and practitioners.

NICEM (National Information Center for Educational Media). NICEM, P.O. Box 8640, Albuquerque, NM 87198-8640. (505) 265-3591, (800) 926-8328, fax (505) 256-1080, http://www.nicem.com/index.html, nicem@nicem.com. A custom search service to help those without access to the existing NICEM products. The NICEM database of 425,000 records, updated quarterly, provides information on non-print media for all levels of education and instruction in all academic areas. Fees are $500 user or multiple user pricing.

Poirier, C., & Feldman, R. (2004, Winter). Teaching in Cyberspace: Online Versus Traditional Instruction Using a Waiting-List Experimental Design. **Teaching of Psychology, 31**(1), 59–62. Research was conducted on students comparing online learning with large traditional introductory courses which are face-to-face. Results showed that online students performed as well as traditional students but their satisfaction rating was significantly higher.

Telematics and Informatics. Elsevier Science Regional Sales Office, Customer Support Department, P.O. Box 945, New York, NY 10159-0945. http://www.elsevier.com/inca/publications/store/7/0/3/index.htt, (888) 4ES-INFO, usinfo-f@elsevier.com. [3/yr.,

$881 inst.]. Publishes research and review articles in applied telecommunications and information sciences in business, industry, government and educational establishments. Focuses on important current technologies including microelectronics, computer graphics, speech synthesis and voice recognition, database management, data encryption, satellite television, artificial intelligence, and the ongoing computer revolution. Contributors and readers include professionals in business and industry, as well as in government and academia, needing to keep abreast of current technologies and their diverse applications.

Videography. United Entertainment Media, 460 Park Avenue South, 9th Floor, New York, NY 10016, (212) 378-0400, Fax (212)378-2160. [Online, no cost]. Ed. Mark Foley, mfoley@uemedia.com, http://www.uemedia.com/CPC/videography/. For the video professional; covers techniques, applications, equipment, technology, and video art.

Witt, P. (2003). Enhancing classroom courses with Internet technology: Are course web sites worth the trouble? **Community College Journal of Research & Practice, 27**(5), 429–439. Examines the communication goals and educational goals of course Web pages as provided as additional information for traditional classes. Some uses are clearly necessary beyond the boundaries of the traditional classroom while other uses do not seem to warrant the time and resources. Suggestions for further research are included.

PROFESSIONAL DEVELOPMENT

Chillarege, K., Nordstrom, C., & Williams, K. (2003). Learning from our mistakes: Error management training for mature learners. **Journal of Business & Psychology, 17**(3), 369–385. Results of a study of adults found error management training resulted in a higher performance than those trained in error avoidance. In additional intrinsic motivation levels were improved.

Continuing Professional Development. Virtual University Press, Brookes University, School of Hotel and Restaurant Management, Gipsy Ln., Headington, Oxford, Oxon OX3 0BP, United Kingdom, (+44) 1642-751168, http://www.openhouse.org.uk/virtual-university-press/cpd/welcome.htm. Ed. Nigel Hammington. [Q., Great Britain $30, US $ $50, US $185 with online access.] Contains book reviews concerning online opportunities for continuing education.

Journal of Technology and Teacher Education. Association for the Advancement of Computing in Education (AACE), P.O. Box 2966, Charlottesville, VA 22902, AACE@ virginia.edu, www.aace.org. [Q., $40 US, $50 intnl.]. Serves as an international forum to report research and applications of technology in preservice, inservice, and graduate teacher education.

Journal of Computing in Teacher Education. ISTE, University of Oregon, 1787 Agate St., Eugene, OR 97403-1923, (800) 336-5191, cust_svc@ccmail.uoregon.edu, www.iste.org. [Q., $29, $39 intl., $42 intl. air]. Contains refereed articles on preservice and inservice training, research in computer education and certification issues, and reviews of training materials and texts.

Kaplan, R., & Kaiser, R. (2003). Rethinking a classic distinction in leadership: Implications for the assessment and development of executives. **Consulting Psychology Journal: Practice & Research, 55**(1), 15–25. Discussions of the "twin pillars" of leadership: task-oriented leadership and people-oriented leadership. Seen as complementary virtues, authors suggests ways to gather data and feedback to ensure balance in leadership.

Kimbrough Kidwell, P., Freeman, R., Smith, C., & Zarcone, J. (2004, June). Integrating online instruction with active mentoring to support professionals in applied settings. **Internet & Higher Education, 7**(2), 141–151. Discusses the use of an online instruction method for reaching distributed educators for professional development updates. Helps ensure consistent methods across locations and dissemination of the latest information to remote sites.

Holzer, E. (2004, Mar). Professional development of teacher educators in asynchronous electric environment: Challenges, opportunities and preliminary insights from practice. **Educational Media International, 41**(1), 81–90. Discusses online learning tools used to scaffold teacher preparation for preservice teachers in graduate programs preparing for rural and sometimes isolated practice.

Jamieson, P. (2004, Spring). The university as workplace. **Quarterly Review of Distance Education, 5**(1), 21–28. Discusses the pedagogical changes in universities worldwide from teacher centered to student centered and the need for professional development techniques to support this change throughout the professorate. Case study highlighted.

Palus, C., Horth, D., & Selvin, A. (2003). **Consulting Psychology Journal: Practice & Research, 55**(1), 26–40. Discusses a theory of "exploration for development" (ED). Its components are as follows: navigating complex challenges, supporting competent shared sense-making, and practicing leadership based on relational principles. Trials of the ED theory were done at a telecommunications company. Results and suggestions included for curriculum development including mentoring and coaching.

Skipton, L., & Maynard, G. (2003). Leadership development as an intervention for organizational transformation: A case study. **Consulting Psychology Journal: Practice & Research, 55**(1), 58–67. Personal development goals are tied to organizational leadership development goals in this case study. No individual skills or behavior changes were achieved; however, the authors maintain organizational functioning was improved.

Society for Applied Learning Technology. Society for Applied Learning Technology, 50 Culpepper St., Warrenton, VA 20186, info@salt.org, http://www.salt.org. Ed. Raymond D Fox. [Q.,]. Provides news, publication reviews, and conference updates for instructional technology professionals

SIMULATION, GAMING, AND VIRTUAL REALITY

Bochenek, G., & Ragusa, J. (2004, June). Improving integrated project team interaction through virtual (3D) collaboration. **Engineering Management Journal, 16**(2), 3–13. Discusses the move away from old systems and models of development to the use of virtual teams and collaborative virtual environments (CVEs) to reduce costs, reduce development time, and improve collaboration among designers.

Dede, C. (2003). Multi-user virtual environments. **EDUCAUSE Review, 38**(3), 60. This article argues that the future holds three environments, other than face-to-face interaction, that will shape our learning and communication: the desktop environment, the portable computing environment, and the virtual world environment. Discusses the impact of these environments on learning and communicating in the future.

Gallus, W. (2003). An example of a virtual reality learning environment. **Bulletin of the American Meteorological Society, 84**(1), 18–22. A pilot model built using photos, computer graphics and experimental data creates a virtual tornadic supercell thunderstorm for student learning. This environment gives students a realistic experience in a safe environment and stimulates critical thinking.

Grady, S. (2003). **Virtual Reality, New Edition: Simulating and Enhancing the World with Computers.** [Book, 208 p., $29.95]. Facts on File, Incorporated. An updated version of the 1998 publication. Covers the history of virtual reality as well as providing a glossary to demystify the language. It features graphs, charts, and illustrations to further explain the text. Primarily written for beginners in the VR world.

International Digital Media and Arts Association Journal. International Digital Media and Arts Association, Florida State University, PO Box 1150,Tallahassee, FL 32306-1150. [New, publication dates undetermined, $95 US] For more information contact Conrad Gleber, Editor. cgleber@mailer.fsu.edu, (850) 766-0188. Focuses on both the use of and the administration of new an emerging technologies such as mobile computing (GPS, personal digital assistants, cell phones), ubiquitous computing ("smart houses," "information appliances"), interactive television, online role-playing games, virtual reality, distributed collaborations.

Joslin, C. di Giacomo, T., & Magnenat-Thalmann, N. (2004, Apr). Collaborative virtual environments: from birth to Standardization. **IEEE Communications Magazine, 42**(4), 28–34. This article provides a 13-year history of the development of CVEs and how standardization is being considered for these programs. Literature review included.

Lahti, H., Seitamaa-Hakkarainen, P., & Hakkarainen, K. (2004, July). Collaboration patterns in computer supported collaborative designing. **Design Studies, 25**(4), 351–372. Research surrounding the use of virtual teams in a design based course resulted in high levels of collaboration, cooperation, and sharing in the joint project.

Rafaeli, S., & Ravid, G. (2003). Information sharing as an enabler for the virtual team: An experimental approach to assessing the role of electronic mail in disintermediation. **Information Systems Journal, 13**(2), 191–207. An empirical study that attempts to quantify the relationship between information sharing via e-mail and group performance. Seventy-six teams were studied as they played a role-playing simulation game called "Beer Game." Results showed correlation between the number of e-mails sent and net team profit or winnings. This was determined to mean improved team performance.

Randerson, J. (2003). Virtual workout beats the boredom for stroke patients. **New Scientist, 177**(2385). Authors discuss their development of freeware for virtual mapping and geologic interpretation. This Internet-based virtual world gives students all the tools needed to perform geologic surveys of the Planet Oit. Freeware available at http://oit. cs.ndsu.nodak.edu/.

Simulation and Gaming. Sage Publications, Inc., 2455 Teller Rd., Thousand Oaks, CA 91320, order@sagepub.com, www.sagepub.com [Q., $94 indiv., $416 inst., $19 single issue]. An international journal of theory, design, and research focusing on issues in simulation, gaming, modeling, role-play, and experiential learning.

Sunrise introduces virtual reality education software. (2003). **T.H.E. Journal, 30**(7), 10. Sunrise Virtual Reality, Inc. has created new educational software that can allow students to explore the Amazon, "touch" the periodic table and interact with molecules, or visit the pyramids in ancient Egypt. The key to its marketability is that the software was designed in cooperation with teachers for easy integration into normal curriculum. Information available at http://www.sunrisevr.com.

Shigeng, P., et al. (2003). Easybowling: A small bowling machine based on virtual simulation. **Computers & Graphics, 27**(2), 231–239. Describes a new extension of the traditional VR bowling game by adding interaction of the players with real bowling balls. Thus exercise is added back into the game. Specific details of implementation and suggestions for future development are included.

Wegerif, R. (2004, Aug). The role of educational software as a support for teaching and learning conversations. **Computers & Education, 43**(1/2), 179–192. Research study was conducted using 119 children in an educational computing context. Computers were programmed to become involved in the conversation as if they were humans. Discusses simulations.

Zyda, M., et al. (2003). Entertainment R&D for defense. **IEEE Computer Graphics & Applications, 23**(1), 28–36. Explains "America's Army," an Internet-based game suite developed by the U.S. Army using VR, modeling, and simulation. Details on each game of the suite and the developers, and general overview.

SPECIAL EDUCATION AND DISABILITIES

Journal of Special Education Technology. Department of Special Education, UNLV, 4505 Maryland Parkway, Box 453014, Las Vegas, NV 89154-3014, (615) 322-8150, http://jset.unlv.edu/shared/volsmenu.html. Eds. Kyle Higgins & Randall Boone. [Q., $40 indiv., $89 inst.]. The *Journal of Special Education Technology* provides "information, research, and reports of innovative practices regarding the application of educational technology toward the education of exceptional children."

Hines, R., & Pearl, C. (2004, Spring). Increasing Interaction in Web-based Instruction: Using Synchronous Chats and Asynchronus Discussions. **Rural Special Education Quarterly, 23**(2), 33–37. Discusses the increased interaction with instructors, other students, content material, and self reflection in the development of Web-based instruction for learners.

Langone, J., Clees, T., Rieber, L., & Matzko, M. (2003). The future of computer-based interactive technology for teaching individuals with moderate to severe disabilities: Issues relating to research and practice. **Journal of Special Education Technology, 18**(1), 5–16. Suggests a community-based approach to teaching technology to those with moderate to severe disability.

Mull, C., & Sitlington, P. (2003). The role of technology in the transition to postsecondary education of students with learning disabilities: A review of the literature. **The Journal of Special Education, 37**(1), 26–32. Provides a review of the literature; suggestions found in the literature primarily centered on helping students make the transition to postsecondary education settings.

Pickering, S., & Gathercole, S. (2004, June). Distinctive Working Memory Profiles in Children with Special Educational Needs. **Educational Psychology, 24**(3), 16. Discusses the use of technology to categorize memory disability areas within children with special learning needs.

TELECOMMUNICATIONS AND NETWORKING

Boardwatch: The Publication for Technology and Business for Internet Service Providers. Penton Media, P.O. Box 901979, Cleveland, OH 44190-1979. [M., $72 US & Canada, $128 International]. The Internet access industry's handbook. Each issue features the leading online editorial covering the Internet, World Wide Web, and the communications industry. Also provides information via its online magazine at http://www. boardwatch.com/.

Canadian Journal of Educational Communication. Association for Media and Technology in Education in Canada, 3-1750 The Queensway, Suite 1318, Etobicoke, ON M9C 5H5, Canada. [3/yr., $75]. Concerned with all aspects of educational systems and technology.

Classroom Connect. Classroom Connect, 1241 East Hillsdale Blvd., Suite 100, Foster City, CA USA 94404, (800) 638-1639, fax (888) 801-8299, orders@classroom.com. [9/yr., $45]. Provides pointers to sources of lesson plans for K–12 educators as well as descriptions of new Web sites, addresses for online "keypals," Internet basics for new users, classroom management tips for using the Internet, and online global projects. Each issue offers Internet adventures for every grade and subject.

Computer Communications. Elsevier Science, Inc., P.O. Box 882, Madison Square Station, New York, NY 10159-0882. [18/yr., $1,342 inst.]. Focuses on networking and distributed computing techniques, communications hardware and software, and standardization.

EDUCAUSE Review. EDUCAUSE, 1112 Sixteenth St., NW, Suite 600, Washington, DC 20036-4823, (800) 254-4770, info@educause.edu. [Bi-mo., $24 US/Canada/Mexico, $48 elsewhere]. Features articles on current issues and applications of computing and communications technology in higher education. Reports of EDUCAUSE consortium activities.

Edwards, M. (2003). The lap of learning. **School Administrator, 60**(4), 6–12. Brings laptop usage in United States up to the date of publication. Lists the advantages of wireless technologies, technology integration for student-centered problem solving, wireless technology planning by school districts.

EMMS (Electronic Mail & Messaging Systems). Telecommunications Reports, 1333 H Street NW, 11th Floor-W., Washington, DC 20005, brp.com [23/yr., $809 in North America, $979 outside of North America]. Covers technology, user, product, and legislative trends in graphic, record, and microcomputer applications.

Demetriadis, S., et al. (2003). "Cultures in negotiation": Teachers' acceptance/resistance attitudes considering the infusion of technology into schools. **Computers & Education, 41**(1), 19–38. Research conducted in a Greek secondary school illustrates that teachers have considerable interest in technology but significant support is required to succeed in integrating technology into classroom teaching. Thus administrators and technology coordinators need to "negotiate" to gain successful adoption within their culture.

International Journal of E-Learning Telecommunications. Association for the Advancement of Computing in Education, P.O. Box 2966, Charlottesville, VA 22901, (804) 973-3987, fax (804) 978-7449, AACE@virginia.edu, www.aace.org. [Q., $85 indiv., $120 inst.]. Reports on current theory, research, development, and practice of telecommunications in education at all levels.

The Internet and Higher Education. Elsevier Science/Regional Sales Office, Customer Support Department, JAI Books, P.O. Box 945, New York, NY 10159-0945. [Q., $79 indiv., $239 inst.]. Designed to reach faculty, staff, and administrators responsible for enhancing instructional practices and productivity via the use of information technology and the Internet in their institutions.

Internet Reference Services Quarterly. Haworth Press, 10 Alice St., Binghamton, NY 13904-1580, (800) HAWORTH, fax (800) 895-0582, getinfo@haworth.com, www.haworthpress.com. [Q., $45 indiv., $75 institutions, $75 libraries]. Describes innovative information practice, technologies, and practice. For librarians of all kinds.

Internet Research (previously Electronic Networking: Research, Applications, and Policy). MCB University Press Ltd., 60-62 Toller Ln., Bradford, W. Yorks. BD8 9BY, England. [5/yr, $1539 US paper & electronic, $369 electronic only]. A cross-disciplinary journal presenting research findings related to electronic networks, analyses of policy issues related to networking, and descriptions of current and potential applications of electronic networking for communication, computation, and provision of information services.

Internet World. Penton Media. Internet World, P.O. Box 901979, Cleveland, OH 44190-1979, www.iw.com. [M., $160 U.S., $200 Canada, $295 elsewhere]. Analyzes developments of the Internet, electronic networking, publishing, and scholarly communication, as well as other network issues of interest to a wide range of network users.

Link-Up. Information Today, 143 Old Marlton Pike, Medford, NJ 08055, (800) 300-9868. [Bi-mo., $34.95 US, $42 Canada/Mexico; $64 elsewhere]. Newsmagazine for individuals interested in small computer communications; covers hardware, software, communications services, and search methods.

Mowen, G. (2003). Adventures in laptop land. **School Administrator, 60**(4), 14–19. Discusses student laptop use and problems. Other issues discuss laptop screen breakage, laptop rules, parent training, wireless programs, and reasons for encouraging laptop use among students.

Network Magazine. CMP Media INC, 600 Harrison St., San Francisco, CA 94107, www.networkmagazine.com. [Mo., $125]. Provides users with news and analysis of changing technology for the networking of computers.

Norris, C., & Soloway, E. (2003). The viable alternative: Handhelds. **School Administrator, 60**(4), 26. Presents handheld computers as a viable option to other technologies, needs for success, advantages for K–12 environment, and the impact of mobile technologies on teaching and learning.

O'Hare, G., & O'Grady, M. (2003). Gulliver's genie: A multi-agent system for ubiquitous and intelligent content delivery. **Computer Communications, 26**(11), 1177–1188. The use of intelligent agents in a wireless system to collect and assemble data for roaming tourists via PDAs. System agents base deductions on a beliefs, desires, and intentions (BDI) scale. Discusses system creation and user experience.

Online. Online, Inc., 213 Danbury Rd., Wilton, CT 06897, www.onlineinc.com/onlinemag/. [6/yr., $110 US, $120 Canada & Mexico, $145 foreign]. For online information system users. Articles cover a variety of online applications for general and business use.

Online-Offline. Rock Hill Press, 14 Rock Hill Road, Bala Cynwyd, PA 19004, (888) ROCK HIL, fax (610) 667-2291, www.rockhillpress.com [9/yr., $66.50]. Examines classroom resources, linking curricular themes with Web sites and other media.

Stewart, K., & Choi, H. (2003). PC-Bang (room) culture: A study of Korean college students' private and public use of computers and the Internet. **Trends in Communication, 11**(1), 63–80. A study was conducted to determine Korean student usage of PC Bangs (college computer labs) and home computers. Results found that most PC Bangs were used by males for gaming, and females tended to use computers at home for e-mail and chatting.

Taylor, L., Castro, D., & Walls, R. (2004, Apr/June). Tools, Time, and Strategies for Integrating Technology across the Curriculum. **Journal of Constructivist Psychology, 17**(2), 121–137. Discusses the results of a grant funded project to develop collaborative designed lesson plans. These resulted in constructivist plans that integrated technology into the classroom and each was positively reviewed by students.

Telecommunications. (North American Edition.) Horizon House Publications, Inc., 685 Canton St., Norwood, MA 02062. [Mo., $130 US, $210 elsewhere, free to qualified individuals]. Feature articles and news for the field of telecommunications.

Trotter, A. (2003). New Web tool calculates costs of school computer networks. **Education Week, 22**(3), 301–304. Discusses a Web-based tool which estimates computer networks for schools. The tool was created by Gartner Inc of Stamford, Connecticut, under a U.S. Department of Education grant. Cost areas include hardware, software, tech support salaries and expenses, indirect support costs for others who troubleshoot computer issues and/or maintain parts of the networked system.

Van Aalst, J., & van der Mast, C. (2003). Performer: An instrument for multidisciplinary courseware teams to share knowledge and experiences. **Computers & Education, 41**(1), 39–49. This article presents an instrument that facilitates both development teams as well as the learner. Tests show success with multidisciplinary development teams.

Index

About the Editors

MICHAEL OREY is an Associate Professor in Instructional Technology at the University of Georgia. Dr. Orey focuses on the application of current models of learning to the teaching process

JO MCCLENDON is a doctoral student in the Department of Instructional Technology at the University of Georgia. She has worked in education as a K–12 teacher, a college instructor, and an academic librarian for more than two decades.

ROBERT MARIBE BRANCH is a Professor of Instructional Technology at the University of Georgia. Dr. Branch focuses on accurate portrayals of complex processes.